Gems of NEW JERSEY

Dedicated to Mort Pye

Editor

The Star-Ledger, which made the GEMS OF NEW JERSEY
newspaper series possible.

Gems of
NEW JERSEY

Written for **The Star-Ledger**
by *Gordon Bishop*

Prentice-Hall, Inc.   Englewood Cliffs, N. J.

Prentice-Hall International, Inc., *London*
Prentice-Hall of Australia, Pty. Ltd., *Sydney*
Prentice-Hall Canada Inc., *Toronto*
Prentice-Hall of India Private Ltd., *New Delhi*
Prentice-Hall of Japan, Inc., *Tokyo*
Prentice-Hall of Southeast Asia Pte. Ltd., *Singapore*
Whitehall Books, Ltd., *Wellington, New Zealand*
Editora Prentice-Hall do Brasil Ltda., *Rio de Janeiro*
Prentice-Hall Hispanoamericana, S.A., *Mexico*

© 1985 by

Newark Morning Ledger Co.

Library of Congress Cataloging in Publication Data

Bishop, Gordon, 1938-
  Gems of New Jersey.

  1. New Jersey—Addresses, essays, lectures.
I. Star-Ledger (Newark, N.J. : 1964) II. Title.
F134.B53 1985   974.9   85-6371

ISBN 0-13-347436-4

Printed in the United States of America

ABOUT THE AUTHOR

GORDON BRUCE BISHOP has been a journalist all of his adult life. Born in Paterson, N.J., on January 1, 1938, he grew up in nearby Hackensack. After high school, he attended the American Academy of Dramatic Arts in New York City (1957–58), where he studied drama and performed in "Come Back Little Sheba" at the Bergen County Playhouse in Oradell.

In 1959, Mr. Bishop joined the editorial staff of *The Herald-News* in Passaic County, where he was an award-winning reporter, columnist and the paper's first drama and movie critic.

While at *The Herald-News*, Mr. Bishop wrote a comedy with his former high school drama teacher, which was produced at the Midway Theatre in Manhattan in 1963. He was graduated from Rutgers University in 1967 with a Bachelor of Arts degree in English.

In 1969, Mr. Bishop began his association with *The Star-Ledger*, New Jersey's largest daily and Sunday newspaper. As Environmental Editor and columnist, Mr. Bishop won more than a dozen national journalism awards and as many state news writing awards.

He is a five-time winner of the Scripps-Howard Foundation Edward J. Meeman Conservation Award, three-time winner of the New Jersey Society of Professional Journalists (Sigma Delta Chi) Distinguished Public Service Award, and winner of six first-place awards by the New Jersey Press Association for Distinguished Public Service Enterprise, Interpretive and Business Writing.

In 1972, Mr. Bishop was one of two U.S. journalists selected by the Institute for International Education, New York, for a scholarship to the University of Manchester in England, where he studied "Social and Environmental Planning."

He was the first journalist in the 80-year history of the New Jersey Society of Professional Engineers to receive that organization's Distinguished Public Service Award.

He is also the recipient of the New Jersey Audubon Society's Conservation Award, the New Jersey Garden Club's Gold Medal, the New Jersey Agricultural Society's Communications Award, the National and State Recycling Awards, the U.S. Environmental Protection Agency's first Special Award of Merit for news writing, the New Jersey Conference of Mayors Good Government Award, the American Planning Association's Annual Planning Award, New Jersey Chapter, and the Association of United States Army Concerned Citizens Award.

Mr. Bishop has been cited twice by the Washington Journalism Center for conservation writing and was given the second-place award in the Ballew/McFarland Foundation's first National Land-Use Competition. He is on the Board of Trustees of the Natural Resources Education Foundation of New Jersey.

In his spare time, Mr. Bishop has written eight short stories about his childhood in Hackensack, published in local papers.

He also wrote, produced and narrated a two-hour documentary film on life in Newark called IT'S MY HOME and broadcast on WNET/THIRTEEN and New Jersey Network. Two of Bishop's half-hour documentaries on ENERGY LIFESTYLE and IMPACT OF RENT CONTROL were seen on New Jersey Network and cable television outlets in New Jersey.

Mr. Bishop recently produced a new musical in Newark, of which he was collaborator on the script and lyrics. Entitled CRISPUS, it is the story of Crispus Attucks, the first person killed in the American Revolution.

Mr. Bishop is married to the former Jeanne Ann Reed of Teaneck. They have two daughters, Jennifer and Elizabeth. Mrs. Bishop is a schoolteacher.

INTRODUCTION

GOVERNOR THOMAS H. KEAN

*F*or a year and a half, readers of the *Sunday Star-Ledger* were treated to a veteran journalist's sweeping story of his homestate—New Jersey.

It was an unprecedented tour de force, taking in almost every aspect of life in the Garden State, from agriculture, arts and aviation, to wildlife, wineries and the "Seven Wonders" of New Jersey: The Pinelands, Skylands, Meadowlands, Palisades, Paterson Falls, Great Swamp and the ecologically unique holly forest at Sandy Hook.

Representing one of the most ambitious projects in American journalism, GEMS OF NEW JERSEY is an extraordinary showcase of our state's finest human and natural resources.

The work stands as the most comprehensive compilation of pertinent information on New Jersey today.

The 72-part series of feature articles, which ran in the *Sunday Star-Ledger* from June 5, 1983 to October 14, 1984, focused on the dynamic diversity which has made New Jersey an "America in Miniature," as *National Geographic* has aptly described this historic state.

Newark librarian/historian Charles Cummings considers GEMS OF NEW JERSEY a "modern encyclopedia" covering everything from dance, diners and music, to lakes, rivers and Nobel laureates.

New Jersey is seven-and-a-half million people living in a remarkably diverse environment embracing mountains and beaches, cities and farms, verdant valleys and dense forests.

We who represent New Jersey—United States Senators Bill Bradley, Frank Lautenberg and myself—proudly call attention to the countless gems that make our state a special place in which to live, work and play.

SENATOR BILL BRADLEY   SENATOR FRANK LAUTENBERG

It is the "Gateway to America" at the Jersey City waterfront—the beautiful Liberty State Park backdrop for the inspiring Statue of Liberty and the legendary Ellis Island immigration clearinghouse.

At the other end of New Jersey is the tourist capital of America—Atlantic City—which currently attracts more than 30 million visitors a year.

New Jersey began as the crossroads of the American Revolution and the cradle of our nation's Industrial Revolution and, 200 years later, is a revolutionary leader in science and technology.

This is our story, one we'd like to share with everyone.

Thomas H. Kean
Governor, New Jersey
1985

ACKNOWLEDGMENTS

The 72-part newspaper series GEMS OF NEW JERSEY that evolved into this book could not have happened without the contributions, talent and vision of these people:

BRUCE COE   **LINDA FOWLER**   **CHARLES CUMMINGS**

Jeanne Reed   **Victoria Schmidt**   **Helen Fenske**   **George Homcy**

Angelo Baglivo	Roy Weaver	Betty Spero
Anthony Villane III	Lynn Price	Monica Maske
Fred Mihelic	Linda Kirchner	Valerie Sudol
Rachelle De Palma	Richard Gebhardt	Eileen Watkins
Phil Alampi	Barbara Dawson	George Kanzler
Edith Ledford	Kerry Ann Kirk	Michael Redmond
Faith Goldstein	Al Oleck	Ike Kuhns
Susanne Hand	Roy Cruitt	Rhebe Greenwald
Nancy Kelly	Pat Yananton	Peter Yuill
Herman Estrin	Dorothy Lupichuk	Harry Stahl
Cintra Rodgers	Arthur F. Lenehan	Elise Levine
Joseph Friedman		

and special thanks to our Prentice-Hall publishing team of Robert C. Martin, James E. Bradler, Robert Shaw, Ron Ledwith, Mary D. Morano, Anne Ricigliano, Catherine Doherty, Maryalice Lento, Deborah Leary, Jean Karash and Joyce Turner.

TABLE OF CONTENTS

ADULT COMMUNITIES

At Greenbriar, biking is a favorite form of recreation for residents.

Courtesy: The Greenbriar Association

A maturing population has brought about a new, invigorating community lifestyle that can be as challenging and fulfilling as student life on an Ivy League college campus.

Spreading like spring flowers across the Garden State are elaborate private enclaves that offer an alternative to crowded cities and repetitious suburban tract developments.

The movement began in the 1960s when New Jersey became one of the first states to introduce the concept of the "adult" community, or the "pre-retirement" community, or the private "balanced" community.

Whatever their names, they seem to appeal to a maturing generation of middle- and upper-middle-class persons who seek a personally rewarding way of life with those sharing similar values. A kind of Puritan work ethic forms the basis of these new communities and relationships.

New Jersey's success in pioneering this new lifestyle has spread halfway around the world to Japan. Developers there have turned to New Jersey to fashion new adult communities to accommodate an increasingly aging population in the land of the rising sun. While in the Japanese tradition senior citizens have lived with their children, a growing number are finding it necessary or desirable to continue living on their own in their latter years—a decidedly Western idea.

To find out what the new lifestyle was all about, Japanese developers have visited Concordia in Monroe Township, a pre-retirement community being developed by Crestwood Village in Ocean County. The Japanese were intrigued with the idea that a retired or semi-retired person can still live an active life almost tailor-made for them in an adult community.

The popularity of private communities for the older generation—usually those over 48 whose children have grown up and gone away—is rooted in a fundamental need for security and renewed satisfaction. Born before the big war, they are affluent and still active couples in the prime of their lives. Many have reached the peak of their careers and want a change of venue, a fresh start. Their old neighborhood has changed, and so have they.

The best adult communities are designed to please the most discriminating and dynamic individuals, those who "have made it" and now want to enjoy it. The "it" is lavish leisure with the accent on activity and artistic achievement.

In a fashionable adult community, one can indulge in physical and creative pursuits throughout the day and into the evenings. Within these security-tight villages are the finest natural and man-made amenities to be found anywhere: Heated Olympic-sized pools set off by spacious sundecks; lighted, all-weather cushioned tennis courts; paddle tennis, bocce and shuffleboard courts; championship 18-hole golf courses with golf observation decks; studios for arts and crafts and ceramics and pottery; photography labs; woodworking and hobby shops; men's and women's saunas and exercise rooms; libraries and medical clinics; jogging trails and pathways for bicycling; basketball courts, volley ball and playing fields; stylized meeting houses and clubhouses or entertainment centers featuring ballrooms, fireplaces, lounges, kitchens, card and game rooms for billiards, ping-pong, movies, dances; greenhouses and gardens; community newspapers, and cable TV.

These modern-day Shangri-Las, nestled in the heart of suburban society, are often surrounded by wildlife preserves and farmlands, or are near the ocean and bays. The housing and other facilities are integrated into the natural environment, where trees, flora, waterfalls, streams, lakes and ponds are protected for fishing, swimming, sailing, boating, ice skating in the winters and, in the mountain region, downhill and cross-country skiing.

More than 50 "separated and sheltered" communities, created for "privacy and elegance," have sprung up during the past 20 years, starting with Leisure Village in the Central Jersey Pinelands. Numerically, the Ocean and Burlington counties' Pine Barrens contain the greatest share of mid-life and retired residents. More than 2 million of the state's 7.5 million population are over 50 years of age.

A sampling of some of the latest and largest communities-within-a-community include Cedar Glen Lakes in Whiting; Clearbrook in Monroe Township; The Club at Galloway outside Atlantic City; Concordia in Cranbury; Covered Bridge in Manalapan; A Country Place in Lakewood; Crestwood in Whiting; Dover Walk in Dover Township; Elm Towne Village in Camden County; Holiday City in Toms River; Leisure Knoll in Manchester; Leisure Towne in Southampton; Fawn Lakes in Mahahawkin; Greenbriar I and II in Bricktown and Marlboro; Lionshead in Bricktown; Mystic Shores in Tuckerton; Panther Valley in Allamuchy; Rossmoor in Jamesburg; Shadow Lake Village and Shady Oaks in Middletown, and Silver Ridge Park in Toms River.

Three of the largest builders of adult communities in America are based in New Jersey: Leisure Technology in Lakewood, Crestwood Village in Whiting, and Hovnanian Companies in Red Bank, situated in a golden-windowed edifice overlooking the Navesink River and Atlantic Ocean.

Hovnanian has built thousands of residences in New Jersey, Pennsylvania, Florida, Texas and Georgia, among them townhouses in Society Hill Club, Morris Township; Society Hill East, East Brunswick; Society Hill near Princeton; The Club at Galloway near Atlantic City; Shadow Lake Village and Shady Oaks, Middletown, and Covered Bridge in Manalapan, in addition to 1,600 single-family homes in Monmouth County.

Leisure Village

New Jersey's first adult community was Leisure Village, established in 1963 in Lakewood. When first unveiled at the Waldorf-Astoria in New York, the plans for Leisure Village, as envisioned by New Jersey builder Robert J. Schmertz, called for a "total retirement community designed to meet the broad spectrum of residential, physical, social and cultural needs of residents in an adult community."

The words "retirement" and "adult" were used interchangeably, indicating that retirement no longer meant 65 and older. Many executives and professionals were retiring long before their Social Security checks started arriving. A new housing trend, catering to what would soon be the bulk of the population, was suddenly under way.

Leisure Village spawned succeeding generations of bigger and better adult communities. The biggest in the state and the second largest in the nation is Crestwood Village in nearby Whiting, a massive undertaking that today represents the largest adult community investment in the East.

Leisure Village pioneered the private retirement parks where safety and security are as important as strolling through a virgin wooded habitat around a golden pond at sunset. The model Lakewood village covers 450 acres and today is home for 3,450 people living in 2,433 dwellings. Streams, ponds and lakes soothe the surroundings, which include two clubhouses and residents' gardens throughout the secured grounds.

Schmertz's second retirement community was Leisure Village East, situated along Route 70 right off the Garden State Parkway at Exit 88 in Ocean County. The year was 1965 and by 1980 Route 70 would become known as the "seniors' thoroughfare" for the motoring residents of a dozen or so adult communities built between the Parkway and the other end of the east-west, two-lane highway in Burlington County, on the way to Cherry Hill and Philadelphia.

The East Village is similar in style and natural features with the original Leisure plan, except the Route 70 tract was scaled down to 226 acres supporting 1,400 adjoining dwellings and a total population today of 2,240. The familiar chain-link fence bordering the property and the guarded entranceway became Leisure trademarks. Even out in the distant Pinelands of Central Jersey, the denizens of Leisure Villages sought a quiet—and safe—refuge.

Farther down the road in Burlington County, more Pinelands were set aside in 1969 for Schmertz's most ambitious adult community—Leisure Towne in Southampton, smack in the heart of the Garden State's most fertile agricultural fields. The 1,230 acres with parks, nature trails and swimming pools serve 6,800 residents living in 4,300 clustered housing units.

Next came Leisure Village West, also along Route 70, complete with a golf course, greenhouses, vegetable and fruit gardens, swimming pools, tennis and bocce courts, two clubhouses and a lake. The 900-acre Piney paradise, opened in 1972, has reached its capacity of 3,200 homes boasting a community population of 5,120.

Manchester Township, a sprawling, sleepy Pines spot on the map, became one of America's fastest growing municipalities, as the senior population in the metropolitan area discovered another place to spend their sunny years without having to move all the way to Florida or Arizona, far from their roots and family.

Schmertz's last effort, in 1973, was Leisure Knoll, also in Manchester Township. Encompassing 422 acres, the Knoll resembled other Schmertz self-contained communities with their clubhouses, pools, lakes and miles of winding trails.

Schmertz firmly established New Jersey as a senior center of America within 10 years after he launched his Leisure Village plans for Ocean County. Had he waited any longer with his innovative idea, Ocean County might not have been the adult community capital of the East, second only to Sun City, Ariz. For in 1975, the state government decided to preserve the Pinelands as a one-of-a-kind ecological habitat, underlain with an estimated 17 trillion gallons of fresh water, the largest aquifer in the eastern United States.

The era of multiple adult communities in the Pinelands came to a close with the adoption of the Pinelands Master Plan in 1979. The Leisure Villages and Crestwood Villages, however, have already turned the Ocean County pines into a landmark "Golden Pond" for generations of youthful and older retirees.

Crestwood Village

Crestwood Village in Manchester ranks, in sheer numbers, as the most populated adult community in the U.S. outside of Sun City, Ariz., where 20,000 people play in a hot, dry climate.

Considering the size of New Jersey—the fifth smallest state in the nation—Crestwood Village is surely the retiring Brobdingnagian of Urban America. Within only 2,000 acres lives a sizable suburban-town population of 15,000 served by two shopping centers, each with its own medical facilities; eight clubhouses for each of the seven distinct villages within Crestwood; several restaurants; eight banks; seven churches, and a long, man-made recreation lake with a bandstand for any outdoor event. The many ponds in Crestwood are graced with their own gazebos.

The summer opens each June with a Crestwood Village Clothesline Art Show, where talented residents display hundreds of watercolors and oil and acrylic paintings, many of them fetching professional prices. There's a nucleus of an art colony nourishing itself and inspiring others to try their hand at personalized arts and crafts.

With time and talent to spare, villagers have organized symphonettes and choral groups. Someday there may be a Crestwood Symphony Orchestra playing at showcase theaters around the state.

The personal touch is evident everywhere in Crestwood, as flower, fruit and vegetable gardens give Crestwood a thriving farmyard appearance. The annual plantings and perennial fruit trees yield a bountiful harvest, providing a source of fresh food and considerable savings to the gardeners.

Large adult communities, especially Crestwood, are an untapped reservoir of brainpower and skills. Whether they are bankers or bricklayers, pilots or professors, they are living longer, healthier lives and are more active and more involved with their hobbies and communities.

Clearbrook and Rossmoor

Clearbrook and Rossmoor are an attractive pair of adult communities set around the famous Forsgate Country Club just off the New Jersey Turnpike at Exit 8-A, between New Brunswick and Trenton.

Builder Ross Corteze began with an ideal farmland site in Cranbury and modified it into a haven for those who relish the good life. At Rossmoor, a 440-acre tract of New England-styled structures was blended into the gently rolling countryside, where green lawns and blue waters dominate the landscape.

Undertaken in 1964, Rossmoor evolved into a community of 4,500 active retirees and commuting executives, managers and professionals. The 2,600 dwellings in Rossmoor represent 12 styles, ranging from rambling ranches to Early American colonials.

The Rossmoor Clubhouse is a 30,000-square-foot colonial mansion with an auditorium, banquet rooms, private social rooms, lounges, and special rooms for art, card-playing, sewing, ceramics and photography, as well as a woodworking shop and lending library.

Outside are an 18-hole championship golf course and pro shop; an Olympic-size heated swimming pool; a shopping center with gift store, delicatessen, bank, barber and beauty shops; tennis and shuffleboard courts, and a New England-styled meeting house, which serves as a town hall for community functions such as concerts, dramas, lectures and civic meetings, as well as religious services for all faiths.

There are also a medical center and mini-bus service.

Clearbrook, founded in 1973 about two miles from Rossmoor, derives its name from a clear brook that meanders through the 440 acres of farmland dedicated as an adult community.

Although the same size as Rossmoor, Clearbrook accommodates 1,000 more housing units, but only 500 more people. Its

The Billiard Room in the Club House at Rossmoor Adult Community, Jamesburg.

Star-Ledger Photo

Photo Credit: The Leigh Photographic Group

A view from the Clearbrook Timberline model dining room to this light and roomy kitchen with its patio.

Residents swinging away on the Rossmoor Adult Community golf course.

Star-Ledger Photo

25,000-square-foot clubhouse contains the same features as the older and larger Rossmoor cultural center. The extra living quarters in Clearbrook meant reducing the golf course from 18 to nine holes. Otherwise, Clearbrook enjoys the same fine reputation for luxury living as its sister community around the corner.

Concordia

Also in Cranbury is a significant new settlement that appeals to the 48 and over group. It is called Concordia and it is being developed by the same planners who created Crestwood Village.

Concordia is different from the earlier villages because it is structured as a "pre-retirement" community. Based on the 1980 census, more than 35 percent of the population is now over 45 years of age. Concordia was conceived with that mid-life market in mind.

Laid out in the same pastoral environment as Clearbrook and Rossmoor, Concordia will have 3,200 housing units on 489 acres when completed. The housing mix includes detached garden homes, two types of one-story attached dwellings and two-story attached condominiums clustered in cul-de-sacs and small connector roads around a regulation 18-hole golf course, or one of several lakes.

A 12-acre tract has been dedicated for a future commercial complex.

Targeting the physically active, Concordia offers a large indoor swimming pool, jogging and bicycle paths, lighted tennis courts and a 20,000-square-foot clubhouse loaded with exercise equipment.

Concordia will connect every dwelling to a 24-hour-manned gatehouse by a computerized electronic security system. Callers will be able to reach police, fire and medical personnel. And when residents are away, a concierge will receive their packages.

Elegant living in one of the many models at Concordia Adult Community.   Star-Ledger Photo

Concordia was designed to impart the ambiance of a New England resort. The external architecture is like a picture out of Yankee magazine, while the interiors are luxurious and spacious. Residents have the best of both worlds: Cosmpolitan Park Avenue and the rustic charm of Martha's Vineyard.

Privacy is paramount at Concordia. The garden homes have attached one- or two-car garages and formal courtyard entryways. The attached twin residences and villas have private rear patios.

Swimming is a refreshing pastime at Concordia Adult Community in Cranbury.   Star-Ledger Photo

Panther Valley

Panther Valley, in the hilly exurbs of Warren County, is an example of an exclusive all-around or "balanced" community where those on the road to retirement, or in retirement, can share common grounds with families of youngsters and teenagers.

Known as "the New Jersey homes for those who can afford to live anywhere," Panther Valley comprises separate neighborhoods of executive-level, single-family homes on landscaped lots and three individual townhome series. Each neighborhood is situated on its own hill or lakeside and includes its own recreational facilities.

The vistas to the west extend from Panther Valley to the Kittatiny Mountains, which stand in the distance above the stunning Delaware Water Gap. Protected by natural woodlands belonging to the New Jersey Green Acres Program and set below high stone walls, Panther Valley, established in 1976, embraces an environment of undisturbed nature and elegantly planned homes.

The single-family, traditionally styled homes have at least three bedrooms, two-and-a-half baths, two-car garages, large family rooms, eat-in kitchens and extensive expansion space for finishing, determined by individual family interests and demands.

In the heart of the 1,500-acre private residential-recreational community in Allamuchy is the Country Club Manor, a former private mansion and one of New Jersey's most prestigious homes. Today, small cocktail parties and elegant banquets for up to 200 guests are held in its intimate dining rooms and lounge. Temperance Hall is the club building composed of a pro shop, locker rooms with Swedish saunas, card rooms, a dining room for luncheons and a bar-lounge, which features an extraordinary fireplace hearth. Outside lies a championship 18-hole golf course designed by world renowned architect Robert Trent Jones. Above the 18th hole are the club cabanas, swimming pool and tennis courts.

The 800 families in Panther Valley enjoy the burst of plant and animal life in spring, followed by fishing, boating and sailing at the scores of deep lakes carved by prehistoric glaciers. Wildflowers bloom near cultured gardens. Hawks and falcons fly high in the clear mountain sky. Deer graze in hillside serenity, and geese descend to the cool waters to join ducks bathing in the lakes.

In winter, skiing reigns over the white slopes. The nearby Great Gorge, Vernon Valley and Snow Bowl areas are the finest in New Jersey. Cool weather activities also include ice skating, ice boating and ice fishing.

Shadow Lake and Shady Oaks

The classic adult community caters not only to an individual's finer instincts, but also respects and even enhances the natural environment. The sister communities of Shady Oaks and Shadow Lake Village strive for such human-natural interaction and compatibility.

They are Hovnanian planned communities along the upper reaches of the Navesink River in sprawling, suburban Middletown by the Jersey Shore in Monmouth County.

As defined by founder Kervork S. Hovnanian, lifestyle is the right combination of the type of ownership, the ease of living, available recreation, location, convenience and the economics of the present and future, as they relate to one's home.

Photo Credit: Ambrose Cucinotta

A peaceful pond mirrors Panther Valley town houses that blend into the wooded hillside.

The Hovnanian community incorporates conservation in its meaning of lifestyle. As important as appearance is the quality of construction, which conserves energy and money. Retired persons on fixed incomes appreciate an energy-efficient domicile. Such structures keep the cost of living in check through such design features as thermal-insulated, dual-glazed windows; vapor barriers; thermal breaks; insulated sheathing; Styrofoam perimeter insulation; insulated expansion joints, and extra-thick attic and wall insulation.

Shadow Lake Village was the first of the Middletown private communities developed by Hovnanian. Begun in 1974 on 160 acres of wooded riverfront property, Shadow Lake today is a village of 2,000 people living in a pleasing variety of terrace homes and townhouses—952 units in all—clustered around the golf course and 1½-mile-long lake known for its excellent boating and fishing.

Residents enjoy their own nine-hole golf course, swimming pool, tennis courts, shuffleboard and clubhouse, which is the focus of social life: Arts and crafts, parties, woodworking, sewing, billiards, exercise room, saunas, card and meeting rooms, and party room-auditorium with kitchen facilities.

When Shadow Lake Village became fully occupied, Hovnanian readied another shore tract for development. Shady Oaks opened on March 1, 1983, featuring six different models with appropriate names such as New Navesink and New Shrewsbury. The 78-acre private community will have 366 homes and a population of about 900. And like its older sister, Shady Oaks will have the same natural and recreational amenities.

ANIMALS

*E*very branch of life has found a special niche in New Jersey, be it reptiles, amphibians, mammals, birds or insects.

While the human population in New Jersey peaked around 7.5 million by 1980, the animal population—from finely bred horses, dogs and cats, to wild birds, reptiles and deer—is making a dramatic comeback as sportsmen and environmentalists encourage the growth of natural habitat and breeding farms throughout the state.

Swimming in Barnegat Bay are Golden Shiners, Fourspine Sticklebacks, Naked Gobies and Shorthorn Sculpins. Flying around Island Beach are Hooded Mergansers, Semipalmated Plovers and regional birds like the Louisiana Waterthrush, Kentucky and Canadian Warbler and the Summer Tanager.

Roaming the hills of North Jersey are black bears, southern bog lemmings, European hares, New England cottontails, Florida packrats and red-backed voles.

Toads and frogs dig in everywhere, while shells wash up on the beaches, such varieties as the Blood Ark, the Amethyst Gem Clam, the Northern Quahog and the Channeled Whelk.

The coyote has returned to the northern slopes of New Jersey, surviving as handily as the familiar masked raider, the raccoon.

The deer are doing so well, with only the licensed hunter as their seasonal predator, that they have become more abundant than in the great forests of Maine and Oregon.

Even a piece of Africa is tucked away in the Ocean County Pine Barrens, where lions and tigers, giraffes and elephants, hippos and rhinos and other creatures large and small have adapted to a four-season habitat at Great Adventure, the world's largest drive-through safari park outside of Africa.

Horses

Green pastures once threatened by suburban tract developments and urban encroachment today are home for a horse population approaching 100,000. This makes New Jersey one of the five leading thoroughbred centers, and the standardbred horse capital of the United States, in terms of the number of tracks, races, horses, purses and patrons making up this lucrative industry.

The horse industry grosses almost $400 million a year. Of the 8,700 farms in New Jersey, about 2,000 specialize in horses. There are approximately 1,000 farms for pleasure horses, 500 for standardbred (harness racing) and 460 thoroughbred farms producing winners at the world's greatest racetracks.

The 1980s began with more than 3,300 standardbred mares registered in New Jersey, making the Garden State a profitably productive breeding ground. Racers are bred largely in Monmouth County, and jumpers and hunters in Morris and Hunterdon counties.

With the opening of the sports complex and Meadowlands Racetrack in the fall of 1976, The Hambletonian has become the world's number one harness race, bringing together tradition, prestige and a piece of good, old-fashioned Americana. The prize money is nearly $1 million.

Harness racing's richest purse is the $2.2 million Woodrow Wilson Pace. All told, more than 40 million fans have passed through The Big M's turnstiles between opening day and mid-1985. Their bets totaled $5.2 billion.

The United States Equestrian Team also has its training center in New Jersey at Gladstone in Somerset County. For 10 years in a row, the Americans have won the international jumping championship at the National Horse Show, and captured the Gold Medal at the 1984 Olympics in Los Angeles.

Naturally, the horse is the official state animal of New Jersey, a recognition that came only a few years ago after public officials realized the growing popularity of horseback riding, fox hunts, county fairs and the increasing interest in the races at The Meadowlands, Monmouth Park, Freehold Raceway, Atlantic City Race Course and the new Garden State Park in Cherry Hill, which opened in 1985.

The New Jersey Agricultural Society is attempting to raise upward of $20 million to establish a State Horse Park on 142 acres of the Assunpink Preserve in Upper Freehold Township, Monmouth County. The first ring is expected to be ready for the first one-day show next year.

The horse park will feature four outdoor show rings, an indoor arena, stables for 800 horses and spectator capacity of more than 8,000. There are also plans for a polo field, show jumping course, steeplechase course, museum and trails.

During the 1970s, developers, speculators, manufacturers and veterinarians bought up old cattle, chicken and dairy farms or idle land and turned them into successful breeding farms, putting New Jersey right up there with Kentucky, California, New York and Pennsylvania as a major horse industry state.

Cowtown in Woodstown, South Jersey, is the oldest weekly display of cowboy skills and spills in the country. The continuous wild west rodeo first opened its white-washed chutes to bull riding and bucking broncs in 1955.

Other equestrian competitions are held at county fairs in Cumberland, Middlesex, Monmouth, Ocean, Sussex and Salem.

Hunterdon County has become an eastern base for American Saddlebred horses usually sired in Kentucky or California. The American Saddlebred is the peacock of the show ring because of its five distinctive gaits and high tail. A world champion, $175,000 stud at Blue Fields Farm in Pittstown sired numerous other champions, including two that were cited at the 1975 Kentucky State Fair.

Record prices have been paid for Jersey broodmares and handsome yearlings. The Garden State Standardbred Sales Co. attracts buyers from Argentina, Australia, Canada and Finland, ringing up sales of $5 million at its annual auction.

In a typical year, 11 winning stallions have been singled out in the gallery of the New Jersey Thoroughbred's directory. Recent winners have been Bananas Foster, Deer Isle, Jimmy Plains, Vis-A-Vis, Czar Alexander, Electrolytic, Marine Patrol, Pontifex, Command Force, Girl's and Regal Tudor.

Port-A-Ferry ridden by Joey Gillet clears one of the hurdles in the New Jersey Hunt Cup at the Essex Fox Hounds Meeting, Moorland Farms, Far Hills.

Star-Ledger Photo

Cowboy stars such as Roy Rogers and Gene Autry have given the palomino a special place in the hearts of western film fans. In 1975, the New Jersey Palomino Exhibitors Association was formed to become the 12th breed group recognized by the state Department of Agriculture.

Palominos are known as a "color breed" and they can be registered without the effort of tracking down a pedigree. The main criterion for acceptance in the national registry is simply an animal's color. Performance classes in palomino shows include western and English pleasure, trail, English road rack, reining, barrels and parade.

The elegant tradition of fox hunting thrives in New Jersey's rolling hills country. In the 1920s, the Spring Valley Hounds was founded by Seth Thomas of the clock manufacturing company. It was a time when New Vernon and its environs were largely farms and estates. Even with the loss of some farmlands during the past 50 years, the Spring Valley Hounds still covers about 10 miles of country.

Other hunts include Monmouth, located in the Middletown area; Essex, based in Far Hills, and Amwell Valley, in the western portion of the state.

The hunt is a social event as well as a sporting one, with its own etiquette and terminology. The early part of the season is devoted to cubbing, when the new foxhounds, or young entries, are indoctrinated in the chase. Hunt subscribers dress in informal tweed coats and brown boots for cubbing, a sharp contrast to opening day in mid-October when everyone turns out in beautifully tailored formal attire.

The scarlet cloth coats, or "hunting pinks"—designed by a London tailor whose name was Pink—are accessorized with black high hats, when worn by gentlemen members of the field, and polished black boots.

In many hunts, foxes have been spared, replaced by a line of fox scent laid across the hills and valleys for the hounds.

Although the number of family subscribers to each club varies, everyone who rides shares the excitement of this aristocratic sport.

Riding centers and riding stables are expanding as quickly as the horse population. In the core of one of the most densely developed regions is the Watchung Reservation riding stables in Union County. Hundreds of families and youngsters enjoy the miles of horse trails in the reservation overlooking Route 22, one of the busiest highways in the state.

Overpeck Farms in Leonia, Bergen County, is a suburban backyard haven for horses and riders. Established in the summer of 1974 by the Bergen County Park Commission, the 15-acre center, now privately owned, shelters 40 horses that are regularly worked out by some 300 riders a week. The 110-by-200-foot indoor arena is comparable in size to the one used for horse shows in Madison Square Garden.

Site of a former county garbage dump, Overpeck's arena is sprinkled with a clean, powdery material made of milled roofing granules, providing good footing and padding for those who occasionally fall from their horses. More youngsters than oldsters and more females than males frequent the Overpeck riding center.

Business executives and grandmothers, students and professionals have all discovered the joys of riding at the Suburban Essex Equestrian Center in West Orange. Sandwiched between the elegant Manor restaurant and a shopping mall on Woodland Avenue, it is an unlikely place to find white-collar workers stopping by on the way to the office for a wake-up ride around the 90-by-200-foot indoor arena.

At 9 a.m., riding lessons begin and continue into the night, until the last horse has been cooled out and rubbed down, the barn doors closing at 11 p.m.

On Wednesday evenings, the Brooklyn Riding Club performs drill routines to music in full parade dress. Friday nights the Hudson Riding Club, which accepts only Swiss-German males as members, rules the ring for an hour of disciplined horsemanship.

Students from Montclair State College, William Paterson College, Fairleigh Dickinson University and the Caldwell Adult School put the horses through their paces, walking, trotting and cantering around the ring, improving their skills for the next show.

Some weekends are show time as some of the 110 horses stabled at Suburban Essex gracefully complete a course of eight jumps up to four feet high. The philosophy of the equestrian school stresses sportsmanship and enjoyment of the horses rather than competitiveness. Many riders don't participate in group sports and tend to be individualistic.

Suburban Essex hosts about 20 shows a year and club riders travel to as many more each year.

Dogs

New Jersey author Albert Payson Terhune popularized the dog in his many books, whose themes related to his Sunnybank Farm in Pompton Lakes. Some of them are canine classics, such as "Lad, A Dog," "Lad of Sunnybank" and "A Book of Famous Dogs."

Terhune bred prize collies and turned out 25 books. His work left a lasting impression on the millions of youngsters and pet lovers who read them. His finest collies took blue ribbon awards at the Westminster Dog Show.

The Westminster Dog Show is America's premier canine competition. More than 2,600 entries compete in 137 classifications, from Affen Pinschers and Viszlas to whippets and Yorkshire terriers.

Each year, about a dozen entries from New Jersey win in one of the various categories of breeds. Recently, New York had the greatest number of entries at 621, followed by 372 canine entries from New Jersey, 184 from Pennsylvania, 178 from California and 72 from Connecticut, to round out the top five, numerically.

New Jersey produces many of the Westminster Dog Show champions, second only to New York in actual numbers. In a typical year, New Jersey may have as many as 14 champion dogs in the Westminster Show. Here's a sampling of some winners, by category, and the animals' names and residences:

• American Staffordshire, won by Champion Frasa's Thunder Battery, from Woodcliff Lake.

• American Water Spaniel, won by Champion Snippet Dark Waters, from Maywood.

• Australian terrier, won by Austwyn Optimum, from Little Silver.

• Beagle, won by Champion Brantwood's Desperado, from Manasquan.

• Belgian sheepdog, won by Champion Solarmarc's Christina, from Watchung.

• Briard, won by Champion Bellesprite Midnight Cowboy, from Titusville.

• Bulldog, won by Hugobulls, The Queen's Lady, from Marlton.

• Curly-coated retriever, won by Champion Hie on Mark Macling, from Bridgewater.

• Japanese Chin, won by Silva-Wyte Hapi Coat, from Denville.

• Soft-coated Wheaten terrier, won by Champion Greentree Man O'Waterford, from Vincentown.

• Standard poodle, won by Champion Longleat Alimor Raisin Cane, from Randolph.

• Tibetan terrier, won by Champion Koba Tackleton's Joshua, from Allenhurst.

• Whippet, won by Champion Jamal's Desert Digger, from Annandale.

• Wirehaired dachshund, won by Champion Solo's Christmas Knight, from Morristown.

The Kennel Club of Northern New Jersey Dog Show has 127 different breeds to judge each year at the Meadowlands Race Track. The number of entries averages 2,000. The show also features a number of exhibits relating to the care of pets and all kinds of novelties.

A special kind of dog is the "seeing eye." The nation's first seeing eye dog school was founded in 1929 in Morris Township. Each year, Seeing Eye, Inc. graduates about 225 blind people and specially trained German shepherds and Golden and Labrador retrievers. Last year, the school graduated some Boxers, which are assigned to those with allergies.

The puppies are raised in 4-H families by children from nine to 19 years of age. The dogs are bred at a scientific breeding station in Mendham.

There's a class of "superdogs," extremely smart and obedient pets that compete each year for the distinguished honor of being the top dog in America.

The 1982 winner of the Gaines United States Dog Obedience Classic was a Golden retriever from Sparta named Charo, owned by Diane Bauman.

Charo, under Bauman's flawless command, achieved the highest average in the prestigious event: 198.83 points out of a possible 200. That record was set in a two-day program involving 39 exercises under six different judges at the Dallas Convention Center.

Charo and Bauman won by a full point over their closest competitor, defeating 189 dogs from 30 states. And entrants in the annual Gaines Classic represent the country's best, having eliminated hundreds of contenders at the local and regional levels. A 193 point score average is required to enter a regional contest.

Charo is also the recipient of the Golden Retriever Club of America's 1981 working dog certificate and Dog World Magazine's 1980 Award of Canine Distinction for achieving the Utility Dog degree in her first three trials with scores of 197, 198, 198.

Bauman and her partner, Ruth Rosbach, operate the Heel 'N Toe Dog Obedience School in Sussex. They average 180 dogs a week and have several full-time instructors.

The oldest kind of relationship between an animal and a human—simply the comfort of having a pet—has evolved into a worldwide organization called Therapy Dogs International (TDI).

Founded by Elaine Smith, a registered nurse from Hillside, TDI has members spanning the United States, including Alaska, and Canada and New Zealand. The organization is growing as applications arrive daily to TDI headquarters at 1536 Morris Pl., Hillside.

TDI is based on the belief that pets can promote emotional health and happiness by reducing loneliness and depression. Smith has recruited dog owners who want to bring pleasure to patients in nursing facilities and to shut-ins elsewhere.

TDI has initiated legislation to permit service dogs to have the same privileges as guide and hearing dogs. Handicapped persons would be given the right to take their dogs on public transportation and into medical facilities.

A service dog is defined as one individually trained to a handicapped person's requirements, including such chores as pulling a wheelchair or retrieving dropped items.

There are hundreds of kennels, clubs and organizations in New Jersey, but the largest clubs are, alphabetically: Boardwalk Kennel Club in Atlantic City; Burlington County Kennel Club; Delaware Valley Kennel Club, serving the Camden area; Gloucester County Kennel Club; Hunterdon Hills Kennel Club; Monmouth County Kennel Club; New Brunswick Kennel Club; Newton Kennel Club; Palisades Kennel Club; Plainfield Kennel Club; Ramapo Kennel Club; Sand and Sea Kennel Club, Ocean County; Schooley's Mountain Kennel Club, Warren County; Somerset Hills Kennel Club; South Jersey Kennel Club, Cape May; Sussex Hills Kennel Club; Trenton Kennel Club; Twin Brooks Kennel Club, serving the Summit-Morris area, and the Union County Kennel Club.

Cats

Cats are enjoying a kind of pet renaissance, as evidenced by the Broadway musical "Cats," which opened in late 1982 to the largest advanced tickets sale in theater history.

At the center of all that cat attention is New Jersey, the cat capital of the U.S.A. The first Cat Fanciers Association was established in New Jersey in 1906, the nation's largest today with more than a half-million pedigreed cat registrants.

Based in Ocean Township, Monmouth County, the association held its first two shows in 1906 in Buffalo, N.Y. and Detroit, and conducted the first of its annual meetings in Madison Square Garden in 1907.

The first Stud Book and Register in the Cat Journal was published in 1909. Volume I of the Stud Book was published in book form that same year.

On Dec. 13, 1913, the Empire Cat Club, New York, was organized and has remained a member of the association through the years as the oldest club.

Club membership in the association today is approaching 700 in the United States, Canada and Japan.

The New Jersey organization has grown in all areas, promoting more than 260 shows each year in the U.S., Canada, Hawaii and Japan.

The association's central Jersey office started as a kitchen-table operation and expanded into a modern, computerized office that occupies more than 3,500 square feet.

The Garden State Cat Club, formed in 1930, is the oldest existing cat club in the state. The club is famous for being one of the first to sponsor major shows and more cats from the Garden State Club have gone on to win acclaim.

Richard Gebhardt of Denville, president of the Cat Fanciers Association for many years and currently president of the Empire Cat Club, was the first American to judge on the Continent and the first international all-breed judge. He is a cat consultant to numerous publications, among them National Geographic, Woman's Day, Cat Catalogue, Champion Cats of the World, The Encyclopedia of Cats and The Standard Guide to Cat Breeds.

Gebhardt, also a specialist in canines, has had several Best of Breed winners at the Westminster Show.

The popular cartoon character, Heathcliff, the cat devoid of any socially redeeming qualities, is the creation of George Gately, a resident of Upper Saddle River.

An estimated 150 million people read Heathcliff, which is rated among the top 10 comics in the United States. Heathcliff also appears in 900 papers every weekday, including 150 in Europe, Japan and South America.

Noted photographers Ted and Creszentia Allen of West Orange are known by cat fanciers around the world for their many fine pictorial books on felines.

The New Jersey member clubs of the Cat Fanciers Association are: The National Burmese Cat Club in Ringoes; the Pier Longhair Society in Bricktown; the International Somali Cat Club, Gillette; the Persian Bi-Color & Calico Society, Freehold; the Midlantic Persian-Himmie Fanciers, Englishtown; the Oriental SH International, Murray Hill; the Sign of the Cat Fanciers, Englishtown; the Metropolitan Cat Fanciers, East Orange; Penn-Jersey Cat Fanciers, Hopewell; Liberty Trail Cat Fanciers, Moorestown and Mt. Laurel Cat Fanciers, all in Mt. Laurel, and the I Love New York Cat Club in Cresskill.

Wildlife

The official state bird of New Jersey is the goldfinch, a hardy little species that adds color and music to woodlands and the tree-lined streets of suburbia.

The goldfinch is one of hundreds of species of birds that have been identified by ornithologists. Sparrows, swallows, warblers, wrens, robins, doves, crows and jays are the most common, but almost as plentiful are vireos, plovers, loons, larks, terns, owls, mallards, geese, gulls and ducks.

Other favorites among bird watchers are swans, grebes, pelicans, herons, scoters, hawks, ospreys, falcons, sandpipers, cuckoos, kinglets, thrushes, flycatchers, woodpeckers and grosbeaks.

Just at one state park, High Point in North Jersey, some 100 "common birds" are listed by the Department of Environmental Protection. They may be common to the veteran birdwatcher, but they are not that familiar to the average person.

Here's a sampling of High Point's "common" birds: Rufous-sided Towhee, Tufted Titmouse, Red-eyed Vireo, Indigo Bunting, Scarlet Tanager, Black-capped Chicadee, White-breasted Nuthatch, Sharp-shinned Hawk, Cedar Waxwing, Ruby-throated Hummingbird and Turkey Vulture.

At Allaire State Park in Monmouth County, naturalists have their choice of birds, mammals, amphibians, reptiles and fish. In mammals, there are longtail weasels and short-tailed shrews, little brown bats and whitetail deer, meadow voles and opossums, plus many others, all sharing space with humans and their motor vehicles and modern paraphernalia.

Among the amphibians are the pickerel frog, the eastern spotted newt, the spring peeper, the lead-backed salamander and fowlers toad.

The 11 reptilian species include the eastern hognose snake, the southern ringneck snake, the red-bellied terrapin, the northern banded watersnake and the bog turtle.

The 22 species of fish in Allaire include shiners and perch, trout and pickerel, brown bullheads, black crappies, carp, eel, herring and sunfish.

The Department of Environmental Protection has compiled a list of species that are either endangered, threatened or declining. An effort is being made to increase their numbers during the 1980s by setting aside places in the state's Wildlife Management Areas to assure their survival in New Jersey. The endangered species are classified accordingly:

- **Fish:** The shortnose sturgeon.

- **Amphibians:** Tremblay's salamander, the blue-spotted salamander, the eastern tiger salamander, the Pine Barrens treefrog and the southern gray treefrog.

- **Reptiles:** The bog turtle and the timber rattlesnake.

- **Birds:** The bald eagle, the peregrine falcon, the osprey, Cooper's hawk, the Least tern and the black skimmer.

- **Mammals:** The Indiana bat.

- **Marine reptiles:** The Atlantic hawksbill, the Atlantic loggerhead, the Atlantic ridley and the Atlantic leatherback.

- **Marine mammals:** (New Jersey's territorial waters extend three miles out to sea.) The sperm whale, the blue whale, the fin whale, the sei whale, the humpback whale and the Atlantic right whale.

Saw-whet owl with its prey.

Geese flocking to New Jersey's numerous waterways.

Star-Ledger Photo

Eastern cottontail rabbits are found in abundance in the Garden State.

Courtesy: N.J. Div. of Fish, Game & Wildlife

Eastern wild turkey flourish in New Jersey's 125,000 acres of game preserves.

Photo Credit: Nick Wheeler

The "first phase" building of Ramapo College
in Mahwah is the work of Mahoney & Zvosec architects.

ARCHITECTURE

$\mathcal{T}$heir materials are earth and stone, wood and brick, glass and concrete, plastics and space-age metals.

With all of that—and a trained eye and unbounded imagination—New Jersey's innovative architects manipulate mass and space, light and color, shaping forms and structuring reality to a scale and proportion that can only be visualized by the human mind.

Their works are everywhere to be seen: A giant white entertainment arena dominating the Hackensack Meadowlands ... a 16th Century Italianate corporate village blending serenely in the Peapack countryside ... a Romanesque redwood cathedral reaching for the stars by the Statue of Liberty ... a plush casino palace glittering by the Atlantic City Boardwalk ... a luxurious mansion hiding in the woodlands of Morris County ... a glass tower mirroring the Newark skyscape ... a massive storage center in Trenton with 32 miles of shelving space ... and every style of college, bank, barn, prison, restaurant, shopping mall, townhouse and conservation greenhouse.

Disciples of Frank Lloyd Wright and a new generation of

solar pioneers practice their multi-media craft in architectural havens in Princeton, Newark and the suburban parks of the Garden State. One Princeton architect is the nation's leading proponent of the post-Modernism movement.

These practitioners of architecture are no longer simply designers of buildings. Some of them are also painters, sculptors and stylists of furnishings and costumes. Their award-winning creations are displayed in museums and art galleries.

With their cruciforms and courtyards, alcoves and atria, piazzas and pitched skylights, they are redoing the cities and changing the suburban landscape for what they believe is a more enriching built environment: Man learning to live in harmony with nature.

Two prominent schools of architecture at Princeton University and the New Jersey Institute of Technology in Newark provide a creative laboratory for student visionaries who will be given the challenge of designing the communities and corporate headquarters of tomorrow.

With the third largest concentration of corporate headquarters in the United States, New Jersey is fertile ground for companies fleeing the onerous rents of New York City. Waiting for them to make the transition to a campus-like lifestyle is a cadre of gifted professionals who imaginatively shape the space we occupy.

Some of the leading architects and design organizations follow.

Michael Graves

Perhaps no other architect in America equals Michael Graves in his capacity for generating discussion and acclaim of his work. Since receiving his master's degree in architecture from Harvard in 1959 and winning the Prix de Rome in 1960, Graves has demonstrated a continuing design brilliance and innovation that ranks him among the world's foremost practitioners, according to the New Jersey Society of Architects.

A creator of the post-Modernism movement in America, Graves already has become a main source of inspiration for an entire generation of architectural students and has cultivated a cult following at Princeton University, where he is Schirmer Professor of Architecture. The young designers are known as "Graves Groupies."

Graves has earned enough awards and honors to fill a room in a mythical Architects' Hall of Fame. A few examples: Eleven Progressive Architecture design awards and four National Ameri-

can Institute of Architects "Honor Awards" for completed buildings. Add to that 19 New Jersey Society of Architects awards and "Designer of the Year" by Interiors magazine in 1980.

That same year, Graves was awarded the Arnold W. Brunner Memorial Prize in Architecture from the American Academy and Institute of Arts and Letters.

His work has been presented at the Museum of Modern Art in seven exhibitions and at numerous other museums and galleries in the U.S. and abroad, including the 1973 Triennale in Milan and the 1980 Biennale in Venice. His drawings, models and paintings are owned by several prominent museums and private collections and he is represented by the Max Protetch Gallery in New York.

Photo Credit: Proto Acme Photo

Princeton architect Michael Graves designed the Entrance Forecourt of the Environmental Education Center in Liberty State Park, Jersey City.

The Hillier Group in Princeton was honored for its Italianate structures for the Beneficial Corporation headquarters in Peapack-Gladstone.

Photo Credit: Norman McGrath

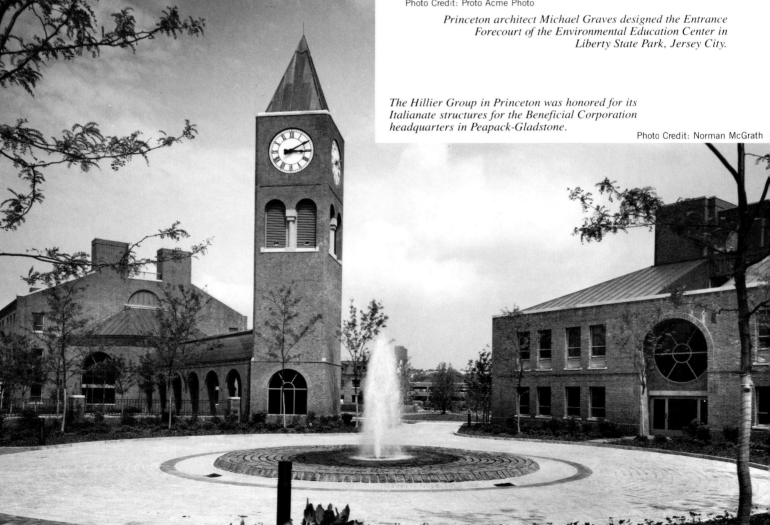

Graves is nothing if not versatile. His portfolio gives him the stature of a Renaissance artist: Painter, sculptor, furniture designer and even costume and set designer for the Joffrey Ballet. He has served as architect-in-residence at the American Academy in Rome, of which he is trustee and president of the Society of Fellows.

A fellow of the American Institute of Architects, Graves likes to emphasize the use of various colors and attempts to adapt and blend the styles of past eras. His most notable and recently completed edifice is the $22 million, 15-story Portland Public Office Building in Oregon, which caught the art world by surprise with its soft pastel hues.

Dedicated in 1983 is his redwood Environmental Education Center at Liberty State Park on the Jersey City waterfront. It resembles a Roman cathedral with a natural beauty that invites attention to Liberty State Park, which furnishes a breathtaking backdrop to the Statue of Liberty and Ellis Island, the historic immigration center. The park center was inspired by the Madonna de Villa in Italy.

Other Graves projects include the Humana Building in Louisville, the Matsuya-Ginza Department Store in Tokyo, a master plan and renovation of the Newark Museum, the San Juan Capistrano Public Library in California, the Cincinnati Symphony Amphitheatre and an addition to the Whitney Museum of American Art in New York City.

Graves' genius is on display in as simple a project as a living room and garden wall to the two-story Schulman residence in Princeton. Cited by the state society, the Schulman project involves three elements of composition linked serially by their progessively decreasing size.

On the garden side, a new center is made by a screened porch connecting the living room addition with a former garage now used for storage. The addition was polychromed to reflect its relation to the garden or landscape.

The Hillier Group

One of the East Coast's most energetic and productive architectural, planning and interior design firms, the Hillier Group in Princeton handles more than $120 million a year in construction design work ranging from New Hampshire to Florida and from Mexico to Vienna.

Listed among the nation's top design firms by both Engineering News-Record and Building Design and Construction, the Princeton group is headed by a design dynamo who in only 15 years turned a one-man, one-room office into an international organization employing a staff of 100, including 35 licensed professionals.

Along the way, J. Robert Hillier's firm accumulated more than 50 state and national awards for outstanding design and enjoys an annual 20 percent growth rate.

"Today's architect has to know about business, marketing and public relations," Hillier says. "The architect is taking on the role of initiator, developer and part-owner of projects because he is the one individual trained to run every phase of a project."

Hillier's clients are the biggest corporations in the world: AT&T, Allied, Exxon, Citicorp and General Foods. In New Jersey alone, Hillier has designed Ortho Pharmaceutical's headquarters, offices for Dow Jones, Applied Data Research, and Carteret Savings and Loan, plus many of the buildings on most New Jersey campuses: Princeton, Drew, Rutgers, Fairleigh Dickinson, Ramapo and Seton Hall.

The Hillier Group's most important work to date is the magnificent Beneficial Management Corp. headquarters in Peapack-Gladstone, Somerset County. The award-winning complex of low-rise, all-brick buildings was fashioned in the Italian Palladian style of the 16th Century and was designed to both humanize the workplace and harmonize with the surrounding rural environment.

The unique corporate village houses some 1,200 employes in a variety of structures tied together by paved and landscaped courts and linked by open and closed arcades. Situated on 30 acres of an 850-acre tract and containing 550,000 square feet of office space, the Italianate village comes complete with an 88-foot campanile (bell tower), atria, courtyards, formal gardens, cobblestone piazzas, alcoves, circular windows and other design nuances.

Underground parking areas, as well as the buildings themselves, are connected below grade by skylit, brick-lined tunnels.

The centerpiece of this elegant tribute to intelligent corporate planning is an octagonal executive edifice with glass dome, marble balconies, brass fittings and a two-story Georgian chandelier.

Among the many awards already bestowed on Hillier and Beneficial are two from the New Jersey Society of Architects, a New Good Neighbor Award from the New Jersey Business and Industry Association and a Land Development Award from the Somerset County Planning Board.

Hillier has also received two national Homes for Better Living Awards.

In association with the Grad Partnership in Newark, Hillier also designed the impressive Richard J. Hughes Justice Complex in Trenton.

The Grad Partnership

In its 77th year, the Grad Partnership is one of New Jersey's most productive architectural firms. The oldest in the state, Grad was started by senior partners Bernard and Howard Grad and today has six partners and a staff of 90 working on some $250 million worth of construction projects a year.

Grad's clients include Prudential, the world's largest insurance company; Nabisco Brands; New Jersey Bell Telephone, and Howard Savings Bank. The Grad has earned 21 consecutive New Good Neighbor Awards from New Jersey Business magazine, published by the New Jersey Business and Industry Association.

Grad projects such as the Meadowlands Arena, the Essex Community College and the justice complex (with Hillier) became immediate landmarks upon their completion.

A pioneer in computer-aided drafting, Grad's success in housing both machines and people in highly functional yet humane workplaces is well displayed in the design of two computer data centers: New Jersey Bell's complex in Freehold Township and the updating of IBM's facility in Franklin Lakes.

Grad's efforts to humanize the prison environment are evident at Trenton State Prison (with the Gruzen Partnership), the Middlesex County Correctional Facility and the Ocean County Courthouse and Jail at Toms River.

Bernard Grad's book, "Adventure into Architecture," defines the role of the architect in modern society. A fellow of the American Institute of Architects, Bernard Grad chaired the Governor's Committee that led to the establishment of the New Jersey School of Architecture at the Institute of Technology in Newark. Peter Pran, Grad's director of design whose projects and drawings have been internationally honored, is on the faculty of NJIT.

The 21,000-seat Meadowlands Arena serves as a total entertainment facility for the New Jersey Sports and Exposition Authority. Designed for versatility, it can be utilized for rock concerts, hockey and basketball games, indoor soccer, boxing matches and for exhibitions and conventions.

The award-winning Howard Savings Bank Operations Center in Livingston steps down with the contours of the land, thus preserving the multi-acre woodlands. The open, airy appearance of the concrete and glass structure is a design response to the Howard Bank's desire to present an attractive "front porch" to the community.

Another Grad masterpiece is the Bergen Community College,

The Meadowlands Arena in East Rutherford is one example of the versatile structures produced by the Grad Partnership.

Another Grad design, the Howard Savings Bank Operations Center in Livingston, opens a "front porch" to the community.

a commuter school sited on a 167-acre former golf course in Paramus. Grad designed a continuous megastructure in order to conserve green acres as well as create a compact campus that encourages student and faculty interaction.

The college is broken down into separately defined units linked by a system of covered walks that serve as "student streets." The campus was designed for an initial enrollment of 2,000 full-time and 4,000 part-time students. Yet the flexible module layout can easily accommodate as many as 5,000 full-time and 10,000 part-time students as enrollment increases.

Park 80 Plaza West II is a landmark office tower at the intersection of Route 80 and the Garden State Parkway. The energy-efficient, 10-story building forms the centerpiece of a pivotal office park. Its dark gray glass walls and terra cotta color bands at the sixth floor are instantly identifiable to Parkway and Route 80 motorists.

Rothe Johnson Associates

Diversity, attention to detail and follow-through are the hallmarks of a Middlesex County company which in eight years has blossomed into the third largest architectural planning firm in New Jersey.

With its founding partners, Edward N. Rothe and Allan R. Johnson, four associates and a staff of 20, Rothe Johnson has generated more than $300 million in construction projects throughout New Jersey and has undertaken work in other states from Connecticut to Florida.

Named Architects of the Year in 1980 by the New Jersey Subcontractors Association for their quality and quantity of work, Rothe Johnson's more notable design achievements also rank among New Jersey's most significant structures.

The award-winning Norman Bleshman State Regional Day School for the Handicapped in Paramus is the only school of its kind in the Garden State. Architects spent time in wheelchairs to experience the obstacles confronted by the handicapped.

What emerged from those real encounters was a compact, 45,000-square-foot structure that earned a New Jersey Society of Architects design award in 1981.

Shaped in a series of four cruciforms, or Xs, the building is easily accessible by a single wide corridor running the length of the complex. Interior and exterior walls are painted in "happy ice cream colors," with numerous skylight-type windows so students in wheelchairs can peer up and see the treetops, sky and clouds.

Star-Ledger Photo

The Norman A. Bleshman School for the Handicapped in Paramus, designed by Rothe Johnson Associates.

The huge Bell Laboratories office-research center in Middletown received the society's highest design award in 1982, "Excellence in Architecture." The 350,000-square-foot facility wraps four, three-story office-research quadrants around two spacious atria. A monumental, grand entry archway frames a sculptural vestibule.

Inside, a cantilevered stairway provides the focal point for two skylit, landscaped atriums, three stories high. Each atrium serves as a meeting place and village green for employes.

The Brookwood Associates Corporate Plaza I in Piscataway is clad in gleaming white, insulated aluminum panels with dark black insulated windows. The 65,000-square-foot, two-story steel frame structure presents a sleek, linear image visible from Route 287.

The main entrance plaza is brick-paved, featuring an exterior balcony and accented by a semi-enclosed courtyard. Inside, a spacious two-story lobby feels like the outdoors with its double-height glazing and courtyard greenery. An all-electric, closed-loop heat pump reduces energy costs and can be adapted for solar heating at any time.

The Gruzen Partnership

Since its inception in Jersey City nearly a half-century ago, the Gruzen Partnership has maintained a long-standing commitment to socially significant issues. Gruzen has won both national and state awards in just about every project area, including residential design and planning, geriatric facilities, hospitals and medical, correctional and judicial facilities, hotels, commercial buildings and housing for the elderly.

With headquarters at Gateway One in Newark, Gruzen also maintains offices in New York and San Francisco.

When Barnett (Barney) Gruzen and Col. Hugh A. Kelly (retired from the Army Corps of Engineers) first joined forces in 1936, it was with a common interest: To provide new public housing for Jersey City and, ultimately, the rest of the state.

Government funding, however, was delayed by the Depression and Gruzen and Kelly designed a White Tower in Paterson, the Kislak Building in Jersey City and a Grand Union supermarket in Paterson (still in use today), as well as the food chain's headquarters. They were also asked to design the first shopping cart as part of the Grand Union assignment.

By 1938, the Federal Housing Act finally opened the way for public housing and Kelly & Gruzen responded with low-cost housing projects in Paterson, Passaic, Harrison and Clark. They were among the first of their kind in the nation and many are still in good use.

Prosperity brought the first four Gruzen-designed luxury residential buildings to Bergen County for the Tishman Co. in 1962. The Horizon Houses rose above the Hudson River in Fort Lee, marking the first silhouettes on the Palisades skyline. Honored by the American Institute of Architects, the Horizon Houses were later joined by two more Gruzen high-rises, Galaxy and Greenhouse.

When Barney's son, Jordan, joined the firm after graduating from the Massachusetts Institute of Technology, the Gruzen firm developed a reputation for state-of-the-art work in prison design. Leesburg was the first of three major prisons done by Gruzen for the State of New Jersey.

Other Gruzen projects include Luther Park, a cooperative housing complex for the elderly in Teaneck, and expansions at Hackensack and Middlesex hospitals and Beth Israel Medical Center in Newark.

Geddes Brecher Qualls Cunningham

This Princeton firm has had an extraordinary impact on architecture—both design and practice—in America, according to the Society of Architects.

Robert Geddes was dean of Princeton University's School of Architecture for 17 years, and many other members of the Geddes firm teach design and design theory at the university level.

The Princeton partnership has been written about or published in nearly every design publication. In 1979, the highest honor bestowed in the profession—the American Institute of Architects "Firm Award"—was presented to GBQC. The award is given to "a firm which has constantly produced distinguished architecture for a period of at least 10 years."

One of the first architectural practices to computerize operations and project data, GBQC was the 1982 winner of the Professional Services Management Association's National Achievement Award.

GBQC's master plan for Liberty State Park on the Jersey City waterfront has been the subject of shows at the Museum of Modern Art and the New Jersey State Museum in Trenton. Combining architectural form, social content and concern for the environment, the Liberty Park 20-year plan (1975-95) aims to transform 600 acres of rotting landfill and derelict piers and shacks into a public urban landscape for a multitude of recreational activities and wildlife.

Two prize-winning projects are Stockton State College in South Jersey and the office and classroom building at Rutgers University, Newark campus.

The Stockton master plan began in 1969 and evolved into eight flexible loft structures that can be used for interchangeable classrooms, seminars, offices or laboratories. Specialized buildings include a theater, library, auditorium, gymnasium, laboratory, swimming pool and a tile-clad student center containing a 400-seat dining hall, a Rathskeller, lounges and game rooms for active and passive recreation.

The Stockton buildings are linked by a two-level spine (interior street) that runs in a linear configuration along the eastern shore of a lake. The campus is in the heart of the Pinelands.

The Rutgers office/classroom building is one of the earliest

The Stockton State College Student Center in Pomona, designed by Geddes Brecher Qualls Cunningham of Princeton. Star-Ledger Photo

and best examples of a "mixed-use" academic facility, having been completed in 1970. Glass-walled, double-height pedestrian galleries and ramps are lively links to classrooms, seminar rooms, student and public "people spaces," and offices. Natural light fills the center of the complex as it steps down a sloping site; each classroom or laboratory has either skylights or outside windows.

Other recent commissions include the State Commerce Building in Trenton, academic offices and dining commons for the Institute for Advanced Study in Princeton (where Albert Einstein worked the last 25 years of his life), two laboratories for Mobil in Hopewell, and a student center for Rutgers.

Geddes Brecher Qualls Cunningham also has offices in Philadelphia.

Eleanore Pettersen

A former apprentice of the eminent Frank Lloyd Wright, Eleanore Pettersen is a precedent-setter who works out of a converted horse barn in Saddle River that doubles as home and office.

Pettersen was the first woman architect ever licensed to practice in New Jersey. She became the first woman president of the 1,000-member New Jersey Society of Architects in 1985.

Directing a staff of eight with some $50 million in construction projects under way, Pettersen, a specialist in residential design, has a long list of impressive credits, from churches, nursing homes and restaurants, to office buildings, resorts and an elegant home in Saddle River presently occupied by Mr. and Mrs. Richard M. Nixon.

After graduating from Cooper Union, the only tuition-free technical school in the nation, Pettersen was one of 50 apprentices selected by Frank Lloyd Wright to live and work at his famous Talisen commune, a 200-acre creative colony in Spring Green, Wis. She later moved on to Knoxville, Tenn., serving as a design architect on the nation's largest power system, the Tennessee Valley Authority.

Pettersen, licensed to practice in seven states, has worked extensively in college planning and was design architect for Sufari Village, a $38 million resort in Ricon, Puerto Rico.

Anticipating the trend toward cluster housing and townhouses because of land limitations, Pettersen put together a 360-unit luxury townhouse development in northern Bergen County.

Pettersen sums up her career this way: "With a lumberman for a father, a painter for a mother, a direction set by Cooper Union and, most importantly, my mentor and inspiration, Frank Lloyd Wright, what could I have been other than an architect who stayed the course?"

CUH2A

When Philip S. Collins won the statewide competition for the New Jersey Pavilion at the New York World's Fair in 1962, an organization with an unmistakable Orwellian code name of CUH2A evolved into the state's largest organization of architects and engineers. CUH2A, based in Princeton, consists of nine partners, eight associates and a staff of 175 in the fields of architecture, engineering, interior design and graphics.

No, CUH2A is not a computer code. It stands for the original principals: Collins, Uhl, Hoisington, Anderson and Azmy (the latter being the 2A).

CUH2A's geographic range extends to the Northeast, Midwest and Sun Belt states. The firm also maintains offices in Egypt and Saudi Arabia.

It has prospered since New Jersey became the setting for corporate headquarters during the past 25 years. A leader in providing corporate headquarters, laboratories, computer complexes and manufacturing and distribution centers, CUH2A serves the giants of American industry: AT&T, IBM, RCA, GAF, Exxon, Mobil, Johnson & Johnson, Pfizer, Squibb, Lockheed, Ingersoll-Rand, Nabisco, American Home Products and American Cyanamid.

Some of CUH2A's ongoing projects are the long-term care facility for the New Jersey Community Corp. in Newark, a laboratory addition to the Waksman Institute of Microbiology at Rutgers University in New Brunswick, and a 448-bed medium security prison in Leesburg.

CUH2A deals with complex technical and environmental problems, which run the gamut from a laboratory layout conducive to interaction among scientists, to a development plan for the Delaware and Raritan Canal State Park.

Recipient of several national awards, CUH2A has been honored for its design (in association with Caudill Rowlett Scott) of the Trenton State College Community Center in Ewing Township. With its comprehensive engineering services (civil, structural, mechanical and electrical), CUH2A delivers state-of-the-art solutions to critical issues in such technological areas as pharmaceutical and chemical research and information processing.

An airy, sunlit space in the Trenton State College Community Center, a creation of CUH2A.

UNIPLAN

For more than 30 years, Princeton architect and urban designer Jules Gregory has championed the cause of cities as an appropriate focus for architects and their profession.

Gregory's extensive involvement in urban planning activities has earned him the American Institute of Architects' two highest honors: The Edward C. Kemper Award for "significant contributions" to the profession of architecture, and elevation to the prestigious College of Fellows.

A widely published author, Gregory has taught and lectured on urban design at Princeton, Yale and Columbia universities and Pratt Institute. He has been a tireless promoter of the concept that the architect's responsibility goes beyond the design of fine buildings to include a leadership role in enhancing the quality of life in America's cities.

A national director and vice president of the American Institute of Architects, Gregory was organizer and chairman of the phenomenally successful Regional/Urban Design Assistance Team (R/UDAT) program. Initiated to achieve new design approaches, the program enables a community with problems to petition its local AIA chapter to bring in a voluntary R/UDAT. Since 1967, more than 80 communities throughout the United States have benefited from the program.

Gregory won the Museum of Modern Arts' "New Talent" competition for his design of a war memorial after graduating from the Cornell University School of Architecture. He subse-quently studied at Ecole des Beaux-Arts in Paris under a Fulbright grant.

Gregory is a principal in UNIPLAN, an association of architects, engineers and planners founded in Princeton in 1969 by the merging of three firms. UNIPLAN has prepared master plans for more than 50 municipal agencies in New Jersey, as well as municipalities in other eastern states.

For its work as part of a team that prepared a three-pronged downtown renewal project for York, Pa., UNIPLAN received a Certificate of National Merit from the U.S. Housing and Urban Development Department (HUD).

One of UNIPLAN's most significant buildings in New Jersey is the William S. Hart Sr. Middle School in East Orange, which received an award from the American Association of School Administrators in 1974. The school serves both the community and 1,800 pupils in grades six through eight.

The roof is a community park reached by public ramps for access when the school is closed. The school roof is a 14-inch-thick composition of insulation and concrete.

Short and Ford Architects

Adapting older buildings for modern use—particularly in the renovation and preservation of historic structures—is the forte of Short and Ford Architects in Princeton. In fact, founding partner William H. Short was elevated to the American Institute of Architects' College of Fellows in 1982 on the basis of his "... significant contributions to historic preservation."

Seven national design awards have been given to Short and Ford for their renovation work for such clients as New Jersey Bell, EMR Photoelectric and municipal governments throughout the state.

The 20-member firm also has designed the headquarters buildings for "Peterson's Guides" (college guidebook publishers), the Nassau Savings and Loan Association and the Wren Associates, a multi-media, audio-visual company, all in Princeton.

Prior to their becoming partners in 1974, Jerry Ford served as a designer on the World Trade Center for the Port Authority of New York and New Jersey, while Short began his career under Frank Lloyd Wright as the supervisor of construction for the Solomon R. Guggenheim Museum in Manhattan.

Short gained national recognition for his design of a condominium conversion for Guernsey Hall, a 40-room Italianate mansion in Princeton. Completed in 1974, the project has become a prototype for the innovative resolution of zoning, economic and preservation issues. It received three design awards.

Harrison Fraker, Architects

Energy involvement could well be the theme of this active Princeton firm, which has gained national prominence for its passive or "natural" solar building designs.

Since its first major commission in 1974 (recognized by an Owens Corning Energy Conservation Award), Harrison S. Fraker Jr., Stanley J. Aronson and Martin M. Bloomenthal have amply demonstrated the appropriate use of solar heating and other alternative energy techniques.

In promoting a conservation ethic, the Fraker family of architects has created an affiliate—Princeton Energy Group (PEG)—which has developed and published numerous sophisticated, solar-oriented computer programs and software for design use in calculators and microcomputers. PEG's purpose is to foster cooperative research on issues involving energy and the built environment, bridging the gap between design research and its timely and appropriate application.

The Princeton Professional Park earned the Passive Solar Design Award for "excellence in the integration of architectural design and passive solar technology in the commercial category" at the fifth National Passive Solar Conference in 1980.

The firm also has won many HUD and U.S. Department of Energy awards.

Described as a "pioneer of the energy conscious design movement in this country" by the AIA, Fraker is a graduate of the Princeton School of Architecture and was an assistant professor at the school for a decade.

Kelbaugh & Lee Architects

After receiving a master's in architecture from Princeton, Doug Kelbaugh founded his environment partnership with Sang Lee (MA, University of Pennsylvania) in 1979.

Kelbaugh was first recognized for having designed one of the first passive solar homes in the United States as his private residence in Princeton. In 1973, the Kelbaugh House was the first in America to utilize a Trombe wall, a mass of concrete for heating or cooling space. The most publicized of all solar houses during the 1970s, the Kelbaugh House has become an architectural solar landmark. The solar house has typically cost less than $100 a year to heat during the cold northeast winters.

HUD granted Kelbaugh and Lee four awards in its 1978 Passive Solar Design Competition, more than any other firm in the country. Their Milford Solar Conservation Center won the New Jersey Society of Architects' highest award in 1981, as well as the 1979 Owens-Corning Conservation Award.

One of their most cherished awards was the 1982 Monroeville, Pa. Civic Center Competition, which had more than 250 entrants nationwide. Their winning design was given the highest award by the Pennsylvania Society of Architects.

Kelbaugh & Lee provide their clients with a diverse range of architectural services, including design, planning, graphics and energy research.

Significant Projects

Ramapo College of New Jersey was one of the first projects to utilize successfully a mirror glass exterior skin. Seven buildings were erected, beginning in 1970, bringing honors to Mahony & Zvosec Architects and Planners of Princeton, and Sasaki Associates of Watertown, Mass.

The college library, completed in 1977, was cited by the Boston Society of Architects, while the New Jersey Society of Architects had this to say about the original campus creation in the Ramapo Mountains of North Jersey:

"This project . . . with its pristine, straightforward, L-shaped structure and mirror glass skin produces a highly successful interplay of transparency against opaqueness. This is a new kind of architecture (1970) which many are experimenting with, but few are able to achieve so successfully."

A more recent award-winning effort by Mahony & Zvosec is its design for the **New Jersey Records Storage Center** and **Library for the Blind & Handicapped** in Trenton. Two functions, a library for the blind and handicapped and a records storage center coexist within 105,000 square feet of space designed to accommodate their separate specialized needs.

Many visually impaired persons are able to experience the effects of natural light and sculpture, or the touch and sound of water, in open courts for outdoor reading activities. Included in the 67,000-square-foot records center is a unique three-tier, three-bay area with 32 miles of shelving space, as well as separate vaults for the storage of microfilm and computer tapes.

Union Gap Village in Clinton is a 438-unit condominium project on 45 rolling acres of pastoral farmland, zoned for a density of 10 multifamily dwellings per acre on property with slopes from five to 10 degrees. Cahill/Prato/McAneny won state honors for preserving the natural integrity of the site by establishing road patterns and fixing building locations compatible with the horizontal contours and vertical slopes.

The one- and two-bedroom condo buildings step vertically and horizontally and blend in with the contours of the site and tree heights. A pedestrian path system meanders past tennis courts and recreation areas, leading to a nine-acre park that terminates at a clubhouse and swimming pool overlooking a retention pond.

Haddonfield Mews was designed by Moorestown architect Herman Hassinger to reflect the growing environmental concerns of preserving existing trees and other natural resources. Some 40 townhouses are situated on a tight two-and-a-half-acre site with a commanding view of Cooper Creek and a county park. Entrance to a row of the townhouses is via a bridge walk over a drainage swale that fills with water during rains and prevents flooding in the area.

The 1976 Bell Systems Award went to Millburn architect James Goldstein for a **National Prototype Facility** in Wayne, Passaic County, housing labor intensive, round-the-clock service operations. The design was created to combat the company's high turnover rate among directory assistance and toll service operators.

The finished product strives to counteract job monotony among employes by combining space for high-technology equipment systems with an unusually colorful and comfortable employe lounge, dining, conference and restroom areas. Reflecting glass is used on exterior walls to mirror the trees and shrubbery during the changing seasons.

A unique example of a New Jersey beach home is the **Diaddorio Thin House** in Ocean City, designed by Radey Associates of Cherry Hill. Radey had to design an attractive summer home on a 20-foot-wide by 100-foot-deep lot on a sandy beachfront.

The zoning required four-foot-wide sideyard setbacks, a 14-foot rearyard setback, a minimum of two parking spaces and an average height of 27 feet above street level with a two-and-a-half story maximum.

The result: A 12-foot-wide, three-bedroom, one-and-a-half bath summer/winter vacation home taking advantage of such setback exceptions as balconies, patios, roof overhangs, chimneys, window boxes, and open stairs and landings to maximize available space and further articulate the facade. Construction is wood frame on pilings with cedar siding.

A stunning, up-to-date version of the Jersey Shore mainstay is the **Glatt Residence** on Long Beach Island, designed by Pleasantville architect Gym Wilson. A large deck off the living room offers 180-degree views and contains a hot tub. The greater part of the top floor is a stepped-back sunbathing bleacher that moves up a full story to a roof deck.

The house contains 2,800 square feet of deck space, compared to 2,200 square feet of interior space. Inside, a loft overlooks the living room. Bedroom and lounge space were designed as sanctuaries away from the festivities, each with undisturbed views of the ocean or bay. Outside, west and north elevations serve as foils to ensure privacy.

The award-winning **Art Gallery Home** designed by Holt & Morgan for a Central Jersey client was organized to provide maximum utilization of wall surface for arrangement and display of a constantly changing art collection and photographic works.

Set in a densely wooded, two-acre lot, the sculptured, multi-level home arranges living areas around a central circulation spine, the west wall serving as a major display area.

The main entrance is from the south at the lower end of the spine, from which visitors proceed through a variety of spatial effects complementing the changing artwork and heightened by a combination of indirect natural and artificial lighting.

Award-winning designs are not limited to huge corporate headquarters, public institutions or majestic homes. Sometimes a

Star-Ledger Photo

Architect Gym Wilson of Pleasantville designed the Glatt residence on Long Beach Island.

simple but well-devised expansion or renovation has a highly beneficial impact on the function of a building and the surrounding neighborhood.

Such is the case of the **Addition to Straley's**, a commercial art supplies store in Livingston. The challenge was to take a rather cluttered old house and add a gallery for display and sale of large paintings and sculptures, reorganize the store and create a positive identification from the street.

A gallery was added to the front of the house after removing an enclosed porch. By removing a front wall, the retail store became a mezzanine or balcony overlooking the gallery. The basement was converted into a framing workshop connected to a small framing department in the gallery. An entry sculpture ccurt brought the building closer to the street and lighting in the court after dark lures passersby.

The Aybar Residence in Ridgefield is architect Romeo Aybar's prize-winning home situated on a mid-sized, triangular-shaped lot that abuts an abandoned street.

Aybar preserved the site's naturally wooded and rocky terrain by "pinning" the concrete foundation to existing rock and eliminating the need to blast. The home's functional open design creates illusions of spaciousness. Generous window placements link the interior and exterior environments.

Star-Ledger Photo

The addition to Straley's art shop in Livingston was given an open look by architects Blender/Feitlowitz, also of Livingston.

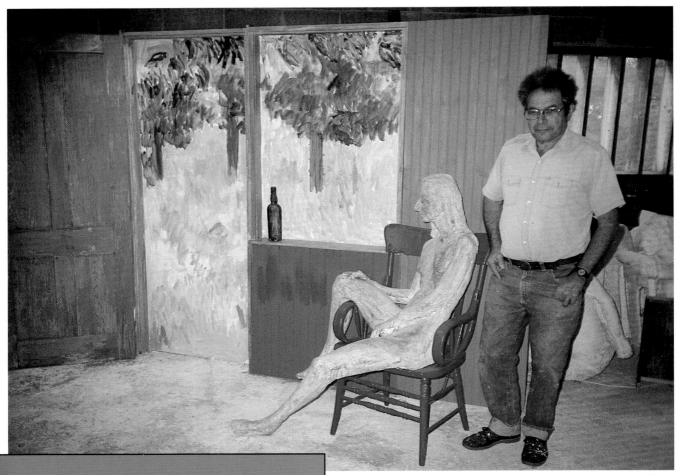

George Segal with one of his famous "plaster people."

ARTS

*M*ore than 30,000 artists make New Jersey their creative studio-home, turning out every conceivable form and image, from tapestries, paintings and woodcuts, to sculptures, stained glass and architectural monuments.

Their diverse works are exhibited night and day at hundreds of art centers, museums, libraries, galleries, bookstores, restaurants, schools and corporate showrooms throughout the state.

They are represented by scores of cultural, academic and professional organizations that have made the Garden State one of the most dynamic art colonies in the United States.

Their range of interests is as unlimited as their collective imagination, and is reflected in their special names: Audubon Artists, Leonardo DaVinci Society, Portrait Society, Printmaking Council, Sculptors Association, Watercolor Society, American Abstract Artists, Society of Arts and Letters, Porcelain Art, Museum of Creative Graphics, Ceramic League, Arts for Fun, Miniature Arts Society, Modern Artists, People for Prisoners Art, Artists for Environment, Business Arts and Teen Arts Festival.

Meanwhile, art colonies are flourishing in Hoboken, Jersey City, Newark, Paterson, Princeton and in Bergen and Hunterdon counties, as emigres from Greenwich Village and the SoHo District in the East, to San Francisco and LaJolla on the West Coast, spark an urban renaissance in America's oldest cities along the historic Hudson, Hackensack, Passaic and Raritan rivers.

The proliferation of artists and outlets for their prodigious expressions is being encouraged by the New Jersey State Council on the Arts and the Federated Art Associations of New Jersey. The two leading umbrella groups share the artist's vision of working in an unfettered atmosphere in which society can interact with the artist, each benefiting from the other.

Artists

There are the human resources, the artists themselves, and the physical resources, their creations and places to view them. Of the hundreds of notable artists in New Jersey, a few have distinguished themselves as innovators in a field where original ideas are almost daily occurrences and are the ultimate measure of any artist.

Among the more celebrated, contemporary New Jersey artists are: George Segal, a figurative sculptor living in South Brunswick; Richard Anuszkiewicz of Englewood, a major "Op" artist; Michael Graves, a Princeton architect; George Tice, an Iselin photographer; Jacob Landau, a painter-printmaker, and

Gregorio Prestopino, a painter, both working in Roosevelt; Clarence Holbrook Carter of Milford, and Leo Dee of Maplewood, both painters, and watercolorist Donald Voorhees of Atlantic Highlands.

• Tony Smith, an abstract sculptor from South Orange, died in 1980, leaving a legacy of monochromatic, Minimalist structures executed on a monumental scale.

Born in South Orange in 1912, Anthony Peter Smith was the oldest son of a manufacturer of waterworks supplies. Bedridden with tuberculosis as a child, Smith spent years in a small prefabricated house on the family property, isolated from his five brothers and one sister.

His earliest attempts to deal artistically with his sheltered reality were converting the small boxes his medicines came in to little "Pueblo Villages."

After studies at Georgetown University and the Art Students League in New York, he landed a job with Frank Lloyd Wright, helping the famous architect design low-cost housing during the Depression. Although he tried his hand at painting, he earned his way as an architect until accepting a teaching post at New York City's Hunter College.

In 1960, Smith started making cardboard maquettes on sculptural projects. He fabricated his first metal sculpture, "The Black Box," in 1962. He turned the back yard of his South Orange home into an informal outdoor sculpture display, slowly refining his highly simplified forms.

By 1964, the curator of the Wadsworth Atheneum show described Smith as "one of the best-known unknowns in American art." He was 52 years old.

The Whitney Museum of American Art has installed a large Smith piece called "One, Two, Three," made up of three related elements. The San Francisco Museum of Modern Art features a 1978 Smith original entitled "Throwback," a version of which is displayed at the New York headquarters of International Paper Co.

Smith's sculptures, modular geometric units packed into tetrahedonal and octahedonal forms, can be found in the collections of Princeton and Rutgers universities, Kean College, the New Jersey State Museum, the Newark Museum and the Museum of Modern Art in New York City.

In the 1970 Los Angeles Expo, Smith was the only artist given an entire plaza level gallery to exhibit a freestanding entity consisting of 3,000 tetrahedra and 1,500 octahedra that required more than 3,000 pounds of cardboard and 150 gallons of glue.

Smith saw his sculptures as presences "isolated in their own environment . . . interruptions in an otherwise unbroken flow of space. If you think of space as solid, they are voids in that space."

• Less abstract and smaller in scale are the creations of George Segal, a post-graduate product of Rutgers University (Master's in Fine Arts, 1963). Segal was described by New York Magazine art critic Kay Larson as "our poet of urban isolation, the man who brought us plaster Pop."

Over the years, however, Segal, who first laid plaster-soaked gauze over live models in 1958, has moved toward Pop traditionalism with what critics call "exotic and marvelous 'Cezanne Still Lifes.'" Others regard Segal as coming close to being an "institution," as his plaster and bronze sculptures are recognizable "landmarks."

Segal's plaster people are intentionally lumpy, crude and ugly, yet, compared with Pop artists Lichtenstein and Rosenquist, his figures retain a certain classical quality, according to Larson. From Surrealism to Cezanne, the plaster look is pure Segal.

Segal was the first artist to launch TIME magazine's "Machine of the Year" cover selection for 1983. It was the first time the magazine did not select a "Man of the Year" for its annual cover the first week in January.

The TIME cover shows a Segal plaster man sitting in a yel-

Courtesy: The Port Authority of N.Y. & N.J.

Sculptor George Segal of South Brunswick waits with "The Commuters," a work he conceived for the Port Authority bus terminal in New York.

low chair staring at a blue-screen video display terminal on a red table. The other half of the pull-out cover shows an equally bland Segal plaster woman lounging in a white wicker chair, white coffee cup in right hand, a video terminal on a blue table next to her.

In choosing Segal as the artist to break the highly recognized TIME tradition, the magazine's publisher, John A. Meyers, wrote: "In search of a memorable depiction of the irresistible invasion of computers into American homes, Art Director Rudy Hoglund approached George Segal, the world-famous sculptor. Segal almost never accepts commercial commissions, but Hoglund thought Segal's 'stark and dramatic settings, in which the eye is drawn to objects,' were perfectly suited to the first Machine of the Year."

Segal's one-man shows have become regular attractions throughout New Jersey. Segal's plaster creations people the exhibition halls of Princeton and Rutgers universities, Douglass College, the New Jersey State Museum and Newark Museum. They have also frequented museums in Switzerland; Rotterdam; Germany; Paris; Brazil, and Belgium, as well as New York's Whitney Museum, the Art Institute of Chicago, the Institute of Contemporary Art at the University of Pennsylvania, the Albright-Knox Art Gallery in Buffalo, N.Y., and the Fogg Art Museum in Cambridge, Mass.

Among the Segal collectors are the Museum of Modern Art, the Guggenheim Museum, the National Collection of Fine Arts in Washington, D.C., and the National Gallery of Canada.

• While Segal is a world famous artist, Michael Graves of Princeton has become an equally recognized designer of buildings.

Michael Graves of Princeton has received international acclaim for his architectural work.

Clarence Holbrook Carter of Milford, standing by his "Eschatos No. 10," has been described as a "homegrown transcendentalist."

Graves is considered by the New Jersey State Council on the Arts as a major influence in American architecture, a view held by those who rank Graves among the best 10 to 15 architects in the country.

Teaching at Princeton University since 1962, Graves has become something of a cult figure there, according to critic Paul Goldberger.

Graves emerged as a national figure in the early 1970s as one of the "Five Architects," a group whose highly theoretical, white buildings explored notions of abstract form. From the drawing board to the building lot, Graves is changing the way people look and think about four walls and a roof.

Progressive Architecture magazine, for example, awarded Graves not one but three prizes in its annual competition in 1980 for modernistic homes he designed and were built in Green Brook, Warren and at the Jersey Shore.

The Kalko house in Green Brook was sited on a slope with a commanding view of the New York skyline. Garages for foreign cars collected by the owner were arranged as a forecourt, with one wall protecting a swimming pool and another opening toward Manhattan.

The shore family wanted a porch to enjoy the sea breezes with a view of the nearby bay. Graves provided them with a lattice-roofed deck attached to the living room for indoor-outdoor living. A two-story pavilion, it also connects with a large garden.

The Plocek house in Warren reflects Graves' interest in classical architecture. The street facade is three stories, delineating the classical levels of basement, piano nobile and attic. In a similar style, a stairwell rising through the house is a formal column divided into base, shaft and capital.

Graves also designed the Environmental Education Center at Liberty State Park on the Jersey City waterfront. The all-redwood building resembles a Roman cathedral and is situated directly behind the Statue of Liberty, a few hundred feet of New York Harbor water separating them.

Graves was the first New Jersey architect to win the American Institute of Architects Honor Award (1975) for the Hanselmann House in Ft. Wayne, Ind. He won his second AIA award in 1979 for renovation of a four-story structure with a neo-Dutch Renaissance facade at 14 Nassau St., Princeton.

• The Op art movement emerged around 1960 with the optical paintings of Richard Anuszkiewicz, who lives and works in Englewood, Bergen County, with his wife, a school teacher, and three children. Of the American artists who rose to prominence during the Op revolution, Anuszkiewicz was perhaps the only one to have held fast to his vision, according to Art News magazine.

New York Gov. Nelson Rockefeller bought one of Anuszkiewicz's first Op pieces in 1960, followed immediately by the Museum of Modern Art and several important public and private collections, including the Whitney Museum, the Albright-Knox Art Gallery in Buffalo, the Aldrich Museum of Contemporary Art in Ridgefield, Conn., the La Jolla Museum, the City Museum of St. Louis, the Dartmouth College Collection, the Yale University Art Gallery, the Joseph H. Hirshhorn Museum, the New Jersey State Museum and the Milwaukee Art Center.

Born May 23, 1930, in Erie, Pa., to Polish immigrants, Anuszkiewicz began drawing as a child on colored papers and pads his father brought home from the factory. After winning a Pulitzer Traveling Fellowship and studying at the Cleveland Institute of Art, Anuszkiewicz refined his vision of optical art at Yale University under the brilliant colorist Josef Albers.

In July 1963, TIME magazine reviewed his work under the heading, "A Painter's Palette in the Age of Science." Two of his most famous optically vibrant creations were analyzed by TIME, the "Knowledge and Disappearance" and "Plus Reversed."

In 1960, the artist began a series of paintings that used only two colors—a "hot" one and a "cool" one. The result: "One part of the painting expands, another contracts, as if the whole canvas were breathing," the magazine's art critic wrote.

Anuszkiewicz was making a historic connection in his dazzling optical paintings. In 1965 Life International magazine defined Op art as "a paradoxical movement dedicated to the practice of fascinating deceptions. It exploits scientific theories about human vision." Life International singled out Anuszkiewicz as "one of the new wizards of OP."

Vogue magazine examined the new perceptual art in its Feb. 15, 1965 edition, recognizing Anuszkiewicz as the leading proponent of color optical effects. And modern art trends forecaster Alfred Barr described an Anuszkiewicz painting in a Look magazine article in March 1963 as a "dazzling shower of discs."

Anuszkiewicz finds children the best audience. "They look at it for what it is. That's really all you have to do," says the Englewood painter. He is now concentrating exclusively on his own work, studying what he has done and using himself as a "growing force."

• From Op art to photography, New Jersey artists have been in the vanguard of their chosen field. Since 1960, George Tice has distinguished himself as one of the most consistently interesting and important photographers working in America, according to the State Council on the Arts.

Tice, a native of Newark, has chosen both nature and the urban landscape as his themes. He has pushed the excellence of printmaking to new highs in order to render the images as perfectly as the medium allows. His darkroom techniques have been featured in the "Time-Life Photography Library Series" and in other leading publications on photography.

Early in his career, Tice documented the simple and seemingly pure life of the Amish: "I saw the Amish farmer as the complete man, self-sufficient and content, dependent only on himself and the earth."

One-man shows of Tice's photographic documentary of New Jersey have been presented at the Metropolitan Museum of Art, the Museum of Modern Art, the Art Institute of Chicago, the New Jersey State Museum in Trenton, and many others.

His many books include "The Amish Portfolio," "Paterson," "A New Jersey Portrait" and "Fields of Peace."

Tice is the recipient of both the National Endowment for the Arts and Guggenheim fellowships. In 1973, he was awarded the Grand Prix Du Festival D'Arles for "Paterson" as the best photography book of the year.

• Then there are artists who do not fit neatly into a particular category. Such is the case of Clarence Holbrook Carter of Milford, Hunterdon County.

Art critics have trouble putting Carter into a nice little inglenook, according to Lawrence Campbell, who sketched Carter's long and prolific career for a restrospective exhibition of paintings and constructions for the New Jersey State Museum in 1974.

Carter, whose first animal painting dates back to 1910, moved to Hunterdon County in 1948 and developed into one of New Jersey's greatest art treasures.

Newsweek magazine in 1971 described Carter as "very much an American phenomenon, a homegrown transcendalist...." The magazine's critic S.K. Oberbeck found a "Magritte kind of mystery in the paintings of Clarence Carter ... meticulously detailed pictures show giant ovid shapes hovering over enigmatic landscapes like the chambered surface of some cosmic pinball machine stretching back to a distant horizon."

The Museum of Modern Art included Carter in its exhibition "American Regionalism and Magic Realism" in 1943 and again in 1968 in "Dada, Surrealism and Their Heritage."

William M. Milliken, former director of the Cleveland Museum of Art, wrote in 1947: "Sincerity shows in the penetrating and persuasive mood which (Carter's) canvases and watercolors cre-

ate. They have clarity, fine color, but they have always, as well, an inner subjective existence, a haunting, sometimes troubling mystery...."

Carter was influenced by the Italian Primitives: Duccio, Benvenuto, Veneziano and Uccello. Museums and galleries throughout the world exhibit Carter's seemingly endless flow of authentic American art.

In its inaugural exhibition in 1979, the Southern Ohio Museum and Cultural Center presented 50 years of Carter's versatile works, noting he is "an intensely American artist and yet he stands outside the mainstream of American art.... He is a 20th Century painter with the sensibility of an 18th Century or perhaps early Italian Renaissance philosopher."

Reviewing Carter's life work in 1969, Joseph McCullough, president of the Cleveland Institute of Art, wrote: "Precision without dryness, analysis without boredom, simplicity without obviousness, impeccable craftmanship always."

• Still another New Jersey treasure is Jacob Landau, the Roosevelt painter-printmaker. Poet John Ciardi, in a 1976 exhibition of Landau's religious works at the ACA Galleries in New York City, immortalized the artist with these words:

An artist of parts, Jacob Landau,
Whose work comes to mind
and to hand now,
Asked the Angel of Days
To show him God's Ways
And show him the Angel did
—and how!

The New Jersey State Museum, a frequent exhibitor of the Roosevelt artist, offered this insight into Landau's consistently exciting prints and paintings: "Distinguished by vigorous creativity and superb craftsmanship, the graphic works of Jacob Landau also reflect his deep intellectual and philosophical concerns as an internationally respected humanist-artist and future-oriented thinker."

Jacob Landau, who lives and works in Roosevelt, has won praise for his interpretations of religious subjects. Star-Ledger Photo

Adds Kneeland McNulty, curator of the Philadelphia Museum of Art: "Perhaps it was Landau's early training as an illustrator that makes him so able to interpret the lives of the prophets; for each of these towering panels (stained glass) encompasses the significance of a man within a single picture . . . . The translation of Landau's original drawings into stained glass is an extraordinary achievement that may well mark a significant moment in ecclesiastical art."

And from Duane Oliver of the Western Carolina University Art Gallery: "Jacob Landau's woodcuts and lithographs . . . display a range, power and versatility that easily demonstrate why he is considered one of the major graphic artists of our time."

Born Dec. 17, 1917 in Philadelphia, Landau has been the recipient of numerous scholarships and fellowships, including the Guggenheim and the Ford Foundation. Individual shows have been at galleries in New York, Paris, Los Angeles, Uruguay, West Germany and major colleges in the United States.

Principal collections of Landau's works are at the Whitney Museum, the Museum of Modern Art, the National Museum of American Art, the New Jersey State Museum, the Library of Congress, the Hirshhorn Museum, the Art Museums of Philadelphia, and the university collections of Princeton, Rutgers, Yale, California, Columbia and Massachusetts.

• Some artists can fool the finest critical eyes searching for new talent. That's what happened to Leo Dee of Maplewood, who submitted a self-portrait, a meticulous pencil sketch, to the Montclair Museum in 1958, for its annual show of New Jersey artists.

Someone from the museum called Dee, then 27, and informed him, "We don't accept photographs." He missed out on the Montclair exhibit, but that drawing, now owned by the Newark Museum, and others have been featured at the Museum of Modern Art, the Whitney Museum, the Smithsonian Institution, the New Jersey State Museum and the Newark Museum.

State Museum Director Leah Sloshberg says critics and laymen alike find Dee's "deft blending of draughtmanship and craftmanship a joy to behold."

Dee's drawings in pencil, colored pencil and silverpoint have been characterized as a "contemporary counterpart to the Flemish and German late Gothic masters." New York City University Arts Professor William H. Gerdts defined Dee's drawings as "deceptively and subtly extremely modern."

Born in Newark and trained at the Newark School of Fine and Industrial Arts, Dee has spent as long as 15 months completing one picture. One silverpoint drawing of a manila envelope is now owned by the Yale University Art Gallery.

• Another Roosevelt painter is Gregorio Prestopino, whose retrospective at the State Museum in 1980 was a "time trip through several artistic eras," according to Eileen Watkins, the Star-Ledger's art critic.

Born in New York City in 1907, Prestopino labored during the Great Depression to capture the dark mood of America on his canvases. The 1950s and '60s saw his work becoming more abstract and hard-edged, while in the 1970s he turned to an entirely different palette and subject matter, Watkins notes.

Between 1943 and 1978, Prestopino had 18 one-man art shows in New York and was also exhibited at the Corcoran Gallery in Washington, the Pennsylvania Academy in Philadelphia, the Golden Gate Exposition in San Francisco, the Chicago Art Institute, and in Paris and Venice. His works have been collected by the Whitney Museum, the Hirshhorn Collection, the Chicago Art Institute and the Walker Art Center in Minneapolis. Prestopino has won many awards, including prizes from the National Academy of Design and the American Watercolor Society.

• Watercolorist Donald Voorhees is the recipient of more than 100 awards from such prestigious organizations as the Hud-

son Valley Art Association, the Salmagundi Club of New York City and the New Jersey Watercolor Society.

Voorhees' exquisite watercolors, many of them depicting life along the Jersey Shore, have been exhibited in museums throughout the United States, including the Frye Museum in Seattle, Wash.; the Edward Dean Museum in Cherry Valley, Calif.; the Central Museum of Wyoming, and the Martello Museum in Key West, Fla. Voorhees has also exhibited with the American Watercolor Society, Allied Artists, Knickerbocker Artists, the New Jersey Watercolor Society, the Hudson Valley Art Association, the National Academy of Design and the National Art Club.

A Voorhees painting, "Beckoning Still," is in the collection of President Ronald Reagan at the White House, and another of his works hangs in the Chilean embassy in Washington, D.C.

The artist, born May 6, 1926, maintains his own year-round gallery in Middletown, Monmouth County. His prints and lithographs are available through a network of more than 500 art galleries and stores nationwide. His original paintings may be seen at a limited number of select galleries throughout the country.

Art Centers

One of the reasons New Jersey is attracting more and more artists is the growing number of places they can exhibit their work. Local and regional art centers are drawing greater public interest, as they are easily accessible and their doors are always open to all art lovers.

* * *

One of the oldest community establishments is the Summit Art Center, founded in 1933 and today supported by more than 2,400 members. The center serves nearly 200 communities throughout northern New Jersey.

When the new half-million-dollar center opened in 1973, original Picassos and Matisses were exhibited, along with drawings, etchings and sculptures by Toulouse-Lautrec, Hopper, Pissarro and Laurencin.

Throughout its history, the Summit Art Center has been basically a school of instruction in the various plastic arts. In 1982, more than 700 students were enrolled in each of the fall, spring and summer semesters. Some 40 instructors, including well-known artists, round out the teaching staff at the Summit center. Studios with 20-foot-high ceilings and full, windowed walls, make the center an exciting place to work for both teacher and student.

* * *

A 19th Century old stone mill is home for the Hunterdon Art Center, founded in 1952 by local civic leaders and businesspeople who saved the mill from being converted into a factory. Standing beside a dam on the South Branch of the Raritan River, the old mill is surrounded by beautiful rolling hills, waterfalls and the Spruce Run and Round Valley reservoirs.

The four-story historic landmark contains 12,000 square feet of space, half of which is used for galleries. The center's services are directed toward the practicing artist and the viewing public. The exhibition schedule is balanced to serve those groups, with 10 to 12 major fine art exhibits a year, as well as quality complementary programs such as lectures, workshops, demonstrations and tours.

In August and September 1982, nearly 6,000 people visited the Hunterdon Art Center. The Stone Mill Shop on the second floor provides a rare opportunity to purchase one-of-a-kind contemporary crafts and prints. Nationally and internationally known craftspeople and printmakers are represented in the shop.

The center offers lectures on such topics as wild mushrooms, sculpture, Anagama kiln building, women artists, and illustrating children's books.

In 1957, trustee and printmaker Anne Steel Marsh was cura-

Star-Ledger Photo

The Hunterdon Art Center, housed in a 19th century stone mill, sits near a branch of the Raritan River in Clinton.

tor of the first National Print Exhibition at the center. The print collection, now numbering more than 150 pieces, has historical significance. One of the center's most popular exhibits was a collection of paintings and photographs from 1850 through 1982 called "Small Towns and Villages."

* * *

The Art Center of Northern Jersey has become a cultural haven for residents of Bergen County. Located in Tenafly, the art center's events take in the full spectrum of cultural activities: Chamber music concerts, gallery exhibits, lectures on Tutankhamen and Picasso, "Heirloom Appraisal Day," a special Museum of Modern Art lecture, an art excursion to the Barnes Foundation and other museums, craft exhibits and gala medieval balls.

Since its inception in 1956, the Tenafly organization has been expanding its program to involve Spanish-speaking students, provide special scholarships for the disadvantaged, sponsor craft workshops and provide tuition-free fellowships for senior citizens.

A faculty of renowned professional artists teaches everything from Chinese brush painting and cartooning to stone and wood carving.

* * *

In 1973, a group of artists established the Printmaking Council of New Jersey at the Ralph T. Reeve Cultural Center in Somerville. The center houses a gallery, studios, a library and an office.

By reserving "studio use" time, artists can extend their own work in two studios and a darkroom. For intaglio printmaking, there is a Charles Brand etching press (bed size 28 by 50 inches), a small side-wheel press, and a full range of related equipment and tools for etching, aquatint, drypoint and other intaglio media.

For lithography, there is a Fuchs-Lang press (bed size 25 by 39 inches), and the necessary equipment for both stone and plate lithography. For relief printmaking, there is a Vandercook proofing press, along with cutting tools, brayers and barens.

For papermaking, there are tubs, screens, felts and a large custom-made blender for pulp.

Classes are offered on a weekly basis in the fall, winter and spring sessions on lithography, etching, relief, collagraph, papermaking and photo-printmaking. Artists give workshops covering a broad range of innovative techniques such as litho-aquatint, monoprint, viscosity, kodalith and individual approaches to traditional media.

* * *

In Essex County, an Army Nike missile base in Livingston

has been converted into the Riker Hill Art Park, providing working space for professional artists and craftspeople. The Essex County Department of Arts rents space to artists in 17 refurbished Army structures on the 41-acre wooded tract.

In 1982, more than 30 artists were working on their paintings, pottery, stones, sculptures and jewelry. Riker Hill is tied in to the county's University in the Parks program, which includes Raku workshops, compositional drawing, jewelry-making, stone carving, oil painting and heads carving. Rutgers University is the program coordinator.

Art Museums

New Jersey is where some of the oldest art museums in the nation began quite humbly in an attic or schoolroom and slowly developed into impressive showcases for American folklore, Indian artifacts and the European masters.

There are art museums in every major New Jersey city and in each of the state's 21 counties, preserving pieces of history and art that tell the story of their own people and places of importance.

* * *

Time and circumstance have put the venerable Newark Museum in the forefront of American cultural centers. Since its founding in 1909 by John Cotton Dana, the Newark Museum has become New Jersey's largest and most prestigious cultural institution.

It is internationally recognized for the quality and diversity of collections in American, Oriental and classical art, ethnology, coins and currency and the natural sciences.

Located at Newark's Washington Park, the museum is housed in a building donated in 1923 to the people and City of Newark by Louis Bamberger.

The museum's collecting philosophy has largely centered on works of American origin. Among its vast holdings, the American painting and sculpture collection with more than 2,000 works is acknowledged as one of the nation's best, representing a complete survey of three centuries of American art dating from Colonial times to the present.

Included in that group are portraits by noted 18th Century painters John Singleton Copley and Pieter Vanderlyn. The epic scope and drama of the native wilderness are vividly depicted in 19th Century romantic landscapes by Thomas Cole, Frederick Church and Asher B. Durand. Later works of the century are represented by portraits by William Merritt Chase and John Singer Sargent.

A pioneer in American folk art, Newark began collecting in 1917 and presented the first two museum exhibitions of folk art in the early 1930s. The outstanding collection includes portraits, landscapes, weathervanes, quilts, decoys, trade signs and samplers made by self-taught artisans.

On display in the Sculpture Garden are works by contemporary artists David Smith, James Rosati, George Segal and Tony Smith, all from New Jersey. A vital oasis in downtown Newark, the Garden provides a tranquil setting for noon-hour picnics and live music, dance and theater programs.

Within this pastoral acre is Newark's oldest schoolhouse, built in 1784, and the Newark Fire Museum, a historical exhibit of fire apparatus and memorabilia.

The largest, single collection—numbering some 20,000 objects—is in decorative arts. The Newark holdings include glass, silver and metalwork, ceramics, furniture, costumes, textiles, dolls, jewelry and household items reflecting the changing styles, various media and the range of technique employed by the world's craftspeople. Some special examples are the English porcelain by the firms of Wedgwood and Spode and 18th Century English silver.

The emphasis of the decorative arts department has been the acquisition of works by American craftsmen, especially those of New Jersey. On revolving display are examples of Victorian silver by Gorham and Tiffany's Newark factory, one of the most complete collections of American art pottery in the United States, and handcrafted 19th Century American furniture by prominent New York cabinetmakers Belter, Roux, Marcotte and Meeks, and Newark's Jelliff & Co.

The museum opened the restored Ballantine House to the public in 1976, returning to the present a part of Newark's rich past. Listed on the National Register of Historic Sites, the house stands as a reminder of late Victorian Newark with its busy commerce and fashionable residential neighborhoods.

The plush home was designed in 1883 by architect George Edward Harney and completed in 1885. Displayed throughout the mansion are many original furnishings, presented to the museum as gifts from the Ballantine Brewery family, as well as period paintings and antiques from the museum's extensive collections.

The Oriental department contains one of the richest and most comprehensive Tibetan collections in the Western Hemisphere. The exotic silver, gold and bronze sculptures studded with precious gems, the magnificent Lamaist altar, ceremonial costumes and rare paintings all represent the Tibetan Buddhist synthesis of spiritual and daily life.

The museum's long commitment to the culture and arts of Tibet began in 1910 with trustee Edward N. Crane and Dr. Albert L. Shelton, a medical missionary, whose efforts formed the nucleus of the collection, which today numbers several thousand pieces. Today's Tibetan treasures include correspondence with the Dalai Lama, ceremonial silver, musical instruments, exotic jewelry, sculptures of deities, dance masks, lavish brocade costumes, appliquéd silk portraits of saints and religious persons, and a grand tent used by aristocratic families for picnics. The museum also houses a Tibetan Buddhist altar.

The Newark Museum showcases black artists, including Charles White, Joshua Johnston, Barbara Chase-Riboud and Romare Bearden. Its African art collection, begun in 1924, contains Yoruba folk art, wool-and-mohair tapestry, and traditional African wood and metal figures.

The George Washington period is well represented in an assortment of coins, medals, documents, paintings, ceramics and textiles. The Hispanic community also can find traditional crafts from New Mexico.

Continuing the tradition of community involvement and educational services begun by Dana, the Newark Museum sponsors a wide variety of free programs, lectures, children's and adults' art workshops, gallery tours and planetarium shows for the general public.

Programs such as the Sunday Afternoon Concerts, the Black Film Festival and the Junior Museum festivals attract new audiences and respond to the tastes and needs of the metropolitan and suburban community.

In 1982, more than 346,000 visitors enjoyed special exhibitions and events. The museum's educational department served another 91,000 individuals by coordinating tours for school children and other groups, and the lending department circulated more than 25,000 museum-quality objects for classroom study in schools and to other institutions throughout the state.

More than 5,000 individuals and families annually support the Newark Museum as members.

* * *

The New Jersey State Museum in Trenton started informally in 1836 when rock collectors began storing their prized pieces in the attic of the old State House. Ceramics were added to the rocks and minerals and the very modest state museum was on its way.

It didn't become the official state museum until 1890 when the Legislature passed a law designating it as such. Two of the country's oldest museums date only from 1870, when both the Boston Museum of Fine Arts and the Metropolitan Museum of Art in New York were founded.

Moved to the State House Annex in 1890, where it shared space with the State Library, the New Jersey museum focused mainly on the flora and fauna in the Garden State. There was a minor interest in porcelains, since Trenton was the site of the nation's finest ceramic and porcelain studios.

For years, the state museum's most famous item was a dinosaur, competing for attention with all kinds of crustaceans unearthed in the Jersey sands. At one time, the eastern half of the state was the sandy floor for the Atlantic Ocean.

In the 1920s, the works of artists of that era, particularly those who were native born, found their way into the museum's expanding storerooms. One of the earliest acquisitions was a marvelous watercolor by John Marin given to the museum by his family.

That period is represented in the state museum by artists in the Steiglitz group. Filling out the '20s period were paintings by Stuart Davis, Charles Burchfield and others. Since 1979, the museum has been buying art of the 1930s, the Depression Decade.

An etching by Auguste Renoir, entitled "Portrait of a Young Girl," was given to the museum as a gift in 1979 by Harriet Whitelaw, a New York patron of the arts and a friend of Barbara Wescott of Rosemont, Hunterdon County, one of the state museum's major benefactors.

The museum today maintains collections relating to art, cultural history, natural science and archaeology/ethnology. Emphasis in collecting, exhibiting and interpreting efforts is directed primarily, but not exclusively, toward examination of New Jersey's heritage.

Current facilities, dedicated in 1965, include a modern, three-level main building overlooking the Delaware River, an adjoining 150-seat planetarium and an adjacent 416-seat auditorium.

The museum shop features a carefully screened collection of museum-related souvenirs, books, jewelry, scientific specimens and collectors' items from around the world at nominal cost.

* * *

The Princeton University Art Museum is one of the oldest university museums in the United States. The museum began with the presentation of the Trumbull-Prime collection of pottery and porcelain, a gift contingent upon the erection of the original building completed in 1888.

Today, the collections run the gamut from ancient to contemporary and, geographically, concentrate on the Mediterranean regions, western Europe, China and the United States.

There is a fine collection of Greek and Roman antiquities, including early ceramics, small bronzes and mosaics from the university's excavations at Antioch. Medieval Europe is represented by sculpture, painting, metalwork and stained glass, an outstanding example of which is a colorful window from Chartres Cathedral.

A large collection of paintings, supplemented by sculpture, reflects the trends of the Renaissance, with emphasis on the Italian school. The French school predominates in 18th and 19th Century painting and sculpture. American art is represented by painting, sculpture, furniture and decorative arts.

The Princeton museum has an outstanding collection of prints and drawings, ranging in time through several centuries and geographically through many schools.

There is nearly a complete set of prints by Jacques Callot and a sizable group of Italian drawings. The now considerable collection of photographs was established in 1971 with the gift of the David Hunter McAlpin Collection and enlarged with the establishment of the Minor White archives, which the artist bequeathed in 1976.

In the Far Eastern field, Princeton has a notable collection of Chinese paintings, sculpture, bronze ceremonial vessels and such examples of the minor arts as bronze mirrors, clay tomb figures and a celebrated collection of snuff bottles. Japanese and Indian pieces augment the selection.

The collection of works of art from Central and South America is extremely fine and includes several pieces of great importance. African art is also represented.

During the 1970s, the museum increased its holdings in 20th Century art, adding works by Duchamp, Johns, Motherwell, Segal and Stella, among others. Not housed in the museum but part of its collections is the John B. Putnam Jr. Memorial Collection of Contemporary Sculpture, with pieces by foremost artists—Calder, Gabo, Lipchitz, Moore, Noguchi, Picasso, David Smith and others—located on the university campus.

* * *

The Rutgers Zimmerli Art Museum was expanded in 1982 from 3,000 to 12,000 square feet of exhibition space. The museum is named in honor of the late Jane Voorhees Zimmerli, a long-time resident of Highland Park.

The new museum opened last February, the inaugural exhibition focusing on Dutch art, "Haarlem: The 17th Century."

A permanent display area is available for the Rutgers art collection for the first time, a collection of some 100,000 works. Nearby Ballantine Hall has been renovated and directly connected to the new wing.

Fourteen printmaking studios, as well as various publishers, artists and dealers, are setting up the Rutgers archives of printmaking studios. Contemporary printmaking material will be available for viewing and research in the David and Mildred Morse Print and Drawing Room. The Morses bequeathed their collection of 19th and 20th Century French art to Rutgers.

The university also is obtaining 100 works by Henri Riviere, a 19th Century French printmaker. Containing watercolors, lithographs and wood blocks, it is the largest collection of Riviere's work outside of Paris.

The Rutgers graphics collection is particularly strong in the 19th and 20th Century French and American prints. The works of artists who have studied at Rutgers—George Segal, Joan Snyder, Lucas Samaras and Charles Simonds—will be collected by the Zimmerli Museum.

The new museum also contains a multi-purpose education room, offices, storage and workshop space, and a sculptured terrace.

* * *

Farther north, the Bergen County Museum of Art and Science, established in May 1956, occupies the ground floor of a colonial building on East Ridgewood and Farview avenues in Paramus.

The remains of the Hackensack mastodon, a massive ice-age relative of the elephant, excavated in 1962-63, and a 10,000-year-old mastodon, the Dwarskill, uncovered in Norwood in 1974, add a striking contrast to the paintings, sculptures and photographs of renowned artists in the arts-science museum. Other prehistoric skeletons and bones from more than 50 species of animals found near an Indian camp are on display.

The Bergen Museum has a Nature Room teeming with fish, frogs, turtles, snakes and plants, and a Discovery Room where everything is touchable, from mooseheads to stones and hats, all within easy reach of visitors.

The museum sponsored "Three Decades of Fine Crafts," a juried show of the New Jersey Designer Craftsmen, marking the 30th year (1981) of the state's largest professional crafts organization. Bergen also presented "The Black Presence in the Era of the American Revolution" in 1982, part of which was created by the Smithsonian Institution.

* * *

The Montclair Art Museum, opened in 1914, is the result of gifts from two benefactors. William T. Evans, one of the nation's first collectors to specialize in American art, offered what would ultimately become more than 50 paintings to the town, then to a private, nonprofit organization that became the Montclair Art Museum. That gift was consummated when Mrs. Henry Rand Lang provided the funds to build a fireproof building to house them, along with her mother's extensive collection of North American Indian art.

The only privately supported, self-governing art museum in New Jersey today, it has evolved into one of the finest small art museums in the country, enjoying wide renown among other art institutions.

The Montclair Museum has a collection of more than 6,000 paintings and sculpture, prints and drawings, constituting a history of American art. There are outstanding collections of native American art, American costumes, English and Irish silver, and Chinese snuff bottles.

About 45 percent of Montclair's schedule is devoted to presenting the work of contemporary American artists and craftspeople, with emphasis on those living or working in New Jersey.

The quality of the programs is enriched by the 10,000-volume art research library, which is also catalogued in the public library for general access. Programs and publications interpret the exhibitions to the public and, through outreach projects, to the schools.

Studio classes use the exhibitions as study resources and stimulus for courses for children and adults. The museum is also engaged in cooperative internship programs with four regional colleges and universities.

Montclair Art Museum serves more than 50,000 people a year. Its services are free to the public.

* * *

The Morris Museum got under way in 1956 and much of its present structure is built around a mansion the museum purchased in 1964 from the Frelinghuysen Foundation. In the beginning, the museum collected "everything and anything," from beautiful pre-Columbian figures to an anonymous gift of dolls and decorative arts materials.

The third largest public museum in the state in terms of volume and service, the Morris Township facility has one of the biggest collections of 19th and 20th Century American costumes. Another major acquisition involved more than 30 African masks and figures from the 20th Century. And 30 prints from contemporary artist Adam Wurtz have been added to the Morris collection.

Publisher Malcolm Forbes turned over his fabulous toy boat collection to the Morris Museum for an exhibit. A contemporary light sculpture show featured eight artists using the theme of light to create colored shadows and patterns through projection, mirror images and indirect lighting.

More than 25,000 youngsters a year participate in scheduled "gallery talks" at the Morris Museum, only one of seven nationally accredited art museums in New Jersey.

* * *

From porcelain to ping-pong, all art is fair game at the Monmouth Museum in Lincroft, home of the largest hands-on museum for children in New Jersey.

Founded in 1963, the independent, private, nonprofit organization was uniquely chartered as a "Museum of Ideas." With no permanent collection, the museum borrows art and artifacts from the nation's leading museums and from galleries and private collections.

More than 50,000 people are directly served each year through exhibitions, bus trips, workshops and outreach programs originating in the Monmouth Museum, whose modern stone building was erected in 1973 on the Brookdale Community College campus.

The Monmouth region enjoys a series of changing exhibitions in the fields of art, nature, science and cultural history. In the children's gallery, space is especially designed for young people to explore, examine, poke and prod various subject areas of interest to them. The human body, environment and non-verbal communication have been subjects of ongoing exhibitions appealing to preschoolers through junior high students.

In 1982, the Monmouth Museum sponsored an innovative exhibit using works of art, artifacts and graphics to explore the influence of trade with China on American decorative art. It was, naturally, called all you wanted to know from "Porcelain to Ping Pong."

The Nabisco Gallery in East Hanover brings art to the workplace in a contemporary, spacious setting.

Courtesy: Nabisco Brands, Inc.

Corporate Galleries

Big businesses' appreciation of art is spreading in New Jersey, as several world corporations set aside space in their headquarters for major art exhibits throughout the year. Names like AT&T, Prudential, Squibb, Nabisco, Campbell Soup, Western Electric and Public Service Electric & Gas Co. (PSE&G) are putting art to work for everyone's enjoyment.

When the Squibb Gallery first opened to the public in October 1972, it was described by one art critic as "the most elegant showcase for art this side of the Hudson."

The 5,560-square-foot, glass-walled gallery overlooks a rooftop garden and 12-acre lake. Exhibitions are mounted on large chocolate brown panels suspended from chrome fixtures in the 11-foot-high ceiling.

That innovative technique affords a variety of arrangements, allowing each exhibition to be displayed and lighted to its best advantage. Walls can be completely removed for sculpture exhibitions.

The gallery is located in the world headquarters of E.R. Squibb & Sons, Route 206, three miles south of Princeton. As many as 10,000 visitors are attracted to each exhibit. Art has ranged from the primitive to the classic to the contemporary—in paintings, sculptures, textiles, ceramics and other art forms.

The Squibb art season runs from September through June, with six professional exhibitions and two employe shows. Squibb assumes responsibility for transporting and insuring the art, and for publicizing the artists' work.

Squibb was honored in 1978 with the Forbes Business Arts Award for its ongoing support of the arts. A recent Squibb exhibition was a striking collection of color photgraphy by the National Park Service entitled "Alaska: The Great Land."

In another artistic event, in cooperation with the City of Venice, Squibb sponsored a recital of Viennese music, benefiting the American Heart Association. Kate Wittlich, internationally celebrated as a foremost interpreter of the Vienna School of Music, performed classical, romantic and modern selections on the piano.

*   *   *

The Nabisco Gallery at world headquarters in East Hanover, was created in 1975 as a way to reach out to its new neighbors. Nabisco had been based in New York.

The food company presented New Jersey sculptors and watercolorists, Waterloo Village watercolor impressions, a career competition in drawing sponsored by the New Jersey Chapter of the National Society of Arts and Letters, and contemporary Canadian art, under the patronage of the Canadian ambassador to the United States, Peter M. Towe, and the U.S. ambassador to Canada, Kenneth M. Curtis.

One of the most memorable exhibits was the Cream of Wheat advertisements from 1900-40, the first public showing of advertising art which Walt Reed, author of "Great American Illustrations," found to be a "microcosm of the whole history of advertising and the art of illustration in America" spanning almost half a century. It is the only complete collection of that medium in existence, according to Reed.

The 95 watercolor and oil paintings were selected from the 700 pieces comprising the total collection. Art for the ads came from some of the nation's most important illustrators: James Montgomery Flagg, famous for the Uncle Sam "We Want You" recruiting poster, and N.C. Wyeth of the gifted Wyeth family.

*   *   *

America's bicentennial celebration led to the creation of the Western Electric Education Center Art Gallery in 1976. About 16 shows a year are presented at the Western Electric Engineering Research Center in Princeton, each lasting six to seven weeks.

The center selects nationally known artists, with emphasis on local individuals who have achieved recognition in their fields. Several exhibits have shown the works of selected up-and-coming artists. Some group shows have given the center's own staff an opportunity to display their best paintings and sculptures.

Western Electric's exhibits often complement national holidays and important events. Exhibits embrace all media: Oils, watercolors, acrylics, prints, metallic intaglios, sculpture in every imaginable material, size and shape, photographs, crafts of fiber and other natural and manufactured materials.

To mark the 10th anniversary of the opening of the research center, the works of world-renowned artist Milton Avery occupied the spacious gallery. Others exhibitors have included Laszlo Ispanky, a Hungarian sculptor; Natalie Best of Westfield, who works in watercolors, and Oliver Rodums, a noted sculptor.

*   *   *

The Campbell Soup Museum in Camden was chartered by the state in 1966 as a nonprofit educational institution. The museum has acquired the most gorgeous tureens made during the past four centuries.

The stunning collection includes soft-paste porcelain tureens, excellent ceramics, silver, gilt and pewter soup tureens. Historic soup plates are from the personal collections of Catherine the Great and from the White House service of Abraham Lincoln. An early 18th Century French or Italian bronze tureen is on display at the world's largest soup factory, as is a silver-gilt tureen with stand and liner from England, 1828-29.

The rare Campbell pieces were gathered from all over the world: A 1750 hybrid hard-paste porcelain tureen with stand from Italy; a 1780 enamel on copper tureen with stand from China; a 1735 tin-enameled earthenware tureen from Holland; a 1730 faience tureen from Spain, plus more than 200 other tureens, soup plates, silver ladles and porcelain spoons.

Prudential Insurance Co. of America, with headquarters in

downtown Newark, owns more than 5,000 works of art, while nearby Public Service Electric & Gas Co., New Jersey's largest utility, has no fewer than 500 pieces worth well over $200,000.

AT&T started buying in 1973 in connection with its Basking Ridge headquarters. All of the giant corporations open their galleries to the public during normal office hours, with hours scheduled on weekends for special events.

Art Galleries

The number of art galleries and organizations in New Jersey continues to grow as more and more artists—and their patrons—build a strong market for buying, selling and bartering their artistic wares.

Each year, another art organization or gallery joins New Jersey's creative family of professional and amateur artists and artisans. A sampling of some of the larger organized activities, commercial and nonprofit, reflects the boundless energies and interests of New Jersey's artistic community.

The **Doubletree Gallery of Fine Art and Contemporary Crafts** in Montclair brings the artist to the community, and vice versa, living up to its name by providing a double service.

Established in 1974 as an alternative to the commercial galleries, Doubletree seeks out professional artists and displays their work under the aegis of "free expression," considered essential to aesthetic growth.

The works of member-artists span the full spectrum, from painting and sculpture to photography, jewelry-making, weaving, ceramics and printmaking. Jurying of new members is an open, ongoing process, as the gallery seeks to recognize those individuals who can contribute to the creative excitement generated by the interaction at Doubletree.

Community service is as important as artistic development. Special events, free and open to the public, feature films, slide-lectures, and exhibition demonstrations of all aspects of the arts: Visual, performing, literary. There are annual salutes to high school art, elementary school programs, exhibits for Montclair State College professors and talented students. There's even an exhibition of prisoner art to round out the Doubletree panoply.

The **America House Gallery** in Tenafly is a showcase for the American craft artist. Betty Turino, gallery director, opened her doors in 1973 with offerings of work by artists from New Jersey and neighboring states. Today nationally known names such as Michael Elkan (wood), Paul Manners (prismatic glass sculptures), Glenda Arentzen (jewelry), Nancy Meeker (potter), Robert Palusky (glass), and Art Reed (glass) can be found on display next to talented newcomers.

City Without Walls is a community-oriented gallery in the heart of Newark, next to "The Rock," Prudential's headquarters. The second and third floors at 140 Halsey St. have been converted into art studios and galleries for exhibiting young, new talent. An artist advocacy organization, City Without Walls is committed to the physical rejuvenation of Newark. Its first book, released in 1982, details "Newark's Architecture: A Study of Steel and Stone."

An urban artist collective, the Newark group presented a major exhibit with Rutgers University, entitled "North of New Brunswick, South of New York." Among the local artists City Without Walls has helped promote are Frank Palaia of Elizabeth, a multi-media artist; Barry Blair of Hoboken, a sculptor, and Bisa Washington, a Newark sculptress and fiber specialist.

The **TWEED Arts Group** in Plainfield began as a subcommittee of the Plainfield Arts Council to study two problems: The lack of public awareness of the many cultural activities in Plainfield, and the demand from working artists for a place to exhibit and work.

The venture is housed in a storefront at 112 E. Front St. It serves as both a forum for artists and a place for the public to participate in arts activities.

Photo Credit: Doug Schwab

Cloisonné necklace, titled "Greek Maiden," by Robert Place of Stewartsville, the 1984-85 recipient of a New Jersey State Council on the Arts Craft Fellowship.

City residents and merchants have discovered that fine art means good business. TWEED is developing into one of the fastest-growing art attractions in New Jersey. Exhibitions have been on new realism, contemporary fiber art, black women artists and photography by a local lensmen, Paul Collier.

The fiber exhibit involved 30 works by seven artists. There were painted silk and quilted vinyl, pictorial wool tapestries, free-standing floor sculpture, modular geometric abstractions and fetish-like wall reliefs.

Among the leading professional galleries are Joseph Dawley in Cranford and the Rossi Gallery in Morristown. Other well-known establishments are Gallery 9 in Chatham, Unicorn Bookstore/Gallery in Hoboken and the Wyckoff Gallery in Wyckoff.

Colleges and universities with active exhibit schedules are Caldwell College, Jersey City State College, Seton Hall University in South Orange, Trenton State College at Hillwood Lakes, Kean College of New Jersey in Union, Montclair State College, Union College in Cranford, Rutgers University's Newark and New Brunswick campuses, and William Paterson College in Wayne.

* * *

In a category by itself is the one-man creation of the world's largest model railroad, some 60,000 pounds of plaster landscape crafted by Bruce Williams of Three Bridges, Hunterdon County.

His 40-year project, about half-completed, covers 13,000 square feet in Williams' five-winged basement. Open to the public for scheduled tours once a year, railroad buffs can wander about 13,000 feet of track, 45,000 feet of wire, a half-million miniature trees, each embedded in plaster hills and mountains, 400 bridges built from thousands of pieces of wood, 950 switches, 500 freight cars and 40 locomotives.

Williams' little railroad world eventually will have 4,500 rail cars and 400 locomotives chugging around his ever-expanding cellar.

The new Atlantic City rising along the world's oldest boardwalk.

ATLANTIC CITY

A tlantic City is America's top tourist attraction, drawing more daily visitors than New York City, Las Vegas or Florida's ever-expanding Disney World.

The world's longest and original boardwalk in Atlantic City has become a gleaming gold coast of modern and historic casino-hotels and convention centers overlooking smooth, sandy beaches and rhythmic whitecaps breaking in a visually endless ocean.

Atlantic City's resurrection in the 1980s as the entertainment mecca of the Western World enhances an already memorable grand tradition of Miss America pageants, the first Easter parades and "Ferris" wheels, the first amusement pier, color postcard and airport—not to mention the most popular family game, Monopoly, in which names like Boardwalk and Park Place have slipped into the language as places of particular significance in our lives.

Atlantic City and its marine environs are even more than that. Their unique kaleidoscopic images reveal sea, sun, surf and sand . . . graceful gulls, sailboats, swimmers and anglers . . . a giant wooden elephant and ancient lighthouse . . . historic villages and museums . . . a wildlife refuge and racetrack . . . wineries and golf courses . . . and the constantly moving sights of joggers, bikers and strollers enjoying a 6½-mile-long, weathered and wonderful boardwalk fronting nostalgic Absecon Island.

To further enrich the Atlantic City experience, there's the exquisite Somers Mansion and a maritime center at Gardner's Basin, boasting the largest tall ship in the United States.

The Fischer Greenhouse showcases America's finest African violets, while the latest aviation and transportation technology is on view at the Federal Technical Center just outside Atlantic City.

And as if that's not enough, Atlantic City's famous Million Dollar Pier has been transformed into "Ocean One," a ship-like structure celebrating Yankee ingenuity, the entrepreneurial spirit and freedom of opportunity.

Visitors can wander directly from the boardwalk into an admission-free central atrium to view a two-level-high neon Statue of Liberty with its grit-and-hope story of the immigrants who settled in America. Or, they can turn on a 14-foot-high "American Ingenuity Light Bulb" and learn about America's greatest inventors.

The $50 million showplace contains 35,000 square feet of exhibits and demonstrations sponsored by major American corporations, plus 120 shops ranging from bazaars and boutiques to books and flowers. The triple-deck ship also has 36 restaurants with an international array of culinary delights from tacos and souvlaki to cheese blintzes and egg rolls.

And, in 1981, a critically acclaimed motion picture starring Burt Lancaster and Susan Sarandon, a Jersey native, depicted a dramatically changing "Atlantic City," giving filmgoers a vivid insight into the nation's oldest *and* newest resort.

Atlantic City is today's largest vacation, entertainment and family resort, receiving more than 30 million visitors in 1984, each spending a day or more at the easily accessible island retreat. That compares to 17 million estimated visitor days for New York City, 15 million for Washington, D.C., and 13 million for Miami during the same period.

Some 52 million people, or 25 percent of the population of the United States, live within a tankful of gas from Atlantic City. By 1986, the number of visitor days to Atlantic City is expected to reach 30 million.

Absecon Island is home, however, for only 120,000 year-round residents. Some 45,000 people work in the boardwalk area, mostly in the nine new casino-hotels that have opened since gambling was legalized by New Jersey voters in 1976. Another six casino-hotels are planning to open by 1986, doubling the work force.

Before legalized gambling, some 2 million visitors a year went to New Jersey's most famous shore resort to watch the Miss America contest, taste some saltwater taffy, participate in a convention for engineers, doctors or teachers, and take the almost ritualistic stroll along the breezy boardwalk.

During its ebbing years, Atlantic City was a place to get away from the noisy drone of metropolitan life. In that relatively quiet phase from 1950 through 1976, life in the Boardwalk Capital of America belonged to the more retiring type. Senior citizens outnumbered everyone.

But Atlantic City was destined to come back from its drowsy, post-war period. An infusion of the right ingredients—mainly capital—was all that was needed to bring the old gray lady by the sea back to life. Everything else in the way of natural leisure and pleasure was already there, the reason for Atlantic City's perennial "fresh air" popularity.

Although situated in a "northern" state, Atlantic City is actually in "sunny" Dixie, being a few miles south of the Mason-Dixon Line that delineates the northern and southern half of the Union. It lies smack in the middle of the vast Boston-to-Washington megalopolis, a sparkling speck of sand supporting the oldest yet newest resort in the nation.

The Lenni-Lenape Indians were the first to be lured to the narrow island by the rejuvenating Atlantic. They called it "Absegami," their word for Little Sea Water. That name was first applied to a small Indian encampment on the mainland now referred to as Absecon.

New England whalers were among the first early white visitors to Absecon Island, having followed the great sea mammals from the cool waters of the North Atlantic to Delaware Bay.

A Quaker, Thomas Budd, purchased the first piece of property in 1695. He was forced to take land he did not want—440 acres of remote sandy real estate at four cents an acre—in order to close a deal for more valued farmland along the nearby coastal plains at 40 cents an acre.

An acre of Boardwalk property went for a minimum of $2 million in 1982.

It wasn't until 1853 that Atlantic City first appeared on a surveyor's map. The name was appropriately imposed over the waves of the Atlantic Ocean by a civil engineer, Richard Boyce Osborne, who was making a survey for the first railroad to the island. Osborne also thought it would be fitting to name the resort city's streets after the states of the Union.

A toy maker then monopolized that idea in a board game that seems to be what Atlantic City is all about today: Building hotels and motels along Park Place, Boardwalk, Illinois Avenue, Pennsylvania Avenue . . . .

The railroad opened Absecon Island and Atlantic City to the throngs from Newark, Philadelphia and New York City.

A conductor on the Camden-Atlantic Railroad, Alexander Boardman, soon became tired of sweeping sand out of his trains from homeward-bound tourists. Boardman talked to some hotel owners and suggested a walk be built to keep the sand out of his passengers' shoes. The hotel operators liked the proposal because it meant less sand in their lobbies and hallways.

A practical solution to an annoying problem led to the development of the world's first oceanfront boardwalk. On Sunday, June 26, 1870, the Atlantic City boardwalk was opened for public use.

It was not meant to be a promenade, business thoroughfare or amusement attraction. It was simply a footpath consisting of boards or planks laid out on the upland beach. The designation "Boardwalk" was not legally adopted until 1895.

The first boardwalk was 10 feet wide, allowing four people to walk abreast, and constructed in 12-foot sections just 18 inches above the sand. It was a mile long. The planks were taken up in September and stored in a barn.

The original wooden walkway, costing $5,000, lasted nine years. It was on that not-too-steady, sandless walk where the first Easter Parade was held on April 16, 1876.

A wider replacement was erected on higher pilings to allow storm tides to flow under without damage to the boards. The 20-foot-wide, two-mile-long boardwalk stood five feet above the beach, without railing. When a hurricane destroyed it in 1889, a sturdier boardwalk was built. That was succeeded by one 10 feet from the ground, 24 feet wide and with solid railings on both sides.

The fifth and final boardwalk was put on massive steel pilings and girders and came with heavy railings. Although other

Bathers teeming in the surf off Yang's Pier in August 1906.

Star-Ledger Photo

seashore resorts have copied the sand-free beach walk, only the original serves four contiguous resorts in one unbroken line, from Atlantic City to Longport, with stops in Ventnor and Margate.

The "Ferris wheel" made its inaugural ride on the Atlantic City boardwalk in 1891—two years before its spectacular "debut" at the 1893 Chicago Columbian Exposition.

Two years earlier, William Somers, grandfather of a recent Atlantic City mayor, created a company to erect an "Observation Roundabout" between New York and Kentucky avenues. It was made of wood instead of today's steel-webbed spinning wheels. On June 22, 1892, a gasoline lamp exploded, turning the giant wheel into a flaming tinder box.

Somers then built a double wheel, side by side, each rotating in the opposite direction. Similar Somers wheels spun thrillfully around at Asbury Park and Coney Island, capturing the public's fancy.

Officials of the upcoming Chicago fair contacted Somers for a wheel of their own. They sent a young bridge builder from Pittsburgh, George W.G. Ferris, to Atlantic City to look at the Somers contraption.

Ferris advised his Chicago patrons to build a steel rather than wooden wheel capable of carrying 1,440 riders. When the Chicago exposition opened, the wheel was the main attraction—and it bore the name of George Ferris.

Somers sued, but Ferris died before it was settled. Somers ultimately won the case, but the name Ferris had been imbedded in the public's mind.

By the early 1920s, Atlantic City was host to the largest convention gathering in the nation. Business leaders decided it was time to build a convention center.

After four years of construction, the largest unobstructed room in the world opened its doors with a stage so big that basketball games can be played on it. The cavernous hall with a capacity to hold 41,000 people, was dedicated on May 31, 1929. It is the home of the Miss America pageant and the summer home of the Ice Capades.

Aviation has been an integral part of Atlantic City's colorful history. The word "airport" was coined in Atlantic City to designate the first municipally operated flying field.

One of the first "air carnivals" was conducted on the beach from July 2 through 12 in 1910. Aviation pioneer Glenn H. Curtiss demonstrated "bombing" by dropping oranges from a height of 100 feet onto a yacht drifting just beyond the surf.

Curtiss also set a world's record for flying time on the opening day of the air carnival. He flew 100 miles an hour for 14 minutes.

The first attempt to cross the ocean by air took place on Oct. 15, 1910 when polar explorer Walter Wellman alighted in his dirigible "America." A storm, however, wrecked the balloon 1,000 miles at sea and a steamer rescued the crew.

The first jet-propelled airplane was a rocket glider that carried William G. Swann, a stunt flier, 1,000 feet from its start on the Steel Pier to a perfect landing on the beach on June 4, 1931.

Aviation continues to play a vital role in the resurgence of Atlantic City. Eleven major air carriers and four smaller jet-prop operators today offer extensive, nonscheduled service from major U.S. cities to the Jersey Shore vacation haven. More than 105,000 people visited Atlantic City in 1982 via air charters.

But the bulk of travelers arrive at the year-round playland by motor vehicle. Autos account for some 12 million visitors; motorcoach charters brought in almost 7 million, and bus lines accommodated another 700,000 during 1982.

Packed with tourists by day and into the wee hours of the morning, Atlantic City nevertheless is just minutes away from sweeping unspoiled wetlands and coastal plains teeming with marine and fowl life. One of the natural wonders of the Atlantic seaboard is the Brigantine National Wildlife Refuge a few miles north of Absecon Island. The 20,229 acres of protected habitat offer an invigorating escape from the glittering environment of Atlantic City.

An appreciation of America's origins can be acquired at Smithville Village, an assemblage of rare Colonial buildings depicting life before the 1776 Revolution.

The Victorian Wheaton Village, once a flourishing glass factory town, stands today as a museum with numerous shops and a crafts arcade showing the evolution of glassmaking in early America. South Jersey remains one of the biggest glass manufacturing centers on the continent.

And then there's Lucy the Margate Elephant—"the only elephant in the world you can walk through and come out alive." The 65-foot-tall, wooden pachyderm, built in 1881 and weighing in at 180,000 pounds, is a National Historic Landmark.

Lucy was the creation of real estate developers who needed a highly visible attraction at a time when the Margate section of Absecon Island was the way the Lenni-Lenape Indians left it.

Guests to Lucy's main hall must walk up a spiral staircase in either of her hefty rear legs. The vaulted ceiling looks like an upside-down boat with its ribbed construction. Stairs lead to Lucy's huge head, where a panoramic view of the coast can be seen through her owlish eyes.

There's also an impressive observation platform on Lucy's back, patterned after the royal Howdah that seats the maharajahs in India.

Atlantic City over the past century has generated a variety of unusual activities, virtually everything from A to Z, from the Atlantic City Race Course to Zaberers, one of the largest restaurants in the United States.

As Atlantic City enters its second century of catering to the tourist, the list of things to do and to see grows almost daily. Already, no other city can offer nine new hotels, each with a minimum of 25,000 square feet of meeting space and no less than 500 guest rooms.

And it's only the beginning. Here's the latest list, alphabetically, representing the ongoing expansion along the boardwalk, still Atlantic City's essential reason for being:

• The Atlantis casino-hotel at Convention Hall and the Boardwalk features a $135 million multi-level casino, rooftop Tahitian Room restaurant, London Arcade shops, full service health club, indoor pool, 1,000-seat cabaret, plus six other restaurants and cocktail lounges. There are 16 different conference rooms for meetings, a spacious ballroom and a direct-access stairway into Convention Hall.

• Bally's Park Place Hotel Casino, a $300 million investment. In full operation since 1979, Bally's has 512 rooms, 13 restaurants, lounges and a cabaret theater. There are 40,000 square feet of meeting space in one park-like level. A major expansion will include a 1,500-seat theater, a 750-room tower, additional restaurants and more meeting rooms.

• Caesars Boardwalk Regency Hotel Casino opened in 1979 at a cost of more than $75 million. An $80 million expansion project was completed in 1985, creating a new facade, a second theater, a new power plant and early Roman decor throughout the public areas. It also increased the casino floor to 60,000 square feet. A new 11-story addition boasts 140 suites, three gourmet restaurants, a health club, a swimming pool and an 8,500-square-foot meeting room, which can be subdivided for various-sized functions.

• Caesars is proceeding with development of a second $200 million casino-hotel on the site of the former Traymore Hotel. There will be more than 500 rooms, 60,000 square feet of casino space, several resaurants, lounges and other facilities.

• Camelot Hotel Casino, a subsidiary of American Leisure Corp., is developing a $190 million complex containing 150,000 square feet of convention and meeting space, including a 40,000-square-foot, column-free ballroom and a 47,000-square-foot exhibit hall capable of accommodating 271 booths. There will be a 1,500-seat cabaret showroom with a major production revue, plus

Star-Ledger Photo

*Singer Steve Lawrence blows on the dice as he becomes
the first to gamble in Atlantic City in May 1978.*

Star-Ledger Photo

*The posh Garden Court of the Golden Nugget Hotel Casino
featuring a mural of Atlantic City at the turn of the century, and
reflecting the opulence found inside the city's refurbished resorts.*

1,000 rooms and suites, seven restaurants, a lounge showroom with 400 seats, two mini-theaters, four tennis courts, year-round ice skating, swimming pools (enclosed in winter), men's and women's health clubs and a 40,000-square-foot shopping arcade, in addition to the 62,000-square-foot casino.

• Claridge Hotel Casino opened in July 1981 with 504 rooms, six restaurants, three lounges, a 650-seat theater and 29,000 square feet of convention space. The cost: $150 million.

• Golden Nugget Hotel Casino, a $153 million venture that began December 1980, is a 22-story structure containing 504 rooms, 25,500 square feet of convention and meeting space, a 524-seat Victorian theater, four restaurants, a pool and a health club. A second casino is in the planning stage.

• Harrah's Marina Hotel Casino opened its doors in November 1980. The $145 million, self-contained entertainment community has 506 rooms, a 44,090-square-foot casino, covered parking facilities for 2,400 cars, an 850-seat theater, five restaurants, five lounges and 25,000 square feet of convention space. Harrah's plans to build a 104-slip marina next to the hotel and an antique auto museum, additional casino space, two new restaurants, plus expanded meeting and convention space. The expansion is more than $12 million.

• Harrah's Boardwalk, a $200 million partnership with Holiday Inns and the Trump Organization, plans to build a 32-story luxury edifice offering 614 rooms and a 60,000-square-foot casino by 1984. It occupies a 2.6-acre tract between the Atlantic City Convention Hall and the Penthouse Boardwalk construction site.

• Hilton Hotel plans to build a $250 million, 634-room hotel-casino near Harrah's. There will be a 60,000 square-foot-casino, plus all of the other amenities.

• Ocean One, a $50 million ship-shaped entertainment and exhibition center, is located on the former Million Dollar Pier.

• Penthouse Boardwalk Hotel Casino is resuming construction of a $200 million complex.

• Resorts International Hotel Casino currently offers 720 rooms, eight restaurants and a 1,650-seat Superstar Theater featuring top name entertainers. There are three entertainment lounges and a health club with a year-round pool and separate health spas for men and women. Resorts was the first casino-hotel to open in Atlantic City in May 1978 at a cost of $122 million.

Resorts plans to develop a portion of its uptown urban renewal property at a cost of $200 million. Phase one will include 1,000 guest rooms, a 75,000-square-foot casino and 60,000 square feet of convention space for meetings, lectures, conferences and ballrooms. Phase two will involve a substantial increase in the number of guest rooms and the amount of public space for various activities.

• Sands Hotel Casino opened in July 1980 with 504 rooms, a theater for 850 people, three restaurants, more than 25,000 square feet of convention and meeting space, an ultra-modern health club featuring enclosed pool, racquetball courts and a Nautilus fitness center. The $70 million investment will grow with anticipated physical changes and expansions.

• Shelburne Hotel, formerly Benihana, is under development at a cost of $200 million.

• Historic Smithville is moving ahead on plans for a hotel, conference center, golf course, tennis complex and swimming pool. Residential housing under construction will number more than 6,850 units. The total development will exceed $300 million.

Star-Ledger Photo

Roulette is one of the many games of chance attracting more than 30 million people a year to the world's most popular resort.

Photo Credit: Tom Cassidy

Sands Hotel & Casino.

• Tropicana Hotel Casino was the most expensive operation at $330 million when it opened as Atlantic City's ninth gaming center in late November 1981. The property consists of a 521-room hotel, 48,000 square feet of casino space, 12 shops, 25,000 square feet of meeting space, tennis courts, swimming pool, health club and six restaurants.

* * *

New housing is also shaping up in the old Atlantic City neighborhoods.

Tannen Towers, the first of the city's new residential high-rises, opened in 1984. Developer Philip Tannenbaum invested $35 million in a 31-story, 292-unit condominium featuring shops, sauna, pool and racquet courts.

Developer Abraham Grunwald plans to put up 214 townhouses on Absecon Boulevard between Tennessee and South Carolina avenues, and Toronto developer Dennis Sutherland wants to build a 22-story, 240-unit condo tower at the corner of Tennessee and Drexel avenues.

Another project completed in 1983 is the McKinley Avenue Townhouses, low-rise family rentals occupying a two-block site on Absecon Boulevard near New York Avenue. Most of the units will be two-bedroom.

Philadelphian Jack Blumenfeld is moving ahead on his Greenhouse, a 34-story, 952-unit condominium at the corner of Atlantic and Michigan avenues. And a 189-unit condo at Illinois Avenue and Bacharach Boulevard is also getting ready for groundbreaking.

The gem of the housing project is the $200 million Ocean Club, a 34-story palace on the Boardwalk at Montpelier Avenue. Amenities range from tennis courts with a resident pro, to limousine and private plane service.

Construction is under way on a 1,200-unit, middle-income housing development, the first of several planned for the "new Atlantic City." The high-rise condominiums are called Marina Club.

In addition, there are nearly 2,000 subsidized living units for the city's senior population, enough for the 1980s, according to the Atlantic City Housing Authority. An attractive senior complex is the Charles P. Jeffries Tower.

Low-income housing is being provided by the authority for some 3,200 families. The authority's executive director, Oscar Harris, considers the low-income dwellings to be among the city's "finest housing stock in stable neighborhoods." They include such public housing projects as Altman Terace, Shore Park and Stanley Homes.

* * *

Atlantic City is coming full circle, having tried gambling very early on. The Thursday, April 10, 1884 edition of the Atlantic Times reported:

"The gambling saloons are running full blast. The Mayor, on being asked why he allows it, answers not a word.

"The Chief of Police says that he has been ill, and besides, he was discouraged by the fruitlessness of his former raids.

"The District Attorney says he can do nothing because the grand jury refuses to indict.

"Meanwhile, the ivory chips clink merrily . . . ."

One hundred years ago, local residents feared gambling would destroy their city. Today, they're hoping casinos will save it.

Star-Ledger Photo   Photo Credit: Gordon Bishop

Poet Allen Ginsberg, a native of Paterson, chants Tibetan mantras during a reading at Tombrock College in West Paterson.

AUTHORS

$\mathcal{T}$hey write about the stars and outer space, presidents and poets, spies and children's fantasies. Nothing escapes their sharply tuned senses. They explore the universe and the mind with equal ease, probing the sources of life and love, war and peace.

They are the wordsmiths linking language with reality in all its abstract and perceivable forms. Their works reflect the deepest dimensions of human expression: The play, poem, novel, short story, movie, biography, history, scientific study, essay, criticism, journalism and the captioned photograph.

They are New Jersey's authors, storytellers and fact-finders, the compulsively curious communicators seeking truth, information and the essence of the physical world.

The best of them have been honored for their literary achievements, touches of immortality for turning an idea into a work of art or a universally scientific application.

Some were born in New Jersey. Others lived and worked here while pursuing their muse. A few prepared for their life's journey by studying at New Jersey schools.

All of them have left something of themselves for history to contemplate.

It took a Catholic schoolboy from Jersey City, **Will Durant**, to write "The Story of Civilization" with his wife Ariel, one of some 20 writing efforts to win Pulitzer Prizes for Jersey authors.

Durant grew up in Arlington, where his father was superintendent of a DuPont branch. His early education was in Roman Catholic schools. He was graduated from St. Peter's College in Jersey City and entered Seton Hall seminary in South Orange. His parents wanted him to become a priest.

Durant served as a Latin and French professor at Seton Hall from 1907 through 1911 and then began traveling abroad. After receiving a doctorate from Columbia University, Durant produced the most popular philosophy book ever published, "The Story of Philosophy."

An innovation in American writing, the book is a comprehensive survey of Western philosophy from Plato to John Dewey in the language of the average man. More than 3 million copies were sold over a 40-year period, liberating Durant from the chores of teaching to earn a living.

In 1935, he began the first of 11 volumes on the complete history of civilization, working seven-day, 56-hour weeks and living an almost monastic life. To write one volume in his story of civilization, Durant had to read some 500 other volumes of information. He turned out 1,000 words a day for the greater part of his life.

Durant died in 1981. His wife and lifelong collaborator died a week after her husband's death.

America's first major novelist, **James Fenimore Cooper**, was born in Burlington, South Jersey, on Sept. 15, 1789. He spent 17 of his most creative and productive years in and around the Burlington area. Cooper's greatest works were "The Leatherstocking Tales," which form an authentic American myth, stories that have appealed to readers at every level of sophistication from Cooper's day to the present.

The tales included "The Last of the Mohicans," "The Deerslayer," "The Pioneers" and "The Prairie." Victor Hugo rated

per higher than Sir Walter Scott, and Joseph Conrad found the Jersey writer "a rare artist . . . one of my masters."

A Princeton-educated writer, **Jesse Lynch Williams** (1871-1929), won the first Pulitzer Prize for "Best Play" in 1917, a three-act comedy that dared to ask, "Why Marry?"

F. Scott Fitzgerald, one of America's greatest novelists, spent three years at Princeton University and talked about his Jersey years in his first book, "This Side of Paradise" (1920). Princeton profoundly disappointed him by not putting him on its football team.

Another part-time Princeton student, **Eugene O'Neill**, won a record four Pulitzers for drama, plus a Nobel Prize in literature.

John O'Hara, who lived most of his life in Princeton, turned out a string of books that became worldwide box-office successes and attained Academy Awards for their stars, including Elizabeth Taylor.

Among the stars in O'Hara's hits were Gary Cooper, Paul

Newman and Joanne Woodward. Some of his bestsellers were "Butterfield 8," "From the Terrace," "10 North Frederick Street," "A Rage to Live" and "Appointment in Samarra."

Albert Einstein, who lived in Princeton from 1931 until his death in 1955, wrote "On the Electrodynamics of Human Bodies" at his office in the Institute for Advanced Study.

George Jerome Waldo Goodman is better known as **Adam Smith**, author of the Wall Street pop books "The Money Game," "Supermoney" and "Paper Money." The Princeton author was a newspaper and magazine writer, editor and screenwriter and co-founder of New York magazine.

A member of Princeton University's economics department advisory council, Smith is the recipient of the G. M. Loeb Award for distinguished achievement in writing about business and finance. Smith's other books include "The Bubble Makers," "The Wheeler Dealers" and "Bascombe."

The real Adam Smith was an 18th Century Scottish political economist and philosopher, whose book "An Inquiry into the Nature and Causes of the Wealth of Nations" exerted a strong influence on economic and political theory and practice.

One of the most popular biblical accounts in publishing history is "The Day Christ Died" by **Jim Bishop**, who is another Jersey City native who lived many years in Teaneck and Sea Bright and produced a series of popular and highly readable "Day" books, such as "The Day Lincoln Was Shot" and "A Day in the Life of President Kennedy."

Bishop, the founding editor of Gold Medal Books and Catholic Digest Book Club and a nationally syndicated columnist, is the recipient of the Encyclopedia Britannica Journalism in Life Award.

A storyteller who didn't turn in his first manuscript until he was 40, **Robert Ludlum** lost no time in writing 13 consecutive number-one bestsellers in 13 years, starting with the "Scarlatti Inheritance" in 1971 and continuing with his 1984 suspense masterpiece, "The Aquitaine Progression." A longtime Leonia resident, Ludlum spent the first half of his life as an actor, director and successful producer at the Playhouse-on-the-Mall, a Paramus theater of which he is a founder.

Among his other books are "The Matlock Paper," "The Matarese Circle," "The Gemini Contenders," "The Bourne Identity" and "The Rheinemann Exchange," a suspense novel set in Germany and made into a television mini-series.

Another storyteller who didn't turn in her first novel until late in life is **Belva Plain** of South Orange. For 30 years she contributed dozens of short stories to McCall's, Redbook, Cosmopolitan, Good Housekeeping and other periodicals before writing

John O'Hara

Belva Plain

William Carlos Williams

Norman Mailer

Sidney Kingsley *John McPhee* *Joyce Carol Oates* *Amiri Baraka*

Star-Ledger Photo   Photo Credit: Thomas Victor   Photo Credit: Jerry Bauer   Star-Ledger Photo

her first novel, "Evergreen," which was published in 1978 and became an instant bestseller.

Like Ludlum, Plain produces one bestseller after another, her second and third being "Random Winds" and "Eden Burning."

The Western novel was popularized by **Zane Grey**, who went to school in the Ironbound section of Newark and played baseball with an East Orange team. The prolific Grey captured the lives of the frontier cowboy and the lawless West when it was being settled by the pioneers. He was an educated Easterner who told the story of how the West was won, and he did it better than any other writer before or after his long publishing career.

Stephen Crane lived to be only 29, but the Newark native wrote the most popular—and considered the best—novel about the Civil War, "The Red Badge of Courage."

The poetic conscience of the Civil War was **Walt Whitman**, whose "Leaves of Grass" is an American classic. Whitman, who lived much of his life in Camden, where he is buried, is regarded by many critics and scholars as the best and most original poet of the 19th Century.

A comparable 20th Century designation has been bestowed on **Allen Ginsberg**, born in Newark in 1926 and raised and educated in Paterson. Son of a poet-teacher, Louis Ginsberg, Allen wrote what is rated as the most important post-World War II poem, "Howl," the story of the Beat Generation of which he was the spiritual voice.

Ginsberg was responsible for getting published Jack Kerouac's "On the Road," which, along with "Howl," documented the post-war period that gave birth to hippies and "Flower Power" children. Ginsberg today teaches at the Naropa Institute in Boulder, Colo.

Ginsberg's mentor was Dr. **William Carlos Williams**, a Rutherford pediatrician who received the Pulitzer Prize in poetry in 1963, the year he died. Opening his practice in 1910, Williams cared for the young during the day and worked long into the night on such memorable poems as "Paterson," an impressionistic piece that mirrored the conditions in the old Silk City from 1946 through 1958.

Williams developed a verse that was close to the idiom of speech, revealing a fidelity to ordinary things seen and heard. He influenced a generation of post-war poets, led by Ginsberg and Gregory Corso.

The biography of another famous poet, Robert Frost, won the 1971 Pulitzer Prize for a Princeton University English professor, **Lawrence Thompson** (1906-1973). Chairman of the editorial board of Princeton University Press in 1959-60, Thompson earned his prize for "Robert Frost: The Years of Triumph (1915-38), Volume II."

Frost asked Thompson to be his official biographer in 1939. Thompson lived near the poet in Ripton, Vt., during many summers and also traveled with the poet to read his poems at a presidential inauguration (John F. Kennedy in 1960).

Two New Jersey authors have each won a pair of Pulitzers for their writings.

George Frost Kennan, a professor at the Institute for Advanced Study in Princeton, received the 1957 Pulitzer for his autobiography, "Memoirs: 1925-50," and the 1968 Pulitzer (in history) for "Russia Leaves the War." Both books also won the National Book Award in the years they were published. Kennan's latest work is "The Nuclear Delusion."

Norman Mailer, born in Long Branch on Jan. 31, 1923, won Pulitzers for "The Armies in the Night" in 1968 (also a National Book Award winner), and "The Executioner's Song" in 1980. Co-founder of the Village Voice, Mailer wrote the widely acclaimed novel on World War II "The Naked and the Dead."

One of the most recognizable scientists in the world today is **Carl Sagan**, whose Pulitzer Prize-winning "Cosmos" became a television event in 1981. Raised in Rahway, Sagan has been a lecturer at Princeton University. The astronomer is based at Cornell University's space science center.

Playwright **Sidney Kingsley** of Oakland was awarded the Pulitzer for best American play in 1934, "Men in White." Kingsley also won the Drama Critics Circle Award in 1943 for "The Patriots."

One of his many hit plays was "Detective Story" in 1949. Kingsley also did the dramatization of Arthur Koestler's brilliant 1941 war novel, "Darkness at Noon," a long-running Broadway show starring Claude Raines.

Kingsley established the New Jersey Motion Picture and Television Commission in 1976, helping to bring the movie industry back to where it began when Thomas Edison perfected the motion picture camera in 1889 in his West Orange laboratory.

Van Wyck Brooks (1886-1963) was a scholar, biographer, sociologist and critic who wrote nearly 30 books, which earned him a preeminent place among historians of literature. Born in Plainfield, one of two sons of a stockbroker, Brooks received his early education in the Plainfield public schools.

Brooks is best known for his five-volume study of American writers begun in 1936 with "The Flowering of New England (1815-1865)," winner of the 1937 Pulitzer in history. He is credited with doing more than any other critic to discover and regain a "usable past" for Americans by recapturing the cultural life of the 19th and early 20th centuries.

Brooks believed that art must have roots in a fertile and receptive native soil, an idea he explored in an early book, "The

Wine of the Puritans," released in 1909.

Brooks also wrote the biographies of Helen Keller and painter John Sloan, both published in 1955, and helped translate 31 French books into English.

Margaret Coit Elwell, a retired professor and author-in-residence at Fairleigh Dickinson University, was awarded the Pulitzer Prize for biography in 1951 for "John C. Calhoun: American Portrait." She also received the Thomas Edison Award for "The Fight for Union."

James Gould Cozzens (1903-79), winner of the 1949 Pulitzer Prize for "Guard of Honor," set his best novels in New Jersey, according to his biographer, Matthew Bruccoli.

A resident of Lambertville from the early 1930s through 1956, Cozzens examined the lives of doctors, lawyers and ministers in "The Last Adam," "Men and Brethren" and "The Just and the Unjust." His most controversial work, "By Love Possessed," was his most popular book and revived an interest in the novelist.

One region of New Jersey spawned—and continues to attract—artists of every ilk and persuasion. Princeton is a historic town where one can live and work and enjoy the pleasant countryside, far enough away from the metropolitan congestion, yet close enough to the capitals of publishing and finance.

Among the hundreds of writers spinning their wordful webs near old Nassau Hall are Peter Benchley, John McPhee, Fletcher Knebel, Joyce Carol Oates, William Goldman, Carlos Baker and Freeman Dyson.

Peter Benchley, born into a family of poets, is the author of three blockbuster novels read and later seen by millions of screen buffs. The first, "Jaws," was released in 1977 and went right to the top of the box-office charts until it was bumped out of first place by another, more distant, creature, "E.T." Benchley's other marine stories transferred to the silver screen were "The Deep" and "The Island."

His prizes include the Fantasy Film Fans International Award and the Golden Eagle Award. Other Benchley books are "Time and a Ticket" and "Jonathan Visits the White House."

William Goldman divided his time between his Princeton studio and his Manhattan apartment, a lifestyle that led to a couple of Academy Awards for the Western classic "Butch Cassidy and the Sundance Kid" starring Paul Newman and Robert Redford, and a second golden trophy for the adapation of "Author."

Redford handed Goldman one of his toughest assignments: The adaptation of the Pulitzer Prize-winning investigative effort on Watergate, "All the President's Men," starring Redford and Dustin Hoffman. Hoffman then took Goldman's novel, "Marathon Man," and asked him to adapt it to the screen, with Hoffman in the title role. It also featured Lord Laurence Olivier.

Princeton Professor **Eric Goldman** (no relation) won the coveted Bancroft Prize for Distinguished American History in 1952 for "Rendezvous With Destiny, A History of Modern American Reform." The Emmy Award-winning moderator of the NBC television program "The Open Mind," Goldman wrote the "Tragedy of Lyndon Johnson" in 1969 while the president was still in office and deciding whether to seek reelection.

Among Goldman's other historical works are "The Crucial Decade—And After, America," "Charles J. Bonaparte," "John Bach McMaster," "American History" and "The World's History" (with F.C. Lane).

Fletcher Knebel began as a journalist working for several newspapers, including the Cleveland Plain Dealer. During his Princeton years he wrote about the issues of his times.

His most popular book was "Seven Days in May," the story of a military takeover of the federal government by an Army general who, in the movie version, was portrayed by Burt Lancaster. Knebel's other books were "The Bottom Line" (which became a catch phrase in business and industry), "Night of Camp David," "The Zinzin Road," "Vanished," "Trespass," "Dark Horse" and "Dave Sulkin Cares!"

Someone once said that **John McPhee** could write a tome on the toothpick and even win the unflinching praise of the most cynical literary critics.

John Angus McPhee, born in Princeton and a lifelong denizen, is a genuine literary resource in every sense of the word. He writes about the common in such an uncommon way that practically every one of his pieces for the New Yorker magazine has been expanded into book form, no matter how narrow the subject matter.

Breaking perceptions down to their finite parts, McPhee, once a television playwright for "Robert Montgomery Presents," has created timeless masterpieces from such improbable subjects as "Oranges," "The Pinelands," "The Deltoid Pumpkin Seed," "The Curve of Binding Energy," "The Survival of the Bark Canoe," "Pieces of the Frame," and "Giving Good Weight."

A graduate of Princeton University, McPhee is the recipient of the Literature Award given by the American Academy and Institute of Arts and Letters. His other works include "A Sense of Where You Are," "The Headmaster," "A Roomful of Hovings," "Levels of the Game," "The Crofter and the Laird," "Encounters with the Archdruid," "Coming Into the Country" and "Basin and Range."

Joyce Carol Oates, a writer-in-residence at Princeton University, has tried many literary forms, most of them successfully. The prolific author has written novels, poems, short stories, essays and criticisms.

Miss Oates won the National Book Award in 1970 for "Them" and the O. Henry Short Story Prize for a collection of stories entitled "By the North Gate." Her plays include "The Sweet Enemy," "Sunday Dinner," "Miracle Play" and "Daisy."

Among her numerous novels are "A Garden of Earthly Delights," "Wonderland," "Do With Me What You Will," "The Assassins," "Childwold," "The Triumph of the Spider Monkey," "Son of the Morning," "Unholy Loves," "Cybele," "Bellefleur" and "Angel of Light." Some poems are "Women in Love," "Expensive People," "Anonymous Sins," "Love and its Derangements," "Angel Fire," "Women Whose Lives are Food," "Men Whose Lives are Money," and "Dreaming America."

As editor of The Best American Short Stories, Miss Oates has distinguished herself in this field, beginning with "By the North Gate," followed by "Upon the Sweeping Flood," "The Wheel of Love," "Marriages and Infidelities," "The Hungry Ghosts," "The Goddess and Other Women," "Where Are You Going, Where Have You Been," "The Seduction" and "All the Good People I've Left Behind."

Carlos Baker, another Princeton University professor, is best known for his many books on Ernest Hemingway, from "Hemingway: The Writer as Artist," to an anthology titled "Hemingway and His Critics." Baker's others books include "Shelley's Major Poetry," "A Friend in Power," "The Land of Rumbelow," and a poetry edition, "A Year and a Day."

Freeman Dyson is affiliated with the Princeton Institute for Advanced Study and is among the leading physicists and mathematicians of the 20th Century. His autobiography and first book, "Disturbing the Universe," was a bestseller and was nominated for the National Book Award in 1981.

John Toland was 42 years old before his first book was published. The LaCrosse, Wis., native spent his early adult years holding a variety of jobs in the Red Bank area and writing no fewer than four novels, 20 plays and 100 short stories—none of which were ever published.

Toland then met an agent who advised him to try writing history books. He won the Pulitzer Prize for general nonfiction in 1971 for "The Rising Sun," a book on World War II in the Pacific, primarily from the Japanese viewpoint. Toland, winner of the Overseas Press Club Polk Memorial Award, authored numerous books, including "The Battle of the Bulge," "Ships in the Sky," "But Not in Shame," "The Flying Tigers," "The Dillinger Days" and "Adolph Hitler," which was honored with a Gold Medal from the National Society of Arts and Letters.

New Jersey's largest city, Newark, also has a long literary history predating Stephen Crane and extending to contemporary authors **Philip Roth** and **Amiri Baraka (LeRoi Jones)**. Prominent on that list is playwright **Dore Schary**, who died in 1982.

Roth, also a writer-in-residence at Princeton, won the National Book Award in 1959 for his first novel, "Goodbye, Columbus," which was made into a major motion picture starring Ali McGraw and Richard Benjamin.

In 1960, the O. Henry Short Story Prize went to the Newark writer. Several of his stories appeared in the Best American Short Stories in 1956, 1959 and 1960. Roth received the Aga Kahn Prize for Fiction in 1958 and the National Institute of Arts and Letters Award in 1960.

His books, many of them bestsellers, include "Letting Go," "When She Was Good," "Portnoy's Complaint," "Our Gang," "The Breast," "The Great American Novel," "My Life as a Man," "Reading Myself and Others," "The Professor of Desire" and "The Ghost Writer."

Poet, playwright and essayist Amiri Baraka received the Off-Broadway Award for best American play, "Dutchman," in 1964. Another play, "The Slave," won second prize in the International Art Festival in Dakar in 1966.

Baraka, who lives in Newark's college compound on Martin Luther King Boulevard, has authored "Blues People," "The Moderns," "Black Art," "Black Music," "A Black Mass," "The Baptism," "Tales," "A Collection of Critical Essays" and "The System of Dante's Hell." His poetry includes "The Creation of New Art."

Baraka founded the Black Arts Repertory Theater School in Harlem and Yugen Magazine and Totem Press in New York City. He also served as the coordinator of the creativity workshops at the Black Power Conference in 1968.

Newark native Dore Schary (1905-1982) was a newspaper writer, playwright, director and producer. From 1926-32, Schary was a screenwriter for various Hollywood studios. He worked for MGM Studios as executive producer in the early 1940s and was vice president in charge of production from 1948-56.

Schary's most successful Broadway play was "Sunrise at Campobello," an early portrait of Franklin Delano Roosevelt. His other dramas included "The Highest Tree," "One by One" and "Banderol." He wrote, directed and produced the movie, "Act One." Schary also adapted Morris West's "The Devil's Advocate" for the stage in 1961.

Schary's books included "Boys Town," "Edison the Man," "Young Tom Edison," "Case History of a Movie," "For Special Occasions," "Heyday" (an autobiography), and "Storm in the West" (with Sinclair Lewis).

A towering literary figure of the 20th Century was **Edmund Wilson** (1895-1972), regarded by his peers as America's leading man of letters. Born in Red Bank, Wilson's father was a prominent attorney who sent his son to Princeton University (class of 1916), where he met F. Scott Fitzgerald. Wilson's third wife was novelist Mary McCarthy. Critic Malcolm Cowley considered Wilson a prolific combination of Carlyle, Dr. Johnson and Sir Richard Burton, the 19th Century British explorer and linguist.

Wilson became known for his monumental works, which required that he learn foreign languages, including Hebrew and Russian, for such books as "Travels in Two Democracies" (1936), "A Window in Russia" (1972) and "Scrolls from the Dead Sea" (1955). His "To the Finland Station" (1940) reflects a broad knowledge of cultural, social and historical subjects.

Wilson served as managing editor of Vanity Fair magazine in 1920-21 and as associate editor of the New Republic from 1926-31. Many of his essays and reviews appeared in the New Yorker magazine.

Norman Cousins, born in Union Hill, is one of America's leading editors and commentators. Editor of the Saturday Review since 1935, Cousins is also editor of U.S.A. and served as editor for several major publications: Treasury of Democracy, The Poetry of Freedom and Great American Essays. Cousins also served as editorial supervisor of March's Dictionary-Thesaurus.

Among Cousins' numerous honors are the Educational Broadcasting Corp. Thomas Jefferson Award, the Benjamin Franklin Citation in magazine journalism, the John Dewey Award for service to education, the Eleanor Roosevelt Peace Award, the Family of Man Award, the United Nations Peace Medal and the National Arts Club Gold Medal for Literature.

His many books include "The Good Inheritance," "Who Speaks for Man?" and "In God We Trust: The Religious Beliefs of the Founding Fathers."

Michael Angelo Avallone is known as "the fastest typewriter in the East," turning out scores of novels and teleplays (television scripts). The East Brunswick resident says a professional writer should be able to write anything—from the Bible to a garden seed catalog and everything that lies in-between.

"Writing is the last frontier of individualism in the world, the one art a man can do alone that basically resists collaboration," says Avallone.

A quick rundown on some of his works reads like a paperback list and TV guide: "Man from U.N.C.L.E.," "Hawaii Five-O," "Mannix," "The Doctors," "The Partridge Family," "The Cannonball Run," "Beneath the Planet of the Apes" and a string of titles familiar to moviegoers and TV watchers, from "Charlie Chan and the Curse of the Dragon Lady" to the "Detective" series.

From 1961-71, Avallone served on the awards committee of the American Mystery Writers.

Kenneth Burke of Andover received the National Medal for Literature in 1981 for a lifelong writing career involving poetry, novels, history, language, translations and editing volumes of books on everything from philosophy to grammar. A music and literary critic, Burke was the recipient of the 1928 Dial Award for Distinguished Service to American Letters and the 1968 New Jersey Teachers Association Poet-of-the-Year Award.

Burke's works include a novel on "Towards a Better Life," "The White Oxen and Other Stories" and "Book of Moments, Poems."

Gay Talese, born in Ocean City on Feb. 7, 1932, is a journalist whose book, "Honor Thy Father," on organized crime families, was an international bestseller and motion picture. Talese's first book, "A Serendipiter's Journey," was published in 1961, followed by "The Bridge," "The Overreachers," "The Kingdom and the Power," "Fame and Obscurity" and "Thy Neighbor's Wife."

Anne Morrow Lindbergh, whose husband Charles was the first person to pilot an airplane across the Atlantic Ocean, in 1927, was awarded the Hubbard Medal of the National Geographic Society for her writings on conservation.

Born in Englewood, Anne Morrow Lindbergh lived many years in New Jersey with the famous aviator, writing "North to the Orient," "Listen, the Wind" and "Unicorn and Other Poems." Her other books are concerned with the global environment: "Gift From the Sea," "Earth Shine" and "Wave of the Future."

Harriet Adams of Maplewood (1893-1982) created one of the most memorable children's series in publishing history, the "Nancy Drew" stories, begun in 1930. The popular series led to the "Nancy Drew Cookbook" in 1973.

Adams' *nom de plume* was **Carolyn Keene**.

Adele De Leeuw of Plainfield has written more than 75 children's books, one of the biggest sellers being "Remembered With Love." More than 15 million De Leeuw books have been printed in several languages.

Judith St. George of Essex Fells also specializes in books for young people, although her writing career began on a historic note, a fictional account of the American Revolution during the winter of 1780-81 in Jockey Hollow, Morristown. The title: "Turncoat Winter, Rebel Spring." Her fifteenth and latest project was aimed at the young adult market—"Do You See What I See? " One of her own favorites is "The Halo Wind."

Judy Blume of Elizabeth was recognized early as a children's writer with her book, "Are You There God, It's Me Margaret," selected as the outstanding children's book in 1970. Some other whimsical Blume creations are "Tales of a 4th Grade Nothing," "It's Not the End of the World," "Otherwise Known as Sheila the Great" and "Then Again, Maybe I Won't."

The New Jersey Literary Hall of Fame each year recognizes authors from the Garden State who have distinguished themselves in their respective literary fields.

The Hall of Fame is located in the Van Houten Library of the New Jersey Institute of Technology (NJIT), Newark. Founder and director of the Hall of Fame is Dr. Herman Estrin of Scotch Plains, a teacher, writer and lecturer.

Newark International Airport.

AVIATION

A century before Wilbur and Orville Wright put wings on people and sent them aloft, the first aerial landing in the Western Hemisphere took place at Woodbury, South Jersey. The year was 1793, signaling the beginning of aviation travel in America.

For the next two centuries, New Jersey was the center of aeronautical developments that contributed to Charles Lindbergh's solo flight across the Atlantic Ocean in 1927, to Amelia Earhart's flight over the Atlantic a year later, to the first rocket engine built at Reaction Motors in Rockaway, and the first landing of a vehicle on the surface of the moon by astronaut Edwin (Buzz) Aldrin Jr. of Montclair in 1969.

The word "airport" came into the language in 1919 when Bader Field in Atlantic City was designated the first municipal airport in the world.

The story of aviation and the role New Jersey played in putting people safely in the skies is vividly portrayed at the Aviation Hall of Fame and Museum that opened last summer at Teterboro Airport in Bergen County.

According to H.V. Pat Reilly, executive vice president of the museum, New Jersey's aeronautical dreams got off the ground when a French balloonist named Jean Pierre Blanchard made the first aerial ascent from within the walls of Philadelphia's Walnut Street Prison. The huge, colorful, hydrogen-filled balloon floated freely over the City of Brotherly Love and drifted 15 miles before gently settling down on a farm in Deptford Township.

President George Washington had given Blanchard a letter of safe conduct to be presented to the first farmer he met in South Jersey. The first airmail letter delivered in the Americas arrived in the Garden State.

The first native American to fly was Charles F. Durant, a resident of Jersey City who sailed his balloon from New York City's Battery Park, across the harbor, landing in then-rural Perth Amboy. It was 1830 and ballooning was becoming more than a daredevil's publicity stunt. By 1855, the first woman soared into the sky in a smoke balloon from Easton, Pa., to Phillipsburg, along the Delaware River.

It wasn't until 1973 that publisher Malcolm S. Forbes of Far Hills became the first man to free-flight a balloon 2,911 miles across the United States.

Forbes followed a long tradition of ballooning in New Jersey. In 1863, Dr. Soloman Andrews of Perth Amboy was the first to build and fly a dirigible balloon in the Western Hempishere.

After the Civil War in 1866, Andrews crafted a larger, elongated triple-balloon called The Aereon. It could fly forward *against* the wind in a fishtail motion, an unbelievable feat at that time.

The first attempt to sail the skies of the Atlantic Ocean was undertaken by Walter Wellman and Melvin Vaniman in 1910. Their twin-engined dirigible lifted from the beach in Atlantic City but was forced down 100 miles at sea. The crew was rescued by a passing steamer.

In 1920, the United States Navy built large airship hangars at Lakehurst and Cape May to accommodate a proposed new fleet of reconnaissance airships, Reilly notes in his account of aviation in New Jersey. Within a few years, Lakehurst became the center of

America's lighter-than-air development and the terminal for the first international passenger air service.

The dirigible service was popular in the 1920s, with the transatlantic flight from Germany to Lakehurst being made in four or five days, proving that commercial flight was feasible and profitable. The airship service ended in 1937 when the German dirigible Hindenberg exploded on landing at Lakehurst.

Fixed-wing aircraft, however, gained acceptance after the Wright brothers demonstrated at Kitty Hawk in 1903 that rather simple technology can resist the laws of gravity. By 1908, the Boland brothers of Rahway were experimenting with fixed-wing flying models and a tailless version was successfully flown by Frank Boland at Iselin in 1910.

That same year, Walter Brookins, a Wright-trained pilot, set an altitude record of 6,175 feet over Atlantic City, while Glenn Curtiss, an aviation pioneer, was demonstrating his flimsy aircraft off the beach of the South Jersey resort. Within five years, the Curtiss Exhibition Co. was carrying sightseers in wooden flying boats off the waters of the Atlantic City Inlet.

While aviation records were being set one after another, New Jersey's aircraft manufacturing companies were creating a new worldwide industry. In 1917-18, aircraft and engine manufacturers in Paterson, Plainfield, Newark, New Brunswick, Elizabeth and Keyport built more than 2,500 aircraft and thousands of engines for the Allies during World War I.

At the same time, the Standard Aircraft Corp. of Plainfield produced the Standard J-1, which became the first commercial

Hot air balloons take to the sky during a meet in Bloomsbury.   Star-Ledger Photo

aircraft in the United States. The little biplanes carried airmail for the postal service between Hadley Field in North Plainfield and Washington, D.C.

In the 1920s, New Jersey's aircraft and engine designers and manufacturers were responsible for opening the skies to commercial aviation, according to the Teterboro museum historian, Pat Reilly. His research shows the undisputed leaders were the Wright Aeronautical Corp. and the Wright-Bellanca Co. of Paterson, and the Fokker Aircraft Corp. of Teterboro.

"It was the development of the Wright Whirlwind J-4 engine that made it feasible for men and women to achieve a new aeronautical horizon," Reilly recounts. "And on all the most historic flights of the 1920s and early 1930s, only Lindbergh's Spirit of St. Louis was not either a New Jersey-built Fokker or Bellanca-designed airplane. Lindbergh's engine, however, was a Wright Whirlwind."

A Fokker F-7 trimotor was used by Richard E. Byrd and Floyd Bennett on the first flight over the North Pole in 1926. A similar plane was used by Byrd and his crew a year later to fly to Europe, a month after "Lucky Lindy's" historic flight. The North Pole plane had been tested and outfitted at Teterboro Airport over a 16-hour period.

Amelia Earhart became the first woman to fly the Atlantic, in a Fokker trimotor, in 1928, and Fokkers were used on Pan American Airways' first international flight, from Key West, Fla., to Havana, Cuba, Reilly relates.

John Ordway Webster was the first to fly air mail from coast to coast in 1921 in a World War I surplus de Havilland DH-4, redesigned and rebuilt by the Wittemann Aircraft Corp. at Teterboro Airport.

The monoplane designed by Guiseppe Bellanca and built in Paterson by the Wright Corp. became the second aircraft to cross the Atlantic, just two weeks after Lindbergh. Pilot Charles Chamberlin and his passenger-sponsor, Charles Levin, flew into Germany, setting a new distance and endurance flight record for that era.

The Paterson-built Bellanca monoplane was also used by Clyde Pangborn and Hugh Herndon in 1931 when they became the first men to fly nonstop across the Pacific Ocean, Reilly's history reveals.

Juan Terry Trippe introduced transoceanic commercial aviation to the United States in 1926 when he formed Colonial Air Transport with a group of friends. Based at both Teterboro Airport and Hadley Field in North Plainfield, the new airline received the first airmail contract awarded to private aviation by the U.S. Postal Service. Airmail Route No. 1 covered the New York-Boston territory. Trippe chose two Teterboro-built Fokker F-7 trimotors and a single-engine Curtiss as the initial equipment for his new airline.

A year later Trippe founded Pan American Airways and bought a Fokker F-10 trimotor to use on Pan Am's first international flight from Florida to Cuba.

In 1965, Trippe negotiated an agreement with the Port Authority of New York and New Jersey for the airline to operate Teterboro Airport for the bistate transportation authority.

Besides Pan Am, other commercial airlines sprang from roots planted in the Garden State. American, Eastern and United Airlines trace their origins to the first major commercial airport in the greater metropolitan area: Newark Airport. Built by the City of Newark in 1928 on 68 acres of swampland, it was the world's busiest airport by 1930.

Newark International Airport today takes in 2,300 acres and represents a billion-dollar investment. Three modern terminals handle more than 10 million passengers and 200,000 plane movements a year.

People Express, the world's fastest growing airline, began renovating Terminal C in 1985 at a cost of $175 million. When completed in 1986, it will give the no-frills airline more space under one roof than any carrier has at any airport, according to Donald C. Burr, founding chairman of People Express.

More than 6,200 people are employed at the fastest-growing airport in the nation. It accounts for much of New Jersey's more than $600 million-a-year aviation industry revenue.

During the bleak Depression years of the 1930s, record-setting speed and endurance flights into Newark and Teterboro airports kept aviation in the forefront of daily events. Famous aviators such as Earhart, Jimmy Doolittle, Howard Hughes and Frank Hawks made aviation history at Newark and Teterboro.

The second leading flying ace during World War II was Maj. Thomas B. McGuire Jr., a 24-year-old former Ridgewood resident who became an instant hero by shooting down 38 enemy planes before he lost his life over the Pacific. McGuire Air Force Base in Wrightstown, Burlington County, is named after the war hero.

Star-Ledger Photo

The Aviation Hall of Fame at Teterboro Airport celebrates New Jersey's aviation heritage from Lindbergh to NASA.

Star-Ledger Photo

Sitting contentedly in his P-38 Lightning aircraft, Pudge, Major Thomas B. McGuire, Jr. flashes the easy smile remembered vividly by his squadron members.

After the war, aviation became big business and the daredevils of the barnstorming era had become little more than pleasant memories. Their death-defying antics, however, are an unforgettable part of New Jersey's colorful aviation past preserved at the Teterboro Hall of Fame and Museum.

Ivan Gates ran the Gates Flying Circus during the "Roaring '20s" and his pilots carried more than 750,000 passengers in their rag-tag collection of World War I surplus planes.

Ivan promoted two National Air Show and Air Circus events in 1927 and '28. Gates' chief pilot, Clyde Pangborn, was the first man to fly an airplane upside-down. When not wingwalking and barnstorming across America, Pangborn advanced the importance of aviation by, among other things, making the first airmail pickup with a hook and tackle at Teterboro, and the first nonstop, transpacific flight in October 1931 from Japan to Washington State in a Paterson-built, Wright-Bellanca airplane.

New Jersey's first director of aeronautics, Gill Robb Wilson (1931-46), organized and commanded the first Civil Air Patrol. He was also co-founder of the Aircraft Owners and Pilots Association.

Royal French Ryder was the first man to test the Bendix hands-off landing system in a B-25 at Teterboro. Ryder joined the Bendix Corp. at Teterboro in 1944 as a test pilot.

When Bendix started experimenting with automatic approach and landing systems during the end of World War II, Ryder was in the pilot's seat of the Bendix B-25 test plane when it touched down without a human hand on the controls.

In 1947, Clifford Evans and George Truman flew two Piper Super Cruisers around the world to and from Teterboro Airport.

That same year, a rocket engine developed and built at Reaction Motors in Rockaway was used to propel Capt. Charles Yeager

Star-Ledger Photo

Radio and early television personality Arthur Godfrey stands next to a vintage Grumman "Widgeon" aircraft during a press conference at Terminal A, Newark Airport, to announce celebration of the facility's 50th anniversary in September 1978.

in the first supersonic flight. Seven years later, Yeager flew an advanced version of the X-1 rocket to the speed of Mach 2.42, more than 1,200 mph.

Radio and television personality Arthur Godfrey, who was born and raised in Hasbrouck Heights, next to the Borough of Teterboro, made his hometown airport a household name when he buzzed the tower in 1952. Before that controversial incident, Godfrey had established himself as an accomplished aviator.

In July 1947, Godfrey set a record by flying solo from Teterboro to Point Barrow, Alaska—and return—traveling 12,000 nautical miles in 62 hours.

The role of women in aviation figures prominently in the history of flying at Teterboro. In 1941, Kay Brick learned how to fly by taking special courses at Teaneck High School, also in Bergen County.

An early member of the Ninety-Nines, aviation's most prestigious women's organization, Brick was responsible for making Teterboro Airport the termination point in the All Women's Transcontinental Race, or Powder Puff Derby. In 1961, Brick was named executive director of the derby and placed the derby's headquarters at Teterboro, where it remained for 14 years.

Throughout the 1950s and '60s, rockets developed by Reaction Motors became larger and more powerful, penetrating the upper stratospheres beyond 60 miles at speeds of 4,535 mph.

The next conquest was outer space. Again, New Jerseyans responded to the challenge by joining the American space program. Walter Schirra of Oradell was one of the seven original astronauts chosen to participate in the space venture. Schirra is the only person to have flown into the Earth's outer atmosphere in three generations of space vehicles: Mercury, Gemini and Apollo.

Buzz Aldrin of Montclair was among the second group of astronauts selected for the National Aeronautical and Space Administration (NASA) moon mission. Col. Aldrin followed Neil Armstrong on to the lunar surface and for two hours and 15 minutes assisted in the collection of lunar surface samples and conducted numerous lunar experiments.

NASA adopted Aldrin's space rendezvous techniques later used on all U.S. missions, including joint projects with Russian cosmonauts.

Astronaut Russell L. Schweickart of Neptune flew on the Apollo 9 space mission, and Kathryn Sullivan of Paterson is in training to become one of the first women to fly in space aboard the shuttle.

Lakehurst in Ocean County is the site of the world's largest, single wooden-arch structures, Hangars 5 and 6. Another hangar is home for an aircraft carrier, Colossus, used for training by the Naval Air Technical Training Center.

The first Navy Parachute Riggers School was also established at the Lakehurst Naval Station in 1924.

Airports and air transportation in New Jersey today represent the most geographically compressed and complex system in the nation, employing more than 26,000 people, including 13,400 military personnel and 2,500 Federal Aviation Administration (FAA) Technical Center employes.

There are 90 public-use airports, 65 privately owned aviation facilities, and more than 400 licensed helicopter landing places supporting power and pipeline patrols, fire fighting, construction, mosquito and gypsy moth control, traffic reporting, medical transportation, storm damage survey, executive travel, law enforcement, charter, environmental investigations, air commuter, bank documents clearing, and emergency missions.

In addition, 24 hospitals have established helicopter landing pads for medical support purposes.

New Jersey's airports range in size from Newark's 2,200-acre international operation to 52 acres at Twin Pines in Pennington just outside Trenton. Newark's parallel main runways are 9,800 and 8,200 feet long, while Twin Pines has a single turf runway of 2,200 feet for small, single engine aircraft only.

Newark International Airport today is utilized by 30 airlines at three modern terminals, and at cargo and other facilities.

Of the 115 airports in New Jersey, eight of them best exemplify the range of services offered, particularly their proximity to the marketplace. Excluding Newark Airport, they are:

• Bader Field, Atlantic City.

Serving the biggest resort in the country in the number of daily visitors, Bader Field occupies 134 acres with a main runway of 2,950 feet and a crosswind runway of 2,600 feet.

Serviced by Allegheny Commuter, as well as air tax, charter and commercial companies, Bader Field is one of two airport facilities owned by Atlantic City.

• Burlington Airpark, Mount Holly.

A parachute jump training center with a drop zone adjacent to it is located at the 120-acre airport three miles southwest of Mount Holly, the seat of Burlington County. A single runway 3,700 feet long is capable of accommodating many types of business and recreational aircraft. It is a privately owned, public use facility.

• Linden Airport, Union County.

During World War II, the General Motors Corp. in Linden was known as Eastern Aircraft. The testing grounds for Eastern's planes along Route 1-9 is now the site of Linden Airport, owned and operated by the city. The airport plays a vital role in supporting the high number of private aircraft and small planes in the New York metropolitan region.

Although jets are not based at Linden, the airport is classified as larger than a general-utility airport and serves as a "reliever" of air traffic congestion at other metropolitan airports.

The busy corporate air terminal lies just south of Newark International Airport.

• Monmouth County Airport, Wall Township.

The largest privately owned, public-use airport in New Jersey, Monmouth airport covers 654 acres and has a main runway 7,000 feet long, exceeded in length only by runways at Newark and Atlantic City airports.

Monmouth Airport houses and is surrounded by aviation-related business and manufacturing companies, including a major producer of airline safety devices.

• Teterboro Airport, Bergen County.

Located in the communities of Teterboro and Moonachie on 878 acres, Teterboro Airport is owned by the Port Authority of New York and New Jersey and is operated by Pan American World Airways Corp.

One of six New Jersey airports with a control tower, Teterboro handles more than a quarter-million takeoffs and landings a year. More than 460 aircraft are based at the Bergen County air transportation hub.

The fully instrumented airport has two runways, 7,000 and 6,000 feet long. The airport is headquarters for the sales, service and training for Falcon Jet Aircraft and is home of the Aviation Hall of Fame and Museum.

Three FAA offices are located at Teterboro. Several national corporations base their flight operations at Teterboro, including American Cyanamid, Texaco, National Distillers, Beechcraft, Executive Air Fleet, Aero Services and Omni Flight Group Helicopter Services.

• Millville Airport, Cumberland County.

A surplus Navy base with three 5,000-foot runways, Millville Municipal Airport is the headquarters of Airwork Corp., a major worldwide overhaul facility for jet turbine engines. It is also the home of Wheaton Industries, a major glass and plastics manufacturer.

• McGuire Air Force Base, Burlington County.

Located at Wrightstown, McGuire is the home of the 21st Air Force Headquarters of the Military Airlift Command (MAC). It is a major East Coast port of embarkation for deployment of military troops and cargo to Europe, Africa and the Middle East. McGuire also houses strategic air refueling and tactical fighter units of the Air Reserve Forces.

The base is named after Maj. Thomas B. McGuire Jr., Congressional Medal of Honor recipient and native of New Jersey.

• Morristown Airport, Morris County.

Located in Hanover Township, Morristown Airport was built by the military in 1941 and declared surplus in 1944. Used by Bell Labs for test purposes, the airport today takes in 600 acres.

Two runways are 4,000 feet and 6,000 feet, the longer one for all-weather instrument landing. Morristown is designated a "reliever" airport for Newark, allowing landings for commercial craft as large as 727s. Morristown handles a quarter-million operations a year.

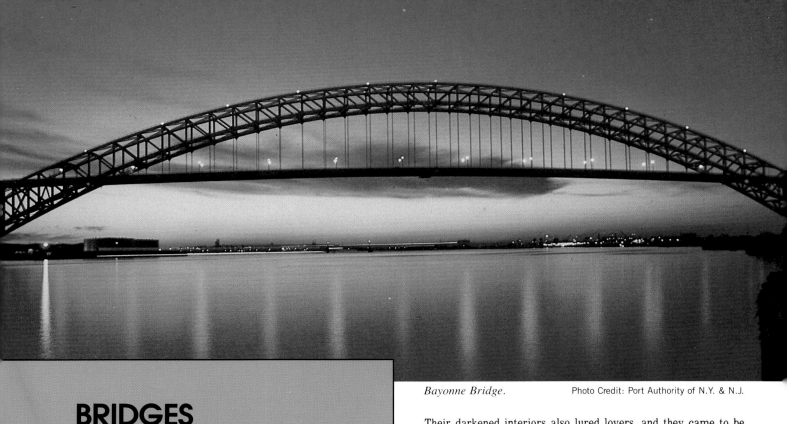

BRIDGES

*T*heir thick steel girders and tightly spun cables weave a massively intricate web of soaring architectural strength over New Jersey's rivers and wetlands, linking the state's roads and railways into a tremendously complex transportation network.

There are more than 6,200 of them, of which a half-dozen are among the most magnificent superstructures in the world.

They are New Jersey's bridges, engineering masterpieces spanning the bistate Hudson and Delaware rivers. Other less imposing yet splendidly sweeping arches and suspensions stretch gracefully across the Hackensack, Passaic and Raritan rivers, while still other vaulting eye-catchers range over the Arthur Kill, Kill Van Kull and lesser waterways.

As a peninsula-shaped state, New Jersey is coursed by more than 6,000 miles of tributaries. And as the most urbanized state in the nation, New Jersey is crisscrossed by tens of thousands of miles of roadways.

To get from one point to another, people and their carriages had either to go over or around the aqueous obstructions. All kinds of bridges had to be built to shorten the distance for weary travelers making their way from Jersey City to Newark and Trenton, or the commuters passing through between New York and Philadelphia and Washington, D.C.

At one time there were some 75 covered bridges in New Jersey, constructed from 1825-75. There is just one left: The quaint Green Sergeants' covered bridge in Sergeantsville, Hunterdon County. The white oaken landmark, hammered together in 1872, spans the Wickecheoke Creek. The original abutments were built in 1750. The single-lane bridge is still in use. It is 81 feet long and 12 feet wide.

Historians say covered bridges served as shelters during storms and were used by farmers to shape their loads of hay. Their darkened interiors also lured lovers, and they came to be known fondly as the "Kissing Bridges."

Unless a bridge is 20 feet long, it does not appear on the state's roster of bridges checked periodically for safety. Although there are about 6,200 bridges in the Garden State at least 20 feet and longer, there are many that have been orphaned by bankrupt railroads and manufacturers that have long gone out of business.

The latest breakdown shows there are 2,383 state-owned bridges more than 20 feet in length ... 2,327 local and county bridges ... 1,422 bridges maintained by private agencies such as the New Jersey Turnpike Authority, the New Jersey Highway Authority (Garden State Parkway), the Atlantic City Expressway Authority and the Port Authority of New York and New Jersey ... an undetermined number of bridges owned or abandoned by Conrail and Amtrak ... and orphaned bridges rotting or rusting away on forsaken industrial sites and fallow farmlands.

Water drew the Colonial settlers to New Jersey and their bridges helped to forge an Industrial Revolution that was ignited in Paterson on the Passaic River when Alexander Hamilton conceived America's first planned industrial city.

Today, New Jersey bridges have made it into the history books for their beauty and unique construction.

The George Washington Bridge is the busiest span in the world and many noted architects believe it is the most beautiful. The "GW Bridge" is also the only 14-lane bridge in the world and was the largest suspension bridge when built.

The Delaware Memorial Bridge is the longest twin-suspension bridge ever erected.

The Bayonne Bridge replaced America's first public ferry, established in 1750. And when erected in 1931, the Bayonne Bridge boasted the longest steel arch on earth.

The first bridge in the United States named after a woman is the Betsy Ross over the Delaware River, connecting Pennsauken in South Jersey to northeast Philadelphia.

Named after the river that George Washington crossed to win a revolution, the Delaware Memorial Bridge, which joins the New Jersey Turnpike with Interstate 95 in Delaware, holds the record for the largest continuous underwater concrete pour for the bridge's anchorage in New Jersey.

The second longest cantilevered highway bridge in the world is the Commodore John Barry Bridge between Bridgeport, South Jersey, and Chester, Pa.

New Jersey's most important bridges follow.

George Washington Bridge

From tower to tower, the George Washington Bridge leaps in uninterrupted splendor for 3,500 feet across the swirling Hudson River some 250 feet below. The mighty towers stand 600 feet like kings of the Palisades.

More than 2 billion vehicles have crossed the GW Bridge since it opened on Sunday, Oct. 25, 1931. Twice as long as the longest suspension bridge ever built at the time, the bistate span remains a marvel of its time, the noblest of all bridges.

Construction began in October 1927. Some 43,000 tons of steel went into the creation of the Hudson River bridge. Once the towers were in place, spinning wheels moved back and forth across the river, weaving a web of steel wires, each thinner than a pencil, until four incredibly strong cables were ready to sustain the roadway. Each cable is a yard in diameter and contains 26,474 wires, which, if stretched end to end, would reach 107,000 miles, nearly halfway to the moon.

The tensile strength of the wire is 225,000 pounds per square inch.

A total of 3,368 cable band bolts hold the cable bands on the 36-inch main cables in place. The cable bands, in turn, support the vertical cables (suspenders).

Steel suspenders hanging from the main cables support the steel-concrete, split-level roadway, 14 lanes in all. Structurally sound, it can remain so indefinitely.

The total weight of the bridge is 600,000 tons.

The original cost of the bridge was $59 million. The Port Authority added a second level and, over the years, has invested more than $241 million in its most treasured bridge.

The largest free-flying American flag ever made (60 by 90 feet) is suspended on holidays and special occasions beneath the arch of the New Jersey tower of the bridge. During the 1964-65 New York World's Fair, the U.S. flag was illuminated at night by a battery of floodlights, a spectacular first that has been repeated for holidays and special events.

The bridge's diamond necklace—148 lights on the cables—

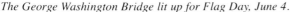

The George Washington Bridge lit up for Flag Day, June 4.   Courtesy: Port Authority of N.Y. & N.J.

glows nightly to outline the graceful curve of the lovely suspension bridge.

The George Washington Bridge has been celebrated in art, photography, poetry and music. William Schuman, who later went on to become president of Lincoln Center, wrote a musical composition, "George Washington Bridge," for symphonic bands.

Designed by the Port Authority's chief engineer at the time, Othmar H. Ammann, the George Washington Bridge has been an emergency landing strip for a small plane and a passageway for animals that have been driven or herded across its traffic lanes.

During the 1981 drought, a 36-inch water pipeline was assembled along the north pedestrian walk to carry water to near-empty New Jersey reservoirs.

The friendly giant started life as "a memorial to friendly cooperation between states" and it remains a symbol of cooperation and unity between the two "new" Colonial sister states of New Jersey and New York.

Pulaski Skyway

New Jersey's first superhighway was, when built, the most spectacular skyroad or diagonal highway in the country, a mammoth viaduct extending 3.7 miles over the Passaic and Hackensack rivers and Meadowlands.

A grand memorial to Gen. Casimir Pulaski, the Polish hero of the American Revolution, the Pulaski Skyway was the "greatest highway project" in the United States when it was built in the early 1930s at a cost of $20 million.

The route used before the skyway opened on Thanksgiving Day 1932 was 4.2 miles long, with two drawbridges that frequently delayed traffic. Those obstacles often made the 13-mile trip from Jersey City to Elizabeth a two-hour ordeal. The skyway reduced traveling time to a few minutes. It was the final link in the 13-mile stretch between Jersey City and Elizabeth that cost $40 million and was the most critical segment of the New York-to-Washington route, the most heavily used in the world.

The project involved two bridges whose cantilevered arches of unornamented steel were linked to the huge concrete-steel viaduct. The New Jersey skyway served as a model for a British project.

The two spans are 135 feet above the tidal rivers and merge into long sweeping lines with the regular deck spans crossing the meadows at a height of 75 feet. Despite its impressive size, the skyway gives an appearance of sturdy grace. The grades are so gradual they do not exceed 3.5 percent at any point along the elevated corridor.

The skyway took 88,461 tons of structural steel to build, or 20,000 tons more than were used in the George Washington Bridge. Fabrication of the members required more than 2 million rivets.

A record depth for pneumatic drilling was established in the excavations for the foundations, which were carried 147 feet below mean high-water level for the bridge piers.

The viaduct is built upon piers of reinforced concrete shafts linked by reinforced concrete and capped by steel "shoes," which support arched spans of lattice steel.

The 550-foot-long spans carry the roadway between the towers, and shafts 90 feet tall stand at each end of the bridge spans to carry the shoes.

Built during the worst economic depression, the $7 million-a-mile project almost became a 10-cent toll road to offset the costs. The Federal Highway Administration and Gov. A. Harry Moore vetoed the idea.

Designed by S. Johannesson under the direction of State Highway Engineer Jacob L. Bauer, the Pulaski Skyway received the fifth annual award in 1932 from the American Institute of Steel Construction for "the most beautiful and monumental bridge built in the United States."

Bayonne Bridge

At the time of its opening, Nov. 15, 1931, the Bayonne Bridge was the longest bridge of its type, anywhere. The bridge's 1,675-foot steel arch is longer by five feet than the similar span of the Sydney, Australia bridge.

Another product of the Port Authority and its chief engineer, Othmar Ammann, the Bayonne Bridge held the record for steel arches for 46 years. In 1977, the New River George Bridge was completed in Fayetteville, W. Va. It was 25 feet longer.

The midspan clearance of 150 feet permits ocean-going vessels to pass under the Bayonne Bridge on their way to Port Newark and the Port Authority Marine Terminal in Elizabeth.

With its symmetrical, 325-foot-high arch, the Bayonne Bridge was voted "the most beautiful steel bridge" by the American Institute of Steel Construction in the prestigious Class A for 1931.

Built for $13 million—$3 million under budget—the Bayonne beauty leaps over the Kill Van Kull, connecting Bayonne to Port Richmond, Staten Island. The Kill Van Kull is the main ship gateway between Newark Bay and the Hackensack and Passaic rivers.

More than 4.4 million vehicles use the toll bridge each year. Not once has the awesome arch been forced to shut down to traffic.

Goethals and Outerbridge

Since the close of the Civil War, the growing populations of New York and New Jersey sought a quicker route to Staten Island than waiting for a ferry.

Consideration had been given to the problem of bridging the Arthur Kill, the narrow tributary separating North Jersey from Staten Island, which, geographically, is an extension of the New Jersey mainland, not New York.

The Port Authority solved the worsening transit problem with the opening of the first two facilities it built: The Goethals Bridge and Outerbridge Crossing.

The two bridges were dedicated on June 20, 1928 and opened to traffic on June 29. The steel truss cantilevered bridges are of similar design. Both are four-lane and span the Arthur Kill with a 135-foot clearance to allow large merchant vessels to move through the congested shipping channel.

The Goethals Bridge, linking Elizabeth with Howland Hook, Staten Island, is a fitting memorial to Maj. Gen. George W. Goethals, builder of the Panama Canal and the first consulting engineer of the Port Authority. The PA was founded in 1921 to manage the movement of people and goods through the port district, a 50-mile radius whose center is the Statue of Liberty.

The Goethals' center span is 672 feet, its truss spans 1,152 feet and the width of the main bridge spans 62 feet. The Port Authority has invested slightly more than $26 million in the bridge since its conception.

The Goethals Bridge connects directly to the New Jersey Turnpike at interchange 13 and is a major route between Brooklyn and New Jersey, a continous ribbon of asphalt feeding into the Staten Island Expressway and Verrazano-Narrows Bridge, the last great span designed by Othmar Ammann, in 1963.

Traffic volume on the Goethals Bridge exceeded 9.8 million (eastbound) in 1984.

The Outerbridge Crossing happens to be the Port Authority's outermost bridge in the port district, but its name is derived not from its geographic location but from the man who served as the first chairman of the Port Authority: Eugenius H. Outerbridge, a prominent Staten Island resident.

Connecting Perth Amboy in New Jersey with Tottenville, Staten Island, the Outerbridge provides a southern link between the island and the Jersey Shore.

The bridge's center span is 750 feet long and its truss spans 2,100 feet. The main span is 62 feet wide. The Port Authority has invested more than $31.7 million in the Outerbridge Crossing, which registered more than 9.8 million toll-paying customers (eastbound) in 1984.

Delaware Memorial Bridge

The twin spans of The Delaware Memorial Bridge are impressive by any architectural standards, but they do not have that stunning, naked-steel look of New Jersey's northern bridges. The four towers are simply sticks of unembellished steel stuck in the water. Impressive—but bland by Ammann's engineering design standards.

The first Delaware Memorial Bridge (named after the bistate river) was opened to traffic on Aug. 16, 1951. The four-lane suspension span joined U.S. 40, 130 and the New Jersey Turnpike with U.S. 13 and 40 in Delaware.

In 1956, the 2,150-foot-long bridge was designated as Interstate 295, a part of the interstate route between Maine and Florida.

In 1962, the Delaware River and Bay Authority, a bistate agency, was formed to operate the bridge and the Cape May-Lewes Ferry.

A twin span was built in 1963. Each structure operates as a one-way facility. The total cost of the original bridge and approaches was approximately $43.9 million. The total cost of the twin span was almost double that, $79.1 million.

Although the two spans are practically identical to the untrained eye, there are considerable differences in the design of the substructures and the superstructures of the suspension spans. In the original bridge, the piers for the towers and anchorages were built on large blocks of concrete resting on stable ground far below the bottom of the river.

In the new bridge, steel H piers with a relatively small concrete cap were used for the Delaware anchorage and both tower-piers. Only in the New Jersey anchorage was a soil bearing foundation used as in the first bridge.

The largest continuous underwater concrete pour ever undertaken created the New Jersey anchorage. It measured 246 feet by 106 feet by 30 feet thick, totaled 27,500 cubic yards of concrete,

and took 14 days of continuous operations to build. That broke the previous world record of 27,000 cubic yards in seven and a half days on the New Jersey anchorage of the first bridge built in 1949.

In the first bridge, each cable contained 8,284 parallel wires, each .196 inches in diameter, wrapped together to form an outside diameter of 19.75 inches. In the twin structure, each cable contains 9,196 parallel wires of the same diameter, wrapped together to form a cable 20.6 inches thick.

The clearance under the first span is 157 feet, and under the second span, 165 feet. The highest point of the first bridge is 585.5 feet and the second bridge, 494 feet.

The first bridge, carrying traffic to New Jersey, cost $43.9 million. The second bridge, moving traffic to Delaware, cost $79.1 million.

A record 19 million vehicles crossed the dual spans in 1983.

Barry, Franklin, Ross, Whitman

The Delaware River Port Authority began in 1919 as a bistate bridge commission of New Jersey and Pennsylvania. Today the authority serves the people of the lower Delaware Valley and owns and operates four bridges: The Benjamin Franklin, the Walt Whitman, the Commodore John Barry and the Betsy Ross.

Its first undertaking was the construction of the Delaware River Bridge, later renamed the Benjamin Franklin Bridge. When opened on July 1, 1926 between Camden and Philadelphia, it was the world's largest, single-span bridge.

The Ben Franklin has been the keystone of the authority's activities. Its headquarters are adjacent to the bridge's toll plaza in Philadelphia. More than 1 billion travelers have passed over the Franklin Bridge during the past half-century.

The Ben Franklin was built in an era when architectural adornments were appreciated, and it has been a landmark in Philadelphia, second only to City Hall's statue of William Penn.

The seven-lane bridge also serves pedestrian traffic and carries the PATCO trains between South Jersey and Philadelphia.

The main span is 1,750 feet and its highest point above the water is 380 feet. The Delaware authority has spent more than $45 million on the bridge, which clocks some 24 million vehicular movements a year.

The Delaware Memorial Bridge.   Star-Ledger Photo

The Ben Franklin Bridge connects Camden with Philadelphia.   Photo Credit: Carlton Read

Revenues from the Ben Franklin made it possible for the construction of the Walt Whitman Bridge, the busiest of the authority's four spans. Its great success and contribution to the area are visibly evident by the development which has sprung up at its feet in South Philadelphia and in Gloucester County. The bridge opened on May 16, 1957.

The volume of traffic on its seven lanes—about 34.5 million vehicles yearly—qualify the Walt Whitman as one of the 10 busiest bridges in North America. At the time of its construction, it was the eighth longest suspension bridge in the world.

Named in honor of the Civil War poet who lived out his life in Camden, the bridge was voted the most beautiful in its class in 1957. It leaves the ground a mile from the river's edge on both sides and gradually sweeps to the 30-story height of the towers, providing a 150-foot high-tide clearance for vessels at its midpoint. The highest point of the structure is 374 feet from the water.

With a 2,000-foot main span, the Walt Whitman, from ramp end to ramp end, covers a distance of 6.5 miles. The authority has put $34.5 million into its construction and maintenance.

* * *

The Commodore John Barry Bridge between Bridgeport and Chester, Pa. opened on Feb. 1, 1974, replacing a ferry service that had operated at the location for more than 30 years.

The Barry serves the rural agricultural region of South Jersey and the heavy industrial area of southeastern Pennsylvania. The five-lane, fixed-span bridge is the second-longest cantilevered highway bridge in the world. It is situated midway on the 30-mile stretch of the Delaware River between the Walt Whitman to the north and the Delaware Memorial's twin span to the south.

Representing an investment of $127 million, the Barry Bridge registers 5.7 million vehicular movements a year. Its main span is 1,622 feet and its highest point above the water is 418 feet. The total length of the bridge project is four miles.

* * *

The Betsy Ross Bridge is the newest Delaware span, opening to traffic on April 1, 1976. The eight-lane span, which looks like a railroad trestle, has one of the widest roadways of any bridge in the world.

A continuous-truss span, the Betsy Ross was the first bridge in the United States named after a woman. The American Revolution folk heroine made her home in Philadelphia.

The bridge's main span is 729 feet and its highest point from the water is 215 feet. The bridge width is 90 feet. The construction-maintenance investment stands at $103 million. More than 4.7 million vehicles cross the Betsy Ross each year.

From Trenton to the Gap

A series of 19 vehicular and pedestrian bridges lunge over the Delaware River between the state capital in Trenton to the scenic Delaware Water Gap at the Pennsylvania-New York border.

The most famous of the 19 steel and wooden crossings operated by the Delaware River Joint Toll Bridge Commission is the lower Trenton tax-supported bridge. An electric sign is mounted on the downstream truss, which reads: "What Trenton Makes the World Takes."

The original upstream section of the piers and abutments were sandstone ashlar masonry and were started in 1803. Piers and abutments were anchored in rock. The original wood arch superstructure and approaches were constructed in 1805-06. It was remodeled in 1848 by removing the wing arches and adding a new and stronger arch rib on the downstream side.

The piers and abutments supporting the present configuration are the original masonry. The section of the bridge serving the railroad remained in service until 1903, when the present stone arch railroad bridge was built and put into service.

The iron bridge built in 1876 on the upstream portion of the existing piers and abutments was removed in 1929-30 after having been replaced with the present five-span steel, Warren truss bridge.

Construction of the present bridge was completed in 1928-30 at a cost of $644,555.

* * *

The commission's six toll-supported bridges, in addition to the above Trenton-Morrisville landmark, are: The New Hope-Lambertville Bridge, the Easton-Phillipsburg Bridge, the Portland-Columbia Bridge, the Delaware Water Gap Bridge and the Milford-Montague Bridge.

The commission also oversees 13 tax-supported bridges, two of them pedestrian overpasses: The Lumberville-Raven Rock Bridge and the Portland-Columbia Bridge.

The Riegelsville Bridge is a wooden remnant serving communities on both sides of the Delaware River having the same name: Riegelsville.

The other tax-supported bridges on the Delaware are: The lower Trenton-Morrisville, the Calhoun Street Trenton-Morrisville, Scudder Falls, Washington Crossing (where the general braved a winter storm to attack the Hessians in Trenton), New Hope-Lambertville, Stockton-Centre Bridge, Frenchtown-Uhlerstown, Milford-Upper Black Eddy, Easton-Phillipsburg, and Belvidere-Riverton.

The Commodore Barry Bridge between Bridgeport, N.J. and Chester, Pa.   Photo Credit: Carlton Read

Homes overpowered with decorative woodwork, such as the famous "Pink House," are typical of the buildings promoted by carpenters during the resort town's heyday, from 1840 to 1910.

Courtesy: N.J. Div. of Travel & Tourism

CAPE MAY

Cape May is pleasantly trapped in a time warp of architectural antiquity, a living museum that originated as the first seashore resort in America and 150 years later became the first community to be designated a national historic landmark.

Strolling down Yacht Avenue or Washington and Lafayette streets, one's eyes are sumptuously treated to the dazzling detail of 19th Century structures reflecting the grand sweep of western civilization.

Intricately complex styles blend and contrast from house to house, block by block, from Greek to Gothic, from Renaissance to Georgian, Victorian to Elizabethan, Italian to Queen Anne, and Swiss chalet to Tudor.

Some 600 in all, they represent the greatest collection of the 19th and early 20th centuries: finely preserved homes, hotels, taverns, churches and beach clubs.

There are the Pink House and the Physick House, the Octagon House and Heritage House, the Mae West House and Skinner House, all expressions of an era of elegance and whimsical romance when southern hospitality, charm and gracious living evoked a sense of supreme confidence in a new country on the move.

Life seemed always ideal at this tip of a peninsula named New Jersey. The Kechemeche, a branch of the Lenni-Lenape tribe, were taken by the moderate climate and abundant wildlife.

After Sir Henry Hudson spotted the cape on Aug. 28, 1609 on the way to discovering the Delaware and Hudson rivers, life on this lovely jut of largely liquid land would remain an escapist paradise, a place to rest and restore oneself.

The cape was named after Cornelius Jacobson Mey, a Dutchman in the employ of the Dutch West India Co. Mey explored the Jersey coast in 1621. Impressed by Mey's description of the cape, two other company representatives—Samuels Godyn and Blommaert—made the first purchase from the Indians, a four-mile tract along the bay from Cape May Point northward and 12 miles inland. The date was May 1630.

The two Samuels firmly established a New Netherlands colony and, within two years, the first resident-landowner, Davi Pieterson, an eminent seaman, settled in Cape May.

Pieterson developed a prosperous fishing industry, the whale being the biggest prize of the daily catch. By 1638, English Colonists had migrated from Connecticut and Massachusetts to expand their whaling industry. They founded Town Bank, or Cape May Town, and eventually assumed control over the area in the 1660s.

A Londoner, Dr. Daniel Coxe, heard about the whalers and farmers working the water and land and improving their lot. Sight unseen, Coxe bought 95,000 acres of the cape in 1688 and made a handsome profit when he sold his holdings to the West Jersey Society four years later. The society delineated that region as Cape May County.

Of the 442 square miles in Cape May, only 172 are firm land for agriculture and development. The meadows, tidal marshes and waterways in time yielded Lily Lake in Cape May Point, Bennett's Bog near the county airport, the Stone Harbor bird sanctuary and a three-century-old holly tree at milepost 23 of the Garden State Parkway.

The cape's most popular attraction, outside the 17-block historic district, is one of the finest and safest stretches of sparkling white beaches in the world, a 30-mile-long strand splashed by a warm, gentle surf in the summer. The water's temperature is a soothing 76 degrees.

Within 400 miles of the cape lives nearly half of the nation's population.

Between the American Revolution and the War of 1812, Cape May was a secluded retreat shared by the seafaring Colonists and the last of the Lenni-Lenapes. After the war with Britain, a steamboat started plying the Delaware waters between Cape May and New Castle, Del., and the nation's first seashore resort was waiting and ready to be born.

The first Congress Hall was built at Cape Island by Thomas Hughes in 1812. Rebuilt in 1816, 1853 and 1879, Congress Hall today is the most important Victorian-type hotel in Cape May. The ornate exterior trim and gaslit interiors made it a sought-after hostel.

A large, L-shaped brick structure with a full-length veranda on three sides, the hall is decked out with brackets designed like stars and affixed to the thick columns stabilizing the walk-around porches.

* * *

Many of the elaborately embellished buildings, frequented by such statesmen as Henry Clay and Presidents Lincoln and Grant, are still intact today.

Where else within a half-hour walk can one find jagsawn bargeboards, brackets and spandrels, or cornices, turrets and Corinthian capitals, and every shape, size and color window, including medieval, stained glass, oriel, bullseye and palladion.

Look up and around for cast-iron widow walks, belfries with old clocks and ells, acroteria and pavilions, balconies, verandas and geometric friezes clinging under eaves and beckoning the wandering eye.

From 1840 to 1910, Cape May reigned as the queen of seashore resorts, to be succeeded by her northerly neighbor, Atlantic City, with its wide, wonderful boardwalk.

The international elite vacationed at the world's largest hotel, the Mount Vernon, built in 1853. Cape May rivaled the posh resorts of Newport, R.I.; Long Branch on the northern Jersey Shore, and Saratoga Springs, N.Y. The cape was the most invigorating spa on the Atlantic in the mid-19th Century.

Many of the wooden summer palaces were consumed in the 1867 fire that leveled two city blocks. Most of the structures built after 1867 today stand as a complete and rare showcase of late Victorian architecture.

The random, eclectic styles so fancied by the newly rich yet unsophisticated American entrepreneur reflect their carefree, almost fairytale view of the world.

* * *

An advertisement from 1853 shows the elaborate Mount Vernon Hotel on the Cape May beachfront. The hotel boasted a bridal chamber; an "exquisite apartment always engaged for weeks before-hand."

Courtesy: Newark Public Library

The Christian Admiral Hotel.

The individual carpenter-builders who conceived and constructed these fanciful creations relied on trade journals and textbooks for their artistic designs. They improvised freely on what they thought were traditional styles: Greek Revival, Gothic, Queen Anne, Italianate, Elizabethan, Eastlake, Mansard . . . and whatever else inspired their boundless imaginations.

Their borrowings, however, were not necessarily accurate, architecturally or historically. These highly personalized statements, unrestricted and romanticized, produced an architectural vernacular that led to the picturesque style Americans believed to be the epitome of fashion.

The more creative cape carpenters and builders began by using the handbooks of construction considered standard reference at the time. Those off-the-shelf "pattern books" were replete with designs, material costs, tidbits on "good taste" and a few pretentious guides to culture.

The parvenue client eager to exhibit his newly found fortunes selected Cape May as the ultimate site for summer living.

Those innovatively expressive cottages, mansions, estates, villas and hotels that survived the periodic fires and battering coastal storms today give the cape a continuing, homogenous architectural character, a truly original man-made environment.

To appreciate the variety of styles and the painstaking detail that went into the 600 structures in the historic district, a glimpse of just some of the more pronounced features should be enough to satisfy the casual history buff.

They are as follows:

The **Victorian Mansion**, built in 1856 by southern planters as a "gentlemen's club," remains in nearly mint condition. Patterned after an Italian villa, the white clapboard building is set off by a ground-floor veranda on three sides with elaborate Corinthian capitals on the front four columns. An attractive cupola is mounted on the roof and a servants' wing extends from the back of the house.

The **Chalfonte Hotel** is the oldest of the large hotels in Cape May, having survived the fire of 1878. Built by Henry Washington Sawyer in 1876, the Chalfonte has retained its fine Victorian qualities. Shaped like a long L, the structure is outfitted with first- and second-story verandas. All of the original trim is intact. On the roof sits an Italian-villa type cupola.

The **Pink House** is one of the most ornate homes in the district. Erected in 1879 by a merchant, the frame Victorian house exhibits one of the most elaborate ornamental porches in Cape May.

The **Christian Science Church**, an exceptional example of Gothic Revival style, was built for the McCreary family in the 1870s. Fancy shingle work on the third floor is complemented by Gothic details on doors, railings and porches. A Mansard roof tops a corner tower with Gothic windows. An oriel window on one side is protected by a balcony decorated with Gothic patterns.

William H. Church opened the **Colonial House** in 1895 after it had gone through various stages of construction beginning in 1874. The original building accommodated 135 guests. A French roof and roomy porches gave the four-story hotel an elegant appearance. Comfort and convenience were enhanced by gas lights, an electric bell system and steam heat.

The Queen Victoria.   Star-Ledger Photo

A Victorian home on Congress Street.   Star-Ledger Photo

The present hotel elevated its image with corner turrets and a striking Mansard roof. Fish-scale shingles, porch brackets and rails remain intact.

It looks like a small railroad station waiting room, but it was probably the office for the Stockton Hotel Bathhouses. The **Beach Club Clubhouse** contains exquisite dormer windows and incised carvings in the hoods over the windows. An intriguing geometric frieze covers otherwise bland space under the roof's eaves. Heavy brackets hold together the sturdy porch.

Eight guest cottages connect to form a lovely string of Victorian row houses. The **Gurney Street cottages** were attached to the **Stockton House**, built in 1869. All but two doors of the cottages welcome guests with entrance fanlights.

One of the most beautifully restored dwellings is the **Brewster House**, with its black shutters set starkly against white clapboard. An oriel window with gingerbread on one side of the house is in excellent condition, as are two acroteria. An acroterium is a pedestal for a sculpture or ornament at each base or at the apex of a pediment.

Green-trimmed medieval windows and simple bargeboards with patterned edges give the **Episcopal Church of the Advent** its distinctive look. White vertical siding with scalloped bases on a fieldstone foundation are reminiscent of the Gothic style so popular when this house of worship was constructed in 1867 as St. John's Chapel for summer visitors.

Durable stained glass and a square corner tower for a belfry with an ancient clock make the 1893 **Methodist Church** a standout example of unity of style despite successive alterations and additions. It is one of the oldest churches in continuous use in Cape May during the past century.

The **Victorian House** is another fine example of the Italian villa influence, a wide veranda running full-length of the first story of this white clapboard, square domicile. Oversized ornate brackets draw attention to the eaves, while a cupola with a catchy ornament crowns the roof. There's also a Victorian outhouse in the Corgie Street side.

A cast-iron widow's walk tops the white with blue-trimmed Victorian **Annie C. Knight House**, while nearby a small turret with lace-like carving and square colored glass in the front window offer an interesting composite of the 1879 **Blake House**.

An odd-looking structure at 8 Broadway is a cross between Greek Revival and High Victorian. Its columned porch is a busy collection of unusual capitals, spindle rails and fancy carpenter's trim. The roof peaks seem to dance with acroteria.

Stick-style double verandas make the **Leslie House** a worthy example of early 20th Century architecture, but the 1910 **Euler House** with its white columned portico is a superb study of early 20th Century re-revivalism, according to the National Register of Historic Places.

The house at 915 Washington St. is another carpenter's conscious reverie standing the harsh test of time. Fanciful woodwork and herringbone and fish-scale shingles provide a stunning background for a bullseye window in one wing.

The **Mae West House** gets its name from two rather large projective bays that fit into this well-proportioned structure with great architectural character. It's an early 20th Century hybrid whose mere presence attracts all passersby.

At 115 Reading St., a startling **Swiss chalet-type** house shouts for recognition. Its odd roof lines set it apart from the other well-preserved homes on Reading Street.

The **Octagon House** is a small, typical, mid-19th Century farmhouse just across the inlet bridge. There are only a handful of these gray clapboard octagon structures remaining today.

A curious looking cupola with an onion dome gives the **Community Center** its unique identity. Used as a church until 1899, the white clapboard building with green shutters has sharp but simple lines, distinguished by Greek Revival trim and keystones in the door and window arches. One of the oldest in Cape May, the religious center was constructed in 1853.

The **Mainstay Inn** at 635 Columbia Ave. was an exclusive, elegant gambling house for gentlemen when it opened in 1872 as Jackson's Clubhouse. A grand villa with sweeping veranda, the spacious interior shows off sparkling chandeliers hanging from 14-foot ceilings in rooms that are richly ornamented with walnut furnishings.

The **Abbey** at Columbia Avenue and Gurney Street was built in 1869 for the wealthy coal baron, John B. McCreary. The stunning Gothic Revival summer villa features an imposing 60-foot tower, stenciled and ruby glass arched windows and shaded verandas. Victorian antiques in the bed-and-breakfast inn include 12-foot mirrors, ornate gas lighting fixtures, tall walnut beds and marble-topped dressers.

Designed by renowned architect Stephen Decatur Button, The Abbey is one of the best examples of Gothic Revival architecture in the East. The graciousness of a bygone era is still alive in this opulent home.

The **Wilbraham Mansion** at 133 Myrtle Ave. overlooks a park that bears the same name. Built in 1840 as a farmhouse by Judith Hughes, one of the many local Mayflower descendants, the property was acquired by John W. Wilbraham in 1900. A wealthy Philadelphia industrialist, Wilbraham "Victorianized" the fairly simple farmhouse by adding a wing, rooms, bay windows and other protuberances.

A visit to the Wilbraham Mansion transports one back to a time when elaborate mirrors, a bedroom suite formerly owned by a Romanian countess, marble fireplaces and high, detailed ceilings were the stuff of romantic yet real-life dreams.

The **Vondrick Cottage** at 726 Corgie St. is one of the last examples extant of a small, private Victorian home in the area. Originally the favorite summer place of Dr. Augustus Bournonville of Philadelphia, the Vondrick Cottage is being interpretively redesigned in the country Victorian spirit. There are four charming bedrooms on the fourth floor.

A luxurious, 23-room mansion at 635 Washington St. next to City Hall, has been turned into **Alexander's Restaurant**. Every detail of food, decor and building restoration is the result of loving respect for the craftsmen of the Victorian era. Sunday evenings, the proprietors offer personally guided tours through their restaurant-home.

The **Emlen Physick Estate** at 1048 Washington St. was the rallying point for preservationists wanting to keep Cape May from mimicking other busy shore resorts with honky-tonk motels and commercial concrete strips slicing through Victorian neighborhoods.

* * *

After the worst coastal storm of this century ripped through Cape May in March 1962, wiping out the boardwalk, city hall and several houses, a local physician suggested the still-standing 19th Century buildings in the center of town be protected as a "Victorian Village," which eventually became a splendid tourist attraction.

Local officials liked Dr. Irving Tennebaum's idea and successfully sought a $3.5 million federal grant to revitalize the downtown district. Cape May was the first small city to receive an urban renewal grant specifically for preservation.

Some residents and commercial interests, however, wanted to raze what they saw as nothing more than dilapidated eyesores. Many unusual buildings were wiped out by the wrecking ball before the wholesale landmarks destruction was halted at the Emlen Physick Estate.

A group of concerned citizens organized the Mid-Atlantic Center for the Arts (MAC), a nonprofit, nonpolitical group. Still unable to deal with indifferent local officials, the members broadened their base of support, singling out the Physick Estate as the cornerstone for the preservation campaign. They also won two seats on the City Council, including the powerful mayor's office.

In April 1972, Cape May was declared a National Historic Landmark. Significantly, the designation includes not only the Victorian vintage structures, but modern buildings and undeveloped land as well.

An old ship's bell welcomes shoppers to Cape May's restored Washington Mall.   Star-Ledger Photo

In 1877, Dr. Emlen Physick contracted Frank Furness, a prominent architect, to design his posh summer home in Cape May. The main house was completed in 1881, a Victorian jewel set amid eight-and-a-half acres of breezy open spaces.

The Physick Estate today is a house-museum chock-full of authentic Victorian artifacts, costumes and furniture, including an original Furness bedroom suite and bookcases, ornate iron grill work and wood paneling. There are 10 rooms on the second and third floors and four rooms and a pantry on the first floor. Another small building displays antique tools.

* * *

Outside the historic district are equally inviting historic settings.

The **Cape May Court House**, finished in 1850, houses a 333-pound bell.

Down at the tip is the oldest lighthouse still actively commissioned by the U.S. Coast Guard, which also makes its headquarters at the cape. Reaching 165 feet above ground level, the **Cape May Lighthouse** was resurrected in 1859, replacing the original tower built in 1823. Part of the foundation of the original lighthouse is still visible at low tide.

A magnificent panorama of the Jersey cape sea, bay and river can be seen by climbing the 183 steps to the top of the lighthouse. A balcony circles the peak just below the light itself. On a clear night, the light can be seen a distance of 19 miles.

* * *

Historic Cold Spring Village, in northern Cape May, is a typical 19th Century South Jersey farm village. The restored village comprises 15 buildings, some dating back to the 1700s, creating a living outdoor museum consisting of craft shops, a country store and the "Old Grange" restaurant.

During the day, craftspeople can be observed working at their various trades and giving lessons on a scheduled basis.

* * *

Thousands of ships have been lost on the Jersey cape beaches and three of them have been memorialized, two at Cape May Point and one in Ocean City.

A rudder control peeks out of the sandy surf at 16th Street in Ocean City, the only visible part of the four-masted Sindia that grounded in a December 1901 storm. Ship memorabilia are preserved in a local museum.

His Majesty's Ship Martin, which blockaded Delaware Bay during the War of 1812, was attacked and stranded on the shoals and then burned in 1813. Exposed by Hurricane Hazel in 1954 on Lighthouse Avenue at Cape May Point, HMS Martin was salvaged, mounted and placed on public display.

The newest and most unusual wreck is the Atlantus just off Sunset Boulevard in Delaware Bay. It was blown aground in a storm in 1926 while lying at anchor awaiting final positioning as part of the principal structure for a ferry wharf.

The Atlantus was one of three experimental ships built of concrete during World War I when steel was in short supply. The bulky ships, however, were difficult to maneuver and the experiment proved to be a costly failure.

Decommissioned after the war, the three concrete hulks were towed to Baltimore and destined for the government's graveyard of ships. Salvaged from the Navy's maritime cemetery in 1926 for yet another sinking mission, the Atlantus and her sister hulks were to be sunk in the form of a "Y" and used as the foundation for a ferry slip.

Beached by a storm on the way to the docking site, the Atlantus was finally abandoned. It was too big and the water too shallow for the Atlantus to ever be floated again. She remained there, gradually disappearing into the sand. What's left of the Atlantus has been declared a historic site by the state.

The threat of German U-boat attacks during World War II gave rise to three submarine lookout towers, which today are reminders of the beachfront blackouts of the early 1940s.

* * *

The Cape May County Historical and Genealogical Society celebrated its 50th birthday in 1976 with a monumental move of its county museum to the John Holmes House, one mile north of the Cape May Court House on Route 9.

The Holmes House is a classic example of Cape May construction during the Revolutionary War era and is listed in the National Register of Historic Homes.

Among the museum's most prized displays are the huge lens from the Cape May Lighthouse, a large collection of instruments and other artifacts from New Jersey's early medical and pharmaceutical development, and many Indian relics, whaling implements, ship models, tools and household utensils dating back 300 years and more.

Travelers along the eastern seaboard can also enjoy the 70-minute "mini-cruise" on the Cape May-Lewes Ferry that connects the two historic towns in New Jersey and Delaware. The Garden State Parkway hooks up with Route 9, which continues via the ferry to Route 13 in Delaware.

The famous Cape May "diamonds" are another curious feature of the southernmost tip of New Jersey. The quartz pebbles can be found on the beach along the Delaware Bay.

The Cape May Geographical Society described the sparkling little stones as bright and clear gems when wet and dull when dry. Pieces of almost pure quartz, they were ground into bits by abrasion by rock and sand over thousands of years. When cut and polished, they tend to look like rhinestones. The largest ever found at the cape weighed almost a pound and was larger than a hen's egg.

Star-Ledger Photo

The Cape May lighthouse keeps vigil over the coastline at the state's southernmost community. On a clear night, its beacon reaches 19 miles.

The Cape May "diamonds" are hand-picked souvenirs that can be set in gold, silver or platinum to make attractive rings, stick pins, bracelets or necklaces.

Autumn is a glorious time of year in Cape May. The thick cape forests gleam with the flaming reds, brilliant oranges, shining yellows and russet browns that are the trademarks of oaks, maples and other hardwoods. The hundred shades of green and cool, crisp blues complete the cape's colorful rainbow.

Meryl Streep.   Courtesy: Paramount Pictures

CELEBRITIES

Sinatra ... Springsteen ... Streep ... Basie ... Alda ... Godfrey ...Sarah Vaughan ... Dionne Warwick ... Flip Wilson ... Jerry Lewis ... Jack Nicholson ... John Travolta ... Brooke Shields ... Michael Landon ... Christopher Reeve.

The roll call of New Jersey's entertainment celebrities reads like a Who's Who of Show Business.

Their names light up the entertainment world like a galaxy of stars, from Sinatra and Springsteen to Travolta and Streep. They sing, dance, act, compose music, write, direct, produce and perform on stage and for the screen and TV.

The seasoned stars have performed in every medium in the United States and around the world: Vaudeville, nightclubs, concerts, radio, stage, television, movies, benefits ....

Their faces have graced the covers of news, fashion, pop and show biz magazines and billboards.

Most have reached the peak of their profession, breaking boxoffice records and hitting the top of the music charts, or sweeping the Nielsen ratings.

The best of them have been honored with Oscars, Emmys, Tonys, Grammys, Obies, Golden Globes, Critics Circle Awards.

Some have been elevated to matinee idol. Others have become faddish and occasionally even enduring cult figures.

The greatest among them are regarded as institutions.

A few are global corporations, their talents and naturally good looks spinning off books, calendars, dolls, pins, posters and other personality products for star-struck consumers.

The gifted are innovators and consummate artists, often writing, directing, producing, promoting and starring in their own TV shows and movies and packaging their own concerts and recordings.

As celebrities, they share a common bond: New Jersey was their birthplace, where they grew up before they became household names ... or they chose to live in the Garden State to raise their families.

Alan Alda, for example, settled in Leonia, Bergen County, in the early 1960s to give his family a permanent home while developing his skills as an actor and director at the Playhouse-on-the-Mall in nearby Paramus, founded by his neighbor and friend, best-selling author Robert Ludlum.

A theatrical pioneer, Alda starred with Diana Sands in the first interracial love story on Broadway, "The Owl and the Pussycat," which had its world premiere in the popular Paramus playhouse in 1964.

Ludlum then handed Alda his first important non-acting assignment: Directing the venerable Fred Clark in "The Midnight Ride of Alvin Blum."

Alda's apprenticeship in Bergen County paid off when he went west and launched one of the most successful series in television history, "M*A*S*H."

The wacky Korean War Army sitcom survived where most experimental series failed because its star was the critical catalyst, keeping the action and wit moving in front of and behind the camera, as script writer, director and creative consultant throughout its long run.

Courtesy: CBS Television Network

Alan Alda, left, who appeared on stage in Paramus early in his career, joins his brother, Anthony, and his father, Robert, during the filming of a 1980 M*A*S*H episode that featured the family of actors.

For most of the series, Alda commuted between California and Leonia, wanting his wife and children to live a normal life in a typical suburban family community.

* * *

Little known quality actors have burst on the scene with such blockbusters as "Jaws," starring Roy Scheider, a native of Orange, and the still number one television mini-series, "Roots," starring John Amos from East Orange in the central role of the African slave Kunte Kinte.

Portraying "Superman" in three box-office sweeps made Christopher Reeve of Princeton a sensation.

John Travolta's "Saturday Night Fever" sparked a disco craze across the land and catapulted the Englewood native to stardom and a permanent place in the Dancers Hall of Fame. Fred Astaire called the macho star of "Grease" the best dancer to light up the silver screen since Hollywood's golden age of musicals.

James L. Brooks, a 43-year-old native of Union County, produced the award-winning "Mary Tyler Moore Show" and was later rewarded with five Oscars for his first feature film, "Terms of Endearment."

Michael J. Pollard, a product of the Passaic Collegiate School, was the sidekick co-star in the Warren Beatty-Faye Dunaway classic, "Bonnie and Clyde." Pollard, "the potato face" kid, then went on to star with Robert Redford in the definitive movie on dirt-bike racing, peculiarly titled "Little Haus and Big Halsey." Pollard played the little guy who beat the supercool golden boy in the big race.

One of the great comedy teams of all time was Abbott and Costello. Lou Costello, the endearing fatso who could do nothing right, was a street-wise scrapper from Paterson.

At the other end of the social spectrum were the Princeton University students who each left a remarkable legacy spanning half a century: Actors Jimmy Stewart and Jose Ferrer and prize-winning playwright Joshua Logan.

New Jersey continues to attract celebrities and stars-on-the-rise, the latest being comedian Eddie Murphy, who lives in Alpine, and actor Ed Harris, who calls Teaneck his home.

The luxurious high-rises along the New Jersey Palisades have also become havens for the famous, including Dr. Joyce Brothers—counselor to the commoners—whose cameo roles on television (playing a psychologist, of course) and perennial guest on talk shows have made her almost as recognizable as Archie Bunker or The Fonz.

* * *

New Jersey's galaxy of stars shines brighter with the discovery of new talents rising on the horizon each year. Among the more prominent who have made show biz history are:

Frank Sinatra, variously referred to as "The Voice" and "Chairman of the Board," grossed more than $30 million in 1983 at an age when most senior citizens are pursuing the leisurely life of golf, fishing and visiting long-forgotten friends and relatives.

Frank Sinatra.   Courtesy: CBS Television Network

Now at the height of a roller-coaster career, Francis Albert Sinatra, "the kid from Hoboken," almost became a newspaperman, working as a copy boy on the now defunct Jersey Observer. But one night he and his fiancee, Nancy Barbato, went to a Jersey City vaudeville house where a crooner named Bing Crosby was singing. Although he could not read a note of music, Sinatra decided he wanted to become a singer. The rest is history.

In 1937, Sinatra and three young instrumentalists from Hoboken won first prize on the "Maj. Bowes' Original Amateur Hour." He developed his style at the Rustic Cabin, a roadhouse near the George Washington Bridge. Harry James, a trumpeter with Benny Goodman's band, heard a radio broadcast of Sinatra from the Rustic Cabin, and hired him to sing with his newly organized orchestra. From there, Sinatra moved to Tommy Dorsey's band, belting out one hit disc after another.

Sinatra watched Dorsey play his trombone as if it were his own voice, the musical notes sliding and pausing in a conversational style. Sinatra would adopt a similar style of pausing, phrasing and glissandi. He learned to control his voice so that it glided effortlessly from note to note without the interruptions of breathing.

Count Basie.   Courtesy: CBS Television Network   *Jerry Lewis.*   Star-Ledger Photo   *Bruce Springsteen.*   Star-Ledger Photo

At the Paramount in New York, Sinatra became the idol of bobby-soxers in 1942-43. The teenagers swooned and a star was born.

A series of motion pictures followed: "Anchors Aweigh," "The Kissing Bandit," "On the Town"—and then a post-war lull that led to an Academy Award-winning performance as the temperamental Italian GI in James Jones' "From Here to Eternity."

A new Sinatra was discovered and Hollywood beckoned with one lucrative offer after another: "The Man With the Golden Arm," "Some Came Running," "Young at Heart," "Guys and Dolls," "The Tender Trap," "High Society," "Pal Joey," "Can-Can" and a string of other boxoffice delights.

Sinatra was an only child whose parents were born in Italy. His father was a fireman and his mother dreamed of being an opera singer. Her son fulfilled that dream, and then some. Even his detractors regard him as one of the greatest show business attractions of the 20th Century.

Sinatra's lifestyle and philosophy are expressed in perhaps his finest recording, "My Way," the story of a man who did it the only way he could, taking the ups and downs of life as they came.

* * *

Another New Jersey legend is Count Basie, whose roots are in Red Bank on the Jersey Shore. Like Sinatra, William Basie's mother was musically gifted, teaching her son how to play the piano. Bill Basie later learned the rudiments of the organ from Fats Waller.

Born Aug. 21, 1904, Basie worked around New York before heading for Kansas City, playing in silent movie houses and in the Blue Devils and Benny Moten bands. When Moten died in 1935, Basie took over the group.

Radio was also Basie's ticket out of Kansas City. John Hammond heard the Basie Band and brought it to Chicago and then New York, where the Count signed his first recording contract with Decca. Within a year, the Basie Band had become internationally famous. It was 1938 and the world was still trying to shake off an economic depression.

Basie's easy elliptical piano style and his band's rhythm section found a receptive audience wherever they played. Through the 1940s, Basie led a band whose contagious rhythmic pulsation and tremendous team spirit set the standard of the jazz age.

Many jazz stars came out of the Count's ensemble: Thad Jones and Joe Wilder on trumpets, Benny Powell and Henry Coker on trombones, Frank Foster and Frank Wess on tenors.

The Basie orchestra won the Down Beat critics' poll in 1954 and the Esquire Silver Award in 1945. As pianist, Basie won the Metronome poll in both 1942 and '43.

Most of Basie's arrangements were by Neal Hefti and Ernie Wilkins.

Basie made his motion picture debut in 1942 in "Reveille with Beverly," followed by "Stage Door Canteen," "Mister Big" and "Crazy House."

Basie also toured with Sinatra and Tony Bennett in the United States and Europe. He had a command performance before the Queen of England and was featured at the Kennedy Inaugural Ball.

* * *

Jerry Lewis, the clown of clowns, picked up where Charlie Chaplin left off.

At Irvington High School, where he is remembered as one of the craziest cheerleaders in the school's history, Jerry (born Joseph Levitch) was nicknamed "Id" by his classmates, short for idiot. By the time he was 15, Lewis had perfected his own comedy routine, that of the dumb clown pantomiming and mutely mouthing the lyrics of popular songs and opera played on a phonograph offstage.

Failing to get the audience to laugh at the Palace Theatre in New York and a burlesque house in Buffalo, N.Y., Lewis tried out his unique record act at Brown's Hotel in Loch Sheldrake, N.Y., where his father was master of ceremonies. Irving Daye, a comedian working for Lewis' father, liked the pantomimes and became his road manager.

In July 1946, Lewis was doing his record act at the 500 Club in Atlantic City when one of the entertainers on the bill suddenly walked out. Lewis suggested that a singer there join him in his act.

When Dean Martin joined Lewis at the Club 500, one of the most successful teams in show business history was formed. Martin and Lewis went on to star in their own television series and several motion pictures before Lewis decided to break up the act in 1956.

Lewis became one of the most financially successful clowns

Courtesy: The Movie Channel

Jack Nicholson portrays a mental patient in "One Flew Over the Cuckoo's Nest."

Star-Ledger Photo

Dionne Warwick.

Courtesy: Gale Agency, Inc.

Sarah Vaughan, "The Divine One" who hails from Newark, chalked up sales of 3 million records by 1950.

to perform solo or in a team. None of his 30 films grossed less than $5 million and his first record sold more than a million copies.

Some of his classics are "The Sad Sack," "Delicate Delinquent," "Rock-a-Bye Baby" "The Geisha Boy," "The Bellboy," "The Nutty Professor" and "The Patsy."

The contract Lewis signed with Paramount Pictures in 1959 represented, at that time, the biggest single transaction in film history: $10 million to star in 14 films over a seven-year period, seven for Paramount and seven for Jerry Lewis Productions.

Since 1957, Lewis has served as national chairman of the Muscular Dystrophy Association of America. He personally raised the entire cost of a multimillion-dollar building for the Institute for Muscle Disease in New York City. The Jerry Lewis telethon has become a national institution.

* * *

Bruce Springsteen was practically unknown in 1975 when his incredible album, "Born to Run," was released to critical acclaim and instant public acceptance. Never before had a rock performer made the covers of Time and Newsweek magazines at the same time, announcing an original American superstar.

His songs of street life and youthful concerns were gleaned from his years of growing up in Freehold and practicing his lyrics and music in late-night bistros along the Asbury Park boardwalk.

Born on Sept. 23, 1949, Springsteen joined his first band at 14 and commuted to Greenwich Village to perform with the Castiles at the Cafe Wha. His first album in 1972 is now the landmark "Greetings from Asbury Park, New Jersey," produced by the gritty musician and his former manager, Mike Appel, whom he met in the fall of 1971.

Springsteen organized his permanent backup group, The E-Street Band, and toured exhaustively up and down the East Coast until "Born to Run" put him in the same deified ranks as Bob Dylan, with whom the New Jersey artist is compared.

Springsteen's next album, "Darkness on the Edge of Town," revealed a maturing songwriter who definitely had something to say.

"Nebraska," Springsteen's 1983 release, was atypical of his gyrating rock themes. The haunting soundtrack of "Nebraska" was painfully realistic, a downbeat commentary on the impact of the protracted economic recession on the average working man. One song was about a worker on an automotive assembly line who went off the deep end after the Mahwah Ford plant closed, throwing thousands of people on the unemployment lines.

Springsteen takes off, as a rock musician, where novelist Jack Kerouac ended his "On The Road" tour of America during the 1950s with another New Jersey artist, poet Allen Ginsberg from Paterson.

* * *

Sarah Vaughan is among America's original great jazz singers. Born in Newark on March 27, 1924, Vaughan has been proclaimed the nation's top female vocalist in polls conducted by Down Beat and Metronome.

"Miss Vaughan," writes critic Leonard Feather in "Encyclopedia of Jazz," "brought to jazz an unprecedented combination of attractive characteristics; a rich beautifully controlled tone and vibrato; an ear for the chord structure of songs...and a coy, sometimes archly naive quality alternating with a sense of great sophistication."

Vaughan sang with Billy Eckstine's band after winning an amateur contest at New York's Apollo Theatre in 1942. The public first became aware of the Newark singer with the release of her hit recording, "It's Magic." By 1950, Vaughan's records had sold more than 3 million copies.

By 1957, Vaughan was getting $7,000 a week for performances at nightclubs, and her rendition of "Banana Boat Song" was one of the nation's biggest sellers that year.

An only child, Vaughan's father was a carpenter and amateur musician and her mother was a laundress who sang in a church choir. While attending Newark's public schools, Vaughan played the piano and organ for school programs and at churches and sang in the choir of the Mt. Zion Baptist Church.

Among her most popular recordings are "Make Yourself Comfortable," "How Important Can It Be?" and "Whatever Lola Wants" from the smash Broadway musical, "Damn Yankees."

Vaughan has also written several songs, including "I'll Wait and Pray," which she recorded with Eckstine's band.

* * *

The most promising actress of the 1980s is Meryl Streep, born in Summit on June 22, 1949 and raised in affluent Basking Ridge and Bernardsville. Her father was an executive with Merck, the Rahway pharmaceutical giant, and her mother a commercial artist. Her mother coined the name Meryl, a shortened version of her daughter's birth name, Mary Louise.

Believing she was "ugly," Streep changed her appearance at Bernardsville High School, becoming a blonde and winning the starring roles in "Li'l Abner" and "Oklahoma!" She was also chosen as the school's homecoming queen.

At Vassar, Streep pursued her dramatic interests and, after graduation, entered the Yale Drama School on a three-year scholarship. At Yale she dazzled her directors by accepting no fewer than 40 separate roles, ranging from the frolicsome Helena in Shakespeare's "A Midsummer Night's Dream" to the wheelchair-bound translator in the world premiere of "The Idiots Karamazov." When she left New Haven, Conn. for New York, she was already something of a local legend.

Streep also took a delicious bite out of the Big Apple, starring in one classical work after another in the New York Shakespeare Festival, the Vivian Beaumont Theatre in Lincoln Center and the Phoenix Theatre. She captured the Critics' Outer Circle Award for best actress for her performance in Tennessee Williams' "27 Wagons Full of Cotton."

Streep made her television debut in March 1977 in the CBS dramatic special, "The Deadliest Season" and received an Emmy Award for her portrayal of a Roman Catholic woman married to a Jewish concentration camp internee in the TV mini-series, "Holocaust."

Her first major movie, "The Deer Hunter," won the Oscar in 1978 for Best Picture. Streep won an Academy Award for her work in "Kramer vs. Kramer" opposite Dustin Hoffman, and received her second Oscar for "Sophie's Choice" in 1982.

The National Board of Review honored Streep for her 1979 films; the New York Film Critics Circle cited her for "The Seduction of Joe Tynan" and "Kramer," and her performance in the latter also earned her a Golden Globe award and a Los Angeles Film Critics award.

Streep received critical acclaim for her roles in "The French Lieutenant's Woman" and Woody Allen's "Manhattan."

* * *

Jack Nicholson, from Neptune, is that rare combination of actor-director-producer who, like Sinatra, does his own thing his own way and has developed into one of the great character actors of the screen.

Nicholson, born April 28, 1937, made his screen debut in "Cry-Baby Killer" in 1958 and appeared in "Ensign Pulver" in 1964.

But it wasn't until 1969 when he co-starred with Peter Fonda in the cult movie "Easy Rider" that Nicholson displayed his real talents as one of the most versatile actors in Hollywood, earning him an Oscar for best supporting actor.

A succession of brilliant films followed: "Five Easy Pieces" in 1970 . . . "Carnal Knowledge" in 1971 . . . "The Last Detail" in 1974, which won the Cannes Film Festival prize . . . "Chinatown" in 1974, which won the Academy Award and the New York Film Critics Circle Award . . . "One Flew Over the Cuckoo's Nest" in 1975, which resulted in an Oscar, Golden Globe and N.Y. Film Critics Circle award for Nicholson.

The former Jersey Shore lifeguard directed "Drive, He Said" in 1971 and "Goin' South" in 1978, in which he also starred. He also produced "Ride the Whirlwind," "The Shooting" and "Head" in 1968.

* * *

The distinctive voice of Dionne Warwick, three-time Grammy Award winner, demolished the barriers that once separated pop, rhythm and blues, jazz and gospel singing.

The East Orange-born singer (Dec. 12, 1941) collaborated with Burt Bacharach and Hal David in the 1960s to create the most catching melodies in the music industry: "Promises, Promises," "Alfie," "Do You Know the Way to San Jose," "What the World Needs Now," "I'll Never Love This Way Again."

Her gold records and platinum albums sold more than 15 million copies, making her one of the most recognizable voices in the recording world.

Warwick's mother was the business manager for the Dinkard Singers, a church choir group composed of family members. The group toured professionally for 27 years and became perhaps the most successful gospel group of its time in America. The Dinkard Singers was the first such group to record for RCA Victor and the first to participate in the Newport Jazz Festival.

In 1954, Warwick, her sister and their cousin formed their own group, the Gospelaires, and sang together as a trio for seven years. Warwick was the natural leader of the group because she was the only one who could read music.

The satin-voiced songstress set out to become a music teacher. She won a music scholarship to the University of Hartford, studying piano, theory and voice.

In singing a solo at the Apollo Theater in 1966, Warwick overwhelmed the musicians with her vocal range. They complained that it was "impossible to have a 5/4 bar, then a 4/4 bar, then a 7/8 bar." After she explained it was just as difficult for her to sing those Bacharach notes as it was for musicians to play them, the band finally mastered the Bacharach-Warwick technique.

Among her other hits are "Reach Out For Me," "Message to Michael" and "Trains, Boats and Planes."

In 1964, Cashbox, a trade magazine, rated Warwick the top rhythm and blues singer recording in the United States.

Her first movie was "Slaves," the first independent production undertaken by the Theatre Guild in 1968.

* * *

Like many of New Jersey's native stars, Michael Landon is another product of a parent who worked in show business. Born Eugene Orowitz on Oct. 21, 1937 and raised in Collingswood, South Jersey, Landon learned at an early age the hardships of the world-of-make-believe from a father who was a publicity agent for a Hollywood studio.

A natural athlete, Landon established a high school javelin mark in 1954 of 193 feet, seven inches. In an AAU meet that same year, he threw 211 feet. Among the 42 athletic scholarship offers he received, Landon chose the University of Southern California.

A torn ligament shattered his hopes of continuing in athletics and proved to be the impetus for an acting career.

Forced to drop out of USC, Landon took a job in a warehouse where a fellow worker, an aspiring actor, asked him to help him with his lines for an audition. Landon's interest was sparked and a short time later he was signed by Warner Brothers to attend its acting school.

Movie audiences first saw the new Landon in the title role of "I Was a Teenage Werewolf," the 1957 horror film that is something of a cult flick today. Landon was also cast in "God's Little Acre" and "Maracaibo" in 1958, "The Legend of Tom Dooley" in 1959 and "The Errand Boy" in 1961.

A few parts on television when dramatic shows were broadcast live, including a role in "Restless Gun," brought Landon to the attention of the producer of "Bonanza," which became one of the longest running series on TV.

While playing "Little Joe," the kid brother of the Cartwright

Star-Ledger Photo

Courtesy: Paramount Pictures Corp.

Star-Ledger Photo

Two cowboy characters who explored the motion picture and television frontiers: At left, Michael Landon, a Collingswood native, in his role as "Little Joe" in the television series "Bonanza"; at right, John Travolta of Englewood as the honky-tonk hustler in "Urban Cowboy."

Brooke Shields.

family, Landon learned how to write teleplays and direct one-hour episodes of the popular western series.

By the time "Bonanza" ran its wagon-train course, Landon had matured into one of television's most handsome leading men. He convinced NBC to launch a new series he created, "Little House on the Prairie," which became that network's most consistently popular show during the 1970s and early '80s.

Besides starring in the story of a midwestern farmer raising his family on the prairie, Landon wrote one-third of the scripts and directed every other episode.

While "Little House" was still on the air, Landon spun off another series, "Father Murphy," which he also created and for which he wrote most of the weekly scripts.

Landon also wrote, directed and starred in the television movie, "The Loneliest Runner" in 1976 and directed the GE Theater production of "It's Good To Be Alive" in 1974.

* * *

Just as youngsters tried to mimic the style of Elvis Presley in the 1950s and that of the Beatles in the 1960s, the soulful "Travolta look" and the strutting "Travolta walk" became the rage among teenagers in the 1970s.

The reason: John Travolta, the Englewood sensation, and his first two starring vehicles, "Saturday Night Fever" in 1977 and "Grease" in 1978.

Tonsorial parlors featured a $25 Travolta haircut and menswear shops sold out the three-piece white suits and accessories of the type worn by Travolta in "Fever."

The slick, quick-stepping dancer became the heartthrob of the teenybopper set as the best-looking of the Sweathogs in the TV comedy series, "Welcome Back, Kotter," which kicked off in September 1975.

Suddenly Sweathog Vinnie Barbarino out-cooled another leather-jacketed look-alike, The Fonz, from "Happy Days."

Except Travolta made the difficult transition from the little tube to the big screen and received an Academy Award nomination for his frenetic exploitation of discomania in "Saturday Night Fever."

As a singer, Travolta's first single, "Let Her In," sold more than 800,000 copies and reached the number five spot on the Cashbox best-seller charts.

The road to fame and riches (he gets more than $1 million per picture) began at Dwight Morrow High School in Englewood, where jumpin' John picked up dance steps and rhythms from black students, developing a "looser style" that served him well in "Fever" and "Grease."

As an actor, he warmed critics' hearts with his sensitive portrayal of "The Boy in the Plastic Bubble," an ABC-TV movie that aired in November 1976.

Born Feb. 18, 1954, Travolta is looking forward to directing as his next challenge, something he's already learning from his latest mentor, Sylvester "Rocky" Stallone.

Travolta's other film credits include the trendy "Urban Cowboy," "Moment by Moment" with Lily Tomlin, Brian De Palma's "Carrie" and "Blowout," and Stallone's explosive "Staying Alive."

* * *

Brooke Shields' career began before she could walk or talk. Not even a year old, she was recognized everywhere as the Ivory Soap Baby, her first modeling job.

Like child stars Judy Garland and Elizabeth Taylor, with whom the Englewood model-actress is often compared, Shields was groomed and promoted by a fiercely ambitious mother, Teri Schmon Shields, who came from a poor, devoutly Roman Catholic family in Newark.

Teri Schmon, a part-time Seventh Avenue model and restaurant manager, married socialite Frank Shields, a 6-foot, 7-inch business executive. His parents were Francis C. Shields, an American tennis champion of the 1930s, and Princess Marina Torlonia of Rome, an international beauty.

Brooke Shields, born May 31, 1965, is one of the most sought-after models in the world, her striking face appearing on almost every popular magazine on the newsstands. She was also seen as the sizzling dungareed doll in the Calvin Klein commercials.

By the time Brooke was 12, she was a controversial celebrity. Her 1978 role of a 12-year-old New Orleans prostitute in director Louis Malle's film, "Pretty Baby," put her up against Jodie Foster and Tatum O'Neal as filmdom's foremost nymphet attraction.

The next year, Shields was playing a pinball hustler in "Tilt" . . . the foot-loose orphan in Peter Fonda's "Wanda Nevada" . . . and a sassy runaway foster child befriended by George Burns in "Just You and Me, Kid."

Shields achieved teenage stardom in two adolescent romance movies, "The Blue Lagoon" (1980) and "Endless Love" (1981). "Lagoon" grossed more than $100 million worldwide, establishing Shields as a "hot property," despite the bad reviews.

As a model, Shields was demanding—and getting—$10,000 a day.

In merchandising her daughter, Teri Shields formed Brooke Shields and Co., which brought about two "Brooke" books and the "Brooke Doll," rivaling the beloved Barbie Doll. Before even going into production, the Brooke Doll, each with 16 fashion ensembles, had generated advance orders of some $1.5 million.

Living in a tudor-style mansion in Englewood Cliffs with her mother, Shields—between assignments—completed classes at the Dwight School in Englewood and enrolled at Princeton University in the fall of 1983.

* * *

If Christopher Reeve does nothing else the rest of his life, he will always be remembered as the cinematic Superman, the man-of-steel from the planet Krypton who actually grew up in Princeton to become a 6-foot, 4-inch-tall model-actor.

Born Sept. 25, 1952, the square-jawed Reeve is the son of Wesleyan professor Franklin Reeve, a novelist and translator, and Barbara Johnson, a writer for a weekly Princeton newspaper, Town Topics. (She later married a wealthy stockbroker.)

While Reeve was attending Princeton Country Day School, a representative from Princeton's McCarter Theatre interrupted a fifth-grade science class to ask if one of the children would like to sing a role in the production of Gilbert and Sullivan's "The Yeoman of the Guard." Reeve volunteered and later starred in every Princeton Day School production and studied stagecraft and makeup at the Lawrenceville School.

An English major at Cornell, Reeve enrolled in his senior year in the advanced drama program at the Juilliard School for Drama in New York City. One of his teachers was actor-director John Houseman.

After graduation from Cornell in 1974, Reeve served a brief stint in the TV soap opera "Love of Life." At the same time he joined such stage troupes as the Circle Repertory Company and the Manhattan Theater Club.

In late 1975, Reeve was the doting grandson to Katherine Hepburn's grand dame in "A Matter of Gravity."

A year later, after doing some bit parts in Hollywood movies, Reeve was interviewed for the role of the first of three Superman films that turned the Princeton actor into a celluloid super-hero.

Not wanting to be stereotyped as a flying, red-caped freak, Reeve returned to dramatic character roles in the Orwellian "Somewhere in Time" with Jane Seymour and Christopher Plummer (1980) and Ira Levin's shocker "Death Trap," with Michael Caine and Dyan Cannon (1982).

Coming full circle, Reeve went back to his first love, the stage, and played in the summer stock productions of "The Cherry Orchard," "The Front Page" and "The Heiress" at the Williamstown Theater, earning, in 1980, the Equity weekly minimum of $225.

Turning down a $1.5 million film deal, Reeve instead starred in the Broadway version of Lanford Wilson's drama "Fifth of July." He portrayed a Vietnam veteran who lost the use of both legs in the war.

The critics hailed his moving, sensitive performance.

* * *

New Jersey cocktail lounges and Catskill resorts were the training ground for Broadway show-stopper Melba Moore, who was raised a Catholic in Newark and Harlem.

Moore attended Waverly Avenue Elementary School, Cleveland Junior High School and Newark's Arts High School, where she specialized in music. After studying voice and piano and majoring in music education at Montclair State College, Moore taught music for a year at the Peshine Avenue Elementary School in Newark.

"Superman" Christopher Reeve comes down to earth after completing a spectacular flight in his glider.

Valerie Harper.

Gilbert Price and Melba Moore sing "Stranger in Paradise" in "Timbuktu!"

Courtesy: Charles A. Pomerantz, Ltd.

Star-Ledger Photo

Star-Ledger Photo

Believing that "God gave me an opera voice," Melba sang and played piano with a group called Voices and tested her talents in solo appearances in cocktail lounges in New Jersey and the Catskills.

In 1968, the composer of "Hair," the American tribal, love-rock musical, cast Moore as a singer in the off-Broadway production that would move to Broadway and give the Newark actress an opportunity to play Lutiebelle and win a Tony Award for best supporting musical actress in 1970. The role had been played, before Moore took over, by a succession of blue-eyed blondes.

The petite chanteuse has been compared to Aretha Franklin and Barbra Streisand, belting out brash Broadway hits or soul tunes.

Born Oct. 27, 1945, Moore is the daughter of singer Melba "Bonnie" Moore Smith and jazz saxophonist Teddy Hill. The singer can speak in an earthy, drawling black vernacular or middle-American English, whatever the role requires.

In its "Salute of the Week," Cue magazine described Moore as "This slender, pixie-faced flashing-eyed girl with the voice like a call-to-arms (which has this super-cool town on its feet, cheering)."

"Hair" led to a role in the film "Cotton Comes to Harlem" and a recording contract. Her first album, "Learning to Give," was released in 1970, followed by "Look What You're Doing to the Man" a year later.

In 1972, the Melba Moore-Clifton Davis Show replaced the Carol Burnett Show for the summer season.

Moore is a frequent star in the lucrative circuit of high-class night and supper clubs, beginning with her first engagement at the Waldorf-Astoria's Empire Room in June 1971.

* * *

To television viewers, Valerie Harper is "Rhoda," that Bronx-bred, Jewish earth-mother who, in real life, was a strictly raised Catholic living in South Orange and Jersey City.

Born Aug. 22, 1940, Harper received three Emmy Awards for her supporting role on the "Mary Tyler Moore Show," playing Rhoda Morgenstern, who eventually had her own half-hour comedy series from 1974-78.

A former dancer and improvisational actress with Second City and Story Theatre, which played Broadway in 1970-71, Harper got her start in the Radio City Music Hall corps de ballet, where she danced behind the high-kicking Rockettes.

Graduating to the chorus line of the musical "L'il Abner" during its Las Vegas run and subsequent Hollywood filming by Paramount in 1959, Harper returned to New York for more chorus jobs in "Take Me Along," "Wildcat" and "Subways are for Sleeping." She studied with actor-teacher John Cassavetes and married actor Richard Schaal in 1964. They moved to California in 1969, where Schaal founded his own theater company.

While acting in Story Theater on the West Coast, Harper auditioned for the part of Rhoda Morgenstern. When "Rhoda" was spun off on its own, she made television history.

"Rhoda's" premiere on CBS-TV on Monday, Sept. 9, 1974, at 9:30 p.m. became the first program ever to capture first place in the Nielsen ratings with its first public exposure. And the special wedding show was probably the most publicized domestic event on TV since the birth of Lucy's baby during the 1950s.

In 1975, Harper won her fourth Emmy Award for best actress in a comedy series.

From stage, to television, to movies, Harper succeeded in all entertainment media. She appeared as the Chicano wife of Alan Arkin in the film comedy "Freebie and the Bean" in 1974 and Neil Simon's "Chapter Two" and "The Last Married Couple in America" in 1979.

She has received a Golden Globe Award for best actress in 1975 and was named the Hasty Pudding Woman of the Year by the Harvard Hasty Pudding Society, also in 1975.

* * *

As is the case with so many New Jersey personalities, John Amos' place in the annals of show business history is secure, firmly fixed by one role: Kunte Kinte. It was th saga of an African slave that caught the world's attention in the runaway best-seller "Roots," the most widely watched television mini-series ever to be broadcast.

As a youngster growing up on Hillside Place, East Orange, in the early 1950s with another talented kid on the block, Dionne

Actor John Amos treats himself to a haircut by Willie Koonce during one of his visits back to East Orange.

Roy Scheider, born in Orange, won acclaim for his role as the tormented choreographer in "All That Jazz."

Susan Sarandon.

Star-Ledger Photo   Courtesy: 20th Century-Fox Film   Courtesy: Time-Life Productions

Warwick, Amos made his first money as a Star-Ledger delivery boy.

New Jersey first heard of Amos as a football star at East Orange High School. Hoping to become a professional football player, Amos headed for Denver on an athletic scholarship.

When he got there, Denver State discontinued football from the school's sports schedule. Amos wound up at Colorado State studying sociology. He eventually was drafted by the Denver Broncos and was cut from the roster after a few games. Amos holds the record for being cut from more teams (13) than anyone in professional football history.

Such persistence is rewarded in show business, where rejection and determination are the chief ingredients of success.

Because steady jobs are few and far between for black actors, Amos tried his hand at writing. He became a principal writer for the "Leslie Uggams Show," the replacement for the canceled "Ed Sullivan Show" on CBS, but the new black format didn't do well in the ratings. America was not yet ready for skits about poor black families living in the New York ghetto.

Amos wrote an episode for the popular "Sanford and Son" TV series starring Redd Fox and supplied some sketches for "Laugh-In." He appeared in a couple of films, "Vanishing Point" and "Sweet Sweetback's Badasssss Song." He starred in Broadway's "Tough To Get Help" in 1972 and in "Norman, Is That You?" in Los Angeles.

It was on "The Mary Tyler Moore Show," playing the TV weatherman Gordie, where Amos began to click as a commercial performer. In 1973, Walt Disney Studios cast Amos as the football coach in "The World's Greatest Athlete," which premiered in 250 cities across America, a first at that time for a feature film.

From there he moved on to his own TV series, "Good Times," opposite Esther Rolle (1974-76), and the TV pilot movie "Future Cop," and stayed on for the series in 1977.

And then came "Roots" that same year, which set all kinds of records and made Amos a famous figure.

* * *

Roy Scheider starred in the biggest boxoffice blockbuster of the 1970s, "Jaws," one of Steven Spielberg's early romps as a filmmaker ("E.T.," "Close Encounters of the Third Kind," and so forth).

Scheider, who played the no-nonsense sheriff in "Jaws" (1975) and its 1977 sequel, was born in Orange on Nov. 10, 1935 and was a history major graduate of Franklin and Marshall College.

Scheider looks more like a street-toughened ex-fighter or longshoreman than the chain-smoking choreographer in "All That Jazz," the bio-flick of Bob Fosse ("Damn Yankees," "Pippin," "Pajama Game," and movie director of "Cabaret" and "Lenny").

As a character actor, Scheider has always found work, from off-Broadway appearances in "The Alchemist," "Sergeant Musgrave's Dance" and "Stephen D.," to Broadway roles in "Chinese Prime Minister" and "Betrayal."

His television performances include the Hallmark Hall of Fame movies, "Secret Storm" and "New York Police Department."

But film is Scheider's favorite medium, keeping him active on a regular basis. Among the movies Scheider has been billed in are: "Paper Lion," "Star," "Stilleto," "Puzzle of a Downfall Child," "French Connection," "The Outside Man," "Marathon Man," "The Seven-Ups," "Sheila Levine is Dead and Living in New York," "Sorcerer" and "The Last Chance."

Scheider won an Obie Award for his 1968 off-Broadway performance in "Stephen D."

* * *

Loretta Swit of Passaic created one of the most unforgettable characters in a television series: Hot Lips Houlihan, the blonde, mouthy Army major nurse in "M*A*S*H," which ran an unprecedented 11 years on CBS.

Like most fine actresses on television and in film, Swit studied at the American Academy of Dramatic Arts in Manhattan and got her first break as the understudy for Sandy Dennis in the Broadway comedy "Any Wednesday."

Swit next portrayed one of the Pigeon sisters in productions of "The Odd Couple," one in Florida starring Marshall and Shelley Berman, and another in California with Ernest Borgnine and Don Rickles.

The role that really boosted her stage career or pared her for "M*A*S*H" was as Agnes Gooch in "Mame." She toured in the musical for a year with Celeste Holm recently chairwoman of the New Jersey Motion Picture and Television Commission, and then re-created the part in a Las Vegas production with Susan Hayward.

When Swit arrived in Hollywood in 1969, she an impressive resume that has kept her busy since. Her film credits include "Stand Up and Be Counted," "Freebie and the Bean," "Race With the Devil" and "S.O.B." She has done several made-for-television movies and has appeared in dozens of TV series and shows such as "The Bob Hope Christmas Special."

* * *

Susan Sarandon, who starred opposite Burt Lancaster in Louis Malle's memorable depiction of life in transitional "Atlantic City" in 1980, was born Oct. 4, 1946 and lived in Edison and Metuchen.

Susan Abigail Leslie's goal as a child was to be an accomplished actress. She received a degree in drama and English at Catholic University and has acted in scores of stage, television and film productions.

Her stage credits include "An Evening with Richard Nixon," "A Stroll in the Air," "Albert's Bridge," "Private Ear, Public Eye" and her most recent successful venture off-Broadway, "Extremities," the story of a rape victim who manages to attack her attacker.

Among the many movies Sarandon has appeared in are "Joe," "Lady Liberty," "Loving Molly," "The Great Waldo Pepper," "The Other Side of Midnight," "The Front Page," "The Last of the Cowboys," "Rocky Horror Picture Show," "King of the Gypsies," "Something Short of Paradise" and "Loving Couples."

Sarandon's television roles have been as varied as a TV Guide listing: "The Last of the Belles," "June Moon," "The Satan Murders," "The Life of Ben Franklin," "The Haunting of Rosilind," and the soap opera serials "Search for Tomorrow" and "A World Apart."

* * *

Melanie was the flower child of the Hippie Generation, which left its indelible imprint at Woodstock in 1969.

Melanie Safka grew up in Long Branch in the 1960s, writing songs and practicing on her guitar. Her mother, Polly, is also a singer, and owner of Paint 'N Place, an arts store at the Monmouth Mall in Eatontown.

Melanie made her recording debut in 1969 and turned out her first hit, "Lay Down," in 1970. Her three most popular songs are "Beautiful People," "Look What They've Done to My Song, Ma" and "Brand New Key."

Melanie's other singles include "Peace Will Come," "Ruby Tuesday," "The Nickel Song," "Ring the Living Bell" and "Cyclone."

Among her albums are "My First Album," "Leftover Wine," "All the Right Noises," "The Good Book," "Gather Me," "As I See It Now" "Please Love Me," and "Arabesque," recorded in 1981.

Last July, Melanie performed her first metropolitan area concert since a 1978 show at Carnegie Hall. During the 1970s, Melanie toured Europe, where she is a genuine American star.

Melanie has been working on a musical, "Ace of Spades," based on the life of the daughter of Calamity Jane. She has written the songs for the production and plans to play the lead role on Broadway.

Melanie.   Star-Ledger Photo

* * *

Connie Francis was the Barbra Streisand of the Fifties, one of the top recording artists of the century whose singles sold in the millions.

Her first hit in 1957, "Where the Boys Are"—the title song of a film in which she played—sold more than a million copies, one of 10 gold records from the Newark singer who started out as an accordionist.

Born in Newark's Ironbound section on Dec. 12, 1938, Concetta Franconero learned to sing in six languages—French, German, Spanish, Italian, Yiddish and Japanese. She is equally adept at rock 'n' roll, swing, popular love ballads and motion-picture theme songs.

Connie's father, who liked to play the concertina, sent his 4-foot, 10-inch daughter to Miss Masciola's Music School in Newark to take lessons on a miniature accordian. When she played her accordian on the Arthur Godfrey Talent Scouts Show on CBS-TV, she won first place under her new name, Connie Francis.

She attended Arts High School in Newark and Belleville High School, graduating as a National Honor Society member. She was also editor of the school newspaper.

From 1955-57, Francis recorded 10 singles, none of which made a hit, and sang on the soundtracks of the movies "Jamboree" and "Rock, Rock, Rock."

Since her first success, Francis has recorded more than 25 singles and 25 albums.

Both her voice and her comedic style won praise from reviewers who saw her first important part in "Where the Boys Are" (1960). By 1962, Francis was earning as much as $12,000 a week for nightclub and hotel engagements. At the pinnacle of her career, she owned four publishing companies and granted licenses to manufacturers of Connie Francis charm bracelets, socks, sweaters, diaries and other name-carrying products.

Francis was named four times as the best female singer of the year by "American Bandstand" (ABC-TV) and was designated most programmed vocalist of the year by Cashbox and best female vocalist of the year by Photoplay magazine.

* * *

Flip Wilson was dubbed Flip (short for "flipped out") by his barracks buddies during a four-year hitch in the U.S. Air Force.

The 10th of 18 children of a destitute family (his father was a janitor), Flip was born Clerow Wilson on Dec. 8, 1933 in Jersey City.

At the age of seven, Wilson went to the Mosque Theatre in Newark (now Symphony Hall) and saw the team of Stump and Stumpy. When he heard all that laughter, he knew he wanted to be a comedian.

A high school dropout at 16, Wilson began writing scripts for himself and developing his own act after his Air Force discharge in 1954. He worked as a bellhop at the Manor Plaza Hotel in San Francisco.

Hitchhiking around the country and barely making a living in low-paying night spots, Wilson gave himself 15 years "to make it." The black comedian Redd Fox cut that schedule by six years when he recommended the witty ethnic monologist to Johnny Carson during a telecast of "The Tonight Show" in 1965.

From the late-night NBC show, Wilson was introduced to the national Sunday night family audience on "The Ed Sullivan Show." Wilson then made the rounds of the TV funny shows such as Rowan and Martin's "Laugh-In."

At the beginning of the 1968-69 season, he hosted his own special on NBC, the network's way of preparing him for his own series. From 1970-74, "The Flip Wilson Show" scored high in the Nielsen ratings.

Wilson starred in the TV special "Pinocchio" and was seen in the films "Uptown Saturday Night" and "Skatetown, U.S.A." His albums include "Cowboys and Colored People," "Flippin'" and "Flip Wilson, You and the Devil."

He received the Grammy Award for best comedy record in 1971.

* * *

Anyone who's ever watched television or gone to the movies has seen the square-faced features of Brian Keith, an actor born Nov. 14, 1921 in Bayonne.

Keith's resume describes him as an "American actor of easygoing types, understanding fathers and occasional villains."

Flip Wilson.   Star-Ledger Photo

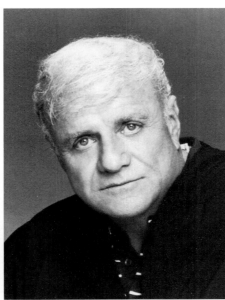

Teenage heartthrob Connie Francis won her first talent competition by playing the accordion for another New Jerseyan, Arthur Godfrey.

Brian Keith. Courtesy: ABC Television Network

Celeste Holm. Courtesy: Donald Smith Promotions, Inc.

Keith's most recent stage appearance was in "Da" in 1979. Here are just a few of his film credits: "The Young Philadelphians," "The Deadly Companions," "Savage Sam," "The Parent Trap," "Moon Pilot," "The Raiders," "Those Calloways," "The Hallelujah Trail," "Rare Breed," "The Russians Are Coming, the Russians Are Coming," "Nevada Smith," "Reflections In a Golden Eye," "Suppose They Gave a War and Nobody Came," "McKenzie Breaks," "The Wind and the Lion," "Nickelodeon," "Hooper," "Meteor" and "The Mountain Men."

His television output is just as prodigious: "Crusader," "The Westerner," "Family Affair," "The Little People," "The Brian Keith Show," "How the West Was Won," "Centennial," "The Seekers," "Power" and "Moviola."

The 1983 television season included yet another Brian Keith series, "Hardcastle and McCormick."

* * *

Arthur Godfrey, "the ole redhead," at one time was king of radio and television, perhaps the best salesman of products either medium ever had.

The entertainer, who sang and played a ukulele, neither particularly well, made a fortune pitching Lipton Tea, Chesterfield cigarettes and scores of other products.

Godfrey, who died in 1983 after a long battle with lung cancer, was born in Hasbrouck Heights on Aug. 31, 1903. He served in the U.S. Navy from 1920-24 and was an accomplished flier, setting a round-trip record between Alaska and Teterboro, where he kept a DC-3 for his weekend flights to his Kentucky horse farm.

Godfrey, who always played himself, was in three movies: "Four for Texas," "Where Angels Go . . . Trouble Follows" and "The Glass Bottom Boat."

Godfrey's homespun humor and philosophy have been preserved in several records and books.

* * *

Celeste Holm, a resident of Warren County, is best remembered for her portrayal of Ado Annie in Rodgers and Hammerstein's "Oklahoma!" and her Oscar-winning performance in "Gentlemen's Agreement," starring Gregory Peck.

A star of stage, screen and television, Holm has turned her attention in recent years to the business side of show business. She is currently chairwoman of the New Jersey Motion Picture and Television Commission and is a member of the President's Council on the Arts.

Holm has received the Actors Studio Award, the Golden Needle Award and was voted the Performer of the Year by the Variety Clubs of America.

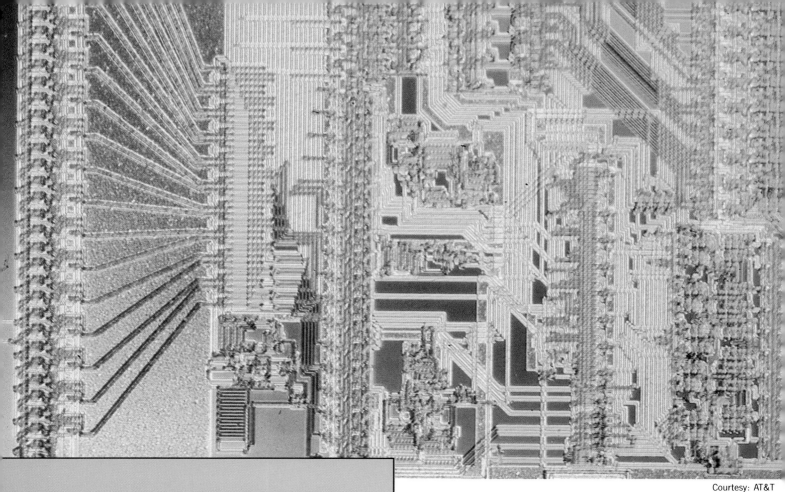

Courtesy: AT&T

For the rest of this century progress in microelectronics will not be threatened by the physical limits of operating such tiny circuits. Shown is the Digital Signal Processor, a general purpose building block suited for numerous telecommunications applications.

COMMUNICATIONS

New Jersey is the nerve center of an international communications network that has brought the world together into an electronic global village.

As civilization enters the computerized Age of Information, New Jersey is leading yet another industrial revolution that began a century ago with Thomas Edison's electric power system and the development of the phonograph, motion pictures, radio and television by the great inventor and scientists at Bell and RCA Laboratories in Princeton, Camden, Newark, Holmdel, West Orange and Murray Hill.

Today, New Jersey is the telecommunications capital of the world, having pioneered and launched the space-age satellite system serving earth's nearly 5 billion inhabitants in any city, hamlet and remote village capable of picking up electronic signals for sound and visual images.

New Jersey's growing communication family is led by AT&T and its Bell research division, and RCA Laboratories, Western Union and ITT (International Telephone & Telegraph Co.).

Scores of smaller, highly specialized electronics companies make up the most comprehensive, diversified communications operations concentrated in one place.

The "solid state" era and the new powerful era of "photonics" both began in the Garden State, as well as the first satellite experiments and the first microwave and cable studies and dis-

coveries, according to William Baker, vice chairman of the New Jersey Department of Education and former research director of Bell Laboratories in Murray Hill.

Even the now obsolete mechanical typewriter—a 19th Century communications breakthrough—was perfected by Edison, who improved the original and unworkable wooden keys by replacing them with metal faces.

Another Edison device was the mimeograph machine, which triggered an informational paper explosion that is barely coming under control with the advent of the VDT—Video Display Terminal.

Guglielmo Marconi demonstrated ship-to-shore transmission on his wireless in Shark River Hills, Neptune. The site where the transmission took place in 1896 was named Marconi Road.

Setting up shop in England, where investors lured the Italian inventor, Marconi inadvertently sparked the creation of the Radio Corporation of America (RCA), a move by the United States government to compete, blip-by-blip, with the British wireless company.

* * *

From the imprinted word to the recent optic fibers carrying messages at almost the speed of light, New Jersey inventors and scientists have refined and redefined the word "communication" during the past century.

And they are now on the threshold of microelectronic systems that will put the world at everyone's fingertips through pocket transmitters and receivers, and advanced visual and verbal formats for the home, office and motor vehicle.

In 1983, New Jersey became the first site for experiments in videotext—a two-way transmission system of textual materials for display on television screens. CBS and AT&T selected the Village of Ridgewood in Bergen County to test their information innovation. Several hundred families in the affluent community used their computer-linked home TVs to call up on the screen restaurant and stock market listings, as well as electronic shopping and banking.

The home banking services of the CBS/American Bell videotex field test allows consumers to purchase products from merchants, view advertising, and pay bills by writing electronic checks.

The new American Bell is also conducting videotext experiments. And Time, Inc. and the Panasonic Co. of Secaucus (and its Japan-based parent, Matsushita Electric Industrial Co.) have entered the teletext business—a one-way service that allows consumers to simply call up listings.

Dow Jones News/Retrieval of Princeton, the largest information service in the world, has added a shopping information service for consumers. Starting out supplying information to the business market, Dow Jones now services some 60,000 users with stock quotes and averages, financial and investment services, such as earnings reports, and general news.

The mobile telephone market, known as cellular radio, got off to a quick start in New Jersey as consumers snapped up the new technology for their vehicles and briefcases.

The name cellular comes from the system in which each city is to be serviced by a network of antennas transmitting low-fre-

quency signals, which are automatically transferred from one geographic "cell" to the next.

Competition is keen among companies seeking cellular radio operating licenses from the Federal Communications Commission (FCC). AT&T, for example, wants licenses in 29 of the 30 major metropolitan markets in which the FCC is accepting cellular radio system applications.

Several New Jersey companies are prominent players in a field that includes MCI Communications, which has key operations throughout the state; Graphic Scanning Corp. of Teaneck, the largest radio paging firm in the business; Metromedia of Secaucus, and Western Union of Upper Saddle River.

Bell/AT&T

When Alexander Graham Bell invented the telephone in 1876, he turned to his tinkering ally Tom Edison to make the receiver work. Working in Menlo Park, Edison implanted a piece of carbon, which converted electrical impulses into recognizable voice patterns. That collaboration gave birth to the Bell System and AT&T.

The American Bell Telephone Co. was founded in 1880 and the American Telephone and Telegraph System was organized five years later. Western Electric became the manufacturing arm of the Bell System in 1882 and a research branch of AT&T's Engineering Department was established in 1911. It was the forerunner of Bell Laboratories, set up in 1925.

Since then, Bell Labs, based in Murray Hill, has produced more than 20,000 patents, among the latest for lightwave communications technology. The R&D operation has averaged a patent a day. Every decade recorded another Bell milestone:

- Long-distance TV transmissions in the 1920s.

- Microwave radio transmissions in the '30s.

- The transistor in the '40s.

- Semiconductor electronics, including the solar cell, in the '50s.

- Communications satellites in the '60s.

- Digital switching in the '70s.

- Lightwave communications in the '80s.

Bell's 20,000th patent, granted on Tuesday, Aug. 9, 1983, was for an etching technique to further advance lightwave technology voice, data and video transmission. Lightwave technology involves laser light pulses that travel through hair-thin glass fibers.

On earth or in outer space, Bell is pushing communications to its limits.

In May 1929, a soft-spoken, 26-year-old Bell Labs engineer recorded the first radio reception from the stars. The discovery of radio emissions from the center of the Milky Way by Karl Jansky spawned the science of radio astronomy, and laid the foundation for a later discovery—"The Big Bang," or the origin of the universe—which brought a 1978 Nobel Prize in Physics to Bell Labs scientists Arno Penzias and Robert Wilson, the fourth Nobel award to Bell scientists.

The three other Nobel Prizes were for:

- The "Wave Nature of Matter" (1937), first demonstrated by Clinton Davisson in 1927 and which became the building block for much of today's solid-state electronics.

- The transistor (1956), invented by Bell scientists John Bardeen, Walter Brattain and William Shockley, making possible today's integrated circuits embodying the basic concepts fundamental to the computer, radio and television and industrial controls of all kinds.

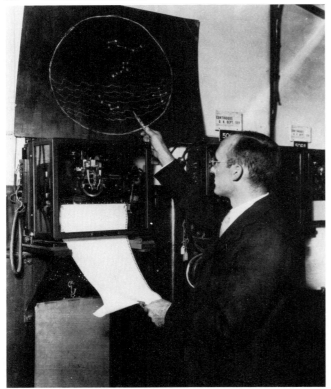

Courtesy: Bell Labs

The late Karl Jansky of Bell Telephone Laboratories is shown pointing to the position on a chart where radio noises from space were first heard. While attempting to pinpoint the source of noise interfering with radiotelephone service, Jansky detected a peculiar hissing sound coming from the area of the Milky Way. Later this hissing was identified as radio signals generated by the natural processes in stars and galaxies. His work resulted in the new science of radio astronomy in which the heavens are studied by listening to radio waves rather than looking through an optical telescope.

• "Improved Understanding of Local Electronic States in Solids" (1977), shared by Bell scientist Philip Anderson for making it easier to work with the electronic structure of glass and magnetic materials.

* * *

In a typical year, Bell Labs technical staff can: Patent more than 300 ideas and applications for the communications industry... produce some 5,700 technical publications and presentations... and receive roughly 90 scientific and engineering awards and 29 additional awards for community and other services.

Although AT&T and the Bell System have been broken up by federal decree, the new AT&T remains one of the biggest companies in the world, with assets of almost $40 billion (about the size of Mobil Oil) and a work force of 376,000.

Much of the communications giant is based in New Jersey. The major operations, in addition to AT&T Bell Labs in Murray Hill and Holmdel, are: AT&T Communications and AT&T International in Basking Ridge ... AT&T Information Systems, Southgate ... AT&T Consumer Products, Parsippany.

The work at **AT&T** Bell Labs represents the greatest communications contribution of the 20th Century—from electron-beam lithography and molecular-beam epitaxy to magnetic bubbles and thermocompression bonding. Some of Bell Labs' more remarkable patents are:

Lasers. The basic principles of the laser, an optical device that transmits light on a single frequency in a highly concentrated beam, were originally conceived by A. Shawlow and C.H. Townes in 1958. Lasers are used for measuring the Earth-Moon separation distance, for fabrication of integrated circuits, as light sources in certain photonic systems, and in eye and ear surgery.

Lightwave systems. Lightwaves carry voice, data and video signals on beams of pulsated light through hair-thin glass fibers. The Bell System installed the world's first lightwave communications system to provide a wide range of customer services. Each pair of glass fibers (one for each direction) can carry 672 voice conservations, or a mix of voice and data, or a video channel. A half-inch diameter cable containing 144 fibers can carry more than 46,000 simultaneous conversations.

Microwave technology. Bell Labs' pioneering work on microwave theory and waveguide propagation greatly aided development of World War II radar and later resulted in the first commercial microwave radio line, which opened in 1948. Bell's contributions to microwave technology include antennas, solid-state oscillators and amplifiers, and other devices.

Solar cell. In 1954, Bell scientists D.M. Chapin, C.S. Fuller and G.I. Pearson invented the silicon solar cell, which converts sunlight directly into electricity. Arrays of these devices serve as batteries to power satellites and as electric-generation sources in remote areas.

Sound pictures. Audio equipment developed by Bell Labs was used to make the first sound motion picture with synchronized musical score ("Don Juan" in 1926) and the first film with synchronized dialogue (Al Jolson's "The Jazz Singer" in 1927). Many advances were patented by Bell Labs during the 1930s and '40s, including new loudspeakers, projectors and optical stereo soundtrack techniques.

Television transmission. In 1927, Bell Labs demonstrated the first long-distance transmission of live television over wires in the United States. Bell System advances in television transmission include design of a national television network using frequency-division diplexing, coaxial cable, international transmission by Telstar satellites, helping televise the Apollo 11 lunar landing, and providing coverage of the 1980 Winter Olympics at Lake Placid, N.Y. and the 1984 Summer Olympics at Los Angeles, by means of a lightwave transmission system.

The System 85 digital terminal data module, from AT&T Systems, allows for the simultaneous transmission of voice and data.
Courtesy: AT&T

Radar. Bell Labs began research on radar in 1938 and designed more than half of all radar systems used by the U.S. in combat. The radar systems were made by Western Electric. Bell developed the first fully automated tracking radar system.

Artificial larynx. The most important link in communications is the human voice. In 1929, Bell Labs developed a reed-type artificial larynx that enabled thousands of people who had lost their voices through disease or accidents to regain the power of speech. In 1960, a transistorized instrument was produced.

Speech synthesis. In the late 1930s, H.W. Dudley built the first electronic speech synthesizer at customer services. Three other Bell scientists then developed computer programs that yielded understandable synthetic speech from an input of any ordinary English text. The program assigns duration, intensity and voice pitch, and then applies the rules of human speech that are dependent on phonetic context.

Computer languages. Bell Labs has designed a number of "high-level languages" such as C language—sets of software instructions that make it easier to use computers in simulating the operation of an electrical circuit. Other applications include the solution of complicated algebraic problems and the control of computer operations through English language commands.

Charge-coupled devices. Invented in 1969 by Willard Boyle and George Smith, these devices have potential applications for imaging, digital memory and signal processing, and have been used in miniature television cameras.

Field-effect transistor. Invented in 1951 by W. Shockley, the metal-oxide field-effect transitor is widely used today in calculators, digital watches, random access memories and video games. A gallium-arsenide variety, developed at Bell Labs in 1947, is used in microwave transmission.

Picosecond switching. Electronic circuits that operate at picosecond (one trillionth of a second) speeds were designed and operated by Bell Labs researchers in 1977. Such circuits operate 10 to 100 times faster than conventional semiconductor switches.

BELLMAC. The BELLMAC-4 is the "computer on a chip," developed in 1978 and containing added memories and circuitry for use in telephone equipment. In 1981, Bell Labs introduced models of the BELLMAC-32A microprocessor—a "superchip" designed to take the place of some 500 separate integrated circuits in future computer systems.

Magnetic bubble. Magnetic bubble memories provide a compact, solid-state alternative for other types of large-capacity memories. Data are stored in minute bubble-like magnetic domains in a thin film of magnetic material. The bubbles are also used for testing microwave transmission systems.

Gemini Electronic Blackboard System. This pressure-sensitive electronic blackboard was developed in 1977 to transmit handwriting and drawings over telephone lines, displaying them on a remote video monitor.

New Jersey Bell

New Jersey residents often are the first to reap the benefits of new technologies tested in their own backyards by the AT&T Network Control Center and 14 AT&T Bell Laboratories sites throughout the state.

To serve the communications needs of the nation's most densely populated state, New Jersey Bell built a local exchange network with closely spaced telephone switching centers. These "central offices" link clusters of telephone customers with others, forming an interconnecting chain that stretches across the state, the nation and around the world.

The proximity of the central offices made New Jersey an economical testing ground for new technology within and between switching systems. Their ability to offer new features and services to customers was first tested in New Jersey.

The earliest vintage of digital interoffice facilities were suited—economically and operationally—to the geography and calling patterns of New Jersey customers. That led to a broad base of digital facilities and the ability to deploy rapidly the latest network developments to the existing New Jersey Bell system.

The Garden State today is traversed by the world's largest lightguide cable route—776 miles—between Cambridge, Mass., and Moseley, Va.

Lightguide, in conjunction with microwave routes using digital technology, forms a backbone digital network interconnected at hub locations by a Digital Access and Cross-connect System. The result is an end-to-end digital pipeline that enables New Jersey Bell to accommodate almost any business data transmis-

Neil Waste and Bryan Ackland use a computer-based system that helps AT&T Bell Laboratories engineers examine new integrated circuits on a color-coded display terminal.

Courtesy: AT&T

Pete Yankura, an AT&T Consumer Products engineer, designs a special terminal at laboratories in Holmdel.

Courtesy: AT&T

Star-Ledger Photo

The C.S. Long Lines, the world's largest cable ship, is shown docked at Port Newark in 1981. The ship is owned by Transoceanic Cable Ship Co. of Morristown, a subsidiary of AT&T. It has laid more than 50,000 nautical miles of undersea cable since 1963.

sion equipment. The digital "interconnectivity" offers New Jersey businesses plenty of room to g w within the state.

In 1984, New Jersey Bell, w   ssets of more than $5 billion, employed a work force of 23,00'   orted by an annual budget of $2 billion.

As a result of the AT&'   iture, a new company was created by the seven regiona   tems, inc   ng Bell Atlantic, which serves New Jersey   urroundi.   tes.

Called Bell Communica   arch, th   technical development arm of the nation   stem is   d in Livingston, with satellite offices i   Townsh   lletown and Piscataway. Bell Research   erate w   8,000 employes.

RCA

When British financial interests brought Marconi's wireless system into being, the United States realized it could not count on another country to control electronic communications beyond America's borders.

It was Franklin Delano Roosevelt, as undersecretary of the U.S. Navy during World War I, who decided a wireless company owned and run by Americans was needed to protect the nation's defense interests.

In 1919, under the watchful eye of Uncle Sam, the Radio Corporation of America was born. RCA, as it was later incorporated, was raised as a sibling of General Electric and Westinghouse. The two powerful parents encouraged their latest subsidiary to grow into a formidable communications empire of its own. By the early 1930s, RCA was big and strong enough to go its way alone, permanently leaving the GE/Westinghouse nest.

Less than a year after RCA was founded as a transatlantic radio communications company, it established its first major research facility on Long Island. In large part through RCA's impetus, the radio industry grew rapidly in the U.S., and in 1929 RCA acquired the Victor Talking Machine Co. in Camden and Radiotron in Harrison.

RCA's founding chairman, Gen. David Sarnoff, was acutely aware of radio's mass appeal. In Newark, for example, Bamberger's department store was selling crystal sets by the hundreds in the early 1920s. One day in 1922, Louis Bamberger, the owner, called in his salesman handling the crystal sets, Jack Poppele, and asked him to set up a radio station on the store's roof. A telegrapher during World War I, Poppele erected two poles on Bam's flat roof overlooking Market Street, strung a wire between them, and WOR went on the air.

Poppele went on to build WOR radio and television into a major broadcast company and became a founding member of the American Broadcasters Association and its first president. Poppele, now retired, lives in West Orange.

Poppele is credited with broadcasting America's first radio show on Christmas Day in 1923—from the rooftop of Bamberger's!

New Jersey, as far as RCA was concerned, was the place to be in the infant days of broadcasting. By the mid-'30s, RCA was pioneering both radio and television broadcasting from its New Jersey laboratories.

In Jersey City, Allen B. DuMont transmitted a crude picture of Mickey Mouse on a 2½-inch disc. It was 1926 and DuMont was developing his Jenkins Radiovisor. (The word "television" had not yet been coined.) DuMont helped to introduce a new visual medium in the infant days of radio.

But RCA was the catalyst in the birth of the television era. Its communications record remains a first in the broadcasting industry, beginning with an inventor and scientist who made television the most pervasive medium on earth.

The year was 1923. Dr. Vladimir K. Zworykin applied for a patent on the iconoscope, the first electronic "eye" of television. In 1930, television was shown on a 6-by-8-foot screen by RCA at RKO-Proctor's 58th Street Theater in New York City. (WOR-RKO today operates in New York and New Jersey.)

In 1933, the first fully electronic television system, employing an iconoscope camera, a kinescope receiver, and an electronic synchronizing generator, was introduced by RCA.

In 1939, President Franklin D. Roosevelt, who originally conceived the RCA communications idea, appeared on camera at the New York World's Fair in a dramatic demonstration of the new medium.

In 1942, RCA consolidated its research operations in Princeton. There, scientists and engineers developed the all-electronic, compatible color television system now used in the United States, Canada, Japan and Latin America and the parent of the systems used throughout the world.

The first public demonstration of an all-electronic system was in 1946. That same year, RCA's 630TS, the first mass-produced television receiver, went on the market to begin the post-war boom in TV. It looked like a little radio set with a 10-inch screen in the center.

RCA organized the first "network," linking its NBC facilities in New York and Washington by coaxial cable, with branches in Philadelphia and Schenectady, N.Y.

In 1953, tape recordings of both color and black-and-white TV were shown at RCA Labs in Princeton. A year later, the first commercial production of color TV receivers began.

Research and development of a marketable video disc system began at RCA Labs in 1965. In 1971, color pictures were achieved on a video disc. Ten years later, RCA introduced the SelectaVision VideoDisc system. Consumers can now watch movies on their TV sets simply by playing what looks like a 33 rpm record.

Radio, and black-and-white and color television have been the hallmarks of NBC and its parent company, RCA.

* * *

RCA is also synonymous with the Space Age. RCA Satcom satellites spinning around the globe carry more hours of nation-wide television distribution than any orbiting carrier in the world.

The first RCA satellite was rocketed into outer space in 1958. On Dec. 18 of that year, President Eisenhower broadcast a message of peace from the orbiting RCA "Score" communications payload. That demonstration of the potential of space communications was the first of many space experiments leading to today's RCA Satcom series satellites.

The latest generation of RCA satellites, designed to stay in orbit for 10 years, was sent aloft in the mid-1970s. RCA Satcom I was launched in 1975 and Satcom II slid into orbit a year later. The third and fourth Satcoms went into operation in 1981 and 1982. The first of RCA's advanced Satcoms lifted off at Cape Canaveral, Fla., in late 1982.

Including RCA's five Satcoms, more than a dozen U.S. domestic commercial satellites soar through space, shrinking the world into what media analyst Marshall McLuhan described as a "global village" connected by invisible electrons.

Spacecraft are handling thousands of jobs, from voice communications and news events televised "live," to telemedicine, data communications and educational programs for remote areas.

Also arriving on the scene are electronic mail, newspaper publishing, video conferences and the exchange of documents over two-way TV screens, library exchange programs, direct-home broadcast and satellite-to-hotel room movies.

The RCA Satcom satellites are built by RCA Astro-Electronics in Princeton. They are operated by RCA American Communications (Americom), also in Princeton.

All RCA Satcoms have 24 channels, each of which can carry the equivalent of 1,500 two-way voice circuits, or one FM/color TV transmission. Each channel can also transmit 64 million bits per second of computer data.

The satellites can cover all 50 states and Puerto Rico. There are an estimated 5,000 earth stations with direct access to these winged, metallic objects that resemble futuristic flying creatures.

Of the 25 million homes served by cable TV, nearly all receive at least one satellite-relayed channel of programs.

RCA Americom is the only carrier with two satellites dedicated to cable TV programming. Satcom III-R and IV provide a programming capacity of more than 1,000 hours a day.

RCA Satcoms are the first of a new generation of communications satellites that have three-axis stabilization, which gives them extra weight and power capabilities.

All spacecraft are controlled from tracking, telemetry and earth stations operated by RCA Americom at Vernon Valley in Sussex County and at South Mountain, Calif.

The efficient RCA Satcom design is a result of RCA Astro-Electronics' long experience in building space vehicles. The organization was founded almost at the beginning of the space age, opening its doors in Princeton in March 1958, only five months after Sputnik went into orbit.

Since then, RCA Astro-Electronics has designed, built and successfully launched more than 110 spacecraft and subsystems.

The color TV pictures sent back from the moon during the Apollo missions were transmitted by an RCA Silicon Intensifier Tube. Such a tube uses a silicon wafer containing 600,000 to 800,000 light-sensitive diodes per one-third square inch, as the tubes target, or "retina." Incorporating a special light amplifier with a silicon target, the tube produces quality TV pictures over a very broad range of light levels, from the dimness of sunrise to the brilliance of high noon. Unlike most imaging tubes, the Silicon Intensifier Tube is essentially impervious to damage by direct sunlight.

Western Union

Founded in 1851, Western Union is the world's senior telecommunications company, having pioneered many, if not most, of the "electronic mail" advances over the past dozen decades.

With headquarters in Upper Saddle River, Bergen County, Western Union operates major New Jersey facilities in Mahwah, Glenwood, Moorestown and Cherry Hill.

Glenwood is the command and control center for Western Union Westar satellite system. All Public Broadcasting Service and National Public Radio programs use Westar, as well as commercial broadcasting networks and several national publications.

In addition, more than 2,000 customer-owned earth stations —including Dow Jones and Time, Inc.—transmit internal communications via Westar.

The heart of Western Union's electronic communications network is InfoMaster, one of the largest computer communications installations in the world. With a consistent record of more than 99 percent reliability, the InfoMaster system provides automatic switching and computer storage for more than 350,000 messages daily.

WU presently records annual revenues of $1 billion a year, employing 14,000 people and operating a nationwide communications complex valued at $2 billion.

Its New Jersey operations employ 3,000 skilled personnel, 600 of them at its Moorestown complex, where various message communications services are handled.

Western Union was the first telecommunications company to employ multiplex telegraphy, microwave transmission, message-switching computers and domestic communications satellites. These technological innovations, coupled with the recent growth of data communications, have placed Western Union in a unique position to capitalize on the explosive growth in telecommunications.

Western Union transmits Telex, public message and private wire services for millions of customers, ranging from individual users to the largest corporations and government agencies.

The company's 10,000-mile microwave radio beam system spans the continent, replacing the poles and wires of a century ago. Integrated with that system are five orbiting Westar satellites, the first launched in April 1974 and the sixth in 1982. Additional Westars will be put into service as demand for telecommunications increases.

RCA Satcom V communications satellite is checked for precise antenna alignment at the company's Princeton facility.

Courtesy: RCA News

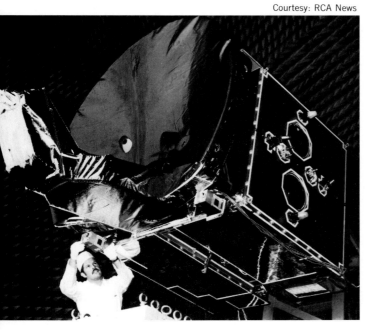

Satellite dishes operate at the Western Union Glenwood Earth Station in Vernon.

Western Union also maintains 8,000 public offices and agencies, where customers can send and receive money orders, as well as Mailgram, Telegram and Cablegram messages.

MetroFone, a rapidly expanding, long-distance telephone service for business and residential users, is another vital Western Union service.

But the most timely development for Western Union is its return to the international record communications marketplace. Beginning in August 1982, Western Union extended its Telex service worldwide.

ITT

International Telephone and Telegraph Co. is a $25 billion a year conglomerate that specializes in making telecommunications equipment outside the United States.

About 7,500 ITT employes work in New Jersey at facilities scattered throughout the state in East Brunswick, Midland Park, Newark, Nutley, Paramus, Paterson, Princeton, Randolph, Secaucus and Voorhees.

ITT—COINS (communications and information companies) has headquarters in Secaucus. COINS, which consolidated its various companies into one management group, provides such services as in-line data bases, yellow pages directories, and printed business and technical materials, as well as productivity improvement training services.

ITT's telecommunications operations include ITT Worldcom, which uses microwave, undersea cable, high frequency radio and satellite transmission to provide international data communications services throughout the United States and between the U.S. and more than 200 companies.

Worldcom is responsible for the direct communications link between the White House and the Kremlin.

U.S. Transmissions Systems, Inc., Secaucus, handles long-distance voice and data communications services in this country. The company owns and operates a major microwave transmission network from which it offers reduced rate, long-distance telephone

service, known as ITT Longer Distance. It also provides private line voice and data communications services for business users.

Since its founding in 1920, ITT has grown into the second largest telecommunications equipment supplier in the world. Its global network of land, undersea and satellite links makes the company's telecommunications operations the largest U.S.-based international record carrier.

ITT companies figure prominently in the U.S. Space Shuttle program. ITT monitors the 4-million-circuit-mile tracking net-

Laurie Cowen of Clifton assembles the control board for a navigation unit being built by ITT Avionics Division in Clifton.

work around the globe, tracking spacecraft to provide telemetry and timing data for flight controllers.

Broadcasters Hall of Fame

There are the Oscar, the Emmy, the Grammy, the Tony, the Obie . . . and now—the Mikee.

It's the latest in a lengthening list of awards bestowed upon entertainers and members of that industry. The Mikee Award is given to those who were part of, or are trying to preserve, "The Golden Age of Radio."

The Mikee and the National Broadcasters Hall of Fame originated in Freehold, Monmouth County, in May 1977, a belated idea conceived by Arthur S. Schreiber, a liquor store owner who realized that radio did not have the same promotional pizazz as movies and television. Yet many of the film and TV greats honed their show biz skills through the popular talking box developed in the 1920s, and which became an original American art form by the '30s, reaching its zenith when television popped on the scene in the early 1950s.

An era of broadcasting genius was fading away when Schreiber, an ex-newspaperman, decided to create the nation's first Broadcasters Hall of Fame above his liquor store at 22 Throckmorton St. in downtown Freehold. It's the only home for radio nostalgia buffs in the land, housed in an old store in an old Revolutionary War town.

Schreiber is searching for a permanent showcase museum for the greatest collection of wireless artifacts extant. He has had a few offers—an abandoned factory in Passaic, a dingy warehouse in another city—but the radio curator is holding out for a special place to display his invaluable memorabilia.

Take the 1922 Atwater Kent radio, one of a handful in working condition from the time when radio was not yet a proven commercial venture. Schreiber has lots of vintage radios, so many in fact that movie producers now tap his supply for scenes from the Depression or World War II period. He loaned 45 radios from the 1940s period to director Sidney Lumet. They became working props in the 1983-released film "Daniel."

Visitors to the Freehold Hall of Fame can find the 1924 Big Box Model 20, the Radiola Series 100 made in 1926, Philcos and RCAs from the early days of radio.

The Freehold museum is the beneficiary of remarkable collections from such radio pioneers as Edward G. Raser, who helped establish Trenton's first radio station, WMAL, in 1922, and worked on the design and construction of the state capital's first 500-watt station, WOAX.

Raser donated more than 200 pieces to the Hall of Fame in 1983, among them a Magnavox amplifier manufactured in the early 1900s . . . a Western Electric cone speaker constructed of papier mache . . . a wireless sending device of the 1910 period . . . a water-cooled transmitting tube used in the early 1920s . . . a Paragon Regenerative Receiver from the same period . . . several spark and coil sets in use before the invention of the telephone . . . one of the first portable crystal sets produced in Jersey City by the Mengel Co.

More than 2,000 items are featured in the museum or stored in nearby garages. There are prized microphones and earphones, rare photographs and posters, classic cathedral-shaped radios and ancient electronic gadgets.

The New Jersey Hall of Fame eventually will show everything in broadcasting from wireless to satellite. Visitors now can see pictures of their favorite radio personalities and hear the voices of The Lone Ranger, The Shadow, Amos 'n' Andy, Ozzie and Harriet, Charlie McCarthy, Baby Snooks, Gene Autry, Kate Smith, Gabriel Heatter, Eddie Cantor and hundreds of radio celebrities now preserved on tape.

The second-floor museum also features an audio-visual slide

Star-Ledger Photo

Arthur S. Schreiber, who founded the Broadcasters Hall of Fame in Freehold, stands with an RCA Radiola III-A.

show depicting the history of radio. It was produced by Schreiber with a New York film company.

In a brochure prepared by Schreiber called "Return to Yesteryear," the golden age of radio is remembered in that innocent age when words alone created clear images of people and places that became imbedded in the minds of listeners. A generation of youngsters grew up humming the Lone Ranger theme song and not knowing it was really the "William Tell Overture."

Each year, Schreiber inducts new members into the Broadcasters Hall of Fame. Recent inductees have included Frank Sinatra, who crooned his way to stardom on radio with Tommy Dorsey and Harry James; CBS broadcaster Douglas Edwards; character actor E.G. Marshall, and radio-television personality Arlene Francis.

American Focus

The most widely syndicated public affairs radio show in the United States is "American Focus," a half-hour program emanating from Princeton and heard every week on some 460 radio stations with an estimated audience of 3 million listeners.

It began in the early 1970s as "Focus on Youth," a program aired on WBUD in Trenton, and orchestrated by high school student Garth Ancier. When he was accepted at Princeton University in 1974, he brought the show with him.

In the beginning, "Focus" was lucky if it could get an assistant sanitation engineer of Mercer County to go on the show. But Ancier managed to convince some local and state officials to appear on his show and, by 1975, he was selling the show to stations such as WNBC in New York. NBC still broadcasts the show at 8 on Sunday mornings.

Today, "American Focus" runs in 70 of the top 100 markets in the United States. The name was changed to "American Focus" to appeal to all formats. Some stations thought that "Focus on Youth" was all about young people.

A production of the Focus on Youth Radio Network, "American Focus" is a nonprofit product. All of the money earned from its sole sponsor, Shell Oil Co., is pumped back into production. Its 1985 budget was $100,000.

Except for President Reagan or Frank Sinatra, there's no one "American Focus" can't get on the air, according to Larry Rosin, executive producer and a student at Princeton University.

Among those who have been interviewed on "Focus" have been Academy Award-winning actor Richard Dreyfuss; Dr. Jonas Salk, who discovered the polio vaccine; Mike Wallace, star of "60 Minutes," the most successful investigative news program in television history; U.S. Sen. Barry Goldwater (R-Ariz.); Presidents Carter and Ford; Henry Fonda; Walter Cronkite; Alexander Haig; George Bush; Nobel laureate and economist Milton Friedman, and actress Jaclyn Smith.

"Focus" is staffed by 35 to 40 students who work in areas ranging from guest relations to tape editing and research. "Focus" is known for its in-depth research before each show.

The Media

Serving the Garden State's 567 municipalities and 21 counties are a far greater number of media outlets—a total of 1,240 by the latest count.

The print medium leads the broadcast industry by an 8 to 1 ratio. There are 100 radio stations, 10 television stations and 49 cable TV systems licensed to operate in New Jersey, as of 1982.

That leaves nearly 1,000 print outlets, from daily and weekly newspapers to state and local periodicals and college publications.

Out front, numerically, are the 323 weekly newspapers circulated in their hometowns, from the big cities and their surrounding suburbs to the rural farm villages.

Their mastheads reflect the weeklies' geographic and special interests, with names such as the Cape May Star and Wave; the Experienced Citizen in Denville; the Town Crier and Herald in Barrington; the Bayonne Facts; the Princeton Packet; the Bloomfield Independent Press; the Community Journal in Berlin; Garden State Nite Life; the Bound Brook Chronicle; the Beachcomber News in Brigantine; the Lower Township Lantern; the Butler Argus; Suburban Trends; the Progress in Caldwell; the Register News in Bordentown; the Record Breeze in Clementon; the Clark Patriot; the Palisadian; the Post Eagle in Clifton; the Weekly Retrospect in Collingswood; the South Jersey Advisor; the News Beacon in Fair Lawn; the Booster News in Farmingdale; the Hunterdon County Democrat, and the North Bergen Free Press.

Also, the Florham Park Eagle and Community News; the Forked River Gazette; the Newark Community Alert; the Sharp Shooter in Newton; the Nutley Sun; Ironbound Voices in Newark; the Record Spirit in Paulsboro; the Atom Tabloid in Rahway; the Randolph Reporter; the Civic Press in Runnemede; the Sampler in Salem; the Monitor in Trenton; the News Transcript in Freehold; the Valley Star in Cresskill; the Store News in Dunellen; the Senti-

nel in East Brunswick; the East Orange Nu-View; the Elmer Times in Elmer; the Review in Glassboro; the Messenger in Garfield; the Forum in Hackettstown; the Observer in Hasbrouck Heights; the Plain Dealer in Kearny; the Hoboken Reporter; the Statesman in Howell; the Lawrence Ledger; County Today in Little Falls; the West Essex Tribune in Livingston; Atlanticville in Long Branch; the Mountainside Echo; the New Brunswick Spokesman; the Sussex Spectator; the Oakland Bulletin; the Advocate, the official newspaper of the Roman Catholic Archdiocese of Newark; the Grafica and the Jewish News, based in East Orange; Lavoz Spanish Newspaper in Elizabeth, and the Italian Tribune News.

There are also some 225 local and state periodicals catering to every whim and fancy, including Angler's News, Bow Waves, China Travel Newsletter, Cockpit, Enjoy, Environmental-Ed, Fit Parade, Fruit Notes, Golden Voice, Heart Beat, Jersey Business Review, Jersey Woman, Lean Lines, Life Line, New Jersey Outdoors, New Jersey Voter, Nursery Notes, People Power, Salad Bowl, Synod Synopsis, Trailblazer, Veterans News and Window.

The more than 80 college publications summon their students' attention with such headings as the Caldwell College Kettle, the Camden County College Common Sense, the Brookdale Community College Stall, the Felician College Encore, the Glassboro State College Whit, the Monmouth College Outlook, the New Jersey Institute of Technology Vector, the Passaic County Community College Kaleidoscope, the Ramapo College Horizons, the Rider College Directions, the Rutgers Gleaner, the Setonian, the Somerset County College Commuter, and the Trenton State College Chimes.

Some internal publications, or "house organs," are Mack Trucks' "Particulars," Elizabethtown Water Co.'s "News on Tap," Christ Hospital's "Synapse," The New Jersey Turnpike Authority's "Pike Interchange," Public Service Electric & Gas Co.'s "Energy People," St. James Hospital's "Pulse," Barnert Memorial Hospital Center's "Floor-O-Scope," and the First National Bank of New Jersey's "Key First News."

Among the 245 nationally circulated publications are Aerosol Age, Bullpen, Classic Car, Drug Topics, Embroidery News, Fashion Perspective, Golf Journal, Hypnosis Quarterly, Industrial Robots International, Jaguar Journal, Katolicky Sokol, Laboratory Equipment, Micro Waves, Netherlands Philately, Ophthalmic Surgery, Public Works, Religious Broadcasting, Society, Tropical Fish Hobbyist, Urban League Review, What's Left?, and Zionism.

The 10 television stations, with the exception of WNET/13, licensed in Newark, are all ultra-high-frequency channels: WWAC-TV (Channel 53), Atlantic City; WAAT-TV (Channel 40), Avalon; WNJS-TV (Channel 23), Camden; WNJM-TV (Channel 50), Montclair; WNJU-TV (Channel 47), Newark; WWHT-TV (Channel 68), Newark; WXTV-41, Secaucus; WNJB-TV (Channel 58), Trenton; WNJT-TV (Channel 52), Trenton, and WRUB-TV (Channel 65), Vineland.

Of the 26 daily newspapers, the leading ones are The Star-Ledger, Newark; The Record, Hackensack; The Courier-Post, Camden, and The Press, Asbury Park.

There are radio stations in scores of communities, from Atlantic City and Avalon to Trenton and Teaneck.

The complete listing of New Jersey's media outlets can be found in "Burrell's New Jersey Media Directory," published in Livingston.

Courtesy: AT&T Communications

*AT&T Communications headquarters building
located in Basking Ridge.*

CORPORATIONS

Demographically in the heart of the greatest marketplace in the world, New Jersey is home for many of the largest international corporations, as well as the place where 90 out of America's 100 biggest businesses conduct operations.

The fourth smallest state in the nation, New Jersey surprisingly is the gateway to the global marketplace, handling more than 80 percent of the tonnage moving through the bustling New York Harbor.

As a corporate haven for such multinational giants as Johnson & Johnson, Prudential and AT&T, the Garden State ranks *first* as the "most likely choice" for company headquarters, according to Fortune magazine's "facility location survey" of the top 1,000 firms in the United States.

These and comparable corporations—the backbone of American enterprise—find New Jersey an excellent environment in which their employes can work, live and play.

As a recognized leader in commerce and industry, New Jersey today boasts the world's largest private research and development laboratory (AT&T), the top insurance company on the planet (Prudential), the number one soup factory (Campbell), the most productive chemical factory (Du Pont), the biggest containerized shipping port (in Elizabeth), the most extensive "piggyback" freight service yard (Conrail in Kearny), the busiest airport in terms of takeoffs and landings (Teterboro), the most heavily trav-

eled toll road (Turnpike), and the largest private business concern on earth (AT&T).

AT&T best exemplifies the recent corporate trend wherein workplaces must be as appealing as an executive's homestead. Over the last 20 years, AT&T has decentralized its vast communications empire, shifting most of its operations to New Jersey.

As one of the state's five largest employers, AT&T has established home bases for its Communications in Bedminster; AT&T International in Basking Ridge; AT&T Bell Laboratories in Holmdel, Murray Hill, Whippany and eight other locations; and AT&T Technologies, whose new headquarters are in Berkeley Heights and whose regional headquarters are in Newark; AT&T Engineering Research Center and Corporate Education Center in Princeton; AT&T Consumer Products Office in Parsippany, and service centers scattered throughout the state. AT&T Technologies (Western Electric) is phasing out its huge manufacturing plant in Kearny.

Even foreign auto makers have set up their North American headquarters in the Garden State, making it the foreign car capital of the U.S. Based in Bergen County are: Rolls Royce and Peugeot in Lyndhurst; Mercedes-Benz and BMW in Montvale; Jaguar, MG, Triumph and Rover in Leonia; Alfa-Romeo and Renault in Englewood Cliffs; Volvo in Rockleigh, and Citroen in Englewood.

Other foreign outlets with a New Jersey mailing address are Germany's American Hoechst and BASF; Belgium's Agfa-Gevaert; the Netherlands' North American Philips; the United Kingdom's famed Josiah Wedgwood & Sons, USA, and France's Parfums Rochas.

Attracted by New Jersey's geological diversity and fiscally

exceptional Triple-A bond rating, more than 5,000 Japanese nationals have settled in the Bergen-Hudson-Essex region, representing firms such as Panasonic, Toyota, Datsun, Sharp, Minolta, Fuji, Yashica and an impressive array of Japanese high-tech companies.

New Jersey is also America's medicine chest, loaded with pharmaceutical industries that include J&J, Hoffmann-LaRoche, Bristol-Myers, Merck, Squibb, Schering-Plough, Ciba-Geigy, Sandoz and Warner-Lambert.

The chemical industry finds the chemistry is just right in New Jersey, with many dwarfing all other corporate operations by the mere presence of Du Pont, Union Carbide, Monsanto, American Cyanamid, Allied, Dow, Sun, Apollo, GAF, Hercules, Stauffer, Reichhold, Olin, Airco and Hooker.

The oil industry began in Bayonne last century when John D. Rockefeller created the world's largest petroleum conglomerate, Standard Oil of New Jersey. Today its successor, Exxon, continues its engineering and research operations at laboratories in Clinton, Florham Park and Linden.

Exxon also operates one of the world's largest refineries in Linden, while four other refineries are run by Mobil, Texaco, Chevron and Hess in South Jersey and Middlesex County.

As the transportation hub of North America (the most heavily used air-water-rail-road interface at Ports Newark-Elizabeth, Newark International Airport, the Turnpike and Rte. 1-9), New Jersey is first in pharmaceuticals, second in chemicals (including the petroleum industry), fifth in rubber and plastics, sixth in instruments and related products, seventh in food and related products, eighth in electrical machinery, ninth in paper and textiles, and 10th in fabricated metals.

With the most productive farmland acreage in the country, New Jersey ranks first in the production of cultivated blueberries and third in cranberries, according to the U.S. Department of Agriculture. It is also the second leading exporter of steel and iron scrap. Altogether, New Jersey ranks fifth nationally in the value of U.S. products shipped abroad, or more than $9 billion worth of merchandise yearly.

One community in Bergen County, Paramus, has the highest per capita retail sales in the United States, making it the shoppers' paradise of the land.

Linden is the Cadillac capital of America, the classy cars being assembled at one of General Motors' most advanced industrial plants.

Corporate names either rooted in New Jersey or linked to major regional offices and plants have become household words or readily identifiable symbols: Mennen, Bell, Prudential ("The Rock"), Nabisco, Campbell Soup, Western Union, A&P, Exxon, Mobil, Westinghouse, RCA, IBM, ITT, GM, GE, Hartz.

Products of New Jersey corporations can be found in any home, office and motor vehicle or almost anywhere goods are sold: Linoleum, Formica, Bakelite, Vinylite, Teflon, Melamac plastic, Band-Aid, adhesive tape, Duco Lacquer, Neoprene, butyl rubber, Plexiglas, Glad bags, Eveready and Energizer batteries, Prestone and Simoniz, Vitamins A, C, B1 and B12, cortisone, Anso IV carpeting, Oreo cookies, Life Savers, Geritol, Di-Gel, Rolaids, Certs, Chiclets, Dentyne, Clorets, Bromo Seltzer, Schick shavers, Mazola corn oil, Hellmann's mayonnaise, Fleischmann's margarine, Pepperidge Farm, V-8 vegetable juice, Swanson's and Mrs. Paul's frozen dinners, Ritz crackers, Baby Ruth and Butterfingers candy bars, M&Ms, Mars bars, Three Musketeers, Maybelline cosmetics, Coppertone, Mueller, Buitoni and Franco-American spaghettis, Vlasic pickels, Skippy peanut butter, Planter's nuts, Daisy air rifles, Jacuzzi whirlpool baths, Dr. Scholl footwear, Valium, Lenox, Old Spice and Pine-Sol... plus hundreds more famous brand names.

The leading New Jersey-based companies are: New Jersey Bell Telephone, Newark; The Prudential Insurance Co., Newark; AT&T's eight major departments and five subsidiaries, including AT&T Bell Laboratories and AT&T Technologies; Supermarkets General Corp., Woodbridge; J&J, New Brunswick; Public Service

Electric & Gas Co., Newark; The First National State Fidelity Bank of New Jersey; Hoffmann-LaRoche, Nutley-Clifton; American Cyanamid, Wayne; Kidde, Inc., Clifton; Merck & Co., Rahway; Schering-Plough, Kenilworth; Great Atlantic and Pacific Tea Co. (A&P), Montvale; Ingersoll-Rand, Woodcliff Lake; Jamesway Corp., Secaucus; Nabisco Brands, East Hanover, and Becton, Dickinson and Co., Paramus.

Also the Campbell Soup Co., Camden; Grand Union, Elmwood Park; Jersey Central Power & Light Co., Morristown; Wakefern Food Corp. (Shop-Rite), Elizabeth; Foster-Wheeler Corp., Livingston; Warner-Lambert, Morris Plains; Mennen, Morris Township; Western Union, Upper Saddle River; United Jersey Banks, Princeton; Mayfair Supermarkets (Foodtown), Elizabeth; Foodarama Supermarkets, Freehold; Allied Corp., Morristown, and CPC International, Englewood Cliffs.

And, Automatic Data Processing, Clifton; Prentice-Hall, Englewood Cliffs; Mutual Benefit Life, Newark; Engelhard Corp., Edison; Airco, Montvale; American Hoechst Corp., Somerville; Atlantic Electric Co., Atlantic City; Inserra Supermarkets, Mahwah; Village Supermarkets, Springfield; First Jersey National Corp., Jersey City; Horizon Bancorp., Morristown; The National State Bank, Elizabeth; Lockheed Electronics Co., Plainfield; Crum and Forster, Morristown; Lenox, Lawrenceville; Heritage Bancorp., Cherry Hill; New Jersey Manufacturers Insurance Co., West Trenton; Perkin-Elmer Data Systems, Oceanport; Sandoz, East Hanover; Automatic Switch Co., Florham Park; Transamerica, Lawrenceville; Howard Savings Bank, Newark; National Starch and Chemical Corp., Bridgewater, and New Jersey National Corp., Trenton.

Companies with significant operations in New Jersey are: RCA, Sears, Exxon, General Motors, Du Pont, Westinghouse, Acme Markets, IBM, Mobil, ITT, Marriott, Ciba-Geigy, Squibb, W.R. Grace, R.J. Reynolds Industries, Stop & Shop Companies, Owens-Illinois, Bendix, Consolidated Rail (Conrail), Combustion Engineering-Lummus, Ford Motor, Union Carbide, Hershey Foods, Litton Industries, Chubb Corp., North American Philips, Pennwalt Corp., General Electric Co., CBS, Anheuser-Busch, Hercules, Owens-Corning Fiberglass, Eastern Airlines, People Express and Amax (U.S. Metals Refining).

Entertainment with a capital "C" (for casinos) is overtaking chemicals and communications as New Jersey's fastest growing revenue generator. In existence only seven years, Resorts International immediately has established itself as Atlantic City's biggest casino-hotel, ranking as New Jersey's 35th largest employer by 1984.

A string of boardwalk casinos suddenly popped on New Jersey's "top 100" employment charts as soon as they opened their doors to gaming and nightclub patrons. They are Atlantis Casino

Autos roll off the assembly line at General Motors New Jersey division plant in Linden.

Star-Ledger Photo

Star-Ledger Photo

Harrah's Trump Plaza, shown under construction on the Atlantic City Boardwalk, is among the casinos ranking high on the employment charts.

Star-Ledger Photo

Robert Ferguson, Jr., Chairman of First Fidelity Bank, points to New Jersey map showing bank locations as Peter Cartmell, Chairman of the former Fidelity Union Trust Co., reviews the merger of the two banks in 1984.

Hotel, Bally's Park Place, Caesars Atlantic City Hotel Casino, the Claridge Hotel and Casino, the Golden Nugget Hotel & Casino, Harrah's Marina Hotel Casino, Resorts International, the Sands Hotel and Casino, the Tropicana Hotel and Casino and Trump Plaza Hotel Casino. Other casinos are joining the list as they get ready for their grand openings during the next five years.

When First National State Bank of New Jersey merged in 1983 with Fidelity Union Bancorp, to become First Fidelity Bank, one of the biggest banks in America was established with assets totaling more than $10 billion. Together, they employ more than 8,000 people in 305 offices throughout the state.

A representative sampling of some of New Jersey's top 100 companies, in terms of employment, reveals the incredible diversity and specialized talents that have made the Garden State one of the nation's most prominent corporate mailing addresses:

* * *

New Jersey Bell, one of the 22 Bell systems divested from AT&T on Jan. 1, 1984, is the state's largest employer with nearly 29,000 workers. New Jersey Bell handles some 38 million calls on an average business day, and the number increases annually.

In the vanguard of the information explosion, NJ Bell is no longer just phones connecting voices, but also a transmitter of television images, graphics and videotext. In 1982, NJ Bell inaugurated service over the state's first lightwave communications route. In a lightwave system, information travels as bursts of laser light through hair-thin glass fibers encased in a cable about the diameter of an index finger.

These fingers can carry many more messages than conventional copper facilities, are immune to electrical interference and require fewer signal "boosters" along the transmission path.

In the next few years, NJ Bell will be enriching its network with sophisticated digital capabilities. To be introduced in 1985 is Local Area Data Transport, or LADT, permitting low- and medium-speed data transmissions to and from homes and small businesses.

With one version of LADT, customers will be able to use their regular telephone lines for simultaneous voice and data communications. A lawyer, for example, could consult with a client on the phone while a clerk in the next room uses a terminal connected to the same phone line to query a remote information base.

Tested in 1983 was another transmission vehicle—CSDC, or Circuit Switched Digital Capability. This system can use regular telephone lines to carry up to 56,000 bits of information per sec-

Won-Tien Tsang of Bell Labs, inventor of the laser, tests the cleaved coupled-cavity laser that he designed.

Star-Ledger Photo

Murray Hill is home base for Bell Laboratories, AT&T's center for research and development.

ond. CSDC can also send a page of facsimile in only four seconds. Or, with a special tele-conferencing feature, a customer can talk on the phone, flip a switch to receive graphics or text on a terminal device, then switch back to the conversation.

A powerful new technology—cellular mobile radio—promises to open a new era of communications to people on the go. NJ Bell is providing transmission and switching systems for Advanced Mobile Phone Service. With AMPS, an area is divided into many geographic units or honeycomb-like cells, each equipped with a low-powered radio transmitter and control equipment connected to a mobile telephone switching office.

As a vehicle moves through an area, electronic switching equipment hands off calls in progression from cell to cell, enabling many people to use their mobile phones at the same time. Future units may be able to receive and transmit data as well.

* * *

Prudential, also with headquarters in Newark, protects more than 26 million people around the world through various life, health, home and auto insurance policies. As the second largest employer in the state (about 19,000), Prudential Insurance Co. of America has assets amounting to more than $77 billion, placing it among the five biggest corporations in the U.S.

In recent years, Prudential has branched into such areas as property and casualty insurance, health care, leasing, investment banking and securities brokerage services. More than 5,500 Prudential agents are licensed to sell mutual funds and other investment-oriented products.

In 1981, Prudential acquired Bache, one of the oldest and largest investment brokerage firms in the world. Prudential-Bache Securities, Inc. now provides clients with stocks, bonds, options, commodities, tax-favored investments and a personal asset management service called the Command Account.

In health care, Prudential administers the federal Medicare program in New Jersey, North Carolina and Georgia, and the Medicaid program in New Jersey.

Concerned over the global energy-environmental dilemma, Prudential has undertaken a revolutionary conservation project at Princeton's Forrestal Center, headed by the distinguished physicist Dr. Theodore B. Taylor. The Prudential-Taylor plan is to use ice made in the winter and hot water made in the summer to cool

The Prudential Insurance Company of America's office in downtown Newark.

and warm buildings throughout the year. By tapping nature's available resources, Prudential is able to cut its heating and air conditioning costs and push America closer to the Solar Age.

* * *

AT&T and **AT&T Bell Laboratories** are two of New Jersey's largest workforces, 17,500 and 12,000, respectively. Most of the newly organized AT&T operations are based in New Jersey, including AT&T Bell Labs in Murray Hill, Holmdel and Whippany, and eight other locations.

After completing the most extensive restructuring ever undertaken by a corporate enterprise, AT&T today consists of seven principal organizations:

• Western Electric, now AT&T Technologies, for manufacturing and supply, with offices in Newark, Morristown, Parsippany and Princeton, and service operations in Union and other New Jersey communities. The Kearny plant, once WE's biggest, will be phased out in 1985.

AT&T Technologies also comprises AT&T Network Systems, AT&T Technology Systems, and AT&T Consumer Products.

• AT&T Bell Laboratories, for research and development.

• A new organization, AT&T Communications, which will encompass but be much larger than the previous Long Lines Department in Bedminster, providing nationwide long-distance service.

• American Bell, now AT&T Information Systems, producing enhanced communications and information services and equipment for business, government and residential customers.

• AT&T International in Basking Ridge, marketing products and services overseas.

The 20th Century "Information Age" is largely the product of AT&T, technology that was invented and developed by AT&T Bell Labs, applied by AT&T Technologies, and channeled to the marketplace by AT&T.

It was at Bell Labs, with the invention of the transistor in 1947, that the revolution in solid-state technology was born. It has developed into microelectronics, software and digital systems, and lightwave communications.

A digital computer memory made at Bell Labs in 1981 uses a quarter of a million transistors on a single chip, while a newer version of the Bellmac microprocessor (actually a computer on a chip) contains 150,000 components.

Construction started in June 1982 on the world's largest laser-powered lightwave system, a 776-mile project extending from Massachusetts to Virginia.

Meanwhile, AT&T is working with government telecommunications agencies in Europe to use lightwave technology for an undersea cable system across the Atlantic Ocean in the late 1980s.

By the end of 1983, AT&T had introduced its Picturephone meeting service (video tele-conferencing) into 42 cities. Business people may use the service to hold face-to-face meetings over a two-way hookup between conference rooms, without having to travel to a distant city for the meeting. Video tele-conferencing is a significant time and energy saver.

* * *

When the **Great Atlantic & Pacific Tea Co.** converted a corner grocery store into a spacious supermarket at the end of the last century, it was the first link in what was to become the world's biggest food chain, known simply as A&P.

Today, the old tea company, which revolutionized the retail food industry, has survived several mid-life crises to become one of New Jersey's marketing success stories. Now number three on the state's food charts, A&P runs its national operation from a central office complex in Montvale.

Its 69 A&P stores in the Garden State, plus another 56 Super Fresh outlets in the South Jersey-Philadelphia region, employ more than 4,000 people. In the U.S. and Canada, A&P today operates about 1,000 supermarkets, many featuring such attractions as specialty food islands, gourmet meats, seafood shops, in-store bakeries and the aromatically familiar, freshly ground Eight O'Clock Coffee coming right out of the grinder.

In the extremely competitive food industry, a relative newcomer has taken a commanding lead in New Jersey—Supermarkets General, based in Woodbridge, which is the parent corporation of Pathmark and Rickel Home Centers. Ranked as New Jersey's fifth largest employer (some 15,000 jobs), Supermarkets General was founded in 1966, and, within two decades, had

Courtesy: AT&T Communications

AT&T Communications network operations center in Bedminster allows managers to monitor the volume of calls and instantly reroute traffic to avoid congestion.

climbed all the way to the 21st largest retailer and 10th largest supermarket company in the United States with sales in excess of $3.25 billion.

Concentrating on larger supermarket-drug stores, Pathmark maintains a strong presence in the Middle Atlantic and New England areas. The bulk of its sales are in the metropolitan tri-state region.

Rickel has built a reputation on do-it-yourself merchandise, brand name tools, building materials, paints, electrical and plumbing supplies and home-related seasonal products.

Rounding out New Jersey's major supermarket operations are Acme, with headquarters in Philadelphia and second only to Supermarkets General in gross sales; Grand Union in Elmwood Park; Wakefern Food Corp. (Shop-Rite), Elizabeth; Mayfair Supermarkets (Foodtown), also based in Elizabeth; Foodarama Supermarkets, Freehold; Inserra Supermarkets, Mahwah, and Village Supermarkets, Springfield.

* * *

The pharmaceutical industry can trace its healthful roots to New Jersey, beginning with Johnson & Johnson in New Brunswick, and branching out over the past half-century to form a flourishing medical tree-of-life.

Today, that firmly planted tree is sustained by J&J; Hoffmann-La Roche in Nutley-Clifton; Merck & Co., Rahway; Schering-Plough, Kenilworth; Becton Dickinson, Paramus; Warner Lambert, Morris Plains; Squibb, Princeton; Sandoz, East Hanover; the Swiss firm of Ciba-Geigy, whose pharmaceutical divisional headquarters are in suburban Summit, and dozens more smaller drug companies.

With sales approaching $6 billion, **Johnson & Johnson** is a growing family of 150 companies from around the globe that took a $100 million commercial disaster—the Tylenol tampering episode—and turned it into a universal safety standard for the pharmaceutical industry. Tylenol changed forever the way medicine is packaged, ushering in an age of unprecedented consumer protection and demonstrating once again J&J's credible leadership in the health products field.

Johnson & Johnson, whose
headquarters is in New
Brunswick, employs 80,000
workers worldwide.

Employing 14,000 in New Jersey, J&J has approximately 80,000 on its payroll worldwide, working in some 200 manufacturing facilities and producing everything from toiletry and baby care items to natural and synthetic fibers.

J&J's most famous product is the Band-Aid, a word with a common meaning that has slipped into the language, even though it's a trademarked brand name. Other Johnson products are: Surgical instruments, fiberoptic and pain control products with trade names such as Classic, Micros and Britelite ... medical devices including intravenous catheters, infusion pumps, sets and filtration apparatus for monitoring respiratory, cardiac and cerebral functions, and sold as Dinamap, Jelco and Cathlon IV ... Devro brand edible protein sausage casings ... suture and mechanical wound-closure products, dispensed as Ethicon, Vicryl, Prolene and Proximate ... extracorporeal technology for blood and other diseases in connection with kidney failure, heart valves and cardiovascular complications, trademarked as TriEx, Intersept, Interpulse and Hancock ... Johnson's baby powder, soap, oil, cream, lotion, shampoo and other baby care products ... and Sundown Sunscreen, Red Cross adhesives, Reach toothbrushes, Sof-Wick surgical dressings, Modess, Stayfree, Sure, Natural sanitary napkins, and dozens of other medical products.

*　*　*

Hoffmann-La Roche, a private company that does not disclose its annual sales or earning figures, considers its mission to be improving standards of diagnosis, therapy and health care through ongoing R&D.

A community of more than 8,000 Roche workers in New Jersey, plus thousands more outside the state, are responsible for prescription medicines, diagnostic test products and services, as well as bulk medicinals and vitamins for the food, pharmaceutical and agrochemical industries.

Roche's strength comes from its original research in biology, chemistry and medicine. The Nutley-based pharmaceutical behemoth focuses its resources on mental disease, cancer and immunology, cardiovascular disease, endocrine and gastrointestinal disorders, dermatology and infectious and inflammatory diseases.

Roche currently sells more than 45 prescription pharmaceutical products, from Librium and Valium to Solatene and Xenon. Roche plans to introduce more than 25 new products over the next eight years.

Roche clinical laboratories in Raritan provide *in vitro* laboratory services to aid in the correct diagnosis of disease. Up to 20 regional labs and a network of 80 collection stations serve much of the United States in the rapid pick-up and transport of biological specimens and prompt reporting of computerized test results. Roche labs offer more than 600 diagnostic tests and profiles. Routine procedures are performed in the areas of blood and urine chemistry, cytology, hematology, immunochemistry, immunochematology-serology, microbiology, parasitology and pathology.

Roche's Fine Chemicals Department is a major supplier of bulk vitamins, colors, acidulants and medicinals to the drug, cosmetic and food industries. Roche also provides liquid crystals to the electronics industry for digital watches, calculators and instruments.

Since 1934 when it was the first company to produce Vitamin C commercially, Roche continues to supply a full line of vitamins A, C, E, the B complexes, biotin, niacin, and forms of pantothenic acid. Major manufacturing plants are located in Nutley and Belvidere.

Roche remains a leader in the development and application of recombinant DNA and related technologies. A new department of molecular genetics was formed to develop proteins and peptides with potential biological significance. Through biotechnology, efficient production of a wide spectrum of compounds, including vitamins, amino acids and antibiotics, is being accomplished.

At the Roche Research Center, consisting of Roche labs and the Roche Institute of Molecular Biology, nearly 1,500 scientists and other personnel are engaged in pioneering biotechnological research. After more than two years of joint scientific collaboration, Roche and Genentech in San Francisco have reached a scientific milestone in the production of two types of human interferon needed to cure cancer.

Roche is currently looking for agents that will have a positive effect on memory and mental performance, and is also studying receptor site mechanisms and identifying enzyme systems in the brain to find new drugs that will affect the central nervous system.

*　*　*

Merck of Rahway is a $3 billion-a-year corporation with

Hoffmann-LaRoche in Nutley-Clifton is a leader in biological, chemical and medical research.

some 33,000 employes in 80 countries. More than 4,500 are located in New Jersey. Merck is known for discovering, developing, producing and marketing products and services for the maintenance or restoration of health and the environment.

The company, which sells more than 1,000 products, is divided into two industry segments: Human and animal health products, and special chemical and environmental products.

Human health products include antihypertensive and cardiovascular products, of which Aldomet is the largest selling, and anti-inflammatory products, of which Indocin and Clinoril are the two largest selling.

Merck's special chemical and environmental products include granular activated carbon, and water-saving equipment such as cooling towers, evaporative condensers and closed-circuit fluid coolers for industrial, commercial and other large cooling, air-conditioning and refrigeration applications. Specialty chemicals are used for water treatment, the manufacture of paints and paper, oil field drilling, food additives and cleaning products.

As a leader in the water-management business, a Merck subsidiary, Calgon, is removing salt from seawater through a highly effective chemical process that already produces more than 100 million gallons of fresh water each day.

A Merck scientist, Dr. Lewis H. Sarett, is credited with the historic synthesis of cortisone in 1944, then considered the most complicated achievement of synthetic organic chemistry. It opened the door to dramatic new approaches to treatment of rheumatoid arthritis and other inflammatory conditions, and other diseases.

* * *

Maybelline, Di-Gel, Coppertone, Solarcaine and Dr. Scholl are just a few of the popular consumer products associated with **Schering-Plough**, the nearly $2 billion-a-year international corporation centered in Kenilworth.

Health and personal care are at the core of S-P's pharmaceutical research efforts, which also embrace new therapeutic agents and immunology and recombinant DNA technologies.

In the field of recombinant DNA, work on alpha (leukocyte) interferon, a substance that holds promise for treating various forms of cancer and viral infections, has resulted in successful, large-scale production.

Schering-Plough's over-the-counter drugs include the Beech-

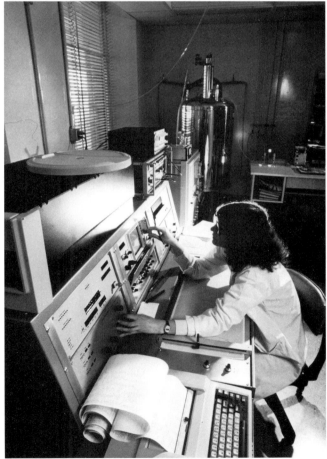

Dr. Sheila Cohen, a researcher at Merck in Rahway, operates a nuclear magnetic spectrometer, which provides information on molecular structure and intra-cell activity.

Schering-Plough's largest New Jersey facility in Kenilworth includes 1.3 million square feet of manufacturing, warehouse and administrative space.

Star-Ledger Photo

man labels, and Chlor-Trimeton, Coricidin and Tinactin. Wesley-Jessen, the company's vision care products division, markets the DuraSoft contact lenses.

Schering-Plough employs 4,200 people at its Bloomfield laboratories and Kenilworth complex.

* * *

Warner-Lambert, Morris Plains, is a $3.3 billion worldwide maker and distributor of health care and consumer products, many of which are household names: Chiclets, Dentyne, Certs, Clorets, Rolaids, Bromo Seltzer, Trident, Listerine, Gelusil, and other popular brand names such as Myadec, Halls throat lozenges and Sinutab.

Warner-Lambert conducts business in more than 130 countries with a work force of 42,000, of which 3,000 are in New Jersey. With more than 100 manufacturing facilities and four major research centers, Warner-Lambert directs its resources to the improvement of health care. Ethical health care lines include pharmaceuticals, diagnostic products, intravenous infusion instrumentation, intravenous catheters and other hospital products and optical and scientific instruments.

Warner-Lambert also is a major producer and marketer of chewing gums, breath mints, shaving products and pet care items.

In 1983, Warner-Lambert completed a $16 million research center at company headquarters in Morris Plains. Its primary interest will be new non-prescription drugs and other consumer products.

* * *

Becton Dickinson began in 1897 with one product—clinical thermometers—and 20 people. Today, the New Jersey firm, with headquarters in Paramus, is the world's leading manufacturer of single-use hypodermic needles and syringes, a market estimated at $650 million.

With sales of around $1.2 billion and a statewide payroll of 3,400, Becton Dickinson (which shares its name with Fairleigh Dickinson University, founded by the same family) today ranks as one of the most broadly based health care companies in the world.

In the field of laboratory diagnostics, BD has built a unique position with capabilities covering three of the major diagnostic disciplines: Immunology, microbiology and hematology.

Courtesy: Warner-Lambert

A Warner-Lambert scientist in the New Consumer Products' Research Center in Morris Plains carrying out work on new mouthwash formulations.

BD's products also span a spectrum of detection technologies, including radiotagging, fluorescence, particle agglutination and flow cytometry. BD's comprehensive approach to health care allows it to serve the different needs of various markets, whether it be the large urban hospital, the decentralized clinical laboratory, a physician's office, or the medical research lab.

* * *

Squibb and Ciba-Geigy can trace their origins to New Jersey. Ciba's roots are in Union County, while Squibb has had its pharmaceutical operations based in the Garden State since the turn of the century.

In observing its 125th anniversary in September 1983, Squibb dedicated its latest manufacturing plant in New Brunswick. Squibb moved its corporate headquarters from New York to the Princeton area in 1983. There are now more than 4,500 Squibb personnel in New Jersey.

Squibb is a $1.8 billion annual sales operation specializing in pharmaceuticals, medical systems and health products. Among its principal products are Theragran vitamins, Sweeta, and Charles of the Ritz, Jean Naté, and Yves Saint Laurent cosmetics.

Ciba, originally from Summit, merged with Geigy, of Ardsley, N.Y., in 1970. It is a publicly owned Swiss company. With annual sales approaching the $2 billion mark, Ciba-Geigy provides jobs for approximately 5,000 New Jersey residents. Ciba-Geigy maintains administrative facilities, regional sales offices and distribution centers in Summit, Toms River, Carlstadt, Hightstown and Paramus.

Ciba-Geigy's Airwick Industries markets such well-known household products as Glamorene, Stick Ups, Air Wand, Carpet Fresh and Chore Boy.

* * *

America's first petrochemical center, New Jersey remains the petroleum and chemical processing complex of the East, second only to the Gulf Coast's oil and chemical operations.

The chemical conglomerates are represented by Allied, Cyanamid, Du Pont, Union Carbide, Germany's American Hoechst

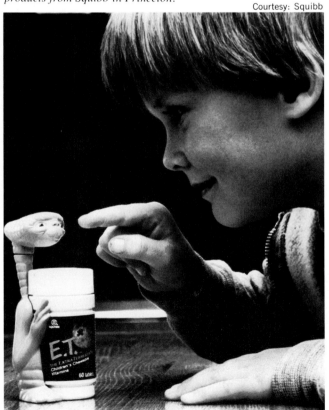

E.T. children's chewable vitamins are one of many products from Squibb in Princeton.

Courtesy: Squibb

based in Somerville, and scores of smaller chemical companies.

The oil companies maintaining refineries and storage facilities in New Jersey are Exxon, Mobil, Shell, Texaco, Chevron and Hess. Chevron runs a refinery in Perth Amboy, making most of the asphalt in the Northeast, while Hess has reactivated a refinery in Woodbridge, where there is also a huge storage tank depot supplying heating fuel and gasoline to customers in the New Jersey-New York region.

Exxon's Bayway Refinery in Linden is the second largest in the U.S. Along with the Mobil and Texaco refineries in South Jersey and the Hess plant, they furnish much of the distillates for the Northeast. Exxon, with roughly 9,000 employes in New Jersey, rates its refinery's plant capacity at 200,000 barrels a day. There are 42 gallons in a barrel.

On the lower Delaware River stand Mobil's 120,000-barrel refinery in Paulsboro, and Texaco's 88,000-barrel refinery in Westville. Texaco also maintains marketing offices in Cherry Hill and a deepwater shipping terminal in Newark.

A sprawling tank farm in Woodbridge contains refined products of Shell Oil Co. Most of the roadways in this region are paved with asphalt produced at Chevron's 125,000-barrel-a-day refinery in Perth Amboy. Hess' 75,000-barrel-per-day refinery in Woodbridge is "cracking" distillates for specialized hydrocarbon markets.

In chemicals, Allied, Cyanamid, Du Pont and Union Carbide synthesize the bulk of the world's hydrocarbons into products ranging from carpets and communications materials to space-age electronic and computer ingredients.

Allied Corp., which acquired the $4 billion Bendix Corp. in 1983, manages its far-flung empire from Morris Plains, directing its human and technical resources in the fields of chemicals, fibers and plastics, oil and gas, electrical and electronic, and health and scientific products.

The Bendix Corp. has businesses in aerospace-electronics, automotive and industrial products areas. Bendix and Allied are responsible for some 7,000 jobs in New Jersey.

One of Allied's most visible products is its luxurious Anso IV nylon carpet yarn.

Cyanamid, of Wayne, is a $3.5 billion corporation involved in chemicals, medical and consumer products, and agricultural technology. Brand names associated with Cyanamid are Old Spice, Pine-Sol, Pierre Cardin fragrance, Breck shampoo and Formica, which can be seen on tables and countertops everywhere. Cyanamid has created about 5,700 jobs in New Jersey.

Du Pont built the world's largest chemical factory in Deepwater, South Jersey, on the Delaware River, known as the Chambers Works. The $23 billion chemical-energy-minerals giant is based in Delaware. Du Pont has eight areas of interest: Biomedical and polymer products, fibers, coal and minerals, agricultural and industrial chemicals, industrial and consumer products, petroleum exploration and production, and petroleum refining, marketing and transportation. Among Du Pont's subsidiaries is Conoco, an oil, gas and coal company.

Du Pont has coined some words that are now part of the consumer's vocabulary: Teflon, Orlon, Dacron and Antron. Du Pont also owns Remington Arms, makers of ammunition and shotguns and rifles used for hunting and target shooting.

Union Carbide is another global Gulliver whose sales have topped $10 billion. Carbide's business turns on chemicals and plastics, gases and related products, metals and carbons, batteries, home and automotive products, and specialty products ranging from agricultural and food processing to electronic components.

Union Carbide's brand names have been seen by practically everyone who's ever watched television or shopped in a store or supermarket: Glad plastic bags, Eveready and Energizer batteries, Prestone antifreeze, Simoniz and Simoniz SuperPoly car wax.

The 2,400 Carbide employes in New Jersey work in plants or offices in Freehold, Bound Brook, Carteret, Clinton, Hackensack, Keasbey, Moorestown, Perth Amboy, Piscataway and Somerset.

* * *

Campbell Soup and **Nabisco Brands** conjure images of appetizing snacks, foods and beverages. Each could easily fill a shopping cart with its assorted brand name products, be it the pickles or peanuts, pastas or pizzas, crackers, cookies or candies.

Starting out 125 years ago canning tomato soup in Camden, Campbell parlayed ripe Jersey tomatoes and tender chickens for instant hot soups into a vast food company of 40,000 employes and 80 manufacturing plants in 12 countries. Campbell products today are in stores and dispensing machines in 120 foreign markets.

Although still called the Campbell Soup Co., the $3 billion-plus food conglomerate sells Prego spaghetti products, Franco-American spaghettis, Swanson's and Mrs. Paul's frozen dinners, Snow King frozen foods, Pepperidge Farm baked goods, Juice Bowl, Vlasic pickles, sauces and bar cheese, and V-8 cocktail juice.

Campbell is also getting into the restaurant business. It has opened several H.T. McDoogal's "theme" restaurants, a few Hanover restaurants on the East Coast, and the Annie A's. Pietro's, the chain of pizza restaurants in the Pacific Northwest, grew from 29 to more than 40 by 1985. To strengthen its Northwest market, Campbell purchased five Engine House pizza establishments from Quaker Oats in 1982.

Campbell has discovered the consumer's "hot buttons" in changing tastes. The winning combination of palate pleasers includes nutrition, convenience, low sodium, price value, quality and uniqueness.

* * *

Nabisco Brands, East Hanover, is even more diversified than Campbell Soup, marketing everything from Oreo cookies and Planters nuts to Ritz crackers and Fig Newtons. Add to that lengthening list Life Savers, Care-Free chewing gums, Baby Ruth, Butterfinger, Chuckles and Junior Mints candies, Triscuits, Premium and Wheat Thins, Royal gelatins and puddings, Fleischmann's and Blue Bonnet margarines, Nabisco Shredded Wheat, Milk-Bone dog biscuits, Mister Salty pretzels, Corn Diggers popcorn . . . and what you have is an endless cornucopia of treats.

And that's not all. Nabisco Brands has brought into its family of foods and home products the Granny Smith's pastry and cake-mix, Dr. Ballard's dog food, Miss Mew cat food, foreign labels such as Walkers Crisp potato chips, Hovis wheatgerm biscuits, French tea bags, and Droste chocolates and coffee.

Nabisco Brands is also the exclusive American distributor of Carlsberg Danish beer and malt liquor, and Moosehead beer.

The $6 billion bakery-based corporation calls New Jersey its home, providing jobs for approximately 4,000 employes.

Nabisco's all-time best seller is America's almost cultish cookie: A creamy mix of calories trapped between two tantalizing chocolate wafers. More than 100 billion Oreos have been stamped out since the first black-and-white one rolled off the confectionary conveyor belt in 1912.

* * *

Farberware, Jacuzzi, Daisy air rifles, PGA golf clubs and balls, all have one thing in common—a parent company in Saddle Brook known simply as **Kidde**.

It's a $2.7 billion outfit with a community of employes numbering 50,000. Kidde's 150 operating units around the world share similar interests: Consumer and recreation products, industrial and commercial products, and safety-security-protection devices and services.

Kidde's consumer and recreation products include Farberware cookware and electric appliances, Progress lighting fixtures, Tucker plastic housewares, Jacuzzi pumps and whirlpool baths, Ertl diecast miniature toy vehicles, Valley pool tables, Bear archery and Universal physical conditioning equipment.

Kidde's diversity is reflected in its industrial and commercial products: Mobile hydraulic cranes; Victor calculators, cash registers and computers; Weber aircraft interior equipment; New Jersey Office Supply; Scott Rice and Ross-Martin office equipment and supplies.

Among the many well-known lines of security gear are Kidde and Fenwal fire protection; Sargent; Arrow Lock; McKinney architectural hardware; LeFebure banking equipment, as well as Globe Security uniformed guard services.

The Jacuzzi company was built around the invention, 62 years ago, of the jet pump, making possible convenient, modern water systems in rural America. Pumps and water-moving equipment still make up a large part of Jacuzzi's business. In 1955, Candido Jacuzzi, concerned about his son's rheumatoid arthritis, invented a portable whirlpool device which, attached to a standard bath tub, provided excellent hydrotherapy. The product was marketed four years later and became an instant success.

Bear Archery equipment, started by Fred Bear in his home, today is the largest company in its field. Daisy has dominated the youth air gun market for almost a century. New Jersey Office Supply publishes a catalog listing more than 100,00 items of office furniture, word processing supplies, custom printed forms and other products.

The history of Sargent is almost the history of the lock busi-

An employee of Nabisco Brands Bakery in Fair Lawn cleans the cookie die used to make Barnum's Animal Crackers.

Star-Ledger Photo

This filling machine at the Camden plant of Campbell Soup Company turns out tomato soup.

Courtesy: Campbell Soup Company

ness in America. As early as 1890, Sargent was one of the largest industrial employers in the country, and the inventor of hundreds of locks, small tools and architectural hardware.

* * *

Western Union touches everyone's lives through its personal and computerized communications network. America's original electronic messenger, Western Union built a reputation on the hand-delivered telegram. Today it can send voices and images into your home TV via a satellite signal.

Based in Upper Saddle River and employing 3,000 people in New Jersey, the billion-dollar company operates an ever-expanding communications system that includes Westar satellites in orbit, a transcontinental microwave transmission line, electronic switching centers, and local transmission lines in major metropolitan areas.

Western Union customers can send the traditional telegram, or a Cablegram or individual Mailgram. Long distance telephone service is supplied by WU's MetroFone. Its WorldWide Telex service was launched in 1982, strengthening its Teletypewriter and other office message services, basically Telex I and Telex II.

Star-Ledger Photo

Western Union's Network Management Center in Upper Saddle River is the heart of America's original electronic messenger service.

* * *

Englehard Corp. is the world's leading precious metals manufacturer, specializing in platinum, gold and silver used in cars, computers and other industrial products.

The $2 billion firm is situated in Edison, where Englehard executives oversee 25 plants and eight principal mines in Alabama, Alaska, Arkansas, California, Florida, Georgia, Massachusetts, New Jersey, Ohio, Vermont, Virginia, Australia, Canada, England, France, Italy, Japan, Mexico and Switzerland, with additional offices in Argentina, Austria, Belgium, Brazil, Denmark, Finland, West Germany, Hong Kong, New Zealand, Singapore, South Africa and Spain.

Englehard specializes in catalysts, paper coatings and fillers, precious metal components and mill products. It also makes products for the electronics, dental and medical fields, as well as sorbents, suspension agents, lime and industrial extenders, and process technology.

Founder Charles Englehard was immortalized by his good friend, author Ian Fleming, creator of the James Bond technological thrillers, whose most memorable fictional character was a

tycoon named Goldfinger. Like Englehard, Bond's nemesis was worth his weight in gold.

* * *

The third largest combined utility in the United States, **Public Service Electric & Gas Co.** is New Jersey's number one utility, serving 5.5 million residents or 1.8 million gas and electric customers within the great urban corridor between Philadelphia and New York City.

Generating revenues of nearly $4 billion and more than 13,000 jobs, PSE&G is the energy pipeline for the state's six largest cities and 300 smaller suburban and rural communities.

Public Service, a spinoff of one of Thomas Edison's companies, has been in the forefront of the electric utility industry in developing load management and conservation techniques. By balancing power demands during the hot summer months and frigid winter months, PSE&G has been able to cut energy costs for consumers.

PSE&G also is the national center for testing large-scale advanced battery systems and power conversion equipment for energy storage. The utility also has introduced a solar water heating program for qualified customers, a $3,500 package installed and serviced by PSE&G for the property owner.

Public Service has been testing electric cars for use by urban/suburban dwellers who work within 30 to 40 miles of where they live. Other projects under way are fish farming at its Mercer Generating Station, taking advantage of recycled warm water to raise rainbow trout, and tapping methane gas in garbage dumps for heating greenhouses producing food year-round.

* * *

The vast bulk of hardcover and paperback books begin their distribution life in New Jersey with countless publishers such as Prentice-Hall, McGraw-Hill, A.S. Barnes & Co., Citadel Press, Dow Jones Books, Hayden Book Co., Littlefield, Adams & Co., Oxford University Press, New American Library, the famed Peterson's Guides from Princeton, and the presses of Princeton, Rutgers and Fairleigh Dickinson universities.

Prentice-Hall, Englewood Cliffs, acquired in 1984 by Gulf + Western, is the $400 million information source for students, professionals, teachers and executives in education, business technology and government.

Some 2,300 writers, editors and staff personnel are stationed in New Jersey, assigned to Prentice-Hall's various publishing ventures, including the College Book Division, Loose-Leaf Services Division, Business and Professional Division and Deltak, which produces video-based, in-house training programs in the data processing field.

Deltak is the world's premier publisher of multimedia information and training materials for data processing personnel. Deltak assists thousands of organizations worldwide in solving productivity problems in high-tech areas.

Prentice-Hall's ARCO Publishing Co. reaches specialized book markets outside conventional trade channels. High school and college students rely heavily upon ARCO publications that help them prepare for College Entrance Examinations, the Graduate Record Examinations, and a number of related tests.

* * *

New Jersey's business environment is strengthened by its endlessly changing kaleidoscope of services, as exemplified by these four companies selected at random from the top 100 employers compiled each year by the New Jersey Business and Industry Association in Trenton:

• ADP (Automatic Data Processing), Berkeley Heights and Clifton. Begun in 1949 in Paterson with a few thousand borrowed dollars, ADP had only 12 clients and revenues of $35,000 when Frank Lautenberg, now United States senator from New Jersey, joined the firm three years later.

By 1985, ADP had sales of more than $1 billion and a worldwide work force of more than 18,000, of which 2,500 are in New Jersey. To more than 125,000 companies and financial institutions, ADP is "The Computing Company." ADP handles payrolls for small companies to millions of processing transactions for large financial institutions.

• Foster Wheeler in Livingston is a $1.7 billion engineering, design and construction firm that entered the energy race in the 1980s. Staffed by 3,100 technical experts and support personnel, Foster Wheeler—builder of massive petrochemical and public utility projects—is now an oil producer and installer of its own power systems. The high-tech company is also into solar development and synthetic fuels (synfuels).

• CPC International, Englewood Cliffs, is a $4.5 billion food Goliath whose labels are familiar to all: Hellmann's and Best Foods mayonnaise, Thomas' English muffins, Skippy peanut butter, Mazola corn oil, Karo corn syrup and Golden Griddle.

CPC operates 104 plants, of which 31 are located in North America, 39 in Europe, 22 in Latin America and 12 in Asia. One-third of the plants turn out wet milling corn products, while half are engaged solely in the manufacture of branded grocery products.

• Jamesway, of Secaucus, operates 65 discount department stores in the middle-Atlantic states of New Jersey, New York, Pennsylvania and Virginia. About 20 are in the Garden State. Jamesway, with sales approaching a half-billion dollars, is one of the nation's fastest growing discount stores, and one of the largest sellers of housewares and gifts, toys, linens and domestics, small electrical appliances and children's wear.

* * *

Like AT&T, many international corporations conduct an increasing amount of their business operations in New Jersey, although their home bases may be in another state or nation.

Among those who have made the Garden State a corporate beehive of activity are RCA, IBM, ITT, GM, GE, Ford, Litton, Lockheed, Westinghouse, Burroughs, Marriott, Hershey Foods, R.J. Reynolds, Anheuser-Busch, W.R. Grace, McGraw-Hill, Dow Jones, Owens-Illinois and Owens-Corning Fiberglas Corp.

They are New Jersey's leading employers, along with the major corporate headquarters of Prudential, Johnson & Johnson, Bell Laboratories, Nabisco Brands and scores more, collectively delivering services and making products ranging from cars and coffee, books and beer, to telephones and satellites.

Their New Jersey operations have led to the development of radio and television, solar electricity, radar, and a sophisticated array of electronic and computerized systems for transportation, communications, education and national defense.

Their fortunes and futures are an integral part of New Jersey's corporate heritage and destiny. Some of the biggest and the best are essential elements in New Jersey's still unfolding corporate story.

RCA R&D team, a move that would change the world of communications. Dr. Vladimir K. Zworykin was the father of television, having perfected the first practical picture tube, the "iconoscope." Zworykin also is credited with creating the first kinescope picture tube.

RCA unveiled the black and white commercial television set at the New York World's Fair in 1939. In 1942, RCA moved its R&D operations from Camden to Princeton and again made history by launching the first commercial color television system in 1953 after five years of planning and discussions with the Federal Communications Commission (FCC). Color television was introduced by RCA's subsidiary, NBC.

In 1981, RCA produced the first major American consumer electronic product since color TV: The SelectaVision VideoDisc system.

RCA today is an $8 billion-a-year communications colossus whose 6,200 engineers and scientists are inventing and improving technologies in the fields of optics, acoustics, electronics and communications. RCA employs about 14,200 specialists and support personnel in New Jersey, many of them located in the Princeton area.

RCA Labs have carried out pioneering work in computer memories and systems, high fidelity stereo recording, lasers, solid-state materials and devices, satellite communications and numerous other achievements spanning the entire electronics spectrum.

During World War II, the Sniperscope and Snooperscope—infrared devices used for night combat and reconnaissance—were a product of RCA's research in optics. Wartime research also led to the development of the "image orthicon," which provided a versatile camera tube for military television systems. For post-war television, its ability to function in low light levels made possible flexible operation in the studio and in the field.

Television display research is improving color picture tubes while exploring new display concepts such as a full-color, flat-panel TV display with a 50-inch diagonal only four inches thick.

New features are also improving the VideoDisc system: Freeze-frame, programmable random access and high-speed visual search.

An infrared camera that detects small variations in heat to create recognizable television pictures in total darkness is being readied for the marketplace. Potential applications include industrial production, medical diagnosis and military surveillance.

Research continues on an optical disc-data storage and retrieval system using a solid-state laser for recording and retrieving information. The system has, among other features, vast memory capacity and quick random access.

Other efforts under way at RCA labs are an experimental system of direct broadcast satellites and ground-support facilities, as well as a new consumer television information service.

In energy research RCA labs is perfecting amorphous silicon solar cells, a major step toward large-scale power production. RCA's solar cells convert common sunlight directly into electric energy for direct use or storage in batteries for nighttime use.

RCA

The Radio Corporation of America was set up in 1919 by General Electric and Westinghouse to protect the United States' interests in the newly emerging communications industry. RCA had taken over the Marconi Wireless Telegraph Co. of America, a British enterprise.

Until the early 1930s, RCA functioned as a joint subsidiary of GE and Westinghouse. It also had links with AT&T. It was a growing company run by a committee.

RCA's now renowned research laboratories grew up in Camden. In 1929, a brilliant Russian electronics engineer joined the

ITT

Another Brobdingnagian business is the International Telephone and Telegraph Corp., a $25 billion enterprise whose simple message is: "The best ideas are the ideas that help people."

With more than 5,500 workers in Nutley, Paramus, Paterson, Clark, Cedar Knolls, Secaucus, East Rutherford and Midland Park, ITT's products and services reach hundreds of millions of people around the world in telecommunications and electronics, natural resources, food, insurance and finance.

From a forester developing a faster growing species of pine to an insurance salesman offering customers a new way to earn

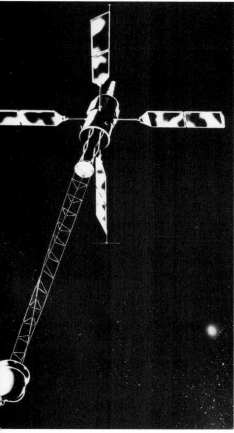

Left, an artist's drawing depicts NOVA, the Navy navigation satellite that guides military and commerical ships. RCA Astro-Electronics in Princeton is building three NOVAs for the Navy.

Right, Sal Galasso of Newark, a mechanical assembler with ITT Avionics Division, Clifton, works on radio navigation systems.

Courtesy: RCA News   Courtesy: ITT Avionics Division

higher interest on their life insurance, ITT North America is a family of 136,000 men and women who generate more than $13 billion in sales and revenues.

ITT is the Continental Baking Co., marketing such staples as Wonder bread and Hostess cakes. ITT is the Sheraton Hotel chain, more than 350 on this continent alone. ITT is the familiar green-and-white Scott lawn products and Burpee lawn and gardening products. ITT is the Hartford Insurance Group.

In natural resources, ITT is Carbon Industries, Eason Oil Co. and Raynoir Inc. They produce cattlefeed supplements made from the byproducts of the pulping process at ITT mills, and are among the leaders in their industries in technology and equipment for exploration, drilling and extraction of fossil fuels.

ITT companies play a vital role in the U.S. space shuttle program. As the second largest telecommunications equipment supplier in the world, ITT oversees a global network of land, undersea and satellite links, making it the largest U.S.-based international record carrier.

Founded in 1920, ITT brings to market such new ideas as microcomputer-controlled, anti-skid braking systems; shock absorbers that tame the pitch and vibration of Formula I racing cars and the new high-speed French trains; submersible pumps capable of handling 24,000 gallons of water a minute to protect dikes against tidal surges, and VLSI circuits, which enable conversion of color TV to digital signal processing.

ITT's Pennsylvania Glass Sand Corp. is expanding the use of its ground silica in the coatings market and as material for glass-fiber-reinforced plastics.

To help meet the continuing demand for vehicle weight reduction, ITT's Thompson Industries introduced lightweight simulated wire wheel covers, as well as a high-strength, lightweight bumper reinforcement that meets all government criteria for impact safety.

ITT's automotive products operations, Alfred Teves, Inc., enjoys a significant share of the disc brake market, supplying pin slide calipers, brake booster systems and brake valves for downsize, front-end-drive cars and light trucks.

ITT's stereo color television is now among the most successful on the European market, and ITT World Directories is the largest yellow-pages producer outside the United States.

ITT's Sheraton owns and operates four hotel-ships that cruise the ancient Nile River in Egypt, a popular tourist attraction in the land of the pharaohs.

IBM

International Business Machines is to computers what Charles Lindbergh is to aviation. Without peer, IBM dominates the computer industry, racking up more than $35 billion in sales, rentals and services worldwide. And that's just for one year.

IBM, rooted in Armonk, N.Y., is in the field of information-handling systems, equipment and services to solve the increasingly complex problems of business, government, science, space exploration, defense, education, medicine and many other areas of human activity.

With more than 6,000 employes in New Jersey, IBM products keep the state's business, government and educational communities humming with data processing machines and systems, telecommunications systems and products, information distributors,

This IBM leased facility in Princeton houses offices for the Systems Supplies Business Unit of the National Distribution Division.

Courtesy: IBM Corp.

office systems, typewriters, copiers, learning and testing materials, and related supplies and services.

IBM maintains three divisional headquarters in Franklin Lakes: Field Engineering, Systems Supplies, Customer Service—and its financial marketing groups in Princeton, as well as branch and regional offices in the state's major cities.

Most products are both leased and sold through IBM's international marketing organizations. IBM is everywhere people are trying to sort through information and solve problems. Some random examples:

• The government of Brazil uses an IBM computing center to process its census of 125 million people, as well as to study the best economic uses of agriculture, transportation, communications and other national resources.

• IBM computer graphics are used by a large U.S. mining corporation to evaluate exploration opportunities.

• The Los Angeles County Fire Department fights fires and meets other emergencies with the use of IBM computers for optimum dispatching of 700 vehicles and 2,200 uniformed employes from 128 fire stations.

• Field surveys of animal and plant life for use in land development are among many government applications of IBM computers serving the growing population of Australia's North Territory.

• An agricultural association in Reims, France, uses an IBM System/38 computer to help more than 4,000 farmers and wine producers, such as the champagne-producing family businesses, efficiently manage all phases of their accounting.

• A wheat cooperative serving 56,000 farmers in Alberta, Canada operates a network of IBM computers installed at more than 120 grain elevators for daily inventory and sales accounting.

• A Pacific Coast aircraft manufacturer has installed 25 IBM Displaywriters for more productive text editing and administrative typing in its advanced technology, computer services, legal and other departments.

IBM systems aid doctors and staffs in hospital departments such as pediatrics, pharmacy, radiology and physical therapy.

The International Committee of the Red Cross, Geneva, Switzerland, uses an IBM computer to keep records that help trace more than a half-million "boat people."

Westinghouse

It's a $10 billion annual operation based in Pittsburgh with extensive activities in the Garden State: Westinghouse Elevators based in Dover, Micarta furniture lamination in East Rutherford, engineering services in Hillside, computer center in Livingston, and a corporate trucking terminal in Edison.

More than 5,000 Westinghouse employes make New Jersey their home, contributing to the success of a company whose catchphrase is, "You can be sure if it's Westinghouse."

Teleprompter, a leader in the rapidly expanding cable television market, is one of the newest members of the growing Westinghouse family. From television programming to electronic control systems, Westinghouse manufactures energy-efficient Life-Line motors . . . radars for the B-1 bomber and the Army's Division Air Defense gun system . . . Tomahawk cruise missile launchers for submarines, adding to the current Trident and MX missile launcher programs . . . and innovative control systems for electric utilities, steel mills and chemical plants.

Westinghouse is also Thermo King, a world leader in advanced truck and trailer and container refrigeration.

Westinghouse is the Longines-Wittnauer Watch Co., and Creative Publications, a leading publisher and distributor of educational materials.

Westinghouse is the Learning and Leisure Group, led by the Beverage Business Unit.

Westinghouse is the Community Development Group, creating living environments in Pelican Bay and Coral Springs, Fla.

Westinghouse is Muzak, the nation's leading supplier of functional music to offices, factories, hotels, restaurants and other establishments. Muzak uses advanced satellite technology to speed new musical selections to its domestic franchises and sub-scribers, while music tape distribution continues overseas.

Westinghouse is electronic mail, voice message switching and personal computers.

Teleprompter operates the largest non-governmentally fund-ed network of satellite receiver stations, with more than 130 cur-rently in use.

Westinghouse, builder of fossil and nuclear power plants, is an engineering-design leader in the utility industry.

Litton

A $5 billion high-tech firm from Beverly Hills, Calif., Litton Industries has a pervasive presence in New Jersey, its more than 2,200 employes working in plants and offices in Morris Plains, Paramus, Newark, Totowa, Passaic, Pine Brook, Belleville and Hasbrouck Heights.

Litton engineers and scientists apply advanced technologies to a broad spectrum of practical and profitable products, from inertial navigation equipment to electron tube devices, from mili-tary command and control systems to seismic exploration tech-niques, and to the frontiers of today's advanced work in digital voice switching and electronic display devices.

Kimball Systems in Paramus is the headquarters for the world leader in inventory control systems, serving retailers, ven-dors and industry throughout the world for more than a century.

Kester Solder has been manufacturing a full line of solders and soldering chemicals in Newark for half a century. Kester's 15,000-square-foot Newark facility houses production and mar-keting personnel whose average length of employment is more than 20 years. Kester's product line serves the industries of elec-tronic components, consumer electronics, telecommunications, business machines, automotive and transport. Kester also pro-vides the hobbyist and craftsman in the do-it-yourself home mar-kets with their distributor line of products.

Robins Engineers & Constructors, located in Totowa, designs and installs bulk material handling systems for the transport and processing of energy resources, from power stations to coal and coke transshipment terminals.

Hewitt-Robins Conveyor Equipment is found in Passaic, the birthplace of the first successful belt conveyor that is now the standard throughout the world. The Passaic plant is the largest producer of conveyor idler assemblies in the world. It also pro-duces mine conveyor systems, other conveyor accessories, and a variety of Tuffgard polyurethane products.

Combined, Hewitt-Robins Conveyor and Robins Engineers & Constructors account for 200,000 square feet of offices, ware-houses and manufacturing facilities in New Jersey, employing more than 300 people.

Sweda International in Pine Brook is a familiar name in electronic and electromechanical cash register and point-of-sale systems around the world. Sweda has sales and service outlets in more than 80 countries.

Sweda is a name found in restaurants, cafeterias, hotels, motels, drug stores, specialty stores and supermarkets. In super-markets, the Universal Product Code printed on most grocery products is read by Sweda's patented laser scanning beam in microseconds.

In a related field is Westrex O.E.M. Products, one of the original equipment manufacturers for cash registers as well as punchtape readers and printers. West Caldwell is the home of Westrex general offices.

Airtron Division has its headquarters and main manufactur-ing facilities in Morris Plains. Airtron operates the largest crystal growing facility of its kind in the world, and is the world's largest producer of single crystal rods for solid-state lasers. Principal uses of the crystal rods include target designators and range-finders for military applications. In commercial markets, they are used for welding, cutting, drilling and scribing.

Airtron also supplies precision optics and dielectric coatings for components used in laser systems.

Airtron is one of the nation's leading suppliers of microwave waveguide transmission lines and components, used primarily as weather radar for commercial airlines. Other uses include coun-ter-measure systems for the military and relay towers and satel-lite ground station systems for the military and for communica-tions.

Yet another Airtron activity is the manufacture of simulated diamonds through its Diamonair subdivision. Diamonair offers the finest cut stones and are priced at just a fraction of the cost of real carbon beauties.

McBee Systems of Belleville is a respected competitor in the world of "one-write" bookkeeping systems. These specialized forms allow various bookkeeping entries and functions to be completed in just one writing. McBee's primary influence is in North America.

Kimball Tag Products, also in Belleville, produces tea bag tags and airline luggage tags. Belleville is the home office for McBee, which is part of Litton's Specialty Paper, Printing and Forms Group. Its products range from removable wallpaper and adhesive drafting film for blueprints, to sterilized surgical pack-aging.

Able-Stik Products, another paper group operation located in Hasbrouck Heights, produces printed and die-cut, self-adhesive labels, which are supplied in sheets, rolls and continuous fanfolds. Able-Stik also supplies stock inventory of data processing labels, file cards and rotary index cards, in addition to other pressure-sensitive paper products.

Litton's myriad operations are indicative of the cross-fertil-ization that occurs within many New Jersey corporations, from division to division, department to department, employe to em-ploye.

Lockheed

Lockheed Electronics Co. (LEC) in Plainfield is a subsidiary of the $6 billion Burbank-based Lockheed Corp. Lockheed, with 1,700 employees, is a leader in the design, development and produc-tion of advanced electronic products and systems for military, government and industrial customers.

Lockheed's New Jersey plants (another is located in Denville) turn out automatic weapon control and air traffic control systems, radars, automatic test equipment, fuses and other ordnance prod-ucts, instrumentation and spacecraft tape recorders, computing registers for fuel oil delivery trucks, and computerized telephone directory assistance systems.

Lockheed Electronics also provides custom design and manu-facturing of microelectronic hybrid circuits, instrumentation cali-bration, and environmental testing services.

LEC's weapon control system is aboard the U.S. Navy's newest, most advanced combat ships: Nuclear-powered cruisers, destroyers and helicopter assault vessels. The Lockheed system contains the latest technology in radar sensors and digital signal processing and is the first digital fire control system deployed by the Navy. The LEC system can control a variety of weapons from 30mm to eight-inch guns, as well as missiles, against air and surface targets.

LEC introduced the first minicomputer-based air traffic con-trol system (ATC). The company developed and installed an ad-vance ATC system for the Kingdom of Saudi Arabia. Newer models are being built for the space shuttle and other future flight missions.

In the industrial area, Lockheed Electronics is helping the telephone industry cope with problems of data retrieval. Lock-heed's RADRU/C (rapid access data retrieval unit/computer)

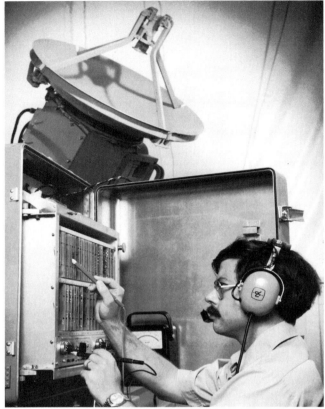

Courtesy: Lockheed Electronics Co., Inc.

Lockheed senior engineer Bill Buntemeyer aligns feedback control for a gunfire system designed by Lockheed for Spanish navy ships.

Star-Ledger Photo

Athletic equipment and clothing fill the Union store of W.R. Grace & Co.'s Herman's World of Sporting Goods.

enables telephone directory assistance operators to respond with accuracy and split-second speed.

W.R. Grace

New Jersey figures prominently in the $6 billion corporate world of W.R. Grace & Co., whose interests lie in chemicals, natural resources and selected consumer services.

Grace, occupying a skyscraper in Manhattan, has established several headquarters in New Jersey: Herman's World of Sporting Goods in Carteret, Channel Home Centers in Whippany, Hooten Chocolate in Newark, Baker & Taylor Book Distribution Center in Somerville, and Elson T. Killam Associates, an engineering consulting firm, in Millburn.

With more than 4,000 employes in New Jersey, the 130-year-old company also operates a chemical plant in Woodbury, and construction products plants in Trenton and North Bergen. Around the world there are about 260 plants and 88,000 workers.

Grace is the leading specialty chemical concern, manufacturing more than 85 major specialty product lines. Including its agricultural chemical business, Grace is the nation's fifth largest chemical company.

Grace's natural resource interests include the operation of contract drilling rigs, the provision of energy services, rental tools and equipment for the petroleum industry, the exploration for and production of crude oil and natural gas, and coal mining.

Grace restaurants include specialty dinner houses, coffee shops and fast-food outlets.

Lummus

In a campus-like setting along the Garden State Parkway in Bloomfield stands the modern headquarters of C-E Lummus, one of the world's largest design, engineering and construction companies.

A subsidiary of Combustion Engineering in Stamford, Conn., Lummus employs about 2,500 electrical, chemical and mechanical engineers and support staff.

Combustion Engineering provides equipment, products and services for oil and gas and other industrial markets, steam generating systems, equipment and services for electric utilities, and engineering and construction services, primarily for the chemical, petrochemical and petroleum processing industries.

Combustion Engineering ($4 billion in annual sales) is made up of 34 business units, with more than 47,000 employes and facilities in 84 countries. Lummus is one of the few contractors in the world that conducts proprietary research into new technologies for petroleum refining, petrochemical processing and development of alternative fuels.

Some 40 percent of the thermal electric power generated in 84 countries is produced by steam generators of Combustion Engineering design.

New Jersey Ballet. Courtesy: N.J. Div. of Travel & Tourism

DANCE

𝒯hey are the great ladies of American dance, innovators in movement and choreography, the standards by which much of today's ballet and modern dance are measured.

Ruth St. Denis of Somerville (1877-1968) is remembered as the "Mother of Modern Dance," having introduced that form at the turn of the 20th Century, and inspired a generation of young dancers, including Martha Graham.

Patricia McBride of Teaneck (born Aug. 23, 1942) is a more recent original, starting out in 1949 at age seven studying acrobatics and tap and toe dancing and becoming "merely the most exciting ballerina in America" by the 1960s, according to critic Arlene Croce.

St. Denis and McBride are perhaps the most famous dance products of New Jersey, although scores more have achieved lasting notoriety, be it in jazz, ethnic or experimental.

McBride has danced in legendary roles fashioned exclusively for her by such renowned choreographers as George Balanchine and Jerome Robbins of the New York City Ballet.

She has danced before presidents in the White House and with superstar Mikhail Baryshnikov.

She has been alternately described in Dance Horizons as "the dancing incarnation of all that is best in the dynamically varied and energetically exciting American character" and as "one of American ballet's most magnificent gifts."

McBride's earliest training from age seven to 13 was at a little Teaneck school run by Ruth A. Vernon. At 18, "Patty" McBride became the youngest principal dancer at the New York City Ballet. The rest is history.

New Jersey's first gift to the world of dancing was Ruth St. Denis. Her ritualistic creations are a unique blend of East, West and down-on-the-Jersey-farm fantasies dreamed up in her early Somerville years.

In the book "The Dance in America," St. Denis is affectionately known as "a little New Jersey farm lass who grew up to become one of the dance geniuses of all time."

The child of an inventor father and a physician mother, Ruth Dennis (her real name) bounded about her Somerset County farm, dancing on the grass, reading "Camille" at eight years old while perched in the crotch of a tree, plowing through Kant's "Critique of Pure Reason" at 11, not fully understanding it but certainly moved by it, and finally tackling the one book that influenced her life for her 91 years: Mary Baker Eddy's "Science and Health."

After a successful European tour early this century, St. Denis returned to America to give this country its first native-born institution of dance training.

During her untiring, prolific career, St. Denis brought her extravagantly theatrical productions to Carnegie Hall and the Metropolitan Opera House. She created a total of 140 dances—from "Cobras" and "Incense" in 1906 to "To a Chinese Flute" in 1957—and performed in them until her death in 1968.

Ruth St. Denis performing one of her works.

Star-Ledger Photo

St. Denis' groundbreaking work led directly to the foundations of modern dance, affecting two latter day giants, Martha Graham and Doris Humphrey.

Today, the Garden State is home for no fewer than 600 dance studios and 50 amateur and professional companies, ranging from theater and gymnastics to movement education and dance therapy for the handicapped and elderly.

Curiously, two outstanding Russian dancers, Leonid and Valentina Kozlov, chose Englewood as their new home after they defected from the Soviet Union in 1979.

A handful of New Jersey dance companies are attracting top performers and national attention. Among the leaders are the New Jersey Ballet Company and the Princeton Ballet Company.

*   *   *

The New Jersey Ballet Company, based in West Orange, gave its first performance in 1958 to a small band of believers who nurtured it into a reputable troupe, with the help of internationally acclaimed dancer Edward Villella, artistic adviser for the last several years.

Supported by 30 percent public funding, the New Jersey Ballet reaches out to the people not only through its masterful performances, but through workshops, classes, lecture-demonstrations, residencies and teacher training in theaters, high schools and colleges in the Garden State and at a festival in West Virginia.

The National Endowment for the Arts and the New Jersey State Council of the Arts contribute to the company's expanding artistic program, which even reaches elementary school students.

New Jersey Ballet has developed a broad repertoire of contemporary ballets and jazz works, from the traditional pas de deux to abbreviated presentations of "Swan Lake," "Don Quixote" and "Peter and the Wolf."

Villella creates some choreography for the company and takes part in special galas. The day-to-day operations are handled by the troupe's executive director, Carolyn Clark, and associate director, Joseph Carow.

Born in East Orange and raised in Livingston, Clark has always been conscious of the role the arts can play in enhancing New Jersey's image, according to the Star-Ledger's dance critic Valerie Sudol.

As a child, she saw her first dance and theatrical productions at Newark's Symphony Hall and the Paper Mill Playhouse in Millburn, two theaters where her company now performs regularly.

The American Ballet Theatre has been the greatest influence on Clark's work with the New Jersey Ballet. Before joining American Ballet Theatre, Clark performed, while still in high school, at Radio City Music Hall and later as a member of the Metropolitan Opera Ballet.

With American Ballet Theatre, Clark toured North America, Europe, Africa and the Soviet Union. In 1959, Clark left the ballet stage to appear in Broadway musicals and television productions, including the prestigious Bell Telephone Hour.

"I have always believed that dance is the most universal of the arts," Clark says. The teacher-dancer is bringing that universal art form into the community through mini-concerts featuring classical and jazz pieces.

*   *   *

Princeton Ballet was selected in 1978 as one of the eight major regional companies in the United States. Princeton was given that distinction by the National Association of Regional Ballet.

Performing since 1963, Princeton Ballet opened the Garden State Art Center's classic season in 1980 with guest artists from London's Royal Ballet. It also has participated in the Dance-at-McCarter Theater series in Princeton. Last spring, Martine Van Hamel and Kevin McKenzie of the American Ballet Theatre appeared in the McCarter production.

In 1954, Audree Estey founded the Princeton Ballet Society. Nine years later the ballet company was formed. Estey served as director until 1982.

Her training ranged from California to Canada with Ernest Belcher and Theodore Koslov. Her personal ambition was to "cultivate and present the finest in the art of ballet for the State of New Jersey."

Judith Leviton is currently director of the Princeton Ballet Society, which supports a professional wing based in New Brunswick, under ballet master Dermot Burke. The society also supports a nonprofessional regional company, Princeton Ballet II, a member of the National Association for Regional Ballet.

The Princeton Ballet Company includes 40 major works and excerpts in its repertoire, from "Don Quixote" and "Cinderella" to "The Nutcracker" and "Sleeping Beauty."

Ballet, modern and jazz are standard fare at the Princeton workshop, which also offers master classes and lecture-demonstrations.

*   *   *

The Garden State Ballet, which originated in Newark, is one of New Jersey's oldest dance companies. It specializes in the works of master choreographer George Balanchine and Peter Anastos, founder of Les Ballets Trockadero de Monte Carlo and who is currently doing free-lance creations for Pennsylvania, Dallas and San Antonio ballets, working with Baryshnikov. Anastos designed the routine for Baryshnikov's last television special and is completing a full-length "Cinderella" for the American Ballet Theatre.

The Garden State Ballet concentrates on contemporary dance and staging revivals of early American ballet from the 1930s and '40s by such choreographers as William Dollar, Lew Christensen and Eugene Loring.

The creative force behind the Garden State troupe is Fred Danieli, who moved to Newark in 1950 after a brilliant career as one of the first to champion the cause of a uniquely American style of ballet.

During the 1930s and '40s, Danieli danced with small touring companies that evolved into America's finest ballet troupes: The American Ballet Theatre and the New York City Ballet.

Danieli made his professional debut in 1938 in the Broadway

The late choreographer George Balanchine rehearses with Patricia McBride of Teaneck and Mikhail Baryshnikov.

musical, "On Your Toes." The following year he appeared in Chicago with Ballet Theatre, the precursor of the American Ballet Theatre.

Just before World War II, Danieli formed his own small troupe, El Ballet de los Americas. After the war, he performed in a CBS television dance series, which included a production of "Crime and Punishment." In 1959, Danieli decided to organize his own ballet school in Newark.

Today, the Garden State Ballet is planning to take up residency at the William Carlos Williams Center for the Performing Arts in Rutherford. As part of the Fairleigh Dickinson University campus, the center will give its new ballet company an opportunity to bring ballet training to the school on a credit-earning basis.

* * *

Other promising groups emerging in the 1980s are exploring new frontiers in places like Atlantic City, Mount Laurel—a pastoral farm community—and May's Landing along the coastal plains of South Jersey.

The Atlantic Contemporary Ballet Theatre is the fledgling product of Phyllis Papa, the first American to be a principal dancer in the Royal Danish Ballet. Papa was a student of the Joffrey and Harkness Ballet Schools and a former performer with the American Ballet Theatre, Royal Danish Ballet and the Stars of the American Ballet, for which she also served as artistic director and ballet mistress.

Papa's choreography has won two grants from the National Endowment for the Arts and the New Jersey State Council on the Arts. Her troupe of 14 dancers, ages 18 to 25, showcase such favorites as "The Growth of America," "Eclipse" and "Mountain Legend," music of the Appalachian springs. She has choreographed "Beatle Music" and has translated John Denver's "Clear Water" into an original expression.

Papa's contemporary ballet theater is the resident group at Atlantic Community College in May's Landing. Her troupe appears at the Tropicana and Claridge Hotel Casinos in Atlantic City.

During the summer, the Atlantic Contemporary Ballet Theatre operates a camp for students and dancers seeking not only a bit of recreation but an opportunity to learn the latest in contemporary dance.

* * *

Community service is the reason for the **Mount Laurel Ballet Company's** existence.

Founded in 1969 by Fern Helfond, who studied under Alfredo Corvino at Juilliard, the grass-roots company contains anywhere from six to 15 performers who learn the strict Enrico Cecchetti method of dancing. Cecchetti's premier American performance was at the age of seven at the Philadelphia Academy of Music.

Supported by local donations, Mount Laurel Ballet covers the gamut of dancing—classical and modern, jazz and folk. The youngsters (ages 12 through 18) perform in schools, hospitals, libraries and parks.

* * *

Another little gem whose origins began quite humbly enough as a social service program is the **Inner City Ensemble Theatre and Dance Company** in Paterson, America's first planned industrial city.

The Paterson troupe—more than 10 students in training, four choreographers and guest artists in repertoire—traces its roots to a theater-oriented social service workshop started in 1973 to help city teenagers grow and develop a positive self-image.

One of the objectives of the dance company is to give city youth an understanding of the needs and feelings of other people in their lives, according to the Dance Council of New Jersey, which has been closely following the growth of the ensemble. The dance component was added in 1977 and "swiftly became a cohesive company of high-energy performers," the council points out.

The touring ensemble has been before some highly diversified audiences: Churches, prisons, festivals, social agencies, high schools and colleges.

The Paterson company toured Puerto Rico twice, appearing before 80,000 people. It has also been seen on metropolitan television.

The Inner City Ensemble is funded by, among others, the City of Paterson and the New Jersey State Council on the Arts.

In 1983, the ensemble acquired from the city an old abandoned church on Broadway for renovation into its first permanent home. The $300,000 project was supported by a $50,000 grant from the Paterson-based Meyer Foundation.

* * *

At the opposite end of the spectrum is **The Westminster Dance Theater** in Elizabeth, a company for ballet, modern and jazz. The former Union County Dance Company offers a repertoire ranging from modern dance to classical and neoclassical ballet, performed by a 10- to 20-member complement.

Westminster appeared in the first New Jersey Dance Festival in 1978 and has been in the entertainment program of the Garden State Arts Center in Holmdel.

Founder and artistic director Karen Battell-Stickles says the company "explores aspects of drama in dance, a sense of theater

Photo Credit: Peter Cool

Dancers of the Princeton Ballet Company show why "The Times They Are A-Dancing."

Courtesy: New Jersey Ballet Company

Former New Jersey Ballet Company dancer Mikifumi Nagata and partner Emilietta Ettlin in the pas de deux from Balanchine's "Stars and Stripes."

Photo Credit: Kenn Duncan

Kevin Santee, a principal dancer of the New Jersey Ballet Company, shown in costume for the ballet "Le Corsaire."

and of innovation." She also showcases young, new choreographers' accomplishments. Battell-Stickles studied at the American Ballet Theatre School in New York and has been a guest artist with the Garden State Ballet and a principal dancer with the Downtown Ballet Company and the Puerto Rican Dance Company in New York.

Westminster is the company-in-residence at the Ritz Theater in Elizabeth.

* * *

The Baron Ballet Company in Waldwick, Bergen County, which is also represented in the National Association for Regional Ballet, features eight to 12 dancers supplemented by guest artists presenting ballet, character and jazz works. Since its debut performance in 1978, the Baron Ballet has appeared in schools and regional dance festivals in Pennsylvania, New Jersey and New York.

Founder Helena Baron studied dance and music in Europe with Victor and Tatjana Gsovksy and Olga Preobrajenska. She has performed with the Deutsche Opera Ballet and the Berlin Ballet.

The narration for the company's lecture-demonstrations is done by Paul Sutherland, ballet master for the Joffrey Ballet in New York City. Sutherland was also a principal dancer with the American Ballet Theatre.

Baron says her company's primary goal is to "cultivate New Jersey's own young talent, while bringing to the people of New Jersey a greater opportunity to view and appreciate dance."

Their repertoire includes "An American in Paris," "Flower Festival" and "Bolero."

* * *

Center Dancers in Somerville is a focus of modern dance activity in Central and South Jersey. The company was organized in July 1979 and made its debut at the New Jersey Center for the Performing Arts, where it became the resident dance company.

Modern dance technique, improvisation and composition form the nucleus of the workshops and master classes. Five danc-

ers from 20 to 30 years of age perform the works of company director Michelle Mathesius and co-director Midge Guerrera, including "Glimpses," "Mood Reflections," "Totems," "Dance Images" and "Accumulation."

Center Dancers collaborates closely with New Jersey musicians and designers who also use the center as their base. Since its inception, the company has been featured in concert in theaters, schools, community centers, galleries and museums throughout the state.

The company has links with the Westminster group and the Mill Hill Playhouse in Trenton. It specializes in dance history projects, reconstructing works of Ruth St. Denis.

Director Mathesius believes that dance "should function as a framework and a vehicle for appreciating movement." She says her repertoire ranges from the dramatic to abstract movements, without excursions into fads or gimmickry. Mathesius' working premise is that the body has a language of its own and it is with this that she experiments.

* * *

The Julie Maloney Dance Company in West Caldwell began performing in concerts in New Jersey and New York in 1975. Maloney's six to eight dancers bring their independent program into schools in northeastern New Jersey and also participate in residencies and community cultural events.

Assisted in 1979 with a grant from the New Jersey State Council on the Arts, the Maloney Dance Company offers a repertoire from classic and swing to abstract and surreal.

* * *

The New Jersey Dance Theatre Guild, Rahway, has focused its efforts on raising the standards of dance education in local communities by means of student examinations and combined dance concerts and workshops.

Until 1964, young talented dancers from New Jersey, aspiring to perform the classics of ballet repertoire, had to travel considerable distances to learn from the best in the metropolitan region. At that time, a concerned group of dance studio directors and instructors combined their resources and formed the guild. In 1978, the guild purchased its present residence at 1057 Pierpont St.

The Rahway center offers students an ideal environment in

which to study, rehearse and prepare a repertoire of classical and modern works under the direction of leading teachers and choreographers. The guild annually awards a minimum of 30 scholarships through the Ballet Proficiency Rating Examinations, the Ruth Ann Deutsch Memorial Scholarship Competition, the male dancers' training program and other programs.

The guild sponsors an annual Youth Dance Concert, exhibiting diversified dance forms, teacher certification classes, summer programs, performing arts competitions, and proficiency rating programs in ballet, tap and gymnastics.

Among the dancers who have been associated with the guild are Rosemary Sabovic of the New Jersey Ballet; Amy Lichardus and Elizabeth Stewart, who danced with the Bolshoi Ballet during its New York appearance; Meg Potter of the American Ballet Theatre corps, and Linda Bechtold, a member of the Joffrey Ballet.

* * *

Les Petites Ballet, Ltd., in Marlboro, is a student group of 24 dancers ranging in age from 10 to 18. The workshops and master classes concentrate on ballet, modern, jazz, choreography and eurythmics, the art of harmonious bodily movements through expressive timed movements in response to improvised music.

Director Linda Leshine, a graduate of New York's High School of Performing Arts, performed with the Joffrey and Metropolitan Opera ballets. Leshine was assistant choreographer to the Brooklyn and North Shore Opera companies.

Les Petites Ballet has been presenting short selections and full-length productions during the past 10 years, among them "The Donkey's Dream" and "A Day at the Circus."

* * *

Another solid student group, according to the Dance Council of New Jersey, is the **Shore Ballet Company**, with studios in Island Heights and Fair Haven.

Some 24 dancers and students from 12 to 30 years old have, since 1972, been bringing such high-quality fare as "Firebird" and "Magic Trunk" to the Monmouth Arts Center, Ocean County College and Artists-in-Schools. The community-based company has been funded by the Exxon Corp. and the New Jersey State Council on the Arts.

* * *

The name **Hortense Kooluris** is synonymous with the art of Isadora Duncan, a major innovator of modern dance.

A resident of Short Hills, Kooluris received her training from two of Duncan's first disciples, Irma and Anna Duncan. Kooluris was chosen to perform in Anna Duncan's documentary film on Duncan dance.

Kooluris co-founded the Isadora Duncan Centenary Dance Company in 1977 to celebrate the birth of the famed dancer. As the leading exponent in the effort to preserve the dances of Isadora Duncan, Kooluris has prepared a lecture on Duncan's life, art and effect on the art world of the 20th Century.

* * *

The leading advocate of dance therapy in New Jersey is **Dr. Agnes A. Hirsch** of Highland Park.

Associate professor of dance at Middlesex County College, Hirsch has become a teacher, performer, choreographer and researcher in several disciplines of dance/movement. Her classes and workshops involve therapeutic use of dance/movement, which she defines as the physical and psychic integration of the individual through movement therapy, stressing body and sensory awareness, energy-blocking, alignment, tension-flow, rhythm and other specific exercises.

* * *

The Dance Council of New Jersey was established in 1978 by the Middlesex County Arts Council to foster programs of the highest aesthetic and educational caliber, and by serving as a clearinghouse through which dancers statewide could centralize and disseminate their activities. The nonprofit organization has headquarters at 841 Georges Rd., North Brunswick.

Dance is being elevated to a more prominent position by the New Jersey State Council on the Arts, which has appointed its first dance program coordinator, Nicholette Birsky, formerly a dancer in the Greenhouse Dance Ensemble, co-directed by Lillo Way of Montclair.

Photo Credit: Paul Kolnik

Dancers of the Garden State Ballet perform "Footage" by choreographer Peter Anastos.

Blue paint is applied to the Cybis Carousel Charger. All Cybis artists mix their own paints so that each sculpture will vary slightly from the others. The color's intensity is muted in the heat of the kiln.

DECORATIVE ARTS

They create the finest china, glass and porcelain from the sparkling sands of Salem to the dull gray clays of Trenton.

It is the oldest of man's art and it has achieved timeless perfection in New Jersey under the masterful eyes and hands of Walter Scott Lenox, Boleslaw Cybis, Edward Marshall Boehm, Alphons G. Muller and Theodore Corson Wheaton.

Their rare earthen works have been collected by presidents and popes, princes and princesses, queens and museums. They are on guarded display at palaces and art galleries, at the White House and the Vatican, the Soviet Union and the People's Republic of China, and at cultural capitals around the world.

Dignitaries and heads of state are regularly presented with precious gifts made by America's best artisans, whose skills have been and continue to be honed at porcelain studios and glass furnaces in Trenton, Flemington, Pomona and in Salem County.

America's first industry, glassmaking, burgeoned in Salem County before the American Revolution. Starting out with sand aplenty in 1739, the New World's glass industry supported more than 100 factories in Salem by the time New Jersey and 12 other Colonies declared their independence in 1776 from the motherland.

Wheaton Village in Millville, South Jersey, is today the largest family-owned producer of glassware in the world, while Alphons Muller's Flemington factory in North Jersey is the oldest continuous glass-cutting operation in the United States and the nation's oldest manufacturer of hand-cut crystal.

Lenox, founded in Trenton in 1889, is America's oldest famous name in fine china and has been the official White House state service since President Woodrow Wilson, a former governor of New Jersey, first recognized the flawless firings of Walter Lenox's custom ceramics early this century.

Boleslaw Cybis, a native of Lithuania, established the nation's premier porcelain studio in Trenton in 1940 and today shares the sculptured ceramic honors with another Trentonian— Edward Marshall Boehm, a naturalist-farmer who opened his basement workshop in 1950 at the age of 37 and within a year was deemed "a natural genius," and whose first animal sculptures were acquired by the Metropolitan Museum of Art.

Lenox, Cybis, Boehm, Wheaton and Muller left a legacy of

excellence that their craft-disciples follow to the minutest detail today, a peerless standard in the earth-to-art medium.

New Jersey's master potters and glassblowers have attracted a new generation of artisans redefining the Old World materials of fiber, wood, clay and glass.

Led by such new masters as porcelain sculptor Laszlo Ispanky of Hopewell and ceramist Albert Green of Westfield, they are pursuing their dreams at places as diverse as Peters Valley Craftsmen at the Delaware Water Gap to the New Jersey Guild of Designer-Woodworkers at Kean College and Whichcraft Studio and Gallery in South Orange.

Lenox China and Crystal

Born in Trenton in 1859, Walter Scott Lenox grew up in one of America's most important pottery centers. Coming home from school he would stop by any one of the ceramic factories and watch the potter at work on his wheel, turning dull clay into shapes and colors that must have seemed magical to a young boy yearning to be an artist.

Lenox would spend hours at a time quietly observing the potters fashioning their wet plastic earth into objects of service.

Although being an artist was his first desire, young Walt realized he had to learn the rudiments of the trade before becoming a designer and decorator. He began as an apprentice in the Ott and Brewer factory and the Willetts pottery in Trenton, mastering the practical details of making bowls, cups and dishes while studying design in his spare time.

As Lenox's artistic talent developed, Ott and Brewer discov-

Vanessa Carder works on a new design for a table setting at Lenox China and Crystal in Lawrenceville.
Star-Ledger Photo

ered their young potter had a natural ability in making ordinary things look exceptionally beautiful. Still in his 20s, Lenox was promoted to the important position of art director at Ott and Brewer.

It was to be a brief opportunity for Lenox, who wanted to do more than make routine ceramic products. At that time, design was crude, expression exaggerated. American-made china did not have the quality or reputation of imported china.

Lenox would change that, but not before—at the peak of his artistic powers—he was stricken with an affliction that left him blind and paralyzed. His life seemed to parallel another great artist, English writer John Milton, who at the height of his creativity became blind and then wrote the longest poem in the English language, "Paradise Lost."

Lenox's moment of glory also arrived late in life, ironically as a blind, crippled man overseeing America's standard-setting ceramics company.

With $4,000 he had saved at Ott and Brewer, Lenox started the Ceramic Art Co. in 1889 with a partner, Jonathan Coxon Sr. It was a risky venture and his backers put up the money only if he agreed to convert his business into a tenement house if it failed.

Within five years, Lenox acquired sole ownership of Ceramic Art and his three-story pottery managed to survive recessions and the overwhelming competition from the imports. No one really believed an American factory could produce china of first quality.

"Often," Lenox once told an acquaintance, "I would sit on the porch in the evening, light my pipe and talk as if the world were mine and rosy with prosperity, even though I was conscious that I didn't have five cents in my pocket."

Lenox strived to produce a rich, ivory-tinted ware known as Belleek, a china that originated in Belleek, Ireland. He brought two Belleek potters to his Trenton factory in the hopes of creating ceramics with a stunningly lustrous glaze.

At one point, when his funds were nearly exhausted, Lenox gave a wealthy Philadelphia visitor a tour of his factory. Explaining the many difficulties in producing fine china, Lenox stopped at a kiln to examine a finished product. He found a tiny, almost imperceptible flaw in every piece. The $2,000 worth of china was immediately destroyed. The visitor was aghast at what he had just witnessed.

Perfection, however, paid off. Lenox and his Belleek potters produced china that could stand up to the best imports. At first, the Trenton ware lacked the durability of the finest foreign products, but Lenox developed his own formula and, by the turn of the 20th Century, he was able to compete with the top-of-the-line imports.

Americans, however, remained skeptical. They preferred the imports to the Lenox china. From the time the master potter became disabled in 1895 to when he formed Lenox, Inc., in 1906, business progressed, yet the recognition Lenox dreamed of as a boy eluded him.

It wasn't until Tiffany's took an interest in Lenox's exceptional china settings in 1917 that his dream materialized. Once Lenox china was displayed in the handsome showrooms of Tiffany stores in New York and Philadelphia, the affluent customers accepted them as the best money could buy.

That same year, President Wilson finally broke the precedent at the White House by ordering a complete service from Lenox, a 1,700-piece dinner set costing $16,000, an investment comparable to a quarter of a million dollars today.

Since 1826, Congress had been on record as requiring that, so far as possible, all equipment for the White House should be bought in the United States. But no President had been able to find American-made china fit for the White House table, until Lenox perfected his Belleek.

Until the day of his death on January 11, 1920, Lenox continued to visit his factory regularly, carried piggyback to his office by his chauffeur. His fingertips served as his eyes, touching the plates, cups and saucers to find the slightest imperfections.

An artist puts the finishing touch on a decorative plate at Lenox.

Courtesy: Lenox

Although Presidents and heads of states ate on Lenox dinnerware at the White House, it wasn't until the 1930s that Lenox, Inc., under the presidency of Harry Brown, broke away from the European design traditions by introducing clean and simple lines in contrast to the elaborate and often rococo style popularized by the old world potters.

Lenox's modern style, particularly the unencumbered decorative motifs against ivory backgrounds created by Lenox's own protege, William H. Clayton, attracted so much attention that by the late 1930s, the Lenox trademark was on perhaps one of every four pieces of chinaware purchased in America.

Production methods, too, have radically improved since Walter Lenox worked the potter's wheel. The wheel is today run by electricity and a weird instrument called a "jiggerblade" vastly speeds the shaping of a plate.

A magnetized trough draws impurities out of the "slip" from which china is molded. Infrared heat now dries the glaze and the ware is baked on a moving table that circles for 30 hours through a huge, 130-foot tunnel, in which complicated pyrometers maintain exact temperatures ranging up to 2,200 degrees Fahrenheit.

And following Lenox's strict standards, no "seconds" are ever sold. All imperfect pieces are destroyed at the china plant.

In the 1960s, Lenox, Inc. expanded its operations by acquiring Oxford Bone China, now widely known for its pure white color, translucency, delicate appearance and remarkable strength. Oxford has become a favorite of American brides.

In 1965, Lenox purchased the oldest crystal glassblowing company in the United States and Lenox Crystal was born. It is the choice of the U.S. Department of State for embassies around the world.

Between 1968 and 1972, the Lenox family continued to grow with the addition of Lenox Candles; Paragon Products Corp., a refiner of custom waxes for Lenox's candle companies as well as for the food and paper industries; Carolina Soap and Candle Makers, specialists in scented candles and soaps and toiletries; Kaumagraph Co., a specialty printer; ArtCarved, Inc., a leading designer and manufacturer of wedding and engagement rings, and H. Rosenthal Jewelry Corp., a prestige distributor of high fashion jewelry.

In 1972, Lenox introduced a versatile line of superceramic,

casual dinnerware with the trademark Temper-ware. The microwave-oven-safe, dinner/cookware combines strength and beauty with a full two-year warranty.

Other acquisitions include the Imperial Glass Corp., a manufacturer of quality cut glassware; Taunton Silversmiths, Ltd., a major manufacturer of fine silver-plated gifts, serving pieces and accessories; the John Roberts Co., renamed ArtCarved Class Rings; Eisenstadt Manufacturing Co., a wholesale distributor of jewlery products, and Lenox Awards, a designer/manufacturer of emblematic jewlery and awards.

Lenox also operates two Latin American subsidiaries producing melamine dinnerware, stainless steel flatware, sterling silver and silver-plated flatware.

Lenox has built a new china plant in Pomona, South Jersey, the largest and most modern of its kind in the world. It is, as Lenox envisioned a century ago at his Trenton potter's wheel, an American shrine to art, to faith . . . and to idealism.

Cybis

If it's a Cybis, it can be found in Buckingham Palace, the White House, the Vatican, or where kings and presidents reside. The name is synonymous with the finest porcelain in the world.

Boleslaw Cybis (pronounced see'-bus) seemed destined for artistic acclaim. His father was a well-known architect who designed the summer palace of Russia's Czarina Maria Fiodorowna.

Born in 1895 of Polish parents in Wilno, Lithuania, Boleslaw Cybis received his early artistic education at the St. Petersburg Academy of Fine Arts. While a student in Russia, the revolution broke out and Cybis sought refuge in Constantinople as an artist, sketching portraits in sidewalk cafes and fashioning peculiar clay pipes, which he soon learned were becoming collector's items.

Returning to Warsaw in 1923 to study at the Academy of Fine Arts, Cybis helped found the Brotherhood of St. Luke, an organization of artists who, reacting to the modernistic trends, dedicated themselves to learning the techniques of the old masters.

After graduation from the academy in 1925, Cybis married Marja Tym, who he met in school and was a talented artist in her own right. For the next 15 years, he and Marja traveled and studied throughout Europe and Africa, applying their skills as painters.

Many of Cybis' paintings were exhibited in Geneva, Krakow, Berlin, Munich, Frankfurt, Moscow, St. Petersburg, Amsterdam and Rome. His ceiling mural in the Polish Pavilion received the Grand Prix. In 1937, he was appointed a professor at the Warsaw Academy.

Several American museums and art galleries exhibited Cybis' works during the 1930s and Studio magazine described his paintings as being reminiscent of Leonardo da Vinci's.

In 1938, the Polish government commissioned Boleslaw and Marja to paint al fresco murals in the Hall of Honor at the New York World's Fair. They extended their visit to America by touring the Southwest and sketching Indians on various reservations.

It turned out to be the turning point in their lives and careers. On the way back to Poland their ship was turned around in the mid-Atlantic. It was the outbreak of World War II.

The couple established Cybis Art Productions in 1940 to produce fine porcelain sculptures in the style of the European studios they remembered so well.

They chose Trenton because of its reputation as the Staffordshire of America. In a converted carriage on Church Street, the Cybises and the local artists they hired worked in rooms where sculptured friezes reminiscent of Greek mythology crowded the cornices and archways.

A porcelain studio is like a symphony orchestra: Many artists, or musicians, are needed to create the final product or musi-

Courtesy: Cybis Studio

*"The Bride," a finely detailed
sculpture by the Cybis Studio, was
presented to Pope John Paul II by the
people of Iowa.*

Courtesy: Boehm

*The Pontiff Iris, created in
porcelain by Boehm, is an example
of the finely shaped flowers that
have become trademarks of the
studio.*

Courtesy: Boehm

*"The Great Egret" by Boehm was
commissioned by the National Audubon
Society.*

cal effect. A subject is sculpted in a clay-like substance called plasteline. The sculpture is dissected into many sections from which plaster of Paris molds are made. The porcelain itself is made by mixing different types of clay with water until a silky smooth liquid the consistency of heavy cream is achieved.

Known as slip, the liquid is poured in the various molds and allowed to remain until a thin shell is formed on the inside of each mold. Each piece must be joined together to form the original sculpture. The sculptures are then fired in kilns at temperatures near 2300 degrees.

A sculpture may go through as many as six or eight firings depending on how many colors are required for the composition.

The mold only produces the basic shape of the sculpture. All of the tiny details, for which Cybis sculptures are valued, are worked into the clay, which when used to make the mold is as fragile as piecrust.

With tools similar to those found in a dentist's kit, the artists sculpt the delicate leaves and flowers, petal by petal, the tiny bows formed from ribbons of clay.

The Cybis Studio is America's oldest existing art porcelain studio. Its character is reflective of the early European ateliers so familiar with the Cybises during their 1930s travels. Although the founders died in 1957 and 1958, the Cybis Studio remains America's premier porcelain showcase.

The present Cybis Studio on Norman Avenue was designed around a courtyard, its gardens changing with the seasons and offering the artists the ideal environment for examining the numerous subjects from nature portrayed in Cybis porcelains.

Among the many Cybis sculptures presented as presidential gifts of state are: A chess set given to the Soviet Union during the 1972 Moscow Summit Conference; an artist's proof is in the collection of the Smithsonian Institution . . . a colonial flower basket presented to Queen Elizabeth II during her Bicentennial visit to the United States in 1976 . . . the doves of peace given to Soviet President Leonid Brezhnev to commemorate the signing of

the SALT II (nuclear arms limitations) Treaty . . . Eskimo mother presented to Prince Charles and Diana, Princess of Wales, to commemorate their wedding . . . the bride presented to Pope John Paul II during his 1979 visit to the United States . . . and the North American Indian series, a complete collection on permanent display at Blair House in Washington, D.C., the official guest house of the United States.

The Cybis Studio is dedicated to preserving porcelain art in America. It has funded several traveling exhibits, including the American Porcelain Tradition, documenting 150 years of porcelain artistry in the United States.

Cybis art is a best seller among fund-raisers, particularly conservationists. Cybis has been selling two limited-issue sculptures to help pay for the $500,000 in repairs to the Calypso, the Cousteau Society's research vessel. Money is being raised through the sale of 1,000 porcelains of humpback whales, each retailing for $1,775, and 500 "Dolphin Rider" creations selling for $575 apiece.

In an age of automation and endless reproductions, art collectors cherish Cybis porcelain sculptures as an American art form capturing the beauty of fantasy of nature and man's highest artistic moments.

Boehm

Boehm is the only American porcelain studio to operate an extra-national subsidiary in—of all places—the most competitive pottery country in the world: England, home of Wedgwood, Doughty and Spode.

The story of Edward Marshall Boehm is something right out of an old-fashioned fairy tale, full of wonder and surprise.

Born in 1913, Boehm loved the land and its natural inhabitants. He learned about animals as a veterinarian assistant and bought a farm near the Delaware River by Washington's Crossing. Until the age of 37, he raised prized cattle and horses and was the first to breed rare birds in captivity in the spacious aviaries he built on his farm.

Filling a need to preserve his beautiful animals as works of art, Boehm started a basement studio in Trenton in 1950 in the ceramic center of America. Neither Boehm nor his wife Helen had any experience in porcelain making or marketing and promoting artwork.

The naturalist-farmer understood animals as well as any talented artist working in the Trenton pottery factories. Boehm began by recreating in miniature detail his beloved farm animals. So lifelike were his first creations that his original bulls and stallions were instantly recognized as "equal to the finest of superior English work" by Vincent Andrus, then curator of the American Wing of the Metropolitan Museum of Art in New York.

Within 10 years, Boehm was represented in 11 other museums, including Buckingham Palace, Elysee Palace and the Vatican. By 1983, Boehm porcelains have been collected by 90 museums and institutions around the world.

Early in 1953, President and Mrs. Eisenhower heard about the New Jersey naturalist sculptor and ordered several of his miniature animals as gifts to visiting heads of state, culminating in the sculpture "Prince Philip on His Polo Pony" given to the queen and prince when they visited the United States in 1957. Every American President since has selected fine Boehm porcelains as gifts for visiting dignitaries.

When Pope John XXIII was presented with several pieces for the Vatican Museum, including "Cerulean Warblers with Wild Roses," he commented: "One hesitates to go too close for fear the birds might fly away."

John E. Hartill, president of the British Manufacturers' Federation in 1966-67 and managing director of Minton China of England, offered this account of Boehm's contribution to ceramic art:

"At one memorable gathering, when a superb collection of Boehm sculptures was presented to a cultural centre, Edward Marshall Boehm was described as the ceramic genius of the age. In more ways than one, he has made ceramic history in the twentieth century, and future generations will recognize his work as an important contribution to the art of our time."

The master porcelain maker died in 1969 and his dynamic studio partner extended her husband's vision of striving to produce the greatest porcelains humanly possible.

Helen Boehm assumed the design responsibility and traveled to England in 1970 to open the first American porcelain art studio and gallery. In just three years, Boehm of Malvern England Limited was carving its niche in the history of fine porcelain.

Under Helen Boehm's brilliant direction, honored commissions continued to come to the Trenton studio. President Nixon placed a major Boehm collection in the Oval Office of the White House and distributed sculptures to the heads of all NATO countries. On his historic trip to China in 1970, Nixon presented Chairman Mao and the Chinese people with a lifesize pair of mute swans called "Birds of Peace."

President Ford brought Boehm porcelains with him on his trips to Russia and China in 1976. He also presented the lifesize Boehm American Bald Eagle to the Smithsonian Institution.

In August 1980, Boehm of Malvern presented to the Queen Mother on her 80th birthday a porcelain replica of the "Rose of Glamis," a new species of rose hybridized in her honor.

A replica pair of the mute swans (only three pairs were made) was auctioned by Sotheby's of London in September 1975 to benefit the World Wildlife Fund. The swans brought $150,000, more than three times the highest auction price of any porcelain made since the turn of the century.

The Boehm Porcelain Guild was founded in 1980 in response to collectors' wanting to organize Boehm chapters throughout the United States.

Combining business with the sport of kings, Boehm mounted its first polo team in 1980. A year later, the Boehm team won the World Cup and Gucci Cup Championships. In 1982, it went on to win the prestigious Rolex Cup and victoriously claimed the Queen's Cup of Great Britain.

The story of Edward Marshall Boehm and his nature reproductions continues to make magic wherever a Boehm porcelain is unveiled. From a cattle farm in New Jersey to the historic halls of the Vatican, the White House and Buckingham Palace, Boehm has left an incomparable and lasting legacy of nature's most beautiful creations.

Flemington Cut Glass

Some 20,000 visitors stream into Flemington's glass district each weekend, searching for something special among the world's largest display of glassware, from rugged utility ware to the most luxurious stem crystals.

The landmark glass factory is a bargain shopper's delight, for it's one of the few remaining places where one can still see glass cutters practicing their disappearing crafts.

The oldest continuous glass-cutting operation in the country, the Flemington factory was founded in 1908 by Alphons G. Muller to produce the finest hand-cut crystal in the world. As many as 65 Old World artisans bent to Muller's cutting wheels to create elaborate table-top elegance during "The Brilliant Period" in cut crystal history. "American Rich Cut Class" was the symbol of ultimate quality and hundreds of Flemington pieces found their way into museum and private antique collections.

With more than 150,000 glassware items in inventory today, Flemington Cut Glass Co. is the largest retailer of its kind in the world with the biggest selection of china, glass and gifts in any one location.

Originally, Muller sold only his own cut glass. But by 1925, he diversified and became a major outlet for the world's finest manufacturers of china and dinnerware.

Visitors are welcome to watch the cutters and glassblowers fashioning full-lead crystals, custom-decorating any crystal pattern one chooses, even monogramming.

Crystal can be made in several ways, the finest being by combining a large percentage of lead with quartz sand. High lead crystal adds weight and strength to permit deep cuttings, a characteristic of "The Masterpiece Collection" made in Flemington.

After the crystal is formed, a batch is taken to a blower, who hand-blows the crystal into the desired shape. The designer then draws the patterns of the cuttings and gives it to a rougher, who makes the first deep incisions on the crystal.

If a rougher cuts too deeply, he can ruin the whole piece. If the cut is perfect, it goes to a smoother, who smoothes the hard edges and cuts smaller incisions.

Depending on the pattern, it takes about 30 hours and 10 artisans to make each piece in Flemington's famous "Masterpiece Collection."

The quality of hand-cut, full-lead crystal can be determined by its ring, brilliance, sharpness and weight.

Some of the glassware specialties sold in Flemington are:

• **Bubble glass**—A glass containing many small visible bubbles deliberately induced for decorative effect.

• **Cased glass**—Glassware in which one layer of glass is applied over another. Several layers may be applied, each of a different color, texture or design.

• **Crackled glass**—Glassware whose surface is marked by a network of tiny cracks purposely induced by sudden cooling to create decorative effects.

• **Iridescent glass**—Glassware with a special coating which, when struck by light, reflects the colors of the rainbow.

• **Pressed glass**—Glassware formed in a mold, the actual

pressing being done either mechanically or by hand. Both shape and design may be molded simultaneously in this method.

• **Bisque ware**—The "body" of the ware after the first firing, before glazing. The origin of the word is said to be from its similarity in appearance to a sailor's sea biscuit.

• **Bone china**—Fine china that contains, in addition to clays, an ingredient that gives it a characteristic whiteness. Bone china was first made in England in the early 1800s by the addition of ox bone ash.

• **Ironstone**—A heavy, durable earthenware.

• **Semi-vitreous ware**—A harder body than earthenware, it is opaque and somewhat porous.

• **Vitrified china**—Nonporous fine china fired at extremely high temperatures, far stronger, thinner and more translucent than ware fired at lower temperatures and for shorter periods of time.

• **Stoneware**—Harder than semi-vitreous ware, it is nonporous and does not have the translucence of china.

The fifth generation of Mullers presently runs the world's largest glass outlet. Because New Jersey is the glass capital of America, it is the home of the national magazine for table-top professionals—China Glass & Tableware—published in Clifton, Passaic County.

Wheaton Village

Down in southern Jersey they make glass . . .
By day and by night, the fires burn on in Millville
and bid the sand let in the light.

When poet-historian Carl Sandburg wrote about Millville's glassmaking industry, it was—and remains—the basis of South Jersey's industrial economy.

The history of glassmaking lives on in Wheaton Village, the largest museum in South Jersey, where 7,000 objects from Mason jars to Tiffany masterpieces are displayed in a 20,000-square-foot elegant exhibit area.

The museum traces the development of American glassmaking from the first glassworks in the 17th Century Colonies when bottle and window lights, free blowing, mold blowing and pressing were all done by artisans who have since been replaced by automation today, except for a handful of isolated crafts studios.

Wheaton glassworks was the vision of Theodore Corson Wheaton, born in Tuckahoe, South Jersey, in 1852. As a youth, Wheaton earned money clamming and oystering in the local bays.

Before becoming an apprentice to a pharmacist in South Seaville, Wheaton sailed for a year on a 400-ton "coaster vessel." At 21, he entered the Philadelphia College of Pharmacy and Science. After graduation in 1876, he enrolled at the Medical College of the University of Pennsylvania, receiving his MD degree in 1879.

Wheaton worked for a druggist before buying a wallpaper and drug store. In 1888, he purchased shares in the newly established Shull-Goodwin Glass Co. in Millville. The glass house started with 25 employes making pharmaceutical bottles and scientific glassware.

The doctor then bought out his partners and renamed the business the T.C. Wheaton Co. Today, Wheaton employs more than 3,000 people in Millville, plus another 700 at factories in other areas. They produce a full range of glass products, making Wheaton Industries the largest family-owned glassware maker in the world.

Star-Ledger Photo

Kontes paperweights, on display in the Arthur Gorham Paperweight Shop at Wheaton Village, Millville, range from $350 to $1,500.

In the T.C. Wheaton Glass Factory, students are invited to witness the transformation of molten glass into items of exquisite beauty. Since the automated production of glassware in the early 20th Century, the glassblower, or gaffer, has almost become extinct as a craftsperson.

Wheaton Village has preserved that craft and one can watch contemporary artisans using century-old techniques to create classic pitchers, bottles, vases and paperweights. In fact, the Arthur Gorham Paperweight Shop in the village offers the finest quality and the largest variety of handmade paperweights in the world.

The Wheaton Village Crafts Arcade presents the individual crafts worker, paying particular attention to native New Jersey crafts.

The Prince Maurice Pottery is in daily operation, making traditional hand-thrown and decorated slat-glazed wares, typical of 19th Century New Jersey.

The General Store features penny candy, a working nickelodeon and hundreds of unique and inexpensive household items. Distinctive gifts can be found in The Brownstone Emporium.

Handcrafted glass, woodcarvings, pottery and weaving articles are available at the West Jersey Crafts Company Store. Freshly dipped ice cream is served up in season at the Pharmacy.

Be entertained by Professor Elias B. Fester's traveling road show, or stop by during the annual Great Victorian Fair and Antique Auto Show. Within the village stands the 1876 Centre Grove Schoolhouse and the 1880 Palermo Train Station. A tour of the 88-acre village with its stately pine and oak trees can be taken aboard a half-scale model of the C.P. Huntington late 19th Century steam locomotive and train.

The Agricultural Center depicts farm life before the Garden State became the manufacturing hub of the Northeast.

Glass, however, is the theme of Wheaton Village: Carnival glass, milk glass, Victorian glass, whiskey bottles, medicine bottles, baby bottles, flasks, carboys, pickle and fruit jars, snuff boxes, ink wells, and every colored and odd-shaped container or vessel for mineral oil and perfumes, hair dyes and barber supplies.

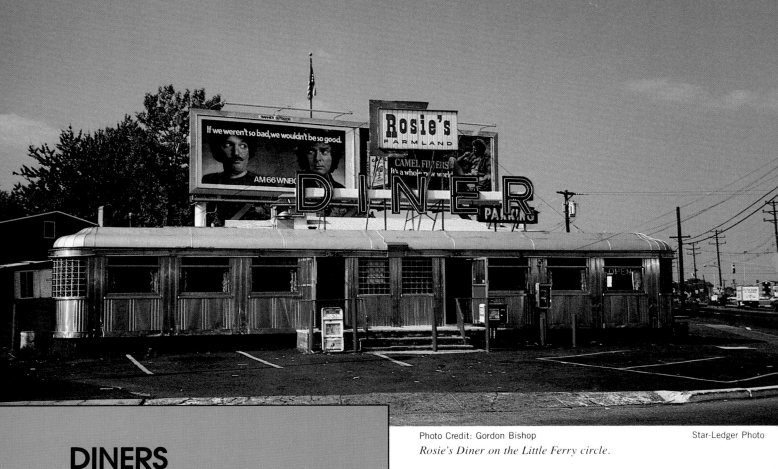

Photo Credit: Gordon Bishop   Star-Ledger Photo

Rosie's Diner on the Little Ferry circle.

DINERS

New Jersey is the diner capital of the world, the home of nearly 2,000 of the nation's estimated 6,000 movable eating places.

The smallest and the largest, the fanciest and the grittiest diners embellish, in their own inimitable fashion, New Jersey's highways and tree-lined suburban streets.

A phenomenon of the East Coast, diners dot the northern coastal states like palm trees soaking up the sun on the lower Pacific coast.

America's landmark diner—Rosie's, on the busy Little Ferry traffic circle in Bergen County—has been seen on TV sets around the globe. The shiny, stainless steel-Formica interior becomes an instant backdrop for such products as Rosie's "quicker picker upper" paper towels and 70 other popular convenience items.

The word "diner" was coined by a Bayonne bar and grill operator who launched America's stainless-steel age of roadside eateries catering to a newly motorized nation-on-the-go. Jerry O'Mahony thought the lunch wagon, as he would shape it, resembled the dining car of a train.

O'Mahony was still working at his father's bar and grill when he decided in 1913, at the age of 33, to build the most attractive and durable lunch cars since Walter Scott first set up his horse-drawn wagon one night in 1872 to feed hungry factory workers in Providence, R.I.

Scott's makeshift street car, the first of many Pioneer Lunch wagons, served up a homemade meal of chicken, ham, boiled egg, buttered bread and a slice of juicy pie: Apple, cranberry, huckleberry, mince and squash.

But it was the Bayonne bartender and his handsome mobile diners that brought about an original American lifestyle for the hungry-on-the-run. By the 1920s, O'Mahony's Bayonne factory was assembling more diners than all other rivals.

O'Mahony's slogan said it all: "In our line, we lead the world."

The feisty Irishman and his competition, notably P.J. Tierney from New Rochelle, N.Y. crafted the best look-alike diners of their day. They had that scrubbed down, spotless look: Long, smooth marble counters, and an eye-catching pattern of ceramic tiles on the walls and floors. The sun's rays streaked through the stark glass skylights and the softly frosted and finely etched windows, and the sun beams bounced off the polished metal coffee cylinders, striking the richly varnished wood or brightly painted metal ceilings.

Their stools were made entirely of white porcelain enamel and often mounted with leather or wooden seats.

It was a time when any style was acceptable, and the more expensively constructed diners became dazzling examples of Art Deco at its outrageous best.

The American diner has been memorialized in movies and books capturing the nostalgia of a bygone era, when the corrugated-stainless-steel highway stop was an American tradition and, in this part of the country, an institution.

The motion picture "Diner" starred an old stainless diner from Oakland, Bergen County, that was moved to Baltimore for the movie set. The Oakland diner depicts life and its infinite social interactions in the familiar roadside refreshers. That special flavor and feeling was also captured in the colorful photographic essay "American Diner" by Richard J.S. Gutman and Elliott Kaufman.

For all of its nostalgic value, the era of the always-open diner is gradually giving way to the McDonald's and comparable, contemporary-styled, fast-food restaurants.

Even the familiar 'round-the-clock diner is undergoing an

architectural and culinary metamorphosis. A diner is not necessarily a diner by today's free-wheeling standards.

A sampling of some of the Garden State's "diners" shows how a word and a concept in public eating can be radically changed to appeal to changing tastes and incomes. Watch the word "diner" carefully in this progression of culinary images:

- Tops Diner in Jersey City.
- The Colonial Diner Restaurant in Woodbury.
- Brooklawn Diner and Restaurant, Gloucester County.
- The Colony Restaurant and Diner in Jersey City.
- Michael's Diner & Bar in Newark.
- The Star Diner and Lounge in Camden.
- The White House Dinette in Hunterdon County.

Pat's Diner in Belmar has evolved, with renovations, into Pat's Riverside Diner-Restaurant.

There are also famous diners that bill themselves as Max's Grill in Harrison, a truly stainless classic . . . Rosie's Pit Stop in Cranbury, not to be confused with the Little Ferry landmark diner . . . White Manna Hamburgers in Hackensack, the small, rounded diner featured in the 1939 World's Fair and the subject of several artists' cameras and canvases.

The recent emergence of diner-restaurants is a logical business development, a direct appeal to all consumers, from those who prefer sitting on a stool, or in a booth, or absorbing the ambiance of a dimly lit dining room.

The diner corridor of America may well be Routes 1-9 between Trenton and Newark, where just about anything and everything that embraces the concept of "diner" constantly vies for the motorists' attention night and day.

Every conceivable configuration can be found among New Jersey's 2,000 or so diners: Barrel tops, trolley-style, modern, Mediterranean, Moorish, Tudor, Spanish, Colonial, the White Castle look, the original stainless steels, and the twin-roofed Monarchs, whose louvered ceilings open and close to control the flow of heat from the kitchen and patrons.

Created for a mobile society, diners change hands—and places. The Frontier in Plainfield is now Victoria's—Yesterday and Today.

And the archetypal American diner, The Gateway, is no longer in Phillipsburg. It has been transplanted to England for the same reasons the London Bridge was brought to Arizona a few years ago. Both countries prize original works of art.

The Gateway Diner was born in the proud tradition of the sleek Silk City diners made in Paterson during the heyday of these fabricated show pieces on wheels. With a standard front door in the middle and rectangular windows dividing the upper and lower halves of the stainless, oversized railroad car, the Gateway Diner was built in 1947 as America entered its greatest period of prosperity.

The nearly forsaken diner was pure Americana, reeking and creaking with post-war nostalgia, just before the advent of rock 'n' roll and the cultural revolution of the Sixties that shocked America out of its sublime innocence.

When Warner Dailey came across the Gateway in 1982, it seemed destined for the scrap heap. The ole Gateway had seen better days and was struggling to stay alive as the McDonalds and Gino's slowly circled it in the Delaware Valley of western New Jersey. Its days as a gleaming diner welcoming truckers and those who enjoy a hearty meal of steak and potatoes were numbered . . . until Dailey and his partner, John Hornby-Smith, gave Gateway a new lease on life. The 20-ton, 40-foot-long, 14-foot-wide, Silk City special cost $50,000 to purchase, ship and set up in the Chelsea section of London near King's Road. Dailey and Hornby-Smith thought so much of their surprise find that they

Armindo Ferreira, one of the owners of Max's Diner in Harrison, shares the news of the day with some of his regular customers. The exterior of the tiny eatery still sports original advertising slogans.

took out a Lloyd's of London insurance policy on the London-bound diner.

Dailey, who has lived in London since 1972, runs an antique shop. Hornby-Smith deals in old cars, planes and oddities in London. The great city had every kind of restaurant, except a bona-fide American diner. Gateway filled the bill.

* * *

No New Jersey diner has yet to be designated a national historic landmark, but there are plenty to choose from if someday historians want to preserve a few to remind future generations what traveling life was like before the fast-food craze and the arrival of the Holiday Inns and Ho-Jo's with their flashy discos and executive dining parlors.

In many cities and out-of-the-way places, diners remain a constant, almost cozy fixture, a kind of social equalizer where school prom couples recuperate in their tuxedos and gowns after an all-night partying spree, along with the truck drivers, salesmen, policemen and anyone in need of an off-hours recharge when the regular restaurants are closed until dawn.

Many towns would be darkened communities without the Main Street diner glowing in the night, offering a warm respite to any weary insomniac or the nocturnal workers who keep the factories humming while the world sleeps.

By definition, a diner is a 24-hour operation and anything else is merely a bland imitation. A diner is also a structure assembled in a factory and hauled to a site on its own wheels, or in sections in a truck. If it's a sectionalized delivery, the sides and roof are bolted together at the site.

The genuine diner contains a counter with stools and a number of booths with individual jukeboxes. Large, fake leather menus offer just about every kind of platter and dessert, all baked on the premises, to qualify as a true diner.

Although not a prerequisite, many diners today are run by Greeks.

Diners often assume the identity of their locale, with some of the best known being the Arlington Diner in North Arlington, the Barnegat Diner, the Bayville Diner, the Bridgewater Diner, the Brunswick Diner in East Brunswick, the Deptford Queen Diner, the Cinnaminson Diner, the Dover Diner, the Edison Diner, the Flemington Diner, the Forked River Diner, Angela's Glassboro Diner, the Hightstown Diner, the Manasquan Diner, the Middlesex Diner in North Brunswick, the Mount Laurel Diner, the Princetonian Diner, the Raritan Diner, the Sandy Hook Diner in Atlantic Highlands, Loupe's Somerdale Diner, the Toms River Diner, and the Vincentown Diner.

New Jersey was one of the original 13 Colonies that formed an alliance and gave birth to a new nation in 1776. That Colonial history is reflected in the names of many New Jersey diners, such as the Colonial Diner in East Brunswick, and the Colony Restaurant and Diner and Colonette Diner, both in Jersey City.

Many diners belie their humble beginnings, as evidenced by these fashionable and sometimes elegant appellations: The Tiffany Diner in East Brunswick, the Regent Diner in Howell, the Windsor Diner in Cherry Hill, the Blue Fountain Diner in Piscataway, the Prince Diner in Jersey City, the Premium Diner in Edison, the Country Club Diner and Restaurant in Camden, the Club Diner in Bellmawr, the College Inn Diner in Princeton, the Court Diner in Morristown, the Parsonage Diner in Menlo Park, and the Heritage Diner and Restaurant in Livingston.

A handful of diners owe their identities to rare jewels, such as the Diamond Diner in Cherry Hill and the Emerald Diner in Edison.

Others remind travelers of the Garden State's agrarian roots and natural amenities: The Country Squire Diner in Wall Township, Jim's Country Diner in Pennington, the Maple Diner in Elizabeth, the Red Oak Diner in Hazlet, the Town & Country Diner in Bordentown, the Village Diner Restaurant in Camden, the Sunrise Diner in Ship Bottom, the Golden Dawn Diner in Gloucester County, and the Park Diner in Harrison.

Highways and trucks made New Jersey the diner capital, and some establishments capitalized on that unique distinction with such names as the Roadside Diner in Wall Township, the Freeway Diner in Deptford, the Cloverleaf Diner in Point Pleasant, the Extension Diner in Trenton, and the Open Door Diner in Newark.

Diners also mirror their special interests: The Tunnel Diner near the Holland Tunnel in Jersey City . . . the Liberty View Diner near the Statue of Liberty by the Jersey City waterfront . . . the Shore Diner in Toms River, the seat of Ocean County . . . the Ocean Queen Diner and Restaurant in Bricktown, on the Atlantic seaboard . . . the Bendix Diner, wedged in the median of Route 46, by the big Bendix plant in Teterboro . . . the Cross Bay Diner in Toms River.

If an owner wants to be identified with the diner, he or she says so in the rooftop signs: Otto's in Jersey City, Olga's in Marlton, Hedy's in Hillside, Ponzio's Kingsway Diner and Restaurant in Cherry Hill, Fisher's in Beach Haven, Jamie's in Toms River, Lido in Springfield, Laura & Charlie's Diner in Dunellen,

The Lido Diner, a popular "island" retreat for motorists, sits amid the bustling Route 22 corridor in Springfield.

Star-Ledger Photo

Pat's in Trenton, Paul's in Secaucus, Swede's in Cranbury, Prout's in Sussex, Jimmy's in Boonton, Bosko's in South River, Chappy's in Paterson, L&M in Ocean Township, and two in South Jersey, Geets', and Barbara.

The most interesting for drivers who break up the monotony of their trips by reading signs are the odd or offbeat names, among them: Miss America Diner in Jersey City, the Spotless Diner in Newark, the Nautilus Diner in Madison, the Tick Tock in Clifton, the Foursome in Rahway, the Flagship in Tuckerton, the Empire in Runnemede, the Copper Bell in Windsor, the Golden Star in Clifton, the White Star in South Plainfield, the two Horseshoe diners in Jersey City, the Atco in Camden, the Arena in Kearny, the Echo Queen in Mountainside, and the Dakota in Montville.

* * *

In their prime during the 1940s, the dozen or so diner manufacturers in New Jersey turned out hundreds of long, short, narrow and wide mobile eateries for a vehicularized society.

Then came the bold golden arches and the Kentucky colonel's golden-fried chickens, changing the eating habits of a new generation of Americans. The quickie hamburgers and finger-lickin' good chickens pushed the diner industry to the brink of extinction.

Two major New Jersey manufacturers made the transition to the diner-restaurant era with its emphasis on brick and stone facades, cantilevered and terra cotta roofs, arched windows, extended entranceways . . . the ultimate effect being that each stands out as an individual personality.

And that is how the Kullman Dining Car Co. in Avenel (Woodbridge) and the Swingle Dining Car Co. in Middlesex continue to produce diners either in their factories or erected on-site. A smaller but highly specialized operation is Musi Dining Car Co. in Carteret.

Kullman and Swingle are down to making, in sections, four or five diners a year. In the boom years of the '50s and '60s, diners came off the assembly line at the rate of 10 to 12 a year. Now, the diners are bigger and more luxurious, catering to businessmen, bankers, lawyers and families.

A diner sold for $10,000 in the 1930s. Today, they can cost $1 million, depending on the quality of the curtains, lighting and designer decorations.

"Greco-glitzy," inside and out, is the way guidebook gourmet authors Neil Weiner and David Schwartz describe the current crop of customized diners. It's what today's entrepreneurs want and what Kullman and Swingle can fabricate, if the price is right.

The Kullman Co. began building diners in a Newark warehouse in 1927. Founder Samuel Kullman expanded the business into the largest in the United States by the 1950s. His grandson, Robert, now runs the family firm.

Kullman was the first to introduce the Colonial and Mediterranean-styled diners in the 1960s, featuring bay windows and coach lamps. The sprawling, anodized brick structures come complete with fine carpeting and plush seating for up to 400 patrons. Regardless of their size, they can be dismantled and moved to another lot as easily as they were first put up.

The diner is delivered as one complete package: All the owner has to do is provide a level lot and the dishes and utensils.

Regardless of size, diners are still manufactured by skilled craftsmen, and rolled to the site.

Unlike the mass produced steel diners, today's models are a collaboration between the manufacturer and the buyer, who decides the layout and the contents, right down to the bars, bathrooms, booths, counters, doors, grills, refrigerators, stoves, tables and seats.

Kullman can build a deluxe model with all the trimmings in 12 to 14 weeks. The big ones are built in 12 sections. Just a decade ago, diners were all the same size, seating about 60 people.

Nine out of 10 Kullman diners are ordered by Greek-Americans who, says Kullman, "want more brick, more stone, more earthy tones, more skylights."

The Swingle Co. was organized in 1967 by Joe Swingle, who married one of O'Mahony's nieces and learned the trade from the nuts and bolts all the way to negotiating long-term bank loans to finance his dream diners. One of his most attractive creations is the Red Oak in Hazlet, which looks more like a country estate than a Route 35 diner.

Swingle was a teacher who worked with O'Mahony until the company was sold in 1952. By then, Swingle had become O'Mahony's business manager.

Swingle's Middlesex factory has launched a "new generation" of diners—which is really a resurrection of the nostalgic classics, but with the latest space-age materials and state-of-the-art technology for the kitchen and heating-cooling-ventilation system.

New Jersey's growing collection of diners represents every configuration ever construed in the name of dining. The most typical of the various modes of diners made in New Jersey range from the stainless classics to the elaborate edifices of recent vintage.

* * *

Rosie's Diner was named after a character in a TV commercial portrayed by veteran stage-screen-television actress Nancy Walker, most recently remembered as the mother of "Rhoda" in that hit CBS comedy series.

When Walker and the video crew showed up at the Little Ferry diner in 1971 to shoot the Bounty paper towel commercial, the place was known as the Farmland Diner. There weren't any pastures or cropland around the Little Ferry circle then, but there were when Tex Corrado established a diner in 1945 at the Route 46-Moonachie Road intersection.

Corrado, who owned diners in Hoboken and Jersey City, baptized his new diner the Old Silver Dollar. Its stainless steel, vertically-corrugated skin was the trademark of the Paramount Diner Co. of Hawthorne, one of the giants of the rust-proof diner era.

When Tex's son, Ralph, took over the Old Silver Dollar in 1961, he recalled those pastoral scenes when his father first opened the diner after the war. He dubbed the sleek diner the Farmland, hoping to recapture the flavor of a long-gone agrarian age.

For 10 years, Ralph and his circle diner prospered under the Farmland logo displayed proudly atop the 60-by-25-foot landmark.

Rosie, the hardworking waitress behind the Farmland counter, would change all that, making the Little Ferry diner the most famous in America. Some 70 products have been identified with Rosie's, and scenes from two movies, "Alone in the Dark," starring Jack Palance and Donald Pleasance, and "Phi Beta Rockers," have been filmed inside and outside of the striking Paramount dining car.

Corrado appeared in both feature films. He expects to be in many more, as well as being a sort of technical consultant on the sets of all those commercials, from Body All to Sanka.

Corrado and Rosie's have become celebrities, as souvenir seekers stop in for a meal—and leave with an autographed menu.

Something of a tourist attraction surrounded by billboards and gas stations, Rosie's is so popular that Corrado sells Rosie T-shirts and sweatshirts to memorabilia collectors from as far away as California.

The interior of Rosie's is pure American diner, from its polished tiled floor to the glistening Formica and marble ceiling, set off by strips of stainless steel. Lighting is furnished by 6- and 8-foot-long fluorescent tubes running down the center of the ceiling.

Thick bottled glass rounds the corners of the diner, allowing light to penetrate, but blurring the view for diners and passersby alike.

The colorful counter top, where most of the action takes

"Rosie's" rules the Little Ferry traffic circle. Actress Nancy Walker has been seen leaning over its polished counter in many a television commercial.

place in both the real world and through the lens of a camera, changes like a Hollywood set, from blue to yellow to butterscotch to whatever hue the next TV or movie director deems appropriate.

What makes Rosie's the quintessence of the American diner is the stainless fan design behind the grill and food preparation and display areas along the wall. That bit of shiny decor gets into every production, even if it's a 15-second TV spot. Without it, Rosie's would be just another glittering highway diner.

For its time, Rosie's was a rather spacious diner, equipped with 24 revolving counter stools and 14 bright red booths. Any bigger, Corrado believes, and Rosie's would lose its "dated" appeal.

Almost as dated are Rosie's breakfast prices. Two eggs, toast and coffee is a bargain $1.45 (March 1985 menu price).

* * *

If big and lavish means better, then the **Tick Tock Diner** on Route 3 in Clifton, opposite Hoffmann-LaRoche, is the ultimate *dining* experience, in terms of decor, square footage and the variety of meals and desserts available 24 hours a day, year-round.

The Tick Tock Diner has more than just kept up with the population growth and changing trends during the past 35 years. It has set the standard for the new American diner.

The original chrome, Pullman-styled Tick Tock Diner was built in 1947 by the now defunct Silk City Co. in Paterson. Its 60 seats and basic furnishings served the motoring public for 23 years, eventually grossing $500,000 annually for its Greek owners, Nick and Katharine Ramoundos.

In 1976, the serviceable Silk City dining car was replaced by a modern stone-glass-steel structure with a 253-seat capacity: 18 at the counter, 75 in the booths and 150 in an adjoining dining room. The new hybrid Tick Tock Diner rings up sales of more than $2 million a year.

Recently, another dining room (200 seats) was added, making the Tick Tock a refreshing businessmen's sanctuary by day and a family and after-party place at night.

Never to be forgotten, the Silk City "starter" diner has been saved in a sentimental sketch by Mrs. Ramoundos. Its indelible, archaic visage appears on the paper placemats.

Once a favorite stop of tractor-trailer drivers, the Tick Tock has sacrificed parking slots for extra seating. The long 18-wheelers rarely roll into the Tick Tock any more, its lot now crammed with cars and vans. The transition has been from blue collar to middle-class, the business types and families accounting for most of the traffic.

The Tick Tock, as its name implies, keeps on ticking, its doors never closed. Ramoundos, in fact, doesn't "even have a key to the front door." His artistic wife, whose paintings of race horses grace the walls for the Meadowlands Racetrack handicappers just down the highway, sums up their working life together: "You don't have a diner, it has you."

The Tick Tock exterior is curiously inviting, its tall rows of curtained windows neatly separated by slabs of maintenance-free, sheared-flat rocks with spiraling black lamps sticking out between every other window.

Around an overhanging roof imbedded with soft spotlights in its underside, rims a black wrought-iron railing resembling the deck of a small cruise ship or an oversized widow's walk.

The giant clock sign on the roof informs motorists: EAT HEAVY. OPEN 24 HOURS.

As many as 40,000 people a week frequent this Greco-American eating establishment, some 2,000 on Friday nights.

About 15 percent of Tick Tock's business involves take-out desserts and breads made fresh on the premises. The chefs prepare not only wedding cakes but divorce cakes as well. The wedding cakes outsell the divorce cakes, Nick-the-family-man happily reports.

The Tick Tock menu, with an original Kathy Ramoundos drawing of the Meadowlands Racetrack on the cover, is another story in itself. Here are a few highlights to show why this Clifton showcase has become a dining delight:

For appetizers: Top necks or cherrystone clams, jumbo shrimp cocktail, marinated herring, smoked whitefish, etc.

Egg and omelets include lox and onion, and 17 other entries.

From the sea is everything from lobsters, salmon, shrimps, scallops, clams, snapper, sole and oysters, plus many more.

From the broiler there are filet mignon, rib steak, sirloin, London broil, ham steak, lamb chops, pork chops and lots more.

There are also all kinds of blintzes—cheese, blueberry, banana, pears, peaches—as well as "health" salads, saute dishes, Italian dishes, cold salad buffet, entrees and roasts, open hot sandwiches, "tasty" sandwiches and club sandwiches, the bagel bin,

Short order cook Andy Eleftherioll of Clifton serves up the familiar cheeseburger platter at the Tick Tock.

Star-Ledger Photo

diet delights, "The Burgery" and plenty of side orders, not to mention Tick Tock's famous desserts, such as fruit cheese cake, nut strudel, baklava, homemade bread pudding, linzer tarts, eclairs, Napoleons, pies, cakes, muffins, danish, cookies and other mouthwatering delights.

Add to all that a children's menu, specials from the fountain and beverages, and one can forget ever having to eat home again.

The original Tick Tock Diner on Route 3 in Clifton beckoned to hungry motorists with a gleaming stainless exterior and eclectic menu. Today it serves as many as 40,000 people weekly.   Star-Ledger Photo

Replica of the first successful Incandescent Lamp Menlo Park, Oct. 21, 1879

Edison's first successful light.

EDISON

Brand-new laboratory... at Menlo Park, Western Div., Globe, Planet Earth, Middlesex Country, four miles from Rahway, the prettiest spot in New Jersey, on the Penna Railway, on a High Hill. Will show you around, go strawberrying.
—Thomas Alva Edison, June 1876

*T*he great inventor wrote that abbreviated description to his patent lawyer after having selected the site of a rambling chicken farm to become the world's first invention factory.

Thomas Edison chose New Jersey as the place from where he would revolutionize civilization, which he largely accomplished within his 84-year lifetime.

Because of Edison's unprecedented application of ideas in New Jersey, beginning in Jersey City in 1869 and continuing through 1931 in West Orange, where he died, today one out of every five jobs in the United States is directly or indirectly related to his inventions.

Just one invention—the electric distribution system—accounts for more than 5 million jobs, according to the International Brotherhood of Electrical Workers.

There were 1,093 Edison patents in all, more than any produced by one person. Among those that changed the face of the earth were the light bulb, the electric power system, the phonograph, motion pictures, storage battery, mimeograph, the carbon telephone transmitter, the modern research laboratory, and the electronic principle of radio and television known as the "Edison Effect."

Besides his own creations, Edison also improved inventions of others, including Alexander Graham Bell's telephone, Marconi's wireless telegraph, and the typewriter. Without the wizard's magic touch, they would have been impractical or useless.

By the time he was 31 years old, Edison was hailed by Scientific American as "one of the greatest wonders of the world" and "the greatest inventor of the age."

Henry Ford, who put the world on rubber wheels and revered the famous tinkerer, called that period of history "The Age of Edison."

At 22, Edison arrived in New Jersey an unemployed telegrapher with no place to lodge and not enough change in his pocket for a meal or carfare.

The road to New Jersey and fame and fortune began on Feb. 11, 1847, in Milan, Ohio, where Edison was born, the seventh and youngest child of Samuel and Nancy Elliot Edison. His father, a prosperous shingle manufacturer, had fled from Canada during the Rebellion of 1837-38.

When he was seven his parents moved to Port Huron, Mich. His father became a lighthouse keeper and later established a grain and lumber business.

Alva, as his mother called him, entered public school and disrupted the class with so many questions the teacher branded the boy "addled." When Alva told his mother what happened, his formal schooling abruptly ended—after only three months.

Mrs. Edison felt learning could be fun and decided to be her son's teacher. By the time Alva was nine, he had absorbed everything his mother could teach him.

At 12, he took a job as "news butcher" on the Grand Trunk Railway, selling newspapers, candy, peanuts and sandwiches on a train running between Port Huron and Detroit.

He worked from 6 in the morning until 11 at night, six days a week. He soon found himself taking "cat naps" on the train's hard seats—a habit that stuck with him the rest of his life. The short dozes allowed him to work 20-hour days.

The train's baggage car served as Edison's first laboratory. He experimented with chemicals and became the first to print a newspaper, The Weekly Herald, on a moving train.

One day, a stick of phosphorus burst into flames, setting the baggage car on fire. The conductor tossed Alva off the train—printing press and all.

When he was 16, Edison met a school teacher boarding in his mother's home. She taught him Morse Code. It inspired him to put together a primitive sending key to learn telegraphy.

After the train fire, Edison sold newspapers at stations along the Grand Trunk Railway. One day, at the Mt. Clemens, Mich. station, the young man saw a freight car rolling toward the station agent's son. He rescued the boy in the nick of time. The grateful station master let young Edison tap out messages on a telegraph key. That qualified him, at 17, to become Port Huron's telegraph operator.

In the winter of 1864, Edison seized an opportunity to gain recognition as a telegraph operator by adding a bit of showmanship to his natural gift of intelligence. An ice storm snapped telegraph wires at Port Huron, cutting the town off from the rest of the world. Edison realized if he could make contact with the other towns across the St. Claire River in Canada, he would be an instant hero.

He told town officials to get a locomotive down by the river. He then advised the engineer to pull the locomotive's whistle in a series of short and long blasts which, in Morse Code, spelled out "S.O.S."

A Canadian telegrapher picked up the distress signal in the air and responded in like kind.

Port Huron was again linked to the outside world—and without wires!

This Edison phonograph sold at Sotheby's in New York for $800.

Edison was rewarded with a better job at the Stratford Junction in Ontario, Canada.

For the next four years, the restless Edison became a wandering telegrapher, drifting through Ontario, Michigan, Cincinnati, Louisville, Indianapolis, Memphis, Nashville, New Orleans and other places where Western Union wires reached.

The four years he spent tapping out messages were not entirely wasted. At 17, Edison had devised a machine that could tape incoming messages and run them back at a slower speed. That enabled him to transcribe messages at his leisure.

At 18, Edison found telegraph wires to be terribly inefficient. He knew messages could be sent both ways on the same wire simultaneously. But when he informed Western Union officials of his idea, they dismissed the teenager as a "damn fool."

In the winter of 1867-68, Edison arrived in Boston, accepting a telegrapher's job to keep from starving. That year he worked to perfect a duplex telegraph, which would send messages both ways on the same wire. Western Union tested his device, but the long-distance wires in use then were unacceptable for dual transmission.

Disgusted, Edison quit and placed an ad in the January 1869 issue of The Telegrapher:

"T.A. Edison has resigned his situation in the Western Union office, Boston, and will devote his time to bringing out his inventions."

While in Boston, Edison had perfected the first invention he attempted to sell. It was an electric vote-recording machine.

Edison took it to Washington and tried to sell it to Congress. After he showed a congressional committee how it worked, the chairman informed the unknown inventor that his machine was the last thing congressmen wanted.

"It takes 45 minutes to call the roll," the chairman told the bewildered Edison. "In that time we can trade votes. Your machine would make that impossible."

Disillusioned by the reaction to his first invention, Edison vowed he would "never again invent anything which nobody wants." From then on, he devoted himself to the "desperate needs of the world."

From Boston, Edison went to New York City and persuaded an employe of the Gold Indicator Co., a stock-ticker firm, to let him sleep in the office. From there, Edison watched a mechanical "Gold Indicator" flash prices of the precious metal to scores of offices around Manhattan.

One day, the machine stopped and customers were infuriated. Several mechanics failed to fix the machine. Edison quietly checked the device and found a broken spring. He replaced it and New York was back on the gold standard.

The office manager immediately hired Edison as supervisor at $300 a month, a respectable salary at the time.

Edison admired an electrical engineer at Gold Indicator Co., Franklin Pope. Before long, Pope and Edison started a small company to produce "various types of electrical devices."

Pope invited Edison to live in his Elizabeth, N.J. home. They operated out of a little laboratory in Jersey City, working 16 to 18 hours a day. Within six months, the Edison-Pope lab was acquired by Western Union. Edison then worked exclusively for his former employer, finding ways to improve WU's communications and profits.

After making considerable improvements on Western Union's stock ticker, Edison was summoned to a top executive's office in the winter of 1870. The executive, Marshall Lefferts, wanted to settle accounts before the promising engineer found out how much he was truly worth.

Edison asked Lefferts to make him an offer. When the retired Army General countered with a $40,000 fee, Edison nearly fainted.

* * *

In his notebook, Edison later recalled he took the money, returned to New Jersey by ferryboat and train and went in business for himself. He was 23 years old.

Edison invested his $40,000 in laboratory supplies—chemicals, equipment, books, burners—and rented two factory buildings at 4-6 Ward St., Newark. Here, he filled his first order of 1,200 stock tickers from Western Union. Edison hired the best mechanical, electrical and chemical engineers he could find.

The fledgling Edison research team called its boss "The Old Man," although at 23 he was much younger than his employes.

On July 28, 1871, Edison started a detailed account of his day-to-day activities, a writing chore that filled 3,400 notebooks in his lifetime. They were used to protect his inventions and patents.

In the summer of 1871, Edison noticed a young woman working diligently at her bench in his Newark factory. Not one for formalities, Edison asked the 16-year-old, Mary Stilwell, if she liked him. When she hesitated, Edison told her not to hurry in telling him, unless she would like to marry him.

They were married in Newark on Christmas Day, 1871. Their marriage produced three children, Marion, Thomas Jr. and William. Edison appropriately nicknamed the first two children "Dot" and "Dash" for his years of service as telegrapher, or "lightning slinger."

* * *

Edison's Newark factory cranked out inventions with almost assembly-line rapidity. T.A. Edison secured 34 patents in 1872 for the monograph and duplex, quadruplex, sextuplex and multiplex telegraph systems.

In 1874, Edison improved the typewriter by substituting metal parts for wood and correcting the alignment of the letters and the distribution of ink. Without those modifications, a person could write faster by hand than on a typewriting machine.

A year later, he fashioned an electric typewriter using a revolving ball. It was the forerunner of the IBM "bouncing ball" Selectric typewriter.

Edison's typewriter, however, lacked sufficient electric current for it to function. He would take care of that later, however, by inventing the electric power system.

The economic depression that hit the nation in 1873 forced Edison to look beyond Newark, a high-rent district, if he wanted to remain in business as an independent inventor.

Before leaving Newark, Edison made one of his greatest discoveries, an electrical phenomenon he described as an "etheric force."

Electrically generated waves, he postulated, would traverse an open circuit. Edison had come upon the principle on which wireless telegraphy and radio are founded. In the early 1870s, the idea that electricity would travel through space was almost beyond belief.

In 1886, the same year he made the telephone practical by adding a carbon transmitter, Edison moved his company to a 3.44-acre tract of land some 15 miles southwest of Newark. On the map it was called Menlo Park—a farming community settled by Cornish copper miners. It was, more importantly to Edison, on the mainline of the Pennsylvania Railroad.

* * *

By Nov. 24, 1887, the move from Newark to Menlo Park had been completed. Edison had all the talent and tools he needed to

Courtesy: The Edison Institute

Edison's Menlo Park laboratory now stands in Greenfield Historic Village in Dearborn, Michigan.

reshape society. It would be here that Edison would establish his lifelong dream of building an "invention factory—the world's first multi-disciplined research laboratory."

At 29, Edison wanted to spend the rest of his years inventing, not manufacturing and inventing on the side. He was already recognized as the best inventor in the United States, and that's all he wanted to do: Turn out "a minor invention every 10 days and a major one every six months or so."

The Edison laboratory was housed in a two-story, clapboard structure, 100 feet long and 30 feet wide. The site, Edison believed, stood on the highest hill between New York and Philadelphia.

He stocked his lab with rare minerals and precious metals, instruments and machines, books and gadgets worth more than $40,000, a considerable sum at that time. Many of his mechanics and engineers lived in a nearby boarding house, while Edison, his wife and children occupied a large frame house two blocks away.

Work began at the lab when the whistle sounded at 7 in the morning and many stayed until after midnight trying to solve a problem before the dawning of a new day.

A year after Edison and his tireless crew settled in Menlo Park, the sound of a human voice was recorded for the first time. It was Edison's most original invention—and his favorite.

On Dec. 6, 1877, the inventor turned a handle attached to a cylinder and spoke into a diaphragm. The first words that came into his mind were: "Mary had a little lamb, its fleece was white as snow."

The next day, Edison took his talking machine to the Scientific American office in New York. T.A. Edison was proclaimed the "Wizard of Menlo Park."

On the evening of April 18, 1878, New Jersey's most famous resident demonstrated his phonograph before President Rutherford B. Hayes and friends. The impossible had become possible. From that day on, thousands of reporters, scientists and curiosity seekers streamed to Menlo Park to catch a glimpse of the wizard at work.

By 31, Thomas Alva Edison had become a legend.

His greatest achievements, however, were still incubating in his remote hilltop lab.

Since the 1860s, electric arc lamps had glowed in lighthouses and were appearing more frequently on streets to light up the nights. But they consumed large amounts of electricity and released noxious odors. They were also impractical; the light was blinding for anyone who got too near one.

Edison envisioned practical lighting on every street, in every room, house and factory, a new form of electric energy for cooking, heating and running motors.

The response from the scientific community was something Edison expected. The reputable English electrician John T. Sprague declared:

"Neither Mr. Edison nor anyone else can override the well known laws of nature, and when he is made to say that the same wire which brings you light will also bring you power and heat, there is no difficulty in seeing that more is promised than can possibly be performed."

* * *

For nearly a year, Edison and his research staff labored on the development of a practical light bulb. The scientific world waited, and most felt Edison would fail.

Edison had worked out a successful principle for the electric light. What he needed was a proper filament, or wire, that gave a good light when electricity flowed through it. In his search for a perfect filament material, Edison sent agents into the Amazon jungles and the forests of Japan.

The missing piece of his puzzle was to be found on his desk. He rolled a piece of ordinary thread in carbon and shaped it into a filament. He then hardened the carbonized thread in a furnace and attached it in the bulb. He drew out the air, creating a vacuum, and turned on the electric current.

The clear glass bulb glowed. It was Oct. 19, 1879. The bulb remained lit all the next day and into the third day, when Edison decided to increase the voltage. At 1:30 p.m, Oct. 21, with a jolt of electricity, the bulb burned out.

Edison had proven his bulb was a practical alternative to the glaring, stinking and expensive arc lamp.

On Dec. 17, 1879, after 260 successful tests of his incandescent lamps, Edison filed his U.S. patent for the electric light bulb.

But a light bulb without a power source is a useless conversation piece. So Edison and his research family set out to create an entire electric production system capable of providing a current for his bulb and any other electric gadgets already in use.

At that time, each electric product had to have its own individual power source, a costly proposition that only the very rich could afford.

To make the clean light bulb and electricity available for everyone, the Menlo Park laboratory turned out generators, conduits, switches, meters, fuses, relays, sockets and insulated wire.

On Dec. 31, 1879, Edison flipped a switch and the main street in Menlo Park lit up, together with the village homes and the wizard's wooden laboratory.

A year later, Edison announced he would light a full square of New York City. The current, he revealed, would come from a central generating station.

Again, the skeptics denounced him as a fake and publicity seeker.

It was certainly one of the most complex engineering feats ever undertaken. Every wire would be in conduits buried under streets, and switches would be installed so that every light unit operated independently of all others.

The world's first central power grid was built at 255 Pearl St. in lower Manhattan, in the heart of the nation's financial district. Those who worked here would profit most from Edison's mind-boggling experiments.

It took almost three years to complete the Pearl Street project, during which time Edison's stock plummeted and his financial supporters wondered if this weren't the wizard's great mistake.

Edison regarded it as his most formidable challenge. He told his fellow workers:

"The Pearl Street Station is the biggest and most responsible thing I have ever undertaken. It is a gigantic problem with many ramifications. There is no parallel in the world . . . All of our apparatus, devices and parts are home-devised and home-made. Our workers are completely new and without experience. What might happen in turning on the big current into the conductors under streets of New York, no one can say. The gas companies are our enemies and are keenly watching our every move, ready to pounce on us at the slightest failure."

On Sept. 4, 1882, a switch was pulled at the Pearl Street Station and 800 lamps suddenly blazed with light in more than 30 buildings.

The Pearl Street experiment was extended and other cities gradually accepted the Edison electric system. Roselle was one of the first.

Edison set up a lamp factory in East Newark (now Harrison) in 1881 and produced 135,000 bulbs the first year. The lamps, by today's lighting standards, were primitive, but they opened the door to a new electronic world without end.

The first to perceive that great untapped potential was Edison himself. During the development of his carbon filaments, Edison was confounded by the black soot that would build up on the inside of his glass bulbs. If he could get rid of it, more light could be radiated from the same electric charge.

Edison had begun in 1880 a series of painstaking steps to eliminate the sooty particles. By 1883, he added a wire to his lamp to prevent soot accumulations. That simple trick, which Edison patented on Nov. 15, 1883, was called the "Edison Effect." The patented electrical indicator was the first application in the field of electronics.

A half-century later, on Nov. 21, 1932, one of Edison's early sooty lamps was inserted in a radio set to replace a by-then advanced radio tube. The radio worked perfectly.

Edison had discovered the basic principle of radio and television transmission—20 years before the first radio tubes were invented.

* * *

Working 16 to 18 hours a day, six to seven days a week, Edison often neglected his family, although his wife and three children enjoyed all the comforts provided by a successful and widely idolized entrepreneur. Edison spent many nights sleeping on a pile of newspapers stacked under a staircase in his laboratory. His wife grew lonely and stout.

Her husband was hardly a romantic companion, as Edison's biographers later noted. He bathed infrequently because he had the notion that any change in his body temperature would affect his health and longevity. So it was not surprising that Mrs. Edison's bedroom door was locked on many nights during the inventor's most creative and productive years.

In July 1884, Mary Stilwell Edison contracted lethal typhoid fever. On Aug. 9, she died in Menlo Park.

Edison's daughter, Marion, 13, found her father "shaking with grief, weeping and sobbing." Edison could not believe his wife had died so young. It affected his concentration and his ability to cope with the growing demands imposed by his unending succession of inventions.

To take his mind off Mary's death, Edison's closest friend set out to find "the old man," now 37, a new wife.

Memorabilia and volumes of scientific works fill the inventor's library in West Orange.

Thomas Edison relaxes on the lawn of Glenmont, his estate in West Orange, where he died in 1931.

A year and a half passed before Edison met Mina Miller, the 18-year-old daughter of a wealthy Akron, Ohio toolmaker. It was the winter of 1885 and Edison was at the home of an old friend, Ezra Gilliland, who had known Edison since their wandering telegrapher days 20 years earlier.

Gilliland had become a prominent Boston businessman and, over the years, journeyed to Menlo Park to help his renowned friend develop projects.

The meeting at the Gillilands seemed to be "love at first sight" for the very eligible widower. Mina Miller played the piano and sang a few songs and Edison was "staggered" by her presence as he recorded in his diary during one of his business trips:

"Saw a lady who looked like Mina. Got thinking about Mina and came near being run over by a streetcar. If Mina interferes much more will have to take out an accident policy."

On Feb. 22, 1886, Thomas Edison, at 39, married Mina Miller, 19, in Akron. They honeymooned in Fort Myers, Fla., where Edison was building a winter home and laboratory.

Before their marriage, Edison purchased a mansion on a mountainside in West Orange (now Llewellyn Park) for $200,000. The 23-room Victorian home on the 13.5-acre Glenmont Estate was a fitting gift to a woman who would begin to polish a rough diamond of a man into a proper gentleman.

In the summer of 1887, Edison erected the first modern research laboratory in West Orange. It was a 250-foot-long, three-story brick building stocked with everything from peacock tails to hog bristles. Four additions to the factory-like laboratory were built to house separate activities in metallurgy, chemistry, woodworking and testing galvanometers.

In the center of the main research building sat Edison's desk, encircled by one of the most comprehensive scientific libraries in the world. Edison wanted his laboratory to be a creative factory to transform the "raw material" of ideas into useful products to attract industry to the pastoral valley.

The valley—and New Jersey—became one of the industrial centers of America. Today, the Garden State remains the most densely industrial region in the United States.

While West Orange prospered from Edison's presence, the inventor's original research lab at Menlo Park eventually was turned into a chicken hatchery.

* * *

On the 50th anniversary of the invention of the light bulb, Henry Ford, who by then had been a hiking companion of Edison, moved the Menlo Park lab—"lock, stock and red earth underneath"—to Dearborn, Mich., where it is known as the Edison Institute. Ford had Edison's personal chair nailed immovably to the lab's worn floorboards.

In West Orange, Edison perfected the motion picture camera, using a new celluloid film developed by George Eastman, founder of the Kodak Co. Edison thought motion pictures would do for the eye what the phonograph did for the ear.

On Oct. 6, 1889, Edison projected an experimental motion picture in his laboratory, giving birth to sound pictures as well. The first movie was actually a "talkie." The moving picture sequence was accompanied by synchronized sound from a phonograph record.

Edison applied for a patent on the motion picture camera on July 31, 1891. The first commercial showing of motion pictures occurred three years later, April 14, 1894, with the opening of a "peephole" Kinetoscope parlor at 1155 Broadway, New York City.

Commercialization of motion pictures as we know it today began on April 23, 1896, at Koster and Bial's Music Hall in Manhattan, where the Edison Vitascope was used. The Vitascope was Edison's name for the motion picture projector. When he added sound, Edison called it the Kinetophone, which he introduced commercially in 1913, or 13 years before Hollywood adopted that means of improving motion picture entertainment.

Movies had their origin in a black, square structure where the first pictures were made under the watchful eye of inventor-director Edison. He saw the new gadget as an educational tool, not an entertainment device.

Edison's studio, dubbed the "Black Maria" for the black police paddy wagons used to pick up prisoners, revolved on wheels to catch sunlight.

Performers streamed to West Orange to participate in this new visual medium. And they worked without pay just to appear before the camera.

Some of the big stars who made their film debuts in West Orange were Buffalo Bill, Annie Oakley and the Gaiety Girls of New York.

Edison developed captions and better projectors and film splicing to produce 14-minute features.

The first story picture ever filmed, "The Great Train Robbery," was shot in the Jersey countryside in 1911 so that it would look like a western setting. It was the birth of the motion picture industry.

During his West Orange years, Edison also raised his second family: Charles, who one day would be Secretary of the Navy and governor of New Jersey; Madeleine, and Theodore, who, like his father, was an inventor and "maverick" and became an outspoken conservationist. Theodore, 87, lives in Llewellyn Park near his father's estate with his wife, a chemist.

On Oct. 21, 1929, the 50th anniversary of the incandescent light, Edison was again honored for his dazzling achievements. President Herbert Hoover, Albert Einstein, Henry Ford and other world figures gathered to reenact the making of the first practical electric lamp.

Shortly before his death in his Glenmont home on Oct. 18, 1931, Edison produced rubber from goldenrod grown in his experimental gardens at Ft. Myers, Fla.

His lifetime embraced three major wars and as many depressions. His mission, as he once reflected late in his life, was "to do everything within my power to further free the people from drudgery and create the largest possible measure of happiness and prosperity."

Edison's unprecedented legacy lives on at the Edison National Historic Site in West Orange. The laboratories and the Glenmont estate are national museums that reveal the life and times of an unschooled inventor whose work improved the fundamental structure of industrialized society.

Star-Ledger Photo

The "Black Maria" studio, nicknamed after police paddy wagons, revolved on a turntable to make the best use of light for Edison's filmmaking activities.

Nassau Hall, Princeton University.

EDUCATION

$\mathcal{T}$he history of higher education in America parallels the birth and growth of two New Jersey institutions and a new nation in quest of independence and knowledge.

Princeton and Rutgers universities, both founded before the American Revolution, helped lay the foundation for a new society's academic, cultural and political future.

More delegates to the Constitutional Congress were products of Princeton than any other school within the Colonies or in England. Princeton also graduated two U.S. presidents—James Madison and Woodrow Wilson—and more than 80 United States senators, the latest being Bill Bradley. More than a dozen Nobel Prize winners have also been associated with Princeton.

Other educational "firsts" for New Jersey are the oldest student literary magazine in the U.S. and the oldest political debating society in the world. The first college football game was played between Rutgers and Princeton in 1869 and the first Catholic diocesan university in the nation was established in the Garden State.

The Mechanical Society of America was founded at Stevens Institute of Technology in Hoboken, and the first commercial college radio station was licensed in New Jersey. A global computer network has been organized by the New Jersey Institute of Technology in Newark, while Fairleigh Dickinson University set up the nation's first overseas campus at old Trinity College

in Oxford, England, as well as a tropical research laboratory in the West Indies.

Over the past two centuries, New Jersey has created an academic environment that has nourished five universities, 23 four-year colleges, 19 two-year colleges, two engineering colleges, a medical college, dental college and seven theological colleges.

From the Assumption College for Sisters in Mendham to Westminster Choir College in Princeton, some 60 centers of higher learning have put New Jersey in the forefront of public and private education. The educational system today serves more than 321,000 college students seeking to enrich themselves in their chosen field of endeavor.

The four-year state colleges are: Glassboro, Jersey City, Kean, Montclair, Ramapo, Stockton, Thomas Edison, Trenton and William Paterson.

The community colleges are: Atlantic, Bergen, Brookdale (Monmouth County), Burlington, Camden, Cumberland, Essex, Gloucester, Hudson, Mercer, Middlesex, Morris, Ocean, Passaic, Salem, Somerset and Union, with plans on the horizon for two more two-year schools in Sussex and Warren counties.

Princeton University

The word "campus" was first used to describe the academic setting at Princeton University, America's fourth oldest institution of higher education, regarded as one of the greatest schools in the world.

Founded as the College of New Jersey in 1746 by charter of King George II, the school was originally located in Elizabeth and later in Newark. In 1756, the New Jersey college moved into its new home in Princeton, Nassau Hall. At the time of its completion, Nassau Hall was the largest public building in the American Colonies.

Nassau Hall witnessed the birth of a new nation, serving as the temporary center of the Continental Congress in 1783 and surviving bombardment during the Battle of Princeton on Jan. 3, 1777, the turning point in the American Revolution. In its first half-century, Nassau Hall, now a National Historic Landmark, housed the entire college: Students, faculty, administration, chapel, library, dining room, kitchen and dormitories.

The legendary stone structure also sheltered the troops of both sides of the Revolution. George Washington routed the British in 1777 and returned in 1783 to receive the thanks of the Continental Congress for his conduct of the war. A commemorative postage stamp was issued to celebrate the 1956 bicentennial of Nassau Hall.

More delegates to the 1787 Constitutional Congress, which formed the United States federal government, were graduates of Princeton than any other American or British university. Since then, Princeton has turned out two U.S. presidents: Madison, one of the fathers of the new democracy, and Wilson, who conceived of a global community that evolved into today's United Nations.

The Princeton campus, an intriguing blend of European Gothic influences and contemporary, modern edifices, covers 2,300 acres of greens and pathways landscaped just enough for that ivy-league, lived-in look. The student body has grown to 4,500 undergraduates and 1,550 post-graduates enrolled in more than 60 departments and programs within three schools: Architecture, Engineering and Applied Science, and Public and International Affairs.

Two baccalaureate, seven master's and one doctoral degree are offered at Princeton. The faculty of 726 includes 328 professors, 64 associate professors, 196 assistant professors, 122 lecturers, 75 visiting faculty, and 16 instructors. There are 110 endowed professorships, plus 367 part-time assistants in instruction, 93 professional librarians and 177 persons engaged in research and related activities.

Undergraduates come from all 50 states, Puerto Rico and 46 foreign countries.

Another notable landmark on the Princeton campus is the Florentine-style Prospect Mansion, home of university presidents from James McCosh to Robert Goheen, the immediate past president. (William Bowen, the current overseer, is the first not to take up residency in the famed mansion.)

The Prospect house, completed in 1849, replaced an 18th Century stone farmhouse built by Col. George Morgan, an explorer of the western United States and an Indian affairs agent who named his home "Prospect" for its commanding view of the Princeton countryside. Morgan's estate was a popular resting spot in Revolutionary times, being visited by such diverse groups as a delegation of Delaware Indians, 2,000 mutinous soliders of the Pennsylvania Line, and members of the Continental Congress.

The Harvey S. Firestone Library is the heart of the university library system, distinguished by its "open stack" design to bring books and students together. There are no call slips to fill out, no long wait for important publications; students simply go to the shelves and find the books they want.

Undergraduates have at their fingertips more than 3.5 million books and microforms, more than 30,000 current journals and documents and other library materials ranging from manuscripts and maps to prints and papyri. These include an enormous wealth of research material, such as the papers of Woodrow Wilson, Adlai Stevenson and John Foster Dulles, and major holdings of American and English writers, including Hemingway, Fitzgerald (a Princeton student), T.S. Eliot and Thomas Wolfe.

The Princeton library houses the archives of the American Civil Liberties Union, and the Gest Oriental Library (in Palmer-Jones Hall), which contains one of the world's most valuable collections of fine and rare Chinese books.

The Seeley G. Mudd Manuscript Library preserves the papers of such 20th Century figures as Bernard Baruch, James Forrestal, Class of 1915, and Adlai Stevenson, Class of 1922.

With more than 100 miles of shelving, some 3,500 study seats, including 1,200 closed carrel seats, and 40 computer terminals, the Princeton Library devotes more than a half-million square feet of space to library services.

* * *

The Princeton campus exhibits a major collection of outdoor sculpture, featuring works by Alexander Calder, Henry Moore, George Segal, David Smith and Louise Nevelson. Pablo Picasso's "Head of a Woman" greets visitors at the entrance of the University Art Museum. Collections range from art of the ancient world, including rare classical, Oriental and pre-Columbian objects, to Renaissance, modern European and American painting and sculpture. There are also outstanding holdings of original prints, drawings and photographs.

The museum's collections have been shaped by the department's curriculum. Representative elements of the collections include Egyptian, Greek and Roman antiquities; Medieval paintings, sculpture and works of art, such as a stained glass window from Chartres, and a large sampling of Renaissance paintings reflecting major artistic trends during that period.

The museum also maintains a collection of French works of the 18th and 19th centuries, and a group of American paintings and sculpture following the development of those arts in the United States.

The Natural History Museum, founded in 1856, is teeming with several hundred thousand archeological, biological and geological specimens. There are samples of most of the world's minerals and gems, fossils brought back to Princeton from expeditions to the Far West and Patagonia, and fossils discovered during excavations for the 150 buildings on the campus.

Among the museum's most popular displays are skeletons of a sabre-toothed tiger, a three-toed horse, a giant pig, a mastodon, and a 75-million-year-old baby duckbill dinosaur, one of 15 found in a nest in Montana in 1978.

Many single specimens and collections, particularly the fossil vertebrates and materials pertaining to the earliest American Indians, are of international fame.

The Woodrow Wilson School of Public and International Affairs, Princeton's only selective concentration, annually enrolls 60 sophomores. The school combines courses in the history, politics, economics and sociology departments for a program preparing students for leadership in public affairs at the local, state, national and international levels.

Founded in 1930 as a joint effort of the departments of economics, history and politics, the school was officially named in 1948 for the 28th President of the United States.

The school's handsome exterior is surrounded by 58 quartz-surfaced concrete columns supporting the bulk of the building's weight. The new school was dedicated in 1966 by President Lyndon B. Johnson.

Undergraduates engage in junior and senior independent work involving a Policy Conference on Public Affairs dealing with a current and controversial topic, and a Policy Task Force, analyzing issues of public policy and recommending lines of action.

* * *

Princeton is a higher learning center that ushered in many "firsts."

A unique hallmark of Princeton's education experience is the preceptorial, a variety of small classes that seeks to avoid professor-dominated instructional settings. A professor of religion, for instance, puts such an emphasis on student participation that each precept is silent until a student initiates the discussion.

Students and teacher come to each session prepared to work together to understand a given problem or thought. Groups are kept small, averaging about 10 students. Most courses at Princeton, both upperclass and underclass, consist of a combination of weekly lectures and preceptorials. As members of the faculty, several deans and the president of the university have led preceptorials in their respective fields.

The American Whig-Cliosophic Society, Princeton's largest extra-curricular organization, is the oldest college political and debating society in the world. Today, Whig-Clio sponsors 16 subsidiary organizations related to public affairs and the development of skills in speech and debate. The speakers' program brings about 20 speakers of national prominence to campus each academic year. They are invited to participate in informal seminars, receptions and dinners with Whig-Clio members, as well as to deliver the traditional formal address.

Some recent participants have been David Rockefeller, John Kenneth Galbraith, George Gallup, Choi Zemin (ambassador from the People's Republic of China), Oriana Fallaci and Brooklyn District Attorney Elizabeth Holtzman.

The Nassau Literary Review is the nation's oldest student-run literary magazine. Published at least twice a year by a staff of 50 and distributed free to undergraduates, its features include creative writing, essays, interviews, drawings and photographs.

The nation's first commercially licensed college station is WPRB, the Princeton student-run outlet founded in 1942 and licensed in 1955. It currently transmits 17,000 watts at 103.3 FM stereo and covers all of central New Jersey and parts of New York and Pennsylvania.

Because the station is a member of the American FM Network, a division of ABC News, it combines the advantages of a national news source with the opportunity, as a student-run station, to be unusually creative in its programming. WPRB's daily schedule includes morning classical and jazz shows, in addition to the progressive rock that composes the majority of the station's air sound. Many students also participate in Focus on Youth, a nationally broadcast program in which the world's most important people are featured regularly.

The Princeton Triangle Club, whose alumni include James Stewart, Jose Ferrer and playwright Joshua Logan, produces and tours an entirely original musical show each year.

The 100-member Princeton Glee Club, founded in 1874, has performed with major orchestras throughout the country and has toured Europe, Central and South America, and, recently, the Far East and the People's Republic of China.

The Tokamak Fusion Test Reactor at the university's Plasma Physics Laboratory, Forrestal Campus, is expected to be the first fusion device to produce energy in any significant quantity by the mid-1980s. Fusion is the chemical process by which the sun generates its heat energy in the hundreds of millions of degrees Fahrenheit.

America's first college football game was played between Princeton and neighboring Rutgers University in New Brunswick. The score of that historic game on Nov. 2, 1869 was Rutgers, six goals, Princeton, four goals. There were 25 players on each team.

Rutgers University

At first a theological school, then a private college, followed by a land-grant institution and, finally, a state university, Rutgers today is a major academic community of 48,000 students and 2,500 faculty members.

It all began in 1766 as a little Dutch Reformed school along the Raritan River in New Brunswick. Named Queens College, its identity was changed in 1825 when a Revolutionary War soldier and philanthropist, Col. Henry Rutgers, donated $5,000 to "Old Queens." The gift also included a charming brass bell, which still chimes in the cupola of the Old Queens Administration Building.

Photo Credit: Jeff Newman

"William the Silent" stands vigil on the campus of Rutgers University in New Brunswick.

Ranked among the foremost universities in the United States, Rutgers has evolved into a major educational-cultural institution whose students and faculty members represent every state in the nation and 64 foreign countries. They can be found at three separate campuses: New Brunswick, Newark and Camden.

The faculty forms the basis of the Rutgers tradition of excellence, as exemplified by the late Dr. Selman Waksman, recipient of the Nobel Prize in Medicine for his discovery of streptomycin, an antibiotic effective in the treatment of tuberculosis.

More than 90 percent of the present Rutgers faculty hold the Ph.D. or equivalent highest degree in their respective disciplines. One professor of English recently won the coveted National Book Award. A university virologist was awarded the 1982 Wolf Foundation Agriculture Prize ($100,000), the highest honor given in that field.

Three current faculty members have been elected to the prestigious National Academy of Science. Another professor, in communications, is chairman of the board of the Motion Picture Association's Classification and Rating Administration. And a humanities professor serves as one of the three distinguished editors of the Library of America, the definitive edition of American literature classics.

The most renowned professors regularly teach undergraduate classes. The student-faculty ratio at Rutgers is about 16 to one.

Each year, the Rutgers campuses host scores of concerts, speakers, exhibits, plays, films, performances and special events. A typical calendar of events would show such luminary figures as virtuoso violinist Itzhak Perlman ... rock performers Jorma Kaukonen and the Allman Brothers Band ... jazz artists Ron Carter, Kenneth Barron and John McLaughlin ... literary voices ranging from Beat poet Allen Ginsberg and feminist author Maya Angelou to critics Hugh Kenner and Richard Ellmann ... a diversity of speakers from U.S. Sen. Bill Bradley to former Iranian hostages Barry Rosen and Kathryn Koob ... annual celebrations such as the New Jersey Folk Festival, Black History Week and Oktoberfest ... special symposiums such as Newark's "James Joyce and Modernism" centennial ... and art exhibits presenting student and faculty shows and major openings such as the "International Works on Paper" on the Camden campus, plus dozens of movies.

Rutgers was cited several years ago for "excellence in academic computing" by a national study funded through the National Science Foundation. The superb facilities at the Center for Computer and Information Services provide centralized batch and time-sharing access and boast large mainframes as well as microcomputers. Computer capabilities can be tapped by students and teachers of history, physics, political science or statistics, practically any subject or theme from A to Z.

The university library is one of the top 15 research resources in the nation; its branches contain more than 3 million volumes and supplementary materials. Electron microscopes can be found at any of the number of extensive scientific laboratories throughout the university. There are also studios for art, dance and music, and several university theaters ranging in design from the traditional to the experimental.

Three Rutgers art galleries hold more than 5,000 paintings, prints and sculptures. More than 20 special institutes enhance the "Rutgers experience," among them the Waksman Institute of Microbiology, the Center for Urban Policy Research, the Institute of Jazz Studies, the Bureau of Engineering Research, and the Eagleton Institute of Politics. The century-old Rutgers Geology Museum features the skeleton of a prehistoric mastodon and an Egyptian sarcophagus among its extensive exhibits.

Many Rutgers students achieve academic distinction. A junior chemistry major has logged more than 500 hours of laboratory research in an independent project to discover a synthetic drug for use in treating cancer. In 1982, another student conducted a complete orchestral performance for the first time in university history. A student from China (who taught herself calculus and physics before entering college), earned straight A's as an engineering major and won a prestigious Bell Laboratory scholarship for graduate study. Another senior, majoring in computer science, received 18 job offers before graduation.

* * *

Undergraduate students at the New Brunswick campus enroll in one of eight colleges. Four are liberal arts schools: Douglass, Livingston, Rutgers and University colleges. Four are professional schools: Cook College, Mason Gross School of the Arts, College of Engineering, and College of Pharmacy.

The colleges are located on both sides of the Raritan River. Within this campus setting are cultural attractions that include the George Street Playhouse, the Crossroads Theater, the Princeton Ballet, and several concert series ranging from symphony to rock.

Douglass, with an enrollment of 3,674, is the nation's largest women's college, founded in 1918 as the New Jersey College for Women. It was renamed in 1955.

Livingston opened its doors in 1965 as a modern college complex whose student body today numbers nearly 3,500.

Rutgers College is the eighth oldest institution of higher learning in America, its past linked with the history of Queens College. The majority of Rutgers College students ranked in the upper percentages of their high school classes. Enrollment has reached 8,360.

University College is one of the nation's few undergraduate evening colleges for adults that is served by its own administrative staff and faculty fellows. Founded in 1934, University College is made up of 3,428 students.

Cook College, with an enrollment of 2,816, boasts the longest history of work in environmental studies of any institution in the country. Founded in 1921 as the College of Agriculture, it became Cook College in 1973 and conducts teaching and research with emphasis in the environmental and agricultural sciences.

The Mason Gross School of the Arts is a recent Rutgers addition, having been established in 1976 as the School of the Creative and Performing Arts. With an enrollment of just 272 students, the school offers degrees in theater and visual arts, music and dance.

The College of Engineering (enrollment: 2,665) was founded in 1864 as the Rutgers Scientific school, while the College of Pharmacy (772 students) was incorporated into the university in 1892.

The Rutgers-Newark campus includes the Newark College of Arts and Sciences, the College of Nursing, University College, and, on the graduate level, the School of Law, the Graduate School of Management and the School of Criminal Justice. Campus resources include special divisions such as the Center for International Business Cycle Research and the Institute of Jazz Studies. There are about 7,500 students at the Newark campus studying in more than 30 fields.

The Rutgers-Camden branch is a commuter campus, attracting more than 5,000 students to the College of Arts and Sciences, University College, the Weekend College, the Graduate School of Law, and the Graduate School-Camden. The campus is set against a backdrop of handsome Victorian buildings and modern edifices erected since the Camden campus became part of the growing Rutgers family in 1927.

Seton Hall University

In 1856, Seton Hall University was founded as the first diocesan college in the United States. A diocese is a Catholic district under the jurisdiction of a bishop. Seton Hall was established as a university in 1950.

James Roosevelt Bayley, the first bishop of Newark and founder of the diocesan college, named the school after his aunt, St. Elizabeth Ann Seton, a Catholic convert like himself. Elizabeth Seton was founder of the first American community of the Sisters of Charity.

The original enrollment of five students in 1856 grew rapidly and four years later the college moved from its first home in Madison (which became the site of St. Elizabeth's College) to its present location in South Orange. Early the following year, the diocesan college was incorporated and chartered by the State of New Jersey.

During the first 12-year period, 531 students entered the college. By the 12th year, the select student body grew to 119; there were 17 seminarians and 16 faculty members, including four priests. Students came from places as far away as Mexico, Brazil, France, Italy, Spain and Cuba, as well as 17 states.

Seton Hall continues to operate under the auspices of the Roman Catholic Archdiocese of Newark. The university, spread out over a 58-acre campus in the Village of South Orange, is composed of six schools: The College of Arts and Sciences, the W. Paul Stillman School of Business, the School of Education, the College of Nursing, and University College, all on the South Orange campus, and the School of Law in Newark.

In addition to more than 40 undergraduate major programs, the university offers 43 graduate programs. Full-time undergraduate enrollment has reached approximately 6,700 men and women. Total university enrollment now exceeds 10,000.

The campus of Seton Hall University, South Orange.

Star-Ledger Photo

Seton Hall offers a "Judaeo-Christian perspective on the long and continuing journey of mankind. To be a Catholic university requires that the constituencies of the university bring such a Judaeo-Christian judgment and choice of values into every aspect of the life of the university, integrating the educational task with faith, hope and charity."

Catholicism at Seton Hall is "for us not a restrictive creed, but an enabling vision calling for all that is best and authentically human." This is the way the university faculty describes its role in the annual Undergraduate Bulletin.

At Seton Hall, the study of ethics, the quest for social and economic justice, the debates of political theories, the analyses of the economic order, the uses of the natural sciences, the conduct of business, the practice of the professions—all are moral efforts. Toward that end, the university's board of regents has approved the foundation of an Institute of Professional Ethics to explore and offer guidance on those issues.

The high caliber of the university's programs is recognized by national accrediting bodies. The W. Paul Stillman School of Business, for example, became the first undergraduate school in New Jersey to receive accreditation by the American Assembly of Collegiate Schools of Business in 1978.

The Stillman Business School publishes the popular, semi-annual Mid-Atlantic Journal of Business. Also an integral part of the school are the Institute of International Business and the Labor Relations Institute, which presents seminars for labor and industry.

Seton Hall College was organized into a university in 1950 and was composed of the College of Arts and Sciences and the Schools of Business Administration, Education and Nursing. The School of Law opened in Newark in 1951. In 1955, Seton Hall launched New Jersey's first college of medicine and dentistry, later taken over by the state.

The Seton Hall Law School is the only law school in New Jersey operated by a private university. It offers the only law school summer session in the state. Total enrollment is 1,000, making it the largest law school in New Jersey and the 21th largest in the nation.

Seton Hall became coeducational in 1968.

Drew University

Founded in 1866 as the Drew Theological Seminary, Drew University today is an independent institution with a College of Liberal Arts, a graduate school, and one of the most distinguished theological schools in the United States.

Students chat outside the gateway to Drew University, a distinguished theological and liberal arts school in Madison.

Photo Credit: Phil Degginger

The liberal arts college was opened in 1928 and the graduate school in 1955. The university presently enrolls 2,500 men and women in all divisions, 300 in the graduate school.

The Drew campus in Madison embraces 186 acres of woodlands and 42 buildings, including one National Historic Landmark. The graduate school occupies the stately Samuel W. Brown Hall, constructed in 1912, whose Great Hall is styled after the one in Christ Church Hall at Oxford.

Home of the renowned Shakespeare Festival of New Jersey, the university has been affiliated with the United Methodist Church since its inception.

Drew Library is the third largest academic library in New Jersey. Its special strengths are in archeology, English and American literature, 19th Century thought, political science and theology.

In 1981, the United Methodist Archives and History Center was added to the library, an acquisition that is expected to make Drew the research center for the denomination. Because Methodism was transplanted to America during the revolutionary era, its history parallels the cultural history of the United States. The archives are a valuable resource for secular studies.

In 1955, the Graduate School Colloquium has attracted prominent speakers from all walks of life. Among the outstanding lecture-scholars who have participated in the Drew Colloquium have been Reinhold Niebuhr, Paul Tillich, Daniel Boorstin, William F. Buckley Jr. and Tom Wicker. They have addressed such topics as "The Future of the Humanities in a Time of Crisis" and "Civil Religion in America."

Fairleigh Dickinson University

The state's newest university is also one of the largest in the nation. The first students were admitted to FDU, then a junior college, on Sept. 12, 1942, at its first campus in Rutherford. The Teaneck-Hackensack campus was opened in 1954 and the Florham-Madison campus in 1958. Graduate studies began in 1954 and the professional School of Dentistry was certified in 1956. The

"The Castle," Fairleigh Dickinson University's first building, located in Rutherford, today houses general administrative offices.

Photo Credit: Junious Jones

FDU extension in Wayne was opened in 1965. FDU attained full university status on June 12, 1956. Today's enrollment exceeds 19,000.

FDU is distinguished by America's first overseas campus, Wroxton College, situated in the ancestral home of Lord North at Wroxton Abbey in Oxfordshire, lying between Oxford and Stratford-on-Avon, England.

A center for graduate and undergraduate study, Wroxton College opened in the summer of 1965. FDU acquired the historic Wroxton Abbey from Trinity College, Oxford University. Students come to Wroxton from a wide range of American universities and participate in an academic program serviced by a resident English faculty and visiting British scholars.

The abbey is an integral part of local life, as students are welcomed into neighboring homes and participate in village activities.

In the fall and spring semesters, undergraduate courses are offered in education, including teaching practice; English literature, which interacts with the Royal Shakespeare Theatre; British history; political science; sociology; economics and fine arts. Graduate courses toward a master's degree in English language and literature are offered during Wroxton College's annual summer session.

Another FDU foreign campus is its West Indies Laboratory, a tropical teaching and research field lab located on the east end of St. Croix, Virgin Islands, facing the coral reef bordering Tague Bay.

The present laboratory includes classrooms, library, research labs, dock-site storeroom, dining hall, dormitory, machine shop, sewage treatment plant and an auxiliary power plant.

The FDU West Indies Laboratory offers graduate and undergraduate courses and provides year-round special projects and research facilities.

* * *

There are three technical institutes in New Jersey—one of them a "think tank"—that are known throughout the world for their exceptional curriculums and pioneering programs in engineering and science. Collectively, they put New Jersey in the vanguard of high-tech knowledge and skills that are reshaping the world, including outer space.

Stevens Institute of Technology

An interdisciplinary approach to technology and science is the basis of the Stevens educational philosophy. Dr. Kenneth C. Rogers, president of Stevens, calls it putting "fundamentals first." All freshmen must take calculus, physics, chemistry, computers, humanities and physical education.

Whether working for degrees in engineering, science, systems planning and management, Stevens students learn the basics before concentrating on chemical, civil, electrical, industrial, mechanical, metallurgical or ocean engineering, computer science, engineering physics, chemical biology, chemistry, computer science, materials science, mathematics and physics.

Stevens was the first major college in the country to require freshmen to have a personal computer. All freshmen are expected to own the Digital Equipment Corp. Professional 350, one of the most sophisticated personal computers on the market, especially for scientific and technical applications.

Use of the personal computer, of the minicomputers on campus and Stevens' mainframe DEC-10, is integrated throughout the entire undergraduate program and helps to bring traditional courses to a new level of sophistication. All of Stevens' computer efforts are directed at turning out students who are computer fluent and who can thrive in a professional environment where the computer plays an increasingly pervasive role.

the first mechanical engineering laboratory named after the famed industrialist-philanthropist.

L. Alan Hazeltine, who taught at Stevens for more than three decades, invented the neutrodyne radio receiver, which neutralized feedback noise and permitted finer selectivity of tuning in early radio.

Professor Kenneth Davidson began to test ship models in the institute swimming pool in the early 1930s. The Davidson Laboratory, the largest campus-based hydrodynamics lab of its kind in the U.S., has included among its investigations the tracking of underwater missiles in anti-submarine warfare, the testing and development of nearly all of the U.S. Navy's torpedoes, and the testing of the Polaris missile.

Star-Ledger Photo

The "Tower" at Stevens Institute of Technology in Hoboken is a focal point of the 55-acre campus overlooking the Hudson.

The history of Stevens, as researched by Rogers, dates back to the American Revolution and the Industrial Revolution. John Stevens, a Revolutionary War colonel, purchased from the state land that today includes the present 55-acre campus on a promontory in Hoboken known as Castle Point, overlooking the Hudson River and New York City.

Col. Stevens introduced the steam ferry to New York Harbor and experimented with the first American steam locomotive, which ran on a track in Hoboken in 1825.

The colonel's son, Robert, invented the T-rail, or solid steel railroad track still used today. With Edwin, another son, Robert built and operated the first commercial railroad in the United States—and they ran it profitably.

On his own, Edwin helped design and build the first ironclad vessels for the U.S. Navy. With yet another brother, John Cox Stevens, Edwin joined the syndicate that built and owned the yacht, America. The sleek vessel defeated all the English contenders to become the first winner of the now coveted trophy known as the America's Cup.

John Cox was the first commodore of the New York Yacht Club, which was organized aboard his schooner Gimcrack, docked at the Hoboken waterfront.

When Edwin Stevens died in 1868, his will provided for the establishment of a college bearing his family's name. The trustees decided to make Stevens an engineering college with a curriculum leading to a single degree they called "Mechanical Engineering."

The first president of Stevens, Henry Morton, already had established a reputation, by age 34, of having been the first to have fully translated the hieroglyphics on the Rosetta Stone.

On the original faculty was the eminent mechanical engineer and pioneer engineering educator Robert H. Thurston, the first president of the American Society of Mechanical Engineers, which was formed at Stevens in 1880. Thurston was responsible for the creation at Stevens of the first mechanical engineering laboratory in the United States.

The movement called "scientific management" had its roots at Stevens, which cultivated the professional engineering entrepreneur. A trustee, Andrew Carnegie, donated the funds for

Courtesy: Stevens Institute of Technology

The rotating arm tests naval ship models in Davison Labs at Stevens Institute of Technology.

The U.S.S. George Washington, the world's first nuclear-propelled, missile-launching submarine, was designed with the help of tests done in the Stevens tanks.

The America's Cup yacht races, identified with the Stevens family since the original 1851 contest, have also figured in the laboratory's history. Since Ranger in 1937, the hull configuration of every America's Cup defender has been model-tested at Stevens.

The Davidson lab also conducts research on such problems as losses in water supply systems, design of drainage systems, and environmental impact of wastes in rivers and bays.

Charles Stewart Mott, Class of 1897 and founder of General Motors, gave the funds to construct the Mott Field House in 1947.

The Samuel C. Williams Library, dedicated in 1961, contains more than 100,000 volumes, and one of the largest and best collections in the United States on Leonardo da Vinci. The library also contains the Stevens Computer Center and is graced by a specially designed mobile contributed by its creator, Alexander Calder, Class of 1919.

Today, undergraduates number about 1,600, of whom 16 percent are women. There are more than 40 special interest clubs, including electronics, sports cars, chess and sky diving.

New Jersey Institute of Technology

Computers have revolutionized modern society and the New Jersey Institute of Technology in Newark is at the crux of that technical revolution.

The "bible" of the new computer industry is being written by Stewart Brand, author of the global best-seller, "The Whole Earth Catalog," published in 1968 with more than 2.5 million copies now in print.

Brand's latest planetary compendium of mail-order tools is "The Whole Earth Software Catalog," published by Doubleday & Co. The key to the new computer catalog's success is a mini-network of computer whizzes sharing informed opinions about software within an international collection of more than 1,900 users called EIES, for Electronic Information Exchange System.

Star-Ledger Photo

Lecture hall/classroom in Tiernan Hall, New Jersey Institute of Technology, Newark.

Star-Ledger Photo

A winding staircase and circular skylight enhance the library on the NJIT campus.

Operated by the New Jersey Institute of Technology, EIES has counted among its membership author Alvin Toffler and former Federal Communications Commissioner Nicholas Johnson. For his latest information tome, Brand tapped the expertise of EIES and invited its entire community to recommend favorite pieces of software to his Whole Earth catalog.

The finished book runs more than 200 pages with 600 recommendations.

The new "computer bible" is just one example of the many innovations at NJIT helping to redefine and improve a rapidly changing, high-tech civilization.

Another is the Institute for Hazardous and Toxic Waste Management. NJIT was the first higher learning center in America to introduce a hazardous waste management program at the postgraduate level in 1981. It brought together under one director the Environmental Engineering graduate programs and the research activities of the Environmental Systems Laboratory, the Air Monitoring Laboratory, the Water Monitoring Laboratory and the Center for Law and Technology. The new institute was organized by Dr. John W. Liskowitz, professor of environmental engineering.

NJIT started life in 1881 as the Newark Technical School. For most of its life it was referred to as NCE, the Newark College of Engineering. The technical complex today occupies a 34-acre campus in Newark's academic hub. Its neighbors are the Rutgers-Newark campus, Seton Hall Law School and Essex County College.

NJIT has been a fertile training ground for generations of technicians, from tinsmiths and harnessmakers to astronauts and inventors. During the school's centennial celebration, noted scientists participated in an international dialogue on "Technology and Society," the impact of man's contrivances on all life on the planet. Among the participants were Nobel Prize-winning physicist Arno Penzias from Bell Laboratories; popular science author Isaac Asimov; Edward Teller, pioneer of atomic and hydrogen energy, and Paul Gray, president of Massachusetts Institute of Technology (MIT).

More than 11,000 students avail themselves of NJIT's diverse technical facilities. Although science and engineering are the mainstay of NJIT, the humanities have also found a secure niche there. NJIT is also the home of the New Jersey Student Poetry Contest, the New Jersey Literary Hall of Fame and the New Jersey Young Filmmakers Festival.

NJIT grants degrees in chemical, civil, electrical, industrial and mechanical engineering; architecture; computer science; surveying; engineering technology; industrial administration, and applied chemistry.

In 1974, NJIT enhanced its traditional engineering mission to include New Jersey's first state-supported School of Architecture. Being the third oldest city in the United States, Newark has become a rich architectural laboratory, loaded with resource materials, design work, research collections and exhibits not duplicated anywhere in North America.

In 1983, NJIT established Third College, which includes programs in management, the humanities, computer and information science and the natural sciences.

The Institute for Advanced Study

It awards no degrees. It has an enrollment of only 200, or less. It has no scheduled courses of instruction. It maintains no laboratories. And its students are also teachers.

It is the Institute for Advanced Study, an academic haven for Nobel Prize winners and the most brilliant thinkers and problem-solvers of the 20th Century. One of its first student-teachers was Albert Einstein, who arrived there shortly after the school opened in 1930 and remained until his death in 1955. During that time, Einstein probed his mind for a unified design of the universe.

A wintry scene of the former Pingry High School campus, now owned by Kean College, Elizabeth.

Star-Ledger Photo

The institute was an idea of Louis Bamberger, the department store magnate, and his sister, Caroline Fuld. "Pure science and high scholarship" are what the Bambergers envisioned. Academic work today is carried out in four schools: Historical studies, mathematics, natural sciences and social sciences.

Among the former members, 14 have been awarded the Nobel Prize; eight the National Medal of Science; 19 the Fields Medal of the International Mathematical Union, the major international prize in mathematics; nine the Dannie Heineman Prize awarded jointly by the American Physical Society and the American Institute of Physics; four the Bancroft Prize in history, and six the Haskins Medal of the Medieval Academy of America.

The Princeton institute is also first among all public and private fellowship programs in the United States in the awarding of residential fellowships. The average is 160 a year.

Work done by visiting members in residence has resulted in more than 5,600 publications to date.

Members of the mathematics school are, for the most part, pure mathematicians, and members of the natural sciences school either theoretical physicists or astrophysicists and astronomers. Some members have worked in other sciences, notably chemistry, biology and psychology.

The School of Historical Studies tends to reflect the interests of the faculty: Greek archeology, epigraphy, Greek philosophy and philology, Roman history, paleography, medieval history, the history of art, modern history, the history of modern philosophy, American intellectual history, and the history of mathematics and the sciences.

Members of the School of Social Sciences have been drawn from the disciplines of anthropology, economics, history, political science, psychology, linguistics and sociology, among others.

The institute, which occupies a square mile of mostly farm and woodland, maintains a productive symbiotic relationship with Princeton University, having access to its libraries and other important resources. The institute has a small, specialized library of about 75,000 volumes, including 1,100 periodical titles. It also has a collection of 3,200 rare books.

Edison, Kean, Monmouth, Trenton . . .

Of New Jersey's 59 schools of higher learning, perhaps four best typify the wide range of interests available to the state's more than 1 million college-bound students.

Edison State College is New Jersey's "college without walls," the only institution of its kind in the country. It was founded in 1972 by the New Jersey Board of Higher Education to help adults earn college credit and degrees without necessarily attending formal colleges.

Edison College has become the lead institution in the State-wide Testing and Assessment Center, a group of New Jersey colleges that support the concept of earning college credits through college-equivalency examinations and assessment of knowledge gained outside the classroom.

Edison is currently participating in the largest educational grant program ever awarded by the Kellogg Foundation. The purpose of the grant is to improve services to the adult learner and Edison State College is responsible for that New Jersey activity.

Edison College is situated near the Capitol complex in Trenton. Commencement exercises are often held at the site of Thomas A. Edison's laboratories in West Orange.

* * *

Kean College of New Jersey receives more than 13,000 undergraduate and graduate students from all of the state's 21 counties. They study in the 60 major areas offered by the college, located in Union.

Founded in 1855 as the Normal School in Newark, the college was named after the Kean family on Oct. 19, 1973. The college occupies 120 acres that were once part of the Kean family estate. Gov. Thomas A. Kean is a member of the Kean family, which has been active in New Jersey's social, political and cultural development since the revolutionary period.

For more than a century, the school provided for the development of leaders in the field of education. Today, about 20 percent of the students are in a specialized education area. More than one-third are in applied disciplines, such as management and computer science, and about one-third are in liberal arts programs.

The Kean Classical Artists Series presents recognized young artists and unusual musical events to audiences from Union and Essex counties. The series is housed in the Wilkins Theatre at Kean College, a fine concert hall in the heart of Union County. The Kean Classical Artists series was founded in 1973 by Professor Herbert Golub, then chairman of the Kean College Music Department. Many major artists have performed in the series, including Marilyn Horne, Ruth Laredo and Jean-Pierre Rampal.

* * *

Monmouth College came into being in 1933 as Monmouth Junior College, one of six experimental institutions established in New Jersey as part of the social movements accompanying the Great Depression. Of the six, only two remain in operation: Monmouth College in West Long Branch and Union College in Cranford.

By 1956, Monmouth College outgrew its "high school home" in Long Branch and moved to the Shadow Lawn campus just down the road in West Long Branch, only a mile from the oceanfront. It now ranks as one of the largest private institutions in New Jersey, its alumni numbering more than 45,000. Students come from more than 20 states and 17 foreign countries.

One of the most beautiful campuses in the Garden State, Monmouth occupies the site of an ornate Victorian seaside resort whose main attraction is a 130-room mansion, selected as one of the top 20 mansions in America ("Great American Mansions and Their Stories," Hastings House, 1963). A National Historic Landmark, the Shadow Lawn mansion boasts 19 baths, 48 varieties of marble, as well as petrified wood, 1,500 mirrors, balconies and pillared entrances, and a 100-foot-long main hall with a Venetian stained-glass ceiling, displaying more than 165 light bulbs. It is an outstanding example of French architecture in the manner of the Versailles Palace.

Woodrow Wilson Hall, as the mansion is now called, served as the site of the most expensive movie musical ever made, "Annie," at a cost of $50 million.

The 125-acre Monmouth campus contains 28 buildings, including one other National Historic Landmark: The Murry and Leonie Guggenheim Memorial Library.

In addition to conferring bachelor of arts and science degrees, Monmouth College awards degrees on the master's level in business administration, electronic engineering, English, mathematics, physics, and teacher education.

* * *

In 1984, U.S. Secretary of Education T.H. Bell observed that "Trenton State College represents the kind of educational integrity that is at the heart of President Reagan's call for a return to excellence in our nation's colleges."

Governor Thomas Kean noted, "I have watched with a great deal of pride and satisfaction during the past few years as Trenton State College—a public institution—has progressively raised its already high standards of admission and retention. Today, it stands among the finest colleges and universities—public and private—not only in New Jersey, but in the surrounding states as well."

Known for beauty as well as quality, Trenton State College today is set in suburban Ewing Township on 225 acres of woodland bordered by two lakes. The campus is just six miles from the state capital.

Founded in 1855 as New Jersey's first Normal School (two-year training for teachers), Trenton State College became a multi-

Star-Ledger Photo

Thespians rehearse in the Fine Arts Theater at Monmouth College, the West Long Branch school whose centerpiece is the 130-room mansion known as Shadow Lawn.

purpose institution by 1972, when 70 percent of entering freshmen were selecting non-teaching majors.

Entering the 1984-85 school year, Trenton State College consisted of five schools: Arts and Sciences, Business, Education, Industrial Education and Engineering Technology, and Nursing.

Its graduate and undergraduate enrollment stood at 9,000. Students may choose to study in any of 27 major fields offering 89 specializations. In all, 68 different baccalaureate degrees are offered.

With a full-time faculty of 355, the faculty-student ratio is 17 to 1. The college's 36 buildings include the Roscoe West Library housing a half-million volumes, an award-winning student center, a 50,000-square-foot student recreation center complete with tennis and racquetball courts, five major computer centers and one of the finest athletic-recreation facilities on the East Coast.

Allen Hall, a lakeside residence hall at Trenton State College.

Star-Ledger Photo

Public Education

In Newark, Portuguese students are learning their ABC's on bilingual computers. In Weehawken, an individualized language arts program has replaced workbooks and textbooks and is now used in 44 states and the Virgin Islands to improve linguistics and writing skills.

The Pollution Control Education Center in Union launched a study of the planet's biosphere in 1974 and today is a national model that has also been adopted in such far away places as Micronesia and other countries concerned about environmental education.

New Jersey's Technology for Children Program is being emulated throughout the United States and several foreign nations, which are establishing "invention contests" patterned after the state's successful experiment.

The "Olympics of the Mind," a competition for gifted children, became an instant media event when first promoted by New Jersey in 1976. The Emmy Award-winning series, "Creativity with Bill Moyers," featured New Jersey's "Olympics of the Minds" in a half-hour show.

One New Jersey high school has developed the nation's only apprenticeship program in industrial repairs training for the handicapped.

Project COED, conceived by state educators, has become the national standard for meeting the needs of the poor and minority youth in the central cities.

New Jersey also instituted the first adult education centers, initially designing more than 25 courses for the state's 1.6 million adults over the age of 25 who do not have high school diplomas.

The national "Model Congress" is now in its 15th year, having evolved from the innovative Institute for Political and Legal Education, where students are turned on to active citizenship.

America's first space colony, a collection of 150 carpenter ants, was aboard the space shuttle Challenger in the summer of 1983, a mission developed by students at Camden and Woodrow Wilson high schools to test the effects of weightlessness on the insects' behavior.

Project ACTIVE, a physical activity training program for handicapped children, has spread to 38 states with 15 satellite centers in such countries as Turkey, Australia, Venezuela and England.

From migrant youths helped by professional athletes to space age learning centers, New Jersey has pioneered an impressive array of educational concepts and projects to reach more than 1 million public school students from at least 125 different language backgrounds, including Arabic, Haitian-Creole, Gujarati and Tagalog.

Lessons are taught in family living centers and barrier-free buildings, as well as conventional schools. With the start of the 1984 school year, there were 597 operating public school districts in New Jersey, more than the number of municipalities in the state, 567. Enrollment, which has been declining in recent years, is now around 1.1 million. Public school pupils are served by an educational staff of some 94,000. The number of instructional rooms now stands at about 69,000.

New Jersey's Bilingual and English as a Second Language (ESL) programs are mandated by law and are considered two of the most comprehensive of their type in the United States. There are about 200 bilingual and ESL programs serving more than 35,000 students from at least 125 different language backgrounds.

Several districts have developed distinctive or "model" bilingual projects, including:

• Union City's Bilingual Special Education Program, which established a bilingual/bicultural Child Study Team and four bilingual classes for the mentally handicapped.

• Newark's Computer Assisted Instruction Program, which adapts technological advances in education for a bilingual audience by exposing students to the computer through a curriculum geared to Portuguese-dominant bilingual students. More than 50,000 Portuguese live in the Ironbound neighborhood of Newark.

• West New York's High School Program, which developed a comprehensive secondary bilingual program that includes "high intensity," or concentrated, English as a second language and the full range of courses designed to meet the individual needs of the student.

Of the 33 language programs accepted into the National Diffusion Network, 12 were from New Jersey. Through those programs, New Jersey has been recognized as a leader in the field of creative educational program development.

* * *

In 1976, New Jersey schools were required to provide educational opportunities for gifted and talented pupils. Since then, the number of identified gifted and talented pupils in special programs has reached 61,000.

Star-Ledger Photo

New Jersey pioneered the popular "Olympics of the Mind" annual academic competitions.

The "Olympics of the Mind" is one of the programs for gifted students that began in the Garden State. Designed to develop student creativity through competitions based on a varsity sports model, the Olympics is offered at the elementary, junior high and high school levels. Schools receive five problems each year, which may be solved by a team of five students assigned to each task. Past problems have included:

• Robby Robot, a project to design and build a robot for less than $10. The robot must move six feet to a dummy, take a cigarette out of the dummy's mouth, put it in a can, pour an ounce of water on the cigarette, speak to the dummy, move again six feet, and stop in a predesignated spot.

• Superstructure, a project to design an 8-inch-high structure from a half-ounce of balsa to support as much weight as possible. The record weight thus far is 900 pounds.

In six years, the "Olympics of the Mind" has been copied in more than 30 states and several Canadian provinces. Finals of the

"Olympics of the Mind" took place in May 1985 at the University of Maryland, where several thousand students who had won their state or equivalent Olympic competitions met for the world title.

Besides Bill Moyers' show on the Olympics, several popular magazines have published feature articles on the competition, including Omni, Psychology Today and TV Guide.

In addition to the Olympics, the State Department of Education has developed similar projects that have regional and national impacts. Among the accomplishments are:

• Managing a five-state consortium to increase the education of gifted students.

• Production of a national award-winning public service TV commercial on gifted children.

• Development of the only federally funded national clearinghouse on the gifted.

• Development of a federally funded national model curriculum (one of four).

New Jersey's Technology for Children Program is one of a kind. New Jersey pioneered this program for elementary and middle school pupils. Its goal is to make children familiar with technology, experienced in problem-solving skills and knowledgeable about the kinds of technical applications done almost routinely by those earning their livelihood.

More than half of the state's school districts have one or more schools participating in the technology experiment. The program offers special "topic workshops" for teachers. The most popular workshops involve micro-computers. Teachers who successfully complete the course may borrow a micro-computer for three weeks. During that time, they try to get other teachers and students to use the little computers.

One Middletown teacher taught her children to invent. It was her method for developing the techniques of problem solving and teaching about inventors. Other teachers adopted the idea and soon the Mini Invention/Innovation Team (MIIT) contest was born.

The MIIT contest, now in its sixth year, received entry applications in 1984 from 2,600 youngsters. Children's inventions, such as biker blinkers for signaling turns and a wind-turbine to generate electricity, often prove to be spectacular solutions to problems that are personal to them.

The invention process requires children to do the research, interview people, write letters, keep logs about their activities and present their findings to contest judges.

Articles have appeared in five professional journals, one publication for children, on four TV networks and in many newspapers. Officials from the Edison National Historic Site in West Orange have invited Technology for Children to exhibit contest winners' inventions at the museum, together with those of the great inventor Thomas A. Edison. Museum officials have developed special tours for the technology students.

* * *

New Jersey set up one of the nation's first Computer Aided Drafting programs, a concept introduced at Hunterdon Central High School in 1979 with the support of RCA, Somerville.

New Jersey was also one of the first states to bring robotics into the classroom. In the Bergen County Vocational-Technical Schools, the robot is used in the electronics program. In the Ocean County Vo-Tech schools, the robot is a learning machine in the Electro-mechanical Equipment Repair program.

The Robot Institute of America predicts that more than 100,000 industrial robots will be installed and operating in American industry by 1990. Training in the field of robotics includes electronics, computers, automated equipment, electromechanical devices, programmable controllers, sensors and artificial intelligence.

The Institute for Political and Legal Education gives high school students practical experiences in politics, government and law. The year-long community-based social studies program was created when the voting age was lowered to 18. Grades six through eight are included in a subprogram called "Law in Action."

Initially started by a staff of teachers for students in 14 New Jersey school districts, the institute curriculum is a balanced mix of innovative printing and audio-visual materials, role-playing, simulation games and experiencing the work-world through internships and contact with community leaders.

The three curriculum components—politics, government and law—are based on five guides: Voter education, the decision-making process, individual rights, juvenile justice, and law and the family.

Crucial to the program's success are the voluntary services of resource people who contribute their expertise, such as the League of Women Voters and the Bar Association.

Refined over a three-year period, the institute's program was validated in 1974 and picked up by more than 40 states, including Hawaii, as well as Washington, D.C., and the Virgin Islands.

This year's 14th annual Model Congress will be attended by more than 500 students.

The Pollution Control Education Center in Union launched "Priority One: Environment" in 1973. It is a 13-unit, interdisciplinary program for elementary, junior high and senior high school classes. The theme of the program is the wise use and preservation of the biosphere, where all life exists in a thin tissue of air, water and soil enveloping the earth.

The Union Pollution Control Education Center made up kits for each grade level. The kits include illustrated student booklets which relate new ideas to the student's own experiences; student investigations leading to pollution control processes; experiment sheets and activity cards enabling a teacher to individualize instruction for specific needs and interests; audio-visuals for pupils to observe phenomena that cannot be duplicated in the classroom; filmstrips and film loops; overhead transparencies, and audio cassettes to aid class discussions.

The subject matter is taught in a one- or two-week unit. Topics include solid waste and sewage treatment, and air, water, thermal, marine, seashore and urban pollution. In other units, pupils are actively involved in the critical environmental problems of open lands, wildlife, wetlands protection, energy conservation, resource management and community response. Each is presented in scientifically accurate and socially responsible settings.

The program can be incorporated into regular science, health and social studies classes, as well as in urban studies or environmental science. The program is currently serving students in 34 states, including Hawaii and Alaska and in Washington, D.C., Puerto Rico, Micronesia and Canada.

* * *

New Jersey is a national leader in adult education, according to the American Association for Adult and Continuing Education. The Garden State ushered in the adult learning centers where adults, lacking a high school diploma and/or basic skills, could schedule their own learning activities and classes. The state is credited with having one of the most cost effective English as a second language programs in the country.

Approximately 250 school districts and county colleges are providing an extensive variety of adult education classes. The classes are designed to help the 1.6 million adults in the state over the age of 25 who lack a high school diploma (33 percent of the adult population). The adult centers also are tailored to improve job skills and to keep pace with the increasingly technical demands of industry and business.

Adult education is the fastest growing sector in public education, with more than 672,000 students enrolled in 1984. Concepts such as flexible scheduling, individualized instruction and programs such as English as a second language were tested and approved with adults long before they were used with children.

Adult education continues to come up with unique and creative educational ideas. The New Jersey Adult Reading Project, for example, has just been validated for national dissemination. Glassboro State College found that "competency assessment tests," which measure the success of the instruction of 24 "key life" areas, can readily be adapted for the teenage dropout. Among the key life factors are: Getting a job, legal rights, parenting, and preparation of income taxes.

Other innovations have been an East Brunswick program to help mentally retarded adults to become self-sufficient, a similar program for deaf adults in Fair Lawn and a volunteer tutor-training program in New Brunswick.

From 1972 through 1982, nearly 160,000 adults earned their high school diplomas through adult education programs in New Jersey.

It's a lengthy title, but it's catching on in more than 40 states, plus Washington, D.C. and the Virgin Islands. "Individualized Language Arts: Diagnosis, Prescription and Evaluation" is the brainchild of the small Hudson River waterfront community of Weehawken. It's used in grades one through 12 and anyone enrolled in the program can learn how to write effectively. The rationale behind the program is that linguistics, the study of language, yields knowledge that can be translated into techniques for improving writing skills.

The instruction uses writing activities in all parts of the curriculum and is organized within a diagnostic teaching framework. Teachers and students have continuous diagnosis of their writing needs and evaluation of results. Writing instruction is related to speaking, listening and reading, as well as to the student's ideas and feelings. It links composition to real-life experience.

The Weehawken student population is highly mobile and for many students English is a second language. The language arts program has completely replaced writing workbooks and textbooks in the schools.

Project COED was conceived as a model for New Jersey and the nation to help the poor and minority youth in central cities to prepare themselves for productive jobs.

COED—the Center for Occupational Education/Experimentation and Demonstration—was established in Newark by the State Department of Education to respond to urban problems that sparked the riots in New Jersey's largest city in 1967.

COED opened in the fall of 1974, serving as a shared-time vocational school for secondary school students in the greater Newark area, and as a statewide development and demonstration center. COED students spend half their day at the center and the other half taking academic subjects at their regular school.

In the 1984-85 school year, more than 575 students from 25 different sending schools were enrolled at COED. The sending schools included 11 regular public high schools in Newark, East Orange, Orange and Montclair; two junior schools; three parochial high schools; five alternative schools, and five special education schools.

Many of the students were on the verge of dropping out when they enrolled in COED. The idea for Project COED stemmed from the success of the Newark Skills Center, which the state inaugurated in 1965. The Skills Center was the first state-operated manpower training center in the nation. It achieved national recognition for initiating programs that combined occupational training and basic academic skills development for out-of-school, unemployed adults.

COED consists of 22 separate programs in 13 occupational clusters. The process involves pre-vocational career exploration and basic vocational skills assessment, which acquaints students with a wide range of occupations and helps determine their interests, aptitudes and deficiencies.

COED's staff and resources have been tapped for a variety of special uses. In 1979, for example, COED conducted a summer-long seminar for counselors from Barringer High School in New-

Another New Jersey innovation is Project COED, which has become the national standard for meeting the needs of the poor and minority youth in the central cities.

ark and Ferris High School in Jersey City. Dropout prevention plans were prepared and the roles of counselors, teachers and parents redefined in channeling students toward a productive life. The joint local-state-federal Youthwork Project resulted in significant and lasting changes at the two cities' high schools.

* * *

The Middlesex County Vocational and Technical High Schools system boasts one of the largest, if not the top secondary vocational operations for handicapped students, not only in New Jersey, but also in the U.S. It has 26 shops serving more than 700 handicapped students in four facilities.

Although impressive in size and scope, the real meaning of success can be measured in the results of its special program. Almost 90 percent of its classified handicapped students who graduate find employment.

Linden High School runs the only apprenticeship program in industrial valve, gauge and instrumentation repair training in the country for handicapped students.

Through the combined efforts of Linden High Vocational School and representatives from local industry, the five-step program prepares handicapped students for entry into the work force, while saving industry the time and money it would have spent training new employes.

Project ACTIVE evolved in Oakhurst, Monmouth County, in the early 1970s to meet the widespread need for individualized physical activity for handicapped children.

The project staff trains teachers of special education, physical education and recreation to prescribe individualized and personalized activities for children from pre-kindergarten through 12th grade.

More than 25 percent of New Jersey's school districts adopted the Oakhurst program, while another 25 percent use materials developed for the program, including 17 manuals that address all types of handicapping conditions.

Nationwide, ACTIVE has been adopted in 38 states and Puerto Rico, with 15 satellite centers established to serve them. Worldwide, ACTIVE has been implemented in Canada, Venezuela, the Dominican Republic and Colombia, whose government has mandated the program for all of that country's schools.

ACTIVE "awareness centers" are operating in England, Australia and Turkey.

Regional Day Schools have been established throughout New Jersey to bring new educational opportunities to the severely handicapped. The schools educate and offer support services to the deaf, deaf-blind, multiply handicapped and severely emotionally disturbed students.

Beginning in 1974, the state built 11 regional schools to serve New Jersey residents who had to go out of the state for special treatment. Pupils today learn basic skills and are instructed in physical education, health and safety, arts and science and career/vocational preparation.

The schools are total learning environments. Each one contains a family living center, equipped with kitchen, laundry, bedroom, living room and bath, in addition to a media center, counseling room, clinic, cafeteria, multi-purpose and physical therapy room.

The schools are also barrier-free. Classroom clusters are color-coded. Walls and floors are covered with varying textures so pupils can recognize different parts of the building through touch.

* * *

New Jersey has been recognized as a world leader in student safety. Protection of the student begins before he or she arrives at the school.

Before 1962, New Jersey school buses were equipped with a four-light warning system for motorists. It was the standard practice throughout the United States. Accident statistics showed the four-light system to be inadequate.

In 1962, the State Department of Education's Bureau of Pupil Transportation redesigned the warning system. The new eight-light system included four amber lights, front and rear, along with four red lights, front and rear. The new pre-warning system alerts motorists of a stopping school bus; the amber lights are activated before a bus pulls to a halt. The red lights are then activated as the amber lights, simultaneously, are turned off.

During the first year of use, accident rates at school bus stops decreased by 68.4 percent. In 1980, at the National Conference on School Transportation, the eight-light system was included in the "Standards for School Buses," indicating nationwide acceptance of a student safety system developed and piloted in New Jersey.

The concept of a personalized school bus was also initiated by the Department of Education, this time by the Division of Finance. In 1970, the department's financial analysts found that the majority of serious school bus accidents occurred while students were waiting at bus stops, crossing roads and after exiting the bus. One statistic stuck out: 95 percent of fatalities happened to youngsters under the age of seven.

Research of available training materials in the United States and Canada found very few programs geared to the interest and understanding levels of primary grade students.

To bridge that curriculum gap, a personalized school bus approach was developed to which children could relate. It came to be known as "Stanley, the Friendly School Bus."

Before this new school bus character could grow into the international status he now enjoys, many innovative steps had to be negotiated. One of the first was to discover what most influenced these primary grade children.

Permission was granted by several school districts to have their second-grade pupils constructively evaluate the "Stanley" program in form and content. Their critical oral and written statements were translated into the animated "Stanley" character so familiar to school bus passengers today.

Over the past 14 years, "Stanley" has been found in almost every state and every Canadian province, including the Canadian northwest territory. Other countries that have also had a visit from "Stanley" include Belgium, West Germany, Ireland and, most recently, Saudi Arabia.

Private Education

Some are as small and cozy as a one-room schoolhouse while others occupy elaborate campus estates enhanced by sparkling brooks, glassy ponds and prized pony paddocks.

They offer everything from forensics and filmmaking to calligraphy and ceramics, and even guitar and yoga—and, that is just the frosting enriching a thick foundation built on the basic "3 R's," the building blocks of human reasoning and understanding.

They are New Jersey's independent or private schools, about 1,000 in all, serving as many as 200,000 students from pre-kindergartners through high school seniors.

More than 95 percent of private school graduates go on to college, an impressive number becoming leaders in business, science, the arts and academia, with a few achieving superstardom.

Superman (as portrayed on the silver screen by Christopher Reeve) is a product not of the planet Krypton, but of the Princeton Country Day School. And Michael J. Pollard, an exceptional character actor who co-starred in the classic film "Bonnie & Clyde" with Warren Beatty and Faye Dunaway, is an alumnus of Passaic Collegiate School.

One private school in Princeton, American Boychoir, is a national institution whose 45 versatile voices have sung at the White House, the Vatican and before kings and heads of states around the world.

Star-Ledger Photo

The contemporary campus of the Pingry School in Bernards Township.

The Pingry School, founded in 1861, recently moved into a new $25 million contemporary complex on a 196-acre campus in Bernards Township. One of Pingry's famous graduates was five-star fleet Adm. William Halsey, whose command was in the Pacific Theater during World War II.

New Jersey's independent schools, the oldest dating back to the 1700s, have been started by Quakers, merchants, musicians, military officers and religious and academic reformers in quest of the ideal environment in which to realize the full potential of the mind, body and spirit.

Private school students come from the 50 states and more than 50 countries, each seeking a special place where both intellectual and physical prowess can be attained in the true Platonic sense.

The private schools, with the exception of the parochial system, which accounts for the majority of the private school population, tailor their scholastic programs for a wide variety of interests. One school may require the study of etymology (the origin of words) in its curriculum; another may offer a range of languages from Greek and Russian to Hebrew and the once universal tongue, Latin. Others may emphasize the development of relationships that focus on the family unit as the basis of society.

A Quaker school founded in 1786 stresses the principles of love, equality, justice and non-violence.

An experimental school teaches through "self-discovery" in which grades, or scores, are less important than solving the problem.

An Englewood school teaches math to youngsters by using a vegetable garden and rabbit hutch, connecting a concrete experience to an abstract number or symbol. Athletics at some schools are downplayed in order to create a more academic atmosphere. And there is a school for those youngsters simply trying to keep up, or cope, with a technical information explosion.

The Peddie School in Hightstown received the largest single donation ever recorded in the history of American private secondary education—$12 million. The funds were given on Oct. 31, 1983, by publishing magnate Walter Annenberg (TV Guide, Racing Form), an alumnus of the 199-year-old school. The Peddie School enrolls 510 young men and women.

In the private school, the student is a special person. Instruction is often given on a one-on-one basis. The pupil-teacher ratio can be 3 to 1 or 10 to 1, depending on the course or the school setup. Catholic schools generally have higher pupil-teacher ratios.

The private schools fill an invaluable niche in New Jersey's educational community. Because they are private, they can explore new directions and, conversely, maintain those ancient and rigorous traditions abandoned by the public schools years ago.

New Jersey's private schools are open to any student who can meet the school's requirements. Many offer scholarships and financial aid to qualifying students. A partial list of private schools reflecting a broad range of learning interests follows.

* * *

The Academy of St. Elizabeth in Convent Station is one of two such schools founded by the Sisters of Charity of St. Elizabeth, the other being St. Vincent Academy in Newark.

St. Elizabeth opened its doors in 1860 as a private Catholic day school. It is situated on a 420-acre campus shared with the College of St. Elizabeth. A small academy enrolling 240 girls, St. Elizabeth is a college preparatory school. Latin is required of all freshmen.

Graduation requirements include four years of theology, English and physical education, two years of American history,

The Academy of St. Elizabeth in Convent Station was founded in 1860 by the Sisters of Charity.

Star-Ledger Photo

mathematics and a modern foreign language, and one year of current world history. Optional trips abroad supplement the foreign language program.

Among St. Elizabeth's diverse co-curricular activities are calligraphy, ceramics, choral, dance, forensics, filmmaking, gourmet cooking, guitar, nutrition, science and yoga.

Academic facilities include an electronic language library, micro-computers, chemistry and biology laboratories, audio-visual equipment and a growing library. Among sports activities available is horseback riding at local stables.

* * *

Admiral Farragut Academy in Pine Beach was the first secondary school to develop a program of naval science approved by Congress and the Department of the Navy.

The academy was founded in 1933 by a small group of experienced educators under the leadership of Adm. S.S. Robinson, who had served as superintendent of the U.S. Naval Academy at Annapolis, and Marine Brig. Gen. Cyrus S. Radford. The school was named in honor of David Glasgow Farragut (1801-1870), a Union commander during the Civil War.

The school, spread out over 35 acres along the Toms River waterfront, opened with 56 cadets in what had been a hotel. Today the academy enrolls 120 boarders and 40 day students, 11 to 19 years of age, in grades five through 12 and postgraduate.

The Corps of Cadets at Admiral Farragut Academy marches in a Sunday afternoon ceremonial parade. The formal processions are held on the Capt. W. Kable Russell field in the fall and spring.

Star-Ledger Photo

The corps is run in much the same manner as the student cadet corps at the U.S. Naval Academy. It has a strong student government and is controlled by the carefully selected cadet officers. The cadet corps is organized as a battalion of three companies, a band and lower school company. Cadets attend weekly chapel, conducted by students and staff, and may also attend local services.

Farragut Academy cadets are expected to have mastered most of the following subjects: English, French, Spanish, world history, U.S. history, American government, algebra, geometry, calculus, trigonometry, mathematics of finance, earth science, biology, chemistry, physics, oceanology, psychology, and science and man.

The naval science curriculum is prescribed by the Department of the Navy for the ROTC and Naval Honor Schools. Cadets are instructed in naval customs, courtesies, orientation, organization and traditions, health and first aid, seamanship, navigation, piloting, communications, radar and sonar, oceanography, meteorology, astronomy, leadership, moral guidance, drill, command, ceremonies and practical boathandling.

The average class has 14 cadets and the student-teacher ratio is 8 to 1. Farragut Hall contains classrooms for naval science, a Naval Museum and administrative offices. The library contains 12,000 volumes.

Waterfront equipment consists of three docks, a boathouse, a 30-foot cabin cruiser, a 19½-foot-long Aquasport, a 25-foot skiff and a fleet of small craft such as rowboats, whaleboats, catboats, Lasers, Penguins, small powerboats and a diesel-powered launch.

Sailing is one of the academy's intramural sports.

* * *

You've probably seen them on television, or heard them on the radio, or listened to one of their popular albums. They are known as "America's Singing Boys" and they have performed in more than 1,500 American cities in 48 states, in the Philippines, Japan, Korea, South and Central America, Europe and Canada.

The choir has sung under the direction of maestros Toscanini, Ormandy, Bernstein, Munch, Mehta and Leinsdorf, and they have appeared at Lincoln Center, Carnegie Hall, the White House, the Vatican and before presidents and kings.

Star-Ledger Photo

Members of the American Boychoir of Princeton, known as "America's Singing Boys," have performed in more than 1,500 U.S. cities.

They are 45 boys, ages eight to 14, from throughout the United States and Canada, and they make their home at the **American Boychoir School** in Princeton. The school is housed in the handsome Gerard B. Lambert Mansion, Albermarle.

In 1937, the Kiwanis Club of Columbus, Ohio organized a choir as part of the club's youth activities. It quickly became, however, an ambitious musical enterprise built around the Kiwanis' day school. Ralph Riley, a prominent Columbus businessman, had wanted to start a city youth band for disadvantaged boys. When he teamed up with Herbert Huffman, a choral director, the Columbus Boychoir was born.

When the famous Vienna Boys' Choir could not tour during World War II, the Columbus Boychoir took its first concert tour, a one-day trip to Cleveland in 1939. Huffman moved the school to Princeton in 1950. In 1980, a $7.5 million nationwide campaign was launched to endow the school as a national institution.

American Boychoir is the only non-sectarian boarding and day choir school in North America. The school is unique in the English-speaking world. New students are selected by audition throughout the school year, while on tour, and at summer camp. Boys are selected on the basis of musical ability, academic aptitude and social adjustment.

The Boychoir is composed of two choirs: The training choir, made up of younger and less experienced boys, and the touring or concert choir. With a scholarship budget exceeding $100,000, American Boychoir has proportionately one of the largest scholarship programs for an unendowed private school in the nation. Some 75 percent of the students enrolled receive some financial aid.

The Concert Choir has completed a major new recording of Handel's "Messiah," with the Norman Scribner Choir and the Smithsonian Chamber Players. During the 1982 holidays, American Boychoir performed before President and Mrs. Reagan at the White House and joined the Smithsonian Chamber Players for two live broadcasts over National Public Radio (NPR) from the National History Museum in Washington, D.C.

On Christmas 1982, the choir was featured on two nationally televised programs, "CBS News Morning" with Charles Kuralt and "ABC World News Tonight" with Frank Reynolds.

* * *

On a 315-acre hilltop overlooking the Village of Blairstown sits **Blair Academy**, just 10 minutes from the Appalachian Trail and the scenic Delaware Water Gap.

In 1848, a group of prominent local merchants and clergymen headed by John Insley Blair got together to start a private school. From 1915-70, the school admitted only boys. It returned to its original coeducational status in 1970.

Today, girls make up about one-third of the school's enrollment of approximately 350. The teacher-student ratio is 1 to 10. The academic year is divided into three equal terms. To graduate, a four-year student must have completed the following required courses: Four years of English, three years of math, two years of modern or classical language, one year of U.S. history and laboratory science.

During the 12th year, a student must take several specialized courses from a list that includes computer science, introduction to law, relief printmaking, music theory and religion as a personal experience.

Blair Academy offers 68 different courses, including 11 advanced placement courses and a wide variety of electives in art, history, music, religion and English.

Ninety-eight percent of Blair's graduates go on to college, including Princeton, Amherst, Bucknell, Cornell, Dartmouth, Vassar and Wesleyan.

The Scribner Library has a collection of more than 19,000 volumes and 2,200 recordings. The Bindeman Music Center contains a small recital hall, classrooms, a seminar room, teaching studios and practice rooms.

Blair fields some 30 separate teams during the academic year, with 24 people involved in coaching. Athletic facilities include three football fields, four soccer fields, 14 tennis courts, a quarter-mile cinder track, a nine-hole golf course, two basketball courts, wrestling and weight-training rooms, and a six-lane pool with two one-meter and one three-meter diving boards.

* * *

During the 1920s at Smith College, Elizabeth Morrow, who dreamed of teaching and having a school of her own, became friends with Miss Constance Chilton, who shared her interest in early childhood education. The philosophy of the school they began in 1930 is best expressed in Morrow's words:

"I wished to steer a middle course between the modern or progressive school and the old-fashioned conservative one and to incorporate in the school, the best of the old and best of the new."

A group of parents who had started a small preschool group in Englewood urged the two Smith graduates to consider that location for their school. On opening day in September 1930, 34 children entered through the doors of an old Dutch farmhouse on Linden Avenue.

There, at the Little School, the new teachers encouraged learning by doing rather than by book work alone. They taught math by having the children lay out and measure a vegetable garden and a rabbit hutch.

Morrow died in 1934 and her sister, Anne Morrow Lindbergh, wife of the famous aviator, was instrumental in renaming the Little School after her in 1948.

The school is now on property that was part of the Dwight Morrow estate. Dwight Whitney Morrow (1873-1931) was a lawyer, financier and statesman who organized the Kennecott Copper Corp. Morrow also served as ambassador to Mexico and was elected to the U.S. Senate from New Jersey in 1930.

The Elizabeth Morrow School has expanded over the years. A separate nursery and kindergarten building was erected in 1972 in honor of Constance Chilton.

With an enrollment of more than 500 students, the Morrow School today remains an independent, non-sectarian, coeducational day school for children two years and nine months to 12 years of age. Through example and direct experience, the three C's—courtesy, cooperation and concern for others—are intertwined in the life of the school.

* * *

As early as 1715, the Religious Society of Friends set up small "schools" in the homes of member-friends. By 1786, the small Quaker community inaugurated the first real school, the Haddonfield Free School, in that region.

From the beginning, the small building on Haddon Avenue, adjacent to the Meeting burying ground, housed the **Haddonfield Friends School**. As it approaches its bicentennial anniversary, Haddonfield Friends School still reflects the educational philosophy of the Religious Society:

"The major purpose of Friends' education is to help the individual develop to the utmost his own potentialities and to grow in the intelligent acceptance of his responsibility to serve his fellow men in accordance with Christ's teaching and example . . . The aim of education is the full and harmonious development of the resources of the human spirit." —"Faith and Practice," Religious Society of Friends.

Over the last two centuries, the Friends School has maintained the tradition of both educating the children academically and training them in religion and philosophy compatible with Quaker beliefs. As education has adjusted to dramatic changes, the little Quaker school has gone through several transitions, from a young men's academy, to a boarding school and, recently, a coeducational day school.

Non-Quakers today constitute a majority of both the student and teacher population. However, students and their parents have long found that Quaker principles are compatible with their own religious views and, in fact, contribute to the development of their own spiritual values. Such Friends' principles as love, equality, justice, non-violence and simplicity are taught. The school week includes attending a Meeting for Worship.

Classes generally have from 14 to 18 students. The school's enrollment is limited to around 200 to allow students to receive the personal attention of their teachers.

Star-Ledger Photo

Preschoolers practice communication skills by sharing experiences at the Hilltop School in Sparta.

* * *

Maria Montessori, the first woman graduate of medicine from the University of Rome, conceived a new approach to teaching in 1912. The method originally had been devised for educating defective children, but the results were so gratifying that the doctor decided to apply the technique to normal students.

The Montessori System involves grouping children of different ages together to solve certain tasks. It's a self-discovery process encouraging freedom of movement in an open classroom, as opposed to an immobile learning environment.

The Montessori approach is practiced at the **Hilltop School** in Sparta, founded in 1967 by a group of parents who rented a room in St. Mary's Church and contributed materials to begin their experiment. The school began with five children, a teacher and an assistant.

Today, Hilltop, set on 13 wooded acres in North Jersey's mountain range, enrolls up to 200 pupils who are taught to be "independent learners."

Benefits of a multi-age level classroom include increased social learning, child-to-child tutoring and academic perspective. Motivated by their own natural curiosity, children spend most of each school day moving freely from one activity to another. Having made their choices, children proceed to do their tasks, singly or together in twos and threes, with the teacher's help as needed.

To complement the high degree of freedom within a Montessori classroom, there is also a high degree of order. Teachers set standards for social behavior. Children are taught to handle materials carefully and to return them to designated places so others may use them. They respect the thoughts and feelings of each student, according to school director Mary K. Thornton.

Since the school's inception, parents have taken dependable, daily part in almost every aspect of Hilltop's activities: Teaching, office work, planning, raising money, maintenance, and other voluntary assignments.

The preschool-kindergarten curriculum concentrates on the practical, the "sensorial" (attractive materials to refine the five senses and help the children to discriminate, classify and compare), language, math, social studies-geography, science, music, art and physical education.

Grades one through seven or eight continue "the basics," adding history and recreation.

Gradually, the Montessori aspect of the curriculum is becoming secondary to a philosophy of education stressing academic excellence and individualized attention.

* * *

The Hun School came into being as a tutoring school for high school students preparing to enter Princeton University. It was established as the Princeton Math School in 1914 by John Gale Hun, an assistant professor of mathematics at Princeton. As colleges introduced higher standards of admission, the Princeton Math School expanded its curriculum and facilities.

In 1924, the school moved to its present location, a 49-acre campus in Princeton's residential western section. Today the Hun School is recognized as an excellent private learning center and for having instituted one of the first foreign student programs in the country.

The Princeton school is also known for its small (limited to 25 students) but pioneering Perceptual Training Program, managed by trained therapists. Qualified students may also take a noncredit course at Princeton or music lessons for credit at the renowned Westminster Choir College, also in Princeton. Classes average 14 students.

A student exchange program is administered by the English-Speaking Union. At Hun, there is an honor code in which students, through school agencies, have a voice in the determination and enforcement of rules. The Student Council makes proposals to the administration about student life, including proposals regarding curriculum changes.

Of the school's 500 students, 8 percent are black, 1 percent Hispanic. Students come from 16 states and 25 countries. Representatives come to Hun from more than 120 colleges and universities to meet with interested students. The 105 graduates of the class of 1985 are attending 80 colleges across the country.

Academic facilities include four science laboratories, a computer center, two photography darkrooms, an art studio, a ceramics and sculpture studio with a potter's wheel and kiln, and a music studio. The library contains 11,000 volumes and a media center.

Students at the Hun School in Princeton learn to use a computer. The school began in 1914 as a tutoring facility for Princeton University graduates.

Photo Credit: Gordon Lutz

* * *

The pastor of a village church was asked to educate the sons of the church elders and, in 1810, the **Lawrenceville School** was born. From those humble origins, Lawrenceville School, just outside of Princeton, has grown into one of the wealthiest private institutions in America, with an enrollment exceeding 650. The school endowment topped $50 million in 1985 and capital gifts amounted to nearly $4.2 million in the 1984-85 school year.

The purpose of the school, as an academic center, is to "offer boys an education that will help them not only gain admission to college, but also become active and thoughtful members of society."

Students can choose from a list of courses currently numbering about 260, plus 27 laboratory courses. Electives include "The Law as Literature," "Genetics," "Advanced Virgil" and "Ecology." Some 15 advanced placement courses are also available to qualifying students. Individual participation is encouraged in small classroom sections averaging 12 students.

One requirement at Lawrenceville is that each student must give roughly 50 hours of service to either the school or a social agency approved by the school.

Students with a particular interest in exploring new fields or in testing themselves against the challenge of a job may apply for Independent Study, off-campus projects, driver training, or a "Term Away" project. Students may also apply to take courses at nearby Princeton University.

Lawrenceville's 1985 graduating class of 180 is represented at 94 colleges and universities, including Harvard, Brown, Carnegie-Mellon, Princeton and Cornell. Students come from 40 states; 7 percent of the enrollment is from 24 foreign countries.

The 30 major academic buildings on the 350-acre campus include the Karl W. Corby Computer Center, the Edith Memorial Chapel, the John Dixon Library, which houses 25,000 volumes, the Pattie T. Helly Gallery of the Arts, the Jansen Noyes Science Buildings, the Allan P. Kirby Arts Center, with a seating capacity of 890, and the Music House.

Lawrenceville's most distinguishing feature is its House System. In each of the 15 houses, the housemaster maintains close contact with the residents. House athletic teams compete intramurally, and house identity is maintained through separate dining rooms in the eating center. The unique system provides a small social environment in which each boy's contribution is important —and measurable.

Lawrenceville has 10 baseball fields, nine football fields, nine soccer fields, a golf course, 23 tennis courts, a quarter-mile, all-weather Tartan track, skeet shooting facilities, and a 200-by-85-foot covered ice hockey rink.

The Edward J. Lavino Field House consists of a main arena with a wood floor surface sufficient for two basketball courts, and a larger dirt floor for indoor football, soccer, lacrosse and baseball practice.

Polo, rugby and cricket are among the many interscholastic sports.

The largest single student enterprise is the Periwig Club, whose dramas, comedies and musicals attract more than a third of the students.

* * *

A thousand energetic children in classrooms, laboratories, lunchrooms and on the fields . . . 135 teachers trained in all the disciplines . . . three campuses, three libraries, three fully equipped academic buildings, three gymnasiums, nine tennis courts and three swimming pools—welcome to the world of **Montclair Kimberley Academy**.

The roots of the academy go back more than 100 years. It was organized by parents who cared deeply about the education of their children.

The student-faculty ratio at Montclair Academy is 9 to 1. The maximum class size is 16, and one-fourth of the seniors are cited for achievement on national examinations.

Each of the three campuses offers a complete liberal arts program.

The Primary School has a faculty of 28 and approximately 250 students from kindergarten through fourth grade. Language arts and mathematics form the foundation of the curriculum.

During the primary grades, students are introduced to the science laboratory, where they learn to explore the world around them. By fourth grade, they are able to discuss in the class the basic aerodynamics of a space launch, the skeletal structure of a dinosaur, and the proper nutrition for a healthy person.

The computer program is extensive, with students using computers for drill, enrichment and stimulation in every subject area. By fourth grade, every child is computer literate and some are writing their own programs. Says one academy father: "I'd love to be able to hire young engineers who understand computers as well as some of these children. They are really learning to think."

The Middle School has an enrollment of nearly 400 students in grades five through eight. In addition to the classrooms and science and computer laboratories, the campus boasts two playing fields, nine tennis courts, two gymnasiums, an auditorium and an indoor swimming pool.

The language arts program in fifth and sixth grades continues the Primary School's fourfold approach: Responding to literature, sustained silent reading, writing and skill development. Ecology, electricity and chemistry form the core of the sixth-grade program. World geography provides the focus of the seventh-grade program.

In eighth grade, earth science classes continue the investigative approach to study the earth and its environment in space. Among the highlights of the eighth-grade English course are "The Odyssey" and the attendant study of Greek mythology.

With a panoramic view of the New York skyline, the Upper School supports the largest student population, more than 400, with a faculty of 45. A series of interlocking buildings house the gym, an Olympic-size swimming pool, science labs, the library, and academic and administrative areas. Additional facilities include a greenhouse, two theaters, a dance studio, computer and word processing rooms and several art studios.

Minimum requirements for graduation include four years of English, three years of a foreign language, three years of math, two years of social studies incorporating U.S. history, two years of laboratory science and one-and-a-half years of fine and performing arts.

Practically all graduates of Montclair Kimberley Academy attend four-year colleges following graduation. Graduates go on to Harvard, Princeton, Smith, Cornell, Colgate, Georgetown, Lehigh, Smith, Skidmore, Tulane, Rutgers and other top public and private institutions of higher learning.

* * *

The second oldest independent day school in New Jersey, **Newark Academy** has been an academic fixture since before the United States became a nation. Founded on March 8, 1774, by a few residents of Newark, the first home of the academy occupied a site on "common land" in the nation's third oldest city. That site today is where a massive granite boulder sits in Washington Park on Broad Street.

Because the two-story, stone schoolhouse was used during the Revolution as a barracks, a guardhouse and a hospital for Colonial troops, a raiding party of British burned the structure to the ground during the night of Jan. 25, 1780.

The next school, a three-story structure, was built at the corner of Broad and Academy streets. In 1857, Newark Academy moved into its third home at High and William streets, later the site of the Newark School of Fine and Industrial Arts. In 1930, a modern, commodious Colonial-type edifice was erected at 215 First St., overlooking Branch Brook Park.

A planned freeway cutting through the city's North Ward forced Newark Academy to relocate in 1964 to its present site, a

Star-Ledger Photo

Dr. Simon Sobering of Maplewood, an instructor at Newark Academy in Livingston, explains the electrostatic generator to student Adam Weiss of North Caldwell.

68-acre knoll in Livingston next to a suburban shopping mall. The much larger facilities allowed enrollment to increase to 480 and offered more than 30 acres of recreational facilities: Six tennis courts, two football fields (one for practice), two baseball fields (one also used for field hockey), two soccer fields, a softball field, an Olympic-sized swimming pool with championship diving boards and a quarter-mile track.

The spacious Livingston plant contains classrooms, an auditorium seating nearly 600, a gymnasium, swimming pool, lounge, meeting rooms and administration offices.

Over the centuries, Newark Academy has been identified by its symbol depicting the academy's pre-Revolutionary origin: A picture of a Colonial schoolboy of the 1770s period, in knee-breeches and cocked hat, with books under one arm and a flintlock over his shoulder. The schoolboy appears ready for an attack by roving British soldiers or lurking Indians. The same symbol, which is now being redesigned, appears on the school newspaper, aptly called "The Minute Man."

Among the academy's graduates have been former U.S. Treasury Secretary William Simon, noted architects Bernard and Howard Grad of the Grad Partnership in Newark; former U.S. attorney for New Jersey Robert Del Tufo and Dr. Brainerd Holmes, former director of NASA's manned space program.

The academy returned to coeducation in 1971. For a time in the early 1800s, girls did not attend the school.

* * *

Rutgers Preparatory School is the oldest independent school in New Jersey. Established in 1766, Rutgers Prep served the New Brunswick area until the opening of free public schools in 1853. Today, students are drawn from more than 60 communities in the Raritan Valley.

For most of its history, Rutgers Prep shared a common board of trustees with Rutgers University. In 1945, Rutgers officially became the State University of New Jersey and "The Prep School" began to chart a separate course. The prep school severed its ties with the university in 1957 and moved to a 35-acre campus in Somerset on the banks of the historic Delaware-Raritan Canal. The campus now houses six buildings, four athletic fields, five tennis courts and a cross-country course.

The Lower School is self-contained in the 18th Century Abraham Beach House (1744) and has facilities for music, as well as its own library. The kindergarten and first grade are located in the Annex, a spacious, four-room building fully equipped for the needs of young children. The Middle and Upper schools share a 5,000-square-foot library and the Upper School contains biology, chemistry, physics and computer labs and a 300-seat assembly hall.

Rutgers Preparatory School has educated three New Jersey governors and numerous men and women recognized in every profession for their quality leadership. Although the majority of the alumni have chosen to enter business, law and medicine, the school counts among its graduates many outstanding educators, including faculty members at Cornell, Dartmouth, Harvard, Tufts, Williams and Yale.

Dr. William H.S. Demarest, Class of 1879, was president of Rutgers College. Dr. Austin W. Scott, Class of 1899, was for many years Dean of Harvard Law School. Dr. Byron H. Waksman, Class of 1936, was chairman of the Department of Microbiology at Yale and presently heads research for the National Multiple Sclerosis Society. Dr. James R. Arnold, Class of 1939, is professor of chemistry and director of the California Space Institute at the University of California at San Diego.

Many Rutgers Prep alumni played pivotal roles in the development of the New Brunswick area: J. Seward Johnson, Class of 1913, of Johnson & Johnson; John W. Mettler, Class of 1895, of Interwoven, and Douglas J. Fisher, Class of 1904, of Sayre and Fisher.

In the arts, Rutgers Prep alumni include the poet Joyce Kilmer, class of 1904; the artist Russell Iredell, class of 1909; the playwright James Shearer, class of 1914, and the photographer Alfred Pach, class of 1931.

Rutgers Prep's K-12 computer literacy approach—featuring a keyboard skills/word processing course—is a model program for other schools. And its foreign language programs offer great opportunities for cross-cultural awareness and enrichment.

In sports, Rutgers Prep fields 40 girls' and boys' teams. The school also is known for its award-winning programs in music, drama and the visual arts.

The 180 Lower School students, 110 Middle School students and 270 Upper School students enjoy a 7 to 1 student-faculty ratio. More than 50 percent of the faculty hold advanced degrees.

* * *

The oldest Methodist secondary school in the nation, the **Pennington School**, was founded in 1838 by the Southern New Jersey Annual Conference of the United Methodist Church.

Established as the Methodist Episcopal Male Seminary, the school become known as The Pennington in 1945. From 1854 to 1910, Pennington was coeducational but reverted to being a boys' school in 1910, remaining so until 1972 when it again accepted girls.

Pennington is committed to educating "the whole person—the mind, body and spirit—by taking the uniqueness of the individual student into consideration."

The 46-acre campus is strategically located in a rural setting within eight miles of Princeton and the state capital of Trenton.

The Pennington School has two special programs: A Center for Learning, limited to 40 students with learning disabilities, and an International Student Program, with a maximum of 14 foreign students.

The faculty consists of 36 men and 23 women, 37 of whom live on campus. The student body numbers 340. Representatives from about 80 colleges visit the campus each year for interviews with students. Juniors must attend a college fair, and each year the school sponsors a career day and "college ahead night," during which students are challenged by a wide variety of professional people.

Pennington does not believe that athletics are of paramount importance, but all students, unless excused for medical reasons, are expected to participate on a team of his or her own ability level. The school does not go out of its way to recruit athletes.

Sports available to boys are football, soccer, cross-country, volleyball, basketball, swimming, wrestling, bowling, baseball, tennis, golf, and track and field. Girls can play in any of the sports, except football and wrestling. They also have their own teams in field hockey, basketball and softball.

* * *

St. Vincent Academy offers the women of Newark the finest alternative education available. The only independent school in Newark with an unbroken history of 114 years, it has been based in the 1850s, Gothic-styled Wallace Mansion on Market Street since 1869. St. Vincent offered both technical training and liberal arts courses as early as 1892, long before they were considered "necessary" for women.

Throughout a century of dramatic change in Newark, St. Vincent has maintained its high standards and Christian philosophy, standing today as a cornerstone of urban education. Located in Newark's Central Ward, St. Vincent is a learning-centered Christian community.

St. Vincent encourages a belief in a rebirth of Newark. Students learn the history of the city and are educated toward neighborhood involvement, legal awareness and community commitment. The family unit is presented as the basis of society. Living skills are explored by the 275 high school students.

In the early 1970s, St. Vincent was one of the first secondary schools to introduce a community service program as a regular part of the curriculum. The current Student-in-Community program services more than 25 nonprofit agencies through the weekly volunteer work of the senior class.

A dual program of courses combines college prep with business training. Small classes, frequent one-to-one instruction and evaluation, and a sequenced monitoring program give each student the benefit of personal guidance.

St. Vincent Academy is owned and operated by the Sisters of Charity of St. Elizabeth, the first congregation of religious women established in New Jersey.

The student body is 76 percent black, 12 percent Hispanic and 8.5 percent Portuguese. About half of the students live in single-parent homes.

* * *

The Winston School in Summit may be New Jersey's newest and smallest independent day school for boys and girls. In 1981, independent school heads saw a need to help those youngsters with minimal learning disabilities.

These experienced educators were concerned about the lack of programs for such disabled students in the Summit area. The Winston School fills that need through specialists who work in modern, bright classrooms that open into a spacious courtyard shaded by lovely old trees.

A Winston School candidate is a boy or girl between the ages of eight and 13 who is average or above average, alert, happy, active, and gets along with others. Except the youngster brings home report cards with such remarks as "doesn't pay attention" . . . "doesn't apply himself" . . . "written work is not neat." These children often have a poor self-image and lack the organization skills necessary for good study habits and social development.

The Winston School program is individualized for each of its 25 students. The program emphasizes reading and related language arts skills. There are also strong programs in math, science, art, music and physical education.

Learning in instructional groups of two to four students per teacher, the child achieves success through overcoming weaknesses. The goal of the Winston program is to encourage motivation and foster the self-esteem of each child.

Boys and girls remain at Winston for varying lengths of time, but most students will complete their individualized program in two or three years.

EINSTEIN

The world's leading scientists, historians and philosophers pilgrimaged to Princeton in March 1979 to honor Albert Einstein, a refugee who made a peaceful town in central New Jersey his home and the place where he pursued a lifelong dream of defining the universe.

Along the way, Albert Einstein, whose 100th birthday was observed in 1979 during a centennial celebration in his adopted hometown, helped change the world—and put Princeton in a perpetual spotlight.

Although he was the world's most famous scientist, Einstein, who died in 1955, effortlessly merged his life and work into the quiet Princeton environment.

The professor was left to his own devices, which were mostly taking long walks along the pleasant, tree-arched streets of Princeton, playing his violin for friends and guests, or riding his bicycle or driving his faded gray Studebaker from his home to the Institute for Advanced Study a half-mile away.

Almost everyone knew the white-haired, mustachioed man with mellow eyes, and they casually accepted him as one of the professors in Princeton, a colonial community made up of students, teachers and some merchants and professionals.

For Dr. Einstein, who had lived throughout Europe and elsewhere, Princeton was a haven of tranquillity, a land where the American Revolution had been fought—and won—and a place where he could go about his business without fear of recrimination or reprisal.

Since Einstein moved to Princeton in 1933 and became a U.S. citizen in 1940, he and his hometown became synonymous. His spirit still pervades the historic, Ivy League town, the center of Einstein's universe during the last 22 years of his life.

It was in Princeton where Einstein worked unceasingly on his theory of the universe: How it all began, why it happened the way it did, and what it all means to the inquisitive mind of man.

When Einstein died on April 18, 1955 in Princeton, he left a unique understanding of the physical universe that stands as a monumental achievement unparalleled in the history of human thought.

Einstein was alternately referred to by his peers and admirers as the father of modern science, the father of relativity, the father of the atomic age.

He reduced our physical reality to an easy equation: Energy equals mass times the speed of light squared.

He fathomed the incomprehensible concepts of time and space, building a bridge between the present and a future many million light years away.

Yet those who worked intimately with Einstein in Princeton found him to be profoundly simple, a bit shy, tender and deeply compassionate.

He was a mathematician and a musician, a poet and a humanist. He played his fiddle with the consummate skill of a professional violinist.

His timeless insights are frequently repeated:

The most beautiful and most profound emotion we can experience is the sensation of the mystical. It is the sower of all true science.

133

My religion consists of a humble admiration of the illimitable superior spirit who reveals himself in the slight details we are able to perceive with our frail and feeble minds.

God is subtle, but he is not malicious.

I have no special gift—I am only passionately curious.

Einstein's reverence for nature and its hidden secrets inspired him to the end of his life to search for the truth, the real meaning of the natural order of things.

Although he suffered from heart disease, which afflicted him in mid-life, he maintained a heavy schedule at his cluttered office at the institute and in the second-floor study of his century-old home at 112 Mercer St., midway between the institute and Princeton University.

When a colleague once asked why he worked so hard when his place in history had long been secured, Einstein replied:

"The only way to escape the personal corruption of praise is to go on working. One is tempted to stop and listen to it. The only thing to do is to turn away and go on working. Work. There is nothing else."

As for his eccentric appearance, such as forgetting to put on his socks, Einstein once told an inquiring writer: "It would be a shame if the packaging were more important than the contents."

* * *

Albert Einstein (he had no middle name) was born March 14, 1879 in Ulm, Germany. His father was a manufacturer of electrochemical products, a technical field Einstein was later to explore and radically improve upon.

He was a slow starter, however. His first words were uttered when he was three years old. An Einstein aficionado once remarked that the child waited until he had something to say.

When Einstein applied to the Swiss Federal Institute of Technology in Zurich, he flunked his entrance exam. He was finally admitted after a year's study at a Swiss high school. At that time he became a citizen of Switzerland.

Einstein's office as he left it shortly before he died.

Photo Credit: Alan W. Richards

Upon graduation in 1900, Einstein earned his way as a tutor, substitute teacher and by computing calculations for an astronomer. He was unable to obtain a teaching post at the university because he had irked his instructors by his nonconforming behavior. One of his teachers called him "a lazy dog."

With a total salary of $675 a year, Einstein managed to support himself and his new wife, Mileva Maric from Serbia. She had studied physics with Einstein at the university.

He continued to study, research and do what he described as his "thought experiments." The mental exercises, which he began at 16, led to his original theories on the nature of the universe.

* * *

In 1905, while working as an examiner in the Swiss Patent Office, Einstein published three now historic papers.

The first, "On the Electrodynamics of Moving Bodies," would become his Special Theory of Relativity.

A study on the "Photoelectric Effect" paved the way for today's electronics and the television tube and solar electric (photovoltaic) systems.

A third paper on relativity dealt with his famous equation.

Einstein discovered that energy (E) and mass (M) were really one and the same. Any bit of matter, he found, contained powerful amounts of energy. The incredibly compact mathematical formula gave birth to the nuclear, or atomic age.

The equation translates to energy equals mass times the speed of light (C) squared, or multiplied by itself. Light travels at 186,000 miles per second.

Einstein had added a new dimension to the physical universe: Time.

He defined gravity not as a force—a principle of Newtonian physics—but as a phenomenon of "space-time." His space-time concept was developed into a four-dimensional world that included not only what we see, such as objects separated by space, but what we don't see: Time.

Einstein's relativity says that time and distance depend on the relative motion of the observer. The only absolute is the speed of light.

If one twin, for example, takes off on a high-speed space journey, he will be younger than his Earth-bound brother when he returns.

Einstein explained that the mass of the spaceship and everything on it appears to double relative to what their mass is on Earth.

Paradoxically, the person on the spacecraft notices no changes; he thinks it is time on Earth that is slowing, and that the masses and lengths on the planet are changing.

Einstein spent most of his life trying to discern patterns of behavior in the universe that would fit into a unified system based on cause, not chance, as scientists of his day believed.

"God does not play with dice," was a favorite expression of Einstein, to which his associates responded: "Stop telling God what to do!"

Relativity, as set forth by Einstein, deals with the physical laws governing the outer universe of stars and galaxies—the macrocosm.

At the other end of the physical spectrum, Einstein's theory of relativity probed the microcosm—the inner, invisible universe of atoms and their neutrons, electrons and protons.

The atom, with its nucleus and orbiting electrons and protons, was a miniature solar system, like the world we live in.

At Princeton, Einstein delved into the two worlds of matter and energy, space and time, hoping to find a unified cosmic theme with which man could relate all of the wonders and mysteries of nature, from the smallest bit of matter to the biggest star in the galaxy.

* * *

Einstein was 26 years old when he offered his theories on relativity and nuclear, or quantum, physics. It was a watershed for both Einstein and science. Soon, the scientific community would put him in the company of Aristotle, Newton and Galileo as among the greatest thinkers in history.

After seven years at the patent office, Einstein moved on to academic posts in Prague and Zurich. In 1914, just before the outbreak of World War I, he became a professor at the University of Berlin and took over the newly established Center for Theoretical Physics at the Kaiser Wilhelm Institute.

A pacifist and socialist, Einstein publicly condemned the war, infuriating the German militarists. His wife and two sons, Hans Albert and Eduard, returned to Switzerland. The separation during the war years led to a divorce. Shortly after, Einstein married his cousin Elsa, a widow.

When Einstein was awarded the 1921 Nobel Prize in Physics for his photoelectric theory, he gave the $30,000 prize money to his former wife and children. Hans Albert went on to be a hydraulic engineer and teacher at the University of California, Berkeley. Eduard went into medicine and stayed in Europe. They died several years ago.

During the rise of Hitler, Einstein became a marked scholar, considered a dangerous eccentric. The Nazis branded him as an enemy of the state who was masterminding a Jewish conspiracy to corrupt science and destroy civilization.

Outside of Germany, Einstein was besieged with requests for lectures, papers, academic positions . . . virtually anything he wanted in his pursuit of what makes the universe tick.

Einstein was at the California Institute for Technology on a visiting professorship when Hitler became chancellor of Germany in January 1933. Einstein never returned to his homeland.

He sorted through scores of offers from the most prominent universities in the world, seeking a permanent place to live and work in an atmosphere of freedom and creativity.

Einstein chose Princeton.

The reasons for Einstein's fateful decision were due to the effects of another individual of German Jewish origins—Louis Bamberger.

When conditions in Germany became intolerable for Jews, Bamberger, founder of the department store chain that bears his name, decided to create a sanctuary for German Jewish refugee scholars, physicists and scientists.

Bamberger selected a site near Princeton University to build his Institute for Advanced Study. It began in 1930 with a $5 million endowment from Bamberger and his sister, Mrs. Felix Fuld.

The rectangular red-brick building with its handsome clock tower sits in spacious surroundings (about a square mile of prop-

Einstein was the first faculty member at the Institute for Advanced Study in Princeton, built in 1930 by Louis Bamberger and his sister, Mrs. Felix Fuld.

Star-Ledger Photo

erty) off Olden Lane, just a few minutes' walk from downtown Princeton.

Einstein, who became the first faculty member at the institute, purchased a white-framed home just around the corner from Olden Lane. It was large enough to accommodate his wife, younger sister, Maja, stepdaughter, Margot, and his personal secretary, Helen Dukas.

Einstein's wife died in 1936 and his sister in 1951. Dukas took up housekeeping and cooking, in addition to being Einstein's secretary. (She had joined him as a young woman in 1928.)

Helen Dukas and Margot Einstein remained at 112 Mercer St., organizing the enormous amount of material that amassed during Einstein's long and productive life. Dukas put in a few hours a day at the institute, preparing volumes of information on the Princeton scientist.

Photo Credit: Gordon Bishop

Einstein's Princeton home at 112 Mercer Street is expected to be designated as a national historic landmark.

* * *

The assistant director of the institute, Mary Wisnovsky, was a friend and neighbor of the famous man, and often joined him on his legendary strolls along the shady streets of Princeton.

"He was a gentle, tender person and spoke with a distinct accent," Mrs. Wisnovsky related during a whispering tour through the monastic-like corridors of the Princeton institute.

"Dr. Einstein was an accomplished violinist. He played chamber music, mostly Mozart and Bach, with my mother (Louise Strunsky), a concert pianist."

On the wall behind Wisnovsky's desk hangs an 8-by-10-inch picture of Einstein, showing him sitting behind a radio microphone wearing a baggy gray sweater, his white hair covering his ears and neck.

The picture is signed, "To Mary and Martha Strunsky, Albert Einstein. 1946." (Martha is Mary's sister.)

The girls' father, Robert, had persuaded Einstein to broadcast a speech from his home on the post-war dangers of the atom bomb. Strunsky, who began his career at Bamberger's, worked at CBS.

Photo Credit: Gordon Bishop

Mary Wisnovsky holds up a prized photo of Einstein giving a radio speech on the dangers of the atomic bomb. She is assistant director of the Institute for Advanced Studies in Princeton.

Ironically, it was a letter Einstein wrote to President Franklin Roosevelt, revealing that the Germans were probably developing an atomic bomb, that prompted Roosevelt to start the secretive "Manhattan Project," which led to the construction and testing of the world's first nuclear device at Los Alamos, N.M. Shortly after, similiar A-bombs were detonated over Hiroshima and Nagasaki, ending World War II.

Einstein's office at the institute has not been preserved as a museum. It has been used continuously by a stream of scholars and scientists since Einstein's death.

"Dr. Einstein would have wanted it that way," Wisnovsky says.

Eventually, Einstein's Princeton home is expected to be designated as a national historic landmark.

A local photographer, Alan Watson Richards, took a picture of Einstein's desk and blackboard as he left it before entering Princeton Hospital for treatment of cardiac complications. He died from an aneurysm and his body was cremated at the Ewing Crematorium. Einstein's brain was removed and analyzed by neuro-specialists seeking clues to his rare intellect.

Richards first met Einstein under quite unusual circumstances in 1943. He recounts it in a book released in time for the Einstein centennial. The book, "Einstein As I Knew Him," was published by Harvest House Press, Princeton.

Richards recalled his first encounter with Einstein:

"A familiar white-haired figure, his face looking straight ahead, was walking along a street in Princeton, seemingly oblivious to the world around him.

"Suddenly, the stooped old man disappeared from view. He had tripped and stumbled into a storm sewer.

"Within seconds, a hand reached out and pulled the fallen man to his feet."

Over the next 12 years, Richards served as Einstein's roving photographer, keeping a watchful eye on him as he made his daily rounds.

The last photograph of Einstein taken by Richards was in the scientist's study in late 1954. Einstein was wearing his usual plain sweater, staring into soft sunlight filtering through the window, a pen in hand. Six months later he was dead.

A favorite of Richards is a bleak wintry picture of Einstein heading down the long path from the institute, a stark, shrinking figure in black coat and hat.

Richards captioned it "The Loneliness of a Long Distance Thinker."

Einstein's favorite candid photo by Richards was one taken on his 70th birthday in his home. It shows Einstein just gazing out into space.

Alan Watson Richards took this photo of Einstein strolling in Princeton. The photographer titles it "The Loneliness of a Long Distance Thinker."

View of Monmouth College's Woodrow Wilson Hall. The West Long Branch campus is the former Shadow Lawn Estate, built during the Depression by Hubert T. Parson.

ESTATES

ome for America's wealthiest, whether a Rockefeller, Vanderbilt or Gould, is a fabled castle or baronial estate hidden in a lush forest with singing streams and meandering footpaths.

Many of America's first multimillionaires found their idyllic Garden of Eden in the pastoral valleys of North Jersey and the gently rolling countryside of Central Jersey.

They built their mansions and landscaped their grounds into grandiose works of live-in art. Most of them still stand as private estates, while others have been absorbed by college campuses or converted into museums and corporate centers. A few were thoughtlessly lost in the suburban development boom.

Early this century, a mile area around Morristown was referred to as "Millionaires' Row," with names like Vanderbilt, Rockefeller and Dodge rounding out the social register. They were later joined by the Dukes, Dillons, Forbes, Fenwicks, Bradys, Englehards and Twomblys in the outlying Somerset-Hunterdon region.

Today, kings and captains of industry continue to be drawn to the land of red foxes, green pastures and historic vistas.

King Hassan II of Morocco paid $7.5 million in February 1983 for the Kate Macy Ladd estate in Somerset County. The 500-acre paradise in Peapack-Gladstone, Far Hills and Bedminster features a 40-room, brick Tudor mansion and eight other buildings for servants, groundskeepers, equipment and animals.

The late Walter G. Ladd was a business associate of John D. Rockefeller.

The Ladd-Hassan transaction turned out to be the biggest real estate sale in the state's history. The previous record had been set by the flamboyant automaker John Z. DeLorean when he bought the Cowperthwaite estate in Bedminster in 1981 for $3.5 million.

One of the king's more famous neighbors is Jacqueline Kennedy Onassis, who enjoys the sport of aristocrats, fox hunting, in rural Somerset-Hunterdon. Other notable residents are former U.S. Treasury Secretary Douglas Dillon and former Secretary of State Cyrus Vance. Farther down the road in Harding Township resides former Treasury Secretary William Simon.

Rock promoter Don Kirshner spent some $5 million to build a dream house in 1978 for his wife in the Morris hills of Harding Township. The Kirshners soon tired of their 17-room contemporary showcase containing a Jacuzzi in every bathroom, an indoor disco ballroom, a completely electronic game room and a movie screening room.

They auctioned off the 29-acre estate in 1982, replete with outdoor disco, swimming pool with underwater stereophonic sound, two greenhouses, two tennis courts, a full-size basketball court, dog run, carriage house and garage space for nine cars.

* * *

The most lavish and expensive estate in New Jersey is the stately "country house" of J. Seward Johnson, whose family fortunes were amassed by the multi-billion-dollar Johnson & Johnson pharmaceutical empire based in New Brunswick.

The Kate Macy Ladd estate, which straddles Peapack-Gladstone, Far Hills and Bedminster, was purchased by King Hassan II of Morocco for $7.5 million. The transaction was the biggest real estate sale in the state's history.

Star-Ledger Photo

Considered one of the 10 most costly residential investments in the United States, Johnson's "**Jasna Polana**" estate in Princeton has a bottom line price tag of $21 million, but with elaborate changes could have cost upward of $30 million during the nearly five years it took to build in the mid-1970s.

The Polish name for the Johnson estate means "Bright Glade." The eight-bedroom mansion is situated on 140 exclusive acres in ivy league Princeton. The 54,000 square feet of living space is larger than a football field. An electrified wire fence rambles 4½ miles around the heavily wooded retreat.

Protecting the mansion is a mile of handcut, pink-and-buff stone wall. The cost of the wall was somewhere around a half-million dollars.

The house is a model for the ultimate creature comforts: Heated marble floors in the bathrooms with heated, gold-plated towel racks, and tubs carved from whole pieces of Italian marble. Windows are bulletproof and even the basement casement windows are crafted from bronze.

A golden floor sets off the enclosed swimming pool. Nearby is an orchid greenhouse that could pass for an astronomer's observatory. An indoor tennis court is also a bowling green. Add to these a reflecting pool, an amphitheater, an herb garden and a two-story breakfast pavilion, and there is no reason ever to venture beyond the hot-wire fence.

And for the family pet, there's a glass-covered, air-conditioned doghouse with a tidy kitchenette. A fancy bronze staircase connects the dog's grounds to the master's manicured lawns and gardens.

* * *

The **Shadow Lawn** estate at Monmouth College in West Long Branch was the site of the most expensive movie musical ever made, "Annie," the comic strip story of Little Orphan Annie and the Wall Street billionaire Daddy Warbucks.

Shadow Lawn was built when the stock market crashed in 1929. The big spender was Hubert T. Parson, then president of the nation's biggest department store chain, F. W. Woolworth Co.

The 128-room, Versailles-styled mansion occupied a 108-acre tract just a mile or two from the Atlantic Ocean. It is ranked as one of the 20 most outstanding mansions in the United States.

The original mansion on the site was the summer home of President Woodrow Wilson. It burned down in 1927. In that shore resort area, several Presidents, including Ulysses S. Grant, vacationed, along with the rich and the famous: Solomon R. Guggenheim, Jim Fisk and James A. Hearn.

After its completion in 1930, Shadow Lawn was like a little city. Lining the great grassy expanse leading to the $10 million establishment (1930 dollar value) are magnificent shade trees, which inspired the name Shadow Lawn. The servants' quarters are as grand as any standard mansion: 35 bedrooms and 12 baths, with a handsome cottage for additional leisure and pleasure. The superintendent and his family had their own 10-room house.

The little city also took in a two-story garage, eight greenhouses, a horse barn with six stalls, a cattle barn with 12 stanchions, a poultry house, a two-story palm house, a bullpen, a ram pen, sheep pens, pheasant pens, rabbit hutches, an icehouse, cottages for the dairymen, the greenhouse keepers and poultrymen, and kennels for the six police dogs that were turned loose on the grounds every midnight.

The property was rimmed with a wrought-iron fence as fine as the one ringing Buckingham Palace.

The French mansion features a three-story-high great hall, a 100-foot-long, leaded-glass skylight set with thousands of electric lights, a four-manual Aeolian organ, a Pompeian swimming pool with filtered and heated water, a Brunswick bowling alley, a theater, gymnasium, golf room, a silver movie screen and two Paramount projectors in a fireproof screening room, a dance floor and a sunken garden surrounded by a tea house.

Parson's designers also laid out a nine-hole golf course and colonnades with electric fountains with alternating lights.

The mansion is constructed of statuary Indiana limestone, steel fireproof tile and marble, of which there are 48 foreign and domestic varieties. There are 17 master suites with 19 baths, each suite in a different period of decoration and furnishings. The dining room is of French walnut.

The estate had its own communal telephone, water, electrical and sewerage systems. There were also five vegetable gardens, flower gardens, raspberry land currant patches, a grape arbor and artificial lake stocked with ducks, geese and swans. In the center of the lake, on a small island, was a small summer house.

* * *

The **Gould Mansion** was erected in the 1890s by George Jay Gould, son of the legendary railroad magnate Jay Gould. The Gould estate is now part of Georgian Court College, a liberal arts school for women in Lakewood, Ocean County.

In early 1896, Gould purchased choice property on the eastern shore of Lake Carasaljo in Lakewood. Gould retained Bruce Price, the noted architect and father of Emily Post, to design the buildings and gardens.

The mansion was completed on Christmas Eve 1898, according to Sister Mary Christina Geis of the college faculty, who researched the history of the Gould property and development. The Sisters of Mercy, founded in Plainfield in 1908, acquired the

Star-Ledger Photo

Another embellished interior is the mansion at Georgian Court College in Lakewood, the former Gould estate.

Gould estate in 1924. Sister Geis offers the following account of the Gould estate:

Gould named the palatial, 200-acre, British-French-Roman estate "Georgian Court." The exterior of his country house was finished in gray stucco with trim in marble and terra-cotta, a charming fusion of Georgian dignity and Norman grace, an English Georgian house with a French chateau roof.

The late 19th Century interior of the mansion is essentially eclectic, displaying fine marbles and woods, hand-painted ceilings, gilded plasterwork decoration, and period rooms.

Guests are greeted in the great entrance hall by huge Ionic columns, a curved marble staircase and gilt rail and balcony balustrade. A French-form chandelier glitters with 150,000 pieces of glass, flooding the hall with soft light.

Three of the most exquisite friezes in America, "The Canterbury Pilgrims," decorate the upper portion of three walls of the great hall. Among the pilgrims are a miller, lawyer, the prioress, the wife of Bath, the knight, the host and 18 other characters who make up the tales of Chaucer. The colors of the frieze blend fittingly with the crimson and gold decor of the hall.

The pine forest around Lake Carasaljo was transformed into spacious Italian gardens set off by urns and statuary. A wrought iron eagle perched on a dragon was mounted on a boulder base and placed at a point where paths converge in the garden. By the lake, a lagoon or inlet was created with an imposing marble esplanade.

Near the lagoon sits an electrical Apollo fountain in a large circular basin. The 10-foot-tall Apollo and a chariot, a colossal nautical shell topped by an octopus, are cast in bronze. Other figures—cherubs, mermaids and seahorses—are carved from white Istrian marble.

An authentic tea garden, a Cha-niwa, was built on a one-acre plot next to the Italian Gardens. A curving path leads to a rustic wall enclosing the front and right sides of the tea garden. The entrance is through a hooded gateway.

A little square teahouse is a genuine Sukiya, identified by its low-pitched roof and overhangs. The Japanese Gardens have the familiar waterfall and stream, wooden bridges, stepping stones, vari-shaped stone lanterns, trees and shrubbery. East meets West where the Japanese cherry trees mingle with the Jersey scrub pines.

* * *

Skylands Manor House was built following World War I by Clarence McKenzie Lewis, a German engineer and financier. Inspired by the ideal combination of sky, lake and mountain beauty of the Ramapos, Lewis planned his magnificent Skylands mansion in 1924 on a high plateau in Ringwood.

The design was influenced by the many appealing styles of the English baronial homesteads. Skylands was built as a summer haven on 1,000 acres of scenic splendor.

Each piece of outer stone quarried from Pierson Ridge above the Emerald Pools on the eastern edge of the estate was cut to exact specifications. The weathered edges were exposed to give the mansion an appearance of antiquity.

All of the exterior iron work is made of non-rusting monel metal. The wrought iron was created by probably the finest smith to have ever worked in the United States: Samuel Yellin, an eminent Czechoslovakian who also designed the iron work for the Princeton University Chapel, the Valley Forge Chapel and the Federal Reserve Bank in New York.

Even the mansion's copper rain pipes and leader heads are reproductions of antique models and are lead-plated to match the historical style.

The dramatic interior of the mansion was decorated like a fancied British castle. Fine-grained English oak doors and woodwork are predominately featured throughout Skylands, and intricately-carved, centuries-old wood panels were brought intact from manor houses and chateaus in Europe.

Many of the passageways are deliberately low and narrow in construction to create the authentic English interior motif. Great halls are placed here and there, replete with imported antique fireplaces and high ceilings. Leaded stained-glass windows are tastefully set with medallions imported from Germany, Switzerland and France. Twisting stairways lead to upper floors and downward to the one-time wine cellars.

The 44-room Jacobean mansion is focalized on formal gardens and athletic fields, tennis courts, two swimming pools, picnic spots, 23 miles of roads and a 35-mile view.

A parlor porch contains weathered teakwood benches and tables built from an old ship. The fireplace in the Great Hall is an exact replica of one belonging to a Scottish nobleman of the 17th Century. The date noted in the fireplace is 1619. The breakfast room was designed in Italian marble. The lavabo, of ancient white marble, was taken from an old Venetian palace.

Skylands was purchased by the state in 1966 and is open to the public.

* * *

Some of New Jersey's most impressive mansions have been preserved as museums and historical-cultural centers. One of the most distinguished is the **Ford Mansion** in Morristown, built in 1773 by Col. Jacob Ford Jr. and used as Washington's headquarters in 1779-80.

The Ford Mansion and the Jockey Hollow encampment where Washington's troops spent the harshest winter of the Revolution became America's first national historic park in 1933. Nearby is **Acorn Hall**, a Victorian architectural masterpiece.

Two Princeton mansions have been designated as homes for the state's governors.

Morven has frequently been described as New Jersey's most historic building. The earliest section of the house was built by Richard Stockton in 1701 on a tract purchased from William Penn in the west Jersey wilderness. Stockton's grandson was one of the signers of the Declaration of Independence.

The Continental Congress met in Princeton in the summer of 1783 under the presidency of Elias Boudinot, brother of Stockton's wife, Annis. Boudinot chose Morven for his official residence and it was there that American leaders gathered to celebrate the signing of the peace treaty terminating the war. Morven, in a sense, filled the role of the first White House of the newly independent United States.

Annis Boudinot Stockton named the mansion Morven, after the home of the ancient Caledonian King Fingal. The Caledonian story contained this passage:

Sons of Morven, spread the feast,
Send the night away with song.

Morven is an early Georgian structure reflecting the classical influence of Italian Renaissance architecture that reached England in the 17th Century. With its meticulously kept gardens and centuries-old trees, Morven today covers some five acres.

The quarters once occupied by slaves still stand behind the main building. A swimming pool with cabanas, as well as tennis courts, have been added this century.

* * *

Drumthwacket, another Princeton mansion, was designated the official residence of the governor this year because it is larger and able to accommodate sizable state functions. The 40-room mansion was built in 1833 by Charles Olden, a state senator who was elected governor in 1859.

Drumthwacket, a Celtic term meaning "wooded hills," was named by Moses Taylor Pyne, who bought the 11-acre site bordering the Princeton Battleground in 1893. Of the 15 main rooms in the original part of the house, 14 contain fireplaces. Six Ionic columns grace the grand front of the Greek revival-styled mansion.

Inside, the stairs and Palladian window are late 19th Century alterations. The flanking 19th Century wings are recessed from the plane of the central house and represent late 19th and early 20th Century colonial revival modifications.

* * *

Two other historic mansions are the **Ballantine House** in Newark and the **Emlen Physick Estate** in Cape May.

Part of the Newark Museum, the elegant townhouse on Newark's once fashionable Washington Park was built by John H. Ballantine in 1883 when he was the "king of brewers."

The Newark Museum rescued the townhouse in 1974 and returned it to its original grandeur. The Metropolitan Society of the Victorian Society in America presented the Ballantine House its 1976 "Preservation Award."

The 8½-acre Physick Estate was restored by the Mid-Atlantic Center for the Arts, which operates it as a community and cultural center. The 16-room house was finished in 1881 for Dr. Emlen Physick, a prominent Philadelphia physician.

The Victorian summer home is one of the few remaining examples by the renowned 19th Century architect, Frank Furness. Evident in the structure is his interest in varied silhouettes, multiplication of gables, hooded dormer windows and massive upside-down chimneys.

* * *

Castles can be seen from hilltops and mountainsides—stark medieval recreations of ancestral originals from England, France, Germany and Italy.

Jane Englehard lives in a Rhine-like castle called **Cragwood** on a 172-acre lofty perch in Far Hills. Former State Sen. Frank "Pat" Dodd once occupied the English-styled **Castlewood** in exclusive Llewyllyn Park, West Orange, where Thomas Edison erected his stunning Victorian **Glenmont** estate a century ago.

There are castles in Flemington and Verona-Cedar Grove, on Lake Hopatcong and on the Rutherford campus of Fairleigh Dickinson University. But the most famous and most visible castle in New Jersey clings majestically to the side of Garret Mountain in Paterson overlooking the Passaic Valley and the New York skyline.

Star-Ledger Photo

Drumthwacket, the official residence of the New Jersey governor, is a 40-room mansion in Princeton.

Garlands of holiday greenery decorate the library of the Victorian Ballantine House in Newark.

Victorian furnishings enhance the family parlor of the Emlen Physick Estate in Cape May. The 16-room manor is maintained by the nonprofit Mid-Atlantic Center for the Arts.

Lambert Castle is the rags-to-riches saga of Catholina Lambert, who rose from a poor delivery boy in his native England to become the silk magnate of Paterson when that old industrial town was the silk capital of the world.

Lambert patterned his fortress dwelling after Warwick Castle in England. By building "Belle Vista," named in honor of his wife Isabel, Lambert was able to relive the glories of English nobility he fantasized about as a youth.

Built between 1890-93, Lambert Castle's most prominent feature is a 70-foot tower made from stone hauled from a local quarry. At the bottom of the central stairway is a picture-frame opening so Lambert could view his wife as she descended the wide wooden steps into the main hall.

Lambert had lived in his castle until his death in 1923. The turreted estate was then acquired by the Passaic County Park Commission and incorporated in the 525-acre Garret Mountain Reservation in 1929.

Opened to the public in 1934, the Lambert Castle Museum has turned into an antiquarian's attic filled with 60,000 silk samples, 20,000 manuscripts, pamphlets and maps, 2,500 rare newspaper editions, and an ever-expanding reference library.

The museum's collections extend from the Colonial and Federal eras through the 19th and 20th centuries—an industrial and technological age associated with the rise of men like Catholina Lambert. Among Lambert's heirlooms is a 1½-ton clock originally built for the Columbian Exposition.

*   *   *

One mansion, in Convent Station, Morris County, is called a castle because of its imposing turrets and embattlements, but the 40-room **Glynallyn** mansion is really an English manor house, a New Jersey copy of Compton Wynyates in Warwickshire.

The Tudor era showcase radiates with stained-glass windows, leaded casement windows and 17 chimneys. On a seven-acre site along Canfield Road, Glynallyn is presently the headquarters for the General Drafting Co., mapmakers and publishers of travel aids and educational material. An old dungeon downstairs with Gothic vaulted ceiling and authentic torch-style lighting has been converted into a company refectory.

*   *   *

The social gem of Morris County, when the area was home to more than 100 millionaires worth in excess of $330 million (well over $3 billion today), was the 750-acre Ruth Vanderbilt Twombly estate named "**Florham**," from the first syllables of family names.

The estate, now the Florham-Madison campus of Fairleigh Dickinson University, was built in 1896 by Miss Twombly's parents. Her mother was Mrs. Florence Vanderbilt Twombly, daughter of William H. Vanderbilt, reputedly the richest man in the world at that time.

The 100-room mansion was modeled after Hampton Court in England. Within the mansion's grounds were a large swimming pool, indoor clay tennis court and a huge carriage house, which FDU converted into eight laboratories and research facilities. The university paid $1.5 million for the historic New Jersey showplace in 1957.

The Florham drawing room was superbly decorated with Louis XIII Barberini-Ffoulke tapestry and the great diamond-shaped tiled hall also displayed fine tapestries on one side and sculpted columns on the other.

A feudal barony, the Vanderbilt-Twombly country home was the scene of lavish parties and musicales featuring Metropolitan Opera stars.

The extensive gardens, greenhouses and model farm for a prized herd of Holstein cows have become the headquarters for Exxon Research Center in Florham Park.

*   *   *

The landmark **Froh Heim Farm** (Happy Home) in Far Hills was assembled in 1882 from nearly 40 farms consisting of more than 5,000 acres. Still privately owned, the Froh Heim estate was put together by Grant B. Schely, who gave Far Hills its name.

The original property contained 24 miles of roads winding through landscaped parks and woodlands, crossing 27 stone bridges built from giant boulders taken from nearby mountainsides. Schely also created many waterfalls and built a railroad spur right to his home so he wouldn't have to drive to the train station. His estate had the telephone number of 1.

Star-Ledger Photo

Lambert Castle in Paterson, built by silk magnate Catholine Lambert, was patterned after Warwick Castle in England. Today it is tended by the Passaic County Park Commission.

The famed farm was noted for its tower, which stood 120 feet above sea level. Designed in the Oriental motif, Schely's estate was used for the filming of scenic backdrops for Mary Pickford's "Madam Butterfly." Another motion picture was also made on the farm, "The Wild Girl," starring Eva Tanguay.

Over the decades, the sprawling farm and squire's country home were restructured along Spanish architectural lines. The grounds were reduced to 360 acres and the refashioned home to 18 rooms with several baths.

* * *

The **Blair Mansion** in Peapack is a French chateau that was once the social and cultural center of Somerset County. Built in 1903 by Clarence Ledyard Blair, "Blairsden," as the locals nicknamed it, commands a breathtaking view of Ravine Lake.

Now occupied as a retreat for religious sisters, St. Joseph's Villa still retains its beautiful limestone, brick and concrete Old World facade. The front doors are iron- and brass-framed, one-inch-thick glass weighing 1,000 pounds each.

A hallway runs the entire length of the chateau. The library, living room and morning room are each the size of a small gymnasium and all finished in different kinds of marble and oak; walnut paneling enhanced by bronze, crystal and silver fixtures, and several fireplaces.

The dining room ceiling is covered by hand-painted murals and each room has its own full-length casement window of plate glass. The second and third floors have 16 master bedrooms and 15 servants' rooms, each with a fireplace, plus nine master baths and several sitting rooms.

An enormous bronze and silver chandelier lights the second-floor landing. Two elevators operate from the ground floor to the fourth level.

To duplicate the Blair mansion today would cost around $30 million.

* * *

The **Massey Mansion** is a 75-year-old, red brick structure that was given a new lease on life this year when it opened to the public as the Lambertville Designer Show House.

The building was featured in the December 1911 issue of House and Garden magazine. The Lambertville house was built by Philadelphia architects C.E. Schermerhorn and Wilson K. Phi-

lips. Restored to mint condition, the Massey Mansion is a fine example of old country charm where comfort and beauty are not overwhelmed by ostentatious decorations.

In Oak Ridge, Passaic County, stands the glamorous 26-room **Ringling Mansion**, built in 1917 of native fieldstone with two-foot-thick walls and 14 fireplaces. Circus king Alfred G. Ringling situated his massively columned home on a 1,000-acre tract along Lake Swannanoa.

A two-story, sunken, walnut-paneled organ room in the south wing adjoins a spacious concrete porch with a view of the major dam of Lake Swannanoa. The centerpiece of the special room was a $26,000 organ, worth a quarter-million dollars today.

Other features of the Ringling Mansion include a $10,000 walnut-and-ebony fireplace mantle imported from Italy, a cupid frieze above the walnut-ebony paneled dining-room walls, and a library finished in San Domingan mahogany.

Ringling entertained such silver screen celebrities as Douglas Fairbanks Sr. and Metropolitan Opera star Geraldine Farrar.

The mansion, an historic landmark, is open to the public.

* * *

Other familiar mansions and estates about the state follow.

Hobart Manor in Wayne is part of a castle constructed in 1877 by a Scottish immigrant, John McCollough, who earned a small fortune in the Paterson wool trade.

Until the 1976 Bicentennial celebration, the fieldstone manor was called Haledon Hall. Of neo-Gothic Tudor design, the 10-room castle boasted two octagon-shaped turrets. They were later replaced with lead-glass bay windows.

McCollough expanded his slate-roofed castle in 1915 into a 40-room mansion with fireplaces in almost every room and a spiral staircase in the main entrance hall. A national historic site, it now houses the administrative offices of William Paterson College.

The **Blauvelt Mansion** on Kinderkamack Road in Oradell was saved from the wrecking ball when an architect decided to make it both his home and office.

The dark brown feudal-looking structure with towers, turrets and high-peaked roofs was built in the 1890s by Kimball C. Atwood, a wealthy insurance executive. The 200-acre estate was acquired in the 1920s by Elmer Blauvelt, who named it "Bluefield," an Americanized version of his Dutch family name.

The Bergen County landmark looming on a hillside looks like a haunted Halloween house, a place where Edgar Allan Poe would probably feel very much at home.

The **Stout Mansion** on the banks of the Navesink River is one of the most expensive estates in Monmouth County. The 19-room house, built in 1917-18 by investment broker Andrew Varick Stout, was sold for the first time this year for nearly $2 million by Stout's son, Bayard.

The wealthy DuPont family visited the Middletown estate soon after it was finished and patterned a staircase in their Winterthur mansion in Delaware after Stout's floating circular staircase.

The secluded, 7.5-acre, wooded waterfront tract is covered with oaks, lindens, dogwoods, firs, giant redwoods and Japanese maples. Designed by John Russell Pope, the architect for the National Gallery, the elegant Georgian mansion features ornate plaster molding, solid brass hardware, six marble fireplaces and detailed cabinetry.

Oak trellis work decorates the brick exterior, along with marble sills and parapets, copper flashing and leaders with a heavy slate roof. The spacious dining and living rooms have manteled fireplaces and floor-to-ceiling windows with a panoramic view of the river.

The kitchen wing is equipped with an elevator, butler's pantry and a silver safe. Sliding glass doors open to a 35-foot brick patio and 20-by-40-foot heated pool.

The Stout Mansion was the subject of a pictorial feature in the March 1921 issue of Country Life, a Doubleday publication.

Courtesy: N.J. Div. of Travel & Tourism

FARMS

It's only a small spot of earth to be sure, but New Jersey was the "Garden of the World" when a new nation called America was being settled by Europeans in the 17th Century. As the largest producer of wheat in the New World, New Jersey was America's first cornucopia.

Although the Industrial Revolution transformed the Garden State from a breadbasket to a leading technological center within a century, New Jersey remains a green, fertile peninsula nourished by the greatest supply of fresh water in the East.

From the rocky hills of Sussex and Passaic counties to the flat coastal plains of Cumberland and Salem counties, the finest horses, bulls and cows graze in pastoral settings as serene and colorful as picture postcards.

Colts Neck stirs up images of sleek thoroughbreds growing up in the central farm belt, while just a few miles to the north fox hunts continue in the grand old tradition in fields and valleys marked by crumbling stone walls.

Holstein cows and modern condominiums coexist peacefully in suburban rural fringes of Burlington, Hunterdon and Somerset counties. Preservation of the countryside has become a Green-Acres obsession in New Jersey, the most urbanized state in the nation. Yet two-thirds of the land is still open for recreation and farming.

Of the 4,813,000 acres in the Garden State, 3 million acres today give New Jersey a predominantly green and invigorating image, with a million acres in agriculture and 2 million acres in forests and woodlands.

Less than 2 million acres are developed for urban-suburban uses, including industry, transportation and commerce.

Just how green is New Jersey's garden after more than 300 years of clearing, plowing, planting and harvesting? Although ranked 45th out of 50 states in land committed to farming, New Jersey is the second largest producer of blueberries, third in cranberries, spinach and summer potatoes, and fourth in asparagus, green peppers, peaches and tomatoes (fresh and processed).

New Jersey's rich harvest includes everything from asparagus to zucchini. The Garden State's bounty is much more than fruits and vegetables, poultry and dairy products. It's oysters and mushrooms, honey and horses, orchids and lobsters.

The most valuable farmland in America lies within the borders of the Garden State, according to the U.S. Department of Agriculture. At $3,148 per acre, it's the richest soil in the country, compared to the lowest per acre price ($165) in Wyoming.

Farming roots run deep in the Jersey soil. Quakers established their first farming colony at Salem in 1675.

New food production techniques were developed in the Garden State, which is home for the world's first frozen food plant at Seabrook Farms (1933), the first American book on fruit culture (1817), the first agricultural society (1781), the first tin can packing of tomatoes (1849), the first organized agricultural commodity association (cranberries: 1862), and the first marketing "cooperative" society (1867).

The world's first cast iron plow was forged by Charles Newbold in Burlington County in 1797. The iron plow, later replaced by steel, improved the efficiency of soil tillage and made possible large-scale farms. Before then, agriculture was inhibited by primitive tillage tools, such as manually operated mattocks and spades.

William Manning, a Plainfield farmer, invented the reciprocating knife blade in 1831. Three years later, Cyrus McCormick adapted Manning's blade to his mechanical grain reaper, thus emancipating farmers from the stoop labor of wielding sickle and scythe.

The disc harrow, variations of which are still basic components of soil preparation machines, was invented by Frederick Nishwitz of Morris County in 1869.

Otto Niederer, a Swiss emigre to Mercer County, invented the mechanical egg grading machine (separation by size) in 1931. That was followed by Niederer's dry cleaning machine for eggs. Both machines took the drudgery out of preparing eggs for market, a manual chore which previously enslaved the egg farmer's wife.

In 1869, Joseph Campbell, a fruit merchant, and Abram Anderson, an ice box manufacturer, formed the first partnership to can tomatoes, vegetables, jellies, condiments and mincemeat. Their first plant in Camden developed into the world's largest soup factory.

Campbell Soup organized the first formal industrial-agricultural research department in 1939. Sales topped $100 million in 1942, $500 million in 1958, $1 billion in 1958 and $2 billion in 1979.

While Campbell's was becoming one of the world's largest food producers, New Jersey farmers were introducing a new approach for selling their agricultural products. The first livestock auction took place near Woodstown in 1926 and two years later consumers found good buys at the first vegetable auction markets in Cedarville and Rosenhayn. In June 1930, eggs were put on the auction block for the first time in Toms River and sold to the highest bidder.

The world's first certified milk was produced on a dairy farm in Fairfield in 1893. Issac Newton of Burlington County founded the Federal Crop Reporting Service in 1866.

Joseph D. Wilson of Stockton initiated the first long distance shipment of chicks in the United States, sending day-old peeps to Chicago by train in 1892.

The first plant patent in the country was granted in 1931 to Henry F. Bosenberg of New Brunswick and assigned to the Somerset Rose Nursery for "Dawn Rose."

Elizabeth White will always be remembered as the Whitesbog woman who developed cultivated blueberries on her plantation in the Pinelands and sent the first shipment to the marketplace in 1916.

Another famous name in agriculture is George Hammell Cook, recognized throughout the United States as an innovative agriculturist, geologist and educator. Rutgers' Cook College bears his name.

Born in 1818 on a small Morris County farm, Cook was appointed professor of chemistry and natural sciences at Rutgers College in 1853. During the next 36 years, Cook established a college farm and put into practice some of his theories about farming.

The New Brunswick campus was the site of the nation's first agricultural experiment station. It was soon copied by agricultural schools throughout the country.

After the Civil War, New Jersey became the chicken capital of the Union. By 1879, the world's largest chick incubator was operating around-the-clock at Cresskill in Bergen County.

The first cooperative artificial breeding association began in 1938 in Hunterdon County. That year, 1,000 cows were bred artificially in New Jersey. Artificial insemination has since become an accepted practice for breeding the best dairy herds in the world.

As land became a precious commodity in New Jersey during the development boom of the '50s and '60s, agricultural production took on a new look. Greenhouses sprouted everywhere and ornamental horticulture bloomed into a profitable business for a new breed of farmer.

The typical farm in New Jersey today is a 130-acre operation run by a family in which the father's age averages out to 58. Some 8,000 farms, plus associated food industries, generate more than $3 billion a year in sales.

"Sweet Jersey Corn," for example, fetched a record high in 1984 of $11.3 million. The state's soybean production topped 4.1 million bushels, netting farmers nearly $26 million, while the wheat crop amounted to 1.7 million bushels worth $5.7 million.

Those juicy Jersey tomatoes brought in a record $20.1 million, with the total vegetable crop, including beans, peppers, lettuce and other fresh produce, tipping the scales at $100 million.

Fruit and berry crops enjoyed a plentiful season with a cash value of $65.1 million, while dairy, livestock, poultry and honey yields exceeded $100 million.

What is considered the best (and also the most expensive) ice cream in the world is made in Woodbridge. It's sold under the Haagen-Dazs label, which happens to be a made-up name that means nothing, except today it means one of the finest ice creams that money can buy.

Another promising agricultural development is the emergence of a wine industry in New Jersey in the 1980s as seven vintners and two farmers sow the seeds and ferment a variety of grapes that will ultimately yield a multi-million-dollar crop. "Chateau Jersey" could someday be the Haagen-Dazs of the wine industry: Selective—and incredibly good.

* * *

Agriculture in an industrialized state is constantly threatened by encroachment and development. Under the 25-year reign of State Agricultural Secretary Phillip Alampi, which ended in 1983, the nation's first farmlands tax assessment act became law (1963), saving thousands of green acres that otherwise would have been paved over instead of plowed each year for their agrarian rather than asphalt value.

To further preserve an endangered way of life, some county park commissions are giving farming a new lease on life. They are doing it by offering the public "living historical farms." Two of them have been established since 1971.

The first was the Longstreet Farm, a living museum of Monmouth County's late 19th Century agriculture. Nestled in the rolling hills of Holmdel Township, the 500-acre Longstreet farmhouse was built in 1775. It is a 1½-story Dutch cottage.

An addition was put on about 1800, reflecting the English

Marilyn Patterson of Middletown looks after one of the horses at historical Longstreet Farm, a 19th century site in Holmdel.

Star-Ledger Photo

Georgian style popular in that period. In the 1840s, a Greek revival porch and decorative architectural features were added. The English-Dutch styled house and barns are well-preserved examples of a two-culture farmstead.

Changing seasons offer visitors the opportunity to experience any number of year-round activities. Plowing, planting, harvesting, threshing, blacksmithing, sheep shearing and ice cutting are among the many farm duties one can learn at Longstreet. There are barn dances and barnyard adventures for "lil' folk" ... corn-husk doll making and cider making ... angel doll making and Christmas wreath making.

For the handy, there's a furniture restorer and antique dealer who gives lessons on construction, finishing and cabinet making and how the techniques have changed over the centuries.

* * *

The other Garden State showcase is The Willows at Fosterfields, a Carpenter Gothic farmhouse maintained by the Morris County Park Commission. A 19th Century harvest festival featuring such rustic arts as basket-making, flour-grinding and chair-building is a regular event at Fosterfields.

Once owned by a grandson of Paul Revere, Fosterfields was purchased by the Foster family in 1881. About seven acres of corn planted in the spring of 1981 was the first use of the farm in 25 years.

Star-Ledger Photo

James Howell stands outside his ancestor's home, the Howell farm in Cedarville. The 150-acre farm dates back to 1697.

Star-Ledger Photo

The Willows, the Gothic farmhouse at Fosterfields in Morris Township, has been restored by the Morris County Park Commission.

Farm director Dan Nordberg of Blairstown harvests the corn with a McCormick-Deering corn binder, built around 1900. The machine is pulled by a team of three draft horses and cuts the cornstalks, bundles them and leaves them on the field to be picked up by another machine. The corn is taken to the Cooper Mill in Chester Township and ground into flour for sale to the public.

The 19th Century farm will have four draft horses, a pair of Jersey cows, two sheep, a sow, piglets and small flock of chickens.

The Morris County Park Commission is restoring the 10-room farmhouse built in 1854 by Gen. Joseph Warren Revere, the grandson of Paul Revere. The dining room is adorned with murals painted by the general, depicting fish and game.

A mural over the fireplace, signed with Revere's initials, displays his family crest of three fleur-de-lis placed diagonally across a shield. The crest is also carved in the living-room mantel and on an ornate marble-topped sideboard.

* * *

The history of New Jersey's farming community can best be told through a dozen or so families whose ancestors first tilled the land and gave New Jersey its enduring image as the Garden State. Each year the New Jersey Agricultural Society presents three or four farming families with the Century Farm Award.

The agricultural stories trace the historical development of New Jersey from the importance of the river and railroad in Burlington County to the canning houses in Salem County.

Probably the oldest existing farmhouse in New Jersey goes back to 1697 when Joseph Sayre of Long Island acquired the original 200 acres of land in what was then part of Salem County, today Cedarville, Cumberland County. The 150-acre farm is only four feet above sea level and produces salt hay, soybeans, alfalfa and beef cattle.

At high tide, farmers found their roads flooded. The Howells solved the problem with manmade dikes or "banks" that protect their cropland. Sluice gates in the banks close when the tide rises, then open as the water retreats.

Today's generation of Howells still remembers when a wagon with a four-mule team picked the milk up daily. At one time or another, peaches, flax, hogs, sheep and vegetables were grown on the Howell farm.

* * *

On Jan. 17, 1702, Matthias Ten Eyck bought 500 acres of prime farmland from John Johnson in Somerset County. The Ten Eycks lived in a 1½-story stone house of low Dutch Style, the upper part used for a grainary, and remodeled it in 1792. The property was taken over in 1899 by Ester Jane Van Nest Van Derveer, niece of Jacob Ten Eyck Jr., who died in 1794, leaving the farm to his three children.

The Van Derveers remain on the land, living in a solid stone house whose long support beams extend from one end of the building to the other, with wide, steel-like wooden stairways between the floors. Livestock is being raised on the farm just off Cemetery Road in North Branch.

Star-Ledger Photo

Generations of Van Derveers have resided in the Dutch stone house that stands in North Branch.

* * *

Cristeon Cummins immigrated to the United States from Austria in 1741, working as a tailor in Philadelphia before investing in a farm in Asbury along the Musconetcong River, Warren County.

Until 1828, the community was known as Cumminstown. It was changed to Vienna, the capital of Austria, from which Cristeon Cummins had come. The sandstone and iron ore stone used in the construction of the original farmhouse was mined locally. The walls of the Cummins farmhouse are two feet thick in the basement and a little more than a foot on the second floor.

* * *

The River Homestead Farm, or the Taylor family farm in Burlington County, was established by Joshua Wright on Aug. 9, 1720. The original tract consisting of 1,000 acres in Chester Township included one full mile of the Delaware River waterfront. Some 90 acres have been dedicated as the Taylor Wildlife Refuge, attracting 180 species of birds.

In the mid-1800s, farm wagons were driven over the riverbank and down the gravel shore into water up to the horses' bellies and right up to the side of the market boat. Loaded on the boats for the trip to the market were watermelons, cantaloupes, apples, peaches, sweet potatoes, tomatoes and firewood.

The Wright family married into the Taylor family in the late 1780s, thus starting the Taylor legacy on the land.

* * *

The 11th generation of Pitneys are living on Pitney Farm in Mendham, settled about 1730. The original tract contained 196 acres.

The fate of a Pitney relative during the Civil War is etched in a fine script on a windowpane of the house. It reads: "Corporal J.S. Watkins Company K-7th Regiment NJV Wounded at the Battle of Williamsburg May 5, 1862. Died May 31, 1862 at Fortress Monroe, Va."

In 1820, Dr. Jonathan Pitney, a relative, rode horseback south to Absecon Island. He declared that only a railroad was

needed to make the island bloom. People were skeptical of the doctor's talk of a prosperous "bathing village." The undaunted doctor did bring the railroad to Absecon Island to a small settlement named Atlantic City.

John O.H. Pitney married Roberta Ballantine of the wealthy Newark beer brewery family. John added 400 acres in the valley and 300 on the hill. The Pitney dairy farm continues to thrive, growing corn and bale hay to feed livestock.

* * *

In 1763, Benjamin Burroughs of Hunterdon County married Mary Van Horn of Trenton and together they rode horseback to Elmer, Salem County, and settled in a log cabin deep in the woods.

Ten years later they purchased 1,500 acres and cleared the land for farming. The Burroughses found axes and arrowheads left by the Lenni Lenape Indians.

The Burroughs farm, called "Mor-Vue," began as a general, all-purpose farm. By the mid-1800s grain and potatoes became the mainstay, followed earlier this century by a small dairy operation with grain, wheat, corn, white potatoes, hay, barley and, by the 1940s, tomatoes.

Beef cattle joined some 50 milk cows and Franklin H. Moore Jr. is now considering starting a horse farm.

* * *

In the mid-1700s, the Snook Farm in Lafayette, Sussex County, began with more than 200 acres. Milk was taken by horse and wagon to the railroad station at Monroe, where it was shipped to New York City.

Butter was shipped in wooden tubs bearing the inscription of "G. Ackerman," the great-great-grandfather of today's Homestead Farm owned by John C. Snook Jr.

The next generation added an apple orchard. A sawmill brought in revenue from logs, and the Holstein herd was expanded from 25 to 40 head by early this century.

The Snook farm will remain in the family, if not as a dairy farm, then in another agricultural capacity.

* * *

In 1824, John Decker bought 30 acres in Boonton and his descendants have farmed it to this day. The primary products of the 80-acre farm, now run by former Boonton mayor Oscar Kincaid Jr., are hay and wood.

Oscar Kincaid Sr. was a member of the Morris County Board

Oscar Kincaid, former Boonton mayor, maintains an 80-acre farm on Powerville Road in Boonton.

Star-Ledger Photo

Sloping lawns and shade trees welcome visitors to Walnridge farm in Cream Ridge.

Star-Ledger Photo

of Agriculture. His wife's family homestead was on the site of the current New Jersey Historical Society building in Newark.

* * *

Seven generations of Sicklers have been raising cows in Woodstown, Salem County, since 1836. The 125 acres consist of pasture, farmland and some woodland.

Holstein cows have been the chief source of farm income for the Sicklers. For many years the Sicklers sold their vegetables, particularly tomatoes, to Heinz and Campbell Soup.

* * *

Some of the finest standardbred horses have been raised on the Walnridge Farm in Cream Ridge, Monmouth County. On June 30, 1830, Nicholas Waln paid $11,000 for 500 acres of land and gave them as a gift to his son, Richard.

The first Waln, Nicholas, arrived in America in 1682 on the ship Welcome with the religious leader William Penn, who settled in Pennsylvania.

About 125 foals a year are born on the Walnridge Farm, now owned by Dr. David A. Meirs, the fifth generation to husband the land and its resources. Meirs has his own equine veterinary practice.

Walnridge has produced some famous stallions, including "Direct Scooter," voted the Aged Pacer of the Year by the U.S. Trotting Association and by the Harness Tracks of America. The horse was syndicated in 1981 for $2 million and commands a stud fee of $5,000.

"Escort," another Walnridge star, was the first winner of the Meadowlands Pace and was bred to more than 150 mares in 1980 alone at a $3,000 stud fee for each.

* * *

In the 1740s, the Indians referred to a medicinal spring in Monmouth County known as the "Spa Spring" on the property that became the Killdee Farm in 1839. The original 176-acre tract has expanded to its present 320 acres.

Seven generations of Stillwells have cared for the land. Potatoes, spinach, tomatoes, cabbage, strawberries, eggplants and carrots were plentiful on the farm and were trucked to the vegetable markets. In addition to asparagus, apples and peaches, the Stillwells tended to some 20 head of cattle, turkeys and pigs.

The fifth generation of Stillwells (Hamilton) always purchased white horses to work on the farm. During the 1930s Depression, Mrs. Oliver Stillwell taught school and from her salary she paid for the seed or a secondhand piece of needed farm equipment.

* * *

"Landseair" means land-sea-air and is the name of a farm that has been in the David Cresse family since 1840. It derives its name from the fresh Cape May environment.

The Cresses farm just about everything, from wood, vegetables, fruits, chickens and salt hay to clams, oysters and crabs from their ponds.

In 1951, Jonathan Cresse began to rehabilitate the land. A hedgerow was planted to stop wind erosion. The soil was rotated and crop cover spread to protect the land. The farm fields are richer today than ever.

A pond with ducks was created to correct a mosquito breeding problem. One acre was set aside for Christmas trees. Numerous artifacts from the family's history cover the wall: An old boat lantern, gear from a horse-drawn wagon, a vintage gun, handmade door hardware, scissors made by Jonathan's grandfather, an antique saw that cut the family's first firewood, and a well-used hay fork.

"Landseair" survives because of the careful management of the Cresse family, while much of Cape May's older farmlands have been washed away by the bay.

* * *

The Lee Turkey Farm in Hightstown, Mercer County, has gone through at least five agricultural transitions since its founding by Richard and Ruth Lee's distant relative, Clement Updike, who began farming in 1843.

The general farming operation evolved into a fruit farm by the 1890s. Lee's Orchard featured apples, although pears, cherries, peaches and even chickens were also prevalent.

The supply of chickens and peach trees increased in the 1920s. By 1964, the Lees stopped wholesaling to the stores in Trenton and auction markets and got into retailing exclusively.

At age 11, Richard Lee became involved in a 4-H project that developed into a major turkey venture. He started with 30 turkeys in 1938 and increased their number to 5,000 by 1951.

Lee's latest venture is a "rent-a-garden." As suburbia closed in on the Lee farm, pressure mounted to convert the valuable farmland into a tract development.

Instead, Lee decided to rent some of his land to his neighbors so they can grow some of their own fresh food. He has turned some city folk into part-time gardeners now seeking to save a vanishing way of life in urban America.

* * *

On Dec. 23, 1660, Gerrit Gerritsen and his wife, Annetje, came to America from their homeland in Holland on the ship Faith and landed in the settlement of New Amsterdam (New York). Being tillers of the soil, it was only natural the Gerritsens moved to the fertile countryside.

They soon settled in Bergen Point, N.J. Their descendants migrated to various parts of New Jersey. One of them, Jacob Garrison (the English form of Gerritsen), lived in Cohansey, Salem County, in 1708. His name is one of the first to appear in South Jersey records.

One of Jacob's grandsons, Samuel, settled on a 40-acre, rented farm near the home of his wife's parents (Reeves) in Hopewell Township. On March 23, 1761, they bought the 200-acre farm in Pittsgrove Township that has remained in the family to the present day.

After the Civil War, an 11-room house was built by that generation of Garrisons on the west side of the Old Burlington Road. The house still stands and the soil still springs forth an abundance of grain, vegetables and other produce.

* * *

Eleven generations of Van Ripers have worked the farm in Woodcliff Lake, Bergen County, since their relative, Garret Van Riper, purchased 160 acres in 1791 and began a legacy on the land.

From the beginning, the Van Ripers specialized in fruits and vegetables, but poultry and livestock were kept on the farm in what was then known as Orville Township. Most of the farm products, including eggs and butter, were sold in the old Paterson market.

By the turn of the 20th Century, the Van Ripers were maintaining four acres of cherry trees, 30 acres of apple orchards, 16 to 20 acres of peach orchards, 2,000 grape vines, and fruits and vegetables. Their products were awarded many prizes at county fairs. One Van Riper, Peter, raised about 75,000 tomato plants a year, 6,000 pepper plants and 6,000 eggplants sold in markets in Paterson, Newark and New York City.

When Garret and his brother Fred took over the farm before World War II, they started a small roadside stand. From then on the Van Ripers believed the consumer should come to the farm to buy fresh fruits, produce and dairy products.

Today two Van Riper brothers own 15 acres and lease another 75 acres, raising egg plants, peaches, apples, tomatoes, squashes—some of the food grown in seven greenhouses. At harvest time, customers from New York City and North Jersey fill both sides of the highway leading to the historic farm site. On a typical Sunday, the Van Riper Farm sells 5,000 gallons of cider.

Two giant trees today grace either side of the farm homestead built in 1860. One is a copper beech, the other a weeping birch, both brought to the land in Frederick Van Riper's knapsack when he returned from the Civil War. The copper beech is one of the largest trees in the Garden State.

The 200-acre Garrison farm in Pittsgrove Township was purchased in 1761.

Peter Van Riper, left, and his brother, Arthur, stand by some of the many plants grown and sold at Van Riper's Farm Market in Woodcliff Lake.

Star-Ledger Photo

Star-Ledger Photo

GARDENS

*A*s the Garden State, New Jersey is ablaze with rainbows of radiant flowers and fragrant scents from spring through fall, climaxing in a dazzling finale of foliage at harvest time.

Azaleas and African violets, lilacs and laurels, violets and zinnias—they all thrive in carefully cultivated beds within formal English walled gardens, under protective acres of glass, or in spacious arboretums.

There are the world famous Hedge Gardens in Cape May ... the nation's largest variety of irises in Montclair ... a bog garden in Basking Ridge, which is really "The Great Swamp in Miniature" ... the "Fern Capital of America" atop a hill in Sparta ... exotic Japanese gardens on the grounds of Prentice-Hall Publishing Co. in Englewood Cliffs ... the renowned and luxurious Duke Gardens in Somerville ... an herb garden at Waterloo Village ... an historic American-Japanese garden path at Macculloch Hall in Morristown ... urban gardens in the heart of downtown Newark ... holly and dogwood gardens at Rutgers University in New Brunswick ... Hidden Gardens in South Jersey ... a stunning rose garden in Glen Ridge ... and the state's largest and most diverse display of greenery and blossoms at Skylands Botanical Gardens in Ringwood.

Gardening and growing flowers and herbs is a way of life in New Jersey, their roots firmly planted by Colonial settlers in backyard survival gardens.

* * *

Tempe Wick Garden at Jockey Hollow Historical Park in Morristown is a restored Colonial garden shaped two centuries ago by the day-to-day necessities: The white-flowering soapwort used to wash woolens and pewter ... pale blue-flowering flax to make linen cloth ... vines of scarlet runner beans ... medicinal herbs ... top onions, horseradish and turnips ... and the usual corn, buckwheat and barley for both man and farm animal.

The Morristown historical garden was first tended by Mrs. Henry Wick, the mother of Tempe Wick (short for Temperence). Henry Wick was a prosperous farmer during the Revolutionary period.

* * *

The **Presby Memorial Iris Garden** in Montclair contains the largest collection of historic irises in the world, with more than 75,000 irises, including most of the 200-plus species (wild varieties) and more than 5,000 varieties from every corner of the globe.

Tall and short, bearded and beardless, the three-petaled flowers are like a master painter's palette, a mix of every hue in the color spectrum befitting Iris, the Greek goddess of the rainbow.

Located in Mountainside Park, this National Historic Landmark is one of the world's finest botanical treasures. In addition

Star-Ledger Photo

Spectacular varieties of irises are found at the Presby Memorial Iris Garden in Montclair.

to being a fine display garden, it serves as a valuable research resource, providing botanical materials to scientists worldwide.

Beds of historic irises preserve root stocks of irises first appearing in written history as early as the 1500s, such as the "Florentina," which flourished throughout southern Europe. The historic beds are arranged in chronological order for ease of study.

The iris is distinguished by designs of threes: Three "standards" (upright petals) and three "falls," (drooping petals). They are classed as bearded or beardless and are crested or bulbous. The beard serves a functional purpose as a landing strip for the bee while pollinating the flower.

The Presby Memorial Iris Gardens are laid out to present each succession of iris bloom to its best advantage. From early spring until the frosts of fall, at least one of the species varieties will be in bloom.

The small irises (species and hybridized) bloom first, sometimes through the snows of early March, like a crocus. The dwarf bearded blooms by the end of April, with the border bearded blooming in May.

The tall bearded varieties bloom from mid-May through mid-June. Some will bloom in May and then again in September. The Siberian, Japanese, Louisana and bulbous irises will bloom during June and July.

Presby Gardens' greatest mass display usually occurs the week before and after Memorial Day when more than half of the irises are in full color.

Each iris in the gardens is identified with a marker having the name of the variety, the name of the hybridizer and the date of official registry. During the peak bloom season, informational plaques provide the visitors with historic and botanical data.

* * *

New Jersey's **Skylands Gardens** is a 250-acre horticultural haven surrounded by orchards, farmlands and woods with vast sweeps of lawns and springs, streams, ponds and six lakes, all commanding a 35-mile view of the Ramapo Mountains and forests.

The Clarence McKenzie Lewis estate, fashioned after an English baronial homestead, is laced with miles of bridle paths, grassy walks and 23 miles of roads. The gardens were designed as a series of terraces serving as a vista toward the distant hills.

Visitors to the state gardens stroll along magnolia tree-lined walks, past an orchard of 260 crabapple trees, a Cupid's garden, an aquatic garden and a lilac garden.

The geometric-shaped annual garden is set off by an old Greek well-head fountain. The special Rhododendron Ramapo is raised in the Octagonal Garden. Experts throughout the world journey to Skylands to see the matasequoi, a genesis of the California Sequoias grown from seed found in North China. Clarence Lewis, an engineer and financier from Germany, was among a limited group that successfully grew the seeds in its tree groves.

When the State Department of Environmental Protection (DEP) acquired the Skylands Manor and Gardens in December 1966, the Skylands International Gardens was established, beginning with the planting of 10,000 tulip bulbs flown in from Holland by special arrangement with the Dutch government. Holland was the first nation to participate with New Jersey in the unique international horticultural project.

Skylands Gardens now displays hundreds of peony bushes, heather, heath, wildflowers, mountain silverbells, plus many specialty trees such as a Chinese Toon and a Kentucky coffee tree.

* * *

Gus Yearick is one of a handful of topiary artists in the United States who sculpts privet hedges into green living monuments. Yearick's **Hedge Garden** in Fishing Creek, Cape May County, has been featured on "Ripley's Believe It Or Not," and in National Geographic, other national magazines and Sunday newspaper supplements.

More than a half-million people from around the world have visited Yearick and his wife Josephine's impressive "Garden of Eden," where they've spent more than 60,000 hours trimming and training little green leafy plants to look like Yankee clipper ships, elephants, Santa and his reindeer, Babe Ruth and Queen Mary.

It all began in 1927 when Yearick started shaping his first figure, Queen Mary, a five-year project that was recognized by National Geographic as an outstanding example of topiary.

Since then, Yearick has cut, snipped and clipped his hedges with hand shears, working seven days a week, eight months a

Star-Ledger Photo

Hedge in the shape of an elephant at Gus Yearick's Hedge Garden.

year. All creations face the sun and first grow upward before Yearick gets them to grow down and around, depending on the configuration he wants.

The elephant, his biggest masterpiece, took seven years to reach its completed stage. Yearick has been working since before World War II on a major display, "The Ball Game," consisting of several baseball players. It takes about 12 years to form one player.

The Yearicks had to build a wall around their garden to prevent accidents as motorists rubber-neck to catch the sights while driving down Fishing Creek Road.

Travel agents include Yearick's amazing Hedge Garden on American tours, listing it as one of the finest ornamental gardens in the country.

* * *

The **Duke Gardens** in Somerville is a study of perfection under glass. Flower fanciers will find the precision of a sculptured French parterre garden, the lush foliage of a tropical jungle, the arid stark beauty of the American desert, the stylized naturalism of Japan and a Chinese garden with a mysterious grotto among the stones.

The Duke greenhouse, an acre of breathtaking beauty, features some of the world's most delicate flowers and greenery, artfully arranged in 11 geographically and culturally distinct gardens.

Originally part of the Duke tobacco family estate built at the turn of the century, the Somerville botanical site was opened to the public in 1964. The greenhouse, shaped like a curved-roof box with open space in the middle for outdoor gardens, features an English garden with a sunburst design planted in succulents and surrounded by a gravel path and sculpted hedges.

Intricate fleur-de-lis designs in dwarf boxwood are changed with the seasons in the formal French garden. The Italian garden is a blend of ferns, acacias and exotic flowering trees from Africa, Australia and South America. The heavy growth partially obscures marble balustrades and sculptures of figures from Roman mythology.

The Indo-Persian Garden resembles the Shalimar Gardens in Lahore, Pakistan. The Edwardian Garden reflects the lush conservatories of the wealthy Americans and Englishmen of the early 1900s.

The American Colonial Garden shows the familiar white latticework and the popular southern magnolias and pink and red camelias. This area also contains palm fronds and tropical trees, a wide variety of orchids and a Cycas or Sago palm, one of the oldest living fossils.

The most stunning formal garden has the scent of a Florida orange grove. Orange trees are joined by grapefruit and cypress trees lining a patterned brick walk leading to a square fountain in the middle of a rose garden. Along the way, one passes through white Arabic archways.

The Duke Gardens are closed Thanksgiving, Christmas and New Year's Day and in the summer months.

* * *

Growing out of a half-acre hilltop in Sparta is a backyard **Fern Garden** with 50 native species of fern and innumerable imports fanning out among wild flowers and indigenous shrubs.

In spring, the fiddlehead ferns stretch out to greet visitors, while the summer and fall months yield the full beauty of the feathery plants. In the winter, the evergreen species, such as the Christmas fern, offer a striking contrast to the sparkling snows.

The Fern Garden was developed by F. Gordon Foster, author of "Ferns to Know and Grow." Foster started his fernery when he moved to Sparta in 1967. He selectively cleared a pile of brambles and rubbish, replanting the sloping rock garden with fern varieties from throughout the world.

Star-Ledger Photo

Duke Gardens in Somerville recreates the world's horticulture in a series of exquisite gardens.

A retired Bell Laboratories engineer, Foster began his fern hobby with a microscope. The flowerless ferns were a complete mystery during the Middle Ages because they did not propagate from seeds but from tiny spores undetectable by the human eye. A spore produces equally small prothallia, which develop into sporophytes. The sporophytes mature into recognizable forms called ferns.

Foster's basement is a spore hatchery with incubators for ferns in different stages of growth. Sterilized conditions are necessary to prevent fungus.

Foster's house is a fern collector's paradise: Large staghorns with sharp antler-like leaves . . . a 1956-vintage bird's nest fern whose leaves measure 20 inches wide . . . climbing ferns, maidenhair, button and Boston ferns.

The American Fern Society in Seattle operates an international spore bank for those wishing to start a fernery.

* * *

The Garden Club of Morristown has restored the **Macculloch Hall Garden**, an historic site first owned by George Perot Macculloch, who in 1823 started construction of the state's first major transportation corridor: The Morris Canal.

Still flourishing from the original Macculloch Hall planting are a large magnolia soulangena, a Japanese Styrax, a sassafras of unusual size and several ancient Norwegian spruce.

Magnificent wisteria once covered the entire side of the hall and a remnant still survives. The wisteria grew from seeds or slips brought to Morristown by Commodore Matthew Calbraith Perry, who opened Japan to foreign trade in 1854.

The Garden Club is slowly reestablishing the fragrant, colorful wisteria. Long paths bordering the orchard have been uncovered and new fruit trees planted. Shrubs of the early 19th Century have been added, including many old-fashioned roses. Spring wildflowers have also been planted in the damp glade on one side of the property.

Iris hybridized by the late Ella Porter McKinney, famed local horticulturist, has been propagated and increased by the Garden Club volunteers.

Macculloch Hall, built in 1806, was restored in 1954 and opened to the public as a museum. A portrait of George Washington by Charles Willson Peale hangs from the wrought-iron bannister of the attractive entrance hall.

* * *

Leaming's Run Botanical Garden is a spot of unsurpassed beauty with Hidden Gardens that will awe your senses. An island of peace in Swainton, Cape May County, Leaming's Run is a masterful mosaic of 27 exquisitely designed gardens interspersed with immaculate lawns and ponds and ferneries.

Leaming's Run was named after a whaler, Thomas Leaming, and a brook, or run, as it was known 200 years ago. The brook runs through the Leaming property. Leaming's house, built in 1706, is the only remaining whaler's house in New Jersey.

The botanical run is a delightful walk along a sandy, winding path through 20 acres of beautiful gardens and spectacular morning glories. Twenty-seven expertly designed gardens lie hidden around a bend surrounding a pond just over a bridge. Each garden has its own aesthetic personality.

The mile-long run reveals a yellow garden, an evening garden, a red and blue garden, an orange garden and other colorful gardens. One of the favorites is the English Cottage Garden bursting with 140 annuals against a rough hewn fence.

Flower scents mix with honeysuckle and pine. The Leaming tract also supports a Colonial farm and herb garden. Specimen gardens of Colonial times include cotton and tobacco. There are also a drying barn and flower shop on the grounds.

* * *

In 1960, on the 100th anniversary of Japanese-American cultural relations, a **Japanese garden** was begun on the campus-like

setting of Prentice-Hall Publishing Co. in Englewood Cliffs along the Hudson River.

Constance Powers, mother of Prentice-Hall president John G. Powers, had sent her son a stone lantern as a gift. Since the publishing house was built in 1954, Powers had wanted to blend the natural beauties of the countryside with the magnificent Allison Park bordering Englewood Cliffs along the Palisades.

The first stone lantern was accompanied by a beautifully illustrated book on Japanese gardens. On a trip to Tokyo, Powers met with one of the most famous makers of stone lanterns in Japan. With his aides, Powers carefully picked piece after piece for their distinctive appearance and beauty. The massive weights were transported to New Jersey and arranged throughout a garden that was literally being carved through the tough rock croppings of the Palisades.

A small stream coursed across the rocky terrain, adding the final touch to the Japanese garden. All that was needed to make it complete was the traditional Japanese wooden bridge. A search ended with the name of "Benkei-Bashi," a bridge built in 1890 to span the moat at the Imperial Palace in Tokyo. It is considered to be the most beautiful bridge in Japan. A model of "Benkei-Bashi" was crafted for Prentice-Hall.

The Benkei Bridge dates back to the 11th Century. Legend has it that the bridge was named after a famed warrior, Benkei, who had fought 999 battles, winning them all. He had the 999 swords of the men he had vanquished and he was determined to have 1,000.

Crossing a bridge, he met Yoshitsune, carrying his sword and set for doing battle. Although Benkei was a strong warrior and Yoshitsune a frail man, the latter outlasted the mighty swordsman. Benkei, exhausted, laid down his sword and said, "You are my master and I will serve you." Thus the bridge got its name, Benkei.

Carved from the woods of Japan, the Prentice-Hall bridge is left in its natural state to blend with the trees, stones and brook. The bronze decorations on the poles of the bridge are of 18th Century design. The bridge stands as a bond of unity between America and Japan.

* * *

The **Frelinghuysen Arboretum** in Morris Township is a green oasis in the rapidly developing hills of Morris County. The 135-

Leaming's Run Botanical Gardens in Swainton.

The Japanese Garden on the grounds of Prentice-Hall, Inc., a major publishing company in Englewood Cliffs, features stone lanterns crafted in Japan.

acre estate of Peter H.G. Frelinghuysen, a former congressman, was dedicated as an arboretum in May 1971.

Each spring, more than 10,000 yellow and white jonquils, purple and white lilacs, silverbells, flowering azaleas and rhododendrons turn the hillside estate into a spectacular kaleidoscope of changing colors. Towering coniferous trees mingle with flowering cherry, crabapple, magnolias, dogwood, red horse, hawthorne and chestnut species.

Overlooking this resplendent bloom of greens and dappled hues is the 15-room Georgian mansion, erected in 1891, that now serves as the administrative headquarters for the Morris County Park Commission. A music room has been converted into a horticultural library. Offices are on the second floor.

Trenton landscaper James MacPherson describes the setting with the white frame house, its entrance flanked by giant Ionic pillars, as "irreproachable." By that, MacPherson means that "in the foreground an open glade of lawn looks down upon a series of pastures . . . beyond are extensive woodlands . . . notable in their season for considerable variety of color. In the distant range of hills is the Town of Boonton."

Behind the mansion are a rose garden and beds of perfect tulips and a greenhouse obscured by shrubbery and trees.

* * *

Although the song says "I never promised you a rose garden," a retired department store executive did exactly the opposite and gave his family a formal 100-by-150-foot **Rose Garden** in Glen Ridge.

Clayton Freeman, once chairman of W.T. Grant & Co., set aside a one-acre corner plot at Hawthorne and Maolis avenues in the early 1930s and filled it with 400 rose plants.

Today, the Freeman Gardens, including a wooded area with footpaths, wildflowers, ferns and several specimen trees such as a Chinese chestnut, is protected by the Borough of Glen Ridge as a public preserve. While formal in appearance, the Freeman Gardens conveys a calming rustic charm. Redwood picnic chairs and tables are shaded by a large apple tree and old logs are stacked by a tool shed. Comfortable white wrought-iron furniture has been provided for senior citizens.

Mrs. Freeman held tea parties in a small, red-brick amphitheater next to the rose garden, now the setting for many weddings.

The block of beauty in the heavily trafficked area was, before the Freemans moved to Glen Ridge soon after World War I, a peaceful cow pasture and later a vegetable garden. It has since become an outdoor laboratory for student nature studies and a quiet retreat for ecologists, ornithologists and those who simply enjoy tilling around a pleasant little garden.

* * *

The resurrected **Cross Estate Gardens** in Bernardsville is an excellent example of a formal English-styled walled garden which, through years of neglect, had become overgrown with weeds before being rescued by volunteers working with the Morristown National Historical Park.

When the park district acquired the Cross Gardens in 1975, the lovely laurel, lilac, holly and azalea collections were choked with vines. By 1982, volunteers had restored the perennial garden by establishing two tiers divided by stone steps and rows of sweet-smelling honeysuckle plants. The higher plane was covered with white, yellow and blue flowering plants, with the lower area supporting a variety of perennial plants.

Discovered in the back of the mansion, buried among some azaleas, was an attractive stone garden pool. Artists now frequent the Cross Gardens, their favorite scenes being a natural blend of lilac and wisteria, which gardeners had allowed to grow together to form interesting random patterns.

* * *

Community gardens are catching on all over New Jersey—in vacant lots in Newark, Paterson and Plainfield, on property donated by churches or colleges or companies such as American Standard in Piscataway or Ingersoll-Rand in Woodcliff Lake.

Some are large, like Denville's municipal gardens, while others are small, like the Covered Bridge garden in Manalapan tended by retired immigrants who spent their lives in the asphalt environments of Brooklyn or Queens.

Denville's dirt paths separating the rental plots (up to $15 a year) have names like Celery Court and Broccoli Way.

One of the most active community gardens in Maplewood features three-foot "bench spaces" at $15 a year to local residents. In 1974, some members of the Maplewood Garden Club put up a 40-by-60-foot greenhouse and established bench spaces for growing everything from jade plants, cactus and lemon trees to culinary and medicinal herbs.

The bench spaces have turned into a social meeting place for the town's "green thumbs," who also donate shrubs, trees and flowers to spruce up the town's train station, public buildings and parks.

* * *

Each year, the **New Jersey Flower & Garden Show** puts on its finest greenery at the Morristown Armory. The themes vary from year to year, each revealing a different aspect of New Jersey's flora and fauna as they relate to the state's contrasting urban, suburban and rural lifestyles.

The Cross Estate in Mendham.

Star-Ledger Photo

Many of the exhibits inspire new landscaping and gardening techniques for amateurs and professionals. For one show, the Metropolitan Chapter of the New Jersey Association of Nurserymen created a children's playground with swings, monkey bars, a slide and a crawling tunnel. For the adults, the playground featured large locust trees, ornamental shrubs, roses and perennials.

Another exhibit was a replica of a gristmill with a working overshot wheel and a millpond surrounded by 30-foot hemlocks and a walk-through "touch and smell" garden for the blind. It was designed by John A. Meeks of Blue Meadow Nursery, Franklin Lakes, for the New Jersey Association of Nurserymen.

Morningside Greenhouses in Haledon provided a profusion of orchids, birds of paradise and other exotic flowers enhancing its tropical gardens.

The County College of Morris imported California-style luxury by fashioning a garden featuring a hot tub enclosed in a greenhouse, including a portable spa.

The Garden Club of New Jersey built six miniature rooms to interpret its theme, "Our Heritage."

The annual New Jersey Flower & Garden Show is sponsored by the New Jersey Association of Nurserymen, the New Jersey State Florists Association, the New Jersey Plant and Flower Growers Association, the Metropolitan Chapter of the New Jersey Association of Nurserymen, Cook College, Rutgers University and the State Department of Agriculture.

* * *

Among the field trips recommended by the Garden Club of New Jersey are:

• The Cora Hartshorn Arboretum and Bird Sanctuary on Forest Drive and Chatham Road, Short Hills.

• The Greenbrook Sanctuary, Route 9W, Tenafly, operated by the Palisades Nature Association.

• The Brigantine National Wildlife Refuge at the southern end of Island Beach State Park.

• The New Jersey Audubon Society's museum and nature trails on Ewing Avenue in Franklin Lakes and at the Scherman Wildlife Sanctuary on Hardscrabble Road in Bernardsville.

• The Herb Garden at Waterloo Village in Byram Township, Sussex County.

• The Tourne wildflower trails on Powerville Road in Boonton, run by the Morris County Park Commission.

• The Home Gardens at Belmont Hill County Park in Garfield, Bergen County.

• The wildflower preserves and pine forest at Washington Crossing State Park on the Delaware River outside of Trenton.

• The Bog Garden, or "Great Swamp in Miniature," developed by Mrs. Tudor Finch, on North Maple Avenue, Basking Ridge.

• The Willowwood Arboretum in Peapack-Gladstone.

• The period garden at historic Acorn Hall in Morristown.

• The Stony Ford Sanctuary, the new National Audubon Headquarters in Princeton.

• The Great Swamp National Wildlife Refuge, located in Harding, Chatham and Passaic townships.

• The New Jersey School of Conservation in Stokes State Forest, Branchville, Sussex County.

• An 1890 working farm, arboretum, hiking and nature trails run by the Monmouth County Park System, Newman Springs Road, Lincroft.

Upper Montclair Country Club.

GOLF COURSES

They are the finely cut emerald jewels of the Garden State, some 260 plush green oases whose sole purpose is to serve the picturesque game of golf.

New Jersey's dramatically differing natural elements give many of these scenic courses their unique distinction: Galloping Hill Golf Course ... Jumping Brook Golf & Country Club ... Nob Hill Country Club ... Skyview Country Club ... Apple Ridge Golf Club ... Orchard Hills Golf Course ... Echo Lake Country Club ... Fox Hollow Golf Club ... Pinecrest Golf Club ... Lincroft Lawns Country Club ... Sunset Valley Golf Course ... Ramblewood Country Club ... Rockaway River Country Club ... Spring Meadow Golf & Country Club ... Tara Greens Golf Club ... Canyon Ridge Country Club ... Alpine Country Club ... Ocean Acres Golf Club ... Shark River Park Golf Club ... Fairway Mews Country Club ... Farmstead Golf Course ... White Beeches Golf & Country Club.

Others have kept alive the state's rich Indian heritage: Shackamaxon Country Club ... Tomahawk Golf Club ... Peace Pipe Golf Course ... Lackawanna Golf Club ... Hackensack Golf Club ... Tamarack Golf Course ... Weequahic Park Golf Course ... Lake Mohawk Golf Club ... Manasquan River Golf Club ... Navesink Country Club ... Packanack Golf Club ... Picatinny Golf Club ... Raritan Valley Country Club ... Roxiticus Country Club.

Some are simply known by their geographic designations: Lakewood Golf Club ... Hanover Country Club ... Paramus Golf & Country Club ... Emerson Country Club ... Essex County Country Club ... Florham Park Country Club ... Maplewood Country Club ... Madison Golf Club ... Glen Ridge Country Club ... Ridgewood Country Club ... Woodbury Country Club ... Plainfield Country Club.

There's also an assortment of odd and catchy names, and abbreviated concoctions of their origins, or whimsical appellations that have made New Jersey a golfer's paradise: Americana, Atlantis, Bey Lea, Baltusrol, Battleground, Copper Hill, Covered Bridge, Fiddler's Elbow, Hollywood, Knickerbocker, Panther Valley, Walkill.

In addition to the engaging public and private courses, New Jersey is headquarters for the United States Golf Association, which operates the official golf museum and library in an elegant mansion in exclusive Far Hills.

Since the golf game was standardized in Scotland in 1754 and introduced in the United States in the 1880s, New Jersey's golf greens and fairways, a few being among the oldest in the country, have attracted a lot of attention over the years.

One of the greatest golf courses in America began as a tennis club. One New Jersey golf course was established by a woman. The most challenging golf course in the world, according to the leading course designers, is Pine Valley in Camden County. One of the first televised golf tournaments took place on a New Jersey golf course in the early 1950s, while others have become the favorites of the top professionals.

U.S. Golf Association

On Dec. 22, 1894, five clubs formed the United States Golf Association (USGA): Newport Golf Club, Rhode Island; Shinnecock Hills Golf Club, Southampton, N.Y.; The Country Club, Brookline, Mass.; St. Andrew's Golf Club, Yonkers-on-the-Hudson, N.Y., and Chicago Golf Club, Chicago.

From those five clubs, the USGA has grown to more than 5,000 clubs. In 1894, two Amateur Golf Championships of the United States were sponsored by Newport and then St. Andrew's. When the USGA was organized, its objectives reached beyond amateur championships. Its primary purpose was to establish uniform playing rules for golf wherever it would be played within the national borders.

The USGA's Far Hills home was designed in 1919 by John Russell Pope, the architect for the National Archives Building and the Jefferson Memorial in Washington, D.C., and the American Battle Monument in France. The spacious red brick, Georgian Colonial mansion features a graceful hanging staircase, which has been photographed and published among a display of classic staircases in several editions of the Encyclopedia Britannica.

An immense fireplace capable of burning seven logs dominates the East Wing. Rough-hewn beams that brace the upper balcony and the floorboards were removed from an old barn. The veranda is enclosed by a glass wall and is decorated with iron lacework.

The golf association acquired the house and 68 acres in 1972.

The USGA library, believed to be most extensive golfing collection in existence, contains some 6,000 volumes. The museum is stocked with artifacts tracing the history of the game from its beginnings to the present through a vast collection of clubs and balls signifying the three distinct stages of the game: The feather ball period, the gutta percha ball period, and the rubber ball period still in vogue.

The artifacts are housed in cabinets in a room off the entrance hall. Here you will find the original constitution and bylaws of the organization and photographs of the winners of three championships conducted by the USGA in 1895. Originally the dining room of the house, it is now the trophy showcase displaying some of the cups held by the USGA from international competitions.

Above the marble fireplace hangs the "moon club" used by Adm. Alan B. Shepard Jr. to play a shot from the surface of the moon on Feb. 6, 1971. Also on display are early Rules of Golf from Scotland, including a facsimile of the first written Rules of Golf from 1744.

The next room contains articles from presidents of the United States who played golf, including an oil painting of the 16th hole of the Augusta National Golf Club done by President Eisenhower. Other presidential items include golf balls used by Warren G. Harding, Eisenhower and Richard Nixon, clubs used by William Howard Taft, Woodrow Wilson, Franklin D. Roosevelt, Eisenhower and John F. Kennedy. There's also a rare photograph of Franklin Roosevelt playing golf before he was stricken with polio.

The library at the end of the hall was the ballroom of the original house. Double doors open onto formal gardens. The painting over the fireplace is a rendition of the first International Match between England and Scotland, done by Allan Stewart.

Next to the library is a room that preserves two exceptional works of art, one an etching by Rembrandt and the other a small oil painting by an unknown artist of a boy playing golf.

The Bob Jones Room contains the 32 medals Jones won in national competition in the United States and Great Britain. Originally the mansion's library, the Jones Room is heavily paneled with centuries-old wood imported from Europe and finished in an egg-and-dart carving motif, the classic theme representative of Georgian architecture in the 18th Century.

From its peaceful perch in the hills of Somerset County, the USGA oversees one of America's most popular pastimes. Some of the most unusual and reputable courses in the Garden State follow.

Baltusrol

Baltus Roll was a farmer who lived on a mountain peak directly behind today's Baltusrol Clubhouse in Springfield. In the early 1800s, Springfield looked exactly like its name: Fields of wheat, corn and cattle and spring flowers growing wild on large vacant tracts.

In the spring of 1895, when the first U.S. Open Championship was played, Baltusrol Mountain became the site of one of America's first and finest golf courses.

When Louis Keller, founder of New York's Social Register, discovered the fertile mountain midway from Morristown and Orange and Newark and Plainfield, he mailed an invitation to his best friends, telling them: "A course of nine holes, averaging two hundred and fifty yards, and with forty-foot greens, has been laid out upon sandy hills, naturally adapted for the purpose, and is now ready for use. An eight-room house on the grounds will be fitted with a grill room and clubhouse facilities. The course has a southern exposure and is adapted for use during the entire year. Annual dues, ten dollars each."

Since then, the 475-acre Baltusrol Golf Club has been the scene of six U.S. Open Championships and the 1983 State Open. Keller's modest nine holes were expanded to 18 and the Women's Amateur Championship first tried it out in 1901. Baltusrol hosted its first National Open two years later. Twelve USGA championships have been played on the venerable courses and the 13th will be played in 1985 when the Women's Open is conducted over the upper course.

A.W. Tillinghast, the leading golf course designer after the turn of the century, laid out a demanding 36-hole complex while keeping 18 holes in play during construction in 1922. Both courses have a normal par of 72. The Lower Course measures 7,076 yards from the back tees and the Upper Course 6,714 yards.

The 1954 U.S. Open ushered in a new era of spectator golf at Baltusrol. It was the first time ropes went up along the fairways to control the gallery, and it was the first such tournament to be televised to a national audience.

The 1967 U.S. Open became another landmark event. Jack Nicklaus set a then record-breaking score of 275 in the U.S. Open Championships. It was in this tournament where Lee Trevino, who finished fifth, established himself as a major figure in golf. Nicklaus' partner in the final day of the '67 Open was the legendary Arnold Palmer.

In 1980, the last time the Open was played at Baltusrol, Nicklaus again broke the record with a 272 score, which still stands.

The pros rate the Lower Championship Course as one of the best in the world. The three most difficult holes, according to the pros, are 6, 10 and 17.

On Number 6, the hardest par 4 in both the 1954 and 1967 opens, the drive must be long and accurate, threading its way through a narrow opening in the trees to an undulating fairway with traps both left and right. The long iron second shot on this 470-yard link is probably going to be played from a hanging lie to a large level green protected by elongated bunkers on either side.

Another tough par 4 link is Number 10, running 455 yards long. It requires the player to favor the left side of the fairway off the tee, flirting with a tall tree and deep rough, to have a straight approach shot to the green. Trees on the right narrow the hole about 275 yards out. A drive hit right invites trouble as it will force the golfer to control a fade around the trees on his second shot to a green amply buffered by larger bunkers on either side.

Number 17 is the longest hole in any Open: 630 yards. The

The stately clubhouse at Baltusrol Golf Club in Springfield is a comforting retreat after a hard game.

Star-Ledger Photo

first of the two par 5 finishing holes demands length if the golfer is to cross the "Sahara Bunker," which splits the fairway from 385 to 420 yards out on his second shot. A long second is also necessary just to set up a grueling third shot to an elevated green guarded by numerous bunkers in front and to the left. The famous 17th will baffle many, resulting in bogies for those attempting to navigate its 11 (lucky number?) bunkers.

Bowling Green

Perhaps the trickiest public golf course in the Garden State, Bowling Green lies peacefully in the Sussex County lake district along School House Road in Milton.

Carved out in the middle of a forest of fragrant evergreens and tall, shadowy oaks, Bowling Green, like so many New Jersey links, grew out of productive farmland. The Milton acreage was owned by Albert Riggs. The club was founded by two pairs of brothers, the Riggses and the Salmons. George Salmon loved to watch the game and in 1966 he saw a lifetime dream materialize into a magnificent golf club when he and the Riggs brothers hired the renowned Geoffrey Cornish to design a championship golf course.

Bowling Green can be played from various yardages of 6,340 to 7,011 for the men and 5,734 for the women. Practically every hole slices through a stand of towering pines and sturdy oaks. The greens are babied to velvety smoothness.

The longest hole measures 611 yards and has been assigned a par 5. Other holes vary from 217 yards (par 3) to 501 (par 5). The 8th hole is the most beguiling. It's a modest straightaway of 217 yards. Simple enough. Except there's a lake and two mammoth bunkers separating the tee from the pin. The steady player can do it in par 3.

Golf historian Red Hoffman found the king-sized tees and ample greens, averaging 7,000 square feet, a pleasure to behold. The par 5 18th hole sprawls more than 10,000 square feet over three levels.

"The strategic placement of sand on 11 dog-holes, coupled with the rifle-barrel aspects of the fairways, make it a true driver's course," Hoffman says of this beautiful par 72 course.

One golfer reviewed the course and had this to say about the 18th hole: "This hole is 611 yards long, a par 5—or so they say. We consulted our score card and figured it out scientifically: Four

wood shots, then a 3-iron, followed by a sand wedge and three putts. Somewhere along the line, the plan collapsed. We shanked the first into a pond, hit three off the tee and ended up in a patch of woods.

"There, we carefully kicked the ball into a decent lie and sent a shot into a trap. Once on the green, we showed how well we can putt—stroking the ball smoothly past the cup time and again. We finally sank a putt. Then we sat down and cried. Price Waterhouse & Co. will have the results next week."

Canoe Brook

Three residents of Summit organized the Canoe Brook Country Club in 1901 on hay fields located in nearby Millburn Township. The hay and shrubs would give way to carpeted fairways, lush greens, misshapen traps and sundry structures that eventually emerged as a recreation retreat by the winding Canoe Brook.

A 133-acre estate was acquired and Jack Vickery and Alex Smith laid out an 18-hole golf course, 5,754 yards in length. Although golf was the initial dominant activity, Canoe Brook was founded first and foremost as a country club catering to the pursuit of recreational activities, including tennis, paddle ball and swimming. Canoe Brook has evolved into a pleasant social club for leisure and competitive fun.

Unlike neighboring Baltusrol, Canoe Brook was distinguished for its annual shad dinners and club dances. The "purists" chased the little white ball at Baltusrol. At Canoe Brook, there were other activities for members, although golf has remained the focal point because of the two fine, par 72 championship courses, North and South, along Morris Turnpike in Summit.

Forsgate

Forsgate Farms was conceived as a completely self-sufficient community. Founded in 1913 by John A. Forster, then president of Crum and Forster Insurance Co., Forsgate at one time was one of the East's leading dairy farms and a showcase for more than 1,000 head of prize Holstein and Guernsey cows.

Forsgate Country Club, which can be seen from the New Jersey Turnpike in Jamesburg, was established in 1931 for the private use of Forster's family and business associates. The course was built by Charles Banks, one of the top course architects of his time.

Each hole at Forsgate is a duplicate of a famous hole on the British Isles. Such great golfers as Ben Hogan, Sam Snead, Julius Boros and David Marr have enjoyed this unique layout that boasts some of the largest greens and traps in the United States.

In later years, Forsgate added an 18-hole West Course designed by noted golf course architect Hal Purdy. Purdy created a fitting complement to the rigorous East Course. The Forsgate member has a choice of two excellent and entirely different courses, which are cut through trees with plenty of ponds.

The New Jersey Professional Golfers Association has held its State Championship at Forsgate an unprecedented 10 times. The Ladies Professional Golf Association (LPGA) has conducted three notably successful tournaments at Forsgate. Amy Alcott won the 1976 inaugural tournament, followed by Kathy Whitworth taking the 1977 title. The 1978 tournament was won by Nancy Lopez, the second win of her record-setting, five consecutive victories as Rookie Player. All three tournaments set LPGA attendance records.

The clubhouse was designed by Clifford C. Wendehack and is a prize example of the architecture of that area of New Jersey. The dining-room and banquet facilities, "country club style," were opened to the public in 1955.

Hominy Hill

Hominy Hill is one of four golf courses operated by the Monmouth County Park System. Situated in the heart of New Jersey's horse country, Colts Neck, Hominy Hill opened in 1965 as a private course for Henry D. Mercer, a shipping magnate who raised championship cattle on his dairy farm. Part of the farm, some 180 acres, became Mercer's private golfing domain, Hominy Hill. Monmouth County acquired the green preserve in 1977 and opened it to the general public.

The agrarian setting for Mercer's golf course was selected as the site of the 1983 Men's USGA National Public Links Competition. The number one handicap hole at Hominy Hill is number 8. It lives up to its reputation as the toughest. The drive must be long and accurate, keeping as close as possible to the left without catching the bunker.

That leaves the golfer with an open second shot uphill to a very narrow green running diagonally from left to right. A bunker protects the front right with a large tree overhanging the back half of the green, making a high, fading long-iron second shot almost a must to break par.

The Monmouth County Park System also operates three other public courses: Howell Park, Shark River and Pine Brook.

Knoll

The Knoll Country Club came into being when 10 millionaires from the Morris County area decided they needed a place to get away and relax and play a quiet game of golf. In 1929, the year of the stock market crash that brought on the Great Depression, they retained the reputable Charles H. Banks, who created an 18-hole championship masterpiece. Banks fashioned an 18th hole that is rated as one of the finest finishing holes in the country.

Knoll survived the hard times and today two 18-hole, full-size golf courses are owned and operated by Parsippany-Troy Hills Township. The 320-acre site is near the Boonton Reservoir.

Before the township took over the posh facilities, the golf grounds and impressive clubhouse were occupied by Bloomfield College. Parsippany-Troy Hills saved the millionaires' playground

from becoming a housing development by purchasing the property in 1976 with a grant from the state Green Acres program. The Knoll's restaurant and bar are operated by a concessionaire.

Montclair

When the Montclair Golf Club took shape in 1894, it was, for the local gentry, an alternative to riding with the hounds. The affluent horsemen did not visualize then that the Montclair Golf Club would someday be the only playing field in New Jersey with "four nines," a numerical arrangement that comes out to 36 holes.

The 13th oldest golf club in the United States (out of more than 12,000), Montclair boasts four equally rated "nines" that begin and end at the prominent clubhouse erected in 1924. The 2,600 members also enjoy seven tennis courts, six platform tennis courts and a competition-size swimming pool, belying its "golf club" image. The club, although named Montclair, is actually in two bordering communities, Verona and West Orange.

Although golf a century ago was more of a man's sport, the Montclair Golf Club was a woman's idea. Mrs. John Wood Stewart, one of the Saturday morning horse riders, happened to see a golf game near Boston. She convinced her riding friends in 1893 to develop a golf course to give them something else to do besides riding with the hounds.

One of the founders was Frederick Merriam Wheeler, whose condenser company grew into the international Foster Wheeler Energy Corp.

Montclair's first nine-hole course ran along the Kimberley Academy's Middle School campus. As Essex County's population spread, the club was forced to move twice, finally settling at its present location in Verona. From 1907-10, Jerome D. Travers, winner of the U.S. Open in 1915 and four-time titlist in the National Amateur and the Metropolitan Golf Association championships, belonged to the Montclair Golf Club.

Charles Banks was called upon to add Montclair's fourth "nine" in the 1920s. From an exclusive golf center, it expanded into a multi-purpose country club. The American Platform Tennis Association has held three national championships at the "golf club." The club, trying to remain true to its name, was the site for the 1985 National Amateur Golf Championship.

Pine Valley

"I think Pine Valley is the finest golf course in the world and the most wonderful and exhilarating place at which to play ... You have to recognize from the beginning that Pine Valley intends to be—and is—the hardest golf course in the world."

So said Sir Peter Allen, a retired chairman of Britain's largest manufacturing company, after playing his first game at Pine Valley in 1933.

Laid out in the sandy pine country of South Jersey, 15 miles southeast of Philadelphia, Pine Valley resembles those courses in a similar environment south of London, places such as Wentworth and Sunningdale. It is New Jersey's most exclusive golf club and considered the best on earth by many professional golfers and leading course architects, including Robert Trent Jones, who had this to say about Pine Valley:

"Few immediately appreciate Pine Valley, that awesome test of golf in Clementon, New Jersey, perhaps the hardest golf course in the world for the average golfer. Nevertheless, with some of the trick features removed, it contains more great golf holes than almost any other golf course in the world."

A few enthusiastic golfers from Philadelphia got together in the fall of 1912 to discuss a place they could play almost any month of the year. The South Jersey Pine Barrens had just the right climate, kept moderate by the Delaware River and Bay.

Star-Ledger Photo

A brook passes by the scenic third hole at the Plainfield Country Club.

From that simple desire, Pine Valley started out as an uncomplicated retreat but soon took on a life of its own. Under the watchful eye of George Crump of Merchantville, Pine Valley turned into an "absolutely uncompromising" golf course, with enormous traps, one covering one and a half acres, traps that were stony, partly bushy and unraked. It was a golfer's delightful nightmare.

From sand, pine and swampland, Pine Valley became a 623-acre sanctuary for golfers and wildlife, the entire property protected by a fence. The golf course embraces 194.5 acres, including bunkers, lakes, roads and buildings. Beyond the fairways and greens thrive virgin woodlands alive with 67 types and varieties of birds.

When George Crump envisioned holes 12, 13, 14 and 15, he sought a better second-shot on No. 13. Originally, Crump planned for a two-shotter straight out from the tee.

One day Crump was on top of the hill where any respectable golfer hopes his drive on the 13th will stop. Crump gazed to his left and spotted the peninsula formation of what is today the 13th green. Calling for a wooden club, he hit a bucketful of balls toward the spot and when the last one had rolled to a stop, he exclaimed: "That's where the 13th green will be."

It proved to be one of the world's greatest two-shot holes, according to the official Pine Valley Golf Club history book.

Before Pine Valley was ready for its first full play, workers removed more than 22,000 stumps; a wooden, 15,000-gallon water tank was constructed on stilts near the 12th tee, and thousands of seedlings were planted to prevent sand erosion.

Its worldwide fame has stimulated informal matches with the Oxford-Cambridge Golfing Society, the Australian Seniors on their way to the World Seniors at Colorado Springs, the Honourable Company of Edinburgh Golfers, the Prestwick Golf Club from Scotland, and a touring group from South Africa.

Plans are projected for home matches with the Royal and Ancient Golf Club of St. Andrew's, Scotland, as well as with Muirfield and Prestwick. And the prestigious Walker Cup was played at Pine Valley in 1984.

Plainfield

Plainfield Country Club offers a truly exceptional—yet unforgiving—18 holes of golf. The Plainfield links are listed among the 100 greatest courses by Golf Digest Magazine. The club hosted the 78th Amateur Championship conducted by the U.S. Golf Association in 1978.

Built like Rome, on seven hills, Plainfield began not as a golf course but as a tennis club with two courts built in 1890. By 1895, when golf started attracting the serious sportsman, the Hillside Tennis Club changed its venue from Plainfield to Edison and established an 18-hole golf course. It was 5,707 yards in length and was played to a par of 36-36-72.

Within 15 years, the rapidly growing club wanted a more challenging championship course. Donald Ross, the Pinehurst, N.C., golf architect, delivered an 18-hole masterwork that was completed in September 1921. It was a test of 6,277 yards with a par of 36-36-72. The 18th hole was a "punishing" 314 yards uphill from a tee near the intersection of Raritan Road and Woodland Avenue. The course has since been extended to 6,435 yards.

Golf historian Red Hoffman, who calls Plainfield his home club, writes: "With the exception of the 5th green, which until (1958) was a 'punch bowl,' and the three holes (replacing the original 16th, 17th and 18th and built by golfers Rowland and O'Loughlin), the greens are those which Ross designed."

Hoffman continues: "Reasonably ample in size—averaging 6,528 square feet in area—with configurations complementing strategic greenside bunkers, the putting surfaces present an imag-

Jack Nicklaus displays a determined look as he lines up his putt on the 10th hole of the final round of the 1980 U.S. Open in Springfield.

inative mix of contours, terraces, crowns and swales, which confront a player with some of the most interesting putting assignments to be found anywhere. Couple these 'within-the-green' features with the location of seven greens—the second, fourth, ninth, 10th, 11th, 17th and 18th—atop hills and fairway cross bunkers on nine others, and you have a golf course which is characteristically Ross and absolutely championship in its requirements."

In addition to its extensive golf complex, highlighted by a handsome, historic clubhouse, Plainfield also serves up a rounded recreation schedule of swimming, tennis, platform tennis and squash.

Somerset Hills

Founded originally in 1898 at another location, the Somerset Hills Country Club in Bernardsville is the secluded home of the rich, an exquisite maze of lawns, trees, traps and water flawlessly executed by A.W. Tillinghast.

The present facility, constructed at this site in 1917, has frequently hosted New Jersey State Golf Association events and the Met Amateur in 1982. The USGA Junior Girls Championship returned last summer for its second play, the first taking place in 1973. The annual Garden State Elizabeth Goss Memorial Round Robin commemorates a top nationally ranked female competitor from the 1930s.

Harry Vardon and Ted Ray are remembered for the exhibition matches played in Somerset Hills in 1920.

The picture-postcard championship course measures 6,512 yards. The front nine is open, rolling topography, while the back nine is wooded and tight with potholes of water. The greens are noted for their undulations and hidden breaks on fast surfaces. Bunkers are deep, filled with fine sand and strategically placed.

Upper Montclair

From a quaint 19th Century firehouse to a posh clubhouse, the story of the Upper Montclair Country Club mirrors the history of America's preoccupation with an indifferent hard ball and hole in the ground.

Founded in 1901, the club's first home was a firehouse next to the Erie Lackawanna railroad station in Upper Montclair, where some of the nation's first multimillionaires lived around the turn of the century. The Upper Ten Club, a social organization that met in the Cliffside Firehouse, teamed up with a group of ardent golfers improving their skills on a makeshift course in nearby meadows. The club's first golf course was that homemade affair consisting of five holes.

By World War I, the club had moved to new grounds and put together an 18-hole course. Many of the holes on that course were designed by Jerome Travers, a National Open and Amateur titlist and a club member.

After the war, the club commissioned a famous local architect, A.W. Tillinghast, to redesign the original 18 holes and add another nine. Soon after completion of the Tillinghast championship course, a new clubhouse was constructed, opening in 1929.

Life on the links breezed by until after World War II when the modern superhighway changed the face of the land, including the Upper Montclair Country Club's. Upper Montclair had abruptly become victim to a couple of imposing transportation corridors —Route 3 and the Garden State Parkway—which placed the tranquil hideaway just 15 minutes from the Lincoln Tunnel and the great metropolis across the river.

The club's east nine holes had to be reshaped after Route 3 claimed a large chunk of property. And in 1955, the Parkway plowed through the heart of the lush green links, resulting in the rerouting of 25 of the 27 holes. Robert Trent Jones was recruited for this assignment.

The new Jones course was ready for play in 1957. From then on, Upper Montclair has made golf history. It was selected as the site of five Professional Golf Association (PGA) tour events, four "Thunderbird Classics" in 1962, '66, '67 and '68, and the 1970 Dow Jones Open, plus four Ladies Professional Golf Association Tournaments from 1977-83. The 1970 Metropolitan Golf Association Championship and numerous New Jersey State Golf championships have been decided on the popular course.

One of the great holes in the world of golf is the 3d on Upper Montclair's South Course. It's a tribute to designer Jones how a well-placed green can survive without a single sand bunker protecting its approaches. Instead, the green is set behind a pond, and a shot that goes into the water is more difficult to handle that one that winds up in the shifting sands.

The fairway doglegs left and slightly downhill through dense meadowland, with high trees bordering both sides. The green, sitting temptingly behind the pond, is walled in by giant oaks. The pond cuts diagonally across the front of the green, and as the hole is moved farther back, the approaches become much more hazardous because of the longer water carry. Gentle mounds frame the green and the putting surface slopes slightly uphill.

During one Thunderbird Classic, Jones reflected on his work at Upper Montclair. "The image of Upper Montclair," he observed, "while not set in such a spectacular environment as Augusta, nevertheless gains its general character and its strength from its similar pattern of architecture: Its plateaued greens, its undulating green surfaces, and its water holes. The fairways are more tightly trapped than Augusta's, and the targets from the tee are, for the pro golfers, more confining... When stretched to its full length and with the rough drawn in, Upper Montclair presents a superb test of golf."

Photo Credit: Erdmute Talle

Petersen House at Smoke Rise.

HOUSING SITES

Albert Einstein lived many productive years in Princeton, as did Woodrow Wilson.

Thomas Edison settled in exclusive Llewellyn Park for most of his life, shuttling between there and his invention factory in downtown West Orange.

Rock superstar Bruce Springsteen lives and works in a modern musical mecca in the pastoral countryside of Rumson, Monmouth County.

Richard Nixon has found a comfortable hideaway in fashionable Saddle River.

The nation's wealthiest are ensconced in elaborate estates in Morris, Somerset and Hunterdon counties.

Entertainment celebrities make their homes high atop the New Jersey Palisades in towering condos and posh apartment complexes.

The most prominent mailing addresses in America are postmarked from such New Jersey communities as Ridgewood, Rumson, Princeton, Deal, Basking Ridge, Bedminster, Bernardsville, Englewood Cliffs, Millburn, Far Hills, Colts Neck, Chatham, Convent Station and Kinnelon, site of the high society Smoke Rise year-round resort.

Around and beyond these rural and suburban enclaves have emerged an incredible variety of new communities, some of them self-contained, all of them offering a lifestyle befitting the "American Dream" of a home in a pleasant setting, complete with the latest amenities.

The residential attractions combine compatible sites—seashore, countryside, lakeside, hills, valleys and woodlands—with a range of personalized housing, from traditional and Victorian to colonial and contemporary. They feature everything from handcrafted or custom-crafted woodwork and cabinets to Jacuzzi baths, cathedral ceilings, skylights, master suites, balconies, redwood decks, executive studies, special fireplaces, and multi-level passive solar heating and cooling.

The hundreds of new housing sites in New Jersey generally reflect the natural conditions within their geographic locations with names like Alpine Estates in Livingston, Aspen Ridge in Clinton, Applewood in Morris Township ... Bay Point Harbor in Barnegat Bay, Bennington Woods in Mt. Olive, Brasch Farms in Middletown, Briarcrest in Howell and Brookside Estates in Bricktown ... Canyon Woods in Old Bridge, Chester Woods in Chester, Country Side Manor in Basking Ridge and Country Woods in Bridgewater ... Deer Brook in Freehold, Deer Haven Farms in Montgomery, Diamond Hill in Berkeley Heights, Deep Run in Old Bridge and Dogwood Meadows in Metuchen ... Evergreen Woods Park in Bricktown ... Fairmount Village in Tewksbury, Florham on the Fairways in Florham Park, Forest Parks in Livingston and Mountain Lakes, and Foxhall in Middlesex ... Glenwood Oaks in

This modern house represents the architectural diversity of Llewellyn Park.

Star-Ledger Photo

Clark . . . Harbor Head in Point Pleasant Beach, Hearthstone in Lakewood, Hickory Knolls in Somerset and High View Estates in Clinton . . . Indian Hills at Sea Pines in Toms River . . . Landing Lanes Estates in Old Bridge, Laurel Hill Estates in Wall Township, Liberty Greens in Convent Station . . . Maplewood Meadows in Readington, Marina Bay Club in Long Branch and Mountain Ridge Estates in Hampton.

Other appealing and intriguing community images include: Old Bridge Mews, Overlook Village in Wharton . . . The Paddock Club in Marlboro, Pond View in Middletown, Point View in Wayne, Prides Crossing in Marlboro, Princeton Landing and Princeton Meadows . . . Quailbrook in Somerset and Quail Ridge in Chester . . . Raintree in Freehold, Riverbend in North Brunswick and Rolling Hills in Andover . . . Seaview Village in Edgewater, Sherbrooke in Bernardsville, Sherwood Court and Club in Matawan, Silver Bay Manor in Toms River, Society Hill in North Brunswick, Stanton Hills and Stonewicke in Clinton, and Sycamore Knolls in Tinton Falls . . . Tiger Hill Estates in Peapack-Gladstone, Timberline in Edison, Timber Hollow in East Brunswick, Trail Wood at Cedar Knolls in Hanover, and Twin Oaks Terrace in Westfield . . . University Heights in Piscataway . . . Vail Estates in Parsippany, Village Green in Hazlet, and Village Harbour in Manahawkin . . . Wharfside in Monmouth Beach, Winchester Heights in Long Valley, Windmill Pond in Morristown, Woodbrook Corners in Metuchen, Woodmont in Lawrence-Princeton, Woodstone in Howell and Wyndham Place in Aberdeen.

These new living centers contrast dramatically with New Jersey's older cities and seasoned suburbs, where occupying century-old brownstones today has become as fashionable as moving into Princeton Meadows. The state's first villages were settled in the 1640s, giving the Garden State the greatest diversity of housing and neighborhoods in the nation.

New Jersey, however, is known for a few innovative communities that have been widely imitated by planners and developers in other states and in countries as different in cultural styles as England is to Japan. The New Jersey landmark communities are Llewellyn Park, Smoke Rise, Radburn (Fair Lawn) and Ocean Grove. Another new community that ranks high on the list of New Jersey housing sites is Urban Farms in Franklin Lakes, Bergen County.

Llewellyn Park

When Llewellyn S. Haskell (1815-72) stood on the southeastern slope of Orange Mountain in the mid-1850s, he was able to see 100 miles, from Sandy Hook and Lower New York Bay to Haverstraw Bay and the Highlands of the Hudson, and of course, the entire metropolitan skyline.

A prosperous New York City medicine importer, Haskell was among those who helped establish Central Park in Manhattan. He loved natural scenery, especially wild forests and mountains. When his health began to decline in the early 1850s, Haskell sought refuge on high grounds with clean air.

He found his lofty retreat 650 feet above the tidal swamps and undulating lowlands of the Passaic-Hackensack-Hudson River basins. There, he created America's first major romantically landscaped residential park.

Haskell acquired Eagle Rock in 1853, a craggy cliff of 40 acres with one old farmhouse on it. The wild, hilly terrain lying south of the great cliff would become Haskell's private residential park, a place for "country homes for city people."

By 1857, Haskell had purchased some 350 acres and the basic design of Llewellyn Park began to evolve. Following the contours of the land, the terrain slowly descended, a mile-long slope marked by a series of natural terraces. The slope was cut diagonally by the irregular course of a plunging mountain brook, whose deep ravines were made into a mountain park of roughly 50 acres. That was the pristine heart of the residential park. Around it would arise rustic homes, cottages, villas, mansions and a haunting medieval castle.

Haskell designated the 50 common acres as "a private pleasure ground . . . to be freely . . . used and enjoyed, as a place of resort and recreation" by the residents of Llewellyn Park.

The Orange Mountain residential park expanded to 750 acres by 1870, about the same size of New York City's Central Park designed by Haskell's friend, Frederick Law Olmsted. Llewellyn Park today embraces approximately 400 acres. The average lot size is about six acres, although the original deed permits homes on one-acre sites.

To outsiders viewing the park for the first time, it looked like a single, handsomely landscaped estate. Llewellyn Park was variously described as a paradise, an Eden, Elysium, a "realization of the Poet's dream," and a fairyland.

Taming and shaping this idyllic wilderness without affecting its natural beauty made Llewellyn Park a model for romantic residential living. Haskell and his landscape sculptors fashioned ponds and waterfalls, rockworks and unexpected glades, and enhanced the native trees and wildflowers with garden beds and thousands of trees and shrubs of native species and rare exotic varieties imported from Asia, Europe and South America. Evergreens and willows proliferated among the flowering trees and profusion of azaleas, magnolias, holly, laurel, dogwood and rhododendrons.

From native rock, Haskell's masons carved an attractive gate lodge set 250 feet back from Valley Road, the main entrance to Llewellyn Park. Visitors were greeted by a picture-postcard fantasy: Glyn Ellyn, a serene scene of man-made ponds, a waterfall, broad paths and a rustic bridge. Leaving what is now simply called "The Glen," one enters a rugged, dark, deep rocky ravine beneath towering oaks, beeches, tulips and chestnuts. Beyond the woodlands ascends the sheer 50-foot wall of the cliff.

The earliest dwellings were of Gothic revival construction with a few Italianate houses and some bracketed cottages.

Two massive towers dominate Castlewood, built in the late 1850s for a local businessman, Joseph C. Howard. Built of rough-hewn traprock from the park's quarries, Castlewood is set into the hill on two levels with a long cloister reaching out toward its stone stable.

The castle was acquired in 1967 by former New Jersey Senate President Frank (Pat) Dodd, a restaurateur, who kept it about 12 years. Dodd had restored the castle and its grounds, improving the fenestration and replacing the bracketed veranda, which dated from early this century. Castlewood is the only remaining example of a castle-type villa designed by architect Alexander Jackson Davis.

Trydyn Terrace, also designed by Davis in 1858, is surrounded by handsome ornamental verandas with decorative spandrels. It was purchased in 1869 by Orson D. Munn, founder of Scientific American magazine.

The most famous landmark in Llewellyn Park is Glenmont, home of Thomas Alva Edison. Designed about 1880 by Henry Hudson Holly and bought by the inventor four years later, Glenmont is a 23-room national shrine containing Edison's library and stacks of correspondence. Edison lived in Glenmont with his family until his death in 1931 at age 84.

Llewellyn Park today continues to fulfill Haskell's dream of the ideal place to live in the midst of a burgeoning metropolis.

Radburn

The mass production of the motor car changed the American landscape and lifestyle. It also gave birth to the first community designed with the automobile in mind.

When created in 1929, Radburn, a section of Fair Lawn in Bergen County, was touted as the "Town for the Motor Age." What made it different from any other town in America—or in the world, for that matter—was its unique "superblock" scheme that kept pedestrians and motor vehicles from interfering with one another. In Radburn, people had their rights-of-way, and the car had its separate place within the residential community.

Designers Clarence Stein and Henry Wright did away with the traditional gridiron street pattern, replacing it with the superblock, their own innovation. The superblock is a large block of land surrounded by main roads. Access roads enter into the superblock from the main thoroughfares, ending in small cul-de-sacs. Houses are grouped around the cul-de-sacs. The remaining land inside the superblock is park area—the backbone of the neighborhood.

In Radburn, which means Saddle River in Old English, the living and sleeping sections of the houses face the garden and park areas, while the service rooms face the little access roads. The Saddle River courses along the eastern side of the Radburn tract.

The walks surrounding the cul-de-sacs on the garden side of the dwellings divide the cul-de-sacs from each other and from the central park area. The walks cross the park where necessary.

To further maintain the separation of pedestrian and vehicular traffic, underpasses and overpasses were provided for people, linking the superblocks.

Radburn was so devised that a pedestrian can start at any given point and proceed on foot to school, stores or church without having to cross a street used by automobiles.

Another Radburn first was that the parks were set aside as a common resource at no additional cost to the taxpaying residents. The savings from not having to pave so many streets and the public utilities that go with such traditional tract developments paid for the parks in Radburn. The area in streets and length of utilities is 25 percent less than in the typical American street plan. The savings also paid for the cost of grading and landscaping the play spaces and green links connecting the central-block commons.

Originally conceived by Stein and Wright to house 25,000 people, the boundaries of Radburn were to the Saddle River on the east, the Erie Railroad on the west, the Glen Rock border on the north, and Saddle Brook Township on the south.

The Old Mill, now part of the Bergen County Park System, was to be the entrance of the new community. The 1930s Depression, however, limited Radburn to its present size of 149 acres, including 430 single-family homes, 60 townhouses, 30 rowhouses, 54 duplexes and 92 apartment units, as well as a shopping center, parks and other amenities.

The Radburn Association manages for the community a park network of 23 acres, two swimming pools, four tennis courts, four baseball fields, three playgrounds, five outdoor basketball courts, an archery plaza, two summer houses, several miles of walkways, a pathway lighting system, an underpass and a community center called "The Grange," which includes offices, a library, clubroom, kitchen, maintenance shop, garage, recreation room and a gymnasium equipped with a stage.

Radburn is a community whose roots were planted in the social as well as physical theories of the Regional Planning Association (RPA). Organized in 1923, RPA promoted new planning environments in harmony with man's social, psychological and biological needs. Members included architects, conservationists, regionalists, realtors and urban critics Lewis Mumford and Charles Whitacker.

In the place of blighted cities and the isolation and squalor of incompletely and poorly developed rural areas, the regional association hoped to create a "middle landscape" whose dimensions and qualities were best displayed in Radburn. Even today, Radburn offers modest housing for most income groups.

Radburn established a real alternative mode of living, one that involved community concern, action and participation.

As America struggled out of the Depression, the influence of Radburn found its way into various Greenbelt communities of Roosevelt's Resettlement Administration and later in Baldwin Hills, Los Angeles, and Kitimat, British Columbia.

The Radburn idea then showed up in England and Sweden at Vallingly, the huge Stockholm suburb. It was copied at the Baron-Backavna Estate, Orebro, and at the Beskopsgaden Estate, Goteborg.

In post-war England, Radburn achieved generic status. The "Radburn Plan," the "Radburn Idea," the "Radburn Layout," appeared first at Coventry and later at Stevenage, Bracknell and Cumbernauld.

It has since spread to Chandigarh, India, to Brazil, to several towns in the Soviet Union, and to a section of Osaka, Japan, which is almost an exact replica of Radburn.

The concept finally returned to the United States at Reston, Va., and Columbia, Md. New towns are being built each year, using Radburn as their model.

Although billed as a "Town for the Motor Age," Radburn turned out to be the "Town for Tomorrow."

Smoke Rise

Legend has it that Smoke Rise was once the happy hunting grounds of the Lenni-Lenape Indians, who gave it the name "The Land Where the Smoke Rises" from watching how the moisture steaming from a glacial lake created the illusion of smoke.

Long after the Lenape left their land in Passaic County, the site was occupied by the Kinney family. Francis S. Kinney built his Kinney Tobacco Co. into a small empire whose most famous brand name was Sweet Caporals. The Kinneys enjoyed Smoke Rise as a self-contained country gentleman's estate, replete with stables, blacksmith shops, greenhouses, piggery, firehouse and ice house.

Kinney built a small chapel on an island in Lake Kinnelon, naming it St. Hubert's, after the patron saint of hunting. Two other Kinney landmarks dominate Smoke Rise today: The stone tower atop Kitty Ann Mountain and the massive stone East Gatehouse.

In 1947, Smoke Rise became a private residential community club, embracing 3,500 acres of scenic, secluded woodlands 1,000 feet above sea level. Within the 24-hour security gates of this elite, lofty retreat lie more than 700 magnificent homes and estates, from ultra-functional styles and quaint New England colonials to California contemporaries and ranches . . . even a palatial English Cotswold Manor estate. Housing sites range from 1.5 to five acres.

Among the homes recently available were a 12,000-square-foot estate with a spectacular atrium, six huge bedrooms, eight baths, an indoor swimming pool, attached greenhouse and passive solar energy system (sale price: $1.4 million), and an executive home with soaring cathedral ceiling for $500,000.

Prominent corporate executives and entrepreneurs have chosen Smoke Rise as their home because of its rustic tranquillity: Century-old trees, wildflowers, natural rock formations, a wooded glen, sparkling streams, ponds and waterfalls, and the wide expanse of the surrounding Pequannock watershed, which offers refuge from a bustling world.

A year-round outdoor playground, Smoke Rise residents can enjoy sailing and boating, fishing and swimming, horseback riding, hiking, trap shooting, hunting, skating, hockey and tennis on 11 courts.

In winter, Hoot Owl Pond is the site of ice skating and informal hockey games. It is also the season to explore Smoke Rise blanketed in crystals of ice and snow.

Miles of hiking trails for both the casual stroller and rugged enthusiast are kept open and free of fallen debris by a committee that also sponsors field trips. The group publishes a Tree Identification Sheet, which is included in the Smoke Rise Nature and Garden Guide. The Garden Club encourages conservation by nurturing wildflowers and assisting residents in improving their grounds and gardens.

With its own stables, miles of tended paths and riding ring with championship jumps, Smoke Rise is a horse lover's paradise. Those who take their equestrian involvement seriously can participate in horse shows, which have brought national acclaim to the Smoke Rise Club.

Cultural events are an intrinsic part of community life. For those who enjoy amateur acting, the Smoke Rise Players provide a chance to entertain or be entertained. Professional theater, ballet and opera performances have a strong following and the club arranges frequent trips to New York City and Waterloo Village.

Urban Farms

A mile-long, spring-fed lake is the refreshing attraction of a 2,500-acre community in Bergen County with the paradoxical

Star-Ledger Photo

The Village Inn in secluded Smoke Rise serves 700 owners of custom homes in the tranquil Morris County community of 3,500 acres.

This home nestled into the woods of Franklin Lakes illustrates the rustic charm of Urban Farms.

Courtesy: Gene Sullivan Assoc.

name of Urban Farms. While "urban" implies city living, "farms" conjures images of pastures, grazing cattle, green fields and rustic barns.

Urban Farms in Franklin Lakes, along busy Route 208, offers the conveniences of modern living in a rural atmosphere preserved by protective zoning ordinances insuring the permanence of property values.

A home in Urban Farms that was worth $50,000 in the early 1960s has a market value today of $250,000.

The four square miles of gently rolling woodlands had been the site of the picturesque John Mackenzie estate. When the financial tycoon died, he willed his property to the Archdiocese of Newark and the Paterson Diocese. The developers of Urban Farms purchased the tract in 1959 and created one of New Jersey's most pleasant neighborhoods.

Occupying about one-third of Franklin Lakes, Urban Farms immediately became an architect's fantasyland. Every home in Urban Farms must be distinct from all neighboring homes in its architectural style.

Land-use controls guarantee scrupulous attention to the preservation of natural beauty provided by ground contours and trees. The regulations and controls set up to insure proper development of Urban Farms grew out of 67 years of experience in construction and real estate.

The three McBride brothers—Frank, Nevins and Joseph—wanted to design a superior community where families could share their recreation as well as living space. Land below 500 feet above sea level is zoned for one acre per dwelling, while land above 500 feet is zoned two acres per dwelling.

The original barn on the Mackenzie estate was remodeled and made into the new community clubhouse. Dinners, dances and movies are among the many regular events conducted by resident-members. There are 13 tennis courts, many of them lighted, plus seven lighted paddle tennis courts, a squash court, a picnic grove, ballfields and a nearby 18-hole championship golf course. The paddle courts are in use throughout the year.

More than 700 homes of the most distinctive design have been built in Urban Farms. Today's homes are larger and more elaborate than those built in the 1960s.

The house of the '80s boasts such features as skylights and 1½-story "Great Rooms" with cathedral ceilings, replacing the paneled family room. The fireplace has become a two-story structure reaching to the roof peak. Master baths have oversize whirlpool tubs and separate showers, and there is more glass in the sliding doors and tall window walls.

In recent years, underground utilities, paved and curbed roads and town water have been incorporated in the development design. Because each house occupies a full acre, advanced septic systems, which recycle water back into the ground, do away with the need for large regional sewer connections.

Typical of the homes being built in Urban Farms today is the Contemporary. Nestled on a hillside acre with a breathtaking view from the many glass doors and large windows in the rear, the Contemporary looks out on a lighted drive that crosses the front door and swings around to a three-car garage. A crushed stone walkway and a planter set off the stone-framed entry with its imported mahogany door.

Visitors are greeted by a two-story foyer and a two-story, step-down living-room with a marble fireplace, above which hangs a mirror. A loft above looks down on this formal setting.

An ultra-modern kitchen with a large breakfast area opens to a deck that runs the entire length of the structure, with several doors opening to it. An indoor atrium invites plantings with its watertight floor and sunny exposure. There are also a huge pantry and powder room.

The West German kitchen cabinets blend in with three ovens, one of them a microwave. The main-floor master suite has a huge walk-in closet and luxurious full bath. The suite is lighted indirectly. On the lower level are a family room with another fireplace, a game room with a wet bar, a study or bedroom, and another full bath. The Contemporary cost $440,000 in 1983.

Courtesy: N.J. Div. of Travel & Tourism

Lake Hopatcong.

LAKES

ike raindrops beading on a fresh green leaf in spring, thousands of lakes and ponds glisten across the Garden State's fertile plains and valleys and rugged mountain terrain.

The great lakes of North Jersey got their start some 50,000 years ago when giant Ice Age glaciers receded to the top of the globe, leaving behind their sculptured earthen works: Pristine rivers, valleys and jagged mountain peaks.

All that was needed to finish off nature's majestic handiwork was a method of turning the glacial rivers and ponds into massive bodies of water.

Eager-beaver industrial man did it practically overnight with his rock-and-concrete dams. Far-flung mirrored surfaces flooded miles of land, giving New Jersey a ready-made recreation haven and a plentiful supply of wet stuff through the changing seasons.

Over the centuries, the ice-carved valleys and natural depressions became Lake Hopatcong, Greenwood Lake, Highland Lakes and Pompton Lakes.

By 1980, the original glacial deposits, fortified with dams, had been transformed, together with new stream- and spring-fed watering bowls, into more than 3,000 lakes, ponds and artificial impoundments in forests, research parks, suburban housing developments and on farmlands.

There are the "cong" lakes—Hopatcong, Musconetcong, Mar-

shipacong—whose names can be traced to the first inhabitants of the land and their attraction to water.

The natives are remembered in lakes with such Indian identifications as Ocquittunk, Absegami, Arapaho, Packanack, Macopin, Mohawk, Ramapo, Watchung, Waywayanda and Kittatinny. And, a lake in the middle of New Jersey's largest city called Weequahic.

Later, settlers and pioneers left their imprint on lakes called Steenykill, Parsippany, Parvin, Atsion, Cupsaw, Sawmill, Shepherd, Shadow, Swartswood, Budd, Bear Swamp and Hooks Creek.

There are also an Echo Lake and an Erskine Lake, a Spring Lake and a Surprise Lake, a Stony Lake and a White Lake.

There are even two Crystal Lakes in Burlington County, an old and a new one, plus a third one in North Jersey.

As for ponds, which can come about by throwing a couple of logs across a stream, they are everywhere in both fresh and salt waters. The more popular ponds are Swan, Duck, Stag, Panther, Sunfish, Sucker, Quick, Parkim, Sally's, Interval, Hopewell and Shotwell.

Not quite as numerous are the bogs, the wet spongy ground that sops up water whenever it rains. They have names, too, like April, Ancora and Burnt Fly.

Finally, the biggest engineering feats have wrought such marvels as Round Valley and Spruce reservoirs, the fountainheads of northwest New Jersey that keep the thirsty cities from drying up during the scorching summer months.

Most of the early impoundments were created for specific uses as reservoirs, mill ponds and furnace ponds. Over the years they were enlarged by higher and stronger dams.

The railroads opened the hinterland and brought more dams to Split Rock, Swimming River, Oradell, Boonton and Tappan on the New York border at Bergen County.

New Jersey's natural lake district, like those in Switzerland and England, are in the mountain region of Passaic, Sussex, Warren, Union and even parts of Essex County, where winter snows and ice melt into cascading rivulets in the sunny spring, filling the dammed glacial lakes and ponds.

Some 70 lakes and ponds owe their existence to glacial action, while another 700 lakes are classified as natural. The majority are man-made.

A survey in 1893 found Sussex County contained more than 50 natural lakes within its 500 square miles. Warren County had 10, Morris and Passaic each an even dozen.

Lake Marcia in Sussex County, a 23-acre glacial lake, has the distinction of being the highest body of water in New Jersey at 1,570 feet above sea level. Round Pond (33 acres) on the mountain above Swartswood Lake, is less lofty, at 1,359 feet. Sand Pond above Coleville, now Rutherford Lake, ranked third in altitude at 1,302 feet, but has the largest water trap: 75 acres.

During the Depression, Highland Lake, created by a real estate developer, became the third highest resort lake in the Garden State.

Some of the larger natural collection basins in Sussex County are Swartswood Lake, 505 acres; Culver's Lake, 486 acres, and Wawayanda Lake, 240 acres.

Since the 1890s, New Jersey's topography has been dramatically altered by bulldozers, dams and tract developments featuring their own instant duck ponds and little spillways.

At last count, Warren County led the lakes and ponds list with 493 impoundments, followed, surprisingly, by Essex County, with 396.

The number of impoundments seems to follow the Garden State's growth pattern during the post-war boom: Monmouth County, 390 lakes and ponds; Morris, 346; Sussex, 227; Hunterdon, 200; Mercer, 173; Burlington, 149; Salem, 114; Gloucester, 104; Camden, 84; Cumberland, 73; Bergen, 69; Ocean and Passaic, each 62; Somerset, 51; Middlesex, 43; Atlantic, 34; Cape May 21; Union, 4, and Hudson, none.

Scattered throughout the northerly region of New Jersey are lakes that conjure up all kinds of colorful and historic images:

Green Pond, Glen Wild, Mount Glen, Deer, Woodcliff, Wildwood, Long Wood, Point View, Cannon Ball, Meadow Brook, Ravine, Silver, Star, Cozy, Wonder, White Meadow, Twin, Shongum, Horseshoe, Denmark, Valhalla and Skyline.

In South Jersey there's a Makepeace Lake and in Central Jersey a Takanesse Lake.

The magnificent triangle of mountain lakes are Hopatcong, Highlands and Greenwood, having opened up the remote mountain chain before the American Revolution.

Lake Hopatcong

Lake Hopatcong is New Jersey's largest and most irregularly shaped natural and man-altered fresh water impoundment. There are more than 30 inlets, coves, bays, crooks, crannies and crevices breaking up the 41-mile-long shoreline.

A summer retreat that long ago gave way to a sprawling bedroom colony, Lake Hopatcong takes in, when filled to the brim, more than 2,500 acres, or nearly four square miles. It's six and a half miles long and two miles wide at its narrowest bend. The depth ranges from five to 25 feet, the deepest hole dropping to 55 feet.

"Honey Water of Many Coves," as the Lenni Lenape described the original, smaller lake, Hopatcong today serves a nine-square-mile lake region embracing four municipalities in two counties, Sussex and Morris.

The lakefront communities are Hopatcong Borough, whose shore residents number about 12,000; Mount Arlington, 5,000 denizens, and Jefferson and Roxbury townships, each adding roughly 4,000 to the regional lake population.

From Memorial Day through Labor Day, as many as 50,000 people will take advantage of the cool Pocono breezes that make Lake Hopatcong a refreshing day or vacation away from the hot, humid cities and suburbs. At 927 feet above the Atlantic Ocean, Lake Hopatcong enjoys the prevailing westerly winds year-round, allowing for excellent ice skating, ice sailing and ice fishing in the winter months.

Three major islands—Raccoon, Indian and Halsey—occupy a large stretch of the lake. The 5,000-foot-long Raccoon Island can be reached by a ferry boat owned and operated by the island inhabitants. About 50 homes, including a few estates, give Raccoon Island a posh appearance. Homeowners on the other islands

Star-Ledger Photo

Sunrise lake, seen from Patriot's Path in Morris Township, is one of about 346 lakes dotting Morris County.

use their own boats to get back and forth between the mainland.

A causeway routes traffic to Bertrand's Island, famous for its amusement park and 78-year-old Lake Hopatcong Yacht Club. In 1880, Ernest Bertrand, a wealthy New York entrepreneur, planned to build a sugar refinery on the island, but the project never left the drawing board. Bertrand's vision also included a German castle and stone embattlement to further isolate himself from outsiders. Only his name remained on the island, along with a few private homes.

The credit for creating Lake Hopatcong as it is known today must go to a Morristown engineer who loved to go fishing there in the 1820s. George Macculloch, like Bertrand, saw the enormous potential of the watershed.

During one fishing expedition in 1822, Macculloch envisioned a canal through North Jersey as a major transportation corridor. The Morris Canal, which would figure prominently in New Jersey's industrial development, was born.

At the site of a five-foot dam built by iron makers in 1750, Macculloch erected a 12-foot-high barrier, raising the level of the lake and furnishing the canal with enough water to hook up Newark and Phillipsburg on the Delaware River.

It was 1831 and the beginning of the American Industrial Revolution. In 1912, Hudson Maxim invented smokeless powder at his Landing laboratory. A portion of Mt. Arlington, where early industry settled, is today a National Historic District.

But it was Macculloch's canal that made it all possible. His channel of locks and rising planes elevated the lake, filling in all of the rocky notches and chinks where fish love to hide and fishermen love to find them.

Once the "Newport of New Jersey," Lake Hopatcong has changed from the days of the steamboats and Gay '90s, when fancy hotels were filled with city folk replenishing themselves in the healthy, "honey" mountain waters.

A historic landmark is the canal-rail junction at Lake Hopatcong. Before the advent of superhighways, passengers arrived by rail and transferred to a small, side-wheeled steamboat. After passing through the Morris Canal lock, the steamboat made stops at the various landings and docks around the lake.

Swimming, fishing and boating are the main activities today. Hopatcong supports the greatest number of pleasure boats of any inland body of water, completely within New Jersey: More than 5,500 motorboats, sailboats, rowboats and canoes.

Keeping the lake fit for recreation and human consumption (Hopatcong has been tapped during severe droughts) are nine rivers and streams and hundreds of springs gushing from the floor of the valley.

Besides the water-oriented activities, Hopatcong offers its residents and vacationers fine golf courses, horseback riding, tennis, handball, hunting and a dude ranch in Succasunna, a section of Roxbury Township.

Roxbury also has another significant lake, Musconetcong, around which a year-round resort community has emerged.

Nearby Mount Arlington has lovely Lake Rogerene, fed by springs and surrounded by forested mountains.

Greenwood Lake

Another sweeping body of water is Greenwood Lake, six miles of shimmering aquamarine liquid shared by New Jersey and New York. Each state claims half of the oak- and hemlock-lined lake.

Like its sister lakes in the mountain chain, Greenwood Lake came into being when debris left behind by a retreating glacier clogged an icy river known today as Wanaque.

The early Colonial settlers took one look at this seemingly endless wedge of water between the mountains and fittingly called it Long Pond. It became much longer when a Colonial iron master threw up a five-foot-high dam, 200 feet wide, to run his furnace in 1768.

The pond again doubled in size when builders of the Morris Canal, constantly in search of more water, built a bigger dam and added 12 feet to the lake's elevation. The last dam to hold back the water rushing in from New York was constructed in 1927.

Today, Greenwood Lake sits more than 620 feet above sea level. The average depth of the New Jersey side of the lake is 10 feet. The deepest is in the northern end on the New York side, where it drops to 60 feet.

There are two versions of how Long Pond became a pretty picture everyone today knows of as Greenwood Lake, or the Little Switzerland of New Jersey.

The earliest source is the Erskine Militia, which fought during the American Revolution. The miners and farmers wore a green uniform and developed a reputation as Robin Hood's band, springing surprise attacks on the enemy in Sherwood Forest. The upper half of Greenwood Lake is buffered by Sterling Forest, with woodlands around the Jersey half in West Milford, Passaic County.

From Robin Hood's green-clad militia supposedly came the designation Greenwood Lake, a sort of warning to the redcoats to stay out of their forest.

The other version has been attributed to the artists and writers who sought a quiet and inspiring place to work not far from New York City. Their paintings glowed a brilliant green, the lake reflecting the quivering leaves. The woods and their green leaves evoked a natural charm for the Hudson Valley artists who made Greenwood Lake their home as long ago as the 1830s.

The 26-mile watershed basin drew artists to the "Beautiful Valley" in the Bella Valle Mountain Range. Tuxedo Mountain on the New York border rises 1,600 feet, while Bearfort Mountain on the New Jersey side reaches 1,500 feet.

Legend has it that anyone who put his feet in Long Pond at some point would live on its shores. One believer is Robert Burrows, executive director of the Greenwood Lake Watershed Management District.

At four years old, Burrows learned to swim in Greenwood Lake during summer trips there with his parents, from Paterson. The Burrows now live by the lake, along with 90 percent of the residents who have moved from metropolitan centers and their suburbs.

The dam at the lower end in New Jersey makes Greenwood Lake the attractive recreation resource it has become during the past two centuries. But the scores of streams and creeks winding their way down the mountain slopes of New York constantly renew it. It's a perfect partnership between two states and the three municipalities that reap its many benefits: West Milford in New Jersey and the Village of Greenwood Lake and Warwick in New York.

Sterling Forest, which has become a corporate convention and research park, also enjoys a bird's eye view of the blue-green, mile-wide lake.

The valley population has stabilized around 22,000, evenly distributed between the two states. As many as 25,000 boats—and a few seaplanes—use the lake for recreation and business.

Two islands break up the sheer, flat length of the lake and give the deer herds somewhere to get away from the residents occupying the thousands of cottages dotting the mountainsides and shoreline. The deer swim to either Storm Island or Fox Island and, in the winter, simply walk across the ice to escape the sounds of the hunters.

Fox Island was acquired by the Fox family and converted into a private, 35-acre resort. Abercrombie & Fitch, proprietors of the famous sporting goods store, built an estate on Fox Island. President Theodore Roosevelt and his son often visited the island, taking a few ducks in season.

One of the many cottages and makeshift docks on Greenwood Lake.

Photo Credit: Bill Leather

Storm Island, just five acres, contains an old farmhouse with a ring of cabins around it.

Frank Sinatra, a native of Hoboken, has a summer home at Greenwood Lake. During the 1940s and '50s, heavyweight boxing champion Joe Louis and middleweight titlist Rocky Graziano worked out at Brown's Hotel on the lake. The original boxing ring can still be found in the weeds and bushes by the hotel, which burned down in 1957.

Another sports footnote has to do with the Sultan of Swat, Babe Ruth. The home-run hitter almost missed a World Series game when his car hit a tree on Tuxedo Mountain at Greck's Maple Wood Inn. The immortal Babe, the story goes, hitchhiked back to the city in time to play nine complete innings.

But Greenwood Lake transcends the Sinatras, Louises and Ruths. In Switzerland, school children learn about the bistate lake because of its striking similarity to Swiss Alps lakes. When visiting Greenwood Lake, the Swiss are amazed at the accuracy of the pictures and descriptions of the Switzerland of the East, according to Burrows.

"Greenwood Lake has become an international resort," he says. "We even have a Bavarian castle on the east shore, serving up the largest hamburger in New Jersey."

The old Continental Hotel, which was gutted by fire in 1931, was replaced by the new Continental Hotel on the west shore. For the French palate, there's the Cafe Du Lac, equipped with greenhouse, also on the west shore. Several other fine eateries cater to international tastes, a pleasant surprise for those who seek more than recreation and solitude.

Happy Landing on the east shore has become a memorable landmark of the days when steamboats with their giltwork and wheelhouse plied the smooth waters of Greenwood Lake. Happy Landing is where the railroad stopped, discharging weary passengers who journeyed five, six, seven hours from Manhattan and cities in New Jersey. The travelers were happy to be at the lake, and their landing still stands as a reminder of the bygone steamboat-railroad era.

In 1983, a powerboat regatta was inaugurated to raise money to maintain Greenwood Lake. The spring boating race, sponsored by the American Power Boat Association, was originated by the Lake Hopatcong Racing Association, which conducts a comparable event each year to pay for the removal of weeds and algae threatening the popular conservation lakes.

Greenwood and Hopatcong are not just important as a recreation resource, but they are part of New Jersey's critical water supply. The waters falling over the Greenwood Lake dam eventually fill the Wanaque Reservoir, one of New Jersey's seven major impoundments serving more than a million consumers in the Passaic Valley region.

Highland Lakes

Highland Lakes in Sussex County are a series of man-made water vessels that came into existence during the Depression and rapidly became a rustic summer resort of log cabins. More than 2,000 cabins and bungalows make up the Highlands community, half of them year-round dwellings and many owned by physicians from the New York-North Jersey area.

Three of the 1,400-foot-high lakes bear the Highland appellation: Highland Lake, Upper Highland Lake and Upper Highland East. The other two are Indian Lake and Little Lake.

The singular Highland Lake is the largest with three beaches and 280 acres of spring- and stream-fed water. A nine-foot-high dam, 400 feet wide, provided an instant idyllic setting for swimmers, boaters and anglers. No fuel-powered craft is permitted on the 2.5-mile-long lake.

Three islands are large enough to accommodate some single-family homes. Six more islands, left in their natural condition, are available for picnics, or for a relaxing stopover during a boat outing.

Upper Highland Lake and Upper Highland East are about a mile round. Upper Highland has one island. Each lake has its own white, sandy beach.

Indian Lake is a finger of water slightly more than a mile in length and from a quarter-mile to a couple of hundred feet wide.

The lush evergreen cover gives Indian Lake exceptional privacy. Hemlocks, mountain laurels and rhododendrons almost hide the homes set back from the lake along the lower mountainsides.

Little Lake is small in name only, as it is about the same size as the other three lakes, roughly a mile around. Active recreation facilities have been built at Little Lake for basketball, handball, volleyball, plus four tennis courts.

The clear spring waters from the Highland Lakes flow into Wanda Lake and Waywayanda Lake, a gigantic impoundment capable of storing an estimated 2 billion gallons of water. Waywayanda was actually two ponds that merged when a 14-foot dam was erected.

Pompton Lakes

Another random collection of mostly artificial ponds in Passaic County are the Pompton Lakes. Waters from the Ramapo Mountains drained into the Pompton region, creating several little pools that the Indians referred to as "round ponds." The first farmers and industrialists added some dams, bringing the total number of collection basins to approximately 25.

The better known ones, in addition to Pompton Lake, are Ramapo and Franklin lakes, and Pines and Glen Wild lakes.

Mohawk to Sunfish

The Wallkill River in Sussex County was all that a real estate developer, Arthur D. Crane, needed to change a mountain wilderness into a fashionable resort community.

A dam at the headwaters of the Wallkill River produced one of the most attractive lakes in New Jersey, the Mohawk.

Construction began in January 1926 during a period of unbounded prosperity, the Roaring '20s. The gates of the 600-foot-long dam were closed on March 17, 1928. By then, a 2,500-acre reservation was ready for development.

The rustic retreat boasted its own country club on a 3½-mile-long lake surrounded by 10 miles of wooded shoreline. Alpine, log cabin, colonial, ranch and split-level homes snuggled into the rocky slopes around the lake.

More than 2,000 families today enjoy all the comforts of resort living: An Olympic-size swimming pool, a yacht club, tennis courts, riding stable, sandy beaches, a golf club and a second country club.

So successful was Lake Mohawk that similar rustic colonies sprang up in that region after World War II: Lakes Saginaw, Seneca, Shawnee, Summit and Winona.

Sunfish Pond sits atop Kittatinny Mountain by the Delaware Water Gap, 44 acres of rare natural beauty that almost became a big tub to be drained every day for its water power.

After a long, political tug-of-war between an electric power company and conservationists, Sunfish Pond and 68 acres around it were saved from becoming part of the the Yards Creek Pumped Storage Electric Generating Project. Sunfish Pond was supposed to be used as an additional 1.3 million-kilowatt power system.

The high-rise power station produces 330,000 kilowatts of electricity by pumping water up Kittatinny Mountain at night when adequate electrical energy is available. Each day when the power demand peaks, the water is run down the mountain through a tunnel to turn turbines, generating electricity.

In South Jersey, the largest body of water is Union Lake, 898 acres of water surface with a maximum depth of 27 feet. Part of the Maurice River watershed, Union Lake was initially used as an industrial water supply source.

Situated in Cumberland County just northwest of Millville, Union Lake offers superb largemouth bass and pickerel fishing. The state's striped bass record for inland waters came from Union Lake in 1978. The linesider was taken by Eldwood Bernat and weighed in at 27 pounds and 12 ounces.

The State Division of Fish, Game and Wildlife is releasing fingerling striped bass in Union Lake in an effort to create a full-scale striper fishery there.

Private man-made lakes are being built every year to satisfy the yearn of homeowners to be near a placid pond or ready-made, miniature wildlife refuge. Shadow Lake in Monmouth County is an example of a recent retirement community catering to outdoor enthusiasts who want a lake, no matter what shape or size, in their own backyard.

Lake Carnegie in Mercer County was artificially created in 1906 through the generosity of philanthropist Andrew Carnegie. The Millstone River was dammed north of Princeton and, voila! . . . a 3½-mile lake took shape. Lake Carnegie today is owned by Princeton University.

Lake Parsippany in Morris County is a 155-acre impoundment encircled by suburban congestion. The artificial lake is

Star-Ledger Photo

Quaint Tudor buildings enhance the boardwalk at the north end of Lake Mohawk, a rustic retreat in Sussex County.

Sunfish Pond, atop a forested mountain in Warren County.

Photo Credit: N.J. Div. of Travel & Tourism

Star-Ledger Photo

owned by the more than 600 member families of the Lake Parsippany Property Owners. An earthen dam reinforced with wood keeps Lake Parsippany from becoming just another segment of a local stream draining the densely developed Parsippany-Troy Hills region.

More lakes are inevitable in a state surrounded by water on three sides—a peninsula streaked with hundreds of waterways, all eventually emptying into the Atlantic Ocean.

A mammoth prehistoric lake that long ago disappeared from the scene may someday return, compliments of modern technology.

Since 1936, residents of the Passaic River Valley have been searching for a method of controlling floods that rage through the most populated region of New Jersey as regularly as the spring rains.

One idea is the rebirth of Lake Passaic, a great glacial depression that dried up for the most part during the last 10,000 years. By placing a dam at the confluence of the Pompton and Passaic rivers, man would be redoing what nature did rather forcefully during the Ice Age.

Should that ever come about, Lake Passaic would return as the largest body of fresh water in New Jersey.

A footbridge links a pathway along the Lake Parsippany dam in Parsippany. The 155-acre lake is owned by more than 600 families living along its shores.

Reminiscent of a medieval country manor, the Skyland mansion towers over Ringwood State Park in Passaic County.

LANDMARKS

As one of the original 13 Colonies, New Jersey today represents living history, life as it was before and during the birth of a nation.

A large part of New Jersey's physical appearance and character comes from its restored historic buildings, preserved neighborhoods, archeological sites, first-of-a-kind commercial-industrial operations, and entire districts designated as national landmarks.

Every one of New Jersey's 21 counties aches with antiquity, pieces of past political and industrial revolutions that changed the world, their origins rooted in Princeton, Paterson, Trenton, Morristown, Freehold, Fort Lee, Menlo Park, West Orange.

Whether it was the longest battle of the American Revolution in Monmouth County, or the cradle of the American Industrial Revolution in Paterson, or the world's first invention factories in Menlo Park and West Orange, New Jersey will always be the place where history was dynamically written.

More than 1,000 historic buildings and sites still cling tenaciously to the present, telling the story of New Jersey's unique mix of people and ideas, drawn together by some intangible need to understand and expand the horizon of knowledge.

Much of this incredibly diverse, 300-year-old laboratory has been saved from the modern wrecking ball. There are ancient lighthouses in Absecon and Sandy Hook, castles in Flemington and Paterson, log cabins in Byram and Swedesboro, tanneries in Elizabeth and Jersey City, row houses in Hoboken and Camden, canals in Passaic and Morris counties, grist mills in Waterloo Village, Tinton Falls and Paramus.

There's a giant wooden elephant in Margate and a rocket launching site in Franklin, a coffee house in Bernards Township and a tollgate house in Upper Deerfield Township, an apothecary in Smithville and a cigar factory in Trenton, a sanitarium in Egg Harbor and an asylum in Newark.

There's even something for pre-history buffs: The first dinosaur skeleton in North America was discovered in New Jersey in 1858, eons of evolution buried beneath the richest soil on the continent.

Princeton-Trenton

The New Jersey Historical Society is the fourth oldest in America. Founded in Trenton in 1845, the society remains the principal conservator and respository of New Jersey's heritage. Its scholarly quarterly journal, New Jersey History, is the second oldest publication in the nation dedicated to history.

Headquarters—a four-story building on Broadway in Newark —houses a superb collection of New Jersey materials, including more than 60,000 volumes and 1 million manuscripts. The museum has become a showcase for works by New Jersey artists.

The New Jersey Department of Education has helped to organize more than 200 Jerseymen Clubs. The society also maintains the five-acre Morven estate in Princeton, built in the early 1950s by Richard Stockton, a signer of the Declaration of Independence. Today, Morven serves as the society's central branch and museum.

But perhaps the most important piece of history, or landmark, would have to be the Princeton-Trenton campaign in New Jersey's heartland. It influenced the direction of the American Revolution and ultimately the course of civilization over the past two centuries.

George Washington scored a decisive victory over the Hessians on Christmas night 1776, and destroyed the British garrison in Princeton that same year. The brutal military campaign forced the British to evacuate New Jersey and demonstrated, for the first time, that the Colonists could win their freedom and independence.

In a retrospect on Washington's Birthday (1983), Time magazine's Hugh Sidey, who writes "The Presidency" column, observed:

"Yet the battle of Trenton might have been as important a battle as this nation ever won. The Trenton victory brought the Revolution back to life. The Colonies dared hope again for independence. France began to look with more favor on the American struggle, and Britain began to lose heart ... Three columns were to have crossed the Delaware River. Only Washington made it across. The gunpowder of his troops was soaked by a freezing rain, so they could not fire their arms. They had to depend on bayonets several times during the night. Washington's officers pleaded with him to call off the attack. The story goes that he stood on an old beehive in a muddy New Jersey field and turned aside every entreaty. The battle of Trenton was won by the determination of one man ...."

The Princeton-Trenton area is saturated with historic monuments and sites, from the 1701 Morven Mansion and 1726 Quaker meeting house, to the 1757 Old Ferry House and pre-revolutionary Thomas Clarke farmhouse.

The nucleus of the Revolutionary War scene is Nassau Hall on the Princeton University campus, built in 1756. The building was occupied by both British and Colonial armies as a barracks and hospital.

Nassau Hall also served as the capital of an infant nation, where the Continental Congress met from June through November in 1783.

In the vicinity are the 1702 Thompson-Neely House and the 1740 Old Grist Mill. Nearby is McKonkey's Ferry House, where Washington rested after crossing the Delaware River before his surprise attack on Trenton.

Also in the state capital is the fieldstone barracks built in 1758 during the French and Indian War to house British soldiers, who were then living in private households.

Outside of Princeton, Washington established a base of operations at Rockingham, an elaborate 20-room farmhouse built in the 1730s. Washington entertained many guests at the Rocky Hill estate, including Alexander Hamilton, Thomas Jefferson and James Madison.

Princeton is also the home of another national historic landmark—the Albert Einstein house at 112 Mercer St., where the mathematical genius lived from the early 1930s until his death in 1955. The Einstein white clapboard house was built in the 1870s.

South of Trenton is the Abbot Farm, the largest known Middle Woodland Village site in the coastal Mid-Atlantic/New England region. The farm played a significant role in the field of archeology and geology, becoming the focal point in a 40-year controversy concerning the antiquity of man in the New World.

In eastern United States prehistoric times, the Middle Woodland (500 B.C.-500 A.D.) was distinguished by rapid and extensive cultural change, characterized by well-developed trade systems and innovations in materials, including elaborate ceramic, lithic and metal items.

Abbot Farms furnished the best evidence for exchange systems in the coastal region, demonstrating some of the most complex and diverse ceramic styles.

Star-Ledger Photo

The pre-Revolutionary Thomas Clarke farmhouse, an historic Quaker dwelling, still stands at 500 Mercer Street in Princeton.

Passaic County

Paterson and its environs were the center of America's pre-Colonial iron industry. Beginning in 1740 with the formation of the Ringwood Co., the first forges and furnaces were of great importance to the Colonies and during the American Revolution. Ringwood Manor served as Washington's headquarters on several occasions and his horses were shod in the old blacksmith shop.

Robert Erskine (Erskine Lakes in Passaic County) was a manager of the Ringwood Mines and Surveyor General for the American Army, preparing many maps which aided Washington in his military campaigns. Washington and his wife planted a tree at Erskine's grave in 1782, closing a chapter in the history of Ringwood. The area is now a state park.

The rambling Ringwood mansion represents the living conditions of three successive families from about 1810 to 1930. The manor contains a valuable collection of Americana amassed by the Cooper and Hewitt families. Cooper founded Cooper Union Institute in New York, the only free-tuition college in the United States. Abram S. Hewitt was America's foremost ironmaster of the 19th Century.

Among the interesting relics of the iron-making days are an anvil and trip hammer from the Hewitt forge, a deck gun from the frigate Constitution, better known as "Old Ironsides," and a Civil War mortar, the carriage of which was made by the Hewitts under a "rush order" issued by President Lincoln.

A huge chain stretches across the front of the manor, reminding visitors of the type of chain pulled across the Hudson River during the Revolution to prevent passage of British vessels.

The Van Riper-Hopper House in Wayne, constructed in 1786, is a fine preservation of New Jersey Dutch architecture. Dutch homes faced south, allowing the sun to beat along the gabled roof and long south wall, heating the house in winter and drying it in summer. There are six fireplaces in the 11-room structure. Large logs were dragged into the house and rolled in the fireplace. The fire was never allowed to die out during the entire year because it would bring bad luck. Only on New Year's Day was the fireplace cleaned and a new fire built. The floors are wide pine planks and the open ceilings are supported by heavy hand-hewn beams. The walls are built of native gray fieldstone.

The Van Riper-Hopper House was dedicated in 1964 as the Wayne Township Museum and is the headquarters of the Wayne Historical Commission.

The American Labor Museum was created in 1982 in the historic Pietro Botto House in Haledon, a silk worker's home which was the center for the weekend rallies of the great Silk Strike of 1913. The Botto House provided a haven for free speech and assembly during the strike involving some 24,000 men, women and children.

Strikers were demanding an eight-hour day, a $12 weekly minimum wage and an end to the four-loom system. Forbidden to assemble in Paterson, workers met in Botto's house in nearby Haledon, across the Passaic River. The balcony of the Botto House provided a stage for John Reed (who was schooled in Morristown and whose life was depicted in the 1981 movie "Reds," starring Warren Beatty) and other labor leaders.

The Botto House features four period rooms representing the lifestyles of immigrant workers in 1913. Galleries portray the events of the Silk Strike and profile the ethnic backgrounds of the workers from Italy, Holland, Germany and Eastern Europe.

An outstanding industrial landmark is the Great Falls of Paterson and the related Society for Useful Manufacturers.

The dam across the river and the buildings that housed a tremendous variety of industrial processes developed over a period of 119 years represent the finest and most extensive remaining collection of engineering, planning and architectural works of that period when the United States was becoming a major industrial nation.

The growth and changes in industrial planning, engineering and architecture that occurred from 1793 to 1912 are vividly depicted in the existing Paterson historic district.

The type and age of historical and architectural documentation cannot be duplicated or replaced for that seminal industrial period, according to the National Register of Historic Places.

Important complexes and sites are the mid-19th Century Danforth & Cooke center, the 1900 trolley barn, the late 18th Century intake basin for L'Infant's water raceway system, the 20th Century Casper silk mill, when Paterson was the silk capital of the world, and several archeological sites yet to be unearthed in the Rogers Locomotive complex (both 1840 and 1870 structures).

A French drawing room in Ringwood Manor captures the elegance of the mid-1800s.
Star-Ledger Photo

Morris County

Another historic setting in New Jersey is Morristown, headquarters for Washington's army in 1779-80 and the first national historic park dedicated in 1933.

The general arrived in Morristown in a severe hail and snow storm on Dec. 1, 1779, and made his headquarters at the spacious home of Jacob Ford Jr. That month, the Continental Army survived the worst winter of the century: 28 blizzards blasting the hills and Jockey Hollow encampment with six-foot-high snowdrifts blocking vital supply lines.

Historic places to visit in the Morristown area, in addition to the Ford Mansion, are: Ft. Nonsense, built in 1777 to protect military supplies and serve as an observation point for enemy movements; the Indian Trading Post in Harding Township where the Lenni-Lenape traded after the Revolution; the 1760 Dixon Homestead in Boonton; the 1693 Martin Berry House in Pompton Plains; the 1794 Melville Mill in Whippany; the 1757 Old Parsonage in Hanover; the 1758 Quaker Meeting House in Randolph; the 1742 Ralston Industrial District in Mendham, and the 1700 Rogerene

Settlement in Mt. Arlington, where the religious leader John Rogers sought refuge for his flock of worshippers.

Morristown is also the site of the Italianate Victorian mansion, Acorn Hall, built in 1853 and named for the largest and oldest black oak tree in New Jersey.

An historic first in Morristown is the Thomas Nast House at MacCulloch Avenue and Miller Road, where the famed cartoonist-illustrator-artist created, among other legendary images, the immortal visage of the jolly, full-bearded Santa Claus whose likeness appears on cards, calendars and yule gifts around the world. Nast lived in Morristown from 1871 to 1902.

Monmouth County

In Central Jersey, the Monmouth Battlefield in Freehold was the site of the longest battle of the Revolutionary War in June 1778. It was also where Molly Pitcher gained notoriety as the woman who took her husband's place on the battlefield when he was felled by a bullet. It may have been the hottest day of the war as temperatures topped the 100 degree mark in the shade.

The Craig Farm House near the Monmouth Battlefield still stands. Built in 1710, the house was occupied by John Craig, paymaster for the militia, who fought in the longest battle while his wife and family remained on the farm. They fled when the British used the farmhouse as a temporary field hospital.

There's mounting evidence that Abraham Lincoln's ancestors landed in New Jersey after their cross-Atlantic sailing journey from Europe. A blacksmith shop in a stone building in Upper

Star-Ledger Photo

Acorn Hall in Montclair is an example of the Italianate style promoted by the Victorians.

Morristown's Ford Mansion, known as Washington's Headquarters, sheltered the general during the harsh winter of 1779. A monument to Washington (inset) stands opposite the mansion.

Inset Photo Credit: Star-Ledger Photo

Star-Ledger Photo   Star-Ledger Photo

The Twin Lights fortification in Highlands has kept vigil over Sandy Hook and the Raritan Bay since 1862.

The Craig Farm House near the Monmouth Battlefield was used by the British as a field hospital during the American Revolution.

Freehold Township is believed to have been operated by Lincoln's great-great-great uncle and namesake.

The stone structure on Burlington Path Road is in sound condition, even though it dates back to 1720. There is a headstone in Assunpink State Park marking the final resting place of six-year-old Deborah Lincoln, daughter of Modecai Lincoln, the president's great-great grandfather who moved west about 1730.

Lincoln's family migrated to Virginia and then to Kentucky, where America's 16th president was born in a log cabin in 1809.

On the coast of Monmouth County, a conspicuous landmark is the Twin Lights fortification atop the Highlands, overlooking Sandy Hook, Raritan Bay, the New York Harbor and lower Manhattan skyline. The double lighthouse was built in 1862 as the first-of-its-kind in the world to guide merchant ships into New York harbor.

Remains of the original lighthouse erected in 1790 are within the three-acre state park. The first building of the U.S. Lifesaving Service, forerunner of the U.S. Coast Guard, is preserved at the Twin Lights site. It was also where Guglielmo Marconi, credited with inventing the wireless telegraph, reported the Americas' yacht cup race.

At the tip of Sandy Hook in the Gateway National Recreation Area stands the oldest, working lighthouse in America. The original lighthouse went up in 1764. It was replaced in 1857. The lighthouse is in the Ft. Hancock and Sandy Hook Proving Ground Historic District. The military mansions at the fort were designed by architect Stanford White at the turn of the century.

Roosevelt Borough in Monmouth County is an intact New Deal planned community of residential, commercial and public structures, integrated into an open space and green belt system. Roosevelt serves as a physical record of important intellectual, political and cultural currents in 20th Century American history.

Roosevelt contained four kinds of communities: Experimental farm colonies, subsistence gardens for city workers; colonies for stranded workers, and, primarily, homesteads for part-time or seasonal industrial workers.

Roosevelt was organized as the only fully cooperative agro-industrial community of the homesteads programs. Its social roots reach back into a long history of Jewish agricultural and industrial colonization.

Roosevelt is the only New Deal community to be settled by a homogeneous population of Jewish garment workers. As early as 1881, an agrarian group called Am Olam began establishing Jewish farm colonies.

The first permanent Jewish agricultural colony in the United States was founded in South Jersey in 1882, at a place called Alliance.

New Jersey became the locus of several enduring colonies started in the late 19th and early 20th centuries, including those at Norma, Brotmanville, Rosenhayn, Carmel, Garten Road, Woodbine (Vineland), Farmingdale and Bound Brook.

The houses at Roosevelt are well-preserved expressions of the "International Style" in the United States. The housing designs —compositions of juxtaposed geometric forms, with smooth concrete surfaces and open planes—follow the stark, functional, unadorned modernist aesthetic.

Hudson County

Hudson County was the site of the first settlement in New Jersey. Bergen, the Dutch word for hill, was settled in 1660 on the banks of the Hudson River. Eventually renamed Jersey City, Bergen later was taken as the name of the county next to Hudson.

Considered the three most prominent landmarks in Hudson County are the Apple Tree House and Old Hudson County Court House, both in Jersey City, and the site of the unlawful duel between Alexander Hamilton and Aaron Burr on the Palisades in Weehawken.

The Apple Tree House, also known as the Van Wagenen Homestead Farm, was built in 1694 and served as the headquarters for Maj. Gen. Marquis de Lafayette during the American Revolution. General Washington conferred with Lafayette many times at the stone house at 198 Academy St., now the Quinn Funeral Home. In the 17th Century there was an apple orchard behind the stone house.

A cane made from a branch of an apple tree was given to Lafayette in 1824. The cane is on display at the Lourdes Museum in Paris.

The Old County Court House at Newark and Baldwin avenues was designed by Hugh Roberts, a resident of Jersey City, and erected in 1910. The Hudson court house rivals the Essex County court house designed by Cass Gilbert, who was the architect of Newark City Hall and the United States Supreme Court building in Washington, D.C.

The gray boulder where Alexander Hamilton fell to his death after being shot by Aaron Burr in 1804 is a national monument overlooking the Hudson River on the Weehawken cliffs along Boulevard East. Hamilton and Burr were revolutionary heroes and political rivals, Hamilton serving as the nation's first secretary of the treasury under President Washington, and Col. Burr becoming vice president under President Thomas Jefferson.

Dueling had been outlawed, but Burr and Hamilton met secretly in Weehawken, then a country retreat a safe distance from New York authorities.

A later Hudson County landmark is the Great Atlantic & Pacific Tea Co. warehouse on the Jersey City waterfront. The A&P was the first nationwide chain, dating back to 1859, 20 years before Frank W. Woolworth founded his variety chain.

The nation's largest retailer in the middle of this century, A&P grew out of a partnership between George Huntington Hartford and George Francis Gilman, son of a wealthy shipowner who opened a hide and leather importing business. Hartford, then 26, worked for Gilman. They began buying tea directly off clipper ships and retailing it along with their leather goods.

By 1860, they opened a tea store on Front Street in Manhattan and two years later abandoned their trade in hides and leather. The Great American Tea Co. was formed in 1864.

This historic Jersey City warehouse is a nine-story reinforced concrete structure of beam and girder construction and brick wall fill. Along each facade, the building's concrete piers and girders divide its face uniformly into bays, almost all of which hold either a double or triple window.

A massive dentiled cornice crowns the warehouse on all sides except the west, which was apparently left plain during the construction. At ground level, three sides display a series of double, warehouse-type sliding doors that open onto a three-foot-high metal-covered shed and a loading dock that passes continuously around the three sides.

The warehouse covers 360,000 square feet of waterfront.

Sussex County

The Old Monroe Schoolhouse is one of some 30 historic landmarks in Sussex County. Situated on one of the country's first toll roads, the Newton-Vernon Turnpike, the small one-room schoolhouse is one of the few in existence made from hand-carved stones.

Star-Ledger Photo

Star-Ledger Photo

Left, Poet Walt Whitman was nursed back to health in Camden, where his home still stands on Mickle Boulevard.

Right, Late 19th century furnishings and memorabilia are preserved in the Walt Whitman House, part of the Camden historical district.

President Grover Cleveland was born in the "Old Manse of Caldwell," right, one of Essex County's cherished landmarks. The interior of the 19th century house features a period rocking chair and spinning wheel, below left, and Cleveland's cradle, placed at the foot of his parents' bed, below right.

Star-Ledger Photo

Dating back to 1819, and possibly earlier, the schoolhouse today recalls a time when school opened with the ringing of the teacher's hand bell, the teaching of the three "R's," and when discipline meant sending a pupil out to cut down his own hickory stick.

Camden County

Camden County accounts for some 30 landmarks, the most prominent being the 1848 Walt Whitman House, the 1726 Pomona Hall and the 1737 Ebenezer Hopkins House.

The gifted 19th Century poet Walt Whitman moved in with his mother and brother at 328 Mickle St., Camden, in 1873. He sought relief from ailing health in the mineral waters around Laurel Springs. He credited the Camden "tonic waters" with curing him from the effects of a stroke. Whitman died in 1892 at age 73 and was buried in Camden.

Today, the Walt Whitman historic district is composed of the last remnants of the neighborhood in which the poet lived. It is an extraordinary example of the typical housing of the 1860s and '70s. The middle-income, narrow lot, three-story houses are similar to the many blocks of row houses that once filled the surrounding Camden area.

Pomona Hall is home for the Camden County Historical Society. The gracious two-story building was built in 1726 by Joseph Cooper Jr., with an addition in 1788 by Marmaduke Cooper. Pomona Hall, an outstanding example of 18th Century residential architecture in the simplified Georgian style, contains a museum and library stocked with 19,000 books and pamphlets, as well as maps, deeds, slides, photographs and genealogical material relating to Camden County and New Jersey.

Ebenezer Hopkins, for whom the Hopkins House in Haddon Township is named, arrived in South Jersey in 1701 to attend to his father's land interest in what was then old Gloucester County. Ebenezer's aunt has been commemorated in Longfellow's "Tales of a Wayside Inn" and in Lydia Maria Child's book "The Youthful Immigrant."

Hopkins House is the only original dwelling extant in Camden County that can be linked to the first generation in America of the Haddon-Estaugh-Hopkins families. The house serves as the headquarters of the Camden County Cultural and Heritage Commission.

The Fairview District of Camden is a workers' neighborhood built just before World War I. It consists of 1,000 homes in sundry combinations of row, detached, duplex and apartment units. Stores, professional offices, a library and church are included in the original construction.

Fairview is completely enclosed by natural boundaries with the exception of the main access route. The street pattern within Fairview is generally circular, with axes leading to the town square. The narrow streets were designed for residents going to work in the factory town.

The buildings are simple and uniform in design. They are brick with Colonial Revival details. The massing of the buildings and detailing are varied to prevent the monotony of uniform style.

Classical features on the housing units vary. The porches, for example, alternate in classical detail, using different forms in columns, roof pediments and door surroundings.

Essex County

The birthplace of President Grover Cleveland—"The Old Manse of Caldwell"—is one of many landmarks in Essex County. Cleveland was buried in Princeton in 1908, site of another national landmark, the 1854 Grover Cleveland Home at 15 Hodge Rd.

Sir Isaac Newton was contemplating his epochal discovery of the "Law of Gravity" when a Puritan minister named Abraham Pierson migrated to a pleasant place along the Passaic River being settled by Puritan leader Robert Treat. The religious community established the First Presbyterian Church on a piece of land that became the center for the third oldest city in America, Newark.

The year was 1666. The Old First Church, as it is known today, stands on Broad Street at Branford Place, a venerable landmark that survived a revolution, civil war and post-war riots.

A family history of business and mechanical acumen dating back to the era of knights and ladies in England continues today at the Watts, Campbell Co., 198 Ogden St., Newark, an industrial landmark and operation founded in 1883. The first Watts invented the shot for weapons. His son, George, left England in the early 1820s to start a smelting and refining business in America.

The Old First Church on Broad Street in Newark, founded in 1666, has stood the test of time.

Star-Ledger Photo

The Watts, Campbell Co. grew from a small firm serving local customers to a sizable plant whose engines were exported all over the world by the 1950s.

The Theophilus Ward/Thomas Force House, built around 1745 and expanded in the early 19th Century, is one of the few early farmhouses in Essex County (Livingston), which has retained much of its original character, craftsmanship and details.

The Clark Thread Co. in East Newark is a historic district representing that period when Clark led the nation in the production of cotton sewing threads.

The district embraces 13 acres and more than 35 multi-story red brick structures erected between 1875 and 1910. The larger manufacturing buildings display open attics and wood truss systems with cast-iron support columns. Most windows are rectangular and set in segmentally arched openings with radiating brick voussoirs and stone sills.

Bergen County

Ft. Lee, settled high on the cliffs of the Hudson River in Bergen County, figured prominently in the British campaign to control New York City and then attack New Jersey.

Shortly after the Declaration of Independence was signed on July 4, 1776, Washington realized that the defense of the Hudson Valley would be essential if the rebellious Colonists were to hold back the redcoats. The British plan was to control the Hudson and split the Colonies in half, bringing an early end to the revolt.

In July 1776, work was begun on a fortification eventually named for Gen. Charles Lee. The largest armada of British ships and troops that had ever left England's shores seized Ft. Washington on the New York side of the Hudson River.

Washington's army, not yet strong enough for a major confrontation with the British forces, retreated from Ft. Lee on Nov. 20. They were the darkest days of the Revolution, causing patriot Thomas Paine to utter, "These are the times that try men's souls." It was the start of Washington's famous retreat across New Jersey.

Ft. Lee's gun batteries and magazine have been reconstructed at the first fortification in New Jersey, today a historic park.

Bergen County, like the Princeton-Trenton-Morristown areas, is steeped in history, having more than 75 historic sites, many with the stone-house theme.

One of the oldest structures on the National Register of Historic Places is the Steuben House on Old New Bridge Road along the Hackensack River. The stone house was built in 1695.

The Old Stone House in Ramsey is a Dutch Colonial farmhouse built in the 1700s of irregular or rubble stone, using a clay mortar reinforced with chopped straw and hog's hair, rather than cut stone. Windows are deeply recessed, consisting of triple panes above and double panes below. One of the original Dutch doors remains intact. Furnishings include a 200-year-old Dutch *kas* (cabinet), a wag-on-the-wall and early American Queen Anne chairs.

* * *

The Zabriskie "Red Mill" on the Saddle River in Paramus was constructed in 1745. It operated as a saw and grist mill. During the Civil War, the saw machinery was replaced with carders and power looms, and did a thriving business as a woolen mill by producing U.S. army blankets for the North.

Two significant historic landmarks in Bergen County are The Hermitage, or the Waldwick Cottage, 335 N. Franklin Tpk., put up in 1845, and the Elizabeth Cady Stanton House at 135 Highwood Ave. in Tenafly, an example of late 19th and early 20th Century architecture.

The revolutionary first call for female suffrage in 1848 was made by Elizabeth Cady Stanton from Tenafly, Bergen County.

She was considered the leading intellectual force in the emancipation of American women. In 1866 she ran for Congress and in 1880 she attempted to vote.

Stanton helped write a history of the women's movement and contributed to the drafting of the resolution that eventually became the 19th Amendment to the Constitution.

The Elizabeth Cady Stanton house was built around 1868. The white-painted frame house is two stories high with a slate mansard roof. Standing on a red sandstone foundation, the house has 11 gabled dormers.

An open Victorian staircase in the front hall is intact. Spiraling in elliptical form to the dormer level, it has a massive, tapered, faceted newel post and turned balusters. The second floor holds four bedrooms.

Radburn, in Fair Lawn, is the world's first community planned with the automobile in mind. Designed by Clarence Stein and Henry Wright in the late 1920s, Radburn was the first community to separate pedestrian and motor vehicle traffic.

That was accomplished by doing away with the traditional gridiron street pattern and replacing it with the "superblock," a large block of land surrounded by main roads. Living and sleeping sections of the houses face garden and park areas, while the service rooms face access roads.

Salem County

In adjoining Salem County, the Hancock House at Hancock Bridge dates back to the land that had been deeded to the Hancock family in 1677. The house was built by William Hancock in 1734.

The initials of William and his first wife, Sarah, along with the date 1734, appear in the patterned brickwork on the south end wall of the original section of the house. The Hancock farm was the scene of a massacre in 1778 when British forces and local Loyalists attacked 20 members of the American garrison, bayoneting them inside the house.

Somerset County

George and Martha Washington gave two Somerville homes a legacy that still stirs public curiosity. The Washingtons arrived at the home of John Wallace, a tea merchant, on Feb. 5, 1779, accompanied by several aides and servants.

Strategies for the spring military campaign were prepared at the Wallace house, built before 1775 by Jacob Hardenberg, minister of a local Dutch Reformed church. Wallace significantly increased the size of the structure with an eight-room center hall addition between 1775 and 1778.

The Old Dutch Parsonage built in 1751 was occupied by Hardenberg when Washington set up shop at the Wallace house next door. The parsonage went on to serve Dutch ministers until the late 1790s when the house was sold to pay off debts.

Union County

Union County has more than 35 historic sites, among the oldest being the 1746 Drake House in Plainfield and the 1750 Boxwood Hall in Elizabeth.

The Drake House, built by Isaac Drake for his son, Nathaniel, was the place where Washington met with his officers for consultation during and after the Battle of Short Hills, fought over the entire Plainfield area on June 25, 26 and 27, 1777.

The original farmhouse was a typical New Jersey one-and-a-half-story structure with four rooms and lean-to kitchen on the

Tea merchant John Wallace lived in this Somerville house when George and Martha Washington paid a visit in February 1779.

first floor, with a loft above. The parlor furnishings represent the late Empire and early Victorian time, circa 1835. The Historical Society of Plainfield and North Plainfield publishes a newsletter and conducts four programs a year of historic interest at the Drake House.

Boxwood Hall, also called the Boudinot Mansion, was erected about 1750 when the seat of Union County was known as Elizabeth Town. Elias Boudinot, American patriot and statesman, purchased the two-story house in 1772.

During the Revolution, Boudinot was commissary of prisoners. On April 23, 1789, Washington stopped at Boxwood Hall on his way to New York for his inauguration as the first president of the United States. A frequent guest at Boxwood was Alexander Hamilton, who stayed there while attending school in Elizabeth Town as a youth.

Boudinot was appointed superintendent of the United States Mint in Philadelphia in 1795. He sold the house to Gen. Jonathan Dayton, a signer of the Constitution, and moved to Burlington.

Hunterdon County

Hunterdon County offers the Flemington Historic District with its famous glassworks, and Dunham/Parry's Mill in Clinton, in continuous operation from 1837 through the 1950s, as one of the major merchant feed and flour mills in northwestern New Jersey.

The square-mile borough of Flemington began as an Indian village, then a farming community and later a resort and railroad hub with renowned pottery and glass industries.

Greek Revival buildings reflect the charm of this small artisan village. They were designed by Mahlon Fisher, a self-taught architect born there in 1810. His works include the Hunterdon County Courthouse, the Doric House and two homes occupied by the descendants of Gov. John Reading and Samuel Southard, also governor of New Jersey and secretary of the Navy for President John Quincy Adams.

The oldest house in Flemington was built by Samuel Fleming, an Irish immigrant, in 1756. Known as "Fleming's Castle," it served over the years as a stagecoach inn and tavern.

A small burial ground contains the remains of Flemington's first white resident, John Phillip Kase, a German immigrant. Also in the burial plot is a native who befriended the original settler, Delaware Indian Chief Tuccamirgan.

Kase bought land in 1738 from William Penn, who founded Pennsylvania. The original Kase log cabin was built near an Indian village.

Although most of the old potteries have closed, the Flemington Cut Glass Co. and the Iorio Studio continue to make Flemington a thriving center for arts and crafts.

Gloucester County

Red Bank Battlefield Park on the Delaware River was the site of Ft. Mercer during the American Revolution. The fort was built during the spring and summer of 1777 by Pennsylvania militiamen under orders of Gen. Washington.

Ft. Mercer on the Jersey side of the Delaware River and Ft. Mifflin on the Pennsylvania side kept the British fleet from supplying its troops in Philadelphia.

Washington wrote on Oct. 9 of the importance of these Delaware River fortifications: "The whole defense of the Delaware absolutely depends on it (Ft. Mercer) and consequently all the enemy's hopes of keeping Philadelphia."

The successful defense of Ft. Mercer against overwhelming odds demonstrated a new spirit and, even before Valley Forge, was a turning point in the war.

In Red Bank Battlefield Park are a display shed for a part of the Revolutionary War and grapeshot recovered from the area, and cheveaux-de-frise, a large wall of wooden stakes imbedded in a body of water and supported by rocks and iron bars to prevent ships from landing ashore. Six cast iron cannons are displayed around a battle monument, a tall stone column surmounted by the figure of a Revolutionary War soldier.

Maps at the time of the Battle of Red Bank show the fort to have been an irregular pentagonal redoubt with parapeted wood palisades, a berme (a narrow terrace between rampart and moat), fraises (sharpened wooden spikes protruding out of the ground), a fosse (dry moat), and abatis (tree branches).

There was a central powder magazine and a sallyport with drawbridge. A larger abandoned outerworks to the north consisted of an irregular bastion with a sallyport to the east.

The James Whitall Sr. House is a fine example of Delaware Valley architecture. Built of brick in 1748, it also has an earlier stone wing with attached stone and brick shed. Most of the original structure is preserved, including the many corner fireplaces, the wide board floors and handsome wood paneling and trim.

Burlington County

The Francis Hopkinson House in Bordentown was built in 1750 by John Imlay, a merchant. Hopkinson was a signer of the Declaration of Independence for New Jersey. He was also a poet, author, composer, artist, inventor, lawyer, judge and politician.

In 1768, Hopkinson, son of a prominent Philadelphia lawyer, married Ann Borden of Bordentown. They took up residence in his father-in-law's house in 1774. Hopkinson was elected to the Continental Congress in 1776.

He was well known for his musical compositions, among them a cantata he conducted titled "Temple of Minerva," to celebrate the alliance between France and the United States.

Some of his most effective writing was in verse. "The Battle of the Kegs" was his best known piece, published in 1778. On his death in 1791, the Hopkinson house passed to his son, Joseph, composer of "Hail Columbia" (1798) and the "President's March."

The L-shaped, two-and-a-half-story brick Hopkinson house is

covered with a dormered roof and a gambrel. The main house, facing west, is about 41 feet, or five bays, wide and 30 feet deep. A two-story brick wing, 16 feet by 30 feet, extends to the rear. A two-story frame wing, 15 feet by 22 feet, is the kitchen and servants' bedroom.

Cumberland County

A classic example of a small cruising yacht, The Spendrift, can be found docked in Fairfield Township, Cumberland County. Built in Falmouth, Mass. in 1882, The Spendrift is believed to be one of the oldest sailing yachts in the United States. In its heyday, under the command of soldier-of-fortune Capt. Henry E. Raabe (1860-1959), The Spendrift was docked in Fair Haven, Monmouth County.

Cape May County

The Philadelphia social set, including Grace Kelly and her family, found a cool refuge from the long, hot summers on a little island off the New Jersey coast called Ocean City. It's a sandy treasure of 19th Century artifacts.

The Friends of the Ocean City Historical Museum have preserved much of this quaint island's heritage. Ocean City abounds in tales of shipwrecks in the vicinity, dating back to pre-revolutionary times. The most famous is the four-masted bark Sindia, driven onto the beach in a gale on Dec. 15, 1901. The museum's Sindia Room helps visitors savor the days of the windjammers through many artifacts, ship models, photographs, sailing papers and pieces of the Sindia's cargo.

Hundreds of pictures, maps, documents and books depict the civic progress and social life of Ocean City since it was founded in September 1879. There are reminders of the old local trolley cars, defunct for about 50 years . . . scenes of early days on the beach and boardwalk . . . valuable glass and china, needlecraft, musical instruments, clocks, mementos of America's wars . . . and a wide variety of seashells and semi-precious stones.

Other Landmarks

An unusual landmark of recent vintage is the United States Animal Quarantine Station in Clifton, Passaic County. During its continuous operation from 1900-79, the Clifton station was the only facility on the East Coast for receiving and isolating foreign animals landing east of the Mississippi River.

Other major landmarks include historic villages such as Waterloo and Batsto, preservation districts such as Hoboken and Paterson, and entire communities such as Ocean Grove and Cape May, which are reviewed in separate sections of this book.

Finally, the State Office of Historic Preservation is designating 60 of New Jersey's 112 railroad stations as landmarks.

Dating back to the 1860s, the 60 stations tell the story of New Jersey's development, from the early factory cities to the post-World War I suburbanization of America.

The rail depots mimicked the architectural trends of the day, from Gothic to Dutch and Colonial to small-town modern.

The first railroad chartered in the United States was the Camden and Amboy Railroad in 1815.

The White House Station, a one-story stone structure in the Romanesque style, gave its name to the sleepy Hunterdon County village. Built in 1892, its Ladies' Waiting Room sported a stone fireplace and curved glass in the windows.

The Madison station was constructed in 1916 in the Gothic style akin to the medieval architecture of such campuses as Oxford and Cambridge in England. Morris County's college campuses today have the same ancient look.

Historic Victorian house in Waterloo Village.

Courtesy: N.J. Div. of Travel & Tourism

Rows of workers' houses line up in historic Batsto Village.

Star-Ledger Photo

Iris willowwood.

LANDSCAPES

Any map of the Garden State reveals a variegated landscape of nature's finest handiwork—natural living sculptures of every size, shape and hue dramatically changing with the seasons.

Many of New Jersey's 567 municipalities reflect their geographic origins in names such as Alpine, Basking Ridge, Beachwood, Cedar Knolls, Cliffside Park, Clover Hill, Deerfield, Glen Rock, Green Pond, Gum Tree, Laurel Springs, Magnolia, Maple Grange, Middlebush, Pine Brook, Riverdale, Rosemont, Victory Gardens and Wildwood.

Attractive gardens and parks adorn every community, from Newark with its stunning spring festival of cherry blossoms—the greatest number in America—to the only wild holly forest in the land on a thin spit of sand stretching out into the Raritan Bay.

But the most magnificent display of outdoor beauty is the annual fall spectacle of foliage—the turning of the leaves in a glorious burst of kaleidoscopic scenes at once both vivid and fleeting.

The colorful show unfolds everywhere in New Jersey, as the maples, oaks, ashes, beeches, birches, chestnuts, hickories, dogwoods, sycamores, tulips and willows surrender their leafy canopy in the frosty mists of autumn.

The rainbowed clusters spread across the hilly terrain of North Jersey, swatches of gold, scarlet and orange reaching a brilliant intensity by early October.

Farther south, the yellows of the ash trees, the reddish purples of the sumac and the bright reds of the swamp maple peak by mid-October. By Halloween, the miraculous little sun-catchers complete their natural cycle and fall to earth to nourish their source of life, fulfilling their mission and assuring another season of renewal.

Of the thousands of species of trees, plants, vines, ferns and flowers flourishing in the Garden State, two are particularly abundant and have been designated as the official state tree and flower: The tall, sturdy red oak and the petite, fragrant purple violet.

The autumnal pageantry is witnessed by millions of people who over the years have discovered the best routes and sights for viewing the Garden State's most colorful changing of the seasons.

From these random vehicular rides along the mountains and through the woodlands have emerged New Jersey's "Fall Foliage Tours." All the spectator needs is a motor vehicle, bicycle or well-conditioned legs to enjoy nature's free outdoor exhibit.

The State Division of Travel and Tourism has mapped out six fall foliage tours, available in a colorful brochure showing where to go and what to see. Provided as a public service to the people, the state brochure begins with:

Autumn foliage along the Musconetcong River in Hackettstown.

• Tour No. 1 through Morris, Sussex and Warren counties, starting in Netcong on Route 206 and heading north toward Andover, taking in historic Waterloo Village along the way. Turning south on Route 517, the traveler will pass Allamuchy, veering right on Allamuchy-Johnsonburg Road to Route 519, and left into Jenny Jump Forest. The forest headquarters there is chock full of extensive panoramas and displays.

Continuing on Route 519 south to Hope, the next turn is at the old Mill, where the road unwinds over the mountain and past the Great Meadows to Route 46, passing America's biggest hatchery at Hackettstown on the way to the starting point in Netcong.

This trip takes in upland forest separated by farmland, with vistas of oak (red leaves), hickories (golden yellow) and beech (pale yellow), with an understory of dogwood (red), birch (yellow) and maples (red, scarlet). In the wetter areas, the red maples dominate. Walkers can choose between trails at Allamuchy Mountain State Park or those at Jenny Jump State Forest.

• Tour No. 2 begins in Newton, also on the circuitous Route 206,which brings the sightseer around Ross Corner, continuing north on 206 through Branchville to Normanock in Stokes State Forest, home of the world's oldest conservation field study center. A map of the forest is available at the entrance to the state preserve.

Leaving the largest public woodlands in North Jersey, Route 206 will take you to Hainesville and onto Route 653, leading to High Point State Park, the highest elevation in the state. Bearing right on Mashipong Road and moving in a southerly direction, the roads merge and finally join with Sawmill Road. A left onto Sawmill connects with Route 23.

One of the places of interest is Franklin, site of the oldest zinc mines in the country. From Franklin, Route 517 and Alternate 517 complete the round-trip to Newton, seat of Sussex County.

This tour crosses rocky farmlands between Newton and Branchville and into the oak-dominant forests of High Point and Stokes. The red, scarlet and orange-red leaves of the oak mingle with the pale yellow of the beech, the yellow of the birch, and the yellow-orange-red of the sassafras trees. There are plenty of hiking trails through Stokes and High Point forests.

• Tour No. 3 embraces Morris and Passaic counties, starting in Riverdale, where Route 511 (Ringwood Avenue) climbs through Wanaque to the national landmarks of Skylands Manor and Ringwood Manor, the famous country home of Alfred North Ringling, the circus pioneer.

Retracing the route to the Village of Ringwood, pick up Route 511 to Hewitt, then turn left on Route 513 for West Milford and Newfoundland, the popular North Jersey lakes region. The next road ahead is Route 23; follow it north to Oak Ridge Road. That becomes Berkshire Valley Road, connecting with Route 15 south to Route 80 east and to Route 287 north through Main Street, Boonton, the old Boontonware pottery center. That will come up to Route 511 for the return to Riverdale.

Athough similar in leaf-turning display to Tour 2, this region differs because areas of evergreen trees break into the sensational show of the hardwoods. There are many undisturbed areas of the state in this tour, as well as pastoral farmlands. Walkers can explore the quiet trails through the gardens in the Skylands and Ringwood State Park.

• Tour No. 4 covers the back country roads of Hunterdon and Mercer counties. Washington Crossing State Park is where this circuitous journey gets under way.

Route 546 east picks up Route 206 north in Lawrenceville for a short distance before reaching Route 569 north to Hopewell. Along these peaceful rural roads you'll be passing over the terrain that was the turning point of the Revolutionary War in the battles of Princeton and Trenton. At Hopewell, take Route 518 west to Route 31 north to the Ringoes, where 31 and 579 fork. Stop in and visit the historic Ringoes tavern.

Bear left on 579 and, at the first intersection out of Ringoes, you'll cross the last remaining covered bridge in New Jersey in Rosemont. Turn onto Route 519 north and at the 519 spur, make a left onto Route 29 along the Delaware and Raritan Canal feeder, following the signs back to Trenton and Washington Park.

This tranquil ride through the Hunterdon-Mercer region engulfs the tourist in woodlands proliferating with red-leafed oaks and dogwoods, yellow maples, and reddish-yellow-orange sassafras. Walkers can choose between the hiking and nature trails at Washington Crossing State Park, or a stroll along the towpath of the D&R canal feeder. Bicyclists may prefer to start at Stockton and take Route 523 north. At Sergeantsville, turn left and ride through the covered bridge to Rosemont and back to Stockton on 519.

• Tour 5 encompasses the southern sector of Atlantic, Burlington and Ocean counties. This scenic drive gets off at the Red Lion Circle, the intersection of Routes 206 and 70.

Moving south on 206 through Indian Mills and Atsion there will be a sign for Batsto, the historic village where iron was forged for military armaments during the Revolution. Route 542 brings you by Batsto on the way to Green Bank, where 536 north brings you into Chatsworth, another historic settlement.

Turning right onto Route 532, continue to Route 72 east until it intersects with 539. Turn left onto 539 and head toward Whiting. Eventually you'll reach Route 70, which takes you back to the Red Lion Circle.

Unlike the hardwoods of North Jersey, the sandy southern half of the state is a mix of soft pines and hard cedars, inter-

Washington's Crossing at the Delaware River in Trenton—the turning point in the American Revolution.

Courtesy: N.J. Div. of Travel & Tourism

Quiet scenes are common in Batsto Village, an historic site in the heart of New Jersey's ecologically unique Pine Barrens.

Star-Ledger Photo

spersed with oaks, red gum with their blood red leaves, the scarlet sumacs, some sassafras and yellow tulip poplars. The reddish maples thrive in the wetter areas.

A special treat for the traveler along Routes 542 and 563 will be the colorfully wild and cultivated blueberry patches and the cranberry bogs along 563. The cranberries will be turning red with floating fruit ready for harvesting in late September and early October. Because cranberry bogs are highly flammable, smoking should be curtailed.

Walkers have a choice of either the hiking and nature trails at Wharton State Forest, or those at Lebanon State Forest. Bikers can go from the Red Lion Circle to Atsion and back in a day.

• Tour 6 lies in and around the Mason-Dixon Line by Atlantic, Cape May, Cumberland and Salem counties. A perfect place to enter this autumnal showcase of foliage is in Buena Vista on Route 557 south. That will go into Route 50 and Tuckahoe.

A sharp right on Route 49 will feed you into Route 548 and the beautiful Belleplain State Forest. A right onto Route 47 will send you into Millville and one of America's first glass works at Wheaton Village. Take Route 49 west toward Bridgeton and then right onto Route 553 north. That will intersect with Route 40, which takes you back to 557 and Buena Vista.

This tour lets you explore the world famous Pine Barrens with its scrub pines and hearty oaks and farmlands. The hardwood fringe of the Pinelands is along Route 553. The oaks and black gums will be radiating their reds, the sumacs their scarlets, the birch their yellows, with the red maples rooting in the wetter low-lying stretches.

Hiking and nature trails crisscross Belleplain Forest and Parvin State Park. By bicycle, prepare for a two-day excursion with overnight camping at Belleplain Forest.

Star-Ledger Photo

*The village of Allaire in Allaire State Park is surrounded
by a remarkable diversity of wildflowers and shrubbery.*

From the Ground Up

The flora and fauna flourishing throughout the Garden State represent thousands of species of plant life, some rare, some common, but all of them making the environment more habitable for both humankind and wild creatures, which still constitute a great portion of the population of all living things.

In Allaire State Park, for instance, there are no fewer than 206 identifiable wildflowers in that Monmouth County open space preserve along the Garden State Parkway. In a stroll through the park one can come across an Arrow Arum or Heartleafed Aster, a Hairy Beardtongue, Blue Curls or Boneset Thoroughwort. How about some Five-Fingers Cinquefoil or Fleabane Daisies? Asiatic Dayflowers will sneak up on you along the dirt footpaths, as will the Downy False Foxglove and Horse Mint.

Other oddities along the shady trails are Indian Tobacco, the Joe Pye Weed, the Whorled Loosestrife, the Monkeyflower, Bittersweet Nightshade, Mottled Pipsissewa, and Queen Anne's Lace.

If you saw these, would you recognize them as the Lady's Thumb Smartweed, or Blue Toadflax? You'd better bring along a plant book to identify the Halberd Leafed Tearthumb, Cut-leafed Toothwort, the Venus Looking Glass or Yellow Rocket.

Add to these 206 species of wildflowers, about 20 different kinds of shrubs, 12 varieties of vines, 50-odd tree specimens and at least 10 types of ferns, and what you have is a spectacular slice of outdoor life in New Jersey, protectively residing within Allaire State Park.

Here's a random sampling of Allaire shrubs: Alder, Azalea

Swamp, Bayberry, Bladdernut, Inkberry, Pepperbush, Spicebush and Winterberry.

Spreading their fingers through the underbrush are such vines as Brier, Honeysuckle, Moonseed, Virgins Bower, Dodder and Trumpet Creeper.

And you'll also find such interesting ferns as Cinnamon, Christmas, Lady, Rattlesnake and Sensitive.

Standing guard over this lush dominion are the grand trees: White Ash, Quaking Aspen, Eastern Red Cedar, Black Cherry, Slippery Elm, Sweet Gum, Mockernut Hickory, Ironwood, the family of oaks (black, chestnut, pin, post, scarlet, scrub, white, willow), the Tree of Heaven, Black Walnut, Pussy Willow and Black Willow.

Island Beach State Park

Allaire State Park, as outlined above, typifies the vast diversity of vegetation thriving in the many public lands set aside for recreational uses in New Jersey. As a peninsula state, however, New Jersey boasts several beachfront parks whose marine environments support forms of plant life compatible with sandy, salty conditions.

Island Beach State Park is an excellent example of what can grow out of dry, salty sand and survive repeated storms and ever-changing littoral configurations. At least 267 species of vascular plants representing 63 different families have been counted on the popular resort island off the Ocean County coast.

Island Beach supports a viable dune grass community and a beach plant community, as well as fresh marsh, wet and dry low-thicket communities. Also abounding are reed grass, salt grass, red cedar and pine woodland communities, and substratum such as laurels and berries, groves of oaks (Spanish and Blackjack), and some individual white and willow oaks.

Meandering around the long, thin island, one will be greeted by delicate ferns (Sensitive, Adder's Tongue, Bog Clubmoss and Flat-branch Ground Pine—to name a few)...plenty of pines (Pitch, Short-leaf, Southern White and Red Cedars)...flowering cattails...pondweeds (Eelgrass, Ditch-grass and Horned Pondweed)...the ubiquitous grass family (Couch and Quitch, Tickle and Bushy Beard, Purple Love and Wooly Panic, Round-fruited and Prostrate Paspalum, and Early Bunch)...the sedges (including Silvery, Prickly, Japanese, Twig-rush, Nuttall's and Creeping Spike)...Duckweeds, Yellow-eyed, Rushes and Spiderworts...lilies (Wild Garlic and Star-flowered Solomon's Seal)...the Iris and Orchis families, the latter represented by Stemless Lady's Slipper, Rose Pogonia and Nodding Ladies Tresses...the families of willow, Wax-Myrtle, Hazel, Beech, Buckwheat, Goosefoot, Amaranth, Pokeweed, Carpet, Pink, Magnolia, Laurel, Mustard, Slundew, Orpine, Rose (including Swamp Shadbush, Chinese Apple and Pasture Rose), Pulse, Flax, Wood-Sorrel, Milkwort, Cashew, Violet and Cactus.

Sharing this limited space are the Spurge, Holly, Male, Rockrose, Loosestrife, Evening Primrose, Parsley, White Alder, Heath, Ebony, Gentian, Morning-glory, Figwort (Blue Toadflax and Butter-and-Eggs), Trumpet Creeper, the Zig-Zag Bladderwort, Madder, honeysuckle and the "Composite Family," whose 40 members include Chicory, Maryland Hawkweed, King Devil, White Everlasting and Spiny-leaved Sow Thistle.

The Little Nature Trail

A walk along any of New Jersey's 4,000 miles of nature trails is an earthy, greening experience.

But a brief look at a backyard suburban trail in Bergen County, just two-thirds of a mile in length, attests to the tropic-

berries and three-lobed, soft, hairy leaves. Reaching 7 feet in height, the maple bushes furnish cover for ground dwellers such as the thrush, ovenbird, junco and foraging squirrel.

A clearing in the woods makes possible a dazzling display of wildflowers: The Pinxter or wild azalea, the Whorled Loosestrife and Blue-eyed Grass, and the low-bush blueberries, which flower and fruit in the summer. The oak seedlings compete for the warming rays with the Witch Hazel, the dominant understory shrub in the upland forest.

The mixed forest is made up of Flowering Dogwoods, Pitch Pines, Ironwoods, Pin Oaks and Chestnut Oaks. The lowlands contain the Cinnamon Fern, the Coast Pepperbush, Spicebush, Shagbark Hickory, Skunk Cabbage, Sour Gum, Wild Grape climbing vine, the common Swamp Maple and the Bittersweet.

You'll see all of this—and more—in a highly-developed bedroom community of Bergen County. It's a compatible blending of man and nature, the housing, business and a steel-concrete infrastructure peacefully coexisting with woods and wildlife.

Princeton's Prospect Garden

University campuses are among New Jersey's most attractive landscapes.

But Princeton University, where the word "campus" was coined two centuries ago, has an exquisite ivy league landscape that rounds out our story on New Jersey's natural outdoor beauty.

The grounds surrounding the Prospect Garden house present a constantly changing array of trees, bushes, plants and flowers, from the commonplace to the exotic. Planting in the garden began right after the house was completed in 1849 with the help of an Englishman named Petrey who brought in the Cedar of Lebanon, the Hawthorn and the Yew.

While the garden has been shaped and reworked over the years by Prospect's sundry owners and residents, many of its trees predate the structure, notably the tulip trees and American beech, which are native to that central New Jersey region. The tulip trees are the tallest in the garden, reaching more than 100 feet and measuring 6 feet in diameter at breast height.

The native trees and the cedar are the oldest in the garden. The Dawn Redwood and Ginkgo are descendants of trees that have been around for millions of years, based on fossil evidence.

Prospect's redwood was planted in 1948 from a seed brought from China and today stands more than 75 feet high with a span of more than 30 feet. Unlike West Coast redwoods, its blue-green leaves turn the same rust-red as the bark in autumn.

The redwood is surrounded by smaller Douglas fir and hemlock. The Ginkgo, or maidenhair trees, are slow-growing and free of pests, contributing to their hardiness and longevity. The tall, straight-trunked trees, which were favorites in Chinese and Japanese temple gardens, show off their fan-shaped leaves and horizontal leaf veins in the summer.

Of the domestic trees in the garden, 19 are native to the Eastern United States, four to the Pacific Northwest, two to the Rockies and one to California.

The many foreign trees are native to such places as China, India and Spain. Included among these are Japanese dogwood, Himalayan pine and European beech. At least one example of each variety of tree is labeled with the botanical and common names.

The flower garden at the rear of Prospect was laid out in approximately its present form by Mrs. Woodrow Wilson, after her husband had the iron fence erected around the garden's perimeter to control student traffic in 1904. Mrs. Wilson supervised the planting of the evergreens, predominately Canadian hemlocks, which serve as a windbreak backdrop for the flower garden.

Star-Ledger Photo

Scenic view of Surprise Lake in Watchung Reservation.

like density and rich variety of plant life in the Garden State. Within this 20-minute leisurely walk, one can view an upland forest, streams and a swamp, each providing a separate set of living conditions and supporting different kinds of plants and animals.

The Bergen County Wildlife Center's Nature Trail in Wyckoff is a quick primer on the unending outdoor assets of New Jersey.

The American Sycamore derives its nourishment from a stream wandering through the Wyckoff wildlife habitat. Growing in a massive column to 100 feet, the sycamores enjoy the cool, moist environment provided by the small, seasonal stream.

The upland forest is aflutter with white oaks, yellow, black and gray birches, red oaks (the state tree) and the rapid-growing tulips. Forming a thick canopy, the mature upland forest allows little sunlight to reach the mulch-covered surface. Small shrubs and wildflowers awaken early in spring, before the trees cast their leafy shadows on the forest floor.

The Evergreen Laurel bushes, mosses and Partridge Berry blanket the ground year 'round in the shaded areas. The American beech with its low, wide spreading branches prefers well-drained soil.

Deer, raccoons and rabbits nibble on the nuts of the beech. They also find the Maple Leaved Viburnum a tasty feast, with its

Courtesy: Newark Public Library

Newark Free Public Library is New Jersey's largest library.

LIBRARIES

hether it is the written or spoken word, the visual image or "touch" reading for the blind, the full sweep of human knowledge is within easy reach in some 60 million books, plus millions of feet of film and video strips, stocked at more than 4,000 public and private libraries in New Jersey.

One of the most comprehensive retrieval systems in the world, the New Jersey statewide library network serves students and scholars, specialists and laymen at 313 free public libraries, 26 area or regional libraries and four major research libraries: Newark Public Library, New Jersey State Library in Trenton, Princeton University Library and Rutgers University Library in New Brunswick.

Some of the oldest and best libraries in America make up New Jersey's verbal and visual network of information, everything from aardvarks and agronomy to plasma physics and zymosis.

And there are networks within networks in the New Jersey library system. At Rutgers, for example, there are 18 libraries within its educational jurisdiction, all of which are available as a research source within the overall state network.

New Jersey libraries house original papers and works, as well as "major holdings" of such historic and literary figures as Woodrow Wilson, F. Scott Fitzgerald, Adlai Stevenson, John Foster Dulles, Ernest Hemingway, T.S. Eliot, Thomas Mann, Thomas Wolfe, Booth Tarkington, Philip Wylie, Allen Tate, Walt Whitman and Noah Webster.

They also preserve the archives of Charles Scribner's Sons and Henry Holt, two important publishers, and the archives of the American Civil Liberties Union.

New Jersey's libraries contain one of the half-dozen finest collections of medieval and Renaissance manuscripts in the world.

The Gest Oriental Library at Princeton holds the largest collection of Chinese rare books outside the Orient.

The biggest collection of Arabic books and journals can also be found in the Garden State, in addition to the greatest examples of early printing.

Princeton University's unique preceptorial study system boasts the highest book circulation rate of any institution in the country.

New Jersey established the first Business Library in the nation in 1903 and started the forerunner of what is today the official "Who's Who," a sort of unofficial listing of the library's original patrons in the 1750s.

An entry of every United States Patent issued—4.4 million to date—has been filed at Newark Public Library, a logical repository of ideas and inventions. Thomas Edison, still the patent record holder, began his career in a four-story factory in Newark in the 1870s. Individual patents are being registered in Washington, D.C. (and Newark) at the rate of 1,200 a week.

Anna Harmyk of Middletown reads to Nichole Gardiner of Shrewsbury in the children's section of the Monmouth County Library branch in Shrewsbury.

The State Library was the first to introduce the micro-automated catalog (MAC) in 1968, and the Newark Public Library was the second public books center in the U.S. to establish a children's section.

From makeshift taverns, church halls, porches and parlors, New Jersey's library system has emerged into a leading information center that has either pioneered or been in the forefront of communications development, leading to phonotapes, phonodisks, microforms, monographs, videotapes, film loops, slides and computer banks listing books, journals, newspapers, magazines, TV and radio news, documents, pamphlets, maps, almanacs, dictionaries, directories, indexes, musical scores, artworks and even papyrus scrolls.

Besides the public, school and academic libraries, there are scores of special libraries in government, industry, corporations, agencies and associations, much of the latter's material open for public perusal.

The 26 area libraries tied into the state network are: Atlantic County Library; Bloomfield Public Library; Burlington County Free Library in Mt. Holly; Camden County Library in Voorhees; Cape May County Library in Cape May Court House; Cumberland County Library in Bridgeton; East Brunswick Public Library; East Orange Free Public Library; Elizabeth Free Public Library; Hackensack's Johnson Free Public Library; Hunterdon County Library in Raritan Township; Jersey City Free Public Library; Linden Public Library; Monmouth County Library's headquarters in Freehold and eastern branch in Shrewsbury; Morris County Free Public Library in Whippany; Newark Public Library; Ocean County Public Library in Toms River; Paterson Free Public Library; Phillipsburg Public Library; Plainfield Public Library; Ridgewood Public Library; Somerset County Library in Bridgewater; Sussex County Library in Frankford Township; Trenton Free Public Library; Wayne Public Library, and Woodbridge Township Free Public Library.

Newark Public Library

Organized in 1888, the Newark Public Library is New Jersey's largest public repository of print and electronic information at the community level. With 1.25 million volumes housed in the main building in downtown Newark and at eight other branches and two storefront outlets, the library of the state's largest city was designated the Metropolitan Regional Reference Center in 1969, with special emphasis on business and art.

The nation's first Business Library was founded in 1903 and today functions in its own headquarters in the heart of the commercial-financial district.

When John Cotton Dana arrived in 1902 to direct the library's

Visitors to the Newark Public Library browse around "The Pyramid," a new method of displaying books of special interest.

growing literary fortunes, he set aside a section for youngsters where they could browse and read at their leisure. Dana had experimented with the first children's section in Denver before accepting the Newark post, where he served until 1929.

Under Dana's direction, the Newark Library issued booklists, articles, bookplates and all sorts of publications that he thought might be of interest to the people of the city. Newark was one of the first to feature American artists.

Extensions were set up where interest could be encouraged. A library print shop influenced the quality of local commercial printing. Pictures and reproductions of paintings were made available for loan, and delivery service of library materials to the schools was arranged with the local board of education. Musical scores were added to the collections when Dana felt the needs of music students became great enough.

Building on that innovative tradition, the Newark Public Library today continues to offer both generalized and specialized services. It is the patent resource center in New Jersey. It has the greatest collection of New Jersey memorabilia. It is the state's language center, offering extensive materials in 25 foreign languages. It is the bilingual center in New Jersey. And it is strong in the humanities, fiction, Afro-American literature and art, and high technology data.

A card holder can check out cameras and computers, films and video tapes. Members are served by the biggest library staff of any municipal or state library, approximately 220 information processors.

New Jersey State Library

It began in 1796 when the state authorized the purchase of 29 books and a bookcase and has, in only recent years, become a highly sophisticated computerized operation involving more than 800,000 titles and the latest technological advances.

Those 29 books and little wooden bookcase, however, did not become known as the New Jersey State Library until 1803. Libraries at that time were a local responsibility and state govern-

ment did not have the funds, or concern, for the public's reading interests. By the beginning of the 19th Century, the state government recognized it should maintain a library in the state capital.

By 1968, the State Library launched the first micro-automated catalog (MAC), an invention of a staff member and an achievement that clearly identified the capital's book-lending institution as a leader in the swiftly changing world of technology. Microfilm copies of the library's catalog, representing more than 800,000 titles, were deposited in the 26 area libraries, along with high-speed microfilm reader-printers.

New Jersey's MAC system has attracted national attention and was used by many libraries prior to the development of computerized bibliographic systems.

In 1900, the State Public Library Commission was created to carry out the growing movement to provide traveling libraries and to promote the formation of county libraries serving rural populations.

A microfilm unit was established by the Archives and History Bureau in 1948. The following year, the Carnegie Foundation-sponsored "Public Library Inquiry" resulted in a move to combine the nation's then 7,500 public libraries into roughly 1,200 regional libraries. New Jersey envisioned a network of area libraries to serve the same purpose: Reaching all residents, not just those in the cities and suburbs capable of supporting their own libraries.

The publication of "Libraries for the People of New Jersey—or Knowledge for All" in 1964 gave New Jersey its first comprehensive plan for library development and satisfied the long-range plan for three interconnected levels of service: The local level comprising the academic, public, school and special libraries; some 20 or more strong area reference libraries, and four large research libraries, including the State Library.

The state created the New Jersey Historical Commission within the State Library in 1967 and, that same year, the New Jersey Library for the Blind and Handicapped materialized.

In 1976, the State Library initiated computerized information retrieval with on-line access to the Lockheed and Systems Development Corp. data banks. And in 1979, New Jersey sponsored its first Governor's Conference on Library and Information Services, adopting 31 resolutions and electing delegates to the White House Conference on Library and Information Services.

Van Remsen of Hamilton Township conducts research with the aid of a microfilm reader at the New Jersey State Library in Trenton.

Star-Ledger Photo

Marie Giadagno of Trenton, and Bob Fortenbaugh of Hopewell are shown working in the interlibrary loan department where Mr. Fortenbaugh is the librarian.

Star-Ledger Photo

Card catalogs fill the reference center in the Firestone Library, located on the Princeton University campus.

Star-Ledger Photo

Today, each of four service bureaus make up the ever-expanding State Library system: Law and Reference Services, Library for the Blind and Handicapped, Library Development, and Technical Services.

The State Library supplies most of its services from a functional, modern, five-story structure just a half-block west of the State House. The 105,000-square-foot facility for the Blind and Handicapped, shared by the Records Storage Center, is a 10-minute drive from the main library, in Ewing Township.

Princeton University Library

The Princeton University library system, which dates back to 1746 as the College of New Jersey founded in Newark, has been specifically designed to bring books and students together. There are no call slips to fill out, no long wait for important books . . . a student or researcher simply goes to the shelves and finds the books he or she wants.

Under this "open stack" arrangement, undergraduates have at their fingertips more than 3 million printed books, more than 30,000 current journals and documents, and other library materials ranging from manuscripts and maps to prints and papyri.

Students involved in special research projects can easily gain access to the rare book and manuscript collections. These include a definitive variety of material, such as the papers of Woodrow Wilson, Adlai Stevenson and John Foster Dulles, major holdings of American and English writers, including Hemingway, T.S. Eliot, Fitzgerald and Thomas Wolfe, as well as graphics by Aubrey Beardsley.

The Firestone Library is the heart of the system, containing more than 50 miles of open shelving, several thousand study seats scattered throughout its seven floors, and more than 500 closed study carrels, many of which are assigned to seniors writing theses in the humanities and social sciences.

By the end of the vigorous administration of Princeton's second president, John Witherspoon, in 1794, the small Presbyterian school already had earned a national reputation. From the students in Witherspoon's term alone were to come a president

(James Madison), a vice president, nine federal cabinet officers, 21 United States senators, 39 congressmen, three justices of the Supreme Court, 12 governors and 39 judges.

Princeton has remained a relatively small institution with a strong emphasis on undergraduate education. The only professional schools are in engineering, architecture and public affairs.

When the Rev. Samuel Davies became president in 1760, he first issued a catalog of the college library. In the preface, he noted:

A large and well-sorted Collection of Books on the various Branches of Literature, is the most ornamental and useful Furniture of a College, and the most proper and valuable Fund with which it can be endowed. It is one of the best Helps to enrich the Minds both of the Officers and Students with Knowledge; to give them an extensive Acquaintance with Authors; and to lead them beyond the narrow Limits of the Books to which they are confined in their stated Studies and Recitations, that they may expatiate at large thro' the boundless and variegated Fields of Science.

When the college moved from Newark to Princeton in 1756, two boxes of books were sent to a room planned as a library on the second floor of Nassau Hall, the newly completed classroom and residential building. During the Revolutionary War, Nassau Hall, the largest edifice in the Colonies, was occupied in turn by British and Continental troops. The large room also served as a meeting place for the first New Jersey Legislature in 1776 and for the Continental Congress for several months in 1783.

In 1873, the Chancellor Green Library, Princeton's first separate library building, was opened. This Ruskinian Gothic octagon with radial stacks was filled to capacity by 1897, when the Pyne Library, a hollow rectangle, was constructed and connected to the Green Library.

Under the preceptorial system of instruction introduced by Princeton President Woodrow Wilson, the library became the center of the educational process. That seems to account for the highest circulation rate per student among the major university libraries of the United States.

Professor Rufus Morey, chairman of the Department of Art and Archaeology, proposed in his "A Laboratory-Library" (1932)

that the library become a workshop rather than a warehouse. The great buildings of the first half of the 20th Century typically consisted of a large fixed-purpose warehouse for book storage, often on multi-tier stacks, closed to most readers, linked to a vast, ornate, high-ceilinged and often ill-lighted reading room.

The Firestone Library, completed in 1948, is much more flexible, with bearing floors throughout which can carry books. There are generally low ceilings and study space scattered throughout the open stacks. Firestone generally houses the university's humanities and social sciences materials.

Among the subjects located outside the Firestone Library, in association with the teaching or laboratory areas, are: Art and archeology, astronomy, biology, chemistry, engineering, geology, East Asia, mathematics and physics, plasma physics, population research, psychology, urban and environmental studies and Woodrow Wilson School.

These libraries range in size from some 300,000 volumes with 150 study seats (art and archeology) down to about 5,000 volumes with 20 study seats (plasma physics).

Although centralized as one library today, there are 17 campus locations where books and staff serve the Princeton academic community.

The emergence at Princeton of new groupings of undergraduates into separate residential colleges in the 1960s led to the creation of two small college libraries, the Julian Street Library of the Woodrow Wilson School and the Norman Thomas Library of Princeton Inn College. These libraries of more than 10,000 volumes each are located in buildings that house dining and social facilities, surrounded by residential areas.

The popularity of the Julian and Thomas libraries brought about the open-stack reserve reading room in 1974, where some 30,000 volumes can be shelved on open stacks surrounded by almost 200 study seats, all within a controlled area.

Princeton Collections

The first major collection to the library of the new College of New Jersey was the gift in 1755 of 474 volumes from Jonathan Belcher, the royal governor of the province. By 1760, the college catalog listed 1,281 volumes and by the end of the century, about 3,000 volumes.

From various sources, particularly from Robert Garrett, have come one of the half-dozen best collections in the country of medieval and Renaissance manuscripts.

The English literature collections have been strengthened by the combined resources of the Morris L. Parish Collection of Victorian novelists, the Rossetti Collection of Janet Camp Troxell, the J. Harlin O'Connell Nineties Collection, the Gallatin Beardsley Collection, and the Miers Collection of Cruikshank.

In American literature, the publishing archives of Charles Scribner's Sons and of Henry Holt have brought a wealth of material to Princeton, as have the files and papers of writers as diverse as Tarkington, Fitzgerald, Wylie and Tate.

The published works of French writers of the 17th, 18th and 19th centuries are well represented in original editions, and the Thomas Mann collection is one of the strongest in America by that author.

The Western Americana and Civil War collections are especially good, and most of the major political and military figures of the 18th and 19th centuries are represented in some depth in the American Historial Manuscripts Collection.

In addition to the papers and files of Wilson, Dulles and Stevenson, are excellent original resources from Bernard Baruch, John Marshall Harlan, James V. Forrestal, George Kennan and David E. Lilienthal.

Princeton has been selective in its emphasis on international or area studies, having developed major graduate programs and

library collections in the East Asian, the Near Eastern and the Slavic areas.

The Gest Oriental Library holds the largest collection of Chinese rare books outside the Orient, and its Japanese and Korean collections have grown substantially since World War II.

The collection of Arabic books and journals is the largest in the U.S., as is the collection of Arabic manuscripts. The Persian collections are exceptional in quality and quantity.

The Marquand Art Library is a treasure house of art history, especially early Christian art, stimulated by the presence at Princeton of the ongoing "Index of Christian Art."

The music collections support a great deal of active musicological research, notably in Bach and Handel. The Hall Handel Collection is the best in the nation.

Curiously, while Princeton is strong in constitutional theory and jurisprudence, it has no law library. The university acquires research materials in biochemistry, but it has no medical library. And it makes no attempt to cover comprehensively the proliferating literature of a host of applied fields such as forestry, nursing, agriculture, education or business administration.

Two great private collections, on indefinite deposit, occupy their own rooms in the Firestone Library. The Scheide Library is unusually rich in the greatest examples of early printing and other landmarks of cultural history, while the Collection of Robert H. Taylor covers in books and manuscripts the sweep of English literature.

The Fine Hall Library of mathematics and statistics has an international reputation, and Princeton's holdings in geology, economics and demography are outstanding.

In the recent field of plasma physics (fusion energy), the analytical catalog of the Princeton collections has been published commercially and its acquisition list is in demand around the world.

The Andrew W. Mellon Foundation Social Science Reference Center, opened in 1974, brings together considerable reference collections in economics and finance, political science, public administration and industrial relations.

Rutgers University Library

The first bequest for what was to become the Rutgers University libraries was made in 1792 by the Rev. Peter Leydt, an early graduate. After nearly two centuries, the number of books at Rutgers exceeds 3 million.

Leydt was an alumnus of Queen's College, the eighth collegiate institution created in the American Colonies and the first to be affiliated with the Dutch Reformed Church. On Nov. 10, 1766, New Jersey Gov. William Franklin granted a charter for Queen's College in the name of King George III of England. The school was named in honor of Charlotte of Meckleburg, the royal consort.

The first classes opened in 1771 on a makeshift campus in a tavern in New Brunswick. The college was renamed in 1825 in recognition of the philanthropist Col. Henry Rutgers, a wealthy New York landowner and Revolutionary War solider who had given the college modest financial assistance (about $5,000) and the bell that still hangs in the cupola of Old Queen's.

Following an agreement made in 1807, the library of Queen's College merged with that of the Theological Seminary of the Dutch Reformed Church. The first librarian was appointed in 1814.

During the early 1800s, the Rutgers' Philoclean and Peithesophian literary societies were organized by students, openly inspired by their professors. The societies were considered secret but not exclusive and, in time, nearly all undergraduates were elected to one or the other. Each society compiled its own library featuring works of literature, biography, history and travel, as

A spacious, contemporary exterior welcomes visitors to Alexander Library on the Rutgers University campus in New Brunswick.

Star-Ledger Photo

well as the leading periodicals. The societies' collections supplemented the meager and more academic holdings of the college library.

On Nov. 23, 1903, the Voorhees Library was dedicated, beginning a new era in library service at Rutgers. More than 46,000 volumes were moved into the new building. By 1927, the number of book titles had tripled. November 1956 saw the opening of the six-story Archibald Stevens Alexander Library with a capacity of 1.5 million volumes and room for 100 readers. It houses the major humanities and social sciences collections.

The Library of Science and Medicine, dedicated in 1970, and the eight specialized science libraries house the science research collections. Together with the Alexander Library, the science libraries contain the bulk of the university's research collections, as well as the materials to support undergraduate instruction.

Like the older Princeton, the Rutgers library system is a network of 18 library units. The libraries add more than 100,000 volumes a year. More than 100 professional librarians and a staff of 250 members reign over libraries on three campuses.

In New Brunswick, there are: The Alexander and Art libraries on the Queen's campus; the Mabel Smith Douglass Library; the Carey Library of the Institute of Management and Labor Relations, and the Agriculture Library on the Douglass and Cook campuses with the Bailey B. Pepper Library (entomology) nearby.

The Kilmer Area Library is located on the Kilmer campus with Livingston College. The Library of Science and Medicine and the collections for Mathematics, Chemistry, Physics, the Center for Alcohol Studies, Microbiology, the Center for Urban Policy Research, the Herbarium and Ceramics are all situated within the Busch campus. These facilities are in the town of Piscataway, across the Raritan River from New Brunswick.

The New Brunswick Theological Seminary, the first established in the U.S., shares its Gardner Sage Library with the Rutgers College community. At Sage, one can browse through Bibles not only in the original Hebrew and Greek, but also in Glagolithic and Hawaiian. Here are church history texts published before the birth of Martin Luther, and books published a year ago—more than 135,000 volumes in all.

In the Rare Book Room at the old Breviary there's a text published in 1480, an extremely rare specimen. The oldest books date from 1472, complemented by first editions by Luther, Calvin, Erasmus and other Reformers.

Outside the Netherlands itself, there is no finer collection of Dutch theology in the world.

The John Cotton Dana Library and the S.I. Newhouse School of Law Library are at the Newark campus of Rutgers.

On the Camden campus are the Camden Law Library and the Camden College Libraries.

Burlington Library

The Burlington "Library Company" came into being during the French and Indian Wars. Its charter is dated Jan. 1, 1758.

The early settlers in the lower Delaware Valley wanted a book place as early as the 1750s. At that time Burlington was the provincial capital of West Jersey, and simply surviving through farming and fighting off the Delaware Indians and French left little time and energy for the pursuit of such leisurely pleasures as reading in the daylight hours or by lamplight before retiring in the evening.

But the Quakers were a hearty, persistent people who believed in the Good Book and its inspiring way of opening up young minds. In the minutes of the Burlington Library Company's first meeting, these God-fearing, land-loving Quakers wrote:

Several inhabitants of New Jersey, thinking a Library Company in the city of Burlington would be of great benefit to the members as well as to the public in general did speak to the number of sixty, who formed themselves into a company and agreed to pay ten shillings per annum in support of the library.

Some 700 books filled the shelves of the first library, which was built in 1757 and opened a few months later, replacing the large south parlor of the home of Thomas Rodman, which served as the area book center. One of the new public library's first books was donated by a local woman, Rebecca Scattergood, and titled "The Government of a Wife, or Wholesome and Pleasant Advice for Married Men."

In 1788, Gen. Joseph Bloomfield (for whom the town of Bloomfield was named) donated a piece of land for the erection of a one-story library at a cost of 50 pounds. That little building on Library Street served the town for 75 years until 1864 when the present structure was built on West Union Street by popular subscription.

The roster of patrons and directors of the Free Public Library of Burlington reads like the first early American "Who's Who." They had dominated the fields of politics, religion and letters.

William Franklin, the Tory son of Benjamin and the last royal governor of the colony, borrowed the first book from the library. Joseph Bloomfield, general, governor, congressman and president elector, was a familiar face at the library.

Elias Boudinot, president of the Continental Congress, was a frequent patron. Boudinot organized the American Bible Society and was the first depositor of the Newark Banking & Insurance Co. Boudinot lived near the library in his retirement. Another book borrower was young James Lawrence, who went on to become captain and a legendary figure in the War of 1812. Lawrence uttered those immortal words, "Don't give up the ship!"

Other library readers included John Woolman, author of "Woolman's Journal" and the first preacher of abolition of slavery. Woolman lived in nearby Mt. Holly. James Fenimore Cooper, America's first major novelist, also enriched the history of the Burlington Library. Cooper, who was born a half-block away from the old library, spent 17 of his most productive years in and around Burlington.

Star-Ledger Photo

The Burlington County Library, located in Mount Holly, was founded by settlers during the 1750s.

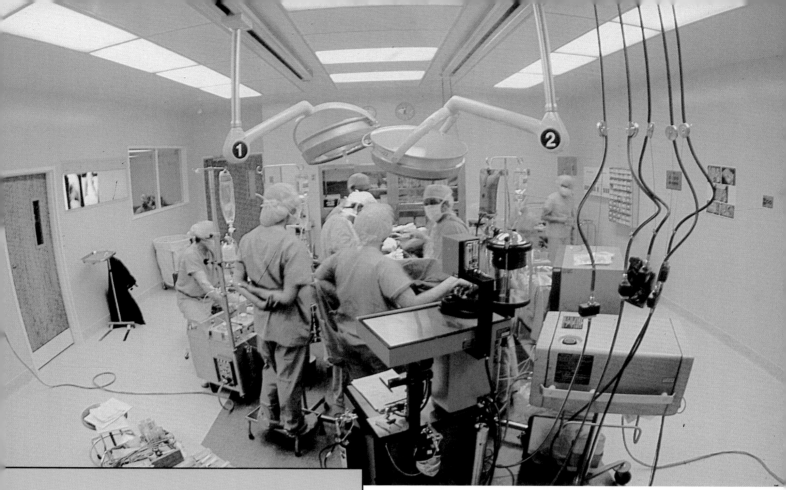

Courtesy: Deborah Heart & Lung Center

Open heart surgery at Deborah Heart & Lung Center.

MEDICINE

Since Dr. William Robinson first practiced medicine in the 1680s in the Union County town of Clark, New Jersey has been the scene of continuing experiments and innovations in the improvement of health care in the New World.

Robinson, whose landmark "plantation" home is one of the finest examples of 17th Century architecture in the nation, was one of the first doctors in the Colonies to conduct dissection for anatomical study and was one of New Jersey's first practicing physicians.

After more than three centuries of pioneering medical care and treatment, New Jersey today offers a highly specialized network of more than 110 hospitals and health centers to the state's 7.5 million residents, in addition to non-residents seeking help in any number of clinics and institutes undertaking revolutionary kinds of surgery and rehabilitation.

Among the breakthroughs credited to New Jersey's medical community are:

• The first cardiac clinic in America established by Dr. Thomas J. White in 1926 at Jersey City Hospital, now the Jersey City Medical Center.

• The first high technology center involving a state agency and private corporation to develop proteins capable of seek-and-destroy missions against cancer.

• "The New Jersey Larynx," for victims of throat cancer and other severe illnesses who otherwise would not be able to vocalize again.

• Rebuilding ligaments and tendons with a patented carbon fiber material.

• The Neville Tube, a prosthetic trachea that is saving lives around the world by creating a new air passage to and from the lungs.

• The Armadillo Connection, which revealed a link between human and armadillo leprosy, leading to a preventative medicine for humans because the armadillo strain of leprosy bacteria, unlike the human variety, can be grown for study in a laboratory.

• The development of two effective vaccines for preventing bacterial meningitis in laboratory animals, with human trials to begin soon. Bacterial meningitis, a crippling and sometimes fatal disease, strikes 10,000 youngsters a year.

• The nuclear heart pacemaker that is implanted in the chest and operates 30 years before having to be replaced.

• The discovery of Streptomycin in the 1940s by Rutgers University's Nobel Prize-winning Dr. Selman Waksman, whose drug practically eliminated tuberculosis and is widely used in the treatment of a variety of other infectious diseases.

• Hundreds of new drugs to fight everything from common infections to complex cancers, led by such pharmaceutical giants as Johnson & Johnson, Hoffmann-La Roche, Schering, Merck and Ciba-Geigy.

• The Middlesex County Homebound Program is the first in the country to be initiated by a county dental society. A cooperative effort has been launched among the New Jersey Dental Association, Middlesex County and the Middlesex County Dental Society to provide dental care to the homebound patient in his or her home.

• The University of Medicine and Dentistry of New Jersey is one of the nation's few institutions offering a prenatal test for detecting sickle cell anemia. The diagnostic procedure is one of the first made possible through recombinant DNA technology, or genetic engineering.

* * *

New Jersey is also a leader in detecting infectious diseases through the combined monitoring efforts of 10 major hospitals. The Inter-Jersey Infectious Disease Group is made up of specialists from the 10 hospitals, who meet on a weekly basis to discuss infectious disease problems and exchange information with physicians and patients.

Besides teaching, the group also conducts research at the infectious disease laboratory at St. Michael's Medical Center in Newark, recognized for its work on new and potent antibiotics.

In 1946, St. Michael's was the first community hospital in the United States to perform open heart surgery. In 1976, St. Michael's formed the first viral diagnostic and treatment center in the state.

New Jersey was the second state in 1969 to establish a program (dialysis) for chronic renal disease patients. There are currently 2,500 patients at 26 facilities receiving assistance.

The first national president of the American Cancer Society was Dr. Robert Hutter, director of pathology at St. Barnabas Medical Center in Livingston.

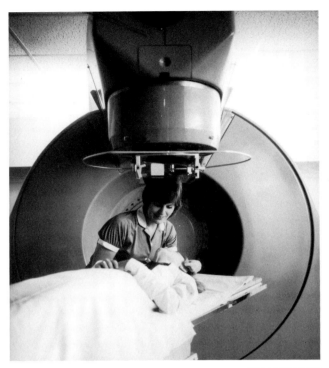

Star-Ledger Photo

Sandra Mazzeo, Director of Radiation Oncology, prepares a patient on the Linear Accelerator in the Clara Maas Cancer Treatment Center.

Advanced medical care for newborns is provided by Clara Maass Hospital in Belleville.

Star-Ledger Photo

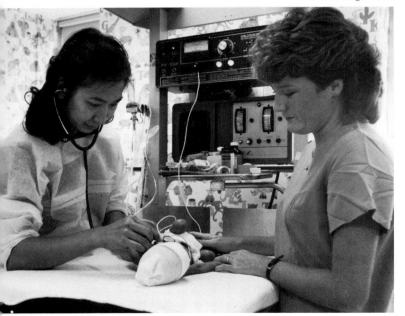

The New Jersey Health Sciences Group, founded in 1973, is a unique consortium of medical, dental, engineering, pharmacy schools and organizations and the pharmaceutical industry, which meets periodically to discuss a broad range of health-related issues and concerns.

New Jersey also has one of the most efficient, cost-effective, and best funded paramedic programs in the United States. The Emergency Medical Services (EMS) system covers almost every one of the state's 21 counties.

Clara Louise Maass is a genuine heroine in the annals of medical history. The East Orange nurse was the first female and American volunteer to die of yellow fever in an experiment in Havana, Cuba to pinpoint the cause of the lethal infection. The Stegomyia mosquito was the prime suspect. Her death on Aug. 24, 1901 ended the experiment and her name has been memorialized by Clara Maass Hospital in Belleville.

Clara Maass is just one of several health care facilities in the Garden State striving for the finest and most advanced delivery of services available in today's high-tech medical community. Here is a sampling of other facilities that reflect the trend toward meeting the community's entire medical needs.

University of Medicine and Dentistry of New Jersey

The state's university medical center is the largest free-standing health sciences university in the United States—and the newest. Its free-standing status allows it to function unattached to another university, which is not the case for most medical universities in America.

The University of Medicine & Dentistry of New Jersey complex in Newark.

Star-Ledger Photo

The medical university is unique for being the only health sciences institution in the U.S. that educates D.O. (doctors of osteopathy) students together with M.D. students in the same classroom. For the first two years of basic study, osteopathic students share learning facilities and experiences with students at the University-Rutgers Medical School.

Established in 1970 by legislative decree, UMDNJ has a current enrollment of some 3,000 students in six health professions schools. There are programs in medicine, dentistry, the life sciences and allied health fields at three medical schools, a dental school, a graduate school offering master's and doctoral degrees in the basic life sciences and a school that offers training in professions relating to health.

The schools are located on campuses in Newark, Piscataway and Camden. Interns, residents, postgraduate students and fellows train at UMDNJ's own facilities and at more than 80 affiliated hospitals and educational centers statewide. These cooperative arrangements have encouraged students to work in New Jersey by allowing them to observe the opportunities and the needs for health care professionals within the state.

Instead of developing health care programs solely to serve the curricular needs of its schools, New Jersey's medical university was created as an active participant in the state's health services industry. The new university was directed to provide services needed by New Jerseyans, both by developing sophisticated tertiary care programs and by offering adequate access to primary care in areas of the state lacking such resources.

Four of the university's schools are based in Newark: The New Jersey Medical School, the New Jersey Dental School, the Graduate School of Biomedical Sciences and the School of Health Related Professions. University Hospital, owned and operated by UMDNJ, is also on the Newark campus, serving as the primary teaching facility for the medical students.

The Rutgers Medical School is on the Piscataway campus and the New Jersey School of Osteopathic Medicine is on the university's rapidly growing Camden campus.

Rutgers Medical School, which trains allopathic physicians, has two campuses: Piscataway and the clinical campus at Cooper Hospital/University Medical Center in Camden.

The New Jersey School of Osteopathic Medicine begins its training of physicians on the Piscataway campus of the University of Medicine and Denistry. Third- and fourth-year students receive their training on the New Jersey School of Osteopathic Medicine's main clinical campus in Stratford, at John F. Kennedy Hospital.

University projects have led to such important discoveries as a prenatal test for sickle cell disease and the development of new prosthetic devices, including replacement ligaments and tendons and an artificial trachea and larynx, improving the quality of life for victims of disease and trauma throughout the world.

Dr. David M. Goldenberg, an internationally recognized pioneer in cancer research, has moved his team from the University of Kentucky in Lexington to the university's medical complex in Newark. Goldenberg's team uses antibodies, products of human and animal immune systems, as a way of pinpointing small tumors in the body. The team is refining that process and is working on the next step: Using the antibodies to seek out and destroy cancer cells.

Dr. David Goldenberg, a pioneer in cancer diagnosis, relocated his research institute—The Center for Molecular Medicine and Immunology—to the University of Medicine and Dentistry of New Jersey in Newark.

Photo Credit: Peter Byron

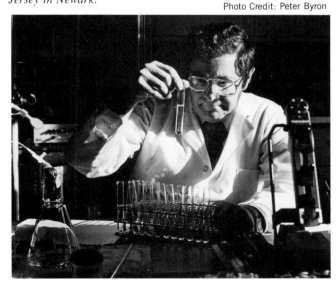

The Center for Molecular Medicine and Immunology was established in 1984 to develop proteins that can find and obliterate cancer cells. It is the first such high-tech joint enterprise between a state agency and private corporation.

Other work being done at New Jersey's medical university includes:

• **The Parkinson's Lookalike.** Some individuals, mistakenly diagnosed as having Parkinson's disease, actually are victims of a nervous system disorder that mirrors Parkinson's. The discovery was made by Dr. Roger Duvoisin, a UMDNJ neurologist known for his role in the development of L-dopa, a drug used to control the involuntary symptoms of Parkinson's disease.

• **Diagnosing heart disease.** A new, painless technique for diagnosing heart disease is being developed by a university cardiovascular specialist working with a team of engineers at Rutgers University. The key to the procedure is a computerized electronic monitoring system that amplifies and analyzes the sound of blood flowing through coronary arteries. The procedure was refined at the university's Piscataway campus in 1982.

• **Protecting artificial implants.** Death from infection is the most significant problem associated with artificial implants such as heart valves and arteries. But university researchers have found these synthetic replacements can be protected if bonded with antibiotics before being implanted. Bonded implants in laboratory animals have demonstrated a high resistance to bacteria.

• **Bone marrow infection.** University researchers have found two new drugs, one a penicillin derivative, effective in treating bone marrow infection in laboratory animals. The bacteria responsible for such infection gradually has become resistant to regular antibiotic treatment.

• **Lasers and glaucoma.** A university ophthalmologist, one of the state's laser surgery pioneers, has adapted laser technology to treat the most common form of glaucoma, known as open angle glaucoma, or "the-thief-in-the-night."

• **Diabetes and exercise.** Another researcher has found that a regular program of physical training among males who became diabetic as adults can reduce some of the risk factors that make them susceptible to premature atherosclerosis, a disease of the arteries that can lead to premature heart disease. The findings have led to a first-of-a-kind program in the state offering diabetics an intensive exercise and education regimen aimed at improving health and self-care.

• **Center for Human Molecular Genetics.** Some of the world's foremost genetics specialists and researchers of connective tissue disease have begun working in the genetics center on the university's Piscataway campus.

• **New Jersey's first Cancer Center.** A major, multi-disciplinary Cancer Research and Treatment Center opened at the university's Newark campus in 1983. The new center features a million-dollar linear accelerator, today's most advanced radiation therapy machine, used to perform a special cancer treatment whereby tumors are surgically exposed to permit more direct and effective radiation. The procedure, called "intra-operative radiation therapy," is available at no more than a half-dozen sites throughout the nation.

• **A statewide Prenatal Center.** The state's most sophisticated program of care for high-risk mothers and newborns was established in Newark in 1981 under the direction of UMDNJ.

• **Regional Trauma Center.** University Hospital was designated in 1981 as the state Regional Trauma Center, serving some 3 million residents with the most advanced approach to diagnosing and treating victims of traumatic (life-threatening) injury.

The second regional trauma center is at Cooper Hospital/University Medical Center in Camden, serving more than 2 million residents in nine counties of South Jersey.

• **Laser Acupuncture.** The University Pain Center has undertaken a major new research initiative—laser acupuncture—to alleviate pain.

• **Diet and Cancer.** A university biochemist, believing nutritional deficiencies play an important role in the high incidence of esophageal cancer in northern China, is focusing on diet as a model for studying the high rates of esophageal cancer among black males in Newark and other urban areas.

• **Urodynamics Laboratory.** The first facility of its kind in New Jersey to offer a complete spectrum of testing for bladder muscle and nerve abnormalities.

• **New Jersey Regional Comprehensive Hemophilia Care Program.** One of the nation's largest, the hemophilia program was established in 1976 under the auspices of UMDNJ-Rutgers Medical School at two primary centers: Middlesex General-University Hospital in New Brunswick, and St. Michael's Medical Center, Newark. Comprehensive, multi-disciplinary care is provided to patients suffering from bleeding disorders.

* * *

New Jersey's medical university is among five nationwide sites where the drug Ketanserin is being tested for treating scleroderma, a baffling connective tissue disease characterized by hardening of the skin.

In Camden, some 2,000 Hispanic children are the focus of a year-long malnutrition study to determine why only some youngsters become malnourished among groups where ethnic, social and economic factors are equal.

The Rutgers Medical School in Piscataway has opened a medical history museum featuring, among other medical paraphernalia, a bloodletting instrument called a scaraficator, an 1825 fever thermometer, and tools used for limb amputation. The rather rare collection was begun in the late 19th Century by Henry Disbrow, head of the Newark Board of Health. It has been augmented by recent gifts, including several from the office of the late Dr. Henry C. Neer, a general practitioner in Park Ridge from 1865 to 1911.

Deborah

Its name is synonymous with humanitarian health care and is known the world over for saving lives at no cost to the patient.

Deborah is more than the sum of its parts, a great tripartite consisting of a heart and lung center, a hospital foundation and a cardiovascular research institute.

Deborah is more than that. It's a philanthropic movement, a kind of medical miracle in an era of unprecedented hospital costs. Deborah is a large family of volunteers dedicated to improving the quality of human life, not through astronomical doctor bills but by contributions as small as a nickel or dime, and by generous donations from those who can afford to say "thanks" in a big financial way.

Deborah started out as a 32-bed tuberculosis sanitorium in 1922 and grew into one of America's leaders in the diagnosis and treatment of heart and lung disease.

The story of Deborah, as pieced together by Clara Franks, a tireless Deborah worker, is made up of two dynamic strands whose joint impact spans over six decades.

One is the medical advances that have occurred regularly since Deborah opened its door to TB victims in 1922, a quiet place

Young beneficiaries of the medical wonders pioneered at Deborah Heart & Lung Center.

Courtesy: Deborah Heart & Lung Center

in the cool, clean New Jersey Pinelands. Geographically, it's Browns Mills.

The other continuous Deborah strand is the incredible philanthropy that runs throughout the history of the remarkable institution. The two strong threads intertwine and form an inseparable bond.

The dedication of the thousands of Deborah Hospital Foundation Chapter volunteers is legendary. That spirit was sparked by founder Dora Moness Shapiro and friends in New York, New Jersey and Pennsylvania.

Mrs. Shapiro and her husband were concerned for the sufferers of the "white plague," tuberculosis. They purchased a private sanitorium in rural Burlington County, South Jersey. They named it Deborah to symbolize the efforts, like those of the Old Testament prophetess, to rescue those in need.

The first of 33 TB patients arrived to stay in a group of four cottages. The main building opened in 1938 and the first nurses' quarters were built in 1941. By 1948, five floors in the original hospital, including a modern surgical suite, were complete.

The development of the facilities was matched by the increase in the number of Deborah chapters. Led by the indefatigable Clara Franks, a cured TB patient who came to Deborah in 1934 and stayed, the corps of dedicated volunteers has reached 70,000 in more than 320 chapters in 10 states.

The new era for medicine and for Deborah was inaugurated on July 28, 1958, when the first open heart operation at the center was successfully performed on a three-year-old boy by Dr. Charles Bailey.

A five-year, $14 million renovation and expansion program was completed and formally dedicated on Dec. 2, 1981 by former President Gerald R. Ford, who now serves on Deborah's Honorary National Advisory Board, along with former Secretary of State and Nobel Laureate Henry Kissinger.

The new $3 million Robert Wood Johnson Jr. Laboratories, opened in 1981, were designed to provide the most modern equipment available under one roof for the Deborah Cardiovascular Research Institute.

Deborah offers the best possible medical and surgical resources at no patient cost, without regard to race, religion, national origin or ability to pay.

A mobile van program began rolling in the fall of 1980, a Deborah Foundation project that offers free blood pressure, lung function and weight testing through computerized technology. The Deborah Van has traveled tens of thousands of miles in five states.

Within the center's 240,000 square feet are housed the medical, surgical and diagnostic and support departments for the cardiovascular and pulmonary services, and the Sylvia Martin's Children's World, which treats young patients from around the globe.

The growing field of nuclear cardiology has a home in the nuclear medicine section at Deborah. Physicians can complete diagnostic studies with nuclear scanning cardiac procedures, nuclear radio-assay drug tests, pulmonary function tests, including nuclear ventilation perfusion ratios, lung scanning and clinical laboratory tests.

Medical expertise and cheerful warmth are blended in the adult and children areas, a setting and a philosophy nurtured by Deborah that encourages patient participation and in-depth education as an integral part of the recovery process. Families are invited to attend classes with the patients.

Kessler Institute

When one thinks of the Kessler Institute for Rehabilitation in Essex County, "a gift of hope" automatically comes to mind. It is a place where those whose lives appear hopeless find they are able to restructure their physical world, while lifting their mental and spiritual outlook in the process.

One of the premier facilities of its kind in the world, Kessler Institute in East Orange and West Orange is the vision of one man: Dr. Henry H. Kessler, who believed "the knife is not enough" in rehabilitating the handicapped.

Since its founding in 1949, Kessler Institute has fulfilled its mission of offering quality care carefully shaped to meet the medical, emotional and social needs of those who have been disabled by spinal cord injuries, brain damage, congenital and acquired amputations, and cerebrovascular accidents (strokes) at the earliest stage in the recovery process.

The Kessler Institute for Rehabilitation offers "a gift of hope" to those disabled by spinal cord injuries, brain damage, amputations and strokes. The East Orange building is pictured above. Below, the Kessler Institute for Rehabilitation, West Orange building.

Today, Kessler Institute is a comprehensive diagnostic, treatment and rehabilitation center with 180 inpatient beds and a daily outpatient population of 300. Treatment is provided by a team of 500 health care professionals, including rehabilitation nurses, physical and occupational therapists, speech pathologists and audiologists, daily live-in therapists, psychologists, social workers, vocational counselors, recreational therapists, prosthetists and orthotists, and other support staff.

Kessler patients come from all corners of the globe. In recent years, the largest percentage have been residents of the greater New York area. Former Kessler patients are active in all fields of endeavor. They are doctors, lawyers, accountants, engineers, computer programmers, electronics specialists, photographers, artists, business executives, sales persons, and even a football coach.

Kessler alumni are living proof that the disabled do return to active, productive lives. They are not burdens on society; they are

people who pay their own way. It is estimated that for every dollar spent on rehabilitation, $8 is returned to the economy.

Kessler Institute evolved from The Hospital for Crippled Children in Newark. Until 1938, the institute's property was owned by a family operating a dairy farm in the Newark area. The institute's original building, the Condit family farmhouse, sat on a strawberry patch in the hills of West Orange.

In 1938, through the encouragement of their Women's Auxiliary, the Children's Hospital purchased the farm property as a country summer home. The two-story building was completed in 1940 and occupied for several years by the hospital's staff and patients.

World War II brought Kessler, surgeon and orthopedist, home to his native Newark from a tour of duty as director of the Mare Island Naval Amputee Center. As chief-of-staff at the Hospital for Crippled Children, Kessler saw the need to establish a community-sponsored rehabilitation center.

With the support of civic-minded friends, Kessler raised the necessary funds to purchase the pastoral summer home in West Orange in 1948. The hospital became the first facility of its kind in New Jersey to provide a comprehensive program for rehabilitation care for several disabled adults and children.

On Jan. 3, 1949, Kessler Institute admitted its first patient. The original building housed 16 inpatient beds, a small dining room, which doubled as the Occupational Therapy Department, and a separate wing for the physical therapy gymnasium.

Kessler's focus has always remained on the *possible*—on what the patient can accomplish—not his disability. The many programs that were developed reflect that philosophy.

• **A Driver Education Program** was created to provide disabled individuals the much needed mobility to regain independent lifestyles. The institute was also one of the first rehabilitation centers in the country to develop a pre-driving evaluation test for perceptually damaged patients.

• A small **Clinic for Amputees** was started in the early years and expanded under the guidance of Dr. Richard A. Sullivan, medical director since joining the staff in 1969. The clinic is now a full-service Prosthetic and Orthotic shop. The department utilizes a comprehensive clinic system for upper and lower extremity amputations and produces sophisticated, customized artificial limbs and braces for the post-operative amputee.

• The **Vocational Services Department** has expanded dramatically since its inception in the early 1950s. A computerized evaluation system correlates information from vocational tests to produce a listing of career opportunities for patients.

• The **Placement Advisory Board** is an employment service for patients, as well as a clearinghouse for member companies interested in employing the disabled.

In 1981, Kessler Institute joined a worldwide celebration to recognize the accomplishments and rights of the disabled. The International Year of the Disabled Person provided the impetus for many exciting activities, including the sponsorship of a road race and wheelchair sports meet, a patient fashion show and a dance marathon. Kessler sponsored the final leg of the "Continental Quest," a 3,400-mile, cross-country journey undertaken by two disabled athletes.

In 1983, Kessler Institute launched a structured Back Pain Program to help patients cope with their back pain through a "team approach" using behavorial and cognitive treatments combined with medical and physiotherapeutic rehabilitation methods. The program also teaches patients to avoid situations that will cause re-injury to their backs. Eight of 10 Americans are afflicted with acute back pain problems at some point during their lives. More than $14 billion is spent treating back pain problems every year.

The institute's Recreational Therapy Department, in co-sponsorship with the Easter Seal Society of New Jersey, inaugurated its own program of wheelchair athletics—Sports On Wheels—during 1983. It began with a basketball wheelchair team playing in exhibition games and the wheelchair league. Other sports are being added, such as archery, track and field, marathon racing, volleyball, softball and aquatics.

Middlesex General

Middlesex General-University Hospital in New Brunswick completed a $65 million building program in 1982. The expanded facilities integrated Middlesex General and the University of Medicine and Dentistry-Rutgers Medical School.

Middlesex General, which celebrated its centennial this year, has become a major academic health center that not only services the residents of Central Jersey, but also provides tertiary services for citizens of central New Jersey.

The Paige D. L'Hommedieu Emergency Suite, which opened in August 1982, is three times the size of the previous emergency unit and is superbly equipped. Features of the new suite include a centrally located nursing station; an ear, nose and throat room; a triage room for assessing patient care priorities; a laboratory, and four trauma rooms for acute cases.

The suite contains the most complete medical communications system to be found anywhere. The new system allows instant contact with rescue squads and makes it possible, through radio contact with paramedics, to monitor vital signs of seriously ill or injured persons before they arrive at the hospital.

The new pulmonary laboratory in the Respiratory Services Department has its own brochoscopy suite for performing tests to determine any impairment of lung functioning. Cardiopulmonary stress tests and sleep apnea studies (for patients who experience brief lapses in breathing during sleep) are two of the procedures done in the pulmonary suite.

Respiratory therapy, another department function, also provides life-support services, including resuscitation and mechanical ventilation. Arterial blood gas studies are done to determine the amount of oxygen and carbon dioxide in the blood.

The Cardiodynamics Department provides a wide range of diagnostic services for heart patients. Non-invasive procedures include exercise stress tests, echo-cardiology, phonocardiography, vectorcardiography and Holter monitoring. A spacious new laboratory for cardiac catheterizations was part of the recent building program.

A state-of-the-art surgical suite covers 36,292 square feet of space and contains 10 operating rooms, including two for endoscopy and cystoscopy. Two of the rooms are equipped with connections for special pumping and suction devices needed for open heart surgery. More than 100 such operations have been performed at the hospital.

Middlesex was the first hospital in Central Jersey to install a CAT scanner in 1977, a remarkable tool that takes thousands of individual X-ray pictures that are processed by a computer into a single image, resulting in something like a three-dimensional X-ray.

More than 150 medical students receive clinical training at the hospital in a typical year. In addition, more than 135 resident physicians complete their training in specialized fields, including medicine, general surgery, pediatrics, obstetrics-gynecology, psychiatry, orthopedics and pathology. There are house staff physicians in the hospital round-the-clock, providing patient care support to faculty and community doctors.

Under the new Diagnostic Related Groups system of paying bills, the patient is charged a specific amount for the illness, rather than for services rendered and days in the hospital. Just about every illness a person can have is assigned to one of 467 categories, and a specific price tag is attached. The new system is designed to promote efficiency since the hospital is paid the same amount regardless of the number of days in the hospital. The system is considered more equitable by insurance underwriters.

Statistics cannot tell the story of a hospital's service to a community, but they can show the scale and magnitude of work performed during a calendar year. At Middlesex, more than 14,000 patients are admitted in a year for everything from a cut finger to open heart surgery. The number of inpatient days of care exceeds 93,000.

There are more than 1,000 births, 25,000 emergency clinic visits, 21,000 home-care visits, 7,000 surgical procedures, 450,000 laboratory tests, 20,000 electrocardiograms, 68,000 respiratory procedures and 16,000 physical therapy procedures. And these numbers are increasing each year at Middlesex General.

Morristown Memorial Hospital

In 1892, Memorial Hospital and All Souls Hospital began life in Morristown. In 1978, Memorial acquired All Souls, creating a comprehensive medical community for a four-county region.

The first operation nearly a century ago was the removal of an infected kidney. A year later the pioneering hospital opened a school of nursing and, since then, this health care center situated in the seat of Morris County has experienced a technological revolution in medical techniques and applications.

The voluntary, not-for-profit hospital today is the central health facility for the people in Morris, Warren, Sussex and Somerset counties, and a medical referral center for all of northwestern New Jersey. Morristown Memorial is also a teaching hospital affiliated with Columbia University's College of Physicians & Surgeons and other prominent medical and educational institutions.

Star-Ledger Photo

Ambulance arriving at Morristown Hospital.

Memorial and Summit's Overlook Hospital are founding members of the Shared Services Consortium, pioneering regionalized health care services in northern New Jersey.

With 689 beds, 1,700 employees, 678 nurses, a medical and dental staff of more than 400, and a spectrum of basic and highly specialized services, Morristown Memorial combines the traditional advantages of a community hospital with the advanced capabilities of a progressive medical center.

MMH has two divisions: 100 Madison Ave., where the emphasis is on acute care, and 95 Mt. Kemble Ave., its center for pre-admission testing, geriatric extended care, outpatient and alcoholic services, and planned facilities for sub-acute and rehabilitative care.

Morristown Memorial's growth parallels the history of modern medical care and treatment. To put the time frame in perspective, All Souls was serving the Morristown community before aspirin was introduced in 1899 and before adrenalin was discovered in 1901.

The Morristown hospital installed its first X-ray equipment in 1903, only eight years after Roentgen announced the discovery of those penetrating rays. The hospital furnished its first pathological laboratory in 1905 and opened its first eye, ear, nose and throat outpatient clinic that same year.

The first motor ambulance went into service in 1915 and the following year the maternity ward opened while the first intern enrolled for training. On the medical calendar, that was the year Vitamin B was discovered.

In 1919, the Havemeyer Pavilion for Contagious Disease admitted its first patients, and in 1924, All Souls was rated as a "Class A" hospital. By 1938, a tumor section was formed for the study and treatment of cancer, and radium therapy was introduced. In 1946, Morristown Memorial became affiliated with the Eye-Bank for Sight Restoration and in 1953 a hemotologic clinic opened.

The year 1957 saw the creation of the hospital's noted Poison Control Center. Today, a Poisindex catalog of more than 160,000 toxic substances and specific treatment instructions is updated quarterly for telephone callers and walk-in patients.

The first heart pacemaker was installed in a patient's chest in 1961, and in 1965 Morristown Memorial inaugurated New Jersey's only cobalt therapy treatment program. The next year, ultrasound equipment was acquired by radiology for brain and cardiac disease diagnosis. By 1971 a pacemaker clinic was established and in 1977 a CAT scanner was "reading" patients' heads for tumors and other diseases.

A Center for Addictive Illnesses opened in 1980 and an argon laser was installed for ophthalmic surgery in 1982.

Morristown Memorial already is planning to replace the magical CAT scanner with a totally new concept: Nuclear Magnetic Resonance. This new approach uses a magnetic field to visualize internal structures and organs, without the hazard of radiation exposure, with a clarity that equals or exceeds CAT scanning and with greater tolerance to motion within the subject being examined.

Some of MMH's specialized services include an alcoholism treatment service . . . ambulatory clinics in 30 specialties . . . audiology and speech therapy . . . a diabetes clinic and classes . . . fiberoptic bronchoscopy . . . a gastro-intestinal endoscopy suite . . . a Helpline mental health telephone service . . . microsurgery . . . stroke unit and rehabilitation . . . tuberculosis clinic . . . and a venereal disease clinic.

Newark Beth Israel
Medical Center

On July 18, 1901, the first official meeting of the medical staffs of the Daughters of Israel Hospital Association and the Hebrew Hospital and Dispensary Association was called to order in Newark.

The aim of these two organizations was to render medical aid to the sick among the Jews and to bring about a harmonious amalgamation for the welfare of what was then termed "the hospital movement."

Newark Beth Israel Hospital was born three months later on Oct. 25. Newark's first new hospital opened on Oct. 27, 1906, a "modern brick building" on Lyons Avenue. That was replaced in 1928 by a fireproof edifice equipped with 350 beds.

Beth Israel in the 1980s is a dynamic health community of 2,300 specialists and staff working in a 545-bed medical center. In its 83-year history, Beth Israel Hospital has been responsible for many New Jersey medical "firsts," including the implantation of the first American-made atomic pacemakers to regulate heartbeats and the first live donor kidney transplant, performed in 1968.

Beth Israel was also the first New Jersey hospital to perform special radioimmunoassay procedures in its Endocrine Laboratory, thus establishing the groundwork for Beth Israel to become a "core" laboratory for special endocrine procedures involving the analyses of tissue samples.

Beth Israel was one of the nation's first blood banks, established in 1937.

The total number of patients and procedures in the Pulmonary Rehabilitation Department has reached an astounding 250,000. More than 420 kidney transplants and 4,000 open heart operations have been performed at the renowned Newark medical center. Beth Israel ranks in the top 5 percent of the nation in the number of open heart surgeries performed annually.

Beth Israel rarely uses freshly drawn blood, preferring to meet the needs of open heart surgery by using blood components entirely. The hospital's "washing machines" were responsible for more than 20,000 blood-cleansing treatments for hemodialysis-dependent patients in 1983.

The hospital performs more than 79,000 diagnostic radiologic examinations a year, nearly 20,000 of which are emergency room procedures.

Beth Israel and Deborah Hospital in South Jersey are the only two state-designated Tertiary Care Cardiac Centers at the present time. The Beth Israel Center is doing 2,000 cardiac catheterizations and about 1,000 open heart cases annually.

Beth Israel is also one of the busiest pacemaker centers in the United States.

Beth Israel has built a reputation on specialized services, four of which best typify the kind of high-tech medical equipment available at the Newark complex:

- **The Flo Okin Oncology Center.** Long a leader in cancer treatment and research, Beth Israel offers a new multi-discipline oncology center under one roof, housing the treatment and administrative areas for medical, surgical and radiation oncology.

Vibrant colors, exciting lighting treatment, exquisite woven graphics and a tree-filled atrium have been thoughtfully fashioned for those who, in a time of illness, become more esthetically sensitive.

The oncology division handles more than 3,000 active cancer patients and adds approximately 1,100 new patients annually. When the division was created in 1970, it was the only fully operational oncology service of its kind in New Jersey. The staff works with clinical research groups at Memorial Sloan-Kettering Cancer Center and Mount Sinai Hospital, as well as the National Cancer Institute.

- **Renal Treatment Center.** Renal medicine has been at the forefront of the multitude of special services provided by Beth Israel since 1963, when the first acute dialysis treatment in the state was performed here.

The renal center offers the complete range of services, including inpatient and outpatient dialysis, home dialysis training, pediatric hemodialysis and an inpatient nursing unit for renal patients. Organ procurement, research and educational activities are being constantly accelerated.

The Ruth Gottscho Kidney Foundation's "Operation Lifeline" provides an organ procurement telephone hotline. The Gottscho Foundation also set up New Jersey's first children's dialysis unit in 1973 at "The Beth."

- **The Nuclear Medicine Center.** The new diagnostic core of the Nuclear Medicine Center enables exploration into areas of

Modern lobby of Beth Israel Medical Center, Newark.

nuclear radiation that had been formerly unavailable. There are now three new cameras, including a portable camera, a stationary computer and a portable nuclear medicine computer, which allows the staff to do comparison studies at bedside and provide computerized images in color.

Active clinical research in nuclear cardiology and in the evaluation of new pacemakers powered by radioisotopes is being pursued, as is the daily use of thallium, the isotope that seeks out the working muscles.

• **The Radiation Therapy Center.** A vital component in the expanded, multi-discipline Oncology Center is the radiation therapy facility, which features a megavoltage linear accelerator. With the accelerator, more than 7,600 procedures were performed in a year. It is no longer necessary to refer radiation patients to other institutions for sophisticated therapeutic treatment.

The cost of the linear accelerator was assumed by the Auxiliary, the only major fund-raising arm of the medical center.

Overlook Hospital

At the turn of the century, Summit was a quiet town of 7,000 residents living in a place largely known as a woodsy health resort. With the building of a rail line to New York came rapid growth and, in 1905, the noted Summit surgeon Dr. William Lawrence responded to the community's booming development and inadequate medical facilities with the creation of a small private hospital.

Lawrence chose a high, peaceful hill overlooking the beautiful Baltusrol Valley, site of the world-famous Baltusrol Golf Club. The original farmhouse on the lofty site had been a hostelry during the Revolutionary War.

On Oct. 1, 1906, Overlook Hospital opened its doors: A brick, three-story structure embodying all the latest ideas in hospital architecture. Over the next four decades, Overlook expanded wing by wing until, today, the modern medical complex contains 551 beds and a staff of 2,500 doctors, nurses, technicians and office personnel. The hospital admits more than 22,300 patients annually. There are 206,100 outpatient visits.

Lawrence's modest hospital on the hill is now home for the state's only Public Health Sciences Library, containing 1,200 consumer publications written in readable, non-technical English, and some 24,350 professional medical publications.

Overlook Hospital in Summit was created by a local surgeon in response to inadequate health care. Open in 1906, today's Overlook Hospital admits about 22,300 patients each year.

Overlook's own anticipation of new directions in health care is perhaps best illustrated by the new $15 million Center for Community Health. Overlook reaches out to the community around it by emphasizing disease prevention and health maintenance through education.

One of its many face-to-face encounters is the "Learn at Lunch" program, which provides to those on their lunch breaks a half-hour presentation by hospital experts in a number of health-related fields. Given on the last Thursday of each month (except during the summer), the Overlook educational pep talks have dealt with such topics as the essentials of safe jogging, avoiding stress on vacations and proper nutrition and diet.

Overlook is also serving the business community with counseling tips to employes with personal problems, ranging from marital and family discord to difficulties with alcohol, drugs and finances. Companies with a combined employe roster of more than 25,000 have signed up for this specialized service.

In conjunction with Morristown Memorial, Overlook Hospital offers the only program in New Jersey in emergency medicine. The two medical centers also cosponsor the Center for Addictive Illnesses, the largest state-licensed, nonprofit inpatient and outpatient facility for treatment and rehabilitation of alcoholism and drug addiction.

Overlook is the only hospital on the East Coast to offer the American Heart Association's computerized interactive CPR learning system. CPR is the life-saving technique known as cardiopulmonary resuscitation.

A $50 million expansion and renovation program was nearing completion in 1985, adding 84 new beds, new surgical suites, intensive care units and emergency and lab facilities.

St. Barnabas Medical Center

St. Barnabas is the largest hospital in New Jersey and is readily accessible, even by helicopter, to the nearly 1.5 million people living in the northern region of the state.

Located in Livingston, St. Barnabas is the major health care provider for 41 communities in Essex, eastern Morris and northern Union counties. The 705-bed medical complex with a 2,100-member staff serves as the major referral center for North Jersey.

As a teaching institution with a century-long commitment to graduate medical education, St. Barnabas physicians share medical expertise with students, residents and fellows in highly regarded teaching programs certified by the Accreditation Council for Graduate Medical Education.

More than 40 laboratory and therapy specialists are graduated each year from six accredited schools in the medical center. These programs are directed by the departments of radiology, pathology, radiotherapy and applied clinical technology.

Each year, more than 100 third- and fourth-year undergraduate medical students receive clinical training in departments throughout the hospital. The center offers approved hospital-operated residences in cooperation with medical schools and research institutions. St. Barnabas maintains affiliation with seven medical schools. The medical center's 10 free-standing residency programs educate more than 100 doctors each year.

The story of St. Barnabas begins in 1865 when it was founded in Newark in a Victorian house. Its first hospital was completed in 1873. Graduate medical education began in 1880. In 1894, a School of Professional Nursing opened.

The first two accredited residencies—plastic surgery and general surgery—were inaugurated in 1947. The 1950s saw a decade of planning for the move to Livingston, which took place in 1964. The first kidney transplant was performed in 1968. Lasers were used for the first time by surgeons in 1972. A kidney center was established in 1973.

Burn treatment service was instituted in 1974 and the state's only certified Burn Unit officially opened in 1977.

By 1980, St. Barnabas was treating more than 110,000 patients a year: 30,000 inpatients, 57,000 outpatients and 23,000 emergency room patients.

St. Barnabas' surgery section is noted for the size and scope of its activities. More than 17,000 operations are performed in the

Burn patients are regularly transported by helicopter to the Saint Barnabas Burn Unit, the only certified burn center in New Jersey.

Star-Ledger Photo

hospital's 14 operating rooms each year. A staff of 126 active surgeons performs advanced procedures such as kidney transplants, cardiovascular and burn-related operations, and complex gastrointestinal reconstructions.

St. Barnabas' reputation as a regional surgical referral center is enhanced by its expertise in techniques of laser instrumentation, esophageal manometry, microsurgery and vascular testing.

and hypertension, including transplantation, hemodialysis, peritoneal dialysis and self-care dialysis. Nephrologists, surgeons, urologists, cardiologists, pathologists, specialized nurses, dieticians and social workers address the varied needs of patients and families. More than 250 kidney transplants have been performed to date.

The kidney center is one of the major outpatient facilities at St. Barnabas. The renal section has treated thousands of patients and currently administers more than 600 treatments every week. St. Barnabas' Satellite Dialysis Center at Pine Brook serves as the primary regional facility for outpatients.

The medical center is a leader in the treatment of the multiple complications of burn victims. As the state's major resource for burns, the St. Barnabas burn team is on call for other hospitals in time of need. Communities across the tri-state area use the medical center's helicopter pad in the transfer of burn victims.

Corporations and institutions receive assistance from the Burn Unit in developing burn prevention and first aid programs. First aid squads, public schools, nursing schools, industrial health professionals and nursing personnel benefit from community education programs.

Valley Hospital

If efficiency is any measure of a hospital's success, then the Valley Hospital in Ridgewood comes out as the leader in New Jersey with an average length of stay for a patient of only 5.6 days.

A relatively small community hospital founded in 1951, the 387-bed facility also boasts the second highest number of deliveries of any hospital in the state, about 3,000 babies a year.

With some 1,600 employes, including 325 physicians and dentists, Valley Hospital offers the residents of the Bergen-Passaic area a wide range of specialties, 17 medical departments in all, from neuroscience and otolaryngology to plastic surgery and urology.

Valley Hospital admitted more than 23,000 patients in 1984 and treated more than 43,000 in the emergency clinic. The number of surgical procedures has approached the 13,000 level.

Among Valley Hospital's community services are:

• **The Raymond E. Banta Valley Center**, which assists young people from eight area towns who have problems concerning drug and alcohol abuse, pregnancy or venereal diseases. The center provides individual and family counseling, as well as crisis intervention. There is no charge for these services.

• **The Northwest Bergen Hospice** is a program of care and

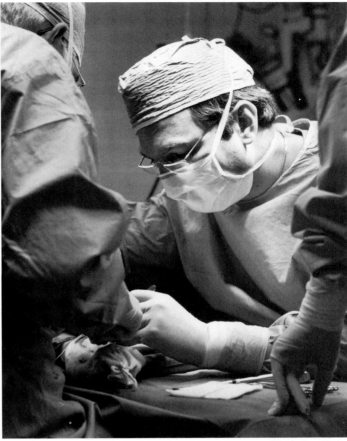

Star-Ledger Photo

Surgeons perform a delicate operation at Valley Hospital in Ridgewood. Valley, which serves the Bergen-Passaic area, has 17 medical departments and a staff of about 1,500.

support for the terminally ill patients and their families. A cooperative effort of Nursing Service Inc., Ridgewood; Visiting Nurses of Northern Bergen County, and The Valley Hospital, the hospice coordinates care through a combination of home and hospital settings with the greatest percentage of care given at home.

• **Tel-Med** is a community service of the Valley Hospital Auxiliary, which funds and staffs this free health information telephone tape library.

• **Tel-Hospital** was instituted in 1979 by the Department of Medical Affairs and Education and is staffed by the auxiliary. Inpatients and outpatients can listen by phone to tapes explaining upcoming medical procedures. The purpose of these tapes is to allay any anxiety a patient may feel prior to treatment.

A memorial to pilot Maj. Thomas McGuire, Jr. stands on the air base that bears his name.

MILITARY

Since Gen. Washington caught the Hessians by surprise at Trenton and captured the British garrison at Princeton—the turning point in the American Revolution—New Jersey has remained a military bastion in the defense of its country.

Economically, the military is the second largest employer in New Jersey, spending more than $3 billion in 1984 in salaries, services and goods.

More than 50,000 personnel work at eight major military installations and related defense operations throughout the state. Another 25,000 residents are retired military employes.

From the beginning of this nation's birth, Jerseyans have left their mark on America's military history.

Major Henry Lee was the youngest and only recipient under the rank of colonel to receive a Congressional gold medal for his daring exploits during the Revolutionary War. A graduate of Princeton University, "Light Horse Harry" was the father of another legendary figure, Civil War Gen. Robert E. Lee.

At 23, Maj. Lee and his cavalrymen raided a British garrison in Jersey City on Aug. 19, 1779, without firing a single shot. Lee's men used bayonets in the sneak attack, humiliating the British.

"Don't give up the ship!" is the rallying cry of the U.S. Navy and it was delivered the first time by Capt. James Lawrence, a resident of Burlington, during the War of 1812. Commanding the Chesapeake off Boston, Lawrence, mortally wounded in a battle with the British frigate Shannon, uttered those final words to his crew.

Princeton native Capt. Robert F. Stockton (1795-1866) was in command of the Pacific coast during the Mexican War (1846-48). He took possession of southern California and declared it a United States territory, setting up a civil government and appointing a governor. The California city of Stockton was named in his honor.

Fleet Adm. William F. Halsey, from Elizabeth, provided cover aboard his flagship, the battleship New Jersey, for Gen. Douglas MacArthur's landing in the Philippines, the beginning of the Pacific Theater victory in World War II. Halsey also led strikes on Marshall, Gilbert, Wake and Marcus islands.

Major Thomas B. McGuire Jr. of Ridgewood, a Medal of Honor recipient, was the second leading World War II flying ace before being killed in action in January 1945. McGuire Air Force Base in Burlington County is named after the famed aviator.

New Jersey has been the scene of many military firsts. During its development, Ft. Dix at one time was the nation's largest military reservation. The Army's first powder factory was built in Dover, Morris County, in 1907. Today it is headquarters for Army armament research.

Ft. Monmouth, the nation's leading military technology and logistics center, designed and built the first radio equipped meteorological balloon in 1928, and developed the first U.S. aircraft detection radar. It also demonstrated in 1946 that space communications was feasible by bouncing a radar pulse off the moon and picking up the return signal.

The world's largest hangar at the Lakehurst Naval Center contains a 450-foot-long aircraft carrier used for training. Lakehurst was also America's dirigible base for transcontinental and oceanic flights.

The U.S. Coast Guard Training Center is in Cape May, and McGuire Air Force Base is the largest military airlift command on the East Coast.

The Navy's only Air Propulsion Center is located just outside of Trenton. The Navy also maintains a huge weapons depot in pastoral Colts Neck, Monmouth County.

There are at least five military museums that trace the history of military developments in New Jersey since Colonial times. At Ft. Monmouth there are the U.S. Army Chaplain Museum, depicting the religious military heritage of the United States, and the Army Communications-Electronics Museum, exhibiting every conceivable communication device, from early wig-wag flags to highly sophisticated electronic gear.

The Sandy Hook Museum was originally the Ft. Hancock guard house and jail, or post stockade, built in 1899. It is now stocked with maps and blueprints of the fort and batteries, military uniforms, weapons and related objects, social history artifacts such as antique bottles, menus, dishes, and cultural artifacts from turn-of-the-century life at a military reservation to a seashell collection and herbarium.

The McGuire Museum, established in 1982, is a memorial to the Ridgewood flying ace who died in action at the end of World War II. A P-38 fighter plane, the kind piloted by McGuire, stands on a pedestal, surrounded by scale models of aircraft used in the Pacific and European campaigns during World War II. From the archives of the Army and MGM motion picture company are 45 minutes of newsreel scenes shot during the war, showing dog fights and the various battles McGuire fought in. The original footage has been transferred to videotape for repeated viewings.

The National Guard Museum at the Military Academy in Sea Girt was opened in 1980 and features military memorabilia spanning more than two centuries, from a Continental Army soldier with his musket and powder horn to a World War I doughboy in his khaki uniform with a field pack. The National Guard owes its origins to Marquis de Lafayette, who commanded a unit called the *Guard National.*

The Air National Guard is based in Atlantic City and at McGuire Air Force Base in Burlington County.

The major military installations in New Jersey follow.

Ft. Dix

Embracing 55 square miles of South Jersey Pinelands, Ft. Dix is buffered by wide flat farms, from watery cranberry bogs to grazing cattle and wheat fields.

Named after Maj. Gen. John Adams Dix, a 19th Century patriot, U.S. senator and New York governor, Dix was first designated a "camp" on July 18, 1917. It served as a cantonment area and training post for troops preparing to fight in the First World War. As one of 16 installations constructed "for the war to end all wars," Ft. Dix rapidly grew into the nation's largest military reservation.

Following the armistice, the camp became a demobilization center. From 1922-26, it was a training ground for active Army, Army Reserve and National Guard units and then remained in caretaker status until 1933. For the next seven years, the post served as a reception, discharge and replacement center for the Civilian Conservation Corps, created by President Roosevelt to put unemployed persons back to work improving the nation's parks, rivers and other natural resources.

In 1939, the camp became a permanent Army installation, or fort. Ten divisions and many smaller units either trained or staged there before assignment on the global battlefields of World War II.

In 1972, the overall training base was reduced from 12 battalions and 60 companies to 10 battalions and 50 companies. Today, the overall budget stands around $1 billion. The Ft. Dix community numbers more than 23,000, of whom nearly 12,000 are military personnel. The fort processed about 27,000 Army personnel in 1984.

Also serving the civilian community, Ft. Dix provided assistance for both the Buffalo blizzard and the Johnstown flood in 1977, two of the nation's worst national disasters. The fort received a Humanitarian Service Medal for its outstanding service.

The symbol of Ft. Dix is the infantryman, considered "The Ultimate Weapon" by the U.S. Army.

Ft. Monmouth

From a tiny cluster of World War I Army tents squatting in a clearing right off the Jersey Shore, Ft. Monmouth has grown into a leader of military technology and logistics. From 1917 to the present, Ft. Monmouth scientists and engineers have ushered in unparalleled advances in military research and development.

In 1928, the first radio-equipped meteorological balloon, a forerunner of a weather-sounding technique universally used today, soared into the upper stratosphere.

A decade later, the first United States aircraft detection

Satellite communications terminals at Fort Monmouth. Star-Ledger Photo

radar was produced at Ft. Monmouth. And in January 1946, the fort's communications specialists bounced a signal off the moon and recorded it for posterity.

Today, Ft. Monmouth is Monmouth County's largest employer, with more than 9,000 civilian employes and a military payroll exceeding 2,000 people. Its annual budget is approaching $2 billion.

Ft. Monmouth began as a Signal Corps Camp in Little Silver, a briar-covered tract that greeted 32 soldiers when they first arrived at the site on June 4, 1917. A battalion training course was started a month later.

The fort today takes in 2,000 acres touching 15 communities. Most of the fort grounds are in Eatontown, Oceanport, Shrewsbury, Tinton Falls and Belmar.

The camp was declared a permanent military post on Aug. 6, 1925. A new home for the Signal Corps laboratories was completed in March 1935.

The outbreak of World War II in Europe in 1939 led to a major expansion that continued through the 1960s. The post is now headquarters for the Army Communications-Electronics Command, which is responsible for all military communications and electronic equipment.

Also based at Ft. Monmouth are:

• Army Avionics Research and Development activity.

• Three Army Electronics Research and Development laboratories: Combat Surveillance and Target Acquisition, working in radar, photography, remote sensing . . . Electronics Technology and Devices, involved in high-speed, low-power, large-scale integrated circuits, and microwave and millimeter wave . . . and Electronic Warfare, concentrating on intercept, direction finding, signal analysis, jamming and signal intelligence.

• Joint Tactical Communications Office, a jointly staffed Defense Department organization hooking up tactical communications and other defense telecommunications systems.

• Army Communications Systems Agency, responsible for strategic communications systems.

• Army Chaplain Center and School, training chaplains who will minister to American soldiers and their families throughout the world.

• Joint Interface Test Force and Joint Interoperability of Tactical Command and Control Systems, which tests and demonstrates compatibility of command and control systems.

McGuire Air Force Base

Covering roughly 3,600 acres in the heartland of New Jersey, McGuire is the only Air Force base in the state and the largest military airlift command on the East Coast. It is known as the "Gateway to NATO," the member countries of the North Atlantic Treaty Organization.

In 1937, there was a single dirt strip runway with a few maintenance and administrative buildings under the control of nearby Ft. Dix. By 1945, it was the western terminus for the return of the wounded from Europe and for those separating from the Army.

On Sept. 17, 1949, the title and function of the base changed, officially becoming McGuire Air Force Base, named after the Ridgewood flyer shot down in combat in 1945. By 1961, there were 1,750 housing units and a continuous construction program for dormitories, officer quarters, dining halls, swimming pools and a gymnasium.

A self-contained community, McGuire's population today numbers 5,200 military and 2,000 civilian personnel and about 8,500 dependents. With assets of more than $820 million and operating expenditures of more than $275 million annually, McGuire also dispenses a combined military/civilian payroll in excess of $100 million a year.

The 438th Military Airlift Wing, host unit at McGuire, is one of five airlift commands on the eastern seaboard under the jurisdiction of the 21st Air Force, also located at McGuire.

The Military Airlift Command controls more than 90,000 active servicemen at installations in more than 30 countries. The 438th's mission is to maintain a constant state-of-war readiness. Activities involve global airlifts of forces and equipment and aerial drops of troops and equipment into combat zones.

The crews of the 438th fly more than 83,000 hours a year on missions to about 50 countries. In an average year, the McGuire Passenger Terminal can serve as many as 310,000 people.

Aircraft from McGuire can fly eastward through Canada,

Left, Coast Guard recruits take daily runs during fitness training.

Right, an instructor supervises cardio-pulmonary resuscitation classes during recruit training at the Coast Guard base in Cape May.

Photo Credit: Ann Everest
Courtesy: U.S. Coast Guard, Cape May

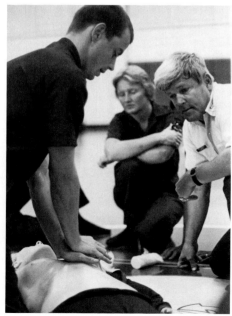

Photo Credit: Debbie A. Berry
Courtesy: U.S. Coast Guard, Cape May

The United States Coast Guard water rescue team stationed at Cape May.

Courtesy: U.S. Coast Guard, Cape May

Greenland, Iceland, NATO Europe, Africa and through the Middle East to the eastern boundaries of Iran and the Arabian peninsula. Southward, the 21st's responsibility includes the Caribbean and South America.

McGuire is also the home of the New Jersey Air National Guard, which operates the F-105 Thunderchief and the 135 Stratotanker. The New Jersey Civil Air Patrol also has headquarters at the Burlington County base. An official auxiliary of the Air Force, it is dedicated to public service, aerospace education and flight training of its cadets.

Coast Guard Cape May Center

The Beach Front Station in Cape May was the start of Coast Guard's activities, in the late 1800s. That station was turned over to the Cape May Kiwanis Club in 1946 for $1.

By that time, the Coast Guard had expanded its operations at the nearby Cold Spring Station, established in 1924 on the grounds of the old U.S. Naval Station. The Recruit Training Center was established in 1948.

The present Cape May station was built by the Navy during World War II as a warehouse and disbursing center. The station is one of the busiest search and rescue operations in the world, averaging more than 1,100 missions a year.

The station also conducts vigorous maritime law enforcement and marine environmental protection programs. The Coast Guard is also responsible for enforcing the 200-mile limit for foreign fishermen.

In 1964, a Sub-Search and Rescue Unit was organized at Fortescue, staffed by a half-dozen men and one boat supplied by the Cape May Station. In its first year, the SAR unit handled 100 cases and in recent years has responded to 250 calls annually.

The Cape May Station maintains a flotilla of small boats to keep the Jersey Shore safe for public use and commercial and sport boating traffic. The vessels include one 44-foot motor lifeboat, three 41-foot utility boats, a 21-foot Boston Whaler Revenge and two trailerable 14-foot Boston Whaler skiffs.

The biggest in the fleet is the U.S.C.G. Alert, a 210-foot cutter with a range of 2,700 miles. Her missions include search and rescue, law enforcement and military readiness.

Some 1,200 personnel are assigned to the Cape May Station and its related operations, with an annual budget of nearly $7 million. Group stations are located at Sandy Hook, Manasquan Inlet, Shark River, Atlantic City, Great Egg, Beach Haven, Barnegat, Cape May, Townsend Inlet, Indian River, Gloucester City and Manasquan.

The Navy and Marine Corps have played a role in Cape May's military development. The first Marine aeronautical company was trained in a seaplane operation at the Cape May Air Station on Oct. 14, 1917.

On Dec. 4, the Navy began to use the site. Seaplane and dirigibles, put into service for anti-submarine patrols, were also based there. The Navy station was called Camp Wissahickon.

The Coast Guard Air Station was founded in 1926, the second in the nation after the Gloucester, Mass. station. In those days the Coast Guard concentrated on rum-running activities.

On June 25, 1935, a national and international speed record was set at Cape May by pilot Richard L. Burke, who reached 174 mph carrying a payload of 2,500 pounds. Two days later Burke set the world altitude record for seaplanes at 18,100 feet.

In addition to seaplanes, the Coast Guard today uses Sikorsky Sea Guard helicopters for rescue and surveillance. An air rescue team is also in Wildwood.

Lakehurst Naval Engineering Center

From takeoff to touchdown, the airplanes bearing the Navy's insignia are put through their aerial and aerodynamic paces at the Lakehurst Naval Engineering Center in Ocean County. From research and development through testing and final evaluation, the Navy's latest flying machines, together with the Air Force's, have given the United States military the critical advantage in the skies.

The most expensive Navy operation in New Jersey is the

The first successful barricade test of an F-18 Hornet took place at Lakehurst.

Military personnel raise the flag at Naval Weapons Station Earle in Colts Neck.

$150 million-a-year Lakehurst Engineering Center, which boasts the largest hangar in the world and, at one time, was the Navy's home of the lighter-than-air "blimps."

Situated on an 11.5-square-mile flat sandy tract in the Pinelands, the naval center is valued at some $350 million. More than 5,000 civilians and military personnel are employed at the center.

There are several testing areas on the base, including helicopter landing pads and impact sites for simulated crashes.

The base also provides rotating classes for training 450 Navy personnel.

The world's largest aircraft—a structure connecting parts of four helicopters with a blimp—was unveiled in 1984 at the Lakehurst center. At 187 feet wide and 110 feet high, the "Heli-Stat" superplane is wider than an aircraft carrier, taller than a 10-story building and 43 feet longer than a football field.

Designed to lift 24 tons, or 8 tons more than military helicopters, the Heli-Stat will be used to harvest timber from remote woodlands in the Pacific Northwest and Alaska that are inaccessible by roads.

Earle Naval Weapons Station

The finest loading pier on the East Coast is operated by the Navy for its weapons depot in Colts Neck, Monmouth County, a picture-postcard venue of thoroughbred horses and prized bulls grazing along a serene countryside.

The Navy chose that 12,500-acre site in 1943 for just that reason: To be away from metropolitan bridges, tunnels, commercial and manufacturing facilities.

The 2.9-mile loading pier at nearby Leonardo, the only one of its type on the Atlantic seaboard, is part of an 8,000-acre waterfront that is home for five ammunition ships: The USS Nitro, Butte, Suribachi, Seattle and Detroit.

Named after Rear Adm. Ralph Earle, chief of the Bureau of Ordnance during World War I, the weapons station is connected to the Leonardo port, with its six deep-water berths, by 14 miles of rail lines and paved roads owned and patrolled by the government.

The $100-million-a-year, round-the-clock operation involves more than 1,000 civilian and military employes. The Navy values the Monmouth County weapons investment at more than $60 million. That includes military laboratories, huge ammunition magazines, living quarters and administrative buildings.

The U.S. Environmental Protection Agency (EPA) operates a 667-foot-long test tank at Earle for oil and hazardous materials investigations. The tank is filled with either fresh or salt water to study the impact of oil and toxic waste spills.

The largest tenant at Earle is the Mobile Mine Assembly Group. MOMAG maintains a stockpile of bottom and moored mines weapons.

Picatinny Arsenal

It has been known by many names, but most Jerseyans still think of it as the Picatinny Arsenal in Morris County.

During the Civil War, the federal government began a search for a depot where explosives could be stored in large quantities and where powder mills might be erected. In November 1879, nine potential sites were narrowed down to one in Morris County.

In July 1880, Congress appropriated $62,750 for the purchase of 1,866 acres in Rockaway Township. It was an ideal site for an arsenal, lying in a 10-mile-long valley between mountain ridges, which served as natural barricades.

The locals called it the Dover Powder Depot, the "Piccatinny" Powder Depot, the United States Powder Depot and, finally, Picatinny Arsenal. Picatinny is an Indian word meaning "peak with broken rocks and cliffs." It is a graphic description of the most prominent mountain peaks.

The area was rich in iron ore and water resources. During the Colonial period, Morris County flourished with mines, forges, furnaces and ironworks. The iron operations helped Washington win the Revolution.

Over the years, the federal government added more acreage to its Picatinny site, bringing it to its present size of 6,491 acres, 308 of which are lakes and ponds.

Construction of the first magazine after the Army took over the property began in September 1880. It was designed to hold 10,000 barrels of black powder and cost $51,700 to build. Four more magazines were built, along with stables, officers' quarters and other service structures.

A few years before the Spanish-American War, the post began assembling powder charges for cannons. The propellant-charge loading in 1898 was Picatinny's first production activity.

In 1902, the Army needed a place to store sodium nitrate used in armor-piercing projectiles. That began Picatinny's second phase of development. Six projectile sheds and some nitrate buildings were erected.

The third phase of the arsenal's development got under way in 1906 with the construction of the Army's first powder factory at a cost of $165,000.

When World War I broke out, Picatinny was producing all sizes of propellant, from .30-caliber to 16-inch for every weapon from the rifle to the coastal gun.

The development and manufacture of pyrotechnic signals and flares in the 1930s took these explosives out of the "fireworks" class.

When the Nazi armies pushed the Allies into the sea at Dunkirk, Picatinny Arsenal was the only plant in the United States

Star-Ledger Photo

A tank is destroyed by Copperhead artillery developed at Picatinny Arsenal.

capable of turning out artillery ammunition, bombs, high explosives, pyrotechnics, fuses and other ordnance items in massive quantities.

Between July 1939 and September 1942, more than 7.5 million bomb fuses, almost 20 million boosters, 44 million artillery primers, 39 million artillery fuses and countless millions of other munitions were manufactured at the Army post.

The largest employer in Morris County, Picatinny today is formally named AARADCOM—the Army Armament Research and Development Center. It is a billion-dollar headquarters employing 6,000 civilians and 200 military personnel.

Among the tenants at the armament center is the New Jersey Civil Air Patrol (CAP).

Naval Air Propulsion Center

Aerospace, chemical and civil engineers and technicians make up the majority of the work force at the Naval Air Propulsion Center just outside of Trenton.

Located on a 77-acre tract next to the Mercer County Airport, the propulsion center employs more than 600 civilian and military personnel with an annual budget of more than $25 million.

The center's mission is essentially the testing of jet engines. Aircraft propulsion sytems, components and accessories are evaluated and tested almost 24 hours a day, in addition to lubrications and fuels used in the systems.

All prototype engines considered for use by the military are sent to the 50-building center for a series of extensive tests and evaluations.

The center also works with propulsion systems considered the "engines of the future," a technology straight out of "Star Wars."

The White House rose garden scene from "Annie" filmed at Monmouth College in West Long Branch. Featured are young Aileen Quinn and Albert Finney.

MOVIEMAKING

Around this rugged Pacific northwestern-like terrain abound quaint New England-type towns, a bustling megalopolis and stretches of solid suburbia.

Next to these stunningly diverse settings lie sleepy villages and farms and a peacefully primitive area reminiscent of the Bayou country.

Adding to that environmental tour de force are low midwestern-style flatlands ... ancient backwoods hiding remnants of hillbilly life ... sandy coastal plains confronting crashing ocean waves ... and the glittering casino and resort capital of America.

Can this be a Hollywood back lot with its mechanically shifting cardboard/plastic scenery vainly imitating America's magnificent natural and man-made wonders?

No, it's New Jersey: 5 million richly contrasting acres that have been aptly described as "America in miniature" by National Geographic magazine, which finds this unique, 50-mile-wide peninsula (home of all of the above plus a futuristic high-tech economy) to be "The State of Surprise!"

So much so, in fact, that New Jersey is once again becoming Movieland, U.S.A.

The motion picture industry began when Thomas Alva Edison developed the movie camera—and first "talkie"—in his West Orange laboratory from 1887-89, also the site of the first movie studio, The Black Maria, so-named because it resembled a police paddy wagon.

The flexible film Edison used in his first "flicker" was invented by a Newark clergyman, the Rev. Hannibal Goodwin. His house still stands on lower Broad Street by the old Erie-Lackawanna railroad station.

The first full-length feature film—"The Great Train Robbery"—was made in Caldwell by director Edwin S. Porter. The 11-minute silent classic was literally cranked out by hand in 1903.

The first western, "A Cowboy Escapade," was produced by Centaur Studio, Bayonne. The year was 1907.

Pathe, the pioneering French filmmaker, set up studios in Jersey City and Bound Brook and produced such boxoffice hits as "The Perils of Pauline," from which the word "cliffhanger" came into the language. Among Pauline's perils was hanging from the Palisades cliffs, the movies' first breathtaking backdrop.

The 1908 motion picture "Biograph" launched director D.W. Griffith's career in New Jersey.

Louis Selznick started his first production company in Fort Lee, as did William Fox (20th Century Fox).

Fort Lee, until World War I, was the motion picture capital of the world. Perfecting their silent, black-and-white picture craft in New Jersey studios were Mary Pickford, Douglas Fairbanks, Rudolph Valentino, Lillian Gish, Lionel Barrymore, Fatty Arbuckle and Pearl White.

The technology and esthetics of filmmaking were experimentally refined in the Garden State.

Even after Hollywood lured filmmakers to a year-round sunny and warm outdoor studio, New Jersey continued to be the preferred "reality" for such gritty storytelling as Elia Kazan's "On the Waterfront," starring Marlon Brando; the offbeat rock musical "Hair;" "Midnight Cowboy;" "Ragtime," and Woody

Allen's "Annie Hall," the first in a series of Allen productions made in New Jersey.

The Monmouth College campus was the site of the most expensive movie musical ever made, the $50 million "Annie," directed by Oscar-winning John Huston.

And, of course, Burt Lancaster's award-winning "Atlantic City" was made in the famous boardwalk resort, co-starring Susan Sarandon of Edison and Metuchen.

Movie/TV Commission

The renewed popularity of New Jersey as an ideal location, replacing the tinseled look of Hollywood, led to the creation in 1977 of the New Jersey Motion Picture and Television Commission.

Pulitzer Prize-winning playwright Sidney Kingsley of Oakland, the commission's first chairman, and Joseph Friedman of Upper Montclair, executive director, can look back within the brief span of seven years at a $150 million motion picture success story.

That investment, as of 1984, represents more than 550 full-length feature films produced in New Jersey since 1977, more than 500 television series and specials, hundreds of shorts and documentaries, more than 1,000 TV commercials and as many as 15 special photography settings a year for still commercials and magazine and newspaper layouts.

Hollywood is keeping its Technicolored eye on New Jersey. The Hollywood Reporter, among other publications, carried this headline recently: "Studio Focus of New Jersey Plans to Attract Filmmakers."

Star-Ledger Photo

Upper right: Actors in "The Perils of Pauline" perch high atop the Palisades while filming the first "cliffhanger."

Right: Elia Kazan, left, directs Marlon Brando and Eva Marie Saint in the 1950's classic, "On the Waterfront," made in Hoboken.

Lower right: A film within a film was shot along the beaches of Spring Lake for "Ragtime," a period movie about life in the 1920s.

Below: Burt Lancaster and Susan Sarandon in Louis Malles' "Atlantic City," filmed on the famous boardwalk.

Courtesy: N.J. Motion Picture & Television Commission

Star-Ledger Photo

Star-Ledger Photo

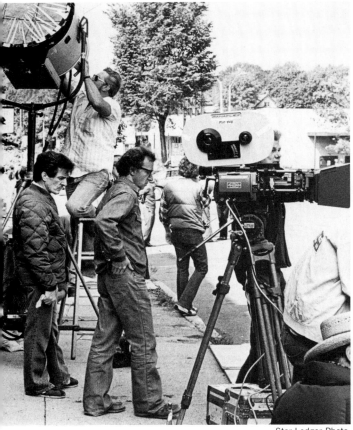

Woody Allen near camera location of film being shot at the Englewood railroad station.

Star-Ledger Photo

Dustin Hoffman, dressed as character Dorothy Michaels, films "Tootsie" at the Plaza West Shopping Center in Fort Lee.

Star-Ledger Photo

Courtesy: N.J. Motion Picture & Television Commission

Mike Antunes and Michael Pare in a scene from "Eddie and the Cruisers," filmed on location throughout South Jersey. Martin Davidson directed this nostalgic musical-drama.

Star-Ledger Photo

Robert Brooks, the director of "Tattoo," watches Bruce Dern as "Karl" walking on the dock during the filming in Ocean City.

The state's own house of horrors, the "Amityville" homestead in Toms River, caused shudders in many a moviegoer.

Star-Ledger Photo

In the planning stage is a $10 million project to convert 80,000 square feet above the Erie Lackawanna train station in Hoboken—just 15 minutes from Times Square—into five or six sound stages.

Hoboken Stages is entering a 60-year lease with the Hoboken Transit Authority. The project is being developed by Jerome Kretchmer, New York City's first environmental administrator in 1970. Kretchmer also wants to form his own production company, to be led by actor-director Patrick O'Neal, chairman of Hoboken Stages.

Friedman says the Hoboken venture will encompass sound studios for recordings, as well as a major video center for television productions.

Jersey Genre

A new American genre of filmmakers finds the real world, especially New Jersey, a favorite working milieu.

John Sayles, a young award-winning short story and screen writer, started his independent filmmaking career from the kitchen table of his Hoboken home. He turned out the nostalgic "Return of the Secaucus Seven" for something like $60,000 in 1981, editing his next-to-nothing budget flick on the kitchen table.

Sayles' next movie, "Baby, It's You," was set in Trenton in 1967 and was released in 1983 by Paramount Pictures. Time magazine movie reviewer Richard Corliss says Sayles' movies, which include "The Lady in Red" and "Alligator," "look as if they were made by a fly on the wall that had an advanced degree in psychology."

The New Jersey writer-director, Corliss adds, is "as always, wise and fair to his mismatched characters."

Filmmakers from Hollywood (Jon Peters and Charles Joffe) and Europe (Dino and Federico De Laurentiis) have come to expect the unexpected in New Jersey.

For openers, they'll find more than 50 identifiable ethnic groups, from Armenians and American Indians to Syrian-Armenians and Ukranians, with their own unique communities and customs . . . a 7,000-seat wooden tabernacle with an accompanying tent colony . . . an authentic Wild West City . . . 72 airports . . . a privately owned rail line . . . auto racing: Stocks, drag, dirt track, midgets, dune buggies . . . an 800-foot-long aircraft hangar containing the deck of an aircraft carrier . . . a rodeo with wild Brahma bull riding, steer wrestling and calf roping . . . more than 1,000 acres of game farms . . . more than 120 standardbred horse breeding farms . . . the largest flea market in the East . . . a modern sports complex with the world's number one harness track . . . a 250-acre fish hatchery with 262 pools and ponds . . . more than 3,000 lakes and ponds and 6,000 miles of waterways . . . a copper mine . . . wagon roads . . . an Indian reservation . . . and America's oldest operating lighthouse.

As Tom Edison discovered a century ago, it's easier and less expensive to make movies in New Jersey than in New York City. And that, commission director Friedman believes, will make New Jersey the place to create cinematic magic in the 1980s.

He points with pride to a growing list of features, commercials and other lens creations being distributed worldwide with that "New Jersey look."

In the feature film category are "Sophie's Choice," starring New Jersey's own Meryl Streep of Bernardsville; scenes from "Tootsie"; "The Amityville Horror," "Amityville: The Possession" and "Amityville 3D," which feature a "haunted" house in Lakewood that has spooked millions of moviegoers; Woody Allen's "Stardust Memories" and "Broadway Danny Rose"; Carlo Ponti's "The Rip-Off;" "Lovesick," starring Dudley Moore; "The Fan;" "The Idolmaker;" "Tattoo;" Martin Scorcese's "The King of Comedy" with Jerry Lewis, a native of Newark, and Robert DeNiro; "Rich and Famous;" "The World According to Garp;" "The Bell

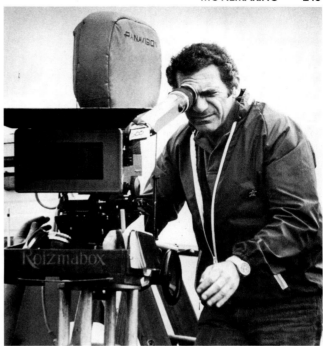

Star-Ledger Photo

Sidney Pollack, director of "Tootsie," views the camera angle for a scene in the Plaza West Shopping Center in Fort Lee.

Jar;" "Mother's Day;" "Friday the 13th;" "Gloria," and Neil Simon's "I Ought to Be in Pictures."

Some television productions (TV movies) have been: "Invasion of Privacy," "Rage of Angels," "Dream House," "The Rules of Marriage," "For Ladies Only," and "Anna to the Infinite Power," starring Dina Merrill.

Among TV series and specials have been: "Walter Cronkite's Universe," "Omni," "The Body Human," "The Right to Know," "A Salute to Mother's Day" and "Clowns."

Television commercials made in New Jersey have promoted just about every consumer product from aspirins to zoos. Just in case you forgot, here are a handful of samplers: Atari Space Invaders, Sony, Hallmark Cards, Chevrolet, Ford, Oldsmobile, Honda, Volvo, Volkswagen, Mercedes-Benz, Jaguar, Toyota, Plymouth, Prudential, Polaroid, Pepsi, Coke, 7-Up, Dr Pepper, Canada Dry, McDonald's, Burger King, Rolaids, Kool-Aid, Hershey's Kisses, Quaker Oats, Birds Eye, Canon and Chinon cameras, Campbell Soups, Tootsie Roll, Gulf Oil, Time-Life Books, E.F. Hutton, Saks Fifth Avenue, Chock Full O'Nuts, Kellogg's, Sara Lee, Old Spice, Geritol, Ivory Soap, Raisin Bran, Lowenbrau, Miller beer, London Fog and Sergio Valente.

The 'Can Do' State

Friedman likes to think of New Jersey as the "can do" state. Quite simply, there's nothing New Jersey cannot do in the way of making a motion picture, Friedman boasts. He cites some dramatic examples:

• A blackout in Hillsdale, Bergen County, for the movie "Alone in the Dark."

• A "controlled fire" in a shopping center in Closter for the same production.

• A chase sequence on Route 9W during midday for "So Fine."

• Finding and delivering thousands of roses for the White House Rose Garden sequence of "Annie."

• A plane flying through a house at Lincoln Park Airport for "The World According to Garp."

• A stuntman jumping free-fall from the top girder of the Dunes Casino-Hotel construction site in Atlantic City for "The Tempest."

• Emergency housing for an entire film crew at a church in Cream Ridge, Monmouth County, during the shooting of "Split."

• Sectioning off an area of Campgaw Mountain County Reservation in Bergen County to film a bear and a wild cougar for a sequence from "The Outdoorsters," which, just coincidentally, reflects the theme of New Jersey's official state magazine, New Jersey Outdoors, published by the Department of Environmental Protection.

The wildlife scene shows the unlimited range of New Jersey's natural and human resources. Although the most urbanized state in the nation, New Jersey is still 60 percent woodlands, farmlands and parklands.

• The rental of a half-dozen four-wheel drive vehicles to maneuver cast and crew members of "Creepshow" through the dunes at Island Beach State Park in Ocean County.

• Filming in residences, office buildings, factories, farms, churches, empty lots, hotels, parks, prisons, courthouses, main streets, theaters . . . the list is as long as the 567 communities and 21 counties that constitute the nation's fourth smallest state supporting the greatest development and population density, including the most number of cars, roadways and restaurants per square mile of living space.

Rave Reviews

Movie fans and critics are perhaps easier to please than those who produce, direct and star in the films distributed by MGM, Paramount, Columbia, 20th Century Fox or Warner Bros.

The most valuable praise that can be bestowed on New Jersey as an historic film colony comes directly from the artists who create the final video, 16mm, 35mm or 70mm product.

After filming all or part of their projects in New Jersey, the directors and producers often critique those who make location shooting possible, from the electricians and carpenters to the meteorologists, who provide the rain clouds and sunshine with a greater predictability than an Atlantic City oddsmaker.

Some of the responses from filmmakers working in New Jersey are:

• **Milos Forman**, director of "Hair": "Why more filming doesn't go on in New Jersey, I don't know. Locations are there and cooperation from the New Jersey film people was tops."

• **Lester Persky**, producer of "Hair": "Not the least of the

Star-Ledger Photo

Actress Sophia Loren arrives on the set of "Firepower," in Clifton, accompanied by the film's director, Michael Winner.

plusses that we got from shooting in New Jersey—and there were plenty—was the money we saved."

• **Federico De Laurentiis**, producer of "King of the Gypsies": "I will strongly recommend to my fellow filmmakers the value of filming in New Jersey."

• **Charles Joffe**, producer of Woody Allen's films: "We had splendid cooperation, and New Jersey is a joyful state in which to work."

• **Ronald Saland and Elliot Geisinger**, co-producers of "The Amityville Horror": "We had a tough location shoot, but because of the professionalism of our director, cast, crew and the great cooperation of the N.J. Film Commission, we wrapped right on schedule."

• **Jon Peters**, producer of "The Eyes of Laura Mars": "We're grateful to (former) Gov. Brendan Byrne and the film commission for their invaluable cooperation during the shooting of 'Eyes.'"

• **Lloyd Kaufman**, producer of "Squeeze Play," shot entirely in New Jersey: "Our TROMA team specializes in cutting costs. That's why we'll be going back to New Jersey again."

• **Joe Wizan**, producer of MGM's "Voices": "The cooperation in New Jersey was fantastic!"

• **Raymond R. Homer**, executive producer of "The Rip-Off": "We save money each day by shooting on this side of the (Hudson) river."

MUSIC

New Jersey Symphony Orchestra.

*T*he sounds of music can be heard everywhere in New Jersey, a state where the beat goes on and on, and it's getting more upbeat all the time.

More than 2,000 bands, orchestras, symphonies, choirs, choruses, chorales, chamber singers and ensembles, opera and music theaters, barbershop quartets, Sweet Adelines, and drum and bugle corps play and perform the full spectrum of vocal and instrumental music in just about every city, suburb and farm community in the Garden State.

In hundreds of auditoriums, stadiums, concert halls and performing arts centers, New Jersey's vibrant musical community presents a year-round festival of natural and synthetic sounds, from pop, classical, jazz, rock, country, folk and ethnic, to spiritual, gothic, baroque, medieval, primitive and futuristic.

In June 1980, a landmark concert at the Meadowlands sports/entertainment complex in East Rutherford made "Country Sunday" the biggest and most ambitious country music event in the Northeast, drawing more than 26,000 spectators of all ages.

Waterloo Village in Sussex County is the host of the official Bluegrass Festival in the northeastern United States.

The Jazz Hall of Fame is a permanent fixture at Rutgers University, while the Rock Capital of America is ensconced at The Capitol Theater in Passaic, under the youthful direction of rock impresario John Scher.

The solid body electric guitar, the dominant rock sound since the 1950s, was invented by Les Paul of Mahwah, a gifted musician who was also the first to do multiple tapings with his singing wife, Mary Ford. Their records sold millions in the 1950s, and their multiple-voice, echo-chamber effect was imitated by recording artists around the world.

* * *

New Jersey is the birthplace of many stylistically innovative singers: Frank Sinatra from Hoboken, Bruce Springsteen, Freehold; Sarah Vaughan, Newark; Dionne Warwick, East Orange; Connie Francis, Bloomfield; Melanie, Ocean Township; Frederica Von Stade, the mezzo-soprano opera star, Somerville, and John Travolta, Englewood.

Capitalizing on New Jersey's dynamic music scene, country singer Johnny Cash has teamed up with rock musician Eddie Van Halen, to take over the Asbury Park Convention Hall and convert it into a musical mecca on the Jersey Shore. It was in the Asbury Park boardwalk bars and bistros where Springsteen developed his earthy, almost spiritual rock style.

One of the most popular patriotic songs of all time, sung perhaps by every pupil in the country, is "America the Beautiful," composed in the late 19th Century by Samuel Ward of Newark.

Over the years, New Jersey has become the testing ground for countless vocalists and musicians working both here and in New York and Philadelphia, resulting in a proliferation of musical groups, most of them professional.

The New Jersey Orchestra Association lists no fewer than 50 community orchestras appealing to almost every musical taste. The Plainfield Symphony is one of the 10 oldest community symphonies in America.

Here's a representative sampling of some of New Jersey's popular musical ensembles, reflecting a broad range of grass-roots support:

The Adelphi Chamber Orchestra of Old Tappan ... the BAC Elysium Chorale with the Battleground Arts Center in Freehold ... the Bergen Philharmonic Orchestra operating out of Teaneck High School and Dwight Morrow High School in Englewood ... the Elizabeth Civic Orchestra from Kenilworth ... the Garden State Philharmonic Symphonic Orchestra, Toms River High School ... the Garden State Sinfonia, Pompton Plains ... Hoffmann La Roche Sinfonietta, attached to the Roche Pharmaceutical Co. in Nutley-Clifton ... the Lakeland Youth Symphony at Mountain Lakes High School ... the Livingston Community Symphony ... the New Philharmonic of Northwest New Jersey in Montclair ... the New Jersey Symphony Orchestra, Newark ... and the Trenton Symphonette.

For opera fans, there are at least 13 specialized organizations offering everything from Mozart's "The Marriage of Figaro" to Wagner's Ring Cycle. Among the diverse groups are Family Opera in North Bergen ... Camerata Opera Theatre in Cherry Hill ... Montclair Operetta Club ... the New Jersey State Opera, Newark ... Opera Classics in Paramus ... and the Ridgewood Gilbert & Sullivan Opera.

Scores of choral groups have brought New Jersey worldwide acclaim, the leading ones being the Westminster Choir and American Boychoir of Princeton, the Newark Boys Chorus and the Masterwork Chorus in Morristown. Others include Abendmusik at St. Paul's Church in Westfield ... Bach Chorale at Trinity Church in Asbury Park ... the Chamber Singers at Middlesex County College in Edison ... the Chorale Polonaise in Hackensack ... the Eatontown Chorallers ... the Elysium Chorale at the Battleground Arts Center, Freehold ... the New Jersey Schola Cantorum in Plainfield ... the Orpheus Club in Glen Rock ... and the Shining Light in Red Bank.

And then there's a variety of "other music" to please any ear for any occasion: The American Legion Band of Hudson County ... the American Guild of Organists in Dumont ... the Bergen Baroque Ensemble, Hawthorne ... the Bergen County Music Educators ... the Cecillian Club of Englishtown ... the Cranbury Consort ... the Dante Alighieri Institute in Jersey City ... the Folk Music Society of Northern New Jersey, Maplewood ... the Gothic Consort Early Music Ensemble, Jersey City ... the Masterwork Music and Art Foundation, Morristown ... the Middletown Folk Festival ... the Monmouth County Wind Ensemble in Red Bank ... the New Jersey Classic Guitar Society, Englishtown ... the New Jersey Jazz Society ... the New Jersey Wind Symphony, West Caldwell ... the North Hudson Girls Fife, Drum & Bugle Corps, Jersey City ... the Ocean County String Band in Toms River ... the Swiss Band of Hudson County in Union City ... the Tic Toc Children's Series in Ridgewood ... and the Unity Institute Concerts in Montclair.

There's even an outfit that bills itself as the Lost Weekend Swamp Stompers.

And then there's the crowd-pleasing Hawthorne Caballeros. Anyone who's ever watched the Macy's Thanksgiving Day Parade, the Tournament of Roses New Year's Parade, or has sat through the half-time of a college or pro football game has witnessed one of the nation's great drum and bugle corps, the Hawthorne Cabal-leros, five times world champions in the American Legion competition and the national champs a record 15 times.

The 128-piece band, smartly dressed in black trousers, red sashes and black sombreros, plays sharp Latin rhythmic pieces dominated by drums, bugles and xylophones. Playing under the direction of James Costello since its formation in 1946, the Hawthorne Caballeros have become America's musical ambassadors, having been sent to Cuba by the State Department in 1955 after Castro's takeover of the Caribbean island. They were also on hand to greet Queen Elizabeth when she visited New Jersey in 1977.

After a long hiatus, the Garfield Cadets were crowned the best drum and bugle corps in the world in August 1983 following the Drum Corps' international competition in Miami.

America's oldest competing corps, with a charter dating back to President Franklin Roosevelt's first term, the Garfield Cadets were recognized as the greatest corps in the land during the 1940s and early '50s. They were the first corps to be inducted into the Drum Corps Hall of Fame.

Along with the Golden Knights of Newark, which won the American Legion national championship and the World Open Contest in 1963, the Garfield Cadets and the Hawthorne Cabelleros have made New Jersey a sort of drum corps capital of the world.

Symphony Orchestras

The New Jersey Symphony Orchestra began as the Montclair Orchestra on Nov. 22, 1922 before 100 listeners at the Montclair Art Museum. It was then a string orchestra under the direction of Philip James.

By the 1927-28 season, the symphony orchestra grew into a full complement of strings, winds, brass and percussion and presented concerts with many distinguished artists. The Montclair Orchestra merged that season with the Haydn Orchestra in East Orange to form the New Jersey Symphony Orchestra.

In 1972, the New Jersey Symphony Orchestra, made up of 82 musicians, was named one of America's major symphonies by the

Tenor George Shirley, artistic director of the New School for the Arts, performs with mezzo-soprano Janice Taylor during a concert at the Montclair Art Museum.

Star-Ledger Photo

Symphony Hall in Newark provides an opulent setting for music performed by the New Jersey Symphony Orchestra.

Star-Ledger Photo

American Symphony Orchestra League, making it New Jersey's leading performing arts institution.

In the spring of 1981, the New Jersey Symphony performed to a national audience in a two-hour special tribute to George Gershwin, carried by the PBS television network.

The New Jersey Symphony has performed at Lincoln Center, Carnegie Hall, the John F. Kennedy Center for the Performing Arts in Washington, D.C., the United Nations in New York and Wolf Trap Farm Park in Virginia.

In a typical season, the New Jersey Symphony will play to more than 150,000 music lovers within the tri-state region. The symphony has been a major attraction at New York City's Harbor Festival, the Garden State Arts Center in Holmdel and the Waterloo Village Festival in Stanhope.

The New Jersey Symphony Chorus, organized in 1966, has developed into the world renowned Newark Boys Chorus.

Many outstanding international soloists have appeared with the orchestra.

* * *

The Greater Trenton Symphony Orchestra is the state capital's oldest cultural institution. Founded in 1921 by Gustav Hagedorn, the symphony's first conductor, the original orchestra contained only 40 players, compared to the 83 musicians on call today.

The construction of the War Memorial Building in 1932, with a seating capacity of more than 1,900, finally gave Trenton a suitable auditorium for cultural activities.

Today, the Greater Trenton Symphony Foundation and Scholarship holds three competitions a year: Gindhart Piano, Hobin Harp and Graham-Stahl Orchestral Instruments. A total of $3,300 is given each year to the winners.

The Trenton Symphony also sponsors free children's concerts each spring for the elementary and junior high school students in the area.

* * *

The Plainfield Symphony Orchestra is one of the 10 oldest community symphonies in the United States. Founded in 1920, the Plainfield Symphony Society was started by local musicians who formed the group and held open auditions. The symphony today numbers 79 musicians.

George Marriner Maull, who holds the baton as music director and conductor of the New Jersey Youth Symphony and as assistant conductor for the Opera Orchestra of New York, took over as conductor of the Plainfield Symphony in the 1982-83 season.

The Plainfield Symphony kicked off the classical music series at the Ritz Theatre in Elizabeth for the 1982-83 season, and has performed with the Garden State Ballet and Lyric Opera Company of Plainfield.

The symphony and opera company, along with Unicorn Productions and the Jinks, Jingle and Jerseymen Jazz Band, share the Tri-County Arts Center, the 90-year-old, Victorian-styled Elks Building in Plainfield.

Members of the Plainfield Symphony regularly get together for special chamber presentations within the community. Six full orchestral concerts are staged each season in the spacious, 1,500-seat Plainfield High School auditorium.

* * *

Garden State Philharmonic Symphony Orchestra is the product of some dedicated musicians, music lovers and some spirited civic-minded residents of Toms River, Ocean County.

Recognizing their area was ready for live symphonic music, they joined forces to organize the Garden State Philharmonic Symphony Orchestra in 1955.

In those days, Ocean County was mainly a place for tourists taking in the sea, sun and surf at the Jersey Shore.

Today, Ocean County is the fastest growing region in New Jersey and is rapidly developing into a cultural haven. The Garden State Symphony performs a fall, winter and spring concert at Toms River High School North on Old Freehold Road. The orchestra consists of 85 members, including professional musicians and others from within the community. Ages of musicians range from 15 to over 70.

In 1969, the Symphony Society organized the Garden State Philharmonic Youth Orchestra. Its 70 members are from 10 to 17 years old and are recruited from 13 communities throughout Ocean and Monmouth counties. The society sponsors annual free Young People's Concerts in area schools in conjunction with a statewide Young Artist Talent Competition.

The 1982-83 season welcomed the arrival of a new conductor, Robert Hall, music director of St. Joseph's Prep School in Philadelphia. Hall has toured with Burt Bacharach and has done recordings with The Jackson Five.

Formerly music director with the La Salle Summer Music Theater, Hall has been the principal trombonist with the Opera Company of Philadelphia and the Philly Pops. Hall has also directed the Rittenhouse Brass Quintet.

* * *

The Livingston Symphony Orchestra, under the direction of Carolyn Hill, was first heard on the evening of June 2, 1956, then playing under the name of the Livingston Community Symphony. The semi-professional musicians accompanied a local performance of "The Mikado" by Gilbert and Sullivan.

What began as a pickup orchestra was more formally organized a few months later by the Livingston High School music director, William Ruch. In the beginning, the orchestra performed for local civic groups and presented small-scale concerts in churches. Its first real public concert was presented in 1960. For its 10th anniversary, the Livingston Symphony Orchestra expanded its season to three full concerts.

Now the Livingston Symphony presents four free concerts each season, plus the annual January children's program, which is so popular that it is given twice in the same afternoon. The children's show features Allegro, the symphony clown.

The semi-professional orchestra consists of 70 musicians. Forty-five experienced nonprofessionals from Essex, Morris, Union and Passaic counties rehearse weekly, September through May, and are augumented during the concert season by 25 professionals.

Since the 1979-80 season, the Livingston Symphony has offered the following program: A Saturday evening concert in November (Thanksgiving weekend), featuring a nationally prominent soloist; a children's concert with two performances on a Saturday afternoon in January; a Saturday evening concert in March featuring the winner of the statewide Young Performers Competition; the Young Performers Competition in April for serious musicians from ages 16 through 20, and a Saturday evening concert in May featuring a special theme or New Jersey soloist.

Director/conductor Hill has been with the Livingston Symphony since 1974. She made her European conducting debut at the Mozarteum Concert Hall in Salzburg, Austria in 1967 and her New York debut at Town Hall in 1972. Hill is the founder of the New York Music Society and serves as director of the United Nations International School music programs.

* * *

The Haddonfield Symphony is an award-winning community orchestra composed of more than 100 playing members from 46 towns in South Jersey, the Delaware Valley and Pennsylvania. The regional symphony is based at Haddonfield Memorial High School.

Founded in 1952 with just 17 players, the Haddonfield Symphony has been under the guidance of Arthur Cohen since 1957. The 60-voice Symphony Chorale was established in 1977.

Star-Ledger Photo

A spray of fireworks provides the background for a concert by the New Jersey Symphony in Princeton. The Symphony's associate conductor, George Manahan, is shown in the inset.

Star-Ledger Photo

Since 1978, the Haddonfield Symphony has been recognized with three ASCAP awards for its "adventuresome" programming. ASCAP is the American Society of Composers, Artists and Performers.

The Haddonfield Symphony presents five subscription concerts during a season, featuring young artists or high school groups in performance with the symphony. Two or more special concerts each season are presented in local colleges such as Stockton, Glassboro and Rutgers/Camden.

The orchestra also sponsors an instrumental solo competition in two age groups for young musicians, the winners then going on to play in concerts with the symphony. Some have even gone on to play with the Philadelphia Orchestra and other leading symphonies in the U.S. and abroad.

A lecture-demonstration team, comprising four musicians from the symphony, gives programs in the elementary schools of Camden County. The musical combo also performs in nursing homes, art galleries and churches.

In addition to the ASCAP awards for innovative programming of 20th Century music, only one of five community orchestras in the United States to be so honored, the Haddonfield Symphony was also selected to represent South Jersey in the Friendship Force Exchange with Italy, and received a grant from Meet the Composer, the only New Jersey orchestra to receive assistance from the New York foundation.

* * *

The New Jersey Pops initiated the concept of free-to-the-public orchestral concerts in the state's shopping centers, bringing popular music directly to the consumer in the marketplace.

The year was 1977, and since then founding director-conductor Michael J. Buglio has done for New Jersey what Arthur Fiedler and his Boston Pops did in the Bay State. In one summer at Waterloo Village in Byram Township, the New Jersey Pops

Star-Ledger Photo
An exuberant Michael Buglio conducts the New Jersey Pops.

attracted some 2,000 concertgoers. The musical fare that summer was Bernstein, Tchaikovsky, Copland, Gould and Sousa.

Besides the suburban malls, the New Jersey Pops has played at the Port Newark Harbor Festival and Liberty State Park on the Hudson River waterfront, as well as at corporate concerts for AT&T and Sandoz, a pharmaceutical company in Florham Park.

The New Jersey Pop musicians are all professional, many of them affiliated with New York and New Jersey orchestras. The Pops has anywhere from 40 to 60 musicians ready to show up for rehearsal.

On Sept. 25, 1982, the New Jersey Pops gave its first performance in the full tradition of the Boston Pops, with champagne bottles "popping" and hors d'oeuvres at Convention Hall in Wildwood. As more than 1,000 people listened to the orchestra at this Burdette Tomlin Memorial Hospital fund-raiser, the organizers of the program decided to make it an annual event.

On July 1, 1983 the New Jersey Pops, with a full complement of 75 musicians, performed at Constitution Hall in the nation's capital, filling an evening with "Americana: Shades of Red, White and Blue."

From four performances in 1977, the New Jersey Pops has scheduled more than 30 performances in its current season. An estimated 10,000 people attended a recent concert in Summit when the Pops appeared with pianist Peter Duchin.

Buglio is a master's graduate of Temple University (trombone and conducting) and is the music director of the Livingston public schools.

* * *

The Cathedral Concert Orchestra, formed in 1983, is the only professional symphony orchestra based in a United States cathedral—Sacred Heart in Newark.

Star-Ledger music critic Michael Redmond found "the effect in the cathedral's cavernous space was no less than hair-raising . . . the sound rolling down the long nave like a tidal wave."

Comprising professional musicians from throughout the area, the Cathedral Concert Orchestra is under the direction of Maestro Thomas Michalak. Michael Pratt of Princeton is the assistant conductor, and Warren Brown of Hillside is the chorus director and organist.

The orchestra is a part of the popular Cathedral Concert Series, which uses the Gothic magnificence of the cathedral for its "concert hall." The orchestra combines with world-class soloists and has brought such artists as Brazilian pianist Arthur Moriera Limba, guitarist Carlos Montoya and jazz man Billy Taylor.

Many composers have had their works premiered at the cathedral. Composer Michael Hoppe of New York City presented the debut of his work "Romance," which was the musical theme for the film "Misunderstood," starring Gene Hackman.

As a multi-cultural program, the concert series also features architectural and art tours of the cathedral before each performance, and provides special programs for children and for young people at the Newark Community School of the Arts. Carole De-Senne of Montclair is the series director.

* * *

The Masterwork Chamber Orchestra is one of the brilliant showpieces of the Masterwork Music and Art Foundation in Morristown. Founded in 1955, the unique foundation is committed to the performance of masterful music, the presentation of visual art, dance and drama programs, and education of children and adults to standards of excellence in a variety of art forms.

The foundation sponsors a professional orchestra, the Masterwork Chorus, a Young People's Choir, the Masterwork Chamber Ensemble, the Masterwork Brass Quintet, the Masterwork School of Arts, and the Masterwork Theater and professional Repertory Company.

There's nothing quite like the Masterwork Foundation anywhere in America.

Since its inception, the Masterwork Foundation has produced more than 250 concerts, 60 Young Artists Concerts, 25 Boy Choir Concerts, 38 plays and 225 summer sings.

The Masterwork Chorus and Orchestra present a rich repertoire, which includes the best of Bach, Beethoven, Berlioz, Brahms, Handel, Monteverdi, Mozart, Purcell, Vivaldi and other equally time-honored composers.

Serious American works are frequently performed, including those of New Jersey composers Walter Giannini, Ulysses Kay, Dorothy Priesing and Ellen Wolcott.

Members of the chorus range in age from mid-teens to the 70s and membership exceeds 650, of whom 125 to 235 will sing at any one time. Masterwork singers come from 15 of New Jersey's 21 counties, while other chorus members commute to weekly rehearsals from Villanova, Pa.; Brooklyn, Kingston, Manhattan and Scarsdale, N.Y.

The Masterwork Chorus has been billed more than 200 times in Carnegie Hall, Avery Fisher Hall in Lincoln Center and New York's Town Hall. It also performs in Newark Symphony Hall, the Garden State Arts Center, the Paper Mill Playhouse and the John F. Kennedy Center for the Performing Arts in Washington, D.C.

The Morristown chorus was chosen by Eugene Ormandy to sing under his direction with the Philadelphia Orchestra in a concert in Newark Symphony Hall and in the New Jersey Bicentennial performance in Princeton.

Music Journal, a national magazine, designated Masterwork "one of the 25 outstanding choruses in America." In addition to concerts and recordings, broadcasts of rehearsals and performances have been heard throughout 76 stations of the National Association of Educational Broadcasters, BBC, Radio France, Rome Radio and WRUL network of South America.

Choirs

The Westminster Choir (and college) in Princeton was the first choir to broadcast from Russia to the United States in 1934 and was the first to appear in a live telecast from Lincoln Center in 1980.

The Westminster Choir, shown at its Princeton home.
Star-Ledger Photo

Founded in 1920, Westminster Choir College occupies a 23-acre campus in Princeton, a place where music greets you from every direction—a choir rehearsal in the playhouse, a voice lesson in a professor's studio in Williamson Hall, piano and organ music from the practice rooms in one of the dormitories.

Everyone at Westminster is a musician, where music is both the medium and the message. A typical student body includes more than 300 enrolled in the four-year undergraduate program, more than 60 graduate students working toward the Master of Music degree, and more than 30 special non-degree students.

At the center of the curricula are the large choirs: The Chapel Choir, Oratorio Choir and Symphonic Choir. Smaller ensemble experience is provided by the Westminster Choir, Westminster Singers and Master Singers.

The Symphonic Choir has performed hundreds of times and made many recordings with the principal orchestras of New York, Philadelphia, Washington, Pittsburgh, Boston and Atlanta. Choir conductors have included Toscanini, Stokowski, Steinberg, Ormandy, Bernstein, Shaw and Mehta.

Westminster holds the distinction of being the chorus-in-residence at both the Festival of Two Worlds in Spoleto, Italy and at the Spoleto Festival, U.S.A., in Charleston, S.C. In 1934, the Westminster Choir singers were the first official American guests of the Soviet Union. They also sang at the dedication ceremonies of the 1938 and 1964 World Fairs in New York.

The 40 choir singers are chosen by audition from the 450 fine musicians on the Westminster campus. The choir's repetoire ranges in style from the Josquin to Messiaen and Penderecki, both a cappella and accompanied.

Under the direction of Joseph Flummerfelt, the Westminster Choir can adapt to a tone or style, be it baroque, romantic, classical, contemporary, folk or spiritual.

The choir has made more than 60 recordings. Messiaen's "The Transfiguration of Our Lord Jesus Christ" won Le Prix du President de la Republique of the Academie du Disque Francais. A recording of the Haydn "Lord Nelson Mass" with the New York Philharmonic won a Grammy nomination for Leonard Bernstein and Flummerfelt.

In 1978, the college established its own Westminster Choir label and has so far released the J.S. Bach "Six Motets," "Christmas with The Westminster Choir," "The Westminster Choir Sings Folk Songs," and Missa "O Pulchritudo" of Gian Carlo Menotti.

* * *

The American Boychoir is another Princeton institution considered to be America's foremost concert boys' choir. The Smithsonian's performing arts division rates the American Boychoir "better than the vaunted boychoirs from across the Atlantic."

Founded in 1937 as the Columbus Boychoir, its classical repertoire has entertained audiences in more than 20 countries on four continents. The Boychoir has been on State Department tours, appeared in some 2,000 towns and cities in 48 states, and has been on national television and radio with major orchestras and in special programs for presidents, popes and royalty.

The only nonsectarian boarding choir school in the western hemisphere, American Boychoir is housed in a 32-room Georgian mansion, the Albemarle Estate, on 18 wooded acres in historic Princeton. Enrollment has reached 56 students representing 11 states and Canada.

Under music director John Kuzma, the 27 choirboys, ages 11 to 14, are booked for 50 to 75 professional concerts a year throughout the United States, including Lincoln Center and Carnegie Hall.

American Boychoir has made 16 recordings, the most recent a complete "Messiah" for the Smithsonian Institution.

In 1982, the Princeton singers participated in a series of performances with the New York City Ballet in George Balanchine's new staging of "Persephone," with music by Stravinsky.

Star-Ledger Photo

President and Mrs. Reagan enjoy a White House performance by the American Boychoir.

Members of the Newark Boys Choir at rehearsal.

Star-Ledger Photo

In March 1983, American Boychoir celebrated the 15th anniversary of its premiere performance of Cantor Charles Davidson's "Only I Never Saw Another Butterfly." A moving cantata based on stories and poems that survived the Holocaust, "Butterfly" exemplifies in music and words the ability of the human spirit to overcome degradation, horror, brutality and even death.

The special concert was presented to educational, religious and cultural leaders, as well as friends of the school. It was dedicated to the lost children of Terezin and their inspiring message.

* * *

The Newark Boys Chorus (and school) started out quite accidentally in October 1966 as an informal group of inner-city boys who were suddenly brought together to sing the "Snowflakes Chorus" in a concert of Tchaikovsky's "The Nutcracker" with the New Jersey Symphony Orchestra and the Garden State Ballet.

Today, the 45 vocalists from diverse socioeconomic and religious backgrounds appear in at least 75 concerts a year, 20 of them in December during the holiday season.

Their repertoire is eclectic, ranging from renaissance, classical, popular, spirituals, folk, African, jazz and show tunes. Contemporary works are commissioned specifically for the Newark Boys Chorus by composer Gian Carlo Menotti and Peter Mennin.

A new commission for the chorus and the Rutgers Jazz Ensemble, "Voices of Jazz" by Paul Jeffrey, premiered March 28, 1982 at Seton Hall University and at St. Peter's Church in New York City.

The Newark Boys Chorus offers the nine- to 14-year-old singers superior academic training in affiliation with Seton Hall, as well as choral and music instruction.

Based at Newark Symphony Hall's new cultural complex, the Boys Chorus was chosen to sing the U.S. premiere of "Children's

Field" (chorus and orchestra), by Japanese composer Michio Mamiya. The work concluded the fourth annual "Music from Japan" concert at Carnegie Hall last February.

The 45 choristers learned to sing in Japanese, which some of the boys had learned during a successful tour of Japan in the fall of 1981.

Under the direction of David Butterfield, the Newark Boys Chorus has performed with leading orchestras, including the New York Philharmonic conducted by Leonard Bernstein and Pierre Boulez, the Philadelphia Orchestra with Eugene Ormandy, the Atlanta Symphony with Robert Shaw, and the New Jersey Symphony with Henry Lewis.

* * *

The North Jersey Philharmonic Glee Club is one of the oldest singing institutions in the mid-Atlantic states. From its beginning in 1939, the all-black chorus was drawn from a cross-section of the Afro-American community, representing different religious persuasions, social classes and neighborhoods.

The glee club was the vision of Dolores Collins Benjamin of Union, who was so moved by a choral festival at the old Newark Mosque in 1938 (today's Symphony Hall) that she asked some of the men to form a chorus.

The glee club's basic repertory includes some 50 songs, which the 36 men, led by a woman, can sing from memory. The woman in front of the all-male chorus is Elaine F. Jones, who started on the piano at age five, graduated from the Juilliard School of Music with a major in the organ, and studied conducting with Harry R. Wilson at Columbia University.

The chorus consists of 12 tenors, 12 baritones and 10 basses. For some members, it's a family affair. Club president Ronald Williams is following in his father's tradition, a bass. Three of Williams' uncles and a cousin are also active members.

The glee club made its New York debut in 1948 at Town Hall. Since the early post-war period, the club has performed on radio and television, in churches, hospitals, shopping centers, outdoor festivals and at Newark Symphony Hall.

Director Jones was the founder-conductor of the Polyphon Chorale and served as musical director of the Rutgers Community Theater. She has also played and sung background music for three TV specials and has performed with the Boatner Chorale.

* * *

Abendmusik at St. Paul's Church in Westfield is the first concert series in the United States to present masterpieces of the baroque with the forces for which they were composed—a choir of men and boys and an orchestra of period instruments.

Abendmusik derives its name from the baroque music series in Luebeck, Germany in the late 17th Century. Johann Sebastian Bach is said to have walked miles to hear the Luebeck concerts.

St. Paul's Choir made concert tours of England in 1966 and again in 1970. The 25 boys and men in the choir sing regularly in the New York Seasons of the Joffrey Ballet. They have also sung with the New York Philharmonic, the American Opera Society and the New York City Opera under Bernstein, Solti, Boulez and Rudel.

The Levin Baroque Ensemble is an orchestra composed of leading instrumentalists from New Jersey, New York and Washington, D.C. About 15 musicians play on original period instruments, the early versions of the violin, cello and oboe.

Among the selections performed by Abendmusik are Handel's "Masque" ("Acis and Galatea"), Bach cantatas, Haydn's "Missa Sancti Nicolai" and Purcell's "The Fairy Queen."

The baroque groups have also done incidental music for a 17th Century adaptation of Shakespeare's "A Midsummer Night's Dream."

Abendmusik was organized by Richard Connelly, the organist at St. Paul's Church.

* * *

Pro Arte Chorale performs regularly at Carnegie Hall and Lincoln Center and in Europe and throughout the United States, but its main concerts continue to take place at its church base in Ridgewood, Bergen County.

Begun in 1964 by John Coulter of Oakland, who saw a need for an amateur singing group to work at a professional level, Pro Arte Chorale consists of 85 voices, whose numbers have increased to 200 for the Festival Chorus. The large chorus has been used to create a rousing climax for Verdi's opulent and rarely performed "Four Sacred Pieces."

Rehearsals take place at the 1,000-seat Our Lady of Mt. Carmel Church in Ridgewood. Members come mostly from Bergen County, although there is a "strong Montclair contingent," plus a couple that travels from Trenton to weekly rehearsals.

The chorale is the resident art group at Bergen Community College in neighboring Paramus.

Star-Ledger Photo

Roger Nierenberg, music director of the Pro Arte Chorale.

Opera

Opera is one of the oldest forms of dramatic musical art; the word itself derives from the Latin term meaning work or labor. The New Jersey opera scene, if nothing else, is a supreme labor of love. It has survived through decades of musical fads, from the swinging band era to today's electronic, decibel-blasting rock incantations.

Keeping opera alive in New Jersey is a handful of artistic companies willing to work countless hours to make one magical moment happen, whether it's in a magnificent symphony hall or in an out-of-the-way, all-purpose community room with folding seats and a cramped stage.

Creating that special magic in New Jersey is a small but dedicated group of artists who have given opera its distinguished place within the state's cultural community.

Led by the New Jersey State Opera, based in Newark, they are the Metro Lyric Opera of Monmouth County, Opera Theater of New Jersey in Middlesex County, the Lubo Opera Company of Morris County, the Trenton Civic Opera, the Suburban Opera Theater in Essex County and Opera Classics of Bergen County.

* * *

The New Jersey State Opera is typical of the way opera has evolved in a state steeped in musical tradition.

The company began as a workshop in 1964, calling itself the Opera Theatre of Westfield. A heavily populated suburb in Union County, Westfield was the home of a number of talented women who had extensive musical training. They had chosen to raise their families rather than pursue a career in music, yet they wanted to use and share their musical talents in the community.

The Westfield women raised funds through bake sales and garage sales and organized their little opera theater, serving as cast, crew, managers and ticket-takers with members of their families.

Before the curtain went up on the first operatic production, one of the group's founders, Sally Schmalenberger, was in Newark singing in a summer concert version of "Die Fledermaus," led by a rising young conductor, Alfredo Silipigni. Schmalenberger asked the talented maestro if he would attend the fledgling opera company's premiere performance in Westfield.

Silipigni liked what he saw and heard and became the company's director. He set out to make it a professional company. The rest is history.

Silipigni prevailed upon a major artist, Salvatore Baccaloni, to sing in Rossini's "The Barber of Seville." An amateur community group overnight became a truly professional company.

From an annual start-up budget of $5,000, the Westfield Opera Company has grown into a $500,000-a-year state institution. The transition took place under the quiet leadership of Vincent Visceglia, a prominent Newark businessman, philanthropist and humanitarian who saw what was happening in Westfield and believed it could be repeated in the state's largest city and financial center.

A member of the Newark Chamber of Commerce cultural committee, Visceglia invited the Westfield group to take up residence at Newark Symphony Hall, a national historic landmark and one of the great concert halls in America.

On Nov. 6, 1968, the curtain went up at Symphony Hall for the production of Gounod's "Faust," starring South Orange resident Jerome Hines, Licia Albanese and Jerome LoMonaco. The Newark debut made the Westfield group a major opera company with statewide appeal. Its name was changed to the Opera Theatre of New Jersey and then to New Jersey State Opera in 1974.

In 1972, Jose Ferrer, star of cinema, Broadway and television specials, tested his enormous talents in "Gianni Schicchi," while other stars lined up for their Newark showcases: Beverly Sills in her first "Norma" performance in the metropolitan area; Richard Tucker's "Cielo e Mar" from "La Gioconda"; the great Italian interpreter of verismo opera, Magda Olivero, first introduced in the New York metropolitan region in her performance of "Tosca"; Birgit Nilsson's last U.S. performance in "Turandot," and fine performances by opera star Placido Domingo.

Always searching for innovative staging techniques, the state opera company imported experimental scenic projectors from Austria for its 1975 production of "Carmen," and commissioned a striking stage set for "Aida" at the Garden State Arts Center in Holmdel.

Today, the company, under the management of Harrison L. Weaver, sees state opera as satisfying the balance between "busi-

Photo Credit: Sedge Le Blang, N.Y.

Opera great Licia Albanese brought her memorable arias to stages throughout New Jersey.

ness artistry and business sense" by getting corporations to support important cultural institutions. The Silipigni-Weaver team has done just that, staging three or four major productions each season and repeating one or more a season at Trenton's War Memorial Auditorium. In addition, summer festival productions have become regular fare at the Garden State Arts Center.

Of the nation's 1,023 opera companies, only 19 have been rated "Class A" by the Central Opera Service of the Metropolitan National Council. The State Opera is one of them.

The New Jersey State Opera is currently expanding its Young Artists Program, conducting auditions throughout the state in an effort to find top quality young singers for the company's school performances and to participate in major productions.

* * *

The Metro Lyric Opera grew out of the Monmouth Opera Festival in 1959, organized by Era Tognoli, a local opera buff. The festival served as a showcase for local talent and to bring live opera to audiences in the Jersey Shore area. At the same time, Tognoli organized the Monmouth Opera Guild to support a new opera company.

In the beginning, a series of summer performances were presented in Asbury Park's Convention Hall on the Boardwalk, with professional artists mostly from New York City, and a chorus made up of talented singers from the shore area. Featured artists included Jan Peerce, Licia Albanese and Mignon Dunn.

Now an opera company in residence at Monmouth College in West Long Branch, Metro Lyric gave many young professionals the opportunity to participate in a full-scale opera production before their debut in major opera companies throughout the world.

Among them are Mignon Dunn of the Metropolitan Opera Company, who performed her first "Carmen" with Metro Lyric; Russel Christopher and Beverly Christianson, who sang with the group before being engaged by the Metropolitan, and Marta Senn, who performed her first "Carmen" with Metro in 1982 and later went on to win competitions in Paris and Baltimore, where she also did "Carmen."

Bolstered by recent successes of "Tosca," "The Merry Widow" and "Carmen," all played before capacity audiences, Metro Lyric Opera launched a special project for the 1984-85 season: A subscription series of three full-scale grand operas staged at the landmark Paramount Theater in Asbury Park. Metro's 1983-84 season offered "Cavalleria Rusticana" and "Pagliacci" at the Paramount.

Several professionals have joined Metro Lyric Opera to augment the elaborate productions. Ida Libby Dengrove, a shore resident and noted artist on the staff of NBC TV, designed and executed the "Barber of Seville" sets for workshop production, and also produced the promotional material for the company.

Anthony Stivanello, stage director, was named "Mr. Opera" by the Metropolitan Opera Company's Opera News. Stivanello is credited by Luciano Pavarotti, in his book "Pavarotti—My Own Story," for having taught him much of what he knows about stage deportment. Stivanello also furnishes Metro Lyric with authentic costumes and scenery.

Another Metro participant is Giampaolo Bracali, conductor of the Rome Opera and a teacher at the Manhattan School of Music, who has recently completed a conducting tour throughout Central and South America. Bracali assumes the responsibility of the Metro Lyric Orchestra. Members of the orchestra are drafted from area symphonies and trained by Bracali.

The New Jersey State Orchestra has collaborated with founder Tognoli in presenting such works as "Tosca" and "The Merry Widow." Tognoli's adaptation of "Madama Butterfly" was presented at Monmouth College's Pollack Auditorium in November 1982.

Metro Lyric Opera also presents workshop programs to senior citizen groups and children, including productions of "Hansel and Gretel," "Jack and the Beanstalk" and "Little Red Riding Hood."

* * *

Opera Theater of New Jersey emerged in 1977 as a training program for unemployed persons. It was originally funded by CETA, the federal Comprehensive Employment and Training Act, which has been largely phased out by the Reagan Administration.

The youthful project, now operating out of New Brunswick, has reached out to more than 100,000 residents and 60,000 school children from Cape May to Hightstown since its inception. The group offers opera, musical theater and arts-in-education programming at reasonable prices.

Artistic director Janet Stewart says Opera Theater "breaks down the myth that opera is only for the elite" by winning new friends of opera wherever her company performs.

Stewart's group, in fact, is the only professional opera company in New Jersey that performs statewide on a 12-month basis.

By the 1981-82 season, Opera Theater, in just four years, had provided more than 200 jobs for New Jersey residents. For the 1984-85 season, Opera Theater presented Donizetti's "Don Pasquale." Its holiday opera continues to be "Amahl and the Night Visitors" by Gian-Carlo Menotti.

The company continues to perform throughout the state in parks, at annual corporate meetings, in street festivals and at labor conventions.

Opera Theater is affiliated with the Middlesex County Cultural and Heritage Commission.

Star-Ledger Photo

Soprano Janet Stewart and baritone Stephen Mosel of Opera Theater of New Jersey.

* * *

Lubo Opera Company was started in 1976 by Jody Lasky, an opera singer from the smallest town in New Jersey, Guttenberg, in Hudson County, "five blocks big" and home of one of the state's most active opera companies.

Lubo, which means love in Bulgarian, came about because Lasky wanted to bring affordable opera-operetta performances into the community, while helping talented American artists unable to find work in a European opera house. Opera in Europe is heavily subsidized by government.

Lasky named her opera company Lubo after singing the lead roles in "Tosca," "Il Trovatore" and "Aida" during a five-week music festival in Sofia, Bulgaria's capital. The Sofia festival was so successful that Lasky returned for several more engagements.

Lasky was selected to sing "Tosca" for the 1974 Winterthur Festspiele in Switzerland. The soprano has always been fond of popular music, having once sang as a teenager with jazz trumpeter Dizzy Gillespie of Englewood.

With headquarters in Guttenberg and offices in Montville, the Lubo Opera Company is the only professional opera-operetta company based in the Morris-Dover area. Lubo also provides professional experience to promising orchestral musicians and classically trained dancers through its own orchestra and corps de ballet.

The company has no salaried staff and all contributions to the nonprofit operation go directly into the cost of staging its productions.

Lubo has mounted productions in Jersey City, Millburn, Morristown, Madison, Boonton, West New York and New York City.

* * *

The Jersey Lyric Opera Company has its origins in the same

community where the New Jersey State Opera was conceived: Westfield.

In its formative stages, the Lyric had no home, moving from auditorium to auditorium before taking up residence at Kean College in Union.

Founded in 1976 by Sonia Lewis, the artistic director, Lyric Opera first presented concert versions, progressing step by step to cameos and finally fully mounted productions with costumes, orchestra and sets. Lewis' goal is to bring the magic of opera, involving all of the performing arts, to the often "opera shy" general public. The company is committed to presenting young professionals with an emphasis on New Jersey talent.

Backstage, onstage and in the orchestra pit, the Lyric has been supported by numerous devoted volunteers without whom the company could not survive. With continuing support from the New Jersey Council on the Arts, Lyric Opera is attracting artists from international opera houses, who are lending their talents at minimal fees to advance the status of the young group and draw larger audiences.

Last April, Lyric presented Verdi's "Rigoletto" at Kean College, starring James Clark of the New York City Opera.

* * *

The Trenton Civic Opera was resurrected in 1979 after a long dormant period when the state capital was still remembered as an opera center during the 1930s and '40s.

The Trenton Opera Association had produced a half-dozen full-scale operas each season for a decade spanning the Depression and World War II years. They were the golden years of Trenton opera, when opera lovers from New York would travel to the city on the Delaware River to hear tenor Giovanni Martinelli and soprano Dorothy Kirsten.

In the 1950s, one production of "Faust" was staged at the War Memorial, starring Ezio Pinza, star of the Broadway musical hit "South Pacific." Performing with Pinza was his daughter, Claudia.

In 1967, Puccini's "La Boheme" was put together by the Greater Trenton Symphony. And area opera fans enjoyed periodic visits by the New Jersey State Opera to the War Memorial.

But it wasn't until the fall of 1979 that opera returned to Trenton as a serious artistic enterprise. Byron and Ernestine Steele were known to Trentonians for their Artists Showcase Opera, a modest company operating out of a renovated church since 1973.

With the advent of Gilbert and Sullivan's operetta "The Mikado," Trenton once again had an ongoing opera company presenting three productions each season. The Gilbert and Sullivan opener was followed by a Christmas production of "Amahl and the Night Visitors" and a spring surprise, Mozart's "The Magic Flute."

* * *

The Montclair Operetta Club predates New Jersey's opera organizations. The club traces its roots back to 1922 when the choir conductor of the Union Congregational Church, Arabella Cole, coached her singers into performing Gilbert and Sullivan's "Patience" at the Commonwealth Club.

Two years later, Cole's church choir staged "The Mikado" for the Woman's Club of Upper Montclair.

The singers finally organized into the Montclair Operetta Club. Its first president in 1925 was Herbert W. Dutch, principal of Montclair High School. The club's first production, "The Pirates of Penzance," opened Dec. 18, 1925. The club's founding membership totaled 24.

For its golden anniversary in 1975, the Montclair Operetta Club pieced together a half-century of operatic vignettes for a three-day gala at Mt. Hebron School, where the club has performed since the school was built in 1931.

A clubhouse was erected in 1950 and expanded in 1967. The sets are constructed in the club's studios on Valley Road.

One life member of the operetta club has been in more than 60 shows since 1945. To become a member of MOC, one has to be 18 years old and have worked in three shows.

Some MOC apprentices have gone on to Broadway assignments and leading opera productions.

Jazz

An original American art form, jazz grew up in New Jersey with the Armstrongs, Ellingtons and Luncefords introducing their experimental black beats and sounds at the Adams, Orpheum and Paramount theaters in Newark.

The history of jazz in America is preserved in the Jazz Hall of Fame at the Nicholas Music Center on the Douglass College campus of Rutgers University, New Brunswick. It was dedicated on March 27, 1983 with the first 11 members inducted into the Hall of Fame, including Louis "Satchmo" Armstrong; William "Count" Basie, a native of Red Bank; Edward Kennedy "Duke" Ellington, one of America's greatest composers; John Birks "Dizzy" Gillespie, who trumpeted in the bebop era; Benjamin David "Benny" Goodman, the "King of Swing," and Charlie "Yardbird" Parker, who revolutionized the jazz vocabulary with his bebop flights.

Each year, 11 jazz artists will be honored as permanent members of the Hall of Fame. This important part of musical history is the work of the New Jersey Jazz Society and the Institute of Jazz Studies of the Rutgers/Newark campus. The institute is the foremost archival collection of jazz and jazz-related materials under university auspices anywhere.

Housed in spacious quarters in Newark, the institute's collection consists of more than 50,000 phonograph records, numerous tapes, cylinder recordings and piano rolls; a library of some 3,000 books on jazz and related subjects, including an extensive reference component; large holdings in jazz periodicals from throughout the world, many of them extremely rare; record catalogs; exhaustive research files; photographs; films; videotapes; memorabilia; sheet music, and a collection of antique phonographs.

The Institute of Jazz was founded in 1952 by the late Dr. Marshall Stearns, a professor of medieval English literature at Hunter College, and the author of the two basic studies, "The Story of Jazz" (1956) and "Jazz Dance" (1968), the latter co-authored with his wife, Jean Stearns. In 1966 the institute's board selected Rutgers as its permanent academic home.

On April 20, 1980, Newark Mayor Kenneth A. Gibson, a former alto saxophonist, declared a Jazz Week in Newark. The major impetus for the annual affair—the first was observed in 1978—was Jazz 88, Newark's public radio station, WBGO, which devotes almost all of its programming to jazz.

The Star-Ledger's jazz reviewer, George Kanzler, has documented the history of jazz in Newark and in New Jersey. Kanzler's research and interviews with leading jazz musicians produced the following portrait of jazz in New Jersey:

• Trumpeter Leon Eason, an Armstrong disciple, led a big band at the Kinney Club (a Newark version of the Cotton Club, complete with chorus line), while Pancho Diggs conducted a big band that played dances every week at Skateland. There were also smaller jazz clubs such as the Picadilly and the Alcazar, where musicians met for jam sessions.

• Saxophonist Bobby Plater composed "Jersey Bounce" and went on to become one of the premier lead alto players in big bands. He held down that chair with Count Basie, until the saxophonist died in early 1983.

Star-Ledger Photo

Star-Ledger Photo

Star-Ledger Photo

• Gil Fuller, a bandleader, became one of the most important arrangers in jazz, orchestrating the intricacies of bebop for Dizzy Gillespie, a resident of Englewood.

• In the early 1940s, saxophonist Ike Quebec emerged from the Newark jazz scene to become a mainstay with Cab Calloway's band. "The Divine One," Sarah Vaughan, who as a teenager sat in the Picadilly, sang with Billy Eckstine and Earl Hines and established herself as one of America's greatest vocalists.

• The Mosque Theater (now Symphony Hall) presented the big bands of Ellington, Woody Herman and Stan Kenton.

• The 1970s saw a resurgence of jazz activity in Newark. Jazz Vespers became a regular Sunday afternoon tradition, now at Memorial West Church under the guidance of Newark's own jazz minister, the Rev. Jan VanArsdale.

• The Key Club and Sparky J's made the corner of Halsey and William streets Newark's own jazz corner of the world during the 1960s and '70s.

The jazz club scene not only revolved around Newark's clubs, but also Gulliver's in West Paterson. Gulliver's is currently without a home—the owner is looking for a new location—and the Newark club scene has ebbed to sporadic presentations.

But there are still clubs that regularly present jazz, with Far & Away in Cliffside Park and Struggles in Edgewater active in the Palisades area of Bergen County, The Cove in Roselle (home of pianist Morris Nanton's fine trio), and, on the edge of Newark, El-C's in East Orange, where a house band plays with guest soloists each weekend.

Although Newark presently lacks a full-time jazz club, the New Playbill Lounge brings in popular acts like Jimmy McGriff, Rhoda Scott, and Houston Person and Etta Jones occasionally. And the vitality of jazz in Newark should improve with the growing activity of a nonprofit organization founded this year, the Newark Jazz Society.

• Both Rutgers/Newark and Essex County College in Newark regularly present free jazz concert series. Arts High School sponsors a big jazz band and drummer-pianist Chick Wing and others teach jazz to children in the community.

Jazz talent of major stature also continues to emerge from Newark, Kanzler reports. Trumpeter Woody Shaw has toured Europe with his own concert ensemble. Organist Rhoda Scott is another major attraction in Europe. The list is impressively long, with names like Schnitter, Davis, Gladden, Johnson and Thomas keeping the jazz beat alive around the world.

Meanwhile, four New Jersey libraries have become jazz producers by supporting new jazz groups and sponsoring concerts and seminars at their libraries in Monmouth, Burlington, Jersey City and Plainfield.

Burlington is using bookmobiles to advertise jazz. Monmouth is presenting free concerts at its eastern branch in Shrewsbury. Free concerts and workshops are hosted by the Plainfield Library, while Jersey City is blending jazz into its "Friends of Art and Music" program.

Unity Concerts

Since its founding in 1920, Unity Concerts of Montclair has brought performances of the world's greatest artists, ensembles and attractions to North Jersey.

The first program to be produced, under the auspices of the Unitarian Church in Montclair, was the "Unity Concert Course," launched on Oct. 28, 1920 by the great violinist Fritz Kreisler. Sergei Rachmaninoff and Pablo Casals also appeared that first season.

In 1923, travel film lectures were added to Unity Institute's offerings, with such notables as poets Robert Frost and Carl Sandburg and aviation pioneer Amelia Earhart. Chamber music recitals were introduced in 1939, featuring the Budapest String Quartet.

The concert series scored the greatest success and became the hallmark of Unity Institute. The concerts have become known for the consistently high quality of the performers presented.

Some of the 20th Century's finest artists and groups have appeared in the Unity Concerts: Rachmaninoff, Heifetz, Horowitz, Padereski, Stern, Segovia, Sutherland, Horne, Rubinstein, Galway, Serkin, Kirsten, Martinelli, the Boston Symphony, the Royal Philharmonic and the Royal Winnipeg Ballet.

Unity's goal is to present popular classical music concerts by famous artists and groups and also to educate all segments of the

Star-Ledger Photo   Star-Ledger Photo

Some of the jazz musicians who put New Jersey on the music map are, left to right: John Birks "Dizzy" Gillespie, performing at the 1981 graduation ceremonies at Fairleigh Dickinson University; composer Edward Kennedy "Duke" Ellington, an honoree of Rutgers University's Jazz Hall of Fame; Louis "Satchmo" Armstrong; William "Count" Basie, a native of Red Bank; and Benjamin David "Benny" Goodman, big band leader.

community in the performing arts and to cultivate future audiences.

Since 1977, Unity has sponsored a series of concerts by the New Jersey Chamber Music Society. For many years Unity has sponsored a series of Symphony Concerts for Young People, with Walter Damrosch conducting the New York Symphony Orchestra.

In 1980, the Montclair cultural organization started producing jazz concerts, presenting such talents as Dizzy Gillespie, Marian McPartland, Bobby Rosengarden and Bob Wilber. Future plans include a contemporary music series and a children's series, both to be co-sponsored by Unity Concerts and the Montclair Art Museum.

In 1982, Unity Institute became a separate, nonprofit cultural organization, ending a 62-year affiliation with the Unitarian Church. Now on its own, Unity has received grants from the National Endowment of the Arts, the New Jersey State Council on the Arts, the Dodge Foundation, AT&T, Prudential and several other New Jersey corporations.

Music, Music, Music

The New Jersey School for the Arts in Montclair is the Garden State's version of "Fame," the popular television series based on the New York School for the Performing Arts.

With $78 and a dream, Patricia Cioffi, a Montclair singer with an operatic dramatic voice, rented a heatless basement in the local First Congregational Church in 1975, and conducted classes in ballet, mime and eurythmics (the art of performing various bodily movements in rhythm, usually to a musical accompaniment).

After two years, Cioffi's hearty young troupers moved to larger quarters in the local YMCA and, in 1979, to Montclair High School.

Today, the New Jersey School for the Arts is teeming with 1,100 students, 900 of whom come from poor families in Newark.

Last month Cioffi's school became the first to present, in English, a Baroque opera, "L'Egisto," a mythological pastoral comedy by Cavalli. It was staged at the Mt. Hebron School in Upper Montclair.

A pioneer in opera education for minorities, the New School for the Arts excels in musical training of all types. There are opera performance workshops scheduled periodically throughout the year conducted by world renowned guest artists.

Students can audition for private vocal technique under the direction of George Shirley. There is private and group coaching in musicianship, and in Italian, French, German and Spanish diction and grammar.

Workshop I in Vocal Technique involves group and individual exercises, using song literature in solving technical problems. Workshop II encompasses interpretive technique and song and operatic literature.

The Teen Vocal Workshop is designed for students ages 10 to 12 in one section and 16 to 18 in another, learning to sight read music.

Music Theory prepares students for sight singing and ear training using a combination of methods including rhythm and melodic dictation, chord progression and the Orff and Kodaly methods.

There are also pre-instrumental courses for students between the ages of four and nine. Instrumental techniques are taught for the piano, recorder and violin.

Funded in part by the National Endowment for the Arts, the New Jersey State Council on the Arts and the Florence and John Schumann Foundation, the New Jersey School for the Arts is developing a reputation as "the Metropolitan Opera of New Jersey."

* * *

The New Jersey Chamber Music Society surfaced in 1974 when pianist Bernice Silk and flutist Peggy Schecter organized what was then called the Montclair Chamber Music Society.

Their goal was to bring a rich variety of the chamber music repertoire to New Jersey audiences. Drawing on the talents of about 20 artist-members, the society has presented programs featuring not only the masterpieces of chamber music literature, but the little known works, both classical and contemporary pieces, using unusual combinations of instruments and the particular talents of the musicians.

The six-concert Montclair series has been the staple of the society's activities. By 1977, the society had to hire its first professional manager and, in 1981, broadened its base outside of Montclair and changed its name to reflect its wider interests.

Star-Ledger Photo

The New Jersey Chamber Music Society, founded in 1974, brings imaginative combinations of classical and contemporary pieces to state audiences.

With the Newark Board of Education, the chamber musicians have participated in a successful 12-part workshop/concert series in the city's public schools.

In 1982, the chamber was chosen to perform an inaugural series at the newly dedicated William Carlos Williams Center for the Performing Arts in Rutherford.

* * *

The Kapelle Woodwind Trio was formed in 1976 and is in residence at the Cherry Hill Mall. Kapelle is an Atlantic Richfield Regional Residency Chamber Ensemble.

The music of the trio ranges from baroque transcriptions of Bach and Telemann to contemporary compositions by Piston and Husa. The repertory includes classical selections by Stamitz and Haydn and works written especially for the Kapelle Woodwind Trio by Randy Navarre, Richard Rudin, Cullen Offer and Alec Wilder.

The trio's concerts are enhanced by some compositions that are influenced by jazz and by the rich variety of duos and solos available to the woodwind instruments.

Kapelle has appeared on radio and television and has performed in many college and community concert series and in concert halls, libraries, churches and schools throughout the eastern states.

* * *

Meet the Composer supports the music of living composers representing the entire musical spectrum: Concert, choral, orchestral, chamber, folk/ethnic, jazz, dance, theater, opera, film, multimedia, electronic and experimental.

The purpose of MTC's award-winning program is to promote the music of our time, develop wider audiences for the works of living composers and generate career opportunities and commissions.

Founded in 1974 by John Duffy, a freelance composer, MTC has supported nearly 20,000 events attended by more than 7 million people, for which 3,461 new works have been commissioned or premiered. The events have been sponsored in the 62 counties of New York, New Jersey, Connecticut, Massachusetts, New Hampshire, Rhode Island, Maine and Vermont. A national expansion to reach all 50 states is under way.

Among the many recipients of grants have been composers whose works have been presented by Atlantic Community College, Dance Collective in Bergen County, Trenton Artists Workshop, Teaneck Artists Perform, Drew, Princeton and Rutgers universities, the Monmouth Jewish Community Center, Monmouth County, Woodbridge and Fort Lee libraries, Friends of Music at Princeton, several YMCAs and scores of music and art organizations.

In 1981, the New Jersey Composers Guild was founded to promote the music of the state's many composers. Honorary president is Roger Sessions of Princeton, a 1982 Pulitzer Prize winner for his "Concerto for Orchestra." The guild currently has 30 members but an estimated 100 composers from New Jersey probably qualify for membership in the guild, according to Robert Pollock of Ship Bottom, a composer, pianist and music teacher at Atlantic Community College.

Courtesy: N.J. Div. of Travel & Tourism

New Jersey's Environmental Education Centers promote the outdoor life, including horseback riding in Mount Airy, Hunterdon County.

NATURE CENTERS

One can explore New Jersey through an easily accessible network of nature centers in the cities and suburbs, along historic waterfronts or in the forests of the Pinelands and Skylands.

In South Jersey, one can find the hawk migration capital of America. In the north, a visitor can see how the Garden State "grows" the greatest number of trout in the nation at the Hackettstown fisheries.

New Jersey's nature centers combine educational with grassroots environmental experiences. From the "Gateway to America" at Liberty State Park in Jersey City to the Washington Crossing State Park on the banks of the Delaware River, more than a dozen nature centers tell the story of New Jersey's incredibly diverse environment and rich heritage.

Whether it's the history of bog iron at Allaire Village or the harvesting of cranberries in Lebanon State Forest, the nature centers have become a great natural resource in New Jersey.

The centers traditionally have focused on flora and fauna, but the total New Jersey environment, including air, water and waste, is being integrated into a statewide program.

The nature centers serve as the source of the most comprehensive environmental-educational material available. The centers are listed here in alphabetical order.

• **Allaire State Park**, Monmouth County.

Nearly 150,00 people last year visited Allaire Village, site of a bog ore furnace and forge where iron was smelted and shaped into horseshoes and utensils.

Originally occupied by a sawmill in 1750, the property was acquired by James P. Allaire of New York in 1822, a brass founder who established the iron foundry in Howell Township.

Allaire Village became a self-contained community with church and school and more than 500 workers, including moulders, ware cleaners, carpenters, pattern makers, wheelwrights, millers, teamsters, ore raisers, colliers, stage drivers, grooms and harness makers.

• **Basking Ridge Environmental Education Center**, Somerset County.

The first fully solar-heated and -cooled environmental education facility in the United States contains classrooms, offices, exhibit areas, audio-visual aids, an auditorium, a laboratory, a bookshop and supportive services.

The regional nature center serves nine counties, 18 Somerset County public school districts with more than 50,000 students, private schools, community college classes, scout troops, adult organizations and families. The 18,000-square-foot center can accommodate nearly 100,000 persons annually. More than 8 million people live within a 35-mile radius of the Basking Ridge solar showcase, situated in Stirling Park off Route 287.

• **Bass River State Forest**, Burlington and Ocean counties.

More than 400,000 people visited this 9,100-acre forest north of Atlantic City during 1984.

A self-guiding trail that begins at the easterly arm of Lake

Star-Ledger Photo

Horse-drawn wagons take children and adults through historical Allaire Village in Allaire State Park, Monmouth County.

Absegami takes a visitor into a transition zone where softwood and hardwood trees merge. The pine and oak woods embrace a small white cedar bog.

Rustic cabins and camp shelters are located along a secluded wooded shore of Lake Absegami. A total of 178 campsites are spaced throughout the wooded environment. There are also six fully enclosed lean-tos along the lake within walking distance of picnic shelters.

• **Cape May Point State Park**, Cape May County.

More than 360,000 logged in at the park and its enviromental-education center last year. The flora of Cape May is among the most diverse in the world. Behind the beach grass community of the dunes are found ponds and marsh of varying brackishness. These grade into viney brambles and thickets, red cedar and wax-myrtle woodlands. On higher ground, small groves of hardwoods abound.

At least 300 species of shrubs, trees, flowers and weeds compete for living space in the park, dominated by the 170-foot-tall lighthouse built in 1859.

There are Japanese Honeysuckle and Southern Arrowwood shrubs . . . Bigtooth Aspen and Sweetbay Magnolia trees . . . Slender Ladies'-Tresses and Mock Bishop's-weed flowers.

The Cape May Point Park is also the migration home of the hawk along the Atlantic flyway.

• **Flat Rock Brook Environmental Center**, Bergen County.

Uniquely situated on the west slope of the Palisades, the Flat Rock Brook Center boasts a wide range of geological features rarely found in one region, from 180-million-year-old volcanic bedrock formations to wetlands, ponds, a cascading stream, meadows and quarry cliffs. Self-guided trails wander throughout the 150-acre, unspoiled native woodlands just four miles from New York City.

"Life in the Pond and Stream" and "Forest and Meadow Ecology" are among the in-depth courses available to the public.

Star-Ledger Photo

Solar panels keep the main building of the Flat Rock Brook Environmental Center in Englewood warm for its visitors. The toad was found in Flat Rock Brook park.

Flat Rock Brook is set in one of the last remnants of the magnificent Palisades Forest, with huge specimens of native trees, myriad colorful native wildflowers and shrubs, and habitats for a large variety of animal life, from frogs to foxes.

The center features a solar-heated interpretive education building, which includes a library, classroom, meeting and display room, kitchen facilities and administrative office. Under development are children's gardens, wildlife habitat areas accessible for observation, plant succession demonstration areas, wetlands, boardwalks and an historical orchard.

• **Hackensack Meadowlands Environmental Center**, Bergen County.

This 52,000-square-foot complex of concrete, brick and wood is situated in the 20,000-acre Hackensack Meadowlands. The $5

Star-Ledger Photo

The Hackensack Meadowlands Environmental Center in Lyndhurst juts into Kingsland Lagoon.

Star-Ledger Photo

Countless trout are "born" at the Hackettstown Fish Hatchery, where special programs are also held for visitors.

The monumental High Point State Park is New Jersey's northernmost recreation retreat along the New York border.

Star-Ledger Photo

million complex sits atop a 30-acre site within a 1,200-acre wildlife preserve providing a variety of recreational activities, including ski slopes, campsites and a tennis club.

Some 247 species of birds and 36 species of fish have been identified in the preserve. More than 200,000 people a year can be accommodated on daily visits to the center, which contains a museum, a 288-seat auditorium, conference rooms and classrooms, an environmental monitoring laboratory equipped to test marine and botanical life, and provisions for handicapped persons. Visitors are welcomed into a sunlit, tunneled area that connects to an octagonal gazebo with a screened deck, which juts out into Kingsland Lagoon.

• **Hackettstown Hatchery**, Warren County.

The goal of the Pequest Natural Resource Education Center is to have a half-million visitors to the hatchery each year leave with a better understanding of the importance of natural resources to New Jersey citizens.

A trail through the hatchery—home for millions of fingerlings each year—features the forestry, geology and land management of the area.

Visitors can see and photograph native wildlife from an observation blind. A system of red lights (most species do not see the color red) allows a visitor to observe many animals after dark in their natural habitat.

There's also a "fish-for-fun" pond, plus fishing instructions.

A natural resource education specialist will coordinate and conduct programs using visual aids, and the museum and the grounds for tips on forestry, soils, water, air, wildlife, energy and geology.

Visitors will see a "living trout stream," the life cycle of fresh water fish from the hatching of eggs through maturity when they are released into healthy streams throughout the state during the angling season.

The Hackettstown Hatchery produces the largest amount of "catchable-size" trout in the country, more than 600,000 a year measuring between 10 and 12 inches in length.

• **High Point State Park**, Sussex County.

Nearly 400,000 people escape to High Point State Park annually to enjoy a 12,686-acre retreat crossed by the Appalachian Trail and topped by High Point Monument, the highest elevation in New Jersey, which is visible from New York and Pennsylvania.

Looking to the northeast, one can see the Catskill Moutains. To the southeast lies the Wallkill River Valley, checkerboarded with farms and woodlands.

Southwest along the Kittatinny Ridge 40 miles away is the Delaware Water Gap. Rising into the sky is Sunrise Mountain at nearby Stokes State Forest.

The High Point Cedar Swamp is virtually an oasis of virgin woodland, supporting a variety of conifers, including large hemlocks, white pine, black spruce and, surprisingly at a 1,500-foot elevation, a sturdy stand of mature southern white cedar.

High Point is a haven for boating, camping, fishing, hiking, hunting, picnicking and swimming.

• **Island Beach State Park**, Ocean County.

The 2,694 acres of Island Beach were once part of an island created in 1750 when the sea opened an inlet between the ocean and Barnegat Bay. The relentless sea, however, closed the inlet in 1812 and it remained that way despite vain attempts by man to reopen it.

One of the few natural expanses of barrier beach left along the eastern edge of the North American continent, Island Beach State Park occupies the entire 10-mile beach strip between Seaside Park and the northern shore of Barnegat Inlet.

Island Beach Park has become an outdoor textbook for scientists and nature lovers. Birds of almost all species common to eastern North America use the park as a rest area during migrations, while many songbirds seek refuge in the briar thickets as a summer nesting ground.

The nature center attracts more than 9,000 people a year. The center features flora and fauna, a "touch table," a mural showing bay-to-ocean ecology and a mounted board with ocean "finds."

Because of the natural values within the beach park, a botanical zone, a recreational zone and a wildlife sanctuary have been set aside. The zones allow the public to enjoy the island's resources and yet conserve them for future generations.

• **Lebanon State Forest**, Burlington and Ocean counties.

The nature center attracts more than 5,000 people who learn about life in the Pine Barrens, from flora and fauna to live amphibians, reptiles and the history of the cranberry industry. There's everything from edible plants to forgotten towns in the 24,413-acre preserve.

The forest derives its name from from the Lebanon Glass Works established about 1862.

An Atlantic White Cedar Swamp is surrounded by a pitch pine forest. Rare orchids and blueberries flourish in the cedar swamp, which supports as many as 4,000 trees per acre.

There are saddle horse trails, hiking, swimming, picnicking, boating, fishing and plenty of space for camping.

• **Liberty State Park**, Jersey City.

The smallest and most popular recreation area in New Jersey, Liberty State Park is visited by a million people a year.

Although only 35 acres of the 800-acre waterfront park are presently open to the public, the new Liberty State Park Environmental Education Center, opened Memorial Day 1983, is attracting both recreationists and historians seeking information on New Jersey's first settlements in Hudson County.

Designed by Princeton architect Michael Graves, the center resembles a Roman cathedral and is constructed entirely of redwood. Three spacious exhibition halls are being used for public displays and meetings. An environmental library, the largest in New Jersey, is also under consideration for one of the three vaulted-ceiling rooms.

The auditorium is being used for slide shows, films and guest speakers.

The waterfront park provides a unique view of the Statue of Liberty and Ellis Island, the legendary immigration center that gave America its late 19th Century nickname, "the great melting pot."

Batona Trail, northern entrance, in Lebanon State Park, is a secluded get-away for hikers.

The Hudson River waterfront area is known as the "Gateway to America."

• **Swartswood State Park**, Sussex County.

Luring 120,000 people a year to its 1,304 acres of water and woodlands, Swartswood Park is an idyllic setting for boaters, bathers and campers. In the winter months, there are snow-shoeing, cross-country skiing, ice boating and skiing. Fishing is a popular pastime at both Big and Little Swartswood lakes. Hunting is also permitted in designated areas, in season.

• **Trailside Nature & Science Center**, Mountainside.

Opened in 1941, Trailside was New Jersey's first nature center. Located in the 2,000-acre Watchung Reservation in Union County, Trailside features 13 miles of marked hiking trails, including the 10-mile Sierra Loop; 30 miles of bridle paths; Surprise Lake for fishing and boating; Seeley's Pond and Blue Brook, stocked with trout annually; a cross-country ski trail, and the county nursery.

Museum exhibits range from taxidermy and game animals, to predators and prey, and rock quarry and minerals. A planetarium, seating 40 people, contains an 18-foot-wide dome, a Nova Star projector and a Unitron telescope.

Science classrooms involve experiments with combustion, water, chemicals, food and other materials. An auditorium seats 259 and the Trailside library contains 550 volumes of environmental and scientific works.

• **Washington Crossing State Park**, Mercer County.

One of the biggest public attractions in New Jersey, Washington Crossing State Park draws more than a quarter-million people a year. The site is where the Revolutionary Army made the historic river crossing on Christmas night, 1776, preceding the battles of Trenton and Princeton, the turning point of the American Revolution.

Continental Lane, over which the American troops marched on that memorable eve, extends nearly the full length of the 807-acre park.

Two unique components of the park are the State Forest Nursery, where forest tree seedlings are raised for reforestation of idle and abandoned lands in the state, and the George Washington Memorial Arboretum of trees and shrubs native to the state.

The visitors center contains an electrified map with slide projection and narration show-and-tell of the troop movements and battles of the "10 Crucial Days."

Displays depicting the evolution of the United States' flag from the days of the early explorers to the present day 50-star flag are housed in a stone barn off Continental Lane. One of the dioramas in the barn portrays the crossing of the Delaware on Christmas night.

The Washington Crossing Open Air Theater is in a unique setting for a cultural and recreational outdoor center. The sloping hillside below Steele Run Pond is terraced to seat 1,000 spectators.

At the nature center, park visitors can observe small exhibits, listen to brief lectures, or go on one of the prescheduled nature tours. A self-guided tour leaflet is also available.

• **Weis Ecology Center**, Ringwood, Passaic County.

The Weis Ecology Center is dedicated to the celebration and preservation of the North Jersey Highlands Region. Bordering 2,000 acres of state forest, the nonprofit, environmental-education-recreation center offers a comprehensive schedule of summer programs: Agriculture, natural history, nature appreciation, orienteering and conservation.

The 160-acre preserve, together with the neighboring Norvin Green State Forest, have more than 40 miles of hiking trails. Whether exploring an abandoned farmstead or a 19th Century iron mine, hikers can link up with the past in North Jersey's last vestige of wilderness.

Each August there is a Highlands Environmental Festival, featuring local folk musicians, poets and performing artists. Activities include a crafts fair, alternative technology exposition, food, games and hikes.

• **Wharton State Forest**, Burlington and Atlantic counties.

More than 10,000 people are drawn annually to the historic Batsto Village in Wharton State Forest. The nature center is at the end of the old iron town, next to Batsto Lake.

The Batsto furnace furnished munitions for the Revolution as well as the War of 1812.

Batsto stems from the word "baatstoo," a steam bath used by the Scandinavians and the Dutch. They borrowed the word from the Leni-Lenape Indians, who referred to the lake as a "bathing place."

Batsto once was a community of nearly 1,000 residents and played an important part in the industrial development of the United States.

* * *

To bring the work of the nature centers to the public's attention, the State Department of Environmental Protection is putting together an Environmental Education Advisory Committee composed of New Jersey environmental educators and natural resource professionals.

An Interdivisional Environmental Education Task Force is also being organized, as well as an Interdivisional Graphic Arts Task Force.

* * *

Although not part of New Jersey's network of nature centers, the Franklin Mineral Museum in Sussex County reveals nature's most brilliant underground marvels.

Known as "The Fluorescent Mineral Capital of the World," the great ore deposits in the Franklin Zinc Mines were depleted by 1954. But its treasured remnants remain a rock collector's and geologist's search-and-find delight.

About 200 kinds of minerals from the Franklin-Ogdensburg mines are on display at the museum, which features a replica mine replete with timber, rails, ore carts, drilling equipment, scoops and other digging paraphernalia actually used in the zinc mines of Franklin Sterling Hill. The bi-level barn-shaped replica depicts the operation of mining zinc ore.

Some 25 minerals from the Franklin-Ogdensburg mines are found nowhere else on earth. Visitors to the museum will see polished and set gemstones, colorful crystals and specimens of great variety, as well as artifacts and curios connected with Sussex County's mining past.

The 35-foot-long fluorescent display room lights up like a rainbow of vivid colors, from the creamy Aragonite to the purple Hardystonite. There are the Axinite and Calcite reds, the Tremolite and Barylite blues, the Percolite and Wollastonite oranges, and the Calcium-larsenite and Smithsonite yellows.

The Franklin ores and minerals, the world's most brilliant fluorescent minerals, are seen under regular light, as well as long and short ultraviolet rays that produce incredible colors.

A billion years ago, an ocean covered the eastern coastal states. Iron, zinc and manganese accumulated and became incorporated in a thickening sequence of sediments and submarine lavas. About 800 million years ago, the accumulations were transformed into the rocks and enclosed minerals seen today at the museum. Many of the rare minerals were formed during the first period of mountain building in the earth's evolution.

Minerals continue to form where weathering can alter the older minerals. The story of the Franklin Zinc Mines is far from completed, and new minerals are being discovered continually.

The museum also contains its own laboratory for the identification and preparation of minerals for display.

Star-Ledger Photo

Visitors to the Basking Ridge Environmental Education Center in Somerset County Park enjoy resting in a gazebo set near the water.

NEW BRUNSWICK

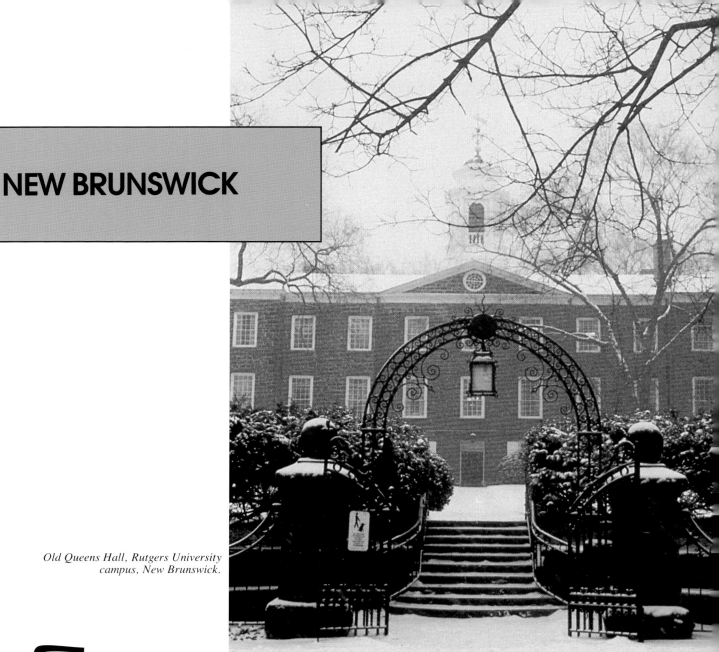

Old Queens Hall, Rutgers University campus, New Brunswick.

*F*ollow the red brick road to a Golden Triangle where "New Brunswick Tomorrow" is coming alive today as an American renaissance city.

From a deteriorating, neglected urban wasteland in the mid-'70s to a refreshing cultural-commercial-academic center today, New Brunswick is New Jersey's central city success story of the '80s.

Several New Jersey cities are starting to make a comeback, especially the Hudson waterfront communities of Jersey City and Hoboken, where being old means being elegant and fashionable as the era of aging brownstones enjoys a remarkable resurgence.

Elsewhere, artisans and craftsmen are rediscovering the rich Colonial history of Paterson and Trenton by rescuing historic factories and warehouses from the downtown demolition squads.

At the same time, Newark, America's third oldest city, is blending antiquity with a modern educational campus setting in the downtown district by preserving the James Street Commons and comparable turn-of-the-century neighborhoods.

Although New Jersey's older cities are refurbishing and re-building their urban image, one stands out as the harbinger of all.

New Brunswick, with its unique location and community chemistry, has come up with the right combination of leadership, corporate clout and academic environment to put it all together this decade.

The home of Rutgers University, founded in 1766, New Brunswick is one of the nation's oldest cities with one of the newest and brightest images.

And yes, there is an attractive red brick road in downtown New Brunswick, fashionably landscaped and lighted and serving the new $3 million George Street Mall with four new restaurants in the four-block heart of the waterfront community.

And, within view of the Raritan River, there is a Golden Triangle, so called because it is bounded by the commercially valuable George and Albany streets properties and the railroad.

Look up and you'll see a 53-foot-high colorful mural along the new Albany Street boulevard, painted by the internationally famed artist Richard Haas. It's one of Haas' popular *tromp l'oeil*, or fool-the-eye, murals commissioned by Johnson & Johnson.

Star-Ledger Photo

"New Brunswick Tomorrow" plans call for the beautification of the once-deteriorating city through a partnership between the public and private sectors. Enhancing the "park city" is a "tromp l'oeil" mural painted on a wall of the Public Service Electric and Gas sub-station on Albany Street.

Rising near the riverbank is the stunningly white Johnson & Johnson worldwide corporate headquarters and luxurious Hyatt Regency Hotel and Conference Center with its grand ballroom, glass elevators and rooftop tennis courts and swimming pool.

Just up the street, the focus of the $15 million New Brunswick Cultural Center is a 2,000-seat State Theater for the performing arts. Around it are the new homes for the George Street Playhouse, the Crossroads Theater, the Mason Gross School of the Arts, the Rutgers Office of Television and Radio, and such resident art groups as the Opera Theater of New Jersey, the Garden State Symphonic Pops Orchestra and the Princeton Ballet.

What is evolving in New Brunswick is "a city within a park, a park within a city," a fitting description of the new J&J headquarters by its world renowned architect I.M. Pei.

The "park city" setting applies equally to this historic hub's rebirth.

It began in 1974 when Richard B. Sellers, then chairman of Johnson & Johnson, decided New Brunswick needed a private helping hand to bring it back to life. Summoning the city's business and institutional leaders, Sellers sought an opinion from an outside authority on New Brunswick's fate. The American City Corp. of Columbia, Md., part of the well-known Rouse Organization, conducted a comprehensive study of New Brunswick for Sellers and his community-minded friends.

In January 1975, American City Corp. found New Brunswick to be a rare old gem in need of a new setting, much like an heirloom waiting to be dusted off and rediscovered.

American City saw an ideal partnership between the private and public sectors, or Johnson & Johnson, Rutgers University and the fading downtown business community. "New Brunswick Tomorrow" was born and a half-billion-dollar private-public investment got under way when Pei was commissioned to develop a land-use blueprint for the restoration of the all but forgotten city lazing wearily by the queen of New Jersey's rivers.

Ieoh Ming Pei, born in Canton, China and educated at MIT and Harvard, was faced with an exodus of businesses and middle-class residents to the suburbs when he sat down at his drawing board to ponder the future of New Brunswick.

The facts were frightening: In 1943, New Brunswick collected $1.8 million a year in constant dollars from the city's central business district. By the time Pei and Sellers arrived to save the patient, New Brunswick was taking in only $300,000 from the same area, not enough to keep the streets and sidewalks clean.

The result of a vanishing tax base was the grim abandonment of businesses and pleasant middle-class homes, whose residents sought greener and more affordable pastures in the suburbs of Middlesex and Mercer counties.

With Sellers and Pei promising a vision backed with hard green currency, "New Brunswick Tomorrow" was officially organized on July 1, 1975. It was a unique urban experiment in which business, government and community leaders founded a nonprofit corporation with a board of directors representing each of those interests. John J. Heldrich, corporate vice president/administration of Johnson & Johnson, has served as NBT's chairman from its inception.

By early 1976, the New Brunswick Development Corp. (DevCo) was formed with Sellers as chairman and William Tremayne, senior vice president of the Prudential Insurance Co. of America in nearby Newark, serving as vice president. Prudential was to figure prominently in the financing of New Brunswick's future.

The resurrection of the business district as a regional commercial and retail center, coupled with neighborhood preservation, was the thrust of the Pei plan.

The architect and J&J braintrust realized the community body could not be revitalized with a diseased downtown economic heart.

The major pieces of this swiftly evolving urban success story follow.

Plaza II

The key breakthrough came in 1977 when a consortium of local lending institutions assured the New Brunswick Develop-

The site of Plaza II, an office building designed by I. M. Pei, was once a littered tract on George Street. Completed in 1979, the center generates $130,000 in local taxes annually.

Star-Ledger Photo

ment Corp. of financing for a $6.5 million office building and parking complex known as Plaza II.

The site was a littered, weed-covered urban renewal tract that had blemished the main thoroughfare, George Street, for more than a decade and sat there as a sad reminder of the failure of the old approach to "urban renewal": Let Government do it!

Pei designed a strikingly modern, six-story office building that looks like a rectangular sheet cake with a swath of tinted glass separating each floor. Ground was broken in September 1977 and the city's first new edifice in recent memory opened in June 1979. An awful eyesore had been turned into an aesthetic asset.

Today, Plaza II is fully occupied and 350 office personnel are bringing life and their consumer dollars back to the downtown district. A fallow block of land now generates $130,000 in local taxes each year.

Route 18

Years of delays over the completion of Route 18 along the Raritan River stalled any hopes of returning New Brunswick to its former glory, when Rutgers University reigned as one of America's most popular schools of higher education.

The turning point for Route 18, a major east-west freeway, was "New Brunswick Tomorrow," which without this vital artery could very well have been "New Brunswick Never."

The U.S. Army Corps of Engineers and the state Department of Transportation finally got off dead-center and gave Route 18 the green light after a decade of exhaustive social and environmental impact studies that led nowhere, until given a new direction by the Pei plan.

The first section of the $45 million, four-lane bypass was completed in 1979, relieving congestion—and unnecessary air pollution from stalled traffic—in the downtown business district. The second phase, a freeway bridge over the Raritan River, was opened on Oct. 1, 1980. The final segment was completed by 1985.

Route 18 was the magic road that led to the redevelopment of downtown New Brunswick. Thriving business and commercial

Johnson & Johnson headquarters, located off Albany and George Streets, overlooks the Raritan River. The "city within a park" includes a 16-story tower and seven adjoining buildings.

expansion would not have been financially or physically possible with streets choked by through-traffic that had no reason to be there, except to get through the heart of New Brunswick to reach Rutgers or Johnson & Johnson.

J&J Corporate Headquarters

Encouraged by the start of Route 18 and the response to the Pei plan, Johnson & Johnson decided to reverse the flight of business out of New Brunswick by announcing on April 6, 1978 that it would erect a $50 million worldwide corporate headquarters near its existing operations.

Pei was again tapped by J&J to design a distinguished complex to complement the downtown plan. A blighted 12-acre tract of mixed uses was chosen for the phoenix-like project. The properties on the site had collectively produced a total of $140,000 in tax revenues for the city. The new J&J center generates more than $1.1 million a year in local taxes and houses some 1,000 corporate executives and support personnel who had been scattered throughout the New Brunswick area.

Overlooking the Raritan River, the J&J "city within a park" consists of a 16-story white tower and seven adjoining low-rise modules graced by lovely trees and plantings. It is the corporate rock of New Brunswick, a solid foundation for the city's promising future.

Middlesex General University Hospital

A significant regional health care resource is the Middlesex General University Hospital, a $65 million expansion and renova-

The new John A. Lynch Memorial Bridge across the Raritan River is a key part of the $45 million Route 18 bypass.

tion of Middlesex General Hospital, to serve as the primary teaching hospital for the Rutgers Medical School.

Dedicated in May 1982, the modern medical complex on the edge of the downtown district employs more than 1,200 people and has made New Brunswick the regional center of highly specialized tertiary medical care for Central Jersey.

Hyatt Regency Hotel/ Conference Center

Pei's blueprint called for a cornerstone at the gateway to New Brunswick in the form of an impressive commercial center. That cornerstone became a $30 million, 300-room hotel and conference center on Albany Street near the Raritan River.

The six-acre gateway site had been a confusing concoction of rundown, mixed residential and business structures, including a gas station and some parking lots.

What stands there today is a V-shaped hotel with a looped entranceway that really looks like welcoming, comforting arms to guests arriving in downtown New Brunswick. Prudential Insurance put up the $30 million in mortgage money in a partnership with the Development Corp. and a subsidiary of Johnson & Johnson. The city also received a $6 million federal Urban Development Action Grant to make the transformation possible.

An additional 100 rooms can be built atop the 300 guest rooms as New Brunswick grows. The conference center features a grand ballroom for up to 1,200 people, a two-level atrium, two restaurants, glass elevators, rooftop tennis courts, a swimming pool, exercise and game rooms and an enclosed garage for 400 cars.

The Hyatt Regency produces some $500,000 in local real estate taxes, as compared to the $30,000 yielded by the previous occupants. The gateway center has stimulated around-the-clock activity and spillover retail business essential to downtown development.

The Hyatt created 239 jobs, of which half had been filled by previously unemployed persons and 42 percent minorities, many of them economically disadvantaged.

New Brunswick Cultural Center

Recycling four existing buildings into a $15 million cultural center will make New Brunswick a highly visible and diverse community for the performing arts.

The centerpiece of the cultural center is the State Theater, a 2,000-seat performing arts hall for symphony, light opera, dance, drama and other classical and contemporary musical events. A new hall would have cost $25 million, compared to the $3 million renovation of the State Theater.

Adjacent to the State Theater on Livingston Avenue are three other buildings: An old YMCA, the Sisser Brothers Warehouse and the former Arnold Constable Department Store.

Conversion of the YMCA allowed a bigger showcase for the George Street Playhouse, increasing its capacity from 269 to 325 seats.

The Arnold Constable Building became the permanent home of the visual arts division of the Mason Gross School, with classrooms, studios, shops and offices.

The warehouse provided plenty of room for the new 300-seat Crossroads Theater, plus the Rutgers Office of Television and Radio, and rehearsal and studio space for resident arts groups such as the Princeton Ballet, Opera Theater, Symphonic Pops Orchestra and organizations that are part of the New Brunswick Arts Resource Center.

The overall plans for the cultural center were developed for the New Brunswick Arts Development Commission by William Wright Jr., director of physical and capital planning at Rutgers.

Along with this cultural boom is the greening of the city center and bringing entertainment outdoors for everyone's free enjoyment.

A fire had blackened a corner of the busiest intersection at George and Albany streets, but from those ashes emerged the Joyce Kilmer Park (the poet of "Trees") in 1977, soon becoming the site of many community events, such as flower shows and noon-time concerts for shoppers and downtown workers.

"New Brunswick Tomorrow" every summer sponsors an outstanding series of free evening musical events in the parks. Thousands of residents and visitors from throughout New Jersey have enjoyed the classics, jazz, bluegrass, gospel and ethnic music under the stars.

Mason Gross School of the Arts

The vacant P.J. Young Department Store on George Street stood as a symbol of downtown decline in the early 1970s. Put up for federal bankruptcy sale in 1976, Johnson & Johnson grabbed it as a potentially strategic location for the new downtown resurgence.

When Rutgers announced it would make the refurbished department store its home for the Mason Gross School of the Arts, Johnson & Johnson sold it to the Development Corp. for the same price it paid to the federal liquidators.

Opening in the fall of 1977, the school of arts has become a vital institution bringing a new dimension of artists, students and faculty into the central business district. The school has grown to nearly 300 undergraduate and graduate students and faculty. Since the Development Corp. leases the building to Rutgers, the property realizes $25,000 a year in taxes.

The school already is outgrowing its department store quarters and is ready to move into more spacious facilities in a new downtown cultural center.

Cast members of "Lorenzo," an original musical presented at the George Street Playhouse, gather for a group portrait. Gov. Thomas Kean has called the playhouse "one of New Jersey's living artistic treasures."

Photo Credit: Suzanne Karp Krebs

Golden Triangle

A $35 million New City Centre, a multiple office-parking-transportation complex, is being developed within the Golden Triangle block bordering the railroad. Architects Rothe-Johnson of Iselin have designed a 10-story office building with 267,160 square feet of space, the structure connected to the downtown railroad station. The project is providing 1,000 permanent jobs.

The $12 million Ferren Parking Deck, opposite the railroad station, opened in early 1983. Sponsored and financed by the New Brunswick Parking Authority, the Ferren Deck, in addition to taking up to 1,250 cars, also contains 68,000 square feet of prime commercial space.

The chief tenant in the Ferren facility is the Rutgers University Book Store, with 19,000 square feet. The move of the book store from the campus to the downtown transportation hub is bringing thousands of students into the business district.

The Old and The New

Both new construction and rehabilitation are radically altering New Brunswick's appearance and character. Not only are the changes dramatically visible, but the 45,000 people who call their five-square mile city home see hope in their future.

A poll by the Eagleton Institute of Rutgers University found that approximately 75 percent of New Brunswick's residents believe their city will be a better place in five years. That September 1982 response was far above the 33 percent average "level of optimism" the pollsters found in surveys of other communities in the New Jersey-New York metropolitan region.

Eagleton reported that 74 percent of New Brunswick's residents are aware of the "Tomorrow" movement and that three-quarters of them approve of it. Johnson & Johnson received an overwhelmingly favorable rating of 86 percent, and Rutgers, 84 percent.

Dr. Cliff Zukin, director of the Eagleton poll, summarized the mood of the waterfront city this way:

"New Brunswick is a city on the move. The momentum can be seen in the visible changes in the physical environment of the city, as well as in the changes in the attitudes of the residents. Since 1976, New Brunswick residents' feelings about their community, as well as their evaluations of specific projects in the city, have become more positive."

With the Golden Triangle, Gateway and downtown revival, New Brunswick has invested or is in the process of spending close to a half-billion dollars to assure a decent quality of life for everyone in the community. For every dollar of public funds going into the golden gateway city, five private dollars are guaranteeing that the money is being carefully and wisely put to use. The five-to-one investment ratio is one of the highest of any cities in America.

Among the other projects moving forward are:

• A $28 million Church Street retail and office complex, balancing 136,650 square feet of property rehabilitation against 136,650 square feet of new construction. The project is being funded by the Church Street Development Corp., a limited partnership headed by New Brunswick architect Don Gatarz and Robert Epifano, president of Epic, a Piscataway contracting firm.

• Three private firms are vying for the role of lead developer in a $27 million operation to develop about 150 units of new downtown condominium housing units and retail space in the Old Hiram Market.

• At a time when many municipalities are closing schools to cut costs, New Brunswick celebrated the opening of the $5 million Paul Robeson School and Community Center in November 1982. The money to build the school was made possible only by the increased municipal tax revenues generated by the new downtown development.

• Another municipal project that has created a strong recreational resource for the community is the $1.2 million renovation of Memorial Stadium, including new football and soccer fields, support facilities and lighting to permit nighttime sports and community events.

New Brunswick also has an ongoing program of upgrading neighborhood parks and playgrounds to provide more and better leisure-time opportunities for all of its residents, young and old.

• In February 1983, Rutgers dedicated the $3 million Jane Voorhees Zimmerli Art Museum, quadrupling the exhibition space and establishing a permanent display of the university's fine art collection.

• A senior citizen housing development sponsored by the United Auto Workers opened last spring. Situated on the fringe of the central business district, the 14-story building provides 214 units of badly needed affordable housing.

• In the neighborhoods, the Development Corp. is acquiring abandoned houses through FHA and VA defaulted mortgages, and then completely rehabilitating and selling the homes, at cost, to people who promise to be owner-occupants, not absentee landlords.

Five two-bedroom townhouses were built in the heart of the city's minority-populated Second Ward. They were sold for under $55,000 each—below their actual cost—to encourage home ownership.

"New Brunswick Tomorrow" (NBT) has concentrated on three critical areas: Jobs and training, improving education and human services.

A unique Career Preparation Center, sponsored by Middlesex County College with NBT, is offering free career, educational and job training counseling to thousands of residents capable of putting in a day's work. NBT has become the catalyst bringing the public, parochial and county vocational school systems together for the first time to work on common problems and solutions.

New Brunswick is building its future on the participation and support of every one of its residents, regardless of their age, education or abilities. It's the only way "Tomorrow" leaders say a community can survive as a family of diverse interests.

Philip W. Anderson, right, Consulting Director in the Physical Research Division at Bell Labs and a professor at Princeton University, shown with co-recipients of the Nobel Prize in Physics, 1977. They are John H. Van Vleck, left, of Harvard University, and Sir Nevill Mott, center, of Cambridge University, England.

NOBEL WINNERS

I rented an old converted barn on six acres in Basking Ridge and began an ongoing love affair with the New Jersey countryside that has been a major force in keeping my family here for nearly 34 years.

—**Philip W. Anderson, November 1982**

*P*hilip W. Anderson, a physicist at AT&T Bell Laboratories, is among 28 Nobel Prize winners who have worked or studied in New Jersey scientific and academic institutions this century.

The New Jersey Nobel club is elite yet growing, and its members include President Woodrow Wilson, Albert Einstein and Eugene O'Neill.

Their ideas span the centuries—and the galaxies. Whether it's tracing the origin of the universe, or creating transistors, lasers or "medical miracles," the Nobel laureates share a common characteristic—an unquenchable curiosity matched only by a rare brilliance to see beyond the unseeable.

The first Nobel recipient associated with New Jersey was Woodrow Wilson, 28th President of the United States, who was selected for the Peace Prize in 1920 for championing world peace and democracy during and after the first global war.

A graduate of Princeton University, class of 1879, Wilson joined the university faculty in 1890 as a professor of jurisprudence and political economy. He was named president of Princeton University in 1902 and was elected governor of New Jersey in 1910. Two years later he was in the White House, the last President to ride to his inauguration in a horse-drawn carriage.

During his second term of office, Wilson guided America through the First World War and established the first planetary peace organization, the League of Nations, in an effort to prevent further international wars. He died Feb. 3, 1924, and is the only president interred in Washington, D.C. A scholar and humanitarian, Wilson is considered by historians as one of the three or four most successful U.S. presidents.

Probably the most popular scientist of all time, Albert Einstein, received the Nobel Prize in physics in 1921 for defining the

241

Woodrow Wilson.

law of the photoelectric effect. The "father of relativity" made Princeton his home from the early 1930s until his death in 1955. Einstein carried on his theoretical work at the Institute for Advanced Study in Princeton.

Owen W. Richardson, professor of physics at Princeton University from 1906 to 1913, was presented with the physics award in 1928 for studying the thermionic effect of electrons sent off by hot metals.

A professor at Stevens Institute of Technology in Hoboken, Irving Langmuir won the Nobel Prize in chemistry in 1932 for his discoveries about molecular films absorbed on surfaces. Langmuir taught at Stevens from 1906 through 1909.

Playwright Eugene O'Neill, who spent a year at Princeton University as a member of the class of 1910, received the Nobel Prize in Literature in 1936. O'Neill was also a four-time winner of the Pulitzer Prize. He lived many years in New Jersey. One of his favorite places was the Point Pleasant area of the Jersey Shore.

Arthur H. Compton, who received his doctoral degree in physics from Princeton University in 1916, shared the Nobel Prize in physics in 1927 for his discovery of the change in wave length of scattered X-rays, now known as the "Compton effect."

Beginning in 1937, a symbiotic relationship evolved between Princeton University and AT&T Bell Laboratories, with headquarters in Murray Hill and Holmdel. Over the years, the "B-P" connection has been responsible for eight Nobel Prize winners (as of 1984). One of them, John Bardeen, was the first to win two Nobel Prizes in the same field (physics). Since Bardeen, only one other recipient has achieved that double distinction, Frederick Sanger (chemistry).

One of the beneficiaries of the B-P connection is Philip Anderson, who shared the physics prize in 1977 for fundamental theoretical investigations of the electronic structure of magnetic and disordered systems.

A Princeton professor, Anderson finds the B-P connection ideal for those who need the freedom to pursue their work. Says Anderson:

"I moved to Morristown in February 1949 with a new degree, a new car, a new baby and a new job at Bell Laboratories. I wholeheartedly expected to leave Bell Labs after a few years for a university position elsewhere in the country.

"A year later, however, I rented an old converted barn on six acres in Basking Ridge (the headquarters of AT&T Communications, another member of the AT&T family), and began an ongoing love affair with the New Jersey countryside that has been a major force in keeping my family here for nearly 34 years.

"The other inescapable magnet for me has been the wonderful research atmosphere at AT&T Bell Labs, which is duplicated at no other industrial lab and at few universities. It is a great advantage for my students at Princeton to be able to interact with the AT&T atmosphere.

"The combination of AT&T Bell Labs with Princeton lends a quality to my life that I can reproduce nowhere else."

The first AT&T Bell Labs Nobel laureate was Clinton J. Davisson, who studied for his doctorate in physics at Princeton University (1911). Davisson shared the Nobel Prize in physics in 1937 for his work at Bell Labs in the diffraction of electrons by crystals. It furnished the first experimental proof that the electron, previously conceived of as a material particle, could also manifest itself as a wave. At Princeton, Davisson prepared his dissertation under the direction of Professor Richardson, the 1928 Nobel winner.

C. J. Davisson, standing next to equipment used in his measurements of electron diffractions in crystals, was a recipient of the 1937 Nobel Prize in Physics.

John Northrop and Wendell Stanley shared the Nobel Prize for chemistry in 1946 for their discovery, with James B. Sumner, that enzymes can be crystallized and for preparing pure enzymes and virus proteins. Northrop and Stanley conducted their chemical investigations at the Princeton laboratories of the Rockefeller Institute for Medical Research, now Rockefeller University, New York City.

Stanley was the first to bring "viruses out of limbo," according to the American Philosophical Society's 1971 yearbook. A crucial change in Stanley's career came in 1932 when he moved from New York to the Rockefeller Institute labs in Princeton. The impact of Stanley's discovery was immense. Viruses had been elusive entities. The idea that a protein molecule could be a virus was, to many investigators, truly shocking, the APS yearbook points out.

The name Dr. John Howard Northrop has been linked with important studies of enzymes, bacterial viruses and experiments of a biological and biophysical nature, according to Roger M. Herriot's biographical sketch of the Nobel winner for The Journal of General Physiology (1962). One of Northrop's ancestors was the Rev. Jonathan Edwards, president of Princeton University in 1758.

In 1950, Edward C. Kendall shared the Nobel Prize in medicine in 1950 for his part in the discovery of cortisone at the Mayo Clinic. Kendall was a visiting professor of chemistry at the Forrestal Research Campus at Princeton University until his death in 1972.

Edwin M. McMillan received his doctorate in physics from Princeton University in 1932 and went on to share the 1951 Nobel Prize in chemistry for his part in the discovery of transuranium elements.

Rutgers University nurtured the 1952 Nobel recipient for medicine. Selman A. Waksman graduated from Rutgers in 1915 and started studying tiny organisms called actinomycetes, which occur commonly in soil. Virtually no one else was concerned with those microorganisms, but they became a lifelong interest of Waksman, who went on to earn his master's at Rutgers and his doctorate at the University of California.

After obtaining his Ph.D., Waksman returned to Rutgers to become one of its most eminent professors. By the 1940s, it was recognized that antibiotics could be produced by those little organisms Waksman had been investigating for 25 years. From a

handful of soil, Waksman and his Rutgers colleagues had isolated streptomycin, an antibiotic that revolutionized the treatment of tuberculosis—and closed many sanitariums.

In 1949, the Rutgers' Waksman Institute of Microbiology was founded and funded primarily from patent rights for streptomycin. Today the Waksman Institute is an internationally recognized research center. Rutgers is building a $7 million wing to house researchers of molecular biology and biotechnology.

AT&T Bell Laboratories scored a triple victory in 1956 when three of its leading researchers won the Nobel Prize in physics for the invention of the transistor, one of the technological marvels of the 20th Century. Replacing large, costly vacuum tubes, the first tiny transistor was less than an inch long and consisted of two hair-thin wires touching a pinhead of a solid semiconductive material soldered to a metal base.

The coveted prize went to John Bardeen, Walter Brattain and William Shockley. Bardeen wrote his doctoral dissertation at Princeton University in 1936 under the guidance of Professor Eugene P. Wigner, who would become another Nobel laureate in physics in 1963.

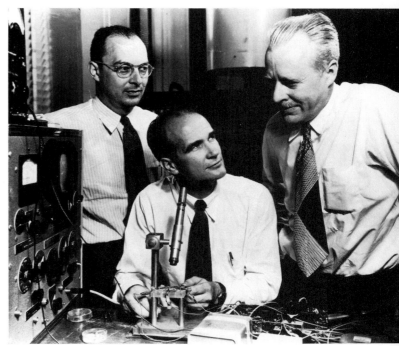

Courtesy: AT&T Bell Labs

John Bardeen, left, William Shockley, center, and Walter Brattain, shown in a 1948 photo taken at Bell Labs, were honored for their work with transistors.

Dr. Selman A. Waksman, seated at a table looking at Petrie dishes.

Courtesy: Rutgers University

Bardeen, who became the first person to win two Nobel Prizes in the same field (1956 and 1972), recalls how it all began:

"My introduction to semiconductors came just after the war, in late 1945, when I joined the Bell Laboratories research group on solid-state physics. Conditions were rather crowded when I arrived at the Murray Hill laboratory. The wind-up of World War II research was still going on. A new building was under construction but was not yet completed, so I was asked to share an office with Walter Brattain and Gerald Pearson.

"... I can still remember the excitement I felt when I first learned of this discovery, which showed definitely that the holes from the emitter could flow appreciable distances through the bulk of n-type germanium."

The breakthrough came in the summer of 1948, eight years before Bardeen, Brattain and Shockley were recognized by the Nobel committee.

Brattain remembered the long, frustrating and sometimes fruitless years of painstaking research leading to the development of the transistor:

"One never knows beforehand if one's research is going to contribute to that understanding, and after 14 years of work I was beginning to lose faith. But I never felt any pressure from management to continue or to change fields. Perhaps the only real threat to my career came in 1932 when I, being a bachelor, would have been the next man in my group to go if the Depression got worse.

"Another incident took place when my laboratory at West Street, New York City, was used to demonstrate C.J. Davisson's experiments on diffraction of electrons from a nickel crystal. That was in 1937 when it was announced that Davisson had won a Nobel Prize. The news services wanted movies and pictures. I was present, taking it all in, possibly with my hands in my pockets and my mouth open. It was hot under the klieg lights and the news people would occasionally let Davisson cool off. During one of these breaks he walked over to me and said, 'Don't worry, Walter, you'll win one someday.' Little did I know that the day would come when he'd be one of the people to nominate us for the prize.

"... The use of the transistor of which I am proudest is in the small battery-operated radio. This has made it possible for even the most underprivileged peoples to listen. Nomads in Asia, Indians in the Andes and natives in Haiti have these radios, and at night they can gather together to listen.

"When I was a boy, the idealists said that the only future for civilization was to see that every child learned to read and write. Even if he never learns to read or write, however, almost every human learns to speak, listen and understand. All peoples can now, within limits, listen to what they wish, independent of what dictatorial leaders might want them to hear, and I feel that this will eventually benefit human society.

"The thing I deplore most is the use of solid-state electronics by rock and roll musicians to raise the level of sound to where it is both painful and injurious."

Shockley was inspired by Bell Labs' first Nobel winner, C.J. Davisson. He recalled:

"One of the inducements (at Bell Labs) was the opportunity to work under the eminent and charming physicist, C.J. Davisson. It is one of the virtues of management at Bell Labs that basic research is encouraged. Two phrases apply: 'Creative-failure methodology' and 'research on the scientific aspects of practical problems.' Our failure to make a transistor was creative. The managerial art of optimizing the interaction between pure and applied research is what makes Bell Labs so eminent a leader in innovation."

The goal at Bell Labs that resulted in the transistor was really a very practical one: Develop technology to serve the telephone system.

In 1961, Robert Hofstadter, another doctoral student at Princeton University (1938), shared the physics prize for his determination of the size and shape of atomic nucleons.

Eugene Paul Wigner joined the Princeton faculty in 1930, became Thomas D. Jones professor of mathematical physics in 1938, and shared the Nobel physics prize in 1963 for his contributions to the theory of the atomic nucleus and elementary particles.

Charles H. Townes, who for many years worked at Bell Labs and then served as a consultant to the world's largest private laboratory, shared the 1964 Nobel Prize in physics for his fundamental work in the field of quantum electronics, which led to the construction of oscillators and amplifiers based on the maser-laser principle.

A maser is an amplifier or generator of electromagnetic waves, which make use of stimulated emission from atoms. In the microwave region, masers are used as highly accurate atomic clocks or frequency standards, and as low-noise amplifiers for weak signals in radar and radio astronomy and ground stations in communication satellites. Townes conceived of the maser in 1951.

Richard P. Feynman, another product of Princeton's doctoral program (1942), shared the Nobel physics award in 1965 for helping to solve the difficulties in carrying out quantitative calculations of the interplay between charged particles. That contribution opened the field of quantum electrodynamics.

The AT&T Bell-Princeton association connected again in 1972, when John Bardeen became the first double Nobel winner in the same field. He shared the award for his work in superconductivity.

Philip W. Anderson, another beneficiary of the Bell-Princeton relationship, shared the 1977 Nobel Prize in physics for his central role in developing a much greater understanding of localized magnetic moments, or atomic-sized magnets that remain fixed at a particular site in a metal.

Anderson's work is being applied in the field of amorphous semiconductors, the basis for a new world energy system: The conversion of sunlight directly into electricity. Solar electricity will eventually replace other conventional forms of power generation, such as oil, coal and nuclear fuel.

Dr. Philip Anderson, using a blackboard at the Bell Telephone Laboratories, shows the equation that helped him win the Nobel Prize for Physics. He has concentrated on research and the study of magnetic fields and solid state materials.

Anderson also was the first part-time professor ever engaged at Cambridge University, teaching theoretical physics in 1967.

The sixth and seventh Nobel Prize winners from AT&T Bell Labs were Arno A. Penzias and Robert W. Wilson. They were cited in 1978 for their 1965 discovery of cosmic background radiation, which confirmed the "big bang" theory of the origin of the universe.

Arno Penzias, left, and Robert Wilson of Bell Laboratories share their 1978 Nobel Prize for discoveries of cosmic background radiation.

Photo Credit: Associated Press

Wilson and Penzias found a residual "heat" that fills the space between all stars and galaxies. In 1963 and '64 they were using the same equipment in a project they hoped would help reveal the origins of the Milky Way galaxy. What first appeared to be bothersome background radiation that interfered with their Milky Way problem was really the remains of a cosmic explosion that give birth to the entire universe some 20 billion years ago.

The "big bang" theory was based on the observation of American astronomer Edwin Hubble that the galaxies are flying apart from one another. Penzias suspected that some of the heat from that explosion should be left over and, therefore, barely detectable with extremely sensitive radio receivers.

Their "listening" to the original sounds of creation was no accident at Bell Labs. It came at a time when the most sensitive radio telescope in the world was assembled at Crawford Hill in Holmdel for satellite communications studies in connection with the Bell System's Echo and Telstar projects.

In 1979, Penzias found evidence suggesting the universe will expand forever. He credits Bell Labs with giving scientists the opportunity to contemplate and pursue such abstract theories on when life in the universe began. He sums up his experience at Bell Labs this way:

"I have been living in New Jersey for over 20 years. When I moved to New Jersey (1962), I was really moving to Bell Laboratories, the place I had dreamt about working ever since I can remember.

"Having lived here for over 20 years, I find lots to like about New Jersey: The people, the beaches, the Pine Barrens— even the weather. Most of all I enjoy living near the center of an extended metropolitan area with a richly diverse culture, encompassing the arts as well as the sciences."

Penzias' partner, Robert Wilson, was also lured to Bell Labs in 1963 for similar reasons. He gives this capsule account of his work and life in New Jersey:

"It was Bell Labs that drew me to New Jersey in 1963. As a graduate student in California, I considered various industrial and academic places to work and concluded that not only did Bell Labs offer an immediate opportunity to continue my work in radio astronomy, but there were also other things going on there that I could be interested in.

"In the years of living in New Jersey, I have grown to love the eastern woodlands with their distinct changes in season. In fact, now that I ski and do radio astronomy at millimeter wavelengths, I look forward to the coming of winter, the best season for both activities."

Another banner year for Princeton University was 1979. Steven Weinberg, a Princeton Ph.D. alumnus (1957), shared the Nobel Prize in physics for his contribution to the theory of the unified weak and electromagnetic interaction between elementary particles. The theory predicts masses of the order of 100 proton masses, but today's particle accelerators are not powerful enough to be able to produce such particles. Weinberg's theoretical conclusions await the development of better technology to prove what his mind believes to exist.

Sir Arthur Lewis, the James Madison professor of political economy at Princeton University, received the 1979 Nobel Prize in economics for his pioneering research into economic development in Third World countries. Lewis has tackled issues that are basic to the causes of poverty among populations in the developing world, according to the Swedish Academy of Sciences, which has been bestowing Nobel Prizes on the world's leading citizens and thinkers since 1901.

Lewis is best known as the creator of the "Lewis Model," an economic theory that describes how traditional societies make the economic transition to modern nations.

The 1980 Nobel Prize for physics was shared by Val L. Fitch, former chairman of Princeton's physics department. Fitch discovered in 1964, while at Princeton, that there was an "implied failure of time reversal invariance" for elementary particles. Physicists pore over elementary particles for clues to the underlying physical laws and symmetries of nature.

One of the deepest of those principles has to do with symmetry under reversal of the arrow of time. The effect is a tiny one, uncovered in a remote corner of physical phenomena, but it was instantly recognized to be of the most profound significance. The Princeton experiment opened a window on the very smallest —and very largest scales—of nature.

Another Bell Labs scientist, Arthur Schawlow, shared the 1981 Nobel Prize in physics for his work on laser spectroscopy. Schawlow was co-inventor of the laser at Bell Labs in the late 1950s.

Star-Ledger Photo

Val L. Fitch, Professor of Physics and Chairman of the Physics Department at Princeton University, explains the "big bang theory," which won him the Nobel Prize in Physics with James W. Cronin.

By beaming laser light at an atom from opposite directions, Schawlow and his colleagues were able to neutralize the Doppler effect, a phenomenon in which atoms absorb either higher or lower frequencies, depending on their direction of movement.

Schawlow, who joined Bell Labs in 1951 and is currently at Stanford University, collaborated with Charles Townes in the development of the laser.

Milton Friedman, winner of the 1976 Nobel Prize in Economics, grew up in Rahway, graduating as the high school valedictorian in 1928. Friedman won the school mathematics and science prizes for four consecutive years and took first place in the oratorical contest the year he was graduated.

A dedicated math buff, Friedman entered Rutgers College at age 15 and was graduated four years later.

Friedman received the Nobel Prize for his achievements in the fields of consumption analysis and monetary theory and history. He demonstrated the complexity of "stabilization theory." Friedman's work repudiated certain Keynesian principles long held to be true. Keynes believed that full employment could be achieved only if governments and central banks deliberately encouraged investment in new capital and goods and maintained a cheap money policy and public investment during a recession.

Friedman favored less government tampering with the economic machine and greater emphasis on free market forces to stabilize the swings between periods of prosperity and recessions.

A Bergen County biochemist, R. Bruce Merrifield, won the Nobel Prize in chemistry in 1984 for his method of creating peptides, protein molecules that are the essence of action in living matter, in his laboratory.

An endocrinologist who raised six children before returning to science, Merrifield was cited by the Nobel Academy for his development of a simple and brilliant rapid automated method to make peptides, the building blocks of proteins.

The method of synthesis has great practical importance for the development of new drugs and for gene technology. The research is used in recombinant DNA, the genetic code of life.

"Without his research, some experiments and processes today done in days would have taken years, even decades," said biochemist Bo Malmostrom, chairman of the Nobel Chemistry Committee.

A Cresskill resident since 1960, Merrifield is a professor at Rockefeller University in New York City. His frontier work on polymers and proteins was completed in 1968.

Landmark Ocean Grove Auditorium and Stokes Statue.

OCEAN GROVE

It began in 1869 as a makeshift tent colony, a small, spiritual community that became "God's square mile of health and happiness." Today, Ocean Grove is a National Historic Site, a unique religious-cultural center still clinging to the Victorian values of faith, morality and common decency.

Until 1979, Ocean Grove, a mile-wide resort in mid-Monmouth County, was closed to traffic on Sundays. But the automobile and time finally caught up to Ocean Grove, bringing the historic religious refuge grudgingly into the 20th Century.

Some 40,000 vacationers enjoy America's Victorian wonderland each summer, escaping into a bygone era that comes alive when 114 colorful family tents spring up around the world-famous wooden auditorium that seats 7,000. It's the season of sun, surf, fun and peaceful reflection, just 60 miles from New York City in the heart of the Jersey Shore.

To visitors young and old, Ocean Grove is a timeless gateway into yesterday.

The narrow, twisting streets with names like Pilgrim Pathway and Mount Carmel Way are lined with the largest assemblage of original, authentic Victorian architecture in America.

Everywhere one looks in this tightly packed home of the Camp Meeting Association of the Methodist Church are enchant-ing balconies and verandas decorated with gingerbread carpenter's lace, spires and towers protuding elegantly above gabled rooftops, chapels, tabernacles, fountains, pavilions and a boardwalk fronting a wide-open beach and ocean free of intrusive buildings so common along the overdeveloped, metropolitan shoreline.

Ocean Grove owes its unbroken tradition of tranquillity and antiquity to a visionary Methodist pastor who lived in nearby Farmingdale. The Rev. William B. Osborn sought spiritual refreshment and fellowship, a place to get away from the pressures and painful memories of the post-Civil War period.

In 1867, Osborn started his search for a site for a camp meeting. With the Rev. J.R. Andrews of Vineland, Osborn came across a remote hideaway near Cape May known as Seven Mile Beach. It seemed like the ideal setting for a religious gathering, except the environment was infested with millions of mosquitoes. The search continued along the Jersey Shore between Sandy Hook and Cape May.

Finally in the summer of 1869, Osborn, in one of his many solo expeditions, found what he wanted: A 300-acre grove of trees, tangled briers and beach plum bushes protected by high dunes, and a noticeable absence of flying pests.

A few footpaths most likely used by Indians all merged into a wagon turnpike, about where Main Street divides the town today.

Rows of tents similar to the ones pitched by Ocean Grove's first settlers line Pilgrim Pathway.

There were four souls living in the secluded grove—Mr. and Mrs. George Rogers and their two children.

To the north was an uninhabited stretch of land later founded as Asbury Park by James A. Bradley, who purchased the first lot in Ocean Grove for $86.

To the south on the other side of Goose Pond was another vacant tract developed by Bradley and named after him, Bradley Beach.

Osborn had no difficulty convincing a group of Methodists of the need for a religious camp for quiet relaxation and wholesome recreation.

The nucleus of the camp meeting consisted of seven ministers, four faithful followers and their families. The 19 founders pitched tents in a clearing near Long Pond, some 300 yards from the sea, and held their first prayer meeting in a candlelit tent on the evening of July 31, 1869. The sermon by the Rev. Ellwood H. Stokes of Red Bank, the district superintendent, was, "In the Beginning, God."

On Dec. 22, 1869, 13 ministers and 13 laymen organized the Ocean Grove Camp Meeting Association of the Methodist Episcopal Church. Soon after, the name "Episcopal" was removed from the corporate title.

The New Jersey Legislature and governor granted Ocean Grove a charter on March 3, 1870 for the purpose of "providing and maintaining for the members and friends of the Methodist Episcopal Church, a proper, convenient and desirable permanent Camp Meeting ground and Christian seaside resort."

The association acquired the 300-acre tract for $40,000. Like the Indians before them, the worshippers from New Jersey, New York and Pennsylvania lived in tents and returned to their permanent inland homes by Oct. 1. Off-season, the grove was watched over by a few caretakers.

In the settling years, there were 200 tents for every summer cottage built for seasonal shelter. By 1875, the railroad extended tracks to the central shore region, bringing as many as 50,000 people to the grove and its gently sloping beaches.

The core of the Methodist community is the solid wood auditorium, a national landmark conceived in 1893 to house the religious and cultural activities of the growing congregation. Fifteen plans were submitted to the Camp Meeting Association, which selected a design by Fred T. Camp of Nassau Street, New York City.

Ground was broken on Dec. 2, 1893. With an average working crew of 36 men, the edifice was erected in 92 days at a cost of $69,112.16. The original plans show that 6,442 cubic yards of earth had to be excavated, or 173,934 square feet. The foundation (broken stone mixed with cement) was poured into 6-by-7-by-9-foot-deep trenches, with a capstone of Pennsylvania granite 2½-by-3½-feet thick.

About 15 tons of stone were placed under each of the seven main trusses, placed 21 feet apart and each spanning 161 feet. The steel and iron reinforcing the wooden structure weighed 550,000 pounds. The building contains 262 windows and doors.

The parabolic-shaped ceiling rises 55 feet from the floor, while the main tower soars 131 feet from the ground.

The overall dimensions are 225 by 161 feet, for a total of 36,225 square feet, covering almost an acre.

Designed to seat 9,600 people using folding chairs and benches, the auditorium today contains 7,000 theater seats.

The triple-towered auditorium, plus belfry, immediately became a favorite stop for eight U.S. Presidents, every state governor since 1894, and famous entertainers, opera singers, evangelists, bands, lecturers, concert artists, statesmen, humorists, astronauts and TV personalities. Among them: Presidents Grant, Garfield, McKinley, Teddy Roosevelt, Taft, Wilson, Eisenhower and Nixon, Enrico Caruso, Marion Anderson, John Phillip Sousa, Billy Sunday and Billy Graham, Nelson Eddy, Duke Ellington, Fred Waring, Victor Borge, Pearl Bailey, Will Rogers, Art Linkletter, William Jennings Bryan, Booker T. Washington, Helen Keller, Lowell Thomas, Baroness von Trapp and Dr. Norman Vincent Peale.

The world's largest auditorium organ was installed in the giant meeting hall in 1907 by Robert Hope-Jones, who is credited with nine-tenths of the innovations in the pipe organ industry during the first decade of the 20th Century.

The four-manual console ranks with the most versatile in the world, producing lightning flashes and thunder rolls, electrical chimes and whispers to accompany soloists. One special key lights up a huge electric flag, which can be made to flutter as if in a breeze, in full view of the 7,000 spectators.

The largest pipe, low C, is 32 feet in length, 12 feet in perimeter and weighs one ton.

The greatest organ stop invented by Hope-Jones was the Diaphone, which generated a tone of great weight. The prototype was built for the Ocean Grove organ in 1908. The enormous pipes were constructed from 2½-inch-thick sugar pine by a lumber company in Asbury Park and hauled to the auditorium by a team of oxen.

The massive organ was installed at a cost of $27,000 and was inaugurated on the evening of July 3, 1908, in a brilliant recital by Mark Andrews of Montclair.

Another treasured landmark in Ocean Grove is the Beersheba, the first well, bored in June 1870. A common pump with a tin cup attached to a chain, the well was improved in 1883 at a cost of $21.30. The fountain is now inside an attractive gazebo in Auditorium Park.

Beyond Beersheba is the Janes Memorial Tabernacle, the oldest building of worship, dedicated on July 14, 1877. The original tabernacle was a second-hand tent purchased for $450. A basket collection was taken to help maintain the camp grounds, the first time money was set aside for that purpose. The amount collected came to $52.

Every weekday morning during the summer, adults gather for inspirational messages. During July and August, a "Preaching Mission" is also conducted in Janes Tabernacle, named after Bishop Edmund Janes.

Thornley Chapel is a living memorial to one of the charter members, Dr. Joseph H. Thornley, who, before his death in February 1889, thought a smaller building was needed to hold many meetings not requiring the space of the tabernacle or temple.

Heck Street is a showcase of highly decorative homes.

Star-Ledger Photo

A scenic boardwalk and rows of Victorian cottages are two hallmarks of Ocean Grove, the tent colony that grew into one of the state's most popular seaside communities.

Star-Ledger Photo

Every weekday morning throughout the summer, Thornley Chapel is crowded with children from two to 12 who come to learn Christian values and enjoy other kinds of activities.

Centennial Cottage, built in 1874, is a museum depicting early life in Ocean Grove. It is an excellent example of carpenter gothic architecture so typical of the Victorian era.

A life-size bronze statue of the Rev. Elwood H. Stokes, the first president of the Ocean Grove Camp Meeting Association, was unveiled in 1905. The Stokes monument stands before the auditorium facing the great Victorian promenade leading to the oceanfront.

The Auditorium Book Store owned and operated by the Camp Meeting Association is stocked with hundreds of Bibles, books, greeting cards, choir festival tapes and gifts of every description for every occasion.

Ocean Grove is also the birthplace of Mrs. Wagner's homemade pies. Mrs. William Wagner founded the famous pie business in the 1890s. Pie ovens were excavated from the site in the 1950s when a new bungalow replaced Mrs. Wagner's two-story frame house and cookery.

Ocean Grove today is a compatible mix of the old and the new. Young artists are taking up residence in refurbished Victorian homes and new art galleries are luring patrons from New York and Philadelphia.

Concerts, film festivals, sand castle contests, college theater and workshops, gospel choirs, string bands, bazaars, lifeguard tournaments, the New Jersey State Opera Orchestra and, yes, even motor car rallies, are all part of Ocean Grove's changing lifestyle.

Outwardly, however, the grove remains a handsome picture-postcard slice of life that has changed little since the Rev. William Osborn started pitching tents and building cottages by the sea more than a century ago.

As Americans rediscover their heritage, the Ocean Grove

experience becomes more and more valuable for historians and artists alike.

One of the world's most popular comedians and filmmakers, Woody Allen, searched everywhere, much like Osborn, for a setting for one of his motion pictures. Allen found what he was looking for in 1979 when he happened upon Ocean Grove. The movie, "Stardust Memories," made at the quiet Jersey resort, is about another time, when life was much different.

Those memories, however, live on in Ocean Grove and in Allen's movie, a reflection of Victorian life, frozen forever.

Ocean Grove's restored Centennial Cottage sports the ornate gingergbread found on many older homes in shore towns throughout the state.

Courtesy: Keyes, Martin & Company

View of Ocean Grove boardwalk.

Star-Ledger Photo

Silas Condict County Park in Kinnelon.

PARKS

New Jersey is an intricate quilt pattern of public parks, forests, marinas, wildlife and natural areas for every conceivable outdoor activity.

With green open spaces in just about everyone's backyard— from local and county to state and federal recreation areas— there's a world of natural and cultural excitement happening at any moment in the more than 600 parks gracing the Garden State's landscape.

There are apple festivals and antique auto rallies ... husky dog sled races and Far East Harbor festivals ... caravans and kennel clubs ... china painters and chair caning clinics ... glass blowers and Colonial candlelight tours ... tea parties and Dixieland bands ... flea markets and scavenger hunts ... square dances and barbershop quartets ... doll shows and ethnic flag-raising ceremonies ... and even edible plant and water ecology walks.

At High Point in the Skylands at the northern tip of New Jersey to Cape May Point in the southern coastal plains, there's an infinite variety of vegetation, wildlife and marine resources awaiting the heartiest adventurer or the occasional explorer.

From America's greatest cherry blossom festival in New Jersey's most populous city (Branch Brook Park, Newark), to the world's only natural holly forest at the Gateway National Recre-

ation Area on Sandy Hook, the abundance of open spaces makes New Jersey a unique environment for both urban man and a growing number of common and endangered species.

New Jersey benefited from the early recreation designs of Frederick Law Olmsted, who is best known for New York City's Central Park. Olmsted laid out Branch Brook Park and Weequahic Park, both in Newark.

Essex County hired Olmsted to plan 19 of the county's parks. The 19th Century architect was responsible for the "overpass" concept that allowed park activities to remain undisturbed by major thoroughfares, which were erected over recreation areas, or, in some cases, tunneled under parks.

In New Jersey, ocean parks, mountain parks and river parks offer visitors and vacationers any outdoor experience, from skiing at Great Gorge and Vernon Valley in hilly Sussex County, to surfing and swimming in the bays and ocean, as well as hundreds of fresh water ponds and lakes.

Two national parks represent markedly contrasting environments, both within an hour's drive from New Jersey's economic-transportation hub, Newark. Interstate 80 is the main freeway to the Delaware Water Gap National Recreation Area in the northwestern corner of New Jersey. The Garden State Parkway is the primary feeder to the Gateway National Recreation Area on Sandy Hook.

Gateway is the most popular beach park in New Jersey, registering more than 2.5 million visitors in 1982. It is the most heavily utilized park, embracing only 1,800 acres on a "spit of sand" jutting out into Raritan Bay along the Atlantic Ocean.

The majestic landmark on Sandy Hook is the lighthouse, the oldest operating one in the United States, built in 1764. The light from the 85-foot tower can be seen 19 miles out at sea.

Since pre-revolutionary times, Sandy Hook has been an island several times as severe storms broke through the narrow neck. The 6.5-mile-long sandbar was formed by glacial deposits left behind during the last ice age 10,000 years ago.

The constantly changing peninsula supports more than 300 marine and bird species, plus the only natural holly forest on the continent. One holly is more than 300 years old. Sharing space with the hollies are eastern red cedars, junipers, willows, bayberry, prickly pear cactus and wild black cherries.

Salt marshes on the bay side of Sandy Hook teem with tiny periwinkles and snails, fiddler crabs and grasshoppers. Spiders, scallops, mussels, sponges and even Diamond Backed Terrapins make Sandy Hook their home, living in salt meadow hay, pickle weed and sea lavender.

The hook's wildlife sanctuary, on the Atlantic Flyway, welcomes the endangered osprey (hawk fish), the great horned owl, great blue heron, snowy egrets, mute swans, buffleheads and clapper rails, which join the night-calling whippoorwill and the early daybreak mourning dove.

On the bay side, boaters can hide in Horseshoe and Spermaceti coves. Plum Island, on the southerly bay side, is a favorite retreat of anglers and picnickers. Before Europeans settled Sandy Hook, the Lenni-Lenape Indians enjoyed the fruit of the beach plum shrub, which abounds on the island.

The history of Sandy Hook parallels the story of a new nation's defense system. Control of the lighthouse sparked several skirmishes between British and Colonial forces. During the 1890s, gun batteries were established on the ocean side.

Fort Hancock became a major military installation during World War I—and a popular duck hunting place for military leaders, including Gen. and President Dwight Eisenhower. The last weapons system installed on Sandy Hook was part of the Nike missile network.

The Defense Department turned Sandy Hook and its attractive officers' mansions, designed by architect Stanford White, over to the National Park Service in 1975. The Coast Guard continues to occupy 200 acres at the northern tip of the hook.

Another historic landmark is the 1899 guard house and post jail, which has become the Sandy Hook Museum. Group tours can be arranged at the visitors center for the holly forest walk, dune walk, beach walk and, in the winter, snowshoe walk.

Some 90 miles from the Gateway salt marshes and dunes sprawls an equally impressive ecological paradise—the Delaware Water Gap National Recreation Area. Covering more than 70,000 acres, the Gap attracts the same number of visitors as Gateway, except there's 40 times more wilderness to get lost in.

The federal government began acquiring land around the Delaware River in 1966 in preparation for the Tocks Island Dam and Reservoir, a 12,000-acre conservation lake that someday may be built if the tri-state region anticipates a prolonged water shortage.

There's much to do and see in the bi-state national park, which has significant scientific and historical value. The nation's oldest commercial road takes sightseers back to the origins of the iron mining industry, connecting pre-Colonial villages in New Jersey with the first settlements in what is today Port Jervis, N.Y.

Geological formations are exposed in the sheer walls of the Gap, gorged out by the Delaware River. From the Kittatinny Point overlook at the foot of Mount Tammany, one can see the

The Barnegat Lighthouse, "Old Barney," stands as a sentinel in this view from the southern tip of Long Beach Island State Park.

last free-flowing river in the East as it races between the rocky walls of the Gap.

Exhibits on the site explain how the Kittatinny Ridge and Water Gap were formed. Trails take hikers all the way to the top of Mount Tammany and Sunfish Pond.

There are also panoramic views of the Gap from Blockhead Mountain. At Resort Point, on the southern edge of the Pennsylvania village by the Gap, stone foundations of the mid-19th Century Kittatinny House are still visible. A small stream once flowed through the hotel kitchen to provide water for cooking and cleaning.

Slateford Farm, at the foot of Mount Minsi and south of Arrow Island, consists of a cabin, shed and springhouse with a stone in its foundation dated 1827. Exposed construction details and authentic country-Victorian furnishings give a picture of life during that period. There are also remains of a slate quarry and a spectacular view of New Jersey Highlands.

Environmental education programs are conducted at Thunder Mountain, Watergate and Sky's Edge for students and teachers. Hidden Lake and Peters Valley, a crossroads village, are havens for artists and artisans. A crafts fair is held annually in late July or early August.

While the Gap and Gateway occupy New Jersey's farthest borders, the state parks generally fan out through the interior, serving every one of New Jersey's 21 counties.

Of the 36 state parks, forests and marinas, 10 nature centers featuring environmental-education programs have been developed at the state facilities. The state recreation areas where nature centers have not yet been established are listed here in alphabetical order.

- **Allamuchy Mountain State Park**, Warren County.

Stretched out along the Musconetcong River, Allamuchy Park takes in 5,046 acres in Warren and Morris counties. Local attractions include the New Jersey State Fish Hatchery, historic Waterloo Village, and the Land of Make Believe.

Within the recreation area are Deer Park Pond and an overlook with sweeping vistas of North Jersey's mountainous terrain. There are 40 sites for trailers and tents, fireplaces, picnic tables, a children's playground and fishing and hiking trails.

The Deer Park natural area contains 2,500 acres of undeveloped woodland open to the public during daylight hours for hiking, bird watching and nature study.

- **Barnegat Lighthouse State Park**, Long Beach Island.

The beacon of the sea is known as "Old Barney," the grand old champion of the tides. Boris Blai, dean of the Tyler School of Fine Arts at Temple University, describes the Barnegat Lighthouse, the centerpiece of the state park, as "a great piece of American sculpture, with the power to move minds and seize hearts . . . a mature work of art as well as a superb piece of engineering."

The lighthouse was the work of Gen. George Gordon Meade. It was built in 1857-58 at a cost of $60,000. The 50-foot tower, its lower half white and its upper a brilliant red, has stood constant and unfailing guard over "The Graveyard of the Atlantic."

Known to every mariner who has sailed the seven seas, Old Barney is open to visitors willing to walk up its 217 steps for a magnificent view of the shoreline and sea.

Barnegat Park provides 2,000 acres of bathing beach, picnic area, dunes and parking for an ideal day at the Jersey Shore. Salt water fishermen have access to the ocean for surf casting, in addition to an inlet bulkhead and stone jetty.

- **Belleplain State Forest**, Woodbine, Cape May County.

Stands of young pine, oak and southern white cedar cover this 12,000-acre forest in the southern coastal plain of New Jersey. Demonstrations of reforestation and silvicultural operations provide continuous harvesting of timber and conservation of forest resources.

Native holly trees and masses of laurel enhance the road-

Canoeists on the Delaware River. Courtesy: N.J. Div. of Travel & Tourism

sides and hiking trails. A six-mile trail connects Lake Nummy and East Creek Lake.

The 26-acre Nummy lake is an abandoned cranberry bog and reservoir. It has been transformed into a magnificent lake surrounded by pine, oak and cedar forest.

It was named in honor of the last Lenape Indian sachem (chief) to rule in that part of New Jersey. The remains of Sachem Nummy are said to have been buried on Nummy Island near Hereford Inlet between Stone Harbor and North Wildwood. The forest was once the hunting grounds for the Lenape Indians.

Besides numerous species of birds, one can find marks of deer, fox, cottontail, raccoon, opossum, red, gray and flying squirrels, muskrat, beaver and many other rodents.

- **Cheesequake State Park**, Matawan, Monmouth County.

Thriving within this 1,001-acre shore preserve are two salt marshes, cedar and cattail swamps, brackish streams, an old clay mine, an old stone dam, an old orchard, an old steamboat landing, Hooks Creek Lake, Perrine Pond, Interval Pond, a nameless pond, miles of trails and a beach-grass restoration area.

Little wooden bridges cross the soggy interface where marsh and land merge. There are 53 sites for trailers and tents and three fields for ball playing. The park is bordered by Cheesequake Creek and the Garden State Parkway. Arts and crafts shows are regular attractions during the summer months.

- **Delaware & Raritan Canal State Park**, on the Delaware River, Hunterdon County.

The Bull's Island section of the D&R Canal Park is home for one of the largest ostrich fern stands on the East Coast. The island also attracts an interesting variety of birds and mammals.

With two unique forest types, the Sycamore River Birch and the Elm-Silver Maple, Bull's Island provides an excellent area for nature observations.

Path worn by visitors near picnic area in Cheesequake State Park.

There's a launching ramp for boats on the Delaware River. Canoes and rowboats may be used in both the river and canal. Power boats are permitted only in the river.

The canal contains catfish, eel, rock bass and trout, while fishermen can take the same species plus smallmouth bass, pickerel, sunfish, suckers, carp and shad from the river.

The 80-acre, water-oriented park provides 75 sites for trailers and tents and facilities for showers, laundry, cooking and picnicking.

Nearby are the famous Flemington Glass Works and Peddlers Village across the river in Pennsylvania.

A festival greets each spring with plant sales, flea markets and arts and crafts displays.

The Kingston section of the D&R Canal Park consists of the Kingston Lock and the tow path used to haul cargo up and down the canal before the age of the diesel-powered tractor-trailer. Canoes can be rented and launched at Kingston. The 25-acre park goes to the Heathcote Brook and Millstone River at the Old Mill Dam.

• Fort Mott State Park, Salem County.

With a 10-gun battery at Fort Dupont on the Delaware Shore and Fort Delaware on Pea Patch Island in the middle of the river, Fort Mott was an important link in the seaward defenses of the Delaware River and early America's first ports.

Located at Finns Point, Fort Mott was first acquired by the federal government in 1838 as part of a master plan to fortify the mouth of the Delaware River. During the Civil War, two acres of the fort were set aside as a cemetery for Confederate prisoners of war who died while interned at the prison camp at Fort Delaware.

In 1875, the burial ground was designated Finns Point National Cemetery and monuments were erected to the 2,436 Confederate and 300 Union soliders buried there.

The 104-acre Fort Mott was first garrisoned in December 1897. During the Spanish-American War, it was manned by the 14th Pennsylvania Volunteer Infantry and Battery L, Fourth Artillery. The main armament of Fort Mott consisted of 12-inch breach loading, rifled coastal defense guns mounted on disappearing carriages. They were exposed to enemy fire from ships for only a brief time.

Following World War II, Fort Mott was decommissioned and the armament removed, never having fired a shot in anger. New Jersey acquired the site in 1947.

Fishing and crabbing in the Delaware River comprise the principal activity within the park, which also caters to family picnics, playfields for games and playgrounds for children.

• Hacklebarney State Park, Morris County.

Along the Black River in a gorge of unusual beauty in Morris County lies the Hacklebarney State Park. Established in 1924 with a gift of 24 acres from Adolphe E. Borie, the park has grown to 574 acres, most of which is a glacial valley fronting the Black River, with two tributary streams, Rinehart and Trout brooks, flowing through the area.

There are two versions of the origin of the word Hacklebarney. One story traces the name to workmen at an iron mine in the vicinity who persistently heckled a quick-tempered foreman, Barney Tracey. "Heckle" Barney in time became Hacklebarney.

Charles A. Philhower, a respected authority on Indian folklore, wrote on the language of the Lenni-Lenape inhabitants of the Delaware Valley:

"'Hackle' is probably a variant of 'Haki,' meaning ground, and 'barney' is a variation of 'bonihen,' (which means) to put wood on fire. Hence, 'Hackiboni,' to put wood on a fire on the ground—a bonfire."

The Hacklebarney streams are stocked annually with trout by the State Department of Environmental Protection and wildlife flourish in this ice-aged-shaped wilderness. Hunting and fishing are permitted in the Class III natural area.

Across the Black River from Hacklebarney Park is a transition forest. The wood is composed of hemlock and mixed hardwoods from the Northern Mesic Ravine to the Northern Flood Plain.

• Hewitt State Forest, Passaic County.

On the map it's just a dot of green, but it's an important spot of open space that comes between Greenwood Lake and Upper Greenwood Lake.

The park is about a mile long and a half-mile wide, big enough to have its own mountain (Bearfort), two brooks (Green and Cooley) and Surprise Lake and West Pond. It's a lovely place to sit and gaze out over the great Greenwood lakes, half of which lie in New Jersey, the other half in New York. The ecologically unique lake forest memorializes Abram Hewitt, the 19th Century iron master from nearby Ringwood.

• Hopatcong State Park, Landing, Morris County.

Located on the largest lake in New Jersey, Hopatcong Park includes a section of the old Morris Canal. The dam and gatehouse controlling the level of the nine-mile-long Lake Hopatcong are within the 107-acre park.

One of the 23 water turbines once used in lifting canal boats over the inclined planes is housed in a concrete structure near the dam.

Beginning in 1832, Morris Canal transportation was the chief means of conveying coal, iron and zinc across the state for half a century. In its best year, 1866, the canal supported 889,229 tons of transported freight.

The canal was 90 miles long and the trip from Newark to Phillipsburg took five days. The carrying charge for coal through to tidewater, including toll, was about $2.25 per ton.

A small cove at the north end of Hopatcong State Park.

Star-Ledger Photo

Hopatcong Park has been dedicated a "no hunting" area. Hunting, trapping and the carrying of firearms or bows and arrows are prohibited.

Charcoal and gas fires are permitted but must be confined to the metal grills provided, or to stoves brought by picnickers.

A well-graded lawn, gradually sloping toward the lake, invites sun bathing.

Like other state parks, Hopatcong is the site of many cultural and artistic events during the summer season.

• **Jenny Jump Forest**, Hope Township, Warren County.

Three trails wind through the 1,118-acre elongated park in northwestern New Jersey. One path goes through an orchard, another through a swamp and the third across a summit nearly 1,100 feet in elevation.

The park's pinnacle is 1,106 feet above sea level. Camping grounds and recreation space separate the Orchard Picnic and Notch Picnic sites.

A nearby attraction is an early Moravian settlement. A Christian demonination descended from the Bohemian Brethren, Moravians emigrated from Czechoslovakia. They hold that the Scriptures are the only rule of faith and practice.

• **Monmouth Battlefield State Park**, Freehold, Monmouth County.

The story of the American Revolution unfolds at this historic site, where the first major engagement in the war took place and made a heroine of Molly Pitcher, the farmer's wife who brought water to the soldiers and loaded cannons and rifles.

The 1,600-acre park was dedicated on the 200th anniversary of the Monmouth Battle—June 25, 1978. A re-enactment of the battle is the main attraction at the museum, which shows miniature soldiers moving across a green board controlled by lights.

Weamaconk Creek and Wemrock Brook traverse the width of the park and feed a small pond. The Molly Pitcher Spring and Well are located between the tributaries. The park is just west of the Freehold Race Track.

• **Parvin State Park**, Elmer, Salem County.

Just 40 miles from Atlantic City, a recreation Mecca for U.S. servicemen during World War II, existed a prisoner-of-war camp for German soldiers. After the war, Parvin Camp was inhabitated for a while by the Kulmuks, descendants of Mongols who fled Siberia during the Stalin era.

Parvin lies between the Pine Barrens and the rich, alluvial Delaware Valley. Along the Maurice River, which meanders down through Cumberland County, are small streams, one of which is called Muddy Run.

Small ponds were formed by damming, the stored water providing power for operation of grist and saw mills, one of which was owned by a family named Parvin.

New Jersey acquired the first piece of the 1,125-acre park in 1930 for $73,677.29. The holdings include 918 acres of forest and 107 acres of water. Parvin Lake is about three times as large as Thundergust Lake, which lies at the easterly end of the arm-shaped park.

A cabin colony was built in Parvin during the Depression by the Civilian Conservation Corps (CCC). Each cabin has its own boat landing.

During the Second World War, German prisoners were allowed to work at various industries in South Jersey, including the P.J. Ritter Food Co. in nearby Bridgeton. The POW camp was equipped with a recreation hall, two large mess halls, a motion picture theater and a store.

Following the war, the camp became a home for displaced Japanese from the West Coast. Many of them worked at Seabrook Farms, the first frozen food plant in the world.

The Philadelphia Zoological Research School has identified 61 different woody shrubs, well over 200 herbaceous flowering plants and 17 ferns and club mosses. The 38 types of trees include ash, birch, cherry, pine, walnut and flowering dogwood.

The park can accommodate 56 places for tents and trailers. Boat and canoe rentals are available, as well as a children's playground, nature area and snack bar.

- **Penn State Forest**, Burlington County.

With the exception of a few sandy footpaths, life in this 5,000-acre wilderness has not changed since the ice age 10,000 years ago. The only human intrusion was a fire tower atop Bear Swamp Hill—elevation 190 feet—which was wiped out by a jet plane in 1971, killing the National Guard pilot operating out of McGuire Air Force Base.

In the core of the Pine Barrens, Penn Forest is truly a place to wander through. The nearest civilization is a gas station and a few houses in Jenkins (pop. 100).

Hunters and horseback riders have discovered its isolated, primitive serenity. Bathing and picnicking along an out-of-the-way beach on Lake Oswego are really the only family-oriented recreation activities encouraged by the state. Visitors can walk or drive through the forest on a half-dozen dirt and sand roads named Sooey, Cabin, Deep Hollow, Lost Lane and Chatsworth.

- **Ramapo Mountain State Forest**, Oakland, Bergen County.

A long sliver of land slicing through the mountainous suburbs of Oakland, Mahwah, Pompton Lakes and Ringwood, Ramapo Forest is a refreshing Green-Acres break in the heavily developed bedroom communities rambling through North Jersey.

Of the 2,500 acres set aside by the state to serve as public open spaces, 1,500 acres have been dedicated as a natural preserve. Only fishing and hiking are permitted in the forest. In the middle of the natural area is the 120-acre Ramapo Lake. Some 18 miles of trails run up and down the nearly five-mile-long green belt.

The state assembled the acreage in 1976, much of it acquired from the MacEvoy Estate. MacEvoy was a wealthy miner and banker.

- **Ringwood State Park**, Passaic County.

Stroll down Honeysuckle Lane and breathe in the beauty of the Skylands Botanical Gardens ... or follow the maze of trails that will take you to numerous ponds, named Swan, Duck, Sally, Gatum, Brushwood, Weyble, Glasmere and Mill ... or enjoy the crystal clear waters of Bear Swamp Lake and Shepherd Lake.

For indoor sights, there are the exquisite Skylands Manor House and the historic Ringwood Manor, where Gen. Washington set up headquarters on several occasions and Robert Erskine, surveyor general for the Continental Army, prepared many maps aiding Washington in his military campaigns.

The 579 acres at Ringwood Park look like a jigsaw puzzle of natural and historic preservation coming together around Cupsaw Lake and Cannonball Pond, which are outside the public recreation area.

The botanical garden is one of the perennial wonders of New Jersey. Flower lovers and photographers can spend a full day examining the combined works of nature and man in the winter garden, octagonal garden, summer garden, perennial garden, annual garden, wildflower garden, bog garden, heather garden, rhododendron display garden, azalea garden, peony garden ... and the cactus rock, the horsechestnut collection and stone eagles.

Ringwood's origins began with the birth of the new world's iron industry in 1740. Three families have occupied the rambling mansion since the American Revolution: The Ryersons, the Coopers and the Hewitts.

Peter Cooper, a philanthropist, founded Cooper Union Institute, a tuition-free school in New York City. A tutor of Cooper's son took over the country residence in 1856 after he married Cooper's daughter. The tutor, Abram S. Hewitt, was America's foremost iron master of the 19th Century.

- **Round Valley Park**, Hunterdon County.

A massive body of water bounded by a green buffer lures recreationists year-round to this 4,003-acre, man-made playground. The oval reservoir was formed by damming the gaps of a natural horseshoe-shaped valley.

Its deepest point is 160 feet. The 55-billion-gallon impoundment, one by three miles, is a delightful fishing, swimming and boating lake, drawing weekend escapists from Newark, Jersey City, Paterson and surrounding suburbs. During the winter, patrons can ice skate, sled, ski cross-country, fish and camp. There are 20 sites for tents and trailers.

Nineteen species of fish flourish in Round Valley. Rainbow and brown trout are stocked yearly by the state. Lake trout were introduced into the reservoir in March 1977. Waterfowl hunting is allowed by boat only during the normal hunting season.

- **Spruce Run Park**, Hunterdon County.

New Jersey's third largest reservoir, Spruce Run, covers 1,290 acres of water surface and 15 miles of shoreline. Opened in June 1973, the recreation area was designed for easy movement by the handicapped, with ramps and paved walks reaching the bathing beach and a fishing pier.

A three-acre-long bathing beach is protected by lifeguards from Memorial Day to Labor Day. The camping area can accommodate 70 setups.

The waters of Spruce Run, along with its two main feeders—Spruce Run Creek and Mulhockaway Creek—offer excellent casting, and catches, for every angler. The creeks are stocked each spring with rainbow and brown trout.

There's a self-sustaining population of large mouth bass, plus other species common to the reservoir: Blue gills, pumpkinseeds, redbreast, sunfish, rock bass, brown bullheads and yellow perch. Fishermen have also come across chain pickerel, northern pike and small mouth bass. The latest addition to the reservoir are tiger muskies.

- **Stokes State Forest**, Sussex County.

One of the most interesting gorges in the state can be found in Stokes Forest, the second largest open space preserve in New Jersey.

Tillman Ravine is an idyllic setting where crystal waters cascade down craggy creeks. The ravine is natural laboratory undisturbed by man, where the forest, rocks and soil as affected by climatic conditions and natural processes may be observed always.

A canopy of towering, graceful hemlocks and other kinds of old growth cover the gorge. The steep banks of the ravine are faced with masses of native rhododendron.

Hidden deep within the 15,000-acre mountainous timberland are the New Jersey State School of Conservation, the oldest environmental field laboratory in the world, as well as a Boy Scout camp and 4-H camp. In the center of the 12-mile-long forest is Stony Lake with its two islands.

An old Indian trail crosses Culvers Gap, one of the 75 miles of footpaths and roads within the forest. Sweeping views of the countryside can be seen from Sunrise Mountain and along the Appalachian Trail, the longest in the United States, running from Maine to Georgia.

Mountain laurels grow profusely in the forest and when in bloom in mid-June present a spectacular blaze of color. Dogwood, azalea and other flowering shrubs and plants blossom through the spring and summer months.

In a large grove of hemlocks, bordering a rippling creek, is Kittle Field, a cool, shady place for picnics.

On the western side of the forest are Kittatinny Lake and Culvers Lake for camping, fishing, swimming and boating.

- **Voorhees State Park**, Hunterdon County.

Tucked away in the northwestern watershed basin by Round Valley and Spruce Run reservoirs is Voorhees Park, another pleasant retreat with scenic trails, an observatory, playgrounds and picnic facilities. It is 516 acres of woodlands welcoming campers and hikers. Tanglewood Trail is a good starting point. Motor vehicles can travel on the scenic road to the observatory and Hill Acres.

- **Wawayanda State Park**, Sussex County.

Laced with lots of challenging trails, including the Appalachian, Wawayanda is one of the four state parks along the New Jersey-New York border. The focal point of the park is Wawayanda Lake, a huge body of water dotted with four islands just north of Highland Lake.

A smaller, narrower yet equally attractive watering spot is Lake Lookout, which can be reached by Lookout Trail. Wawayanda Lake is surrounded by four trails—Wingdam, Double Pond, Pump House and South End. Other trails within the 12,000-acre nature park are the Cedar Swamp, Turkey Ridge, Old Coal, Laurel Pond, Red Dot, Banker and Hoefferlien.

- **Worthington State Forest**, Warren County.

Some of the most rugged terrain in northern New Jersey, along the Kittatinny Mountain overlooking the Delaware River, make up this densely wooded forest. On the top of the mountain sits Sunfish Pond, a glassy-looking glacial lake about 1,400 feet above sea level.

The forest extends six miles along the crest of the Kittatinny Ridge and, except for the fields along the Delaware River, is completely wooded.

The river valley is rich in Indian lore and arrowheads and pieces of old pottery have been unearthed by visitors. Old Mine Road, the nation's first commercial road used by the iron industry, passes through the forest and along the river.

Dunnfield Creek falls 1,000 feet from Mount Tammany to the Delaware, its banks lined with hemlock, maple and birch. The stream is one of the few in New Jersey supporting native brook trout.

An abandoned road, departing from the Appalachian Trail above the Delaware River, follows the creek for two-thirds of its length, then climbs a ravine to rejoin the Appalachian. The white and pink bloom of the mountain laurel in the spring make the trip especially worthwhile.

From high atop Worthington Forest, one can see five islands in the Delaware River as it bends around the park. The islands are Tocks, site of the proposed dam and reservoir project; Labar; DePue; Shawnee, and Arrow.

Finally, cabins are available at eight of the state parks and forests: Bass River, Belleplain, High Point, Jenny Jump, Lebanon, Parvin, Stokes and Wharton. Rates range from a low of $10 a night to $70 a week, and a high of $25 a night to $168 a week.

Star-Ledger Photo

A trail in Lebanon State Park in the area of Routes 70 and 72 in Ocean County.

Courtesy: The Victoria Foundation

Youths learn the principles of geometry at The Victoria Foundation's geodesic dome.

PHILANTHROPY

*W*ithout their quiet generosity, the quality of life in New Jersey would be greatly diminished.

They are in the business of giving—to the arts, to the poor, to the sick and handicapped . . . and to a voiceless environment in need of protection from man's thoughtless activities.

The givers are New Jersey's philanthropic foundations—themselves products of wealth and fortunes—whose only purpose is improving the human condition and the physical world we all must share.

Philanthropy is a democratic society's way of trying to balance the scales of social inequality: Helping the less fortunate to help themselves realize their full potential in a free land.

No gift is too small nor any task too large for one who cares about life and its endless opportunities. Whether it's reaching for the gifted child in the inner city or saving a remote wildlife habitat from industrial destruction, New Jersey's philanthropic foundations serve as the guardians of our endangered human and natural resources.

They are often the conscience of corporate America and a bureaucracized government, leading such initially unconventional causes as consumer and environmental protection, planned parenthood and the worker's and public's right to know on issues involving occupational health and safety.

When a need or a problem surfaces, the community's benefactors respond by pooling their resources, no matter how limited.

In 1979, for example, more than 30 New Jersey corporations united to form the Business Arts Foundation to support the state's arts, jeopardized by double-digit inflation and the start of what turned out to be a long recession. The $1 million fund-raising campaign kept many flourishing art organizations afloat during the worst economic times since the Great Depression of the 1930s.

Back in 1972, when a dollar was worth more than twice today's currency, the Johnson Foundation in New Brunswick established the National Center for the Prevention and Treatment of Child Abuse and Neglect with a grant of $588,000.

The Johnson Foundation has given more than a half-billion dollars to reduce human suffering for millions of people. Johnson is second only to the Ford Foundation in annual donations, primarily in health-related fields.

Wealth alone does not inspire a charitable deed. Little contributions from grateful graduates giving $5 or $10 a year as expressions of appreciation can make a big collective difference.

Rutgers University, for example, received a record $7.4 million in 1982, according to Bruce D. Newman, executive director of the Rutgers University Foundation.

New Jersey's foundations are committed first to making the community work as viable neighborhoods and families. For a community is only as healthy as its residents and businesses concerned about one another's well being.

The following are among the most active of the more than 100 foundations in the Garden State.

Geraldine R. Dodge Foundation

Bits of light . . . points of truth is what the Geraldine R. Dodge Foundation in Morristown searches for in giving $4 million a year to worthy causes and projects, mostly in New Jersey. It's a tough assignment, as the foundation's executive director, Scott McVay, has learned:

"Almost too easily one can picture a number of dark trends in society: Rising military expenditures, inflation, joblessness, spread of totalitarian regimes, violence, unwanted children, loss of farmland and topsoil, depletion of moist tropical forests harboring diverse habitats and fabulous species, the massive production of hazardous wastes that contaminate the soil, ground water and air, acid precipitation, and the list goes on . . . the insistent drumbeat of growing numbers of us—at nearly a quarter million souls a day—puts more stress upon the already strained biological resources upon which human well-being depends: The croplands, grasslands, forests and fisheries."

The Dodge Foundation, organized in 1977, focuses on teenage pregnancy, toxic wastes, farmlands, the Pinelands and the arts. The teenage problem received six grants totaling $225,000 just in 1981. Since 1977, the Dodge Foundation has contributed $560,445 (through 1981) to assist in the development of the comprehensive management plan for the Pine Barrens.

In addition, $158,000 went to implement the landmark plan, "Agriculture for New Jersey," by the State Department of Agriculture, the New Jersey Conservation Foundation and the Middlesex-Somerset-Mercer Regional Council.

Six grants amounting to $170,000 went to New Jersey theaters, for such productions as "Paul Robeson" at Crossroads in New Brunswick, "Cymbeline" at the New Jersey Shakespeare Festival in Madison, "Overland Rooms" at Stage II McCarter Theatre in Princeton, "Out of the Night" at the George Street Playhouse in New Brunswick, and the videotaping of Crossroads' production of "A Love Song for Miss Lydia" by Trenton playwright Donald Evans for broadcast by New Jersey Network.

Following are a random sampling of some of the recipients of Dodge grants.

The Middlesex County Cultural and Heritage Commission—to help sponsor the New Jersey State Teen Arts Program. County and state festivals are held each spring as well as year-round extension projects. Young people exhibit and perform, are sensitively critiqued and work directly with professional artists in workshops. More than 10,000 students from across the state participate in the teen arts festival.

Chesire Home—a residential health care center in Madison for mentally alert young adults with severe physical disabilities. Men and women enjoy participating in a friendly community offering attendant care as well as opportunities for the development of skills for independence and employment.

Among 200 Chesire Homes worldwide, four are in the United States. All have been created through renovation of buildings. The Madison home is the first expressly constructed and designed for wheelchair-bound persons.

Project U.S.E.—to organize youngsters, both middle-class and urban poor, to explore locales in the state and foster a pioneering spirit in students. U.S.E. stands for Urban Suburban Environments. The Dodge grant allows the Newark Wilderness Coali-

Participants in the 1979 New Jersey State Teen Arts Festival hoist a giant puppet during the celebration. The arts festival is supported in part by the Geraldine R. Dodge Foundation, organized in 1977.

Courtesy: Geraldine R. Dodge Foundation

Courtesy: Geraldine R. Dodge Foundation

The generosity of New Jersey foundations is not confined within state lines. Here a youngster learns the dairy business at Macomber Farm in Massachusetts, a 46-acre farm and entertainment center that receives funds from the Dodge Foundation.

tion to participate in the outdoors learning laboratory conducted by Project U.S.E., based in Long Branch.

ISLES—to help impoverished areas help themselves through programs in housing, economic development and community-based technologies. ISLES, in Princeton, is establishing a Community Land Trust in a section of East Trenton, allowing the working poor to acquire home ownership and control the destiny of their neighborhood.

Literacy Volunteers of New Jersey—to help illiterate persons to read via one-on-one tutoring. An estimated 138,000 adult New Jerseyans cannot read well enough to fill out a driver's license or follow a simple recipe. The Princeton organization's goal is to wipe out illiteracy in New Jersey.

Aspira, Inc.—Established in Newark in 1968, Aspira of New Jersey is a community-based agency devoted to reversing the current trend in which more than 63 percent of the 100,000 Hispanic students in New Jersey will not finish high school, and only 10 percent will go on to higher education. The Dodge grant supports a creative arts program offering biweekly workshops in the performing and visual arts to Hispanic teenagers in Essex, Passaic and Hudson counties.

Instructions, Experiences, Exposures—for the Newark-based group of educators who have developed a Saturday program of classes for inner-city gifted and talented elementary school students.

Centrally located at Essex County College, IEE serves 85 students, each enrolled in at least two courses within a wide range of disciplines: Social studies/humanities, art, mathematics, biology and creative writing. Participating in the program are Rutgers University, the New Jersey University of Medicine and Dentistry, Newark Public Library and the Newark Museum.

Recycling Railroads—With nearly 700 miles of abandoned railroad rights-of-way in New Jersey, RR of Newton is a pioneering group trying to turn old roadbeds into recreational parks. With a view toward the possible need for restoration of rail service in the future, Recycling Railroads is working in the northwestern corner of the state to create linear parks and to promote the "rails-to-trails" recreational program.

Peters Valley Craftsmen—In 1970, a little crossroads hamlet in a valley of the Kittatinny Mountains in Layton was transformed into a community of skilled artisans.

Among the craftsmen's gallery exhibitions was a mounted show entitled "Seven Photographers: The Delaware Valley." A Dodge grant paid for a catalog—"a gallery between two covers"—that preserved the eloquent visual interpretations of life in the valley. Proceeds from the catalog sales paid for the costs of circulating the exhibition to museums around the state and country.

Architects' Community Design Center—With a professional staff and eager student apprentices, ACDC of East Orange provides poor communities with free or low-cost planning services.

Parks, playgrounds, day-care centers and neighborhood revitalization plans have been among its projects. With a Dodge grant, the community center set up a nonprofit business component, offering services for a fee to the professional field and government agencies, while fulfilling its traditional role of upgrading impoverished neighborhoods.

The Fund for New Jersey

Charles F. Wallace, an inventor and industrialist from Westfield, died in 1964, and his family established a fund to benefit worthy New Jersey projects. With grants approaching the million dollar-a-year mark, the Fund for New Jersey, with headquarters in East Orange, supports efforts that seem to be "tilting at windmills," according to its director, Robert P. Corman, a former state deputy public advocate.

In 1972, the fund joined the New Jersey Coalition for Fair Broadcasting in its fight to increase the quantity and quality of broadcast coverage in New Jersey. The battle is still going on, with some measurable progress.

Since 1974, the fund stood behind the Fair Housing Council of Bergen County's legal challenge to the racial-steering practices of that county's real estate industry. In 1980, a historic federal court settlement with state and national implications was signed.

In 1977, a special fund was started to assist the pre-casino residents of Atlantic City, its aged and poor, in protecting their homes, jobs and community from an impending massive physical transformation. The Neighborhood Technical Assistance Corp. of Atlantic City today is building a community-support structure serving needy residents.

In 1973, the Fund for New Jersey sought to establish a Newark Community Foundation to address the city's many social-economic problems. By the end of 1979, the Greater Essex Community Foundation became a reality, generating assets of nearly a quarter-million dollars.

Among the fund's grant recipients are:

ACORN—The Association of Community Organizations for Reform Now was started in Jersey City to help citizens participate in policy decisions affecting their daily lives. Since 1981, a $25,000 grant has helped ACORN organize more than 800 families and has established seven new community organizations in Jersey

City. Reflecting the recent change in public aid, ACORN is now generating 60 percent of its revenue from member dues.

BISON—Business in Support of Neighborhoods is the first attempt by a nonprofit group to serve as a liaison, both financially and technically, between the corporate and grass-roots neighborhood communities. BISON is in Princeton.

Family Life Education Network came into being in 1981 to combat the unacceptable levels of adolescent pregnancy, drug abuse and juvenile delinquency. The fund provided a $28,000 grant to help a network of more than 20 statewide organizations assist school districts and communities in these efforts. The Rutgers University Department of Community Education in New Brunswick houses the family life project.

INFORM—a public interest research organization known for its responsible and excellent reports on corporate practices relating to toxic wastes, INFORM conducted a study on the extent to which the state's chemical industry is making efforts to reduce the volume of its hazardous discharges.

The New Jersey Coalition for Battered Women is a volunteer organization of service providers and concerned citizens acting as a clearinghouse and advocacy arm for abused women seeking help. The grant was used to broaden the coalition's membership and fund-raising efforts. Courtney Nance Esposito of Pennington is the project coordinator.

The Clean Water Action Project is one of New Jersey's most successful water pollution control efforts. More than 200 volunteers walk the state's streams and identify improper and illegal disposal of hazardous or toxic wastes.

State and federal environmental agencies are then pressed to take enforcement action against violators. The streamwalkers are under the jurisdiction of the Public Interest Research Group in Trenton, a student-consumer group founded by Ralph Nader.

Hoffmann-La Roche

One of the world's largest pharmaceutical companies, Hoffmann-La Roche in Clifton-Nutley, has one of the most active community affairs programs in New Jersey. Although Roche does not disclose how much it invests in community activities, the amount runs into the millions of dollars.

The key to the corporate program is linking the Roche community with the outside community. A group of employes from the maintenance department, for example, have "adopted" a cottage of retarded women in a state institution. The Roche employes provide social and recreational experiences for these women, who otherwise would remain institutionalized around the clock.

The Roche Research Chapter of Sigma Xi, the Scientific Research Society of North America, sponsors a number of programs with high schools in the Nutley-Clifton area. The students are part of the scientific community, with Roche engineers and scientists serving as role models for students, while also providing professional support for teachers.

A recent program is bringing the Roche Hispanic scientists into schools with significant Hispanic populations.

Community health nurses from several municipalities can continue their education under a program arranged by Roche with the New Jersey Department of Health.

The Roche Engineering Department invites young women pursuing a career in engineering at Stevens Institute of Technology in Hoboken to meet women engineers at Hoffmann-La Roche for a "Women in Engineering Day."

Roche also accepts management interns from local colleges: William Paterson, Montclair State and Bloomfield.

With the cutbacks in health care coverage, Roche decided to fund two local area projects for teenagers from 15 to 18 years old

on learning self-health care. In collaboration with a group of institutions and agencies, Roche is creating a model project for community agencies.

Awards, to date, have been made to the Greater Paterson General Hospital in Wayne, and the Protestant Community Center in Newark.

Roche also produced 10 14-minute films focusing on illness prevention and alternative health care in the home. The films will be used by all American Red Cross chapters.

The pharmaceutical company is also coordinating a curriculum of genetics education for middle-school grades. Under the heading of "Genetics: Investigating the Mosaic of Life," the lessons build on the natural fascination with life and heredity, which begins early with children.

While teachers recognize the value of genetics, they often have difficulty handling the complexities of the material. As a leader in genetic research, Roche developed the program to assist both students and teachers.

The Hyde & Watson Foundation

Improving the physical condition of schools, theaters, hospitals and buildings occupied by humanitarian groups is the sole function of the Hyde and Watson Foundation in Chatham.

With assets of $30 million, the foundation invests up to $2 million a year in capital improvements in facilities and structures within a 50-mile radius of Newark-New York. Such projects include relocations, alterations, expansions, equipment and generally increasing the efficiency, quality or capacity of important programs and services meeting social needs.

The Hyde Foundation was created in 1924 by Lillia Babbitt Hyde, daughter of B.T. Babbitt, a 19th Century industrialist. It was based in Elizabeth until 1966. The Hyde Foundation has assets of $19 million.

The John Jay and Eliza Jane Watson Foundation was established after the death in 1949 of John Watson, a brilliant troubleshooter for International Minerals & Chemicals. The Watson Foundation has investments totaling $11 million.

In 1983, the two foundations merged under a new administrative headquarters in Chatham. New Jersey is a major beneficiary of the combined foundations because the staff members who review the grant proposals live in the Garden State.

Both foundations have been guided by the same philosophy: "To meet the needs of our fellow man in education, health, religion, social services and the humanities and thus to grow in usefulness in perpetuity."

Examples of the Hyde & Watson Foundation funding priorities are:

Metamorphosis—a Princeton group that established the pilot Elizabethport Woodshed Projects, providing job training experience and employment opportunities for ex-offenders.

Newark Recycling, which received a grant for purchase of a forklift truck and canvas laundry carts to improve its vocational training program—involving ex-offenders—in the recycling of waste paper, glass and aluminum.

New Jersey Science/Technology Center, which created a center to enhance public understanding of the values of science and technology and the contributions made in New Jersey.

Miss Mason's School in Princeton, which produced a film and text for its expository English curriculum for use in public and private elementary schools nationwide.

Camp Nejeda Foundation, Newark, a grant to build, furnish and equip office facilities at its camp, which serves diabetic children.

Circus Arts Center, Hoboken, which purchased tools and equipment to help establish a unique training program in the circus arts for youths and adults.

The Hyde and Watson Foundation gave a grant to the Circus Arts Center in Hoboken for outdoor rigging equipment.

Westminster Choir College—a grant for alterations of the undercroft of its Bristol Chapel to provide an organ studio, five seminar rooms and a classroom.

Frost Valley YMCA, Montclair, a grant for building improvements of the Straus National Training Center for the new national "Healthy America Campaign" for community leaders and families.

Hand In Hand, Woodbridge, a grant for new programs for the mentally handicapped.

Calvary Episcopal Church, Summit, a grant for building improvements to increase operating efficiency and energy conservation.

The Robert Wood Johnson Foundation

Gen. Robert Wood Johnson was born and lived most of his life in New Brunswick. He built a family-owned business into one of the largest corporations in the world, Johnson & Johnson, based in Middlesex County.

When Johnson died in 1968, he left a foundation named after him with assets of about $1.2 billion, an amount exceeded only by the $3 billion Ford Foundation.

The Johnson Foundation disburses about $40 million a year

with a singular objective: To make health care more efficient and effective and less costly.

The Johnson Foundation's goal has been to find ways to prevent senile dementia, arteriosclerosis and cancer, so that a person may live out his or her full biologic lifespan with minimal deterioration.

Between 1954 and 1968, there was a 14-year period with little change in age-adjusted death rates. However, since then, America has seen a steady reduction in deaths due to a wide group of diseases as dissimilar as coronary artery complications and peptic ulcers—indeed, a drop in death rates for 11 of the 15 major killers of Americans.

Every year, 75 out of 100 Americans see a doctor. Twelve of those 100 will be hospitalized. Less than one in 100 will die.

The Johnson Foundation supports a variety of studies and demonstrations designed to help people to maintain or regain maximum attainable functions in their everyday lives. From 1968 through 1985, the foundation has invested more than a half-billion dollars toward improving the human condition.

Here's where the funds are allocated:

• Developing and testing new ways of providing health care services—52 percent of the annual appropriations.

• Helping health professionals acquire new skills needed to make health care more accessible, affordable and effective—17 percent.

• Conducting studies and evaluations to improve health care—30 percent.

• Other projects, including donations in the New Brunswick area where the foundation originated—1 percent.

Here's just a handful of representative projects and programs funded by the foundation:

• University of Medicine and Dentistry of New Jersey, Newark, $199,559, for a program to prepare minority students for careers in the medical profession.

• Case Western Reserve University School of Medicine, Cleveland, $149,909, for an evaluation of family dysfunction as a factor in moderate infant growth failure.

• Maine Medical Center, Portland, $145,794, for a study of causes and interventions related to falls by elderly people.

• Middlesex County College, Edison, a grant for a refresher course for registered nurses . . . Plainsboro Rescue Squad, South Jersey, training equipment . . . Salvation Army, New Brunswick, assistance to the indigent . . . St. Peter's School of Nursing, New Brunswick, a nurse training program . . . St. Vincent de Paul Society, Highlands, assistance to the indigent . . . United Way of Central New Jersey, Milltown, $200,000.

The Prudential Foundation

Since the Prudential Foundation in Newark was created on Dec. 27, 1977, it has concentrated on solving a broad range of social problems, from health, education, urban and public affairs to conservation and culture.

Its first president, William H. Tremayne, senior vice president of public affairs, instituted a new concept of "cooperative funding" in 1981. A multiple-year grant of $120,000 was awarded the Neighborhood Reinvestment Corp. to bring together residents, local government financial institutions, insurance companies and a cadre of volunteers whose common goal is urban rehabilitation.

With assets of more than $40 million for 1985, Prudential is increasing its grant activities each year, the 1985 level exceeding $8 million.

Among the hundreds of projects the insurance company is involved in are:

Renaissance Newark—support of public/private efforts to redevelop areas in downtown Newark, New Jersey's largest city and the state's financial-transportation hub.

Ironbound Educational and Cultural Center, Newark, a tool-lending library, giving Ironbound residents the opportunity to maintain and improve their homes and neighborhoods.

La Casa de Don Pedro—social, educational and recreational services to a predominately Hispanic Newark community.

The Family and Children's Service of New Jersey—a pilot program of protective services for the elderly.

University High School, Newark, supporting an alternative secondary school serving Newark's gifted and talented students.

Kessler Institute for Rehabilitation, West Orange, expansion and renovation of facilities to help disabled persons return to independent living.

Ethical Culture Society of Essex County—completion of a housing rehabilitation project on Lenox Avenue, Newark.

Leaguers of New Jersey—multi-service programs for youth.

Milford Reservation, the Pequannock Watershed in Passaic County owned by Newark, development of a Solar Conservation Center, a meeting and camping facility for the handicapped, urban youth and others.

Urban Land Research Foundation—identify and encourage programs that enhance and protect land undergoing development.

Morristown Beautiful—capital improvements to restore the Morristown Green.

Americans for Indian Opportunity—Indian participation in the political and economic decisions affecting Indian populations.

Public Technology, Inc.—to help local governments improve services and cut costs through practical use of applied science and technology.

The Schumann Foundation

John and Florence Schumann lived in Montclair and started their foundation in 1962. John was a top executive at General Motors and Florence was the daughter of A. Ward Ford, one of the founders of IBM (International Business Machines), the biggest computer company in the world.

With assets of $50 million, the Schumann Foundation set out to strengthen communities in which people help themselves toward a better life.

Foundation trustees favor organizations exhibiting a broad base of community support as evidenced by a measure of self-sufficiency. No grants are made to individuals or for permanent endowments, and general operating support is limited to a few compelling requests.

From the first day, the Schumann Foundation has placed special emphasis on Essex County. In the early years, funds were directed to institutions in Montclair and the neighboring communities of West Essex. In the late 1960s, a sizable portion of funds went to Newark following the 1967 riot.

One project Schumann is particularly proud of is St. Benedict's Prep in Newark, an alternative to urban schools confronted with insufficient funds, parental protests, student rebellions, teachers seeking transfers, absenteeism, vandalism and drug and alcohol abuse.

About 35 percent of the foundation's funds are committed to educational institutions. Grants have been made to schools with diverse purposes: Public, storefront preschool programs and preparatory, alternative, and prestigious universities.

St. Benedict's is a shining example of an inner-city educational success story. Serving 310 boys in grades seven through 12,

Photo Credit: George Kemper

Courtesy: The Schumann Foundation

Above, St. Benedict's Prep in Newark prepares urban youngsters for college and careers.

Below, The Child Development Center in Bloomfield is one of the many educational projects sponsored by the Schumann Foundation.

St. Benedict's is an eight-acre retreat of red brick Victorian and modern utilitarian structures circling a 113-year-old Benedictine monastery along Martin Luther King Jr. Boulevard (High Street) in Newark, a neglected neighborhood in transition.

The student body is one-quarter white and three-quarters black and Hispanic. St. Benedict's offers a curriculum that is both traditional and innovative. Most of the students enroll at the finest colleges after graduation: Holy Cross, West Point, Rutgers, Bowdoin.

The heart of St. Benedict's, spiritually and physically, is the Newark Abbey, housing 23 monks, 15 of whom teach at the school.

The Benedictine Order is 1,500 years old and maintains a tradition of strict discipline and scholarship.

The great school was forced to close in 1972 as urban blight spread to High Street and students fled to the suburbs with their families.

A 1963 graduate of St. Benedict's, Rev. Edwin Leahy, rescued the school from the ghetto and oblivion. Under Leahy's enthusiastic and optimistic leadership, St. Benedict's reopened its thick wooden doors in July 1973 with an all-black enrollment of 90 pupils.

When word of the school's scholastic success filtered into the community, whites from within the city—and some who now lived in suburbia—gradually returned to St. Benedict's.

Today, Leahy's special school operates 11 months a year, starting in July with a required six-week summer school of remedial and enrichment courses.

The Turrell Fund

Born in Newark, Herbert Turrell made his fortunes in pharmaceuticals and cosmetics. He was chief executive of OXZY Co., which was acquired by American Home Products Corp.

The fund was founded by Herbert and Margaret Turrell in 1935 and its assets today stand at $49 million. More than $3 million a year in grants are awarded to disadvantaged youth in New Jersey and Vermont. The primary emphasis is on the needs of the urban areas centered in Essex County.

The Turrell Fund believes the focal point of its philanthropy should be the family: How to keep it intact, how to create a kindly and constructive atmosphere, and how to meet its financial and other problems.

There has been a continuing need for residential care for children who cannot be cared for in their natural families. There are differing views on how to provide this care: Large institutions, group homes, foster homes, or through adoption.

The New Jersey Department of Corrections sought the assistance of the Turrell Fund in setting up the Jamesburg Training School for Boys and Girls. A $35,000 grant was given to assist in the start-up costs of the Jamesburg project.

Ranch Hope for Boys in Alloways, South Jersey, is a residential treatment facility with a full educational program on site. A $30,000 grant was invested in a new school building at the ranch.

St. Timothy's in the Ironbound section of Newark was begun in 1962 with Turrell Fund help. Assistance continues today, as St. Timothy youngsters attend schools in the community and participate in neighborhood activities.

Of the programs receiving Turrell funds, the least restrictive one furnishing out-of-home placement for children is the Host Homes Program under the auspices of the Ocean County 4-H Youth Development Task Force.

One of the largest funding projects ever undertaken by the Turrell Fund was the construction of a gymnasium at the East Orange Branch of the YMCA of the Oranges, Maplewood, West Essex and Sussex. Grants totaling $445,000 were committed to the new building, which was dedicated in 1980.

Although the Turrell Fund prefers grants for direct service to children, it does at times recognize the importance of the physical environment for youngsters. The Elizabethport Presbyterian Center and the Youth Consultation Service in Newark have both embarked upon neighborhood improvement projects with Turrell assistance.

The Elizabethport Center engaged youth in an energy conservation program. The project produced a rare combination of benefits: Employment and educational experience for the teen participants...fuel savings and warming living quarters for the families...and a small contribution to a major social-economic problem.

In Hoboken, the Hudson School was formed by parents anxious to see that the full potential of their children be realized. The small school, with an enrollment of 51, has sparked student interest by an unusual approach to staffing. The teachers often have other occupations, providing them with a variety of perspectives to bring to the classroom.

For example, a radio producer, an architect, an engineer, and a professional chef bring their daily experiences into the classroom, making the learning process much more relevant.

The Victoria Foundation

One of the oldest philanthropic organizations in the United States, the Victoria Foundation in Montclair was established in 1924 by Hendon Chubb, an insurance magnate who named the foundation after his mother.

With assets of more than $17 million, the Victoria Foundation generates about $2.5 million in grants annually. It is a recognized leader in the fields of education and community improvement.

In 1963, Victoria initiated a program to enrich educational offerings and achievements in basic subjects in the inner-city public school. Newark's Cleveland School became that central city model of educational excellence.

The foundation has invested hundreds of thousands of dollars to develop the "Newark Victoria Plan." Resources are committed for experimental programs, summer remedial sessions, arts, crafts and recreation, scholarship programs and testing.

The Victoria Plan anticipated by several years the federal "Head Start" program launched by President Johnson to combat illiteracy in urban public schools.

Another Victoria first was the start of a stonework apprenticeship for New Jerseyans under the coordination of the Greater Newark Urban Coalition. In conjuction with nine foundations and six corporations, Victoria put stonework apprentices to work at Manhattan's Cathedral of St. John the Divine, the largest gothic cathedral in America and the only apprenticeship of its kind in the nation.

A dying art was revived and unemployed men and women gained skills, which created a new market in refurbishing neglected landmarks.

At the same time, Victoria has been assisting the New Jersey Marine Sciences Consortium in order to develop and coordinate studies in marine sciences throughout the state. The consortium's success as a leader in protecting marine resources is evidenced by the fact that it has been awarded a grant to engineer a tri-lateral agreement among the United States, Israel and Egypt to revitalize and protect the southeastern shore of the Mediterranean Sea.

But almost all of the Victoria Foundation's work involves New Jersey's urban community. Two outstanding examples are the Tri-City Citizens Union for Progress, which is reclaiming abandoned homes in Newark's West Ward for families who then live in them, and the North Ward Cultural Center, a modern-day melting pot in Newark's predominately Italian North Ward.

Families and neighborhoods remain the overriding concerns of the Victoria Foundation, as reflected in these diverse interests:

Coalition Six—a neighborhood group composed of six adjacent church parishes along the border of Newark's Central and South wards.

New Ark School—a neighborhood self-improvement project at the eastern edge of Newark's Central Ward.

Different Strokes in Orange, an agency reaching out to, counseling and providing high school equivalency tutoring to dropouts with a record of antisocial behavior.

Spaulding for Children—a grant for the cost of publishing manuals on dealing with hard-to-place children by an adoption agency that has placed more than 600 in the last decade.

Kids Corporation—remedial training and cultural trips during the summer for youth from 27 Newark agencies.

Project Link—a community middle school serving dropouts and other post-sixth-graders with educational problems.

Project Quest—a non-sectarian program run by the Catholic Youth Organization (CYO) and offering career guidance field experiences, particularly in the communicating arts.

Second Chance—an agency dealing with physical and vocational needs of newly released ex-inmates of Caldwell Prison.

Montclair Grassroots—year-round support of an agency that uses local facilities (schools, parks, library) to conduct programs for underprivileged youth in Montclair.

Project USE—a grant to provide one- and two-day survival experiences in the forests of northern New Jersey for 140 Newark teenagers.

City Without Walls—an artists' cooperative that conducts art classes, holds exhibits and seeks to attract aspiring young artists within Newark.

Wetlands Institute in Stone Harbor, $25,000 to complete baseline studies on plant nutrients in tidal creek areas and for materials and equipment needed in citizen education programs.

YES (Youth Environmental Society), New Brunswick, a grant to produce a citizens' primer on the New Jersey Pinelands and to help defray operating expenses of the student ecology group.

Star-Ledger Photo

Since 1969 the Victoria Foundation has given more than $300,000 to F.O.C.U.S. (Field Orientation Center for Underprivileged Spanish), including the downpayment for their headquarters in Newark. F.O.C.U.S. responded by including the foundation's name in its title.

The Victoria Foundation supports diverse projects, including environmental protection efforts of the Wetlands Institute in Stone Harbor, South Jersey.

Star-Ledger Photo

The Cathedral of the Sacred Heart in Newark is a French Gothic masterpiece whose spires reach higher than those of Notre Dame. It is the center of the Archdiocese of Newark, which serves about 1.4 million parishioners.

Star-Ledger Photo

RELIGION

New Jersey's origins as a wilderness settled by Quakers and Puritans, wanting only the freedom to express their religious beliefs, are manifested today in the nearly 4,000 houses of worship reflecting a common faith in God.

Almost 4 million of the state's 7.5 million residents belong to some denomination, be it Baptist, Buddhist, Catholic, Episcopal, Jewish, Methodist or Presbyterian.

New Jersey's two oldest and most prominent academic institutions—Princeton and Rutgers universities—started as religious schools for the training of Presbyterian and Dutch Reform ministers, respectively.

They continue to be among the world's most prestigious learning centers for the ministry and other intellectual interests.

Religious congregations, moreover, have been responsible for some of New Jersey's finest works of art:

• The Cathedral of the Sacred Heart in Newark, a French Gothic masterpiece whose soaring spires are taller than the Notre Dame Cathedral in Paris or Westminster Abbey in London.

• The Temple B'nai Jeshurun, a striking modern ark with its eternal light reaching out from a hillside in Short Hills.

• The Byzantine-styled Greek Orthodox Cathedral in Tenafly, constructed in the form of a cross and crowned by a brilliant dome symbolizing "Heaven with Christ," the entire structure anchored on the towering Palisades like a beacon of hope.

• The Trinity Episcopal Cathedral, built over an underground crypt where worshippers once prayed in the center of Trenton, contains what is believed to be a fragment of the stone rolled away from Christ's tomb in Jerusalem on Easter morning.

Early America's venerable seminaries were also initiated by the Dutch Reformed Church at Queens College, now Rutgers, founded in 1766, and at Princeton College, organized in 1746.

The New Brunswick Theological Seminary was formally established at Rutgers in 1810, while the Princeton Theological Seminary was dedicated two years later.

They were followed by the Immaculate Conception Seminary for Catholic student priests, begun in 1861 in South Orange; the Drew Theological School in Madison, 1866, a Methodist seminary that houses the United Methodists Archives; the Rabbinical College of America in Morris Township, 1956; the Northeastern Bible College in Essex Fells, 1950; the Lamaist Buddhist Monastery of America in Washington Township, Warren County, 1958, and St. Sophia Ukrainian Orthodox Theological Seminary in South Bound Brook, 1975.

* * *

Cathedral of the Sacred Heart is the honored seat of Catholicism in New Jersey, the state's dominant religion, accounting for more than 40 percent, or 1.4 million, of the state's 2.8 million Catholic population.

Sacred Heart is the home of the archbishop, the highest ranking Catholic priest in New Jersey. The state's first Catholic diocese, or jurisdiction, was established by Pope Pius IX in 1853, the first bishop being James Roosevelt Bayley in 1859, a convert from the Anglican Communion and the nephew of St. Elizabeth Ann Seton, after whom Seton Hall University in South Orange is named.

Today, the Archdiocese of Newark serves 1.4 million parishioners in Essex, Bergen, Hudson and Union counties, a collection of 125 municipalities, 245 parishes, 199 Catholic elementary schools and 42 high schools, with a total enrollment of more than 75,000 students.

The balance of New Jersey is served by four Roman Catholic dioceses, in Trenton, Paterson, Camden and Metuchen, and an eparchy in Passaic for Eastern Rite Catholics.

Although the Newark archdiocese is geographically the smallest in the nation, covering only 541 square miles, it is served by one Catholic university (Seton Hall), three colleges (St. Peter's in Jersey City, Caldwell College and Felician College in Lodi), as well as the Immaculate Conception Seminary in South Orange.

The archdiocese also serves the medical community with eight Catholic hospitals, ranging from Holy Name in Teaneck to St. James in Newark.

The Newark archdiocese network is made up of 1,285 priests, 236 deacons, 183 religious brothers and 2,483 religious sisters.

Sacred Heart Cathedral remains an active urban parish for some 500 families in Newark, but its immense grandeur has made it a stunning showcase for the arts in recent years. The Cathedral Concert Series is a popular attraction featuring organ recitals, choirs, the Newark Boys Chorus, the Archdiocesan Festival Chorale, a candlelight carol sing, handbell ringers, original dance presentations and premiere performances such as "Dreamscapes" by the Caldwell College Theater.

The cathedral organ sends out a four-second reverberation in the 40,000-square-foot interior, producing a powerful acoustical effect. The organ contains nine divisions and 140 ranks, is located in the triforium, and is played from a three manual movable console. Of all the stops on the organ, the most brilliant is the *trompette-en-chamade*, a horizontal set of reed pipes installed directly over the high altar.

The great church measures 365 feet in length, with a width of 165 feet in the transepts. The front towers extend 232 feet into the air, 28 feet higher than Notre Dame and seven feet higher than Westminster Abbey. The copper-green spire, or flech, which tops the cathedral at the intersection of the nave and transept, soars 260 feet.

Originally conceived in the English-Irish Gothic style, the Newark cathedral gradually evolved on the drawing boards into a French neo-Gothic creation. The 200-by-800-foot plot for the new church was purchased on January 2, 1871 for $60,000. Excavation of the site took two years, 1875-76. Work on the foundations and piers, however, did not get under way until January 1898.

Newark architect Jeremiah O'Rourke selected Vermont Rockport granite as the exterior stone for the walls and towers. The cost of the cathedral was not to exceed $1 million. It cost at least 10 times that amount to finish over a 75-year period. As one of the most valuable landmarks in America today, Sacred Heart Cathedral is a priceless treasure.

The cathedral's incredible weight, including a steel-supported slate roof, is held up by 24 nave and ambulatory columns. The vaulting and clerestory rest on the giant pillars.

The altar, handcarved from Italian Pietra Santa marble, is topped by an imposing Botticino marble canopy standing 39 feet high. At the apex of the canopy is a figure of the cathedral's patron, the Sacred Heart of Jesus.

The focal point of the altar complex is the burnished bronze crucifix with light green onyx marble inlays and lifelike figure of

A view of the interior of the Cathedral of the Sacred Heart shows the massive stained glass window designed by Franz Zettler of Munich. Building the edifice was a 75-year project concluded in 1954.

Star-Ledger Photo

Christ carved from a solid block of Portuguese light rose marble, with garments of Carrara marble.

The finely detailed, handcarved woodwork surrounding the sanctuary was fashioned from Appalachian oak, which can also be found in the pews and ambulatory screens.

Ringing the main altar are five chapels dedicated to national saints representing the various ethnic groups that make up New Jersey's Catholic population.

The stained-glass windows, considered among the greatest in the world, were designed by renowned craftsman Franz Zettler of Munich, Germany. The thick bronze doors were made in Rome and installed in 1954, the year the cathedral was completed. It was dedicated on Oct. 19.

The pealing of the bells is a familiar sound in the city's North Ward and to visitors of Branch Brook Park, which serves as a lush green backdrop and mirrored lake image to the magnificent Gothic cathedral. There are 14 bells in the west tower, all cast in Padua, Italy, and tested by Vatican bell experts. The bells can be played from a small keyboard next to the master organ console in the south gallery, or automatically from a panel in the main sacristy.

The altars, mosaics, wood and stone carvings of New Jersey's most beautiful cathedral are not merely decorations displaying man's handiwork and ingenuity, they are, according to the Catholic church, "statements of an ageless Faith which continues to transcend the test of time . . . ."

* * *

Temple B'nai Jeshurun is a contemporary ark-like structure serving more than 1,200 families in the Essex area. B'nai Jeshurun, which means "children of the upright," is a reform synagogue situated on a heavily wooded 40-acre hillside in Short Hills.

Designed by the Gruzen Partnership of Newark and architect Pietro Belluschi, dean of M.I.T.'s School of Architecture, the superstructure is clad inside and out with a smooth-face, purple-brownish brick.

An exquisite stained-glass window rises 80 feet to the full height of the building. The only other natural light entering the temple filters through a 12-foot skylight across the ceiling of the sanctuary and a slit of glass between the brick facade and dark brown copper roof.

The tall colorful mosaic, fronting a landscaped courtyard with fountain, tells the story of the Ten Commandments. Inside, the 1,000-seat sanctuary is dramatically elevated by 11 burnt-orange carpeted steps approaching the Ark of the Covenant. Therein lies the sacred Torah, the five books, or Law, as written by Moses: Genesis, Exodus, Leviticus, Numbers and Deuteronomy. The scrolls, on fine parchment, contain the words of Moses, penned in Hebrew by a special scribe using a quill and ink.

Two French-woven tapestries, highlighted with Hebrew letters and designed by famed New Jersey artist Ben Shahn, enhance the Ark.

A 350-seat chapel to the left of the Ark is for bar mitzvahs, weddings, funerals and smaller services.

Every detail, inside and out, contributes to the ark's spiritual function. Even the lights in the parking lot have been designed with seven branches resembling the Menorah, the traditional symbol of Judaism, the Jewish faith.

The 20 classrooms are shaped like a conversation pit in the form of an octagon, with a lowered floor and raised ceiling.

The ancestors of B'nai Jeshurun lived for more than 1,000 years in Germany and Eastern Europe and built their temples wherever they settled. One group of about 20 German Jews fled the repressive conditions there, arriving in Newark in 1848. They were known as the "Forty Eighters" and they prayed in rented rooms on Harrison, Washington and Mulberry streets. They called their temporary house of worship B'nai Jeshurun.

After 10 years, they built a temple on Washington Street and Maiden Lane. During this period of their development, B'nai Jeshurun organized the Hebrew Orphan Asylum, which led to the establishment of the Jewish Child Care Association. It is now part of the Jewish Counselling Service Agency.

The Newark "Forty Eighters'" second home was built on

Designed by the Gruzen Partnership of Newark, Temple B'nai Jeshurun is situated on a wooded, 40-acre tract in Short Hills.

Photo Credit: Gil Amiaga

temple have been: Pulitzer Prize-winning composer Aaron Copland; Dr. Abraham L. Sachar, chancellor of Brandeis University; Dr. Jerome Wiesner, provost at M.I.T., and Rear Adm. Ross Trower, chief of chaplains, U.S. Navy.

A special musical Sabbath, "The Compassion Cantata," also premiered at the ark, a work by the synagogue's composer, Dr. Fred Picket.

* * *

The conception of **Trinity Episcopal Cathedral** in Trenton traces back to 1832 when the second Episcopal Bishop of New Jersey first envisioned a cathedral church for his growing diocese. More than a century would pass, however, before Bishop George Washington Doane's dream would become a stone-and-mortar house of worship.

The Episcopal Church has been a spiritual and social part of West Trenton community life since 1894. On Oct. 7 of that year, a modest gathering of Episcopalians met for evening prayer and Sunday school in a room of the old Cadwalader Mansion. Heirs of the Cadwalader estate gave land for a church at West State Street and Overbrook Avenue. All Saints Church was dedicated on Easter Day 1897.

It wasn't until 1930 when a diocesan convention spearheaded by Bishop Paul Matthews sought to make Trinity Church on Academy Street in the heart of the state capital as the site of the diocese's cathedral. Matthews led the movement for the construction of the new cathedral at the site of Trinity Church, founded in 1858.

The bishop and a friend, Ferdinand W. Roebling Jr., of the Roebling family that built the Brooklyn Bridge, made the initial donations for the building of the cathedral crypt. Completed on Dec. 31, 1936, parishioners of Trinity Cathedral worshipped in the underground crypt.

Work on the superstructure began in November 1952. The first service was held in the finished cathedral on Jan. 24, 1954.

Since 1960, an educational building has been added to the cathedral complex. It is the home of the Cathedral Day School, the

Temple B'nai Jeshurun in Short Hills welcomes its congregation with a 1,000-seat sanctuary of contemporary design. The Eternal Light hangs over the bronze doors of the Ark.

Washington and William streets in 1868. On July 19, Joseph Leucht was installed as rabbi, cantor and teacher.

By 1905, B'nai Jeshurun had grown into a large congregation capable of supporting a major temple at High Street and Waverly Avenue. The Newark temple served the childen of the upright well until their new Ark was built in Short Hills in 1968.

In June 1981, Barry Hewitt Greene was installed as the fifth senior rabbi of Congregation B'nai Jeshurun.

The Short Hills ark has been the setting of many cultural, artistic and historic events. In May 1971, more than 20,000 people filled the temple's grounds for the B'nai Jeshurun Israel Expo '71. It was one of the greatest Israel Fairs ever held in the United States.

Among those who have participated in special events at the

Trinity Episcopal Church, seen from State Street, traces its origins to 1894, when a small gathering met in a room of the Cadwalader mansion.

only Episcopal, church-based school in New Jersey offering classes from pre-nursery through sixth grade.

A memorial garden has been established at the cathedral. And a new chapel, St. Helier's, has been created in the north transept of the cathedral. It contains the 11th Century altar stone from the Isle of Jersey.

There is also a reliquary (a container for religious relics) preserving a fragment of the stone rolled away from Christ's tomb on Easter morning. The sacred stone was given to the church by the Armenian Patriarch of Jerusalem, who vouched for its authenticity.

More than 1,400 communicants belong to Trinity Cathedral. A Society for the Performing Arts has been organized to present the full spectrum of cultural events benefiting the church and the greater Trenton community.

On the first Sunday of each month from October to May, the society sponsors organ recitals featuring performers from churches in the New Jersey-Pennsylvania-New York region.

Thanksgiving at Trinity Cathedral is celebrated every year to the sound of bagpipes, honoring St. Andrew, whose name day is close to the annual Pilgrim's harvest-time ritual.

* * *

The Greek Orthodox Cathedral of St. John the Theologian in Tenafly is the latest expression of a 2,000-year-old religion which, like its Roman Catholic counterpart, began with the teachings of Jesus Christ.

For the first 1,000 years, the Christian church, both East and West, was united. However, the faith began to develop differently in the West. Eventually, those differences culminated in an East-West schism of the church. From then on, the Western Church was called Roman Catholic and the Eastern Church continued as Eastern Orthodox, Greek Orthodox and Apostolic Church.

It was in the Eastern city of Antioch that Christ's followers were first called Christians and where Peter became the first bishop. Greek was the universal language of the New Testament, as well as the writings of the early church fathers and the first ecumenical councils.

Eastern Orthodox worldwide membership today stands at approximately 350 million, of which 9.5 million practitioners reside in the United States.

The Greek Orthodox community in northern Bergen County took root in 1952 when a group of orthodox Christians were granted a charter by the Greek Orthodox Archdiocese of North and South America to establish a church in Fairview.

Under the leadership of Father Socrates Tsamutalis, a centralized parish and community center was built in 1968 and 1969 on 11 acres of land along the Palisades cliffs. The church seats 650.

Over the church's main entrance, there is a huge painting depicting Christ, the Mother Mary and St. John the Baptist. Parishioners are then led into the narthex, the first of three main sections of the church. The narthex is the area of preparation. Here, the catechumens remained during the liturgy of the faithful. It is here that the Orthodox Christian lights a candle, venerates the holy icons, and prays.

The nave, the main part of the church, is where the faithful gather to worship every Sunday and on feast days. In the Byzantine style of architecture, an icon screen (the Iconostas), divides the nave from the sanctuary. The sanctuary represents the presence of God in the church.

Immediately before the Iconostas is the solea, a platform representing the meeting place of God and man, of heaven and earth. There are three permanent appointments on the solea: The pulpit, the bishop's throne and the cantor's lectern, all representing the means through which the word of God is taught.

On April 5, 1979, the Tenafly church was elevated to the status of Cathedral of the Diocese of New Jersey, with Metropoli-

An exquisite dome towers above the altar in the Greek Orthodox Cathedral of St. John the Theologian in Tenafly, which accommodates 650 worshippers.

tan Silas as the Bishop. The 60-foot-tall cathedral, built in the shape of a cross, serves 700 families. The parish family is represented by the philanthropic organization of Greek Orthodox Ladies Philoptochos, St. Philothea Chapter; an active Acolyte program; a vibrant Sunday school; a community choir; a Mr. and Mrs. Club, and an enthusiastic youth program comprising Boy Scouts, Girl Scouts and Junior GOYA, as well as a Young Adults League.

Teachers of 'The Word'

When the Puritans arrived in North Jersey and the Quakers in South Jersey more than 300 years ago, religion was the dominant force that shaped their lives and the places they chose to settle. A church was the first community structure built by members of the faith, who made Sunday services the center of the family's religious and social activities.

They shared a Christian philosophy that stood for honesty, humility and hard work, as reflected in the life of Jesus Christ.

Fleeing from religious hostility and persecution in Europe, the Puritans and Quakers sought refuge in the New World, finding it in places like Newark and Salem, South Jersey, their new Edens for worship and for living an exemplary Christian life.

By the mid-18th Century, the first pastoral schools in the Colonies were being organized by the various Christian denominations. Some of the first religious academic institutions were founded in New Jersey.

* * *

Princeton University began in 1746 as the College of New Jersey, although the college was established primarily to educate Presbyterian and other ministers.

In 1812, the Princeton Theological Seminary was established by the General Assembly of the Presbyterian Church to prepare pastors "with various endowments suiting them to different stations in the church of Christ, may all possess a portion of the spirit of the primitive propagators of the Gospel."

The Princeton Seminary has one of the largest and most outstanding theological libraries in the world, a distinguished and experienced faculty and a spacious campus containing more than 20 buildings occupying 30 acres in the heart of Princeton.

Relations between Princeton Seminary and Princeton University have always been cordial and reciprocal. Seminary students, for example, enjoy the privileges of the extensive Firestone Library at the university and may take certain graduate and upper-division undergraduate courses.

Affiliated from the beginning with the Presbyterian Church and the wider Reformed tradition, Princeton Theological Seminary is today a denominational school with an ecumenical, interdenominational and worldwide constituency.

As one of the oldest seminaries in America, Princeton has graduated more than 16,000 alumni. One out of 10 graduates has served outside the United States.

In recent years, seminarians have come from more than 400 colleges and universities, as well as from 90 other seminaries and from 80 denominations, including nearly all Protestant varieties, in addition to the Roman and Eastern Orthodox Catholic churches. More than 60 students from other lands are registered at the seminary in various degree programs.

* * *

New Brunswick Theological Seminary, the first in the United States, was started in 1784 to train ministers for the Reformed Church in America. The seminary has been located in New Brunswick since 1810 when it was moved to the campus of Queens College (Rutgers), founded in 1766 under the aegis of the Dutch Reformed Church.

For half a century the two institutions shared facilities. The present site, two blocks from "Old Queens," was occupied in 1856.

Because of its long history, size and location, New Brunswick Seminary offers an exceptionally high student-faculty ratio of approximately 8-1, allowing for both individual and small group instruction.

Community living is an integral part of theological education at New Brunswick Seminary since many students and faculty members live on the eight-acre campus.

The Gardner Sage Library, dedicated in 1875, contains more than 134,000 volumes, including more than 340 periodicals on current subscription. More than 2,000 additional publications are accessioned annually.

That rich collection of theological works is supplemented by unusually strong resources in the classics, fine arts and social sciences.

As the official depository of denominational archives, the Dutch Church Room is a rare resource for the study of history and doctrine of the Reformed Church of America.

Seminary students also have access to the 1 million volumes of Rutgers' Alexander Library, just a five-minute walk from Zwemer Hall, the main building of the theological school.

Although a Reformed Church seminary, New Brunswick is ecumenical in its outlook and in its multi-denominational enrollment policy.

The faculty of New Brunswick Seminary enjoys a partnership with the faculty of the Princeton Seminary in a program of

Members of the Princeton Theological Seminary worship in Miller Chapel, which was built in 1834 and "Victorianized" in 1874.

study for the Doctor of Ministry degree. New Brunswick participates in the administration, admissions, instruction and evaluation of the program on a continuing basis.

In addition to the traditional theological courses at New Brunswick are several elective subjects such as "The Urban Church and Its Mission," "The Dynamics of Marriage and Family Relationships," "Theology and Problems of Death and Dying," and "Current Issues on Disarmament."

* * *

Drew University, founded in 1866 as a Methodist seminary, takes in a 186-acre, oak-forested campus in Madison, Morris County. The university today enrolls 2,300 men and women in an independent college of liberal arts and in the graduate and theological schools. There are 200 full-time students in the theological school and another 200 in the off-campus doctor of ministry program.

Before Drew was a university, it was a seminary started by the Methodist Church to prepare persons for "intellectually distinguished service in Christian ministry."

About 75 percent of the theology school's 3,000 alumni have made careers in the United Methodist Church, most of them as pastors. Two hundred Drew graduates are currently serving as church administrators, 18 as bishops of the church, 43 as district superintendents and seven as bishops of other denominations. More than 90 are with faculties or administrations of theological schools and about two dozen are chief executive officers of schools or colleges.

Drew alumni can be found in Canada, the Philippines, Korea, Japan, Australia, New Guinea, Norway, Greece, Lebanon, Thailand, India, West Pakistan, South Africa and Mexico.

Although 70 percent of Drew's enrolled students are United Methodist, the rest are from the Baptist, Episcopalian, Presbyterian, Roman Catholic, United Church of Christ and other denominations.

Student ages range from 21 to 65, with the median being 28. Geographically, a typical class represents 11 states, and about 10

Students take advantage of spring weather by meeting for class on the grounds of the Drew Theological School in Madison.

Star-Ledger Photo

percent of the students come from other countries, mainly Asian and West African. The enrollment of the Theological School is evenly divided between men and women.

Among those who teach in the theology school are a Mennonite from India and a Benedictine priest. The 26 teacher-scholars represent 10 denominations.

Drew's Urban Theology Unit provides for a year of study in Sheffield, England, where some of the most advanced work in urban ministry in the world is being carried out.

In 1981, the United Methodist Archives were housed in a new building adjacent to the Rose Memorial Library, making Drew the research center for the denomination.

Drew is one of the four American universities housing the Oxford Edition of John Wesley's works, and the Methodist Librarian at Drew is editor of the Methodist Union Catalog.

Among the many groups on campus are:

• The Women's Resource Center in Wesley House, which provides special programs in film, dialogue and worship and serves as a gathering place to discuss issues concerned with women in theology and ministry.

• A Black Ministerial Caucus, which provides the community with special opportunities to experience black worship, with special courses and projects to meet the needs of black ministerial candidates. Each fall the Black Caucus holds a preaching revival in Craig Chapel, with choirs from local black churches participating in the meeting.

• The International Students Organization, a voluntary gathering of students from the three schools of the university seeking to furnish fellowship and assistance to one another during the year, meeting weekly for a fellowship meal and educational program.

* * *

The Seminary of the Immaculate Conception was founded in 1861 in South Orange by James Roosevelt Bayley, the first bishop of the Diocese of Newark. The seminary was located on the cam-

pus of Seton Hall College until 1926, when it moved to a 459-acre wilderness tract in the Ramapo River Valley, Mahwah.

In January 1983, the Newark Diocese sold the rural country estate to a private developer for $8.6 million, returning the seminary to its home base at Seton Hall this year.

The Immaculate Conception Library contains 69,282 volumes, along with a current subscription to 648 periodicals, journals and newspapers, a cassette tape collection of 200 titles and a microfilm library of 290 reels covering 20 periodical titles. The main reading room has 34 individual study carrels. The library is exclusively a professional one with special strength in Biblical studies, liturgy and church history, a select collection of Jewish studies and a periodical section with particular emphasis on theological journals.

The seminary's mission is to "teach and witness to the Word of God and to serve His People by fostering their growth and renewal through prayer, study and Christian community."

The 1984-85 enrollment at Immaculate Conception was 80 seminarians (men in formation) and 75 nonseminarians (sisters, priests, brothers, lay persons). There are 26 members of the faculty.

Since 1861, the seminary has ordained more than 2,000 priests.

In 1976, the Institute for Priests was established at the request of the bishops of New Jersey in response to an increasing need of priests for "continuous ministerial development in these changing times which call for personal, spiritual and professional renewal." A four-week residency is designed especially for priests who have been active in the ministry for some time and who seek a brief sabbatical interval, freed from the pressures of pastoral responsibility.

The more than 100 biblical, theological and historical courses offered at Immaculate Conception span the full spectrum of human history. Some course titles: "Christ: The Future of Humanity," "The Mystery of Faith," "Experience and God," "Christian Values in Sexual Morality," "Community Aspects of Alcoholism and Drug Abuse," "The Parish Priest in the '80s," "Confrontations with Death: A Shell of Hope," "Understanding Stress in a Spiritual Context," and "Pastoral Psychology of the Handicapped."

* * *

The Rabbinical College of America came into being in 1956 with 10 students studying in a small, one-family frame house in the heart of Newark. The college moved to a 15.2-acre campus in rural Morris Township in 1971, its enrollment having grown to 200 full-time and 100 part-time students.

The campus has three magnificent Gothic-styled stone buildings housing classrooms, dormitories, administrative offices, library, auditorium, dining room and kitchen, synagogue and public rooms. The campus also has tennis courts, an athletic field, a gymnasium and an outdoor pool on handsomely landscaped grounds.

The Rabbinical College is an affiliate of the worldwide Lubavitcher Movement founded in the 18th Century in the town of Lubavitch, Russia. The Lubavitcher Movement maintains a network of Chabad Houses on college campuses throughout the country. They are directed by rabbis ordained at the Lubavitcher institutions. The Rabbinical College of America is an integral part of that network.

The principle of Chabad is the philosophy of the Lubavitcher Movement and is the motivating force behind the studies at the Rabbinical College.

The term Chabad is an acrostic of the Hebrew words for three general segments of the intellect: Chochma (wisdom), Bina (understanding) and Daat (knowledge).

Baruch Klar and Moshe Morgenstern spend some time studying in the library of the Rabbinical College of America in Morris Township.

Star-Ledger Photo

The movement has as its cornerstone the doctrine of Ahavat Yisroel: The love of one's fellow Jew. Although its adherents are observant, Chabad-Lubavitch recognizes no difference between Jews, concerning itself with both the spiritual and material welfare of every Jew.

Emphasizing education, Lubavitchers maintain nurseries, summer camps, primary and secondary schools and colleges for the study of advanced fields of Jewish education.

More than 20 million volumes have emanated from the Lubavitcher Movement in recent years. Printed in more than a dozen different languages, they are designed for all levels of religious education, from those versed in Torah and Jewish knowledge to those requiring an explanation and interpretation of the basic teachings of authentic Judaism.

The Rabbinical College publishes a semi-annual scholarly journal, Pirchei Ha-t'mimim, which contains the findings of Talmudic research conducted by faculty and students. It also issues a periodical, He-oros Ha-t'mimim, a compilation of original contributions by students of Chabad Chassidic philosophy. Students of the New Direction publish Nefesh (the Jewish Soul) in newspaper format. Some 100,000 copies are distributed on college and university campuses throughout the United States.

An extensive library contains a collection of the basic texts of Talmud, Jewish Codes and Jurisprudence, Responsa, Homiletics, Kabbalah and Chassidus.

The college sponsors a Community Outreach program, which sends students out into the community to help break down barriers separating Jews from each other.

Not all students elect to enter the Rabbinate. A number of students enter the teaching profession, while others become social workers in urban communities in the U.S. and abroad.

Students from 10 countries and almost two dozen states were studying for ordination last year. There are 11 full-time faculty members and six visiting professors.

If the student body continues to increase at its present rate, there should be some 600 students in the degree program within 10 years.

At the Rabbinical College, a 50-week-a-year curriculum embraces traditional theological studies, Biblical interpretation, the Law of the Talmud, ethics and philosophy.

* * *

St. Sophia Theological Seminary was instituted in 1975 in the Archdiocesan Center of the Ukrainian Orthodox Church in South Bound Brook.

Archbishop Mstyslav, Metropolitan of the Ukrainian Orthodox Church of the United States, established the Archdiocesan Center as a symbol of religious freedom and a memorial to those who gave their lives for the self-determination and liberty of the Ukrainian nation.

The seminary's name, St. Sophia, stands for "holy wisdom" and exemplifies that which all priests strive to attain. St. Sophia also relates to the great centers of Orthodox Christianity: St. Sophia in Constantinople and St. Sophia in Kiev, Ukraine.

St. Sophia Seminary is the educational arm of the 100-acre Ukrainian Archdiocesan Center in South Bound Brook. The seminary is a spacious, three-story Colonial structure consisting of living quarters, classrooms and chapel.

A program of academic cooperation between Rutgers University in New Brunswick and St. Sophia Seminary permits students to pursue degrees at the New Brunswick Theological Seminary.

Through an educational consortium of three schools—St. Sophia, New Brunswick and Drew University—a doctoral program in liturgics has been formed.

St. Sophia Seminary Library is located in the Home of Ukrainian Culture and contains centuries-old works dedicated to the ancient traditions of the orthodox church.

Other buildings within the archdiocesan center are St. Andrew's Memorial Church, the church consistory, museum, memorial cemetery, the Metropolitan's residence, and residences of clergy and laity assigned to the center.

The grounds of the archdiocesan center are historically significant. Events leading to the American Revolution and the Declaration of Independence occurred at the South Bound Brook site. The consistory is one of the oldest historical monuments in Somerset County and was the home of the American patriot Henry Fisher.

Among the accredited courses offered at St. Sophia's is one on The Festive Cycles, the Paschal and Nativity cycles, including the Feasts of the Theotokos, Lent, Holy Week and Pentecost. Another course is on "Cosmology, Ecclesiology and Salvation," an examination of the creation of the world; the angelic, material and animate worlds; man, paradise and original sin; the church and her sacraments; the spiritual life; death and resurrection; heaven and hell, and the final judgment.

* * *

Northeastern Bible College modestly appeared in 1950 with six students in a class at Brookdale Baptist Church in Bloomfield. Within two years, Northeastern acquired a 17½-acre campus in Essex Fells, where its founder, Dr. Charles W. Anderson, presided until 1980.

The Bible college is a professional, uni-purpose school: Everyone majors in the Bible. In fact, "Majoring in the Word of God" is the school's academic theme.

The course of study at a Bible college develops three major concerns simultaneously. In addition to Biblical studies, there are professional and general studies to prepare ministers and Christian workers for their service to God and humanity.

One-third of the courses required for graduation are Bible or theology subjects. All areas of study recognize "revealed truth" in their disciplines.

Christian service is the second goal of a Bible school student. Courses at NBC are particularly geared toward life ministries in the pastorate, in the mission field, in Christian education, elementary education and music.

The third aspect of Bible school training is "spiritual lifestyle." Many campus activities, including daily chapels, special conferences and the Student Missionary Fellowship, are designed to help students with their Christian development.

The college's philosophy is directed at helping the student to "recognize the Holy Spirit as the ultimate Teacher and the Bible as the supreme authority." Northeastern exists to "nurture these qualities in an atmosphere of faith, scholarship and caring."

The student body numbered 279 this year, with a faculty of 29 teachers. Many of the courses at Northeastern relate to the dynamically changing conditions in the lay world, such as "Applied Anthropology," "Afro-American History," "Earth Science," "Existentialism," "Public Speaking," "Urban Sociology," "Beginning Sign Language," "Marriage and Family," "Cults," and "Church Recreation."

* * *

The Lamaist Buddhist Monastery of America has its Western origins in the Kalmuck-Mongolian community of Freewood Acres in Howell Township, Monmouth County.

The Venerable Geshe Wangyal founded the first Tibetan Buddhist Monastery in the United States in 1958 because of the Kalmucks living in New Jersey who wished to maintain their traditional Buddhist worship.

The Geshe, a lama or "spiritual teacher," laid the groundwork for the spread of Buddhist teachings to Americans. The first monastery was constructed in Freewood by Wangyal and his students. The Howell Township property was sold in 1977, the monastery moving to Washington Township, where a retreat house had been built in 1968.

To replace the property in Freewood Acres, the monastery purchased a large, three-story brick house in New Brunswick in 1979 for use as a residency with a small chapel. In October 1982, the New Brunswick house was formally presented to the Tibet Fund as a gift to His Holiness, the Dalai Lama.

Wangyal was born in Kalmuck, Mongolia, in 1901. At 20, he went to the Drepung Monastery in Tibet and received the geshe degree, representing the highest level of scholastic and spiritual knowledge. Wangyal studied extensively in Tibet, China and Mongolia, arriving in the United States in 1955.

Geshe-la, as he is known, founded and directed the monastery and lectured at Columbia and Princeton universities. He also translated two books from Tibetan into English, "The Door of Liberation" and "The Prince Who Became a Cuckoo, A Tale of Liberation."

Geshe-la died on January 30, 1980. In 1982, the Dalai Lama spoke of him as the "pilot" of Buddhism in America, during the Lama's first appearance at the Labsum Shedrub Ling Monastery in Warren County.

In 1966, '72, '74, '78 and '82, Wangyal had brought more geshes from the East to the New Jersey monastery. Some are now teaching Buddhism, Tibetan and Sanskrit at the monastery.

Through a grant from the Institute for Advanced Studies of World Religions, the Lamaist Monastery translated major Tibetan works into English, representing a significant portion of the primary Indian writings of Buddhist psychology and philosophy.

Public instruction has been given at regular intervals at the monastery's Washington facilities. The subjects taught include Tibetan, Indian, Theravada, Chinese Buddhist philosophy, ethics, logic, psychology, history, and Tibetan, Chinese and Sanskrit languages.

Seminars also have been given on Himalayan and East Asian art, yoga and planetary consciousness.

Recently, resident geshes and scholars at the monastery have given public lectures and courses at Princeton and Rutgers universities and the New Brunswick Theological Seminary.

The monastery observes the traditional Buddhist holidays and, beginning in 1966, established the Festival of Maitreya (The Coming Buddha), held one afternoon during the month of August. The festival is held in commemoration of Lama Dorjieff, the Venerable Geshe Wangyal's former spiritual teacher, a religious assistant to the 13th Dalai Lama.

Dorjieff brought the Buddha's teaching to Kalmuck country, where he founded the festival in 1905. The event is usually attended by 300 to 500 friends of the monastery.

Lobsang Jamspyal, a Lamaist monk, leads a processional during the Maitreya Festival at the Lamaist Buddhist Monastery.

Bally's Restaurant, Atlantic City.

RESTAURANTS

You can dine in a 1736 farmhouse or at a 1778 stagecoach stop.

For those with loftier tastes, there are wide-windowed bistros atop hotels with sweeping vistas of the Atlantic Ocean, Appalachian Mountains and majestic Palisades.

The more formal can be treated like royalty in elegant mansions and estates with manicured gardens, romantic waterfalls and splashing fountains.

The more casual can feast in those ubiquitous hamburger havens where peanut shells can be flipped onto the floor with mischievous delight.

The more curious can enter a turn-of-the-century clam bar and glide lightly over sawdust swept away every morning after the last patron leaves, a ritual since the heyday of the Hudson River waterfront when sailors and longshoremen gulped steaming clams, mussels and lobsters downed with steins of frosty beer.

Some can drop in out of the sky and park their seaplane at a steakhouse on the Hackensack River just nine miles from the George Washington Bridge.

Others can board an ancient barge or relax on resort boardwalks and piers supporting deliciously nautical dining rooms and bars along the coast and up the many inland waterways.

Anyone can bask in the warm glow of a solar greenhouse—The Sea Loft—on the Jersey Shore oceanfront, or be caught up in the luxurious trappings of the world's number one harness racing track while sipping and supping in an elevated eating palace.

The intimate privacy of a railroad car or quiet wine cellar offers an enchanting respite from home or business.

For the more outgoing, there are exotic belly dancers and spontaneous dancing in the aisles in Mediterranean-styled restaurants.

New Jersey restaurant menus appeal to every palate, from Portuguese and Spanish to French and Oriental, Italian and Indian to American and Continental.

More than 10,000 restaurants in New Jersey welcome the hungry, from the selective gourmet to the salesman-on-the-go. They range from the Aratusa Supper Club in the Meadowlands and Archer's in Fort Lee, to the historic Smithville Inn and Zaberers in Atlantic County.

Many are landmarks known throughout the country, while others have been recognized for their award-winning entrees and delicacies.

Here's a random sampling of just some of the renowned restaurants in New Jersey, reflecting either the finest fares or

275

classic settings. They are simply representative of the hundreds of excellent New Jersey restaurants listed in American Express, Mobil or other travelers' and hospitality guides.

The Manor

The Manor in West Orange is a unique statement in dining. A striking three-level complex covering 185,000 square feet, The Manor is everything to behold, everything, that is, except modern.

An opulent blend of classical and romantic styles, The Manor is a nonstop community of 300 waiters, waitresses, chefs, bakers, bartenders, musicians, electricians, carpenters, plumbers, painters, gardeners, florists and office staff, all working to satisfy the senses.

The Manor is the lifelong dream of Harry Knowles Jr. who, after returning from World War II, learned the food service business from the bottom up as busboy, waiter, bartender and banquet manager. His career began at the Robin Hood Inn in Clifton, next to his hometown of Montclair, where his father was the chief of police.

Knowles saw too many society parties, weddings and elegant affairs being booked in the fashionable New York restaurants, leaving the New Jersey outlets with the routine traffic. The enterprising waiter would change much of that high society scene by buying the Moresque from Ida Berg in 1957. He dropped the medieval image from the three-room Moorish restaurant, and The Manor was launched. The six-acre site grew into a 22-acre dining mecca for those seeking something different, something better.

Although exquisitely lavish, The Manor is an original in every detail, from the crystal and silver place settings to the display of Limoges china. The 11-room Regency-style mansion can accommodate up to 2,000 patrons seven days a week. On an average day, 1,200 customers have their lunches, dinners, meetings or parties at The Manor.

The nine banquet rooms, with names like Imperial, Minuet and Regency, are individually appointed with genuine marble, brass, silver, crystal, velvets and woods. Two public a la carte dining rooms, the Terrace and Manor seat 146 and 200 respectively. More than 150,000 lobsters are consumed annually and 45 telephones are within a few strides of any dining table.

The Manor family fusses over its showcase tables and dining rooms. A wrinkled tablecloth, for example, will bring frowns to Knowles' omnipresent face.

Knowles gets many of his decorating ideas from a book of drawings and photos on "The White House and Its 33 Families." That is why there's a diverse mixture of styles inside and out, starting with a curved driveway and circular, partly-trellised dirt path that begins with a wrought-iron gate and features a gazebo, fountain and a Villa D'Este waterfall adorned by gargoyles. Ornamental trees, shrubs and flowers bloom into scented rainbows from April through October. Hanging planters bring the colorful gardens indoors for year-round pleasure.

The newest addition is the 100-seat Le Dome nightclub with a grand Victorian chandelier, an Italian marble bar and brass and stained-glass decor.

The executive chef presides over a carpeted kitchen staffed by skilled cooks. Another four cooks work the banquet kitchen, while five more make cakes, rolls, pastries and ice cream in the bakery.

The Manor is the recipient of numerous culinary awards, including twelve consecutive Travel-Holiday Awards for Dining Distinction, the only New Jersey restaurant so honored; the Business Executives Dining Awards from Restaurant Business magazine and Sales and Marketing Management magazine; the National Restaurant Association's Great Menu Award, and the International Geneva Association's Restaurant of the Year Award.

The Manor is also considered the most popular restaurant in New Jersey, based on recent media polls.

The Manor—the "Mecca" for New Jersey dining.
Star-Ledger Photo

A model of the original Pals Cabin stands on the site of the expanded restaurant in West Orange.

Pals Cabin

A pianist named Walter Liberace got his start at one of America's first roadside restaurants, and the King of Swat, Babe Ruth, loved the hamburgers and frankfurters and cold beer at a place called Pals Cabin in West Orange.

The famous hot dog-hamburger stand opened its shutters and blinked its eyes at the world on May 18, 1932, a 10-by-12-foot refreshment "shack" where a dime bought you a juicy hot dog or burger.

Two pals, Marty Horn and Roy Sale, "squatted" on a vacant lot on the corner of Prospect and Eagle Rock avenues on a bleak day during the depths of the Great Depression. Horn, who went on to develop Pals Cabin into a landmark establishment, had been a bank messenger, a department store clerk and a printing salesman before settling on the great American repast as his life's investment.

Long before "fast food" became an American tradition, Pals Cabin was catering to the motoring public. "You just parked your car, stepped up to a little window, plunked down your dime and bit into the best juiciest hamburger we knew how to make," Horn recalls.

Within two years, the white-suited pals with their black bow ties were serving up charcoal broiled steaks at 50 cents apiece. By 1936, Horn and Sale decided to build "the longest and biggest bar" in New Jersey, resulting in the popular Pine Room. Customers, Horn discovered, were more interested in the special steak than the beverages that accompanied them. A "Cabin Special Filet Mignon" was listed under entrees at $1. A sirloin steak for two went for $2.90.

In 1941, Sale was killed in an auto accident and Horn turned to his sister, Jo Simmons, to help him run Pals.

Horn adopted a slogan, "Good Food for Good Health," which he incorporated into a system of aging meat naturally in scientifically controlled aging boxes. No artificial tenderizers are ever added, no frozen meat products ever purchased.

Pals Cabin offers five dining areas. The counter section, where patrons may dine on anything from broiled lobster to a hot dog, maintains the informal atmosphere of the original shack. The Cabin and Oak rooms are two more casual areas, while the Winchester and Tap rooms offer more formal dining.

On the parking lot level, a handsome Pub Room is used for private functions, and a Gourmet Shop is open to customers who want to take out Pals' foods.

Diagonally across the street from Pals Cabin stood an old farmhouse that had been converted into a restaurant. Founded in the 1920s as Mayfair Farms, it had been closed when Horn purchased it in 1942 and, after refurbishing, opened it on Dec. 7, 1943.

Mayfair Farms is one of the largest banquet centers in the East, capable of seating 1,500. The central room can seat 850. The original farmhouse, built before the American Revolution, is a national historic landmark.

Within Mayfair is an a la carte restaurant specializing in Continental and gourmet foods. Pals Cabin continues to offer steak and seafood, staples of the American diet.

Pals Cabin is steeped in nostalgia, having given a teenage pianist his first break at $40 a week. When Walter Liberace asked Horn for a $10 raise in 1941, and the boss turned him down, Liberace left. He went on to become one of America's greatest entertainers. Other famous faces at Pals were comedians Jackie Gleason and Henny Youngman.

In 1940, Horn joined the Newark Diner Association and when asked to serve as its president, Horn accepted under one condition: That the organization expand to include all types of restaurants in the state.

Thus was born the New Jersey Restaurant Association, its first president serving from 1942-48. Horn's son, Marty Jr., and another son, Donald, have also served as president of the state association. Young Marty also was elected president of the National Restaurant Association in 1970.

Larison's Turkey Farm Inn

Going to Grandma's on Thanksgiving for good old-fashioned country cooking is the theme of Larison's Turkey Farm, a historic landmark where highways 206 and 24 cross at Chester.

The 650-seat restaurant dishes out 1,350 meals on a good Sunday, as customers arrive at the 250-year-old farmhouse as early as 10:30 in the morning. More than 85 percent are waiting to order the Country Style Turkey Dinner, a Sunday spread that costs less than $10 (1985 prices).

The original two rooms of the farmhouse were built in 1736. The structure was expanded in 1800. Kerosene lamps dating to 1850 hang in one of the four dining rooms. Century-old furnishings sustain its early American heritage and create a homespun agrarian atmosphere.

Two authentic wooden cigar-store Indians greet patrons at the entrance of the spacious waiting room. Outside, farm animals wander about the 62 acres of sloping pastures, the turkeys outnumbering the horses, cows, sheep and guinea hens. A pen holds some 1,800 gobblers.

Willis Larison, who ran the restaurant/farm from 1941-75, is still in charge of the barnyard. The turkey inn was sold to Arthur McGreevy in 1975.

On the way to the upstairs restrooms, one passes two bedrooms filled with big game trophies—tigers, grizzly and polar bears, caribou.

McGreevy is developing a picnic catering service on the grounds of the turkey farm. He also owns three other restaurants: In Morris Plains are Llewellyn Farms, a 400-seat establishment that serves caviar and champagne; Brook Tavern, a 75-seat eatery specializing in sandwiches and hamburgers and catering to business clients and the youthful set at night, and the Black Bull Inn on Route 46 in Mountain Lakes.

The Brook Tavern was a turn-of-the-century ice cream parlor whose wooden floors and high wooden ceilings remain intact.

The Ryland Inn

On the wagon trail between New Brunswick and Easton, Pa., the stagecoaches stopped at a place in Whitehouse to rest the horses and the passengers. That was during the American Revolution (1770s); the stagecoach stop today is the Ryland Inn.

Built around 1778 by Col. David Sanderson, who operated the stagecoach run, the Ryland Inn (named after the original owner) lies in a picturesque grove of 19th Century oak and beech trees whose trunks are three to four feet thick and whose branches reach 75 feet high.

The old country inn, set amid 50 acres of farmland, is basic early American architecture. White stuccoed walls and heavy black beams give it a plain and sturdy down-on-the-farm feeling.

The landmark inn seats 265 in six separate areas: 125 in the banquet or Hunterdon Room, and 140 in the dining area, which are five cozy sections named the Colonel Sanderson Room, the Readington Room, the Lamington Room, the Ryland Room and the Tap Room.

William (Jette) Black, vice president of the Ryland Inn, served as the 1982-83 president of the New Jersey Restaurant Association. Black's in-laws opened the Ryland Inn in 1935.

Black's wife, Phyllis Ryland Black, received the International Geneva Association's Restaurateur of the Year Award in 1980. The award, begun in 1877, honors restaurateurs for maintaining the highest degree of excellence in their overall operation. Mrs. Black is the founding officer of the Hunterdon-Princeton Chapter of the Chaine des Rotisseurs and has served as vice conseiller culinaire of the organization.

The Clam Broth House

Slide on the sawdust in the Men's Bar of this world famous seafood restaurant and spot a famous face in the crowd. Since 1899, the Clam Broth House on Newark Street in Hoboken has been sought out by sailors and dock workers and celebrities who love good food in a salty waterfront atmosphere.

A maze of corridors guides customers to nine dining rooms that can handle from one to 650 people at a time. Known for its "steamers" and roast beef sandwiches, the Clam Broth House has many well-known friends: Frank Sinatra and his family (the singer's father was a Hoboken fireman), Tony Bennett, Brooke Shields, Ruth Warwick, Telly Savalas, Veronica Lake, rock star Pat Benatar, novelist Jerzy Kosinski and Lee Meredith.

The Serventi family sold the Clam Broth House to Arthur Pelaez in August 1975. Pelaez changed nothing, except perhaps adding to the number of fine wines and champagnes stocked in the labyrinthine cellars. And cocktails are still made to the exact specifications of the customer.

Imitation being the highest form of flattery, Clam Broth House II has opened in New York City, a copy of the New Jersey original.

Shadowbrook

Construction of Shadowbrook began in the 1880s as a summer home for a Manhattan neurosurgeon. Completed in 1907, the 100-acre estate in Shrewsbury, Monmouth County, was turned into a fashionable restaurant in 1942 by Dr. Fred Thorngreen.

It changed hands in 1958 when Rod Keller Sr., a noted restaurateur, managed the Shadowbrook with his family until 1971. The Zweben family—Sidney, Sandy and Robert—have owned and operated it since 1971.

A one-third-mile-long, tree-lined drive that opens into a circular driveway is the main road into the elegant estate. Set among 20 acres of formal gardens, terraces, lighted fountains and colonnades, Shadowbrook is laden with history, its spacious rooms chocked full of arts and antiques. The lavish Oak Room with its 14-foot ceiling beams and English paneling has a picture window view of the resplendent foliage and flowers.

Shadowbrook contains seven fireplaces, grand spiraling staircases, chandeliers from the Paramount Theater and Biltmore in Manhattan, ceiling panels from the Valard Houses in New York and fine works of art from around the world. There are six private rooms for social functions for 10 to 400 people.

The cuisine is Continental and American. Its renowned Boun-

Gardens, courtyards and statues embellish the Shadowbrook Restaurant in Shrewsbury.

Star-Ledger Photo

The opulence of the "Gay 90s" is found in the railroad cars and Victorian decor of Rod's 1890s Ranch House Restaurant in Morris Township.

Star-Ledger Photo

tiful Board Buffet and English Hunt Buffet are a culinary exposition. The nearby Monmouth Park racetrack has influenced the menu, which offers such entrees as the "famous daily double" and the "seafood trifecta." The gourmet can select from a versatile menu that features Chateaubriand Jardinier, Caponette Kiev and Shellfish Fra Diavolo, topped off with elaborate Viennese pastries.

Rod's 1890s Ranch House

Relive the "Gay '90s" and the Gilded Age of America at Rod's Ranch House and Madison Hotel in Morris Township, within the campus setting of Drew and Fairleigh Dickinson universities and St. Elizabeth's College.

Once "The Street of 100 Millionaires," Madison Avenue is the site of the Madison Hotel, a Georgian Colonial hotel with its massive clock tower and Rod's 1890s restaurant featuring five unique dining and entertainment atmospheres, including "The Whiskey Palace" and two antique parlour (railroad) cars. Wake up to breakfast in the Solarium and work out on the jogging track, tennis courts and golf course and unwind in the Jacuzzi.

The 14 private rooms in Rod's restaurant can seat from 10 to 450 guests. The hotel has 195 guest rooms and suites. The two railroad cars are for private parties of up to 18 people. The restaurant and hotel specialize in both American and Continental cooking.

Rod's also caters to breakfast meetings, and brass deli carts carry cold cuts during small, quiet business meetings.

Le Delice

A first class act is Le Delice in Whippany, the only French restaurant in New Jersey to receive the coveted dining award from Travel-Holiday Magazine in 1981 and 1982.

Chief chef and owner John Foy opened Le Delice in 1979 after a successful debut with The Tarragon Tree in Meyersville,

now run by his brother at its new Chatham location. Foy learned his culinary skills as a saucier at New York's prestigious 21 Club. From there he started his first business, The Tarragon Tree, and proved himself an innovator in the nouvelle cuisine, a French school of cooking that encourages experimentation and creativity.

Foy could have been a wealthy accountant, having worked for Price, Waterhouse in Belgium and later joining Arthur Young & Co. with the intention of becoming a partner in one of the nation's largest accounting firms.

His accounting experience has carried over into his restaurant business, in which he has developed a private mailing list of more than 4,000 corporate executives, entrepreneurs and professionals, and the growth of a wine cellar that began with labels from 45 vineyards in 1979 and now numbers more than 125.

Le Delice is a turn-of-the-century farmhouse that was known as The Barnyard, a "speakeasy" during Prohibition. Foy refurbished the entire structure in salmon pink and French blue with stunning mirrored walls and beautiful flower arrangements on each table. Diners sit down to a splendid setting of hand-painted damask linen, artistically shaped napkins and superb dinnerware.

The Star-Ledger's restaurant critic rates Foy's nouvelle cuisine as the finest in the Garden State:

"There is a style here, a charm and a sense of joie de vivre. Its manner and cuisine are decidedly French, but it is neither foreboding nor uncomfortably haughty. We found instead a rare blend of decorum and fun...The menu, incidentally, is written entirely in English."

The first floor dining area seats about 60 persons, and two small, private meeting or dining rooms on the second floor can accommodate about the same number.

Recipient of the 1979 Societe Culinaire Philanthropique Award for his work in pates and classical buffet, Foy has fashioned a menu that numbers 10 dishes for the first course, 10 fish and 10 meat dishes for the main course, 10 desserts and a cheese and salad course.

Foy has even contracted a private California grower to raise for Le Delice an oyster mushroom, which has a grayish-blue shade and will be available during the cold months of the year. Among the seasonal specialties are ragout of duck, fresh salmon from Norway, baby pheasant and shad and roe.

Patrons at the Pegasus Restaurant have a picture-window view of New Jersey's Meadowlands Racetrack.

Star-Ledger Photo

Nanina's in the Park

A fish store in Newark's "Little Italy" prospered in the 1920s. On weekends, the store's owner, Nanina Gaeta, started cooking some of her fish for friends and customers.

The little fish store/eatery outgrew its Newark premises near Bloomfield Avenue, and Nanina moved to larger quarters in Belleville in 1955.

The Mediterannean-styled restaurant with tiled roof and white porch has been a culinary landmark ever since. Now open seven days a week, Nanina's offers fresh fish, of course, plus pasta, veal and a wine list of more than 300 selections.

One can dine on northern, central or southern Italian specialities in the a la carte Park Room, which seats 78, or indulge in a nine-course, seven-wine dinner in the "Cellar in the Park," which comfortably accommodates from eight to 16 patrons.

The Mari Room books banquets for parties from 50 to 150 people.

Molfetas 46

Begin with the hors d'oeuvres with names like *ktapodaki ladoksido* (baby octupus in wine sauce) and *taramosalata* (creamy red caviar mousse).

Move on to the seafood selections with such foreign tongue twisters as *kalamarakia me horta* (fried tender baby squid with dandelions) and *tsipoura ladolemono* (broiled porgy with lemon sauce).

Try one of the eight entrees: *Arnaki aniksiatiko me aginares* (spring lamb with artichokes and egg-lemon sauce), or *moussaka* (a light combination of eggplant, meat and bechamel sauce).

Have a *horiatiki* salad and a slice of *kaseri* cheese before finishing your meal with a *galaktobouriko* dessert (honey-dipped, cream-filled pastry shells).

Watch out for the vibrant belly dancers and folks kicking up their heels in the aisles.

Welcome! You are in the dynamic Greek world of Molfetas, a pure ethnic restaurant along Route 46 in South Hackensack, just a few wingspans from Teterboro Airport, one of the state's busiest flyways.

Opened in 1973 by Spiro Molfeta, who has been in the food catering business since 1933, Molfetas 46 doesn't have a "bad table view" in its three-tiered dining room, for everyone wants to see Molfetas' famous international floor show and erotic belly dancers.

The front of Molfetas is graced by sparkling fountains and finely sculptured Greek statues reminiscent of the golden age of Athens.

The South Hackensack Mediterranean showcase is the recipient of the Global Menu Award.

Pegasus

The mythical Greek winged horse is the symbol of one of the most popular restaurants in America.

Pegasus, which opened on March 7, 1979, has become the best trackside dining facility in the land, according to Restaurant Hospitality magazine.

The $10 million Pegasus is perched high atop the Meadowlands Racetrack in East Rutherford, an opulent edifice faced with brass, marble and cut glass. Three enclosed elevators take patrons to the top floor, overlooking the Palisades and the New York skyline.

Three sizable dining rooms complement four bars, two saloons and an oyster bar. Pegasus East and West are the windows of the world's most popular harness track.

Pegasus East seats 425 and offers an international buffet that changes every two weeks, from German to Hungarian to Italian to Swiss to Spanish . . . .

Pegasus West seats 435, the a la carte menu served by black-tie waiters.

The Hambletonian Room can serve up to 200 with a choice of buffet or sit-down menu. The three rooms are equipped with 200 color television sets for viewing the thoroughbred and standard-bred races.

The Hambletonian is the richest racing purse in the United States, at $1.5 million. It is the middle jewel of trotting's triple crown and the most prestigious event in harness racing. Started in 1923, the Hambletonian was moved to the Meadowlands in 1981.

Knife and Fork Inn

Susan Sarandon—who grew up in Edison and Metuchen—and Burt Lancaster lunched in the Knife and Fork Inn in the film "Atlantic City."

The landmark restaurant is the last ornate structure left intact in what has become America's most popular tourist attraction, drawing more than 30 million day-visitors in 1984.

The plush Flemish white-stuccoed castle with its peculiar stair-step roof is Atlantic City's most lavish restaurant. The familiar crossed knife and fork is the sign of great seafood cooking near the Golden Nugget, the southernmost casino hotel along the world-famous boardwalk.

Its shellfish and finfish menu is perhaps the finest on the New Jersey seashore. Its predominately Victorian interior comes alive with brilliantly colored fresh flowers, hand-painted ceilings and Currier and Ives prints on the walls.

The construction boom is evident in the barroom, where hard-hats hang prominently over the stools and stock of liquor. Jackets are required at the Knife and Fork, whose intimate glass-enclosed porch and dining room create a quietly pleasant atmosphere.

Established in 1927, the Knife and Fork is managed by the founder's sons, Jim and Mack Latz. The new Atlantic City has enriched the Latz family fortunes. The Knife and Fork site is today valued at $6 million.

Ho-Ho-Kus Inn

On the banks of the Ho-Ho-Kus Brook stands a 200-year-old Dutch Colonial homestead made of Jersey sandstone. Its character is authentic American, from the wallpaper, window swags and curtains to the table linens and dinnerware.

The menu of the Ho-Ho-Kus Inn is also all-American: Steaks, pork and lamb chops, lobsters and scallops. The specials of the day offer something different: Veal paprika, coq au vin, or sauerbraten. Smaller portions at reduced prices are also available.

The inn can seat 135 in a truly historic setting.

Winkelmann's

Hermann Winkelmann opened a roadside butcher shop in 1966, making his own sausages and storing his hams and bacon in his own smokehouse. In Germany, a combination butcher shop and restaurant is as common as America's golden arches and ubiquitous ground beef patties.

Winkelmann added a restaurant to his Lakewood meat store in 1974, and in a short time his five-course Bavarian dinner became the talk of the old Pine Barrens resort in Ocean County. It is one of a select group of restaurants in New Jersey to be given the highest rating by reviewers.

Trained as a butcher in the old European tradition, Winkelmann stays true to his German heritage, from the beer steins standing at attention to the murals bringing scenes of his homeland into his 300-seat dining room. The sounds of folk and waltz music slip softly out of ceiling speakers, while an accordionist makes his way around the tables at dinner time, playing "Tales of the Vienna Woods."

The menu is right out of the fatherland: Wiener schnitzel, pumpernickel bread, sauerbraten, bratwurst, German mushroom soup, Black Forest cherry cake or hot apple strudel, with a bottle of Schneider Liebfraumilch, or hearty dark beer.

For the epicurean, there are a cheese shop and wine and spirits store and, of course, Winkelmann's original roadside butcher shop.

Wortendyke Inn

Built in the 1890s, this part Colonial-part Victorian country home in Midland Park, Bergen County, is operated by Steve Leanhart, who established his reputation with the 35 Club and the Tavern on the Mall in Paramus.

Leanhart's international menu is known for its fresh seafood, fancy prime beef and pastas, pastries and cakes all baked on the premises by his Milano cook.

The dining room is formally finished in brick and glass, and a woodlands mural covers one wall. Leanhart is particularly pleased with his collection of paintings by Fried Pal, a protege of Monet. The dozen or so Pal originals focus on fishermen, ballet dancers and scenes of Monte Carlo and Lisbon.

Glittering cut glass sparkles at the Crystal Bar and from nine chandeliers throughout the dining areas. Each table has fresh-cut flowers. At the piano, classical and contemporary melodies set the nostalgic mood of the evening.

The house's foundation is built like a fortress with two-foot-wide bricks thicker than cobblestone. It is an excellent place to store wines, which now number some 150 varieties, from $8 good table wine to more than $300 for a rare French vintage.

Leanhart is noted for his improvisational style. "We'll make you anything you want, just ask," he says. "If it's not on the menu, we'll put it together."

The Lobster Shanty

Jack Baker's father was a commercial fisherman, so it was only natural that the son would inherit the sturdy wooden boat, nets, lobster traps and dock at Point Pleasant Beach.

Jack and his family made a living selling the fish they caught each day. It was on their back porch that Jack started selling lobster dinners in 1955. Within a few years, the demand for their fresh fish led to the first of a string of Lobster Shanty restaurants on the East Coast.

Baker formalized his back porch enterprise into Chefs International, whose sales skyrocketed from $2 million in 1977 to more than $25 million in 1984.

Chefs International has patterned its successful lobster chain on the Point Pleasant restaurant constructed from raw driftwood, pieces of piers and other nautical effects that make the dimly lit eateries look like waterfront shacks. With four locations in New Jersey, eight in Florida, one each in Delaware and Maine, the Lobster Shanties have made Baker wealthy and something of a celebrity. He appears in his own shanty ads in newspapers and on television.

The fisheries have allowed Baker to branch out and finance a new line of La Crepe restaurants, opening four to date.

Baker's restaurants have been cited for numerous awards, including the Golden and Silver Spoons in Florida and Florida

The original Lobster Shanty, forerunner of the seafood chain, stands in Point Pleasant Beach.

Star-Ledger Photo

Trend magazine's "Top 100," plus top ratings from New Jersey and New York restaurant reviewers.

Baker still loves to go deep sea fishing between business trips and golfing. Since 1980, he has sponsored the Lobster Shanty 100 power boat race, which is run on the Toms River in August.

Geneva Winners

The International Geneva Association was founded in Switzerland in 1877 and its New Jersey Chapter in 1905. The fraternal organization represents the hotel, motel and restaurant industries and is allied with purveyors of food and beverages.

Membership consists of owners, managers, maitre d's, chefs, stewards, wine stewards, bar managers and waiters, captains and students and faculty of the culinary arts schools.

As of 1983, the New Jersey chapter has awarded special grants to 27 students pursuing the culinary arts in New Jersey vocational, technical and culinary schools.

Geneva's aim is to uphold and further the high standards of service to guests. The emphasis is on service, as the finest gourmet dinner prepared by a master chef becomes meaningless if not served properly by highly trained dining-room personnel, according to the organization's charter.

Since 1966, the state chapter has honored a restaurateur each year. The winners have been: Albert Stender, Robert Treat Hotel, Newark; Martin L. Horn, Mayfair Farms, West Orange; Gerard (Rod) Keller, Rod's Ranch House, Convent Station; Steven Morland, The Chanticler, Millburn; Ned Bowen and Andrew Pastene, The Opera, Englewood Cliffs; Peter Kooluris, The Stage House Inn, Scotch Plains; Dienhard Loess and David Rimokh, The Playboy Club Hotel, Vernon; Harry Knowles Jr., The Manor, West Orange.

Also, Frank J. Monica, The Molly Pitcher Inn, Red Bank; William and Elizabeth Motter, The Tower Steak House, Mountainside; Arthur McGreevy, Llewellyn Farms, Morris Plains; Victor J. Avondoglio, Perona Farms, Andover; Phyllis R. Black, The Ryland Inn, Whitehouse; Louis Jean Todeschini, L'Auberge De France, Wayne; Rolf R. Gaebele, Chanticler-Chateau, Warren, and Jacque H. Labye, Jacque's Restaurant, South Plainfield.

Ramapo River. Photo Credit: Tom Cassidy

RIVERS

They twist, curve, tumble and otherwise squiggle their way along the path of least resistance, running for 6,500 miles through cities, suburbs, forests and farmlands, down mountains and valleys and across wide coastal plains.

If unwound end to end, they could span the American continent twice with plenty of wet channels to spare.

They are New Jersey's babbling, trickling and always-on-the-go waterways, from the fresh inland streams and creeks to the salty tidal tributaries racing to the sea.

Like ancient trees spreading out to catch the sunlight, New Jersey's dozen or so significant rivers resemble giant trunks whose serpentine roots and branches search for water in the ground while collecting surface runoff and linking lakes with mill ponds, reservoirs and post-storm puddles.

A waterway flows through or past every one of New Jersey's 567 municipalities, from the wide border rivers in the Hudson and Delaware valleys to the tiniest rills that overflow their shallow banks after a pleasant passing rain.

One-fourth of the state sits atop the largest fresh water aquifer on the East Coast, its deep springs filling the Cohansey, Mullica, Maurice, Tuckahoe and other sandy depressions, reaching for the Atlantic Ocean on the one side and the Delaware River and Bay on the other.

In the great drainage basins of North-Central Jersey, above Toms Rivers, mill towns sprouted along the Raritan, Passaic, Hackensack, Rockaway, Ramapo and Musconetcong rivers during the 17th and 18th centuries. The rush of water over stone-built dams did much of the work of man and beast.

The rivers were the first transportation routes for the Indians and European settlers who converted many of the waterways into mill towns. The map shows seven Milltowns in New Jersey, plus three Millstones, three Millvilles and two Mill Brooks. There are also a Millboro, Milldale, Millhurst and a Mill Creek Cove. And of course there's a river named Millstone, as well as a Mills Creek.

Of the largest rivers and their hundreds of tributaries, the best known are the Hudson and Delaware, shared by New York, Pennsylvania and Delaware.

The Raritan is the longest river within the state, running 90 miles from the northwestern end of New Jersey in the rolling hills country of Mendham through the thick of the industrial corridor before opening into a bay where it merges with the Atlantic Ocean at Perth Amboy. At that point it is an arm of the lower New York Bay.

Hudson River

The English explorer Henry Hudson sailed into what is today the New York Harbor on Sept. 9, 1609. Under contract to a Dutch trading company, Hudson had been wending his way along the New Jersey coast, sighting "three rivers" in the general area of Perth Amboy.

Historians examining Hudson's logs from his rugged little ship, Half Moon, believe the famous explorer had seen, from the vantage point of the New York Harbor, the Shrewsbury and Navesink rivers in Monmouth County, and a third tributary bisecting Sandy Hook, a spit of land jutting out from the Highlands. Over the centuries, the powerful Atlantic tides have ripped through Sandy Hook, creating a quarter-mile-long waterway between the ocean and the bay side of the hook.

The Hudson River originates in a string of post-glacial lakes near Mount Marcy, the highest point in New York State. From Lake Tear of the Clouds on Mount Marcy in the Adirondacks, the Hudson begins its 306-mile-long journey to the sea. For 150 miles from its mouth, the Hudson is a drowned valley, an extension of the Atlantic Ocean.

Geologists have described the Hudson Canyon, where the river and sea become one, as a subterranean mountain range as magnificent as the Grand Canyon.

Where the river separates New Jersey from New York, a series of transportation crossings have been built during the 20th Century. Arching above the deep dark river are the Tappan Zee and George Washington bridges, and burrowing beneath the riverbed are the Lincoln and Holland tunnels, all incredible engineering feats in their day.

One of the geological wonders of the world is the Palisades on the New Jersey side of the Hudson River. A sheer rock wall rising 350 to 550 feet north of Fort Lee, the Palisades are an intrusion of molten material that hardened into a black sheet. The columnar structure of the cliffs came about during the gradual cooling of the hot rocks.

The lower Hudson River and Bay became one of the world's greatest ports, site of the towering World Trade Center and the Statue of Liberty. The Hudson River waterfront along New Jersey is one of the most valuable pieces of real estate on earth.

The 19th Century romantic era that inspired the Hudson River School of Painting and such legends as Washington Irving's Rip Van Winkle can be recalled today as the Clearwater sloop plies the historic waters from Albany to Sandy Hook. The double-masted, 106-foot teakwood sloop is ushering in a waterfront renaissance, bringing back a more gracious time when sailing, fishing and swimming in the Hudson River were simple pleasures enjoyed by all.

Clearwater's goal is a fishable, swimmable Hudson River by the end of this century. Oysters some day may be harvested again from the shores of Jersey City and the nearby Ellis and Liberty islands, the Gateway to America.

Delaware River

From the head of its longest branches to the lower tip of the cape at South Jersey, the Delaware River runs a wild and sometimes tortuous course, traveling 410 miles from upper New York State along the Pennsylvania-New Jersey border toward Delaware.

Before it disappears into the Atlantic Ocean, the Delaware River snakes through the most scenic sights on the Eastern seaboard, flowing around nearly 100 islands between Trenton and two wild streams in upstate New York, where it originates. The Indian creeks, Mohocks on the west and Popaxtunk on the east, unite to form one of the most limpid waterways in America.

Also discovered by Henry Hudson, the quad-state river was named after English Baron De la Warr, who governed that Colonial region from Virginia during the early 17th Century. De la Warr never saw the river named after him. Previously it was known as South River.

The Delaware River cuts through the Catskills, descends into the Appalachian valleys and skirts the Kittatinny range, crossing it at the Delaware Water Gap between vertical sandstone walls, and then settling down as it passes through pastoral farmlands and primitive woodlands.

The Gap is one of America's natural spectacles. The river bends below Schellenburger Island and the mouth of Brodhead Creek, slicing more than 1,400 feet down into the Appalachian spine by Kittatinny Mountain. From Mount Tammany one can view the grand geological interplay between bubbling water and jagged rock.

A long time ago the gorges were choked with ice or debris, the obstruction forming a great lake backing the water on both sides of the river for many miles. Either by erosion or the collapse of the natural dam, the area drained and the river returned to its current condition. The Indians noted the change in the water level, referring to it as the "Minisinks," meaning "The water is gone."

A canoeist can come across a deer drinking from the shallows around Wallpack Bend or near Bulls Island above Lambertville, while gliding over a silver mirror of solitude through a lush canopy of gold and green foliage.

Challenging the canoeist are whitewater rapids at Lambertville, where the bass and the shad seek protection around glistening boulders.

Canoeist-conservationist Jon Kauffman, an authority on scenic rivers, considers the Delaware the "finest" canoeing stream in the East.

Rafting was once a popular sport on the Delaware. As many as 2,000 rafts made up of mostly boards, planks and other sawed-off stuff skidded down the river in one season. The year was 1845. Canoeing is now the preferred method of navigating the river, but power boats occasionally cause a racket on the last major free-flowing tributary in the East.

The river meets tidewater at Trenton, and from there on drifts lazily to the sea, passing graceful fields and quiet marshes. At the Trenton tidal fall line, boaters and commercial traffic were once greeted with a gigantic sign that read "Trenton Makes, the World Takes."

Contributing to replenishing the Delaware's supply of water are three important tributaries draining the western hills and marshes of New Jersey—the Musconetcong and Maurice rivers and Rancocas Creek, near the state capitol.

A vital man-made addition to the Delaware Valley is the Delaware and Raritan Canal, completed in the summer of 1834. The 44-mile-long canal connects Trenton with New Brunswick and the Raritan River and Bay.

A heavily used shipping corridor for nearly a century, the 8-foot-deep, 75-foot-wide canal was dug out by hand and horse-drawn scrapers. Today it's a perfect path for canoeing and hiking, as well as for moving water to the thirsty inland industrial cities.

A comparable canal joins the Delaware and Chesapeake bays.

Perhaps the most historic picture of the Delaware River is the one of Gen. George Washington crossing the ice-clogged tributary on Christmas night, 1776, surprising the British troops wintering in Trenton. The successful attack was a critical turning point in the war, demonstrating that the Continental Army could retake land it had lost to the enemy.

Commemorating the Battle of Trenton, the state has dedicated the waterfront area as Washington Crossing Park.

Mountains and valleys frame the scenic Delaware River, which winds through the gap between New Jersey and Pennsylvania.

Raritan River

The Raritan is the majestic queen of New Jersey rivers, being the largest within the state and being fed by several impressive streams and numerous brooks.

The Raritan River drainage basin embodies a 1,105-square-mile area that is 50 miles long and averages 27 miles in width.

The Naraticong Indians of the Raritang tribal nation called the unobstructed tributary the "Laletan," which means "forked river."

The fork is where the two main arteries of the Raritan—the North and South branches—join below Somerville. For the Naraticongs, it was the Tucca-Ramma-Hacking, "the meeting place of the waters."

Part of Budd Lake breaks out into the South Branch, winding southeasterly for 43 miles through Long Valley, Clinton and Flemington toward the watery meeting place at Raritan, now a growing industrial city. The Black River is a tributary of the South Branch.

The North Branch comes alive in Ralston, Morris County, where a few small lakes spill enough water to generate a stream. The North Branch slips 25 miles through Peapack, Gladstone and Burnt Mills before losing its identity to the catch-all Raritan.

The Raritan drains the most fertile valleys in the East. Much of the farmland, however, has given way to intense industrial development, making the Raritan a prospering commercial corridor also tapped for its abundant water supply.

The Indians loved the land and grew their maize, beans, pumpkins and other fruits in the rich Raritan Valley, according to Cornelius van Tienhoven, one of the first Dutch settlers in the region in the mid-17th Century.

Writers and poets have praised the glories of the queen river. English poet John Davis wrote in 1806 in an "Ode to the Raritan, Queen of Rivers":

> *All thy watery face*
> *Reflected with a purer grace,*
> *By many turnings through the trees,*
> *By bitter journey to the seas,*
> *Thou queen of rivers, Raritan.*

The Raritan basin also takes water from the Millstone River, which flows in a northerly direction, joining at a point about eight miles below the junction of the North and South branches.

Lawrence Brook has its source near Monmouth Junction and also moves northeasterly for eight miles before merging with the Raritan. It drains 45 square miles and is a source of water for New Brunswick.

South River starts in the vicinity of Freehold and flows about 20 miles northward to the Raritan. It is tidal and navigable to Old Bridge.

Bound Brook and its principal tributary, Green Brook, are engulfed in suburban development. The stream flows 14 miles to the Raritan, draining that region of Somerset County.

Middle Brook drains an area of 18.7 square miles and gives Bound Brook its water supply.

Passaic River

A description of the Passaic River in "Dobson's Encyclopedia" (Philadelphia, 1798):

Passaik or Pasaick, is a very crooked river. It rises in a large swamp in Morris County, New Jersey, and its course is from W.N.W. (west northwest) to E.S.E. (east southeast) until mingles with the Hackinsak at the head of Newark Bay. The cataract, or great falls, in this river, is one of the greatest natural curiosities in the State. The river is about 40 yards wide, and moves in a slow, gentle current, until coming within a short distance of a deep clift in a rock, which crosses the channel, it descends and falls above 70 feet perpendicular, in one entire sheet, presenting a most beautiful and tremendous scene.

The new manufacturing town of Patterson is erected on the great falls of this river; and its banks are adorned with many elegant country seats. It abounds with fish of various kinds. There is a bridge of 500 feet long over this river, on the postroad from Philadelphia to New York.

In 1798, when that resource description was written, the Dutch already had been living in the Passaic Valley for 120 years, having founded the City of Passaic. The Great Falls in Paterson were as famous then as Niagara Falls are today.

Fishing and farming originally attracted the Old World settlers to the pristine waters of the Passaic and its myriad offshoots.

The Passaic sprang from the Great Swamp in Morris County, itself the remains of a glacier that left behind Lake Passaic, a massive, prehistoric basin that silted up millenia ago.

From the Great Swamp, the river drops south through Basking Ridge and Millington, swinging north through Berkeley Heights, Hanover and Signac.

Its first sheer descent is at Little Falls, plummeting 40 feet. That plunge will double in height when the Passaic cascades over a traprock precipice in Paterson, a few miles from Little Falls.

The Passaic River and the Great Falls became the home of the Society for Establishing Useful Manufactures, conceived by Alexander Hamilton and several speculators who sparked a new nation's industrial revolution in Paterson.

New Jersey's second largest river, looping 85 miles from the Great Swamp to Newark Bay, drains one of the nation's most flood-prone valleys. Should a dam ever be placed across the confluence of the Passaic and Pompton rivers at Two Bridges in Wayne, Lake Passaic would reappear as the biggest man-made reservoir in New Jersey.

Early industrialists built the Dundee Dam across the lower river between Clifton and Garfield.

The Passaic and its tributaries—the major ones being the Whippany, Rockaway and Pompton—form a 935-square-mile watershed.

Along the riverbanks in Passaic, Rutherford and Newark, there is an effort by local and state officials to create a linear park, opening the entire waterfront to recreation and modern marinas.

Hackensack River

The flat, shallow Hackensack River skims 45 miles over a muddy bottom from its source in Spring Valley, N.Y. through the jigsaw puzzle towns of Bergen County and the wandering, brackish meadowlands, finally coming to a sluggish end at Newark Bay.

The languid river is affected by the tides all the way to River Edge, north of Hackensack. Ocean-going vessels can move up the river to Kearny, while tugs and barges can get through to Hackensack, the seat of Bergen County.

Settled by the Dutch in 1647 as a trading post by the river, Hackensack is the site of the landmark First Dutch Reformed Church built in 1696.

Named after the Ackenack Indians, the town was officially listed as New Barbados until 1921, although it went by the handle "Hackensack" since the days of the Dutch.

The upper river has been dammed to form three reservoirs; one, in Oradell, serves a rapidly developing county composed of 70 municipalities.

The precolonial natives referred to the waterway as "the river of many bends." It runs a fairly steady southerly course with

Star-Ledger Photo

A small boat basin is tucked inside the banks of the Passaic River in North Arlington.

just enough curves and indentations to arouse any weekend explorer's curiosity.

Investigating the hidden creeks in the Hackensack Meadowlands is a rare urban ecological experience. Obscured by marsh reeds and mounds of machine-contoured garbage, the turbid creeks are an integral link in a slowly recuperating wildlife habitat.

Overpeck, Sawmill, Berry's and Bellman's creeks have become home for snowy egrets, turtles, reptiles and fish, surviving together with a new riverfront community called Harmon Cove, several corporate world headquarters and a sports-entertainment complex next to the New Jersey Turnpike, which splits the meadowlands in half.

It's an awesome yet fragile mix of man and nature, nothing quite like it anywhere on the planet.

Rockaway River

The circuitous fingers of the Rockaway River curl deep into the northern hills beyond the Watchung ridges, once the gateway to the vast iron mines of Morris County.

Little Lake Madonna on 1,200-foot-high Sparta Mountain is where the Rockaway takes root. From there it rambles along 40 miles of rough and tumble rocky stairways, falling 1,000 feet to its junction at the Whippany River at the Pine Brook-Hanover border.

Along its splashy way, the Rockaway fills enough depressions to form a number of lakes—Arrowhead, Rainbow, Indian, Ideal, Surprise, Fayson, Valhalla and Estline. The largest Rockaway impoundment is the Jersey City Reservoir in Boonton.

Split Rock Reservoir is also fed by the Rockaway's sister streams.

The Indians were impressed with "roga weighwero," which the settlers construed as Rockaway. "Roga weighwero" means "running out of a deep gorge."

Green Pond Mountain separates the East and West branches, which form the headwaters of the Rockaway.

Two and a half miles long at the base of a mountain sharing the same name, Green Pond spawned East Branch. A mile-long granite cliff rises 150 feet from the glacial lake. Leaving the lake, the brook rushes through a boulder-studded ravine between steep rock walls, dropping 300 feet in less than four miles in a series of cataracts and waterfalls.

Midway between Green Pond and Lake Denmark, a waterfall 100 feet high thunders into the brook.

A mile and a half from forested Lake Denmark is Lake Picatinny, whose history has been associated with an Army arsenal and munitions factories dating back to the Colonial iron centers in the area.

The West Branch of the Rockaway emerges from Lake Swannanoa in the northwest corner of Morris County. Swannanoa and nine other lakes lured mining interests and today represent an irreplaceable recreation resource.

Dams in Rockaway and Powerville control the swiftly moving stream, creating moments of quiet water shaded by riverbank trees, whose branches often meet overhead.

South of the river around Denville, log cabins and summer bungalows, as well as year-round dwellings, huddle around a handful of lakes. East of the river, between Denville and Boonton, another cluster of lakes has become a fashionable bedroom community with a post office address of Mountain Lakes.

The Rockaway provides another picturesque waterfall in Boonton, where it takes a modest 22-foot plunge as it heads for a rugged gorge.

South of Boonton, the Rockaway replenishes the Jersey City Reservoir. The impoundment flooded old Boonetown, an important iron town in the early 19th Century.

After resupplying the reservoir, the Rockaway bends northward for a short stretch and then turns abruptly southeast through flat meadowland to meet up with the Whippany River.

Pinelands Rivers

In the million-acre Pine Barrens preserve in South Jersey, hundreds of primitive creeks and streams create a bewildering web-like anatomy unlike any aqueous habitat in America.

Estuaries, marshes, bogs and swamps laden with lush freshwater and salt-water vegetation, and laced with incredibly intricate tributaries, offer the best canoeing adventure in the East.

A dozen of the main arteries penetrating the pine forest have been charted by canoeists and conservationists, and collectively come under the heading "Pinelands rivers."

A colorful pictorial map of the Pinelands rivers is available from the State Department of Environmental Protection. The most popular streams for exploring the Pine Barrens are:

The **Atsion River**, which has two distinct branches poking almost entirely through Wharton State Forest. The upper branch begins at Route 534 (Jackson Road), and travels six miles to Route 206 at Atsion Lake Dam. The narrow, winding channel is protected by densely wooded shorelines.

Breaks occur at Goshen Pond, a state camping area accessible by motor vehicle, and at Atsion Lake, where a campground has been developed for swimming and picnicking.

There's a canoe landing at the lake. The lower end of the river from Route 206 to the confluence of the Batsto River, just below Pleasant Mills, is the best wilderness area in the state, safely beyond the sounds and sights of human activity. A primitive group campground lies midway in the 14-mile canoe run.

The **Albertson Brook** and **Nescochague Creek** are choked by overhanging vegetation and fallen trees between Paradise Lakes campground and Route 206. Yet the twin tributaries offer an exciting six-mile canoe run, starting at the Palisades Lake Dam and extending to the Mullica River access point at the Route 542 bridge in Pleasant Mills, just beyond the creek's confluence with the lower Atsion.

With the exception of two private campgrounds, the canoeist can enjoy a true wilderness experience.

The **Batsto River** slips serenely through 13 miles of mostly pristine wilderness, starting at the Hampton Furnace in Wharton Forest and connecting with the Lower Atsion Branch at Sweetwater. Along the way one sees low marshy banks, abundant Atlantic white cedars, a natural group camping area at Lower Forge and the Batsto Historic Village near the confluence of the Atsion River.

Within walking distance of the village, at the upper end of Batsto Lake, a canoe landing is available. Landing at the village is not permitted.

Cedar Creek is known for the purity of its water plus a wonderful 14-mile canoe ride along primitive shores for most of its length, with stands of Atlantic white cedars interspersed with thick lowland vegetation.

The ride begins at Lacey Road, just below Bamber Lake, and winds up at Route 9, less than a quarter-mile before Cedar Creek empties in Lanoka Harbor. On Cedar Creek was a bog iron forge and pond developed by the first settlers in the Pines. There's also a historic district in Double Trouble State Park.

Great Egg Harbor River is the longest of the Pinelands' canoeable waterways. The first eight of its 50 miles take the canoeist through areas that have remained in their natural state since the dawn of mankind. These conditions are contrasted with man's intrusion in the Pinelands, intensely developed waterfront complexes leading to the harbor south of Atlantic City.

The western 29-mile stretch above the Lake Lenape Dam at

Mays Landing is the preferred canoe route, with the upper 10 miles often clogged with collapsing vegetation, making travel difficult. The tidal waters below the dam are heavily used by motorboats.

The mainstream of the **Mullica River** is a boater's paradise. The upper four-mile segment from the Batsto River confluence to the Route 563 crossing near Greenbank is shared by both canoeists and powerboaters.

To its confluence with the Great Bay 18 miles downstream, the Mullica River becomes wider and less attractive for canoeing. The extensive salt marshes at that point in the river are more popular with hunters, fishermen and motorboaters than canoeists. One federal and two state fish and wildlife refuges are situated along the river. Historic sites near Port Republic relate to the region's Revolutionary War involvement.

Perhaps the most scenic of the Pinelands waterways is the **Oswego River**, which swirls eight miles through the most magnificent Atlantic white cedar stands in the northern United States. The most popular runs start at Oswego Lake and terminate at either Harrisville Lake Dam or at the Beaver Branch canoe landing, a mile south of the Wading River confluence.

At Harrisville, the ruins of an old paper mill are still visible. Just before reaching Harrisville Lake, the Oswego River passes through Martha Pond Natural Area, displaying the Pine Barrens' extensive flora and fauna.

Rancocas Creek breaks out into four major tributaries—the North, South, Southwest and Mount Misery-Greenwood branches. Together, they provide more than 70 miles of smooth canoeing, half within the Pinelands.

The North Branch, the best known of the Rancocas family, is a pleasant trip for more than 20 miles from the Route 530 bridge in Browns Mills to its confluence with the Rancocas Creek mainstem at Rancocas Woods. The river is interrupted by several small dams, but they are worth the slight delays as this section has high, firm banks uncommon in the Pinelands. Large stately trees line the high riverbanks.

The 12-mile Mount Misery-Greenwood Branch can be explored in one day. Mount Misery Road is a good starting point, as well as the Route 70 bridge one mile downstream. The New Lisbon Road bridge is an easy place to leave the narrow stream, with its many bends and a couple of small ponds created for a now abandoned cranberry farming operation. Less popular are the 19-mile South Branch and the eight-mile Southwest Branch.

One of the longer canoeable rivers in South Jersey is **Toms River**, an unusual wilderness-urban waterway that wends through the woody Pinelands and the densely developed industrial seat of Ocean County, where it empties into the sea. From the Route 528 bridge in Cassville to the bus station boat launch in Toms River, the 23-mile tributary offers constantly changing scenery.

The upper reaches are thin and bent to fit the coastal contour as the water finds its way to the ocean. Low branches and fallen trees are natural navigational hazards to keep the canoeist alert at all times. Farther down river, the channel widens and nature's debris disappears, cleared by commercial and industrial development.

Through the town of Toms River the shoreline is enhanced by numerous holly trees.

Tuckahoe River is a significant tributary that attracts a variety of recreationists: Canoeists, water-skiers, powerboaters, hunters and anglers. The lower 15 miles of the Tuckahoe, from the Route 49 crossing to the confluence with the Great Egg Harbor River, offer the most enjoyment for families and soloists alike. The river passes through extensive salt marshes and a state fish and wildlife management area.

The greatest number of canoeists in the Pinelands can be found on the **Wading River**. There are some 15 miles of fascinating canoeing from the Route 563 bridge at Speedwell to the Beaver Branch canoe landing.

A shorter run stops at Evans Bridge on Route 563, north of Maxwell. Although shorter than the great drainage rivers, the Wading River is larger, wider and straighter, giving novice canoeists an ideal place to practice and develop their skills.

Three state campgrounds are situated along the relatively primitive shorelines. The tidal influence reaches to just south of Bodines Field. That area is heavily used for fishing, waterfowl hunting and powerboating.

Other rivers in the region worth a day's outing are Hospitality Creek and Deep Run, offshoots of Great Egg Harbor River; the Ridgeway and Davenport branches of Toms River; Oyster Creek, Forked River, and the upper reaches of the Tuckahoe, Batsto, Wading, Oswego, Atsio and Great Egg Harbor rivers.

Legends like Black Beard and Captain Kidd are associated with the Cohansey River in Cumberland County. Pirate treasures are said to have been buried in the little islands of the upper meadows of the Cohansey during the time when the river was on the sailing maps as the "Cohanzick," the Indian chief who made the Cohansey basin his happy hunting ground.

Black Beard, legend has it, supposedly boasted that when he stashed his treasure, he always buried two dead men to guard it.

The name also was given to the Cohansey Aquifer beneath South Jersey, the largest block of fresh water on the East Coast.

The Cohansey is 31 miles long and drains a 100-square-mile basin in Salem and Cumberland counties, the beneficiary of all that fresh water being the lower Delaware River.

Rivers, Rivers Everywhere . . .

As a peninsula, New Jersey has more passageways to major rivers and an ocean than any state its size.

Along the Hudson-Atlantic shoreline, moving southward, the major tributaries are the Hackensack, Passaic, Kill Van Kull, Arthur Kill, Raritan, Navesink, Shrewsbury, Shark, Manasquan, Kittle, Toms, Forked, Oyster, Mullica, Great Egg Harbor and Tuckahoe.

On the Delaware River and Bay side, heading north, are Fishing Creek, Dennis Creek, West Creek, Maurice River, Dividing Creek, Oranooken Creek, Nantuxent Creek, Cedar Creek, Cohansey River, Stowe Creek, Hope Creek, Salem River, Game Creek, Oldmans Creek, Mantua Creek, Rancocas Creek, Crossway Creek, Assunpink, Rockaway River and Musconetcong River.

Wriggling around inland are the Pequannock, Wanaque, Ramapo, Rahway, Styx, Lamington, Neshanic, Pequest, Capooling, Millstone, Saddle, Swimming, Wallkill, Manumuskin, Middle and Flat Brook rivers.

Some of the umpteen brooks are Beaver, Bear, Black, Den Hill, Peapack, Burnt Meadow, Indian, Mill, Peters, Troy, Pine Brook, Deep Vaal, Loantaka, Singac, Sleeper, Wrangle, Stone House, Garden, Peckman, Slough, Smokis Voll, Hohokus, Musquapsink, Masonicus, Mingamahone, Squankum, Timber, Ridgeway, Burrs Mill, Webbs Mill and Harrison's.

Among the countless creeks are Lockatong, Wickecheoke, Muskee, Manantico, Nescochaque, Talpehoken, Assicunk, Babcock, Friendship, Big Timber and Tenakill.

And finally there are strips of water called runs, such as Lubbers Run and Cool, Deep, Still, Scotland and Miry runs.

Courtesy: N.J. Turnpike Authority

*Gateway to the East: New Jersey Turnpike Interchange 10
connects with I-287 crossing over the Turnpike amid a macadam
maze of ramps.*

ROADS

ew Jersey is tied tightly together by more than
30,000 miles of undulating ribbons of asphalt and
concrete which, if unwound end to end, could circle the earth and then some.

Forming the transportation hub of the East—where road,
rail, sea and air unite to create a dynamic grid for moving travelers and cargo—New Jersey's highways and byways lead
the nation in use.

The New Jersey Turnpike is both the busiest all-purpose and
safest toll road in America, while the Garden State Parkway is
considered to be one of the most scenic, as well as being the gateway to Atlantic City, the nation's number one tourist attraction.

New Jersey roadways roll and zig-zag over and through
marshes and rivers, bays and beaches, cliffs and mountains, woodlands and farmlands, cities and suburbs.

Lacing the landscape are the sleek Interstates—78, 80, 195,
295, 280, 287—which, in turn, are criss-crossed by the old state
arteries, Routes 10, 15, 24, 35, 45, 49, 57 and myriad numerical designations in between.

The great commercial strips interlock at Routes 4 and 17, the
shopping center capital of the U.S . . . while Routes 22 and 46 compete for the most congested "consumer corridor" of New Jersey,
along with Routes 1-9 between Trenton and Jersey City.

Like Routes 202 and 206, Route 9 snakes up and down and
around the Garden State, offering the most beautiful vistas and
driving challenges for motorists.

Routes 70 and 72 penetrate the primitive Pinelands, while
the Palisades Interstate Parkway rides high on the Hudson River
Palisades.

* * *

When it comes to moving people and goods, New Jersey does
it bigger and better than anyone.

The Turnpike is the widest road in the land, climaxing an
evolution of transportation that began with the first paved road in
the country, built by the Dutch through Warren and Sussex
counties in 1664.

The first public road act was formulated before America's
birth—a publicly built road from Middletown to Piscataway in
1673.

The first road-sheet asphalt pavement was laid down in Newark in 1870.

The traffic circle and jughandle were original New Jersey
creations to improve movement and safety. Camden installed the
first traffic circle in 1925, followed soon after by the now
standard cloverleaf design first used in Woodbridge for safety and
timesaving.

The concrete divider down the middle of highways began as
the "Jersey Barrier."

America's only 12-lane thruway: The New Jersey Turnpike's dual-dual stretch.
Courtesy: N.J. Turnpike Authority

At $7 million a mile, the Pulaski Skyway over the Passaic and Hackensack rivers and meadows was the most expensive and impressive engineering feat of its time when built in the early 1930s.

Four spectacular roadways have helped shape New Jersey's image and character over the past 30 years. All of them were built after World War II and they have collectively contributed to the state's phenomenal growth during the 1950s and '60s.

They are the New Jersey Turnpike, Garden State Parkway and Atlantic City Expressway—the state's three toll roads—and the Palisades Interstate Parkway along the Hudson River between the George Washington Bridge and the New York State border near Bear Mountain.

New Jersey Turnpike

Pop-rock ballads have commemorated New Jersey's most famous highway, a 131.5-mile swath between the sports complex in Bergen County to the Delaware River in South Jersey, plus an elevated 10-mile spur between Newark and the entrance ramp of the Holland Tunnel in Jersey City.

The New Jersey Turnpike is everything anyone has ever said about it, from a paved commuter corridor connecting New York to Philadelphia, bypassing the Garden State along the way, to a fuming gasoline alley cutting through America's industrial heartland.

From four to 12 lanes, the 117.5-mile main stem is the most vital transportation artery in the eastern megalopolis, where about half of the nation's population lives, works and plays in the Boston to Washington corridor.

More than 127 million vehicles clocked nearly 3 billion miles on the New Jersey Turnpike in 1984, making it the number one thoroughfare in the western world, used by cars, trucks, buses and motorcycles.

Only the Garden State Parkway, which restricts trucks and certain kinds of oversized vehicles, caters to more cars.

The Turnpike has introduced many "firsts" since the main stem was begun in January 1950 and opened to traffic two years later on Jan. 15. Among them:

• The first to install guard rails along its entire length, pre-

venting head-on and crossover median accidents and reducing serious injuries and fatalities.

• The first to install in 1962 a radio sign control system, by which speed limit and emergency warning messages are activated by radio at 107 locations along the Turnpike. The illuminated signs, controlled at Turnpike headquarters in East Brunswick, alert motorists to reduce speed because of congestion, accidents or weather conditions.

• The first to provide right-hand safety shoulders on its major bridges.

• The first anti-noise regulations, which went into effect on Oct. 1, 1974, one year before the federal government's law against loud exhaust systems, "singing tires" and other noise-producing equipment.

• The first in toll road history to allow charter bus stops at service areas.

A system for automatic traffic control and surveillance became operational in January 1976. On the widened, computerized Turnpike, sensing devices provide complete control of all roadways by remote control and computer systems. Changeable message signs are situated at all strategic locations to balance traffic flow and close any roadway for emergency purposes.

A laser-type sensor activates the signs that are mounted on overhead structures. Traffic monitors ensure accurate counts for all vehicular movements on all ramps and roadways.

A unique feature of the New Jersey Turnpike is the "dual-dual" stretch between New Brunswick and the northern terminus. It carries six lanes of traffic in each direction.

The 35-mile, 12-lane super-road is another engineering first. The outer three lanes in each direction are reserved for trucks and buses, and the inner three lanes are for cars and motorcycles. Operators of passenger cars and cycles, however, can choose to use either the inner or outer lanes. Drivers of the smaller vehicles generally prefer the more homogeneous inner lanes, if for no other reason than to travel in safer company.

The dual-dual contains more than 100 bridges and overpasses of all kinds, including 10 different spans across the highway for the exclusive use of State Police, maintenance and other Turnpike officials.

In all, the Turnpike Authority maintains some 500 bridges, the longest being the Newark Bay span.

The original highway was built at a cost of $2.2 million a

mile in the early 1950s. The widening in the mid-1960s cost $16.6 million a mile.

To expedite design and construction, the Turnpike Authority divided the alignment into seven sections. Some 260 structures and five major bridges were built.

Patterned after the fast-moving freeway, the Turnpike incorporates the latest safety features, including:

• Crossroads and rail lines, which are grade-separated by bridges, permitting the continuous flow of through traffic.

• Opposing directions of traffic, which are segregated by a median strip, with a continuous, double-steel guard rail.

• Long-sight distances, which allow the driver to make curves very gradually, the result of flattening vertical curves at crests of hills.

• Safety havens, in the form of 12-foot-wide, right-hand shoulders for the full length of the Turnpike, including all bridges, for disabled vehicles and maintenance equipment.

The fully controlled access highway has 28 interchanges. Acceleration and deceleration lanes are 1,200 feet long at interchanges and at the 14 "food and fuel" service areas. The approach lanes allow traffic to merge safely on the 55 mph roadway.

With the opening of its first park-and-ride facility in East Brunswick on Feb. 7, 1972, the Turnpike launched a historically important conservation program nearly two years before an oil embargo made such facilities a necessity.

The concept worked so well that an additional park-and-ride lot was opened on July 8, 1974 at the Vince Lombardi Service Area in Ridgefield, Bergen County, serving some 1,000 cars. Another 580-space lot at Interchange 10 in Edison is on the drawing boards.

To eliminate visual pollution and minimize headlight glare and on-the-road distractions, the Turnpike Authority planted more than 78,000 trees and shrubs in 1981, mostly in the heavily industrialized northern portions of the state. Plantings will continue through the 1980s until the beautification program is completed from end to end.

The names of the Turnpike's service areas read like a "Who's Who" of American notables, all of them associated with New Jersey from birth or having distinguished themselves while living and working in the Garden State. They are, beginning in South Jersey and heading north:

• The Clara Barton Service Area—named for the founder of the American Red Cross.

• The John Fenwick Service Area—founder of Salem County.

• Walt Whitman—the 19th Century poet who lived his later years in Camden, where he died.

• James Fenimore Cooper—the novelist who grew up in Burlington County and whose father founded Cooperstown, N.Y.

• Richard Stockton—a signer of the Declaration of Independence and former United States senator, after whom Stockton State College is named.

• Woodrow Wilson—president of Princeton University, governor of New Jersey, president of the United States and architect of the League of Nations, forerunner of the United Nations.

• Molly Pitcher—Revolutionary War heroine who fought at the Battle of Monmouth, the first major military confrontation between the British and Continental armies.

• Joyce Kilmer—New Brunswick poet best remembered for his poem "Trees."

• Thomas A. Edison—the world's greatest inventor, from Menlo Park and West Orange.

Courtesy: N.J. Highway Authority

The Garden State Parkway lives up to its name by giving motorists a green view of New Jersey with its tree-lined median.

• Grover Cleveland—president of the United States.

• William F. Halsey—World War II Navy hero.

• Alexander Hamilton—architect of America's first planned industrial city, Paterson. He was killed in a duel with Aaron Burr in Weehawken.

• Vince Lombardi—legendary football coach after whom the Super Bowl Trophy is named.

• Peter Stuyvesant—the director general of New Netherlands who founded Dutch settlements in North Jersey.

Garden State Parkway

From the New York State border to the Cape May Ferry at the southern tip of New Jersey, the Garden State Parkway is exactly what its name implies—a long green park for motorists who get to see New Jersey's freshest scenery.

Its sculpted, landscaped median mirrors the Garden State's image of grassy knolls and carefully placed plantings of weeping willows and bending birches. They are interspersed with wildflowers, mountain laurels and New Jersey's familiar marshy sentinels—the tall, reedy cat o' nine tails and quivering foxtails.

Dafffodils adorn the grounds in springtime at the Garden State Arts Center in Holmdel.

The Garden State Parkway is more than a pretty toll road. It's a cultural magnet drawing more than 325,000 patrons to the Garden State Arts Center, a stunning saucer-shaped amphitheater atop Telegraph Hill in picturesque Holmdel, at Exit 116.

Under its open-air, column-supported dome, the space-age Parkway center can pack in 8,000 spectators in seats and on the surrounding lawn to see and hear such stellar performers as Bob Hope, Luciano Pavarotti, Tony Bennett, Rodney Dangerfield, Ray Charles and dozens of other superstars, as well as the London Symphony Orchestra, the New York Philharmonic, the Boston Pops and similarly outstanding symphony orchestras.

Its classical program and potpourri of popular artists are further enhanced by Heritage Festivals presented by New Jersey's Polish, Italian, Ukrainian, Jewish, Slovak, Scottish, German and Irish communities. There are also "Night and Day at the Races," tennis and golf tournaments, and free daytime shows for a quarter-million senior citizens.

From four lanes in Cape May County to the 11-lane Driscoll Bridge spanning the Raritan River, the 173-mile toll road may be New Jersey's best transportation bargain. When the Parkway was built in 1952-53 and the first toll opened in May 1954, a pack of Life Savers was a nickel and a quarter got you through a toll gate. Parkway tolls are still a quarter but Life Savers are 30 to 35 cents a roll.

The $330 million garden corridor either goes under or crosses over 425 waterways and roads. Eight restaurants and nine fuel stations serve the nearly 245 million vehicles that use the Parkway each year. That comes out to something like 3.6 billion vehicle miles traveled—a lot of tire wear and fuel consumption.

With the opening of park-and-ride lots for more than 2,300 vehicles, the Parkway has become a commuter road catering to vanpools, carpools and buses.

Casino gambling and entertainment in Atlantic City have made the Parkway the second most heavily traveled road in America. Record-high numbers were reported in 1984. The month of August reached an all-time high of 30,304,950 vehicles. The

biggest week to date was Aug. 13-19, which tallied 6,923,483 motor vehicles. The record weekend was Aug. 17-20, when 4,158,878 vehicles headed for the Jersey Shore, the state's leading tourist attraction.

The busiest record day on the Parkway was Aug. 18, 1984, a Saturday, when 1,131,338 vehicles filled up the five lanes in each direction between the Asbury Park and the Essex toll plazas.

The Parkway takes in about $95 million a year in quarters (or tokens worth that much). The arts center grosses around $4 million from May through September.

Cars account for 98.5 percent of the tolls, the balance being cars with trailers, buses and trucks. Trucks must enter and leave the Parkway at the Eatontown-Long Branch Exit 105.

Emergency aid to disabled vehicles involves about 75,000 calls recorded annually from motorists calling P-A-R-K-W-A-Y.

Palisades Interstate Parkway

Dynamite was destroying the craggy ancient face of the Palisade Cliffs at the turn of the century, as 12,000 cubic yards of rock were blasted away each day in a Fort Lee quarry for use as filling for road beds and massive earthen works.

The jagged Palisades were in danger of disappearing when concerned conservationists from New York, who enjoyed the soaring black backdrop from their side of the Hudson River, saved the New Jersey natural wonder with a Christmas gift in 1900.

The holiday donation led to the acquisition of the Palisades by a group that ultimately became the Palisades Interstate Park Commission.

In 1901, the New Jersey State Legislature appropriated $50,000 and New York another $400,000 for additional land purchases. They paid from $200 to $500 an acre for land valued at least 200 times that much today.

A 42-mile-long park from the top of the Palisades in Fort Lee to Piermont Creek (near Bear Mountain) in New York was set aside for public enjoyment. The most spectacular view—the 11.5 miles in New Jersey—preserved the Palisades in perpetuity. Two-thirds of the Palisades Park, or 30.5 miles, is in New York.

The Parkway, built from 1947 through 1958, cost $47 million. When opened, the Parkway was ready to carry more than 12 million cars a year, or about one-fourth of all the George Washington Bridge traffic.

The park commissioners decided the best way to protect the Palisades in their original grandeur would be to build a controlled public roadway. They wanted to keep intact the natural Palisades skyline by capping the crest of the cliffs with a beautiful parkway.

The Palisades Parkway became a scenic route restricted to cars and pleasure vehicles, with all crossings eliminated by the attractively designed stone-faced bridges. A great woodland park was created for use by motorists and recreationists.

Rights-of-way average 400 feet in width. Opposing traffic lanes are separated by wide landscaped malls and are, wherever possible, at different levels to eliminate headlight glare.

Mountable reflector-type curbs define the edge of the pavement, and unobstructed 10-foot grass shoulders provide space for repair of disabled cars. Minimum sight distances are 1,000 feet, horizontal curves are more than 2,500 feet and are banked for driving comfort, while accelerating and decelerating lanes at interchanges ease traffic on and off the Parkway.

The Parkway represents perhaps the most successful cooperative venture between the sister Hudson River states, New York benefiting from the view and New Jersey gaining an essential public roadway for residents of Bergen County and the motoring tourist.

Atlantic City Expressway

The southern gateway to America's boardwalk city-by-the-sea is the Atlantic City Expressway, a 44-mile modern toll road between the Atlantic Ocean and the Delaware River near Camden and Philadelphia.

It, too, is flourishing because of the jam-packed casino hotels that have taken over this once lazy, quiet retreat on Absecon Island.

Driving on the expressway, however, is like taking a ride through history. The expressway's 13 exits lead to historic shrines, museums and points of interest. Some of them follow.

The New Jersey Liberty Bell in Bridgeton, which rang out on the signing of the Declaration of Independence . . . the Chestnut Neck 1778 Monument, commemorating the British attack on the villages of privateers who practiced piracy on the high seas. The villages and 10 vessels were destroyed . . . the Hancock House at Hancock's Bridge in Salem, scene of the Patriot Massacre in 1778 . . . the Greenwich Tea Party, in honor of the patriots (disguised as Indians) of Cumberland County, who burned British tea near this site on the evening of Dec. 22, 1774. The teas were taken from Capt. Allen's Brig Greyhound. The monument was erected in 1908 . . . the house of poet Walt Whitman at 330 Mickle St., Camden . . . the Batsto early iron-working community in Wharton State Forest, where there is a restored manor house . . . scene of the 1777 Red Bank Battlefield . . . the Absecon Lighthouse at the tip of Absecon Island in Atlantic City . . . the Cape May Court House Historical Museum . . . the 1716 Friends Meeting House in Seaville . . . the restored Wheaton Glass Village . . . Smithville Inn and Old Village.

The longest, first leg of the expressway was laid down in 1964 over a 37-mile-long course. The seven-mile segment into Atlantic City was completed a year later. The total cost of the project was $33 million.

The four-lane superhighway set another record in 1984, as 35.3 million vehicles (33.4 million of them autos) used the Atlantic City-Camden-Philadelphia link. The vehicle miles traveled ran over the half-billion-mile mark in 1984, clocking a total of 590 million miles.

There are 27 overpasses and underpasses on the state's newest toll road.

In 1981, the Atlantic City Expressway was rated one of the safest toll roads in the U.S.

*The Great Swamp in Morris-Somerset counties, a vestige
of the last Ice Age.*

SEVEN WONDERS

A great swamp surrounded by suburbia.

A thundering falls cascading through the gut of an old industrial city.

A volcanic sheer rock wall descending to the depths of a grand glacial river.

A wild holly forest isolated on a spit of sand sticking out of the seashore.

A magnificent mountain range nourishing hundreds of sparkling lakes and streams and lush, pastoral valleys.

A meandering marsh supporting a rare wildlife habitat in the midst of the newest, most dynamic commercial complex in the country.

A million-acre oasis of pines and pure water lost in time in the middle of America's mighty megalopolis.

They are New Jersey's seven natural wonders, the unmatchable handiwork of eons of geologic upheavals that have shaped the face of this variegated, peninsula state.

They are the Great Swamp, Passaic Falls, Palisades, Sandy Hook Holly Forest, Skylands, Meadowlands and Pinelands.

If one were to compile a list of New Jersey's natural wonders, those seven unique attractions would have to be on it. There are others, of course, from Long Beach Island off the Jersey

Shore to Liberty and Ellis islands (the "Gateway to America") in the New Jersey waters of the New York Harbor, just a stone-skimming throw from Liberty State Park on the Jersey City waterfront.

But no list would be complete without New Jersey's special seven natural resources, which, when looked at as a miraculous mosaic, make the Garden State the most interesting and most diverse environment on the continent.

Pinelands

In the most densely populated and developed state in the nation lies a 1.3-million-acre wilderness that has remarkably survived as the largest open space preserve in the crowded Boston-to-Washington urban corridor.

Sometimes called the Pine Barrens, its sandy mix of soft-wood and hardwood trees spreads for 80 miles from Cape May to Monmouth County, a pristine swath 30 miles wide embracing most of Atlantic and Ocean counties, much of Burlington County, and portions of Cape May, Cumberland, Gloucester and Camden counties, with fringes fanning out to Salem and Monmouth counties.

The unique blend of vegetation, sandy soils, fresh water, Colonial villages and a constantly changing wilderness character are an anomaly in the metropolitan Northeast, where the population exceeds 25 million.

Designated as America's first National Reserve, the Pinelands has also been picked as a "biosphere reserve" by the United Nations, a special recognition that will increase international scientific study of the primitive land of the fire-ravaged scrub pines.

The United Nations Educational, Scientific and Cultural Organization (UNESCO) selected the Pinelands as one of only two regions on the South Atlantic Coastal Plain that contain valuable ecosystems.

The Pinelands is a fragile environment possessing unusual plants and animals, such as the curly grass fern, the pygmy pine trees and the rare Pine Barrens treefrog.

Just a few feet below much of the Pinelands is the Cohansey Aquifer, a formation of unconsolidated sands and gravel functioning as a vast underground reservoir containing more than 17 trillion gallons of fresh water, the single largest source on the eastern seaboard.

The shallow aquifer pushes water to the surface, producing bogs, marshes and swamps and feeding the maze of streams in the Pinelands. The rich organic contents seeping out of the soils give the Pinelands streams their dark, tea-colored look.

Accounting for 20 percent of the state's total land mass, the Barrens constitute low, dense forests of pine and oak trees, ribbons of cedar and hardwood swamps bordering drainage courses, pitch pine lowlands, and bogs and marshes, a collection of flora and fauna unsurpassed in the Northeast.

The 12,000 acres of pygmy forest are a one-of-a-kind stand of dwarf pine and oak smaller than 11 feet. Along the streams and in the swamps, southern white cedar and swamp magnolia flourish. Rooted tenaciously in the infertile drier soils (hence the name "barrens") are red maples, gray birches and sour gums.

The forest floor is covered by thickets of woody shrubs—sweet pepperbush, buttonbush, shad bush, staggerbush, Virginia creeper and poison sumac—and berries—blue, huckle, choke, bear, green and winter—all sharing the limited nutrients.

Added to that hearty ground canopy are plentiful sand myrtle, sweetfern, sheep laurel, leatherleaf, viburnums and azalea.

More than 850 plant species somehow thrive in the Pine Barrens, providing shelter and food to more than 350 species of birds, mammals, reptiles and amphibians.

Many plants genetically know their weather-line boundaries. Some 109 southern plants and 14 northern species reach their respective geographic limits in the Pinelands. Any farther north, the southern species would perish, and the converse is true for the northern varieties.

The cyclically destructive fires that keep the Pinelands' growth in check are nature's way of assuring the survival of the forest. From the acid ashes rise another generation of scrubs and their leafy neighbors struggling for light and life in the rather inhospitable barrens environment.

This "island habitat" teems with botanical wonders at such places as Atsion, Double Trouble, East and West Plains, Forge Pond, Goose Ponds near Egg Harbor City, Hampton Furnace, Lower Forge, Martha Furnace, the savannahs along the Wading River, Quaker Bridge and Sims Place.

In the cedar swamps, soggy ground is strengthened by the cedars' buttress roots matted with sphagnum mosses. Occupying the less popular shady areas are the tough vines, dainty ferns, less sensitive shrubs and moisture-seeking flowers that enjoy this darkened, humid niche.

Although civilization seems to have bypassed the Pinelands, early settlers attempted to tame this forsaken wilderness. Log-

Star-Ledger Photo

Rare Pigmy pines in New Jersey's famed Pine Barrens as viewed from Routes 70 and 72 in Ocean County.

gers cleared stands of pines, cedars and oaks, hauling the lumber to nearby shipyards. Hostelries sprang up along the sandy trails to serve the rugged pioneers, who came to be known as the "Pineys."

During the Revolutionary War, forges and furnaces were established on the major rivers and their tributaries to produce bog iron needed for wheels, weapons and ammunition. The Pinelands' iron industry peaked in the 1850s.

A new nation's glass industry emerged in South Jersey and thrived because of abundant supplies of fine silica sands. Paper mills also dotted the waterways, using salt hay for fiber.

Their legacies are the ghost towns that have become fascinating tourist draws. The most famous is the Batsto iron works, begun in 1765 a few miles from the salt reaches of the lower Mullica River in Burlington County. Preservationists have managed to save the core of the Batsto community, including the big house where the master lived, several workers' cottages, the general store and post office, the sawmill, gristmill and a number of Colonial period structures.

By the end of the 19th Century, the cranberry industry rivaled glassmaking as the dominant activity in the Pinelands. Unthreatened by development until the 1950s, the Pinelands put New Jersey near the top of the berry industry. The Garden State still ranks second in blueberry production and third in cranberries. The Pinelands also contributes one-fourth of the state's agricultural income, despite its impoverished soil.

The Pinelands' population has climbed to 400,000, most of that being senior citizen developments carved out of the wilderness during the 1960s and '70s along Routes 70 and 72, the major east-west arteries cutting through the Barrens.

Municipal densities range from 10 people per square mile in parts of the still mysterious interior to 4,000 people per square mile in towns such as Lakehurst, a large Naval base, and Medford Lakes, a growing senior community.

Where black bears, panthers, timber wolves and bobcats once roamed freely, newcomers are now learning to live with the remaining wildlife. Among the more numerous are gray foxes, raccoons, opossums, weasels, rabbits, deer, beavers, shrews, moles, squirrels and some mink.

Other natives of the Pinelands are snakes, turtles, toads, frogs and salamanders.

A paradise for photographers and naturalists, the Pinelands is crisscrossed by extensive waterways and myriad ponds and lakes. The more popular canoeing rivers are the Batsto, Cohansey, Great Egg Harbor, Maurice, Mullica, Oswego, Tuckahoe and Wading.

The more sizable ponds and lakes are, in Burlington County: Absegami, Atsion, Batsto, Browns Mills, Centennial, Chatsworth, Etna, Goose, Harrisville, Oswego and Pakim... Ocean County: Barnegat, Carasaljo, Colliers Mills, Deerhead, Horicon, Manetta, Pines and Success... Atlantic County: Goose, Hammonton and Lenape... Cape May County: East Creek and Nummy... Gloucester County: Malago and Wilson... Middlesex County: Manalapan and Spotswood... Salem County: Willow Grove.

The origins of the Pinelands inhabitants, their occupations and sentiments, are often expressed by the names of their communities or the places they congregate. Some of the more curious appellations still found in the Pinelands are: Apple Pie Hill, Bread-and-Cheese Run, Chicken Run, Comical Corner, Double Trouble, Gum Spung, Head of Snag, Hundred-Dollar Bridge, Long Cripple, Mecheseatuaix Creek, Mount Misery, Ong's Hat, Stormy Hill and Tub Mill.

Skylands

Within an hour's drive of the Pinelands ascends New Jersey's mountainous lakes district, ranging across the northwestern region. In the hidden valleys and rocky terrain, history was made when Gen. George Washington set up camp in Jockey Hollow and directed the Revolutionary War from his Morristown headquarters.

The Skylands, or Highlands as they were first known, prevented the British from conquering the Colonies, for the early settlers knew this rough territory whose harsh winters finally broke the spirit of the Redcoats.

The oldest rocks in New Jersey make up the sweeping mountain range extending in a northeast-southwest direction across northwestern Passaic, Morris and Hunterdon, and southeastern Sussex and Warren counties.

The ridges of the 600-million-year-old metamorphic rock formation are about 23 miles wide along the New Jersey-New York border, narrowing to about eight miles where the Precambrian mountains are cut through by the Delaware River.

The Ramapo and Passaic mountains crest at heights of 1,200 feet, sloping to 800 to 1,000 feet west of Bernardsville and High Bridge. The highest point is at Bearfort Mountain—1,491 feet—midway between Vernon and Canistear in Sussex County. Several peaks on the Hamburg and Wawayanda mountains exceed 1,400 feet.

The Musconetcong, Pequannock, Rockaway, Wanaque and

A section of the Skylands Gardens in Skylands, part of Ringwood State Park near the northern New Jersey/New York state line.

the North and South branches of the Raritan have carved verdant valleys in the basins between the ranges.

One valley ends at the South Branch of the Raritan River, which plunges into the Lockwood Gorge, leaving the Skylands at 230 feet near High Bridge. The gorge is a picture postcard sight that lures anglers during the fishing season and outdoor lovers year-round.

The principal ranges on the Highlands' westerly side are Allamuchy, Hamburg, Wawayanda, Sparta and the Upper and Lower Pohatcong mountains. In the central region are the Bearfort, Bowling Green, Copperas, Green Pond, Kanouse, Musconetcong and Schooley mountains.

Within this massive body of Precambrian rocks are the remnants of glacial lakes, the two biggest being Greenwood and Hopatcong. Human industry created the scenic Highland Lakes in Sussex County, home of summer vacationers.

This solid resource also contains the Franklin Zinc Mines, a treasure chest of minerals for modern technology.

Prominent features are the spectacular Delaware Water Gap... High Point, with its panoramic view of three states (New Jersey, New York and Pennsylvania)... and the Appalachian Trail, its entire 70-mile, 400-foot-wide right-of-way through New Jersey protected by the state, the only such intact segment of the nation's longest public trail crossing 2,050 miles through 14 states between Maine and Georgia.

The fluvial Skylandscapes also embrace the thrilling ski slopes of Great Gorge and Vernon Valley... the historic Waterloo Village in Byram Township with its 18th Century grist mill, stagecoach inn and craftsmen plying their Colonial trades... America's earliest settlements in Clinton and Lambertville... Flemington's glass and fur centers... the fabulous Duke Gardens in Somerset's fox country... the restored Speedwell Village in Morristown... one of the nation's largest fish hatcheries at Hackettstown... the old Dutch parsonage in Somerville... and Netcong's Wild West City.

The Franklin Mineral Museum puts on a colorful fluorescent rock show in which select pieces of Franklinite, Willamite and other local minerals glow in soft ultraviolet lights. Rock hunters and collectors are also welcome at the Evans Street museum off Routes 23 and 517.

The centerpiece of Skylands are the botanical gardens in Ringwood State Park. Visitors can browse through the Skylands Manor and stroll through the Skylands Gardens, losing themselves along Magnolia Walk and Honeysuckle Lane, or wander around the Bog Garden or Dry Meadow. Plan for a full day to take in all 36 botanical attractions, from the West Terrace and East Lawn to the greenhouse and nursery.

Meadowlands

Crisscrossed by a maze of highways, cut through by the New Jersey Turnpike, home of the greatest sports-entertainment complex in the country, headquarters for some of the world's leading corporations, looking out against a spectacular Manhattan skyline, an immense expanse filled with waterways, wildlife, marshes, and a giant green park fashioned from a massive garbage heap . . . all of which can be best described as the "Meadowlands Miracle."

The Hackensack Meadowlands is a precious open space preserve in the center of the New York-North Jersey metropolitan region, some 19,730 acres of valuable real estate consisting of a lazy meandering river and streams, and tidal flow lands mixed with marsh, meadows and woodlands.

Ignored in the 1960s as a messy place to dump society's wastes, this 32-square-mile eyesore in the middle of 10 million people is being transformed into the most diversified human and natural habitat, teeming with fish, fowl, amphibians, reptiles and four-legged creatures such as muskrats and meadow voles.

They share this tidal ecosystem with the human species and its imposing, built environment: A football and soccer bowl, a sports-entertainment arena, a hospital, hi-tech edifices, riverfront townhouses, clubhouses, marinas, theaters, hotels, concrete cloverleafs, an environmental center standing on stilts, and the world's largest garbage baler.

The most remarkable feature of the Meadowlands is the mountain of waste—more than 10 million tons piled 150 feet high—which is being contoured and landscaped into ski slopes and trails and embellished with tennis courts, camp sites, softball and football fields, and launches for boats.

Pipes are being stuck in the beautified mound to tap the methane gas produced by the decomposition of organic refuse. The siphoned-off gas is being used to heat and cool buildings and generate electricity for the state's largest power company.

The rising 2,000-acre urban park is surrounded at its base by the Sawmill Creek Wildlife Management Area. Learning a lesson from nature, modern man found a way to reclaim a filthy legacy, the cycle of life coming full circle along the muddy banks of the Hackensack River.

Today, more than 50,000 people either live or work in the Hackensack Meadowlands District, the nation's first successful regional planning effort in which 16 separate geopolitical entities surrendered their individual interests for the common good of a single ecosystem.

By 1985, the Meadowlands represented an investment exceeding $1 billion, and is still growing. Its future is evolving into an intricate construction as rich and as strong as its past.

What is geologically known as the Hackensack Basin was scoured by advancing ice sheets, sometimes a mile thick, which reached its southernmost point some 20,000 years ago. As the Wisconsin Glacier receded during a global warming trend, it left behind boulders, gravel, sand and silt. The terminal moraine—a high pile of such debris stretching from Long Island across Staten Island to Perth Amboy—trapped and dammed the melting water, creating Glacial Lake Hackensack.

Fresh water clays and organic silts then began being deposited in layers on the lake's bottom. Vegetation took hold on the damp ground that became exposed as the lake drained. The ocean, continuing to rise from the flow of melting ice, entered the lower reaches of the former lake bed, now coursed by a winding river whose entire watershed had been sculpted by the glacier.

River and sea met. Fresh water mixed with salt. Grasses sprouted at the tenuous and changing meeting places of land and water.

Thousands of years ago, the Hackensack marsh estuary was born. For a while, time stood still. Upon the arrival of the Dutch in the 17th Century, the serene, salty meadowlands became subdivided into 14 municipalities in two counties, Bergen and Hudson.

Waterways in the Hackensack Meadowlands.

Star-Ledger Photo

In 1922, a dam was built across the upper Hackensack River at New Milford, creating Oradell Reservoir. The dam cut off much of the fresh water supply to the Hackensack River, changing the mixing patterns of water within the estuary.

From then on, the Meadowlands gradually filled with roads and refuse until, in 1968, the state created the Hackensack Meadowlands Development Commission. It was an unprecedented land-use experiment that proved man could work with nature to restore the Meadowlands to a healthful condition.

Success is measured not by man's improvement of this beleaguered resource, but by nature's contributions, which come without price tags. The variety of wetland vegetation strengthens the meadow's ecosystem, assuring its continued survival.

An inventory of the six distinct biozones in the Hackensack Meadowlands indicates life is flourishing once again. Plant life includes reeds, cord grass, salt hay, the Common Threesquare Bulrush and Softstem Bulrush, the Dwarf Spikerush, the Tide Marsh Waterhemp, the Salt Marsh Flebane, the Narrow-Leaf Cattail, the Arrowhead, Duckweed, Glasswort, Horned Pondweed and plenty of marine algae.

Some of the 204 water-loving birds are the Least Tern, the Snowy Owl, the Common Loon, Pied-Billed Grebe, Snowy Egret, Yellow-Crowned Night Heron, Glossy Ibis, Whistling Swan, Snow Goose, Green-Winged Peal, Greater Scaup, Hooded Merganser, Marsh Hawk, Marbled Godwit, Ruff, Sanderling, American Avocet, Laughing Gull, Bonaparte's Gull, Long-Billed Dowitcher, Clapper Rail, Common Gallinule, American Coot, Black-Bellied Plover, Ruddy Turnstone, Whimbrel, Knot, Pectoral Sandpiper and White-Rumped Sandpiper.

As water quality improves, fish find their way back into the protective marine nursery. A few of the returning species are the American eel, American shad, rainbow smelt, carp, Satinfin Shiner, Yellow Bull Head Catfish, Silver Hake, Atlantic Tomcod, Three-Spined stickleback, white perch, striped bass, Pumpkinseed, bluefish, weakfish, butterfish, Striped Sea Robin, Tautog, Hogchoker, Crevalle Jack, and spot and winter flounder.

A sampling of reptiles includes the Diamond Back Terrapin, Snapping Turtle and Northern Water Snake. Amphibians are represented by the Leopard Frog and Green Frog, while the mammals' population consists of the meadow vole, muskrat and Norway rat.

There are numerous invertebrates, such as Conrad's False Mussel, Seaweed Hopper, Tadpole Snail, Amphritrite Barnacle, Dagger Shrimp, Marsh Fiddler Crab, and jellyfish.

Ecologists, biologists and marine scientists consider the Hackensack Meadowlands to be the most exciting natural-human environmental laboratory to evolve in the 20th Century. As the interface between the two deepens, the Meadowlands laboratory will become even more important in the unending study of the relationship between man and nature.

Great Swamp

Like the yule tune about a partridge in a pear tree, there can be found in the Great Swamp of North Jersey painted turtles sunning, Canada geese flying, wood ducks swimming, wildflowers blooming, duckweed floating, white-tailed deer foraging, red-necked pheasant fluttering, cattails quivering and chipmunks scurrying . . . in a perfectly peaceful setting.

They—and scores more species—make their home in the Great Swamp in Morris County, a glacial remnant steeped in history and preserved as a National Wildlife Refuge and Landmark.

Spreading out over 6,778 acres in Bernards, Harding, Passaic and Chatham townships, the Great Swamp is another invaluable vestige of the last ice age. Roughly 40,000 years ago the Wisconsin Glacier began grinding and gouging its way down from the

Star-Ledger Photo

The Great Swamp has boardwalks through its 6,778 acres in Morris County.

arctic dome. As it inched its way south, the mammoth glacier gathered thousands of tons of gravel, sand and boulders in its bulk, carrying this cargo along its chilly path.

After 15,000 years, the great ice wall reached its southernmost destination, and stopped. As the earth entered another warming cycle, the great block of ice on a line along Morristown, Madison and Chatham slowly retreated, leaving its glacial till in long ridges, one of them damming an ancient river basin in the vicinity of Short Hills.

Melting its way north behind this natural dam, the glacier fed melted water in the basin to form a giant lake 30 miles long and 10 miles wide. After forming Lake Passaic, the retreating glacier uncovered a second outlet at what is now Little Falls Gap. The lake waters drained out along the present course of the Passaic River.

Lake Passaic disappeared, evaporating into an extensive matrix of marshes and swamps. Black Meadows, Great and Little Piece Meadows, Troy Meadows, Hatfield Swamp, and Great Swamp are what's left of this glacial lake bed.

Great Swamp, an oblong-shaped basin seven miles long and three miles wide, is interspersed with low-lying ridges, knolls, hummocks and open fields. About 240 feet above sea level, the swamp is engulfed by 200-feet-high hills composed of basalt from lava flows eons ago. The bedrock is made of shales and sandstones laid down in the Triassic period (195 million years ago). Basalt ridges are found within these formations.

The swamp floor consists of several feet of peat and organic muck overlaying a thin sheet of sand. The sandy ridges are generally narrow and no more than a few hundred feet long, although they sometimes join one another to form a more extensive chain of dry land. These woodlands compose about 20 percent of the swamp, while the remaining 80 percent is made up of wooded swamp and marshland.

The wetlands are connected with four brooks and their tributaries, which carry water in and out of the swamp. The Great, Black, Loantaka and Primrose brooks form a watershed that includes Morristown National Historical Park and parts of four municipalities.

In 1708, the Delaware Indians deeded a 30,000-acre tract, including the Great Swamp, to English investors. In return, the natives received a barrel of rum, four pistols, four cutlasses, 15 kettles, 30 pounds cash and other goods.

Settlements sprouted in the lake basin, and during the Revolutionary War settlers fashioned wagon-wheel parts with wood cut from the Great Swamp.

By 1844, farms dominated the logged-off lands, as farmers drained marshlands and harvested "foul meadow hay."

The small farming operations soon became uneconomical and vanished from the old lake bed. Much of the cleared upland returned to woods and the lower flats reverted to swamps.

In modern times, the Great Swamp has been eyed for flood control (the 1920s) and drainage projects (1930s).

Suburbia slowly closed in around the swamp and, in 1959, the flat stretch of land looked like an ideal site for a future jetport. That issue became the catalyst for a national environmental campaign to Save the Great Swamp as a natural habitat. Headed by a housewife named Helen Fenske, the Great Swamp campaign was organized at her kitchen table in a Green Village farmhouse and led to the designation of a 6,778-acre swamp as a National Wildlife Refuge.

Fenske's kitchen headquarters has matured into the New Jersey Conservation Foundation, one of the nation's most successful land-banking organizations, based in Morristown.

During the past 20 years, naturalists have come across 204 species of birds, 30 species of mammals, 24 species of fish, 21 species of reptiles and 18 species of amphibians in the wildlife refuge.

The western third of the refuge has been set aside as a Wildlife Management Area, which is timbered, brushed, mowed, farmed and manipulated to maintain habitat for a wide variety of wildlife. Shrubs are planted, water levels regulated and nesting structures provided for wood ducks and other birds.

In the 3,600-acre core of the refuge, no man-made structures, motorized vehicles or equipment are allowed. The National Wilderness Preservation System serves as an outdoor laboratory, providing a primitive outdoor experience for the public. Limited public parking and access for hiking on more than 10 miles of trails are permitted at several points, including the northeast end of White Bridge Road and the Morris County Outdoor Recreation Center (Laurel Trail).

A wildlife observation center is located off Long Hill Road, where a mile of trails, interpretive displays and blinds for observing wildlife are available.

Trails are open to foot travel only. Bicycles and horses are not permitted. Wildlife have no restrictions. People, as visitors, are regulated.

The Great Swamp Outdoor Education Center of the Morris County Park Commission is located on the eastern side of the refuge off Southern Boulevard in Chatham. The center offers a varied natural science program of classes and guided tours, as well as a mile of trail and boardwalk for the public.

The Somerset County Lord Stirling Park is situated on the western border of the refuge. The park has a variety of environmental education courses, guided field trips and 5½ miles of walking trails.

The Great Swamp Refuge Headquarters, located on Pleasant Plains Road, is open from 8 a.m. to 4:30 p.m., Monday through Friday.

Palisades

It's simply a slab of rock sheared off by a cutting glacier that carved out the Hudson River Valley millions of years ago. But it's the best example of a thick diabase sill (volcanic rock formation) in the United States and is considered preeminent among features of its kind in North America.

Yet this sheer, 500-foot-tall cliff that extends 13 miles along the western bank of the Hudson River from the George Washington Bridge in Fort Lee to Sparkill, N.Y. is a magnificent geological marvel. This 3,158-acre product of molten lava and glacial ice is technically called the "Palisades Sill," and it displays what geologists describe as "excellent examples of columnar jointing, olivine formation, thermal metamorphism and glaciation."

Trees and undergrowth struggle for survival along the ragged ridges of the Palisades Cliffs in Bergen County.
Courtesy: N.J. Div. of Travel & Tourism

In other words, it's a breathtaking beauty to behold. To keep it that way, the U.S. Department of the Interior, which is responsible for preserving national treasures, has designated the Palisades as a National Natural Landmark. It is listed in the National Registry of Natural Landmarks, along with the Grand Canyon, Old Faithful and other one-of-a-kind indigenous works of art.

The Palisades sill is responsible for a genuine American word, "cliffhanger." That's how moviegoers rated the famous silent flick "Perils of Pauline," made in the days when the motion picture industry was centered in Fort Lee. A terrified Pauline clung to the edge of the cliffs until, at the last second, she was rescued by her heroic sweetheart.

For those who study the earth's formation and geologic changes, the Palisades sill has become a global reference for scholars in search of an "intrusive body of igneous rock" known as diabase, or dolerite. It forms a prominent ridge for some 50 miles along the New Jersey-New York Hudson River waterfront, curving westward away from the river at Haverstraw, N.Y. Throughout its range, the sill is 750 to 1,000 feet thick.

The magma that formed the black, dark-greenish rocks was one of a series of lava flows intruding and extruding during the Triassic period (195 million years ago) in the eastern United States. Rock hounds know that the igneous rock crystallized into a coarse-grained quartz diabase. The mineralogic composition is generally plagioclase feldspar, augite, hornblende, magnetite and quartz.

The face of the cliff illustrates a classic section of a differentiated sill, with "chilled borders," varying in composition. An olivine layer of green crystals lies compressed about 40 to 60 feet from the base. The varying compositions and the olivine layer represent stages of cooling. In many places, contact between the underlying red Triassic sandstones and shales can be seen. Here, heating of the sedimentary rocks resulted in metamorphism of the shales to hornfels.

Inclusions of the sedimentary bedrock can be found within the sill. They are known as xenoliths, or a rock fragment embedded in the mass of another rock. They were often metamorphosed by the heat of the molten rock.

The incredible columnar structures were created by shrinkage as the magma cooled. The resulting joints are quasi-hexagonal in form, creating vertical columns that periodically break away from the cliff face to form a talus (anklebone) slope below.

The Palisades region was covered by glacial ice during the Pleistocene Epoch 1 million years ago. This epoch was characterized by the rise and recession of continental ice sheets and by the appearance of the homo sapien species. The top surface of the cliff and its face were eroded away and scraped clean by the moving ice, which then left erratic boulders of Triassic sediments of diabase, or hornfels. Exotic rock from the Highlands to the north is also scattered throughout the surface.

The northern end of the soaring site is formed by Sparkill Gap, a two-mile section of the sill that rises 150 to 190 feet above sea level. North and south of the gap the sill forms uplands more than 500 feet high.

Geologists believe the lower surface of the sill was the original course of the Hudson River and had been cut down to the present level during regional uplift, when mountains were shaped by the shifting continental plates.

Later, the Hudson River was captured by headwater erosion of a south-flowing stream and the broad Sparkill Gap was abandoned to become the present "wind gap."

Afterward, regional uplight reversed the drainage in the gap and Sparkill Creek cut a steep, narrow valley through the sill almost to sea level. The gorge, 750 feet wide and 4,500 feet long, follows a northeast trending cross-fault, which has offset the sill more than 900 feet.

The New Jersey portion of the Palisades Interstate Park contains 2,451 acres, while the New York section takes in 707 acres.

Holly Forest

On a fragile spit of sand jutting out into the New York Harbor and the Atlantic Ocean stands a wild, hearty holly forest. Nearly 100 acres, the bayside holly forest is the largest of its kind along the East Coast. It is also the oldest, predating New Jersey's becoming one of the original states of a new nation, in 1787.

Now part of Gateway National Recreation Area, Sandy Hook itself is something of a littoral anomaly. The most northerly tip of New Jersey's oceanfront, the 1,600-acre hook is attached to the mainland just south of the Atlantic Highlands. Extending six miles into the sea, the shore peninsula reaches almost halfway to Brooklyn.

Formed by the constant buildup of sand from eroding beaches in Monmouth County, Sandy Hook is a recurved spit within the Inner Coastal Plain where the topography is flat.

Since the Sandy Hook Lighthouse was erected at the northern end in 1764, drifting sands have extended the tip to where the beacon is now 1½ miles from the water's edge. The hook has been lengthened by about 35 feet a year during the past two centuries. The thin stretch of sand has also been split in half at least twice since explorer Henry Hudson first spotted the hook in 1609.

In this urban marine setting thrive thousands of holly trees towering above a forest canopy of green brier and Virginia creeper harboring a secluded heron rookery. The osprey and great blue heron highlight the holly forest with 53 other species of birds, among them the snowy egret, common crew, black-capped chickadee, house wren, gray catbird, white-eyed vireo, American redstart, common grackle, cardinal and the ubiquitous gull.

Star-Ledger Photo

Holly grows in the dense forest at Sandy Hook.

Battered by storms, the Sandy Hook forest is naturally reinforced with red maples, wild cherries, hackberries and red cedars. The fierce "nor'easters" have served as a barrier to the spread of oaks and similar species from the mainland which would, under

The Passaic River Falls in Paterson plunges 77 feet.

normal conditions, force out the hollies. Facing Spermaceti Cove on the Sandy Hook Bay side, the forest is somewhat shielded from the turbulence of the open sea.

Another factor contributing to its survival on an infertile finger of sand is the holly's tolerance to salt spray and its ability to regenerate in a mature forest.

Some hollies have reached a height of 50 feet with trunk diameters of 24 inches. The rate of growth has been less than an inch in diameter in 12 to 15 years, according to holly expert H. Harold Hume. At that rate, a 20-inch-wide tree trunk would be 240 to 300 years old.

While the old-growth hollies will eventually die, the understory contains a healthy supply of saplings to replace them. The vegetation already is at the "climax" stage and the forest should maintain itself indefinitely without the need for special management techniques, according to the state Department of Environment Protection.

As the most highly developed holly forest in the East, the Sandy Hook woodland supports a community of shrubs and herbs, in addition to 12 species of trees. Some of the 18 varieties of shrubs are honeysuckle, cactus, cashew, rose, lily barberry, heath, grape and sweet gale.

Among the 73 herbs identified in a 1962-64 botanical survey are the mustard family, milkweed, goosefoot, figwort, spiderwort, bean, spurge, pea, plantain, buckwheat, nightshade, pink and mint.

Because it sticks out into a bay and ocean, Sandy Hook is a great shell collector. A random sampling shows there are bubbles, chinks, periwinkles, wentletraps, odostomes, clams, mussels, scallops, cockles, tellins, verticords, slippers, saucers, shark eyes, moon snails and oyster drills.

Passaic Falls

Early settlers traveled by foot, wagon and horse to see the spectacular Passaic River Falls in Paterson. New Jersey's greatest cataract plunges 77 feet from a rocky shelf into a vertically walled chasm. A steel footbridge spans the 280-foot-wide gorge, but it has been closed to the public due to structural weakness. An adjacent shelfland, once a popular picnic ground, is accessible to sightseers.

Had it not been for the action of the glacier that left behind Lake Passaic and blocked the old outlet of the Passaic River some 20 miles southwest of Paterson, neither the falls nor the river would exist today.

Like Niagara Falls, Paterson's cascading waters ranked as one of early America's majestic wonders. The earliest printed account of the falls was that of two Dutch missionaries who visited the misty site with an Indian guide in the spring of 1680. Jaspar Dankers and Peter Sluyter are believed to have been the first white men to see the powerful, roaring scene.

In the "Journal of a Voyage to New York and Several of the American Colonies in 1679-80," written in Dutch, Dankers and Sluyter recount their first impressions of the falls:

After we had traveled good three hours over high hills, we came to a high rocky one, wherein we hear the noise of the water, and clambering up to the top, saw the Falls below us, a sight to be seen in order to observe the power and wonder of God.

In 1798, "Dobson's Encyclopedia," published in Philadelphia, describes this wondrous natural resource serving North Jersey:

Passaik or Pasaick, is a very crooked river. It rises in a large swamp in Morris County, New Jersey, and its course is from W.N.W. (west northwest) to E.S.E. (east southeast) until mingles with the Hackinsak at the head of Newark Bay. The cataract, or great falls, in this river, is one of the greatest natural curiosities in the State ... The new manufacturing town of Patterson is erected on the great falls of this river; and its banks are adorned with many elegant country seats. It abounds with fish of various kinds. There is a bridge of 500 feet long over this river, on the postroad from Philadelphia to New York.

When the United States' first treasurer, Alexander Hamilton, toured the falls area, he proposed the new nation's first planned industrial city, built around the free water power—more than 1 billion gallons a day.

Paterson was conceived in 1778 as the cradle of the American Industrial Revolution. The land circling the falls was named after William Paterson, one of the signers of the Declaration of Independence and a governor of New Jersey.

Hamilton's Society of Useful Manufacturers fulfilled America's industrial dream. Today, the Great Falls industrial area is a historic district, its factories, homes, streets and parks covering a 119-acre tract just three blocks from downtown Paterson. They tell the story of America's industrial might from just after the Revolutionary War through World War II.

The tightly knit complex of architecturally impressive structures is connected by an intricate network of water raceways. Each of the 60 buildings in the falls district has figured prominently in America's industrial development.

During the Golden Age of Paterson, all of the sails in the American Navy were made in the city. It was a leading textile center and the locomotive capital of the country and, by the 1880s, the "Silk City of the New World." Samuel Colt, whose father helped establish the hydropower system for the manufacturers' society in the late 18th Century, invented the revolver named after him in 1836. His workshop was by the river.

By 1900, the power of the Great Falls had made Paterson the 15th largest city in the United States, quite a feat for a commercial hub without a port. It remains the third largest city in the state, after Newark and Jersey City.

Some of the features of the Falls Historic District, which has come full circle and is now turning into an artists' haven, are:

• A hydroelectric power plant built in 1912 and containing four giant turbines that once generated 21 million kilowatts annually. The plant has been refurbished to provide electricity to the entire falls district.

• The last of the channels constructed from 1828-46 to harness water for the foundries, forges and mills huddled along the riverbanks. They are being restored and landscaped into the Upper Raceway Park.

• At the base of the upper raceway is the Ivanhoe Wheelhouse, the only building remaining of the Ivanhoe Paper Mill Complex. Constructed in 1865, it housed the 87-inch Boyden water turbine that surged power to William Butler's famous paper mills, which produced paper for the foremost publishers in the country, including the American Bible Society.

• A section of the original "Yellow Mill," built in 1803, is now part of the Essex Mill, bought in 1870 by Robert and Henry Adams, textile innovators.

The Great Falls Park and Historic District are becoming a dramatic backdrop for boutiques, restaurants, artists' and craftsmen's studios and lofts, and high-quality merchandise outlets.

Trees, freshly paved streets, benches, ornamental lighting and walkways along the raceway are enhancing the historic district, as New Jersey's most famous falls once again lure the creative and visitors alike to a vital natural resource.

Photo Credit: Patrick Yananton

Scuba diver investigates the shipwreck "Pinta,"
eight miles off the shore of Asbury Park.

SHIPWRECKS

*T*here are at least 5,400 of them off the Jersey Shore, the remains of sunken vessels in Neptune's greatest graveyard of ships lost to the sea.

Since Columbus discovered America in 1492, a stretch of the Atlantic Ocean between Sandy Hook and Cape May has become the shipwreck capital of the seven seas.

Piling up on the ocean floor like eerie artificial reefs are the broken, twisted hulks of every size and shape of craft that has ever plied the coastal waters of New Jersey, the busiest shipping corridor in the world.

The soggy derelicts attract marine life and divers from all over the Western Hemisphere, the former seeking sheltered habitat, the latter searching for ancient treasures.

Some ships are just a few hundred feet from the sandy beaches in 30-40 feet of water, while others went down a few miles from shore in depths up to 300 feet.

There are all kinds and makes: Derrick barges, passenger liners, tankers, freighters, sailboats, tugboats, clamboats, schooners, sloops, trawlers, whalers, brigs, transports, drill boats, lighthouse ships, yachts, China junks, Spanish galleons, barks, concrete vessels, destroyers, submarines, subchasers, and all sorts of other floatable configurations of wood, iron, steel and plastic.

They have names such as Henry Clay, Malta, Matilda, Adonis, Clyde, Yankee, Reform, Pocono, Burnside, Park City, Vega, Ruth Shaw, Panther, Anastasia, Oklahoma, Gloria, Guadaloupe, Betsy, Manhattan and Ft. Victoria.

Although abandoned, they now fill a vital niche in the marine environment: A protective place for sea life to propagate. The barnacle-encrusted vessels are laden with lobsters, finfish and shellfish and crawling crustaceans.

Several of the biggest ships were sunk by German U-boats (submarines) during World War II. Some of them were loaded with military hardware—jeeps, tires, ammunition, guns—on their way to troops in Europe and North Africa.

Older sailing vessels, capsized during storms, may have contained precious cargo in the form of gold and silver coins and rare artifacts from the 16th, 17th and 18th centuries.

One of the most knowledgeable treasure hunters on the Jersey Shore—Deborah Whitcraft of Long Beach Island—says she has retrieved, among other items, silverware, plates, buttons and Spanish coins dated 1709 . . . and the heaviest haul of all—an 8,000-pound anchor from a three-masted British Barkentine sailing ship.

Whitcraft, who is compiling a book on New Jersey ship-

An early photograph of the "Fortuna" shipwreck is on display at the Long Beach Island Historical Museum in Beach Haven.

Photo Credit: Star-Ledger Photo (copy of photo on display at Long Beach Island Historical Museum)

wrecks, says only 10 percent of the 5,400 documented sinkings have been located. When a diver finds a shipwreck, its whereabouts are supposed to be entered into a navigational log kept by the U.S. Coast Guard and made available to those with marine interests.

Most of the artifacts on display at the Long Beach Island Historical Museum in Beach Haven have been donated by local divers and salvagers.

Scuba diving and salvaging are growing activities—and businesses—along the Jersey Shore, where more than 20 party boats take teams of divers to underwater sites as far out as 15 miles.

Members of the Eastern Dive Boat Association have rescued from aqueous oblivion such prized pieces as rusting locks, portholes, bells, steering wheels, silver services and utensils, gold pocketwatches, and colorful bottles valued as antiques.

Patrick Yananton of Point Pleasant, skipper of the 38-foot wooden Seafarer, has recovered candlesticks, plates, porcelain, buttons, silver creamers, 1810 padlocks, prongs, spikes, latches, big brass portholes, captain's bells, handles, doorknobs, fasteners and wall coathangers.

Yananton, a former senior microbiologist at Hoffmann-LaRoche in Belleville, has the only underwater television camera along the Jersey Shore for surveying the ocean depths. Besides probing wrecks, the immersible eye has been used by the Coast Guard to determine the cause of shipwrecks.

Dennis Bogan, who pilots the Paramount II out of Monmouth County, has raised the only brass cannon ever to come off a New Jersey wreck. Three feet long and weighing 100 pounds, the 1888 deck cannon was discovered south of the Manasquan Inlet.

The East Coast Diving Service in Morganville charges about $25 for a scuba-diving treasure hunt, renting various party boats on the Shark River Inlet, Belmar, including Mickey Treska's popular rig, the Jackpot. Like many other boat owners, Treska makes his living elsewhere, in recent years working for the New Jersey Turnpike Authority.

The variety of vessels and their vast cargoes offer adventurers the best opportunities for rewards and enjoyment than anywhere else, even more than the clear, warm Caribbean with its jeweled islands, according to Bill Cleary of the East Coast Diving Service.

"A diver can see and do more in the waters off New Jersey than they can in five years in the Caribbean or Mediterranean," Cleary, a 20-year veteran, enthuses.

"I've seen divers bring up toilet bowls simply because it's a piece of nautical history. But the real finds are the ship's wheel, propeller, bell, emblems, gauges, dead-eyes and sextants."

Divers in spongy black wetsuits plunge into the cool Atlantic equipped with up to an hour's supply of oxygen in their bright yellow tanks, plus a knife, a net for holding their artifacts or fish, and often a spear to bring back a sizable meal—a flounder, fluke, bass, mackerel, porgy, whiting, weak or tuna.

Lobsters, hiding in a ship's labyrinthine carcass, are as numerous as starfish gliding across the sandy sea floor. Anything more than a pound is fair game.

So are the valuable antiquities. New Jersey is one of the few places where divers are permitted to take whatever they find. Much of it, fortunately, is turned over to historical and archeological societies for study and public exhibit.

Professional Divers in Neptune, one of a dozen private scuba schools along the shore, can train and outfit a person for about $250. Because diving is a relatively inexpensive endeavor, once the equipment is purchased, it is attracting more and more fishermen and surfers who want a little more excitement out of life than casting a baited hook or riding the waves on a slick laminated board.

A typical outing will have from 10 to 20 divers aboard a party boat. Age is not a factor, except instructors prefer the "buddy system" so one diver can help another in an emergency. Teenagers and retired persons exploring the same wreck is not uncommon. More and more married couples are also diving together, the husband usually going for the heavy artifacts while his partner picks up the knives, forks, plates and service accessories.

Of the hundreds of New Jersey wrecks known to divers, a few have become the favorites of novices and veterans because they are easy to anchor onto and often yield surprising delights, either edible or archeological.

Following are some of the more popular shipwrecks off the Jersey Shore.

* * *

Adonis and **Rusland** met the same fate at the same site just 600 feet off Takanasse Beach in Long Branch.

The Dutch bark Adonis was the first to go down on March 3, 1859. It was carrying a cargo of lead ingots and grindstones. The ingots weighed 115 pounds each and were stamped "Locke Blackett." The Adonis has settled deep into the sandy bottom, today revealing only some wooden beams and ribs.

The steamer Rusland was heading for New York from Antwerp when it ran into the remains of the Adonis on March 17, 1877. The Rusland crashed through Adonis' hull, creating a unique underwater partnership that has pleased snorkel and scuba divers for more than a century. The Rusland's ribs and beams, as well as hull plates and boiler, can be easily seen in the sometimes turbid surf waters.

The dual wrecks can be reached by divers from the Takanasse Beach, where priests spend relaxing hours meditating at San Alfonso Retreat overlooking the oceanfront.

Since party boats anchor on the wrecks for fishing, divers must put out a warning flag or float to protect themselves and their life-sustaining equipment from the angler's sharp hooks. The wrecks lie in shallow waters just beyond rows of stone jetties and pilings jutting out 300 feet from the beach.

* * *

The English ship **Western World** was another victim of shallow waters, having beached itself about 600 feet off Spring Lake on Oct. 22, 1853. It now lies off the tip of a jetty in 30 feet of water.

The Newark Museum of Natural History has been the lucky beneficiary of Western World's unusual cargo, including finely preserved china plates made in Burslem and Turnstill, England, by Felspar.

Other interesting artifacts rescued by divers have been powder flasks, drawer handles, cowboy spurs, latches and files.

* * *

The 200-foot-long English Privateer **Thistle** disappeared in 1813 in only 20 feet of water. Broken up by strong storm tides, the Thistle now lies roughly a half-mile north of the Manasquan Inlet. Divers have come up with handfuls of oddities: Combs, buttons, silver bells and brass pots.

* * *

German U-boats hid behind the mammoth **S.S. Mohawk** to escape detection while waiting to torpedo military ships leaving the New Jersey-New York ports with troops and armaments during the early stages of World War II. When the U.S. Navy discovered the U-boats were using the 500-foot-long Mohawk for cover, it blew the nearly 6,000-ton steel vessel apart, scattering it across a half-mile area.

Many lives were lost when the Mohawk collided with the Norwegian freighter Talisman on Jan. 2, 1935. The Talisman made it to port but the Mohawk came to rest in 80 feet of water about eight miles east of Mantoloking.

Hauling Malaysian tin ingots weighing a little more than 100 pounds apiece, the Mohawk has given up several engines and parts and a plentiful assortment of Clyde Line dinnerware.

Rising 20 feet from the ocean floor, the Mohawk has been systematically stripped of many of her removable parts.

Patrick Yananton of Point Pleasant inspects some of the artifacts he has salvaged from the immersed vessels.

Photo Credit: Gordon Bishop

* * *

Of recent vintage, the Dutch freighter **Pinta**, a 1,000-ton, single-screw motorship, suffered the same fatal affliction as the Mohawk. On May 8, 1963, the 10,000-ton City of Perth British freighter hit the Pinta broadside, sending her to Davy Jones' locker in less than an hour.

Arriving from ports in Central America, the 194-foot-long Pinta now lies completely intact in 85 feet of water, seven miles off Belmar. Her cargo of lumber did not help her stay afloat following the collision.

Artificial flowers from the captain's table were among the first items taken from the Pinta. Also missing are her screw and some hinges and latches. The captain's bell, clearly marked "Pinta 1959," found a home at a marine supply company.

* * *

The steamer **Pliny** was filled with an array of goods when she ran out of steam in 25 feet of water some 500 feet from the Asbury Park shoreline. The sinking occurred on May 13, 1882. Divers have made off with parts of the steam equipment.

* * *

The S.S. **Delaware** is another Clyde Line steamship that has taken on a second life as a flourishing reef three miles off the shores of Bay Head. A fire on the 1,646-ton wooden ship ended its service with the Clyde Line on July 9, 1898.

Record-sized lobsters have taken up residence in the Delaware, reposing handsomely in 68 feet of water. When conditions are clear and bright, the Delaware is an underwater photographer's delight. Dinner ware and utensils are the treasure hunter's catch-of-the-day.

Rumor has it that the ship's strongbox contains a significant amount of money.

* * *

The 616 passengers and 460 crew members of the queen of Israel's merchant marine, Shalom, will never forget that foggy Thanksgiving morning in 1964 when the luxury liner split in half a Norwegian tanker, **Stolt Dagali**, brimming with oil.

The sea claimed the tanker, its slick cargo and 19 of the Stolt's seamen. One stewardess on the Shalom was injured. The stern of the 12,723-ton tanker went right to the bottom; the half-submerged bow was towed to port. The crash site was 17 miles northeast of Barnegat Light.

The French-built Shalom had been in service for only seven months. The 629-foot, 25,338-ton liner managed to make it back to New York Harbor under her own power, just three hours after leaving the port for a 10-day holiday cruise to the West Indies. The Shalom sustained a 40-foot gash in her bow.

The Stolt's stern rests on her port side, protruding 70 feet above the sea floor. The "S" on the tanker's stack has been blanketed by marine growth.

* * *

The first time a life-saving gun was used to rescue passengers from a shipwreck was on Jan. 12, 1850. The Scottish brig **Ayshire**, carrying 201 English and Irish immigrants, took on water off Long Branch.

A ball and line fired from a powerful gun were used as a rescue device to bring in stranded immigrants, demonstrating for the first time that that kind of equipment was effective. The ball and line that saved the immigrants were turned over to the National Museum in Washington, D.C.

A New Jersey congressman was instrumental in organizing 14 boat houses and rescue stations along the Jersey Shore in 1848. Each station was equipped with surf boats, a life car, surf guns and shot lines. The stations served as the forerunner of the U.S. Coast Guard.

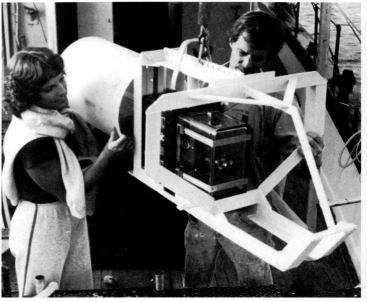

Photo Credit: Patrick Yananton

Michele and Peter Lewis lower a camera for filming an undersea exploration.

* * *

A rare relic from a bygone era is the central attraction in Barnegat's Main Square. A cannon that fired four-pound balls from a sailing vessel was picked up by the New Jersey Skindiving Club from a wreck about eight miles from Barnegat Lighthouse. The 1962 diving exhibition resulted in the naming of the unknown ship the **Cannon Wreck**.

In the same area are three other marine curiosities: The **Spanish Wreck**, the **Magnolia**, and the coal barge **Charles J. Hooper**. No one knows when the three-masted Spanish ship sunk in 75 feet of water, but her timbers and ribs invite underwater explorers to wonder about her ill-fated past. The Magnolia is in 80 feet of water and has become a recent curiosity of sport divers. The Hooper barge made its last voyage on Nov. 7, 1948.

* * *

Another successful target of the killer-shark U-boats was the 422-foot-long freighter, **Arundo**. The 5,163-ton Dutch steamer was torpedoed in 140 feet of water on April 28, 1942, about 15 miles from Belmar. The freighter, with a 55-foot beam, was weighted down with Army vehicles and war material.

* * *

A 19th Century sailing vessel named **Cadet** made her final run around 1880. The rather large vessel (her beam is nearly 35 feet) and sizable capstan are intact in waters about three miles from the Manasquan Inlet. A capstan is a large, spool-shaped cylinder with a cable wound around it. Bethlehem Steel has analyzed several wrought iron spikes that kept the wooden ship together to determine its age and where it was built.

* * *

Three tankers tell the story of maritime life during World War II. The **R.P. Resor** and **Gulf Trade** were knocked out of service by U-boats, while the **Maurice Tracy** wound up on the losing side of a collision.

Standard Oil Co. owned the 7,541-ton Resor, which was torpedoed on Feb. 27, 1942 in international waters 32 miles from Barnegat. While the giant tanker burned off 4.4 million gallons of oil and buckled from the extreme heat, photographers captured the tragic moment in what has become a classic photo essay of a maritime disaster.

The U.S.S. Sagamore tried to tow the tanker to the mainland for possible salvage, but the Resor gave up the day after the explosion, slowly descending to the 100-foot-deep ocean bottom. Divers have attempted to remove a spare propeller in her hold.

A U-boat scored another hit when the Gulf Trade took a torpedo between the bridge and the main mast on March 10, 1942. Also off Barnegat (about 14 miles), the 7,677-ton Gulf Trade was ripped in half. Both sections floated as the 3.4 million gallons of oil blazed across the horizon, the stern finally sinking in 72 feet of water. The bow sank closer to shore. The 1920 ship was 423 feet long with a 59-foot beam.

The wheel, anchor and helm are among the ruins that have been salvaged after the 253-foot-long Maurice Tracy collided almost six miles from Seaside Park on June 17, 1944. The rest of the 2,488-ton tanker remains in 60 feet of water, teeming with fish and luring party boats out of Monmouth and Ocean counties.

* * *

Cannonballs and Italian marble are hidden among the wrecks off Sea Girt and the Manasquan.

Divers have surfaced with cannonballs and valuable artifacts from an old, unidentified wreck a few thousand feet east of the Sea Girt Firing Range, home of the New Jersey National Guard.

The **Civita Carrara**, a sailing vessel stocked with expensive marble, never made it to its destination somewhere along the East Coast. The Civita got as far as a mile from the Manasquan Inlet when it went down in 1862. The heavy marble slabs are still there for those with strong backs or special salvaging gear.

* * *

The 329-foot **Sindia** sunk in shallow waters 200 feet off Ocean City beach. After 82 years, the four-masted bark now lies under 30 feet of sand. Only a portion of the ship's tiller arm juts above the surf at low tide.

The steel-hulled vessel was on the last leg of its final voyage from the Orient to New York when it ran aground during a coastal storm in December 1901. Beachfront owners have staked a claim to the ship's cargo, estimated to be worth $20 million.

A former U.S. Navy diver, Edward Michaud, has spent three years and more than $700,000 trying to recover the Sindia's treasures of trinkets, china and other artifacts. Michaud will be using specially designed dams to hold back the shifting sands as divers dig toward the lower decks of the bark, where the fortune is believed to be trapped.

Photo Credit: Gordon Bishop

A New Jersey diver prepares to take the plunge during an expedition to retrieve nautical artifacts.

Courtesy: N.J. Highway Authority

The Garden State Arts Center in Holmdel, Monmouth County.

SHOWCASES

$\mathcal{T}$hey have names like Waterloo and Orrie De-Nooyer and they attract lots of attention with names like Frank Sinatra, Luciano Pavarotti, Bruce Springsteen and a galaxy of superstars who have made New Jersey a cultural showcase for the arts, from opera and pops to country and jazz.

These performing arts centers range from modern architectural marvels to art deco monuments that epitomized America's unabashed display of affluence, energy and artistic power during the Roaring Twenties.

New Jersey's popular cultural centers are situated accessibly in some unusual places: In the heart of the Hackensack Meadowlands . . . on a hilltop in Holmdel . . . along boardwalks in Atlantic City and Asbury Park . . . next to an old canal towpath in Sussex County . . . in a vocational-technical high school . . . in a theme park in the Pine Barrens . . . in a quiet suburban campus community . . . and in the central cities of Newark, Passaic, New Brunswick and Elizabeth.

Some just came on the scene, while others have been around since the 1920s. A few are just getting off the ground as restored landmarks saved in the nick of time from the urban-renewal wrecking ball.

Most are familiar to those seeking entertainment in all of its endlessly changing forms, from virtuoso piano recitals to electrifying rock 'n' roll.

Among the more prominent showcases of the stars are the Garden State Arts Center in Holmdel, the Meadowlands Arena in East Rutherford, Waterloo Village in Byram Township, Newark Symphony Hall, The Capitol in Passaic, the Orrie DeNooyer Auditorium in Hackensack, the Englewood Plaza for the Performing Arts, The Ritz in Elizabeth, Great Adventure Theme Park in Jackson, the William Carlos Williams Center for the Arts in Rutherford, the Convention Hall home of the Miss America Pageant in Atlantic City, the Asbury Park Convention Center being refurbished by singers Johnny Cash and Van Halen, and the New Brunswick Cultural Center scheduled for completion in 1987.

* * *

The Garden State Arts Center has played host to millions of summer visitors since its opening on June 12, 1968. The round, white, concrete umbrella, designed by renowned architect Edward Durrell Stone, sits on Telegraph Hill like an eerie flying saucer, a scene right out of "Close Encounters of the Third Kind" or "Star Trek."

The circular amphitheater, with its massive roof supported by eight exterior columns, rests comfortably within grassy knolls that form a natural bowl, which shelters audiences from the vagaries of the weather while also providing excellent acoustics. The columns are hollow, cleverly concealing the spotlight and sound systems from the partrons' eyes.

The open-sided saucer seats more than 5,000 people, with additional lawn space for another 4,500 persons under twinkling stars. At night, colored lights illuminate the entire hill with its squat, round structure, a magical setting further enhanced by carefully cultivated gardens in bloom from early spring through fall.

A mall area in front of the theater features a beautiful fountain sending jets of water high above the shrubs and flowers edging the round basin. Hanging baskets of flowers line the sidewalks leading to the mall and theater.

Following its policy of "something for everyone," the Garden State Arts Center presents a varied and stellar assortment of talent aimed at all tastes. Among the perennial favorites are Bob Hope, Tony Bennett, Dinah Shore, Victor Borge and Liberace. Also appearing on the giant amphitheater stage have been Sinatra, Leonard Bernstein, Rodney Dangerfield, Harry Belafonte, Beverly Sills, Pavarotti, Liza Minnelli, Joel Grey, Johnny Mathis, Andy Williams, Dionne Warwick, Burt Bacharach, Steve Martin, Barry Manilow, Perry Como, Mac Davis, Lena Horne and Paul Anka.

A Cultural Center Fund was established at the time the Parkway-operated center opened. The fund gives New Jersey residents —who might otherwise not have an opportunity to see live entertainment—their day of special programs at the arts center. Every season hundreds of thousands of senior citizens, the disadvantaged and the handicapped and underprivileged school children enjoy programs of cultural and educational value.

School children, for example, have been treated to everything from "Gilbert & Sullivan" to "Peter Rabbit" and "Susan B. Anthony." And senior citizens have been given special performances by Dinah Shore and Liberace and concerts by the United States Army Field Band and Soldiers Chorus.

A popular free program has been the annual Talent Expo Showcase of Stars. Performers are New Jersey teenagers selected through a series of regional auditions and competitions in vocal and instrumental music and the dance.

Many of New Jersey's ethnic communities also support the Cultural Center Fund by celebrating their respective cultural backgrounds with colorful Heritage Festivals on the arts center grounds and stage. Alive with dazzling costumes and the aromas of ethnic foods, the mall may be transformed into a village square in Italy or a Scottish meadow.

Since 1971, the Heritage Festival program has made the term "melting pot" more meaningful to thousands of Jerseyans who trace their roots to all corners of the globe. Among the ethnic festivals at the arts center each year are the Polish, Scandinavian, Scottish, Baltic, Jewish, Irish, Italian, German, Byelorussian, Ukrainian, Slovak, and Hungarian.

New Jersey artists and craftspeople also exhibit their work before each performance.

* * *

The Meadowlands Arena stands like a sculpted modern mammoth along the New Jersey Turnpike's northerly exit, an entertainment complex that was an instant success the moment Monmouth County rock star Bruce Springsteen christened it with his electric chants on July 2, 1982.

The 20,000-seat arena, next to Giants Stadium, has had sellout concerts by almost every pop performer and group: Kenny Rogers, John Denver, Neil Diamond, Rod Stewart, Willie Nelson, The Rolling Stones, the Beach Boys, Van Halen, plus many others.

The world premiere of Disney on Ice led a long and varied list of family entertainment, including Ringling Bros. and Barnum & Bailey Circus, Holiday on Ice and the inaugural Toyota Tennis Championships.

The New Jersey Devils recorded four sellout crowds of 19,023 in the 1981-82 hockey season, the largest crowds in the history of the National Hockey League's Patrick Division.

The Meadowlands Arena is also the indoor home field for the New Jersey Cosmos and Rockets soccer teams, and the home base for the New Jersey Nets basketball team.

The top college basketball match-up of the '81-82 season was

Courtesy: Byrne Meadowlands Arena

The Meadowlands Arena in East Rutherford provides 20,000 seats for concerts, spectaculars and sports events.

played out in the arena between number one ranked North Carolina against number two Kentucky.

The National Basketball Association's All-Star Game was played before a sellout crowd of 20,149 in January 1982.

The arena's surprising shape is dramatized at night by uplighting that emphasizes the pitched skylights of the concourse. Visitors enter from four corners onto a ground-level concourse. Tiered seats lie above and below the concourse, with no seat more than 200 feet from an entrance. The steel and concrete structure has a sweeping oval interior that yields unobstructed views of the action.

Designed by The Grad Partnership in Newark, the building steps down with the contours of the land and presents an attractive "front porch" to the community with its open, airy appearance. The area is roofed with a clear, continuous skylight. The cafeteria is the centerpiece of the complex with its 23-foot-high ceiling, curving glass walls looking out over a park and spiral staircase.

Since its opening in 1981, the Meadowlands Arena, named after former Gov. Brendan T. Byrne (1973-81), was host to more than 8 million spectators who filled the facility for 838 events, from rock concerts and family entertainment to the best indoor professional and amateur sports.

* * *

Waterloo Village is becoming New Jersey's most popular historic cultural center, a place where the past peacefully meets the present along the banks of the Musconetcong River and the Morris Canal, one of the state's first major transportation projects after the American Revolution.

Pastoral Waterloo Village in Stanhope is the setting for seasonal arts festivals.

Waterloo Village was established in 1967 to develop a deeper appreciation of the American cultural tradition by presenting our living heritage of music, dance, opera and fine arts.

Registered as a National Historic Site in 1968, Waterloo Village in Byram Township, Sussex County, contains 30 buildings housing antiques and folk arts from the 18th and 19th centuries. From May through October, the Festival of the Arts presents a diverse cultural program featuring classical and contemporary music, dance and opera, as well as crafts and antiques exhibitions.

A five-week summer music school is conducted for 75 gifted artist-students who study and perform classical works under full scholarships with a distinguished international faculty led by conductor Gerard Schwarz.

The classical music series directed by Schwarz has featured, with the Waterloo Festival Orchestra, renowned soloists such as Pablo Casals, Van Cliburn, Byron Janis, Isaac Stern, Andre Watts, Emanuel Ax and Marian McPartland, "The First Lady of Jazz."

For the 1983 summer program, Waterloo hosted, in conjunction with the Wagner Society, the United States premiere of Wagner's opera, "Das Liebesverbot." In 1984, a Strauss arrangement of Gluck's "Iphigenia aus Aulis" was presented. For 1985, the Waterloo Festival Orchestra presented the Beethoven-Weingartner "Hammerklavier Sonata, Opus 106."

Waterloo is one of the venues for the Kool Jazz Festival, and the Waterloo Bluegrass Festival is the official event of its kind in New Jersey and is acclaimed as a major cultural attraction in the northeastern United States.

A $76 million Waterloo Master Plan, prepared by the Hillier Group of Princeton, a prestigious architectural firm, is currently under development. Key projects in the plan include a permanent 4,000-seat performing arts amphitheater with lawn seating for 5,000 ... a 110-room conference center for housing the music school, future fine arts and humanities programs, plus corporate retreats ... restoration of the Andover Forge, which supplied munitions for Gen. Washington's soldiers ... and making a part of the Morris Canal system operational again with a working lock and inclined plane.

Attendance reached a new high in 1984, as more than 150,000 visitors trooped to Waterloo Village to hear the stars under the stars. More than 3,000 people visited the village between Christmas Eve and New Year's Day 1984.

* * *

Newark Symphony Hall, New Jersey's largest, oldest showplace, also enjoyed a record-setting year in 1984, as 200,000 people attended cultural, educational and entertainment events. Symphony Hall audiences welcomed such famed artists as Isaac Stern, Barry White, Victor Borge, Yehudi Menuhin, Millie Jackson, James Cleveland, John Amos—star of television's most popular mini-series, "Roots"—plus the regular productions of the New Jersey State Opera, the New Jersey Symphony Orchestra, the Newark Boys Chorus and the Theater of Universal Images (TUI), the state's oldest black theater.

Newark Symphony Hall occupies "a central place in the cultural history of New Jersey," according to architectural historian Donald Geyer, whose investigation of the hall led to its listing in the National Register of Historic Places in 1975. The historian found Symphony Hall to be "one of the few surviving creations of an important era in American cultural development."

Seating 3,365, the Newark theater is larger than Carnegie Hall, Lincoln Center's Metropolitan Opera House or Philharmonic Hall in New York City. Tests by Bell Laboratories in 1965 put Newark Symphony Hall's acoustics on a par with Boston's renowned Symphony Hall.

Originally called the Salaam Temple, the Broad Street edifice was designed by three architects—Frank Grad, Henry Baechlin and George Backoff—for the Ancient Arabic Order of the Nobles of the Mystic Shrine, commonly known as the Shriners. Ground for the Shriners' temple was broken in April 1922; an inaugural performance was held on Sept. 8, 1925. The theater in the temple was known as "The Mosque." It became a famous showcase during the vaudeville era.

The style of Symphony Hall is Neo-Classical Revival. The design motifs are an eclectic mix, primarily inspired from Greek and Egyptian examples, with some Roman influence. The interior is Classical Renaissance on a grand scale. The 70-foot stage is flanked by two huge baroque doorways, each framed by two wide, spiral-fluted Ionic columns supporting an elaborately ornamented and statued acroterion.

The walls enclosing the orchestra area are rimmed by arcades, which are surmounted by balconies with colonnades of Corinthian columns. Medallions grace the walls between the arches. The colonnade supports a full entablature, whose frieze is decorated with angelic figures separated by scroll work and panels. Between the columns hang exquisite chandeliers of an art nouveau style. From the center of the ceiling hangs the palatial, 3,000-crystal chandelier.

The friezes, capitals and most inside ornamentation are gold-leafed, and the balustrades and columns are carved from white marble. With the red carpeting, the total effect is luxurious, almost opulent.

The opulent interior of Newark's Symphony Hall reflects a number of architectural styles, especially Neo-Classical.

Among the historic figures who have performed at Newark Symphony Hall are Rachmaninoff, Rubenstein, Horowitz, Gershwin, Toscanini, Eugene Ormandy, Lily Pons, and the Columbia, Boston and Cleveland symphony orchestras, in addition to the Metropolitan Opera National Company and the Ballet Russe de Monte Carlo.

Symphony Hall also houses a television and recording studio and a black theatrical company, The Theatre of Universal Images, founded by Clarence C. Lilley in 1970.

To increase attendance, the Symphony Hall Corp. is developing a 500-car parking garage next to the state's premier showplace. Also in the works is the formation of a New Jersey School for the Performing Arts.

In the last six years, more than $56 million has been invested within a three-block radius of Symphony Hall for the construction or renovation of 1,057 apartments for senior citizens and another 338 units of family housing.

The Lincoln Park neighborhood across from Symphony Hall has been formally nominated for historic district status because of its many valuable brownstone dwellings built at the turn of the century.

* * *

The Capitol in Passaic has become the mecca for rock 'n' roll music with the longest running concert series in the country.

Rock impresario John Scher resurrected The Capitol—a vintage movie-vaudeville theater—on Dec. 16, 1971, after promoting concerts in barns, stadiums, gymnasiums and anywhere else he could set up seats and put up a wooden performing platform.

Scher was just a kid right out of high school when he discovered that rock 'n' roll was being stereophonically inundated by psychedelia, disco and pop glitter. Scher searched for a showcase that would make New Jersey the rock 'n' roll capital of America.

With the closing of the famous Fillmore East in Manhattan, Scher made his move. He found what he wanted in The Capitol, a 3,000-seat theater in the heart of a once-thriving downtown Passaic. He brought the Fillmore's innovative "Pig Light Show" to Passaic and continued the Fillmore's tradition of showing cartoons and film clips between performances.

The rest is history. Downtown Passaic immediately started attracting tons of attention from the thousands of rock fans who faithfully pilgrimaged to The Capitol for each sold-out concert, spotlighting such superweights as Springsteen, The Rolling Stones, The Who, Stevie Wonder, Linda Ronstadt, Bette Midler, The Allman Brothers Band, The Eagles, Seals and Crofts, Hall and Oates, The Bee Gees, Alice Cooper, Arlo Guthrie, Sha Na Na, Jackson Browne and other major recording stars.

In 1972, Scher's production company, Monarch Entertainment, bought The Capitol for $160,000. The art deco monument to America's silent film era is now the showcase headquarters of Scher's expanding rock empire. The young entrepreneur also books concerts in the Meadowlands Arena, Giants Stadium, Madison Square Garden, on the Boardwalk at Asbury Park, Rutgers University and The Beacon Theatre in New York City.

The Capitol has come full circle since it packed them in for those foot-stomping, catcalling vaudeville and burlesque shows long before radio and television revolutionized the music industry and rendered those art deco showpalaces obsolete, except for a handful of landmark survivors.

* * *

The William Carlos Williams Center for the Arts is a bold experiment in community culture. Just down the road from the Meadowlands Arena, The Williams Center—named after the Pulitzer Prize-winning Rutherford poet and pediatrician (1883-1963) —is an outgrowth of the sprawling Rutherford campus of Fairleigh Dickinson University.

Former State Sen. Fairleigh S. Dickinson Jr. launched a $5 million restoration drive to convert Rutherford's ornate Rivoli Theater into a 1,516-seat concert hall for orchestra, opera and dance. The refurbished center features a 48-foot proscenium stage with 66 feet of fly space and an orchestra pit for 52 musicians.

The 1922 vaudeville house was used to show movies until 1977 when a fire forced its closing. The complex now contains two movie theaters and a cafe at the basement level, and a 166-seat recital hall, office space and a lobby at ground level.

Since its official opening on Aug. 27, 1982, the elegant Williams Center has been presenting chamber music, jazz concerts, poetry readings and other events. The movie theaters and cafe are also in full operation.

In 1984, more than 80,000 people attended recitals and 95,000 checked in at the cinema.

* * *

The Englewood Plaza for the Performing Arts is a luxurious, late-Victorian picture palace that opened as a silent movie house on Nov. 22, 1926. The lavish art deco theater with 2,000 plush seats and a $50,000 Welte-Mignon organ was built by the Walter Reade Chain as a movie-vaudeville showcase. In the 1930s it was known as the Fox Plaza and during the '40s and '50s it was operated by the Skouras Theatre chain.

In 1963, the Plaza was remodeled at a cost of $100,000, featuring rich red upholstery and aisle carpeting. To accommodate a new wide screen, 400 seats in front of the stage had to be removed.

From 1967-73, United Artists managed to keep the doors open. Television finally took its toll and for three years the Plaza was darkened.

In 1976, John Harms, an organist, chorale director and concert master, brought the old palace back to life, restoring the handsome marble lobby and swank marquee to its original condition. The new red, blue and gold color scheme was designed by Op artist Richard J. Anuskiewicz of Englewood; the artist has done work at Lincoln Center. Painter Johann Ankarian created the hand-sponged effects on the light gold ceiling.

Impresario Harms believed the acoustics at the Plaza to be better than Carnegie Hall's. He chose as the theater's new logo the Griffin, the creature that drew the Greek god Apollo's mythological chariot.

Since its opening on Oct. 10, 1976, the John Harms Plaza has played host to a constellation of world-famous performers: Isaac Stern, Richard Tucker, the Boston Symphony Orchestra, the Beaux Arts Trio, the Vienna Boys' Choir, jazz great Marian McPartland, the Dance Theater of Harlem, folk artist Don McLean, the Norman Luboff Choir, Marilyn Horne, the National Symphony and the Joffrey Ballet.

* * *

The Ritz in Elizabeth is another impressive restoration project, reflecting the desire by older cities to preserve a prized piece of their past.

The 1920s Fabian Ritz was part of that fabulous vaudevillian circuit that turned comic troupers into movie stars, from the deadpan Jack Benny to the irrepressible George Burns and Gracie Allen. The Ritz marquee was also aglow with the names of Betty Grable, Desi Arnaz and the Little Rascals, the small-fry version of the Dead End Kids.

The Ritz on East Jersey Street was boarded up in November 1979, another big movie house victim of television and smaller suburban multiple-movie houses the size of "screening rooms" used by reviewers. The Ritz's orchestra pit had been planked over and the pipe organs at the balcony level removed.

The interior paint in the blue and beige RKO colors had curled and the elaborate ceiling moldings, silk brocade wall fabric, art deco lights and sparkling chandeliers had become faded and dusty. The iridescent fabric decorated with tulip and shell patterns has been restored. The one good feature of The Ritz was its padded walls, still in good condition, making the hall ideal for concerts by keeping sounds from reverberating.

The marquee's Italian Renaissance trim needed cosmetic retouching and new burgundy-colored tapestry had to be installed. The rest of the work involved a lot of cleaning, scrubbing, stripping, painting and hauling away boards and junk cluttering and hiding The Ritz's glorious past.

Reopened in November 1980, the 2,772-seat theater is bringing live entertainment back to Elizabeth and Union County with such solid fare as Ray Charles, comedians Redd Foxx, Rodney Dangerfield, Buddy Hackett and George Carlin, trumpeter Chuck Mangione, The Temptations, The Marshall Tucker Band, Merle Haggard, B.B. King and the Blue Band, and Ricky Skaggs and The Whites.

The spring '85 concert agenda saw the Oak Ridge Boys, country-western favorites; country star Lee Greenwood; a 1950s "oldies" show featuring Little Anthony and an all-star lineup including the Coasters, the Platters and Hank Williams Jr., and a Westminster Dance Theater recital.

The Ritz is rebuilding an audience around comedy, country music and jazz, and is pleasantly finding that live entertainment is one way to bring new life back to a tired downtown business district.

* * *

The New Brunswick Cultural Center is an ambitious $15 million undertaking that's central to the city's renaissance effort.

A cultural center is being created around the State Theater on Livingston Avenue in downtown New Brunswick where City Hall and the Post Office are located.

The State Theater, owned by the city's Development Corp. (DevCo) and projected for a 1987 opening, is being renovated into a 1,800-2,000-seat performing arts hall for symphony, light opera, dance, drama and other classical and contemporary musical events. The theater will be the new home of the Princeton Ballet, Opera Theater of New Jersey, the Garden State Symphonic Pops Orchestra, plus a regional base for the New Jersey Symphony Orchestra, which already performs in New Brunswick.

Next door, the YMCA has been converted into the new home of the George Street Playhouse, with housing for students of the Rutgers Mason Gross School of the Arts on the upper floors. The new playhouse has 325 seats.

The Arnold Constable building is occupied by the Mason Gross School's division of visual arts, with classrooms, studios, shops and offices. The facility is linked to an 800-seat proscenium theater, the only new construction in the four-faceted project.

The Sisser Brothers warehouse is being transformed into an administrative arts and media center. It is the new 300-seat home for Crossroads Theatre, a professional black theater company.

The spacious warehouse would provide offices for Rutgers Television and Radio, and rehearsal and studio space for the resident arts group performing at the State Theater.

By recycling the downtown buildings into a cultural center, the city estimates it saves from $30 million to $35 million.

The Capitol in Passaic—the "Fillmore East of New Jersey"—has welcomed many famous guests to its stage, including rock superstar Bruce Springsteen.
Courtesy: Capitol Theatre

The New Jersey Nets in action
at the Meadowlands Arena.

Photo Credit: Tom Cassidy

Modern sports grew up in the Garden State when most games were played in backyards and on the streets or in open pastures bordering the big cities.

Baseball and intercollegiate football made their debut in New Jersey during the last century and world-class professional soccer was first introduced in the Hackensack Meadowlands in 1977.

But as far back as November 1885, the first international soccer game in the United States was played on a grassy field near East Newark. About 2,000 soccer fans witnessed the defeat of the local all-star team to the rough-playing Canadian national team. The score: 1-0.

Pioneers and visionaries, New Jersey athletes also organized the U.S. team for the first modern Olympics game in 1896, while such legends as Vince Lombardi (whose name is honored in the Super Bowl Trophy) and Pele, the world's greatest soccer player, found the Garden State an ideal environment in which to demonstrate their natural talents and genius in competitive play.

Today, six professional teams make New Jersey their home

base, drawing millions of fans to the greatest sports complex on the continent. The Hackensack Meadowlands has become the playing center for the football Giants, Jets and Generals, the world famous Cosmos soccer team, the Nets basketball team, and the Devils ice hockey franchise.

The Meadowlands Sports and Entertainment Complex, featuring a magnificent stadium, arena and racetrack, also hosts tennis championship matches, the United States Grand Prix, and the world's richest harness purse: The $2 million Woodrow Wilson Pace.

The world's number one harness track attracts more than 3 million seasonal fans who wager nearly a half-billion dollars during 182 standardbred races.

Not to be outdone, the thoroughbreds draw more than 1.5 million to the fast track, producing a handle of $205 million during a 98-race season.

The 270-acre site by the Hackensack River boasts a bowl-shaped, 76,891-seat stadium, a sleek 20,000-seat arena, a sweeping racetrack that can accommodate up to 40,000 spectators, and a restaurant called Pegasus that seats 1,200, three-fourths of them for trackside viewing.

The annual Meadowlands "Kickoff Classic" has become a national event, as two of America's top college football teams compete each opening season for that momentary ranking of "Number One" before their regular schedules start. The University of Miami upset Auburn in the 1984 contest, played at Giants Stadium.

And another world-class event was inaugurated in 1985 as the New Jersey Waterfront Marathon jogged into sports history on May 5 at Liberty State Park in Hudson County.

The year 1985 also saw plans for another magnificent stadium in the Meadowlands area—the new home of two baseball clubs, one from the American League, one from the National League.

But long before there was a world-renowned Meadowlands Complex, sports history was being made in New Jersey. Some games, in fact, were invented on corner lots and the playing fields of the oldest schools in America.

The birth of baseball occurred on a balmy day in Hoboken when the Knickerbockers and the New Yorks took to the field and scored 24 runs in just four innings. The winners of this first baseball game on June 19, 1846 were the New Yorks, who left no doubt they were the best team around. They drove home 23 runs to the Knickerbockers' sole run.

The first organized baseball game lasted only four innings because the rules in those days stated that the first team to score 21 runs was the winner.

The amateur teams played on Hoboken's Elysian Fields under rules devised by an amateur athlete and surveyor, Alexander J. Cartwright, who also umpired the game. Cartwright determined the field's playing dimensions. The amateurs went on playing for 23 years until the city of Cincinnati decided to field a team—and professional baseball was born.

The Babe Ruth League—the largest regulation amateur youth baseball program in the world—was organized in Hamilton Township, outside of Trenton, in 1951. Based in nearby Lawrence Township, the Babe Ruth League has spawned more than 2,900 leagues and 1,750 teams nationwide. More than 300,000 youngsters between the ages of six and 18 presently play in the Babe Ruth League. In New Jersey, there were 103 leagues and 700 teams as of 1984.

George Herman (Babe) Ruth, the Sultan of Swat, vacationed at Greenwood Lake in New Jersey during his New York Yankee playing career and also frequented "speakeasies" in North Jersey during Prohibition. The Babe also played some exhibition games in New Jersey.

America's first intercollegiate football game was played in New Brunswick on Nov. 6, 1869. The teams, then 25 on a side, were fielded by Rutgers and Princeton universities, then arch rivals in private school competition. Rutgers won, 6 to 4, before a small stand of students and family members rooting for their playing relatives.

Robert Garrett, captain of the Princeton track team in 1896, wanted to compete in the first modern Summer Olympics that year. But Garrett couldn't convince his teammates to join him at the games in Greece—until he volunteered to pay their expenses.

With three other Princetonians, Garrett organized America's first Olympics team. The last time the Olympics had been held was during the Golden Age of Greece about 1,500 years ago.

The original U.S. Olympic Team consisted of Garrett and his

A capacity crowd of more than 75,000 watch the world-champion Cosmos soccer team play in Giants stadium.

Courtesy: N.J. Div. of Travel & Tourism

three classmates—Herbert Jamison, Francis Lane and Albert Tyler—a Harvard student and five athletes from the Boston Athletic Association whose members attended Yale, MIT and Boston College.

In Athens, Garrett captured first place in both the shot and the discus, and placed second in the broad jump and third in the high jump. Jamison took second place in the 400-meter race, while Tyler was runner-up in the pole vault. Suffering from illness, Lane came in fourth place in the 100-meter race. The Princeton Tigers went home with 11 olive branches—the most of any national contingent.

The final scorecard showed the first U.S. Olympic Team won nine of the 12 track and field events.

In the 1984 summer Olympics, the world witnessed a historic performance by a superathlete from Willingboro, in South Jersey. Carl Lewis surpassed his idol, Jesse Owens, in the record books by winning four gold medals, in the long jump, the 100 and 200 meters and the relay.

Star-Ledger Photo

Carl Lewis, originally from Willingboro, won gold medals in four events, including the long jump, at the Los Angeles Olympic Games in 1984.

Raised in Levittown (later renamed Willingboro), Lewis broke the nation's prep long-jump record three times while a senior in high school. He soared 26 feet, a foot-and-a-half past his contemporaries.

The United States Equestrian Team, headquartered at Peapack-Gladstone, also captured the gold and silver medals for jumping at the Los Angeles '84 Olympics.

New Jersey schools and teams have produced some of the greatest stars in collegiate and professional sports, among them:

• Bill Bradley, now a United States senator representing New Jersey, was an All-American basketball player at Princeton University and a Rhodes Scholar who played on two world championship teams for the New York Knicks (1969 and 1973).

Star-Ledger Photo

U. S. Senator Bill Bradley was an All-American and Rhodes Scholar at Princeton University before playing with the world champion New York Knicks.

• Paul Robeson, an All-American football player at Rutgers in 1918-19 who went on to become a prominent stage and screen actor. Born in Princeton, Robeson was an exceptional athlete at Somerville High School.

• Billy Austin, an All-American tailback at Rutgers in 1958, and Phil Sellers, an All-American forward in 1975-76 for Rutgers' undefeated basketball team, earned fame and glory at New Jersey's state university.

• Alex Kroll, Rutgers' All-American football center in 1961, became president of Kenyon & Eckhardt, one of the world's largest advertising agencies.

• In college football, the Heisman Trophy is awarded to the best player each year. Named after John Heisman, football coach at Stanford University in the 1930s, the trophy was won by Nebraska's tailback Mike Rozier in the 1983 season. Rozier—like his teammate, wingback Irving Fryar—is New Jersey born and bred.

Joe Theisman, Washington Redskin Super Bowl quarterback.

Mike Rozier, Heisman Trophy Winner.

Jersey Joe Walcott, Heavyweight Champion.

Rozier perfected his moves in Camden and Fryar prepared for his college triumphs in nearby Mount Holly.

• Dick Kazmaier won the Heisman Trophy while playing for Princeton University in 1951. Notre Dame quarterback Angelo Bertelli received the Heisman Trophy in 1943 and settled in Clifton in 1950, where he operates a lucrative chain of liquor stores.

• Joe Theisman, South River High School's class of 1967, is a Heisman runner-up who quarterbacked his Washington Redskins team to the Super Bowl in 1983, defeating the Miami Dolphins in the classic.

• Another South River favorite, Drew Pearson (class of '69), was, until his retirement in 1984, the wide receiver for the Dallas Cowboys, considered one of the best professional football teams of the Super Bowl era.

• A high school standout, South River has won or tied for 19 state championships. The Rams have had nine unbeaten football seasons.

Alex Wojciechowicz, a National Football League Hall of Famer, played for South River, class of '34, and was one of the "Seven Blocks of Granite" at Fordham University in the mid-1930s. The granite wall, which included Vince Lombardi and Ed Franco of Jersey City, was then the most feared line in college football.

Franco, inducted in the Football Hall of Fame, captained the Fordham freshman football team.

* * *

For sports lovers, there's life beyond football, baseball and basketball. New Jersey athletes have also achieved success in the water, in the ring and on the tennis courts.

Elaine Zayak of Paramus won the World Figure Skating Championship in 1982.

Dick Button won a gold medal in the 1948 Olympics for figure skating, scoring the highest number of points in Olympic history up to that time—994.7 for compulsory figures and 191.77 for free skating. A week later the Englewood youth won the World Figure Skating Championship, receiving 5.9 out of a possible 6 from the judges.

Practicing at the Riverdale skating rink near his Bergen County home, Button was the first American to hold a European figure skating title.

Following in Button's brilliant figure-eights is another Bergen County skating whiz, Elaine Zayak of Paramus. Born 18 years after Button made his mark, Zayak won the United States championship in 1981 at the age of 15.

Since then, Zayak has changed the sport. Her famous triple jumps are now a necessary part of any skater's routine in order to finish in first place. Zayak, a human gyroscope, executes seven triple jumps, or axles, in her performance, the first skater in the world capable of completing seven such spins in a program.

Those incredibly difficult jumps, landing on one foot, enabled Zayak to win the world championship at Copenhagen in 1982. She started doing triples when she was 10, despite an accident at three years old that sheared off three toes and part of her foot when she stepped into a rotary lawnmower.

Althea Gibson of East Orange was the first black tennis player to win the prestigious Wimbledon singles championship, in 1957. Along the way, she won the French Open, the U.S. Open at Forest Hills and the National Clay Court Championship.

At the peak of her playing career, Gibson was voted Woman Athlete of the Year in the Associated Press Poll. The former state athletic commissioner joined the Ladies Professional Golf Association in 1963. Author of "I Always Wanted to Be Somebody," Gibson also played semi-pro softball and basketball.

Star-Ledger Photo

Althea Gibson was the first black player to win Wimbledon. Miss Gibson, from East Orange, also won the U. S. Open.

Merchantville, in South Jersey, was where Jersey Joe Walcott developed his pugilistic skills, becoming the oldest boxer to win the world heavyweight championship in 1951. He floored champion Ezzard Charles in the seventh round in Pittsburgh. Born

Arnold Raymond Cream, Walcott, after retiring from the ring, served as state athletic director in New Jersey. He was elected to the Boxing Hall of Fame in 1969. Walcott has lived most of his life in Camden, organizing youth programs.

Other Boxing Hall of Famers from New Jersey are: Freddie Cochrane of Elizabeth, welterweight champion; Johnny Dundee of East Orange, junior lightweight and featherweight champ whose lifetime career fights reached an exhausting 320 bouts; Tippy Larkin of Garfield, junior welterweight champ; Gus Lesnavich of Cliffside Park, light heavyweight champ; Mickey Walker of Elizabeth, welterweight and middleweight titlist; and middleweight champ Tony Zale, who regained his title by knocking out Rocky Graziano in three rounds in Newark in 1948.

Boxing's first $1 million gate took place at Boyle's Thirty Acres in Jersey City in 1921. Jack Dempsey knocked out France's Georges Carpentier in the fourth round.

With the advent of casino gambling in Atlantic City, New Jersey is being touted as the boxing capital of the world. World championship fights are regularly held at the popular casino-hotels along the most famous boardwalk by the sea.

A peninsula state, New Jersey promotes many water sports, from the Benihana Power Boat Race off the coast of Asbury Park each summer to seasonal sailing meets. Only four people have attained All-American sailing honors three times, according to the U.S. Yacht Racing Union. Three of the four are from New Jersey: Gary Jobson and William Campbell of Toms River, and Alex Smegelski of Lake Hopatcong.

The America's Cup was conceived in 1851 by the Stevens brothers: John Cox, the first commodore of the New York Yacht Club, founded in Hoboken, and Edwin, who joined in the syndicate that built and owned the yacht America. Edwin Stevens also founded the Stevens Institute of Technology in Hoboken in 1870.

The America's Cup was the longest winning streak in sports history. The coveted trophy was a permanent fixture at the New York Yacht Club for 122 years until Australia won the cup in 1983 after going the full distance—seven nip 'n tuck races off Newport, R.I.

Bike racing was once more popular in Newark than baseball. Frank L. Kramer of Newark was the world sprint champion in 1912 and the American champ from 1901-16 and 1918-21.

Kramer and other racing greats popularized the sport at the Newark VeloDrome, opposite Vailsburg Park. The board-track center burned down in 1930.

Other New Jersey natives who made the biking record books were the Goulet brothers, Frank and Alfred. Fred Spencer was champ from 1925-28 and Albert Sellinger was the amateur American sprint champion in 1935 and rode in the Olympic games in 1936.

Edward J. Littig, also a national road champion, still holds the single and tandem bike records from New York to Philadelphia. Littig, of Lakehurst, is a past president of the New Jersey Beekeeper's Association.

* * *

Modern football's most prominent figure was Vince Lombardi, a guard on the Fordham University football team.

After winning three football letters at Fordham from 1934-36, Lombardi sold insurance until landing his first coaching job as an assistant football coach at St. Cecilia High School in Englewood. His annual salary in 1939 was $1,700. He also taught physics, chemistry, algebra and Latin in order to fulfill his dreams as a football coach.

Lombardi perfected the T-formation offense and his football teams won six New Jersey state championships. At one time, his team won 36 consecutive games. In 1942, Lombardi became head football, basketball and baseball coach at St. Cecilia. In 1945, his basketball team won the New Jersey parochial school championship.

"Winning is the only thing"—Vince Lombardi began his successful coaching career at St. Cecilia High School in Englewood. He went on to coach at Fordham and West Point before moving to the professional ranks with the New York Giants.

His final and greatest success came as coach of the Green Bay Packers where his teams won the first two Super Bowls and he became a legend in his own time.

Star-Ledger Photo

After eight years at the Englewood school, Lombardi returned to Fordham, serving as freshman coach. In 1949, he became assistant coach at West Point. Five years later he made the big move to professional football, signing up with the New York Giants as offensive coach.

In 1956, the Giants won their only NFL championship since 1938. The following year they won the Eastern Conference championship and, in 1959, Lombardi signed a five-year contract as head coach and general manager of the Green Bay Packers. The rest is football history.

Lombardi's Packers won three straight championships in 1965, 1966 and 1967. His Packers also won back-to-back in 1961 and 1962.

The Packers won the first two Super Bowls, in 1967 over Kansas City (35-10), and in 1968 over Oakland (33-14).

For his phenomenal gamesmanship, Lombardi's name lives forever in the Super Bowl Trophy that honors his unparalleled record in football.

Tennis

The game of tennis also was popularized in the Garden State at the turn of the 20th Century. The Orange Lawn Tennis Club emerged in 1880 as one of the charter members of the U.S. Lawn Tennis Association. The South Orange club produced a few illustrious members during tennis' fledgling years.

William A. Larned was ranked among the top five players in the U.S. a record 19 straight years, from 1894 to 1912. Larned was ranked No. 1 eight times: 1901 through 1903 and 1907 through 1911. Larned was also a perennial Davis Cup player during his prime.

Holcombe F. Ward was ranked among the top 10 U.S. players seven times and reached the No. 1 designation in 1904. He won the national doubles title three times with Dwight Davis, father of the Davis Cup, and three more doubles championships with Beals C. Wright from 1899 to 1905.

Davis Cup players and U.S. Tennis Association presidents (1937-47), Larned and Ward were both elected to the Tennis Hall of Fame.

Dick Savitt, born in Bayonne and raised in Orange, won Wimbledon and U.S. championships in 1951. A member of the U.S. Davis Cup team and ranked No. 2 in the U.S. and the world in 1951, Savitt is also in the Hall of Fame.

Ham Richardson, a native of Westfield, was ranked among the top 10 U.S. players a total of 11 years. He was No. 1 in the U.S. in 1956 and 1958 and No. 3 in the world in 1956 behind Lew Hoad and Ken Rosewall.

Eddie Moyland, a resident of Trenton for many years, was ranked among the top 10 U.S. players in the 1950s, his best year being 1956 when he was ranked No. 4.

Current tennis stars from New Jersey include Peter Fleming of Chatham, Sandy and Gene Mayer of Wayne and Mendham, Pam Casale of Fairfield, and Caroline Stoll of Livingston, who played in the women's pro circuit from 1977-82.

Fleming, NCAA singles runner-up, has been ranked No. 8 in the world. He is a three-time Wimbledon doubles champion and three-time U.S. Open doubles champion with his superstar partner, John McEnroe. They are considered the greatest doubles team in professional tennis, having won seven consecutive Master's doubles, and reign as America's undefeated Davis Cup pair.

Gene Mayer ranked five times in the top U.S. players, while his brother Sandy made the top 10 twice.

In her first pro year, Pam Casale reached No. 16 in world rankings in 1981 and was among the top 10 players in the United States.

Stoll's highest ranking in the U.S. was No. 7 in 1979 and she ranked as high as No. 15 in the world in 1980. In doubles, Stoll ranked No. 2 with partner Kathy Harter in 1979.

Left, Peter Fleming of Chatham has been ranked as high as No. 8 in the tennis world, and No. 1 in doubles with his partner John McEnroe.

Right, Pam Casale of Fairfield ranks among the top 20 women's tennis players in the world.

Star-Ledger Photo

Star-Ledger Photo

Tennis tournaments of note in New Jersey go back to the 1890s when the Middle States Championships were first held at the Orange Lawn Tennis Club. Larned won the title eight times between 1901 and 1909.

The Orange Lawn annual invitational was held from 1920-40. The tourney was won 11 times by future members of the Tennis Hall of Fame during the 1921-33 period—four times by the incomparable Bill Tilden, three times by John H. Doeg, twice by Manuel Alonso and once each by Vinnie Richards and Wilmer Allison.

From 1930-35, the East vs. West team tournament was held at Orange Lawn and such greats of the '30s as Don Budge, Gene Make, Frank Parker, Fred Perry and Jack Crawford were regular crowd favorites.

The Eastern Grass Courts started its run of almost four decades at Orange Lawn in 1946. It was known as the second most prestigious tourney in the U.S.

Orange Lawn hosted the Davis Cup matches between the U.S. and Mexico in 1946. The Americans, sparked by Bill Talbert, Frank Parker and Gardnar Mulloy, won 5-0.

The $100,000 Mutual Benefit Life Open Championships were held at the Orange Lawn Tennis Club from 1976-83. That tournament now resides at Newark Academy in Livingston as the North American Tennis Open.

The $100,000 Volvo Women's Cup was played at Ramapo State College in Mahwah from 1979-82. Ramapo also was the site of the 1983 $100,000 Virginia Slims of New Jersey competition.

The $100,000 Toyota Women's Championships were held at the Meadowlands Arena in East Rutherford in 1981 and '82.

And the $150,000 Computerland U.S. National Women's Indoor Championships were hosted by the Four Seasons Racquet Club in East Hanover in 1984.

Golf

Like tennis, the gentleman's sport of golf was neatly perfected on New Jersey golf courses at the turn of the century by some of the greatest players in the game. Alphabetically, here are a few of the best:

• Willie Anderson, the first pro at the Baltusrol Golf Club in 1898, won four U.S. Opens, including a record three in 1903, '04 and '05. His first win was in 1901. Anderson also worked at the Montclair Golf Club in 1892.

*James Barnes,
golfing great.*

Courtesy: Wide World Photos

• James (Long Jim) Barnes, who finished his career as a pro at the Essex County Country Club, won the first PGA (Professional Golf Association) tournament in 1916, winning it again in 1919. Long Jim also took the U.S. Open in 1921 and the British Open in 1925.

• Al Besselink, born in Merchantville, won the 1953 Tournament of Champions and is believed to be the first winner to give his first prize money to charity: The Damon Runyon Cancer Fund. "Bessie" also won five other major events from 1952-57.

• Wes Ellis Jr., a pro at Mountain Ridge during the 1960s, won the Canadian, San Diego and Texas opens and was only one of two golfers to claim the "Jersey Slam" by winning the State Open, PGA and Met Open in the same year—1963.

• Johnny Farrell, the Baltusrol pro for 38 years, retiring in 1972, won the 1928 U.S. Open at Olympia Fields, when he beat Bobby Jones in a 36-hole playoff. Farrell also won five tour events in 1926 and seven the following year.

• George Fazio played out of Pine Valley after World War II and won the 1946 Canadian Open. Fazio, who lost the 1950 U.S. Open playoff to Ben Hogan, became one of the foremost golf course architects from the links. The first course Fazio designed in 1963 was Atlantis in Tuckerton.

• Marty Furgol, the Wildwood Country Club pro in the early '60s, won three tour events from 1951-54: The Houston and Western opens and the National Celebrities Invitational.

• Vic Ghezzi, born in Rumson and a pro at the Rumson and Englewood clubs, won the 1941 PGA when he beat Byron Nelson on the 39th hole in the final. Ghezzi also won 10 other tour events.

• Johnny Golden, a North Jersey pro, was a PGA pioneer who won four tournaments in the 1920s and was a member of the first two Ryder Cup teams. Golden, who also played in the early Masters, was one of only two players ever to win the New Jersey Open three straight years, 1927-29.

• Ralph Guldahl, a pro at Braidburn in 1938, captured the U.S. Open in 1937 and '38 and the Masters in 1939. Guldahl also holds three Western Open titles.

Baseball

A purely American concoction, modern "team" baseball not only began in New Jersey but many of its best players were born in the baseball state and many of the game's brightest stars were discovered while playing school ball here.

Johnny Vander Meer, a product of Midland Park, remains the only pitcher in professional baseball to hurl two consecutive no-hit games. The "Wild Dutchman," whose ball had a terrific hook, blanked the Boston Braves 3-0 on June 11, 1938. Four days later, he shut out the Brooklyn Dodgers 6-0. Vander Meer made sports history in a Cincinnati uniform.

The Newark Bears was considered the greatest minor league team of all in 1937. Yankee slugger Charlie Keller (1930s-40s) was recruited from the famous Bears.

Hall of Fame pitcher Walter Johnson managed the Bears in the early '30s. Three other Hall of Famers playing in Newark were outfielder Tris Speaker and pitchers Rube Waddell and Ed Walsh.

Newark also played in the ill-fated Federal League in 1915, finishing in fifth place with a season record of 80-72. The Newark club was managed by Bill Phillips and the lineup included Hall of Fame outfielder Eddie Roush and pitching sensation Ed Reulbach, who had a 20-10 record that year.

A walk through the Hall of Fame at Cooperstown, N.Y., reveals many New Jersey natives immortalized in metallic plaques, including Leon (Goose) Goslin from Salem, an outfielder with the Washington Senators, and Billy Hamilton of Newark, the base-stealing record holder who played with the Boston Braves before the turn of the century.

Other New Jersey baseball stars include Don Newcombe of Madison, the pitching ace of the early 1950s Dodgers who started his pro career with the Newark Eagles of the Negro League... Larry Doby, Paterson Eastside High's all-state great who played outfield for the Cleveland Indians from 1947-55 and after that for the Chicago White Sox and Detroit Tigers... Ron Perranoski of Paterson, the Dodgers' steady relief pitcher in the early '70s... Hank Borowy of Bloomfield, the only pitcher in the majors ever to win 20 games in one year between the American League and the National League, attaining that distinction in 1945 with the Yankees and Chicago Cubs... Jim Bouton of Newark, the Yankees pitcher whose controversial book "Ball Four" took fans from the ballfield to the locker rooms and into the private lives of baseball's biggest names of the '60s and '70s... Al Downing of Trenton, who pitched with the Yankees and Dodgers in the '60s and '70s... Andy Messersmith of Toms River, pitcher for the Dodgers and Angels in the '70s... Joe Cunningham of Saddle River, hitting star of the Cardinals in '50s and '60s... George Case of Trenton, base-stealing star of the '40s... Doc Cramer of Beach Haven, hitting star of the '30s... Kid Gleason of Camden, manager of the Chicago Black Sox in 1919.

After signing with the Giants out of the Negro League, Willie Mays began his career with a Class B baseball team in Trenton, where the amazing slugger hit .353 in 83 games in 1950.

Yankee scout Paul Krichell first saw, and later signed, Lou Gehrig when the pin-striped immortal was playing against Rutgers in New Brunswick. Gehrig was a Columbia University player when Krichell spotted his special talents on the New Brunswick campus ballfield.

New York Yankee players have had a long association with New Jersey. Mickey Mantle lived in River Edge during his playing years with the Yankees, catcher Elston Howard resided in Teaneck and ran businesses in Nutley and Belleville, and the inimitable Yogi Berra raised his family in Montclair and established a successful soft drink company in Garfield called Yoo-Hoo.

Whitey Ford pitched a season at Ft. Monmouth in 1951 in his Army uniform.

Besides the Federal League, New Jersey's other brush with the majors occurred in 1957, when the Brooklyn Dodgers played three "home games" in Jersey City's Roosevelt Stadium to bolster the club's waning attendance in New York.

Perhaps baseball's most enigmatic player was Moe Berg, a native of Newark and Princeton University alumnus. Berg assumed several guises over the years. Besides his fame as a major league catcher (Dodgers, White Sox, Red Sox), Berg was also a scholar, linguist, lawyer—and World War II spy.

Off seasons, Berg, who was fluent in 10 languages, earned a law degree and studied at the Sorbonne in Paris. During the Great Depression, Berg was a member of a distinguished entourage, including Babe Ruth and Lou Gehrig, which toured Japan, promoting America's greatest sports export: Baseball.

Berg's scholarship intelligence and linguistic skills were put to use by Uncle Sam, who sent the little catcher to South America on a fact-finding mission. Shortly after, Berg was working for the Office of Strategic Services (OSS), the United States' global intelligence organization. The baseball star's most exciting adventure was to uncover information about Germany's atomic bomb efforts.

In one undercover operation, Berg posed as a German businessman and tailed a top German nuclear scientist to Switzerland, where he was scheduled to give a talk. Berg managed to obtain duplicates of vital documents related to atomic projects. He then helped to bring European scientists to the United States.

After World War II, Berg was recommended for the Medal of Merit, the highest honor awarded to civilians during wartime. He declined to accept the award, and refused to say why. He died in Newark in 1972.

Football

Like baseball, football is taking over a bigger chunk of the calendar year with the addition of another league and more franchises, including the Jersey Generals at the Meadowlands stadium.

The Garden State has been producing football stars since the early days of the game. Amos Alanzo Stagg, a product of West Orange (born 1862), is regarded as the granddaddy of all football coaches. The historic sports figure is in both the football and basketball halls of fame.

Alexander Moffat, a Princeton Hall of Famer (1881-83), revolutionized the art of punting by inventing the spiral kick in 1881.

Charlie Berry of Phillipsburg was an All-American at Lafayette and played professional baseball from 1955-62 before becoming a big league umpire.

Roosevelt (Rosie) Grier, from Linden, was a Penn State All-American who played for the Giants and was one of the Rams' "Fearsome Foursome." Grier made the transition from grid star to movie star.

Mount Holly's Franco Harris bulldogged his way to fame at Penn State and playing fullback with the Pittsburgh Steelers. He played on the Steeler teams that posted a record-breaking four consecutive Super Bowl victories.

Lydell Mitchell of Salem, not far from Harris' home turf, teamed with his fellow Jerseyan at Penn State and later played for the Colts.

Jim Kiick of Boonton became the brilliant half of the Miami

Courtesy: New York Yankees   Courtesy: New York Yankees

Left, Elston Howard resided in Teaneck while playing, and later coaching, for the New York Yankees.

Right, Yogi Berra of Montclair has managed the New York Yankees baseball team.

Courtesy: Associated Press

Franco Harris of Mount Holly won four Super Bowl rings with the Pittsburgh Steelers and is one of the leading all-time rushers in professional football.

Star-Ledger Photo

Walter Dukes, a 7-footer, played for Seton Hall in South Orange and the New York Knicks.

Star-Ledger Photo

Frank Tripucka of Bloomfield was an All-American quarterback at Notre Dame in the 1940s. His son Kelly was a basketball star under the Golden Dome and now plays for the Detroit Pistons.

Dolphins' famed "Butch & Sundance" backfield combo during the 1970s.

Frank Tripucka was Bloomfield's All-American quarterback at Notre Dame from 1945-48, and his son, Kelly, is one of the top scorers on the Detroit Pistons basketball team.

Alex Wojciechowicz, another of South River's enduring dynasty, was one of Fordham's fabled "Seven Blocks of Granite."

Phil Villapiano of Long Branch was a linebacker for the Raiders, and Alex Webster of Kearny, a Giants fullback in the '50s, went on to become his team's coach in the '70s.

Basketball

All-American and Rhodes Scholar Bill Bradley is New Jersey's most famous basketball player, compiling impressive records at Princeton University and with the New York Knicks, and is now making it in the world of politics as a United States senator with a promising future as a national leader.

Bradley represents the culmination of a long basketball tradition in the Garden State that auspiciously started with the Passaic High School "Wonder Team," which won 159 straight games in 1919, including the finals of New Jersey's first state tournament. Coach Ernest Blood was responsible for 147 of those games.

Richie Regan of Newark was a 1951-53 All-American at Seton Hall University in South Orange, where he now serves as athletic director.

Another Seton Hall star of the 1940s is Bob Davies, who turned pro with the Rochester Royals and was voted into the Hall of Fame.

Walter Dukes, the 7-foot center at Seton Hall in the early 1950s later played with the New York Knicks.

Tom Heinsohn of Union City is regularly seen in the light beer commercials with other famous sports figures. Heinsohn was a star at Holy Cross from 1954-56 and was a player and subsequent coach with the Boston Celtics in the 1960s and '70s.

Rick Barry of Elizabeth was a pro star for the Nets and Golden State Warriors who earned his playing credentials at Roselle Park High School and Miami University.

Another Elizabeth son, Eddie Donovan, played and coached at St. Bonaventure in the late 1950s and early '60s. Donovan eventually became general manager of the Knicks and Buffalo Braves of the NBA.

Mo Layton pursued a pro career with the Phoenix Suns after putting Newark's Weequahic High School on the basketball map in the 1960s.

Twins Johnny and Eddie O'Brien of South Amboy starred in the college ranks with Seattle University in the 1950s, and John (Honey) Russell coached Seton Hall to a string of victories twice: From 1937-43 and again from 1950-60, leaving the South Orange university with a 294-129 record.

Hockey

Princeton's All-American football star Hobey Baker pioneered ice hockey in the U.S. in that game's infancy. Regarded as the finest American ice hockey player of all time, Baker played for Princeton's Tigers from 1910-14. He never played professional hockey, for his career was cut short in a plane crash during World

War I while flying for the elite Lafayette Escadrille in France. Baker made it into the Football Foundation Hall of Fame and the Hockey Hall of Fame.

In track and field, some notable athletes in the record books are Mel Sheppard of Almonesson Lake, a middle-distance runner in the 1908 and 1912 Olympics . . . Carl Lewis of Willingboro, the 1984 Summer Olympic champion . . . Bill Bonthion, Princeton running star of the '30s . . . Marty Liquori of Montclair, Essex Catholic and Villanova middle-distance runner in the '70s . . . Don Bragg of Penns Grove, pole-vaulting star of the '50s . . . Eugene Orowitz (actor Michael Landon) of Collingswood, the national high school javelin champion in 1954 . . . Milt Campbell of Plainfield, the decathlon star of the '50s . . . Tom Courtney of Newark, a middle-distance runner of the '50s . . . Mark Murro of Newark, javelin star of the late '60s . . . Dave Sime of Paterson, a leading sprinter of the '50s.

Polo

And then there's the aristocratic sport, polo.

The Far Hills Polo Club in Bedminster Township is developing into one of the world's most exclusive polo centers. The Far Hills Polo Club was known for more than a half-century as the Burnt Mills P.C. because the entrance to its two regulation fields is on Burnt Mills Road in Pluckemin.

Operated by area enthusiasts primarily as a hobby, the Far Hills club today maintains a five-month schedule of matches and champagne and black-tie affairs. Its international team played the All Ireland polo team in 1983 for the first time in several decades on New Jersey ground.

Polo ponies cost an average of $4,000, but the top ones in competition are worth far more. Two stallions owned by one player—Zografus, winner of more than $450,000 in purses, and Bold Destiny, a son of Bold Ruler (Preakness winner, 1957 Horse of the Year and sire of Secretariat)—are among the most successful sires in racing, judged on their percentage of winning offspring.

The Far Hills Polo Club is growing because players wintering in Palm Beach, Fla., are looking for places to play in the summer. The club is beginning to draw royalty, world-class competitors and others in the active Palm Beach circle.

* * *

The most popular place in the New York-North Jersey metropolitan region is the sports complex, a giant magnet in the Hackensack Meadowlands drawing millions of people to its football stadium, hockey and basketball arena and the richest purse racetrack in America.

Six professional teams make the Meadowlands their home-games headquarters: The world famous Cosmos soccer team, the New Jersey Nets basketball franchise, the fledgling New Jersey Devils ice hockey players, the United States Football League's New Jersey Generals, and two New York additions to the Garden State's 78,000-seat bowl in the Meadows—the National Football League's Giants and the Super Bowl-winning Jets.

Cosmos

History was made when the Cosmos moved from New York to Giants Stadium in the spring of 1977. Led by Pele, the world's greatest soccer player, the Cosmos won the North American Soccer League Championship in 1977, '78, and again in 1980 and '82. The Cosmos made it to the finals in 1981, and lost.

Established in 1971, the Cosmos became the most famous sports team in the world, as well known in Europe, South America, China and Africa as they are around their impressive Giants Stadium.

In 1980, the Cosmos completed an unprecedented tour of six continents in one year, and in 1982 they carried the North American soccer banner on an undefeated tour of Australia, Japan and Korea, the club's most successful international journey ever.

Pele joined the club in 1975 and West German superstar Franz Beckenbauer joined in 1977, making it the year of the "Cosmos Phenomenon" at the Meadowlands stadium.

The Cosmos claimed their fourth crown in 1980 behind an amazing 18-goal playoff performance by the North American Soccer League's all-time scoring champion, Giorgio Chinaglia.

Nets

Like the Cosmos, the Nets have played on both sides of the Hudson River until finding a permanent home at the Meadowlands Arena.

The Nets began life in 1967 as the New Jersey Americans, a new American Basketball Association franchise. Their first home was the cavernous and drafty Teaneck Armory in Bergen County. A year later they became the New York Nets, settling in Commack, on Long Island. That year, Bobby Lloyd of Rutgers hit 49 free throws in a row over a 13-game span for a new ABA record.

Moving into the Nassau Veterans Memorial Coliseum in Long Island, the Nets advanced to the ABA final round in 1971-72, capturing their first Eastern Conference crown.

Julius (Dr. J.) Erving led the Nets to their first ABA championship in 1973-74, the good doctor averaging 27.4 points per game during the regular season, winning the most valuable player award.

Erving added to his personal accomplishments in 1974-75 by setting a single-game scoring record and personal career high game of 63 points. Dr. J took his Nets to the ABA championships again in 1975-76, winning it all.

In 1977, the Nets shifted their operations to the Rutgers Athletic Center in Piscataway and became the home team at the Meadowlands Arena upon its opening in 1981-82, when Bernard King and Darryl Dawkins joined the Nets roster.

Devils

What's in a name? In the Devils, it's everything! It's New Jersey folklore and fantasy, the story of a spooky demon who stalked the pygmy forest of the Pine Barrens, scaring the early superstitious "Pineys" out of their backwoods wits.

It's also the name of New Jersey's only hockey franchise.

Before there was a Devils team tearing up the ice at the Meadowlands Arena, there was a franchise born in 1974-75 as the Kansas City Scouts. They tested America's heartland for pro hockey, an effort that lasted just two years. They then tried their luck as the Colorado Rockies from the 1976-77 through 1981-82 hockey seasons.

A half-continent away, a native New Jerseyan, Dr. John J. McMullen of Montclair, decided it was time the Garden State had its own hockey team. The Rockies headed East and became the Devils in 1982-83.

A young team, the Devils are here to stay, according to McMullen and his partner, former New Jersey Gov. Brendan Byrne.

The Devils are a fire-and-ice combination at the arena, generating fan support in their debut years in the Meadowlands. The Devils often sell out the house, all 19,023 seats, when playing their Hudson River rivals, the New York Rangers, or the other metro teams, the Philadelphia Flyers and the Long Island-based Islanders.

McMullen is committed to building a winning franchise, a

Star-Ledger Photo · Star-Ledger Photo · Star-Ledger Photo

Representing some of New Jersey's home teams are, from left: Pele, the former Cosmos Star, Darryl Dawkins, New Jersey Nets, and Nick Beverly of the Devils.

process that takes four to five years for any club. Then watch out for those Jersey Devils!

Generals

Their 1984 season got off to a record start, as 62,300 fans (a new high for the infant U.S Football League) watched the New Jersey Generals grind the Birmingham Stallions into the ground at the Alabama stadium. It was an opening game victory, 17-6, for New Jersey's first grass-roots, pro football franchise.

As in the case of the Jersey Devils, the Generals are a team that's a-buildin'. And they're doing it around an awesome machine called Herschel Walker.

The All-American and Heisman Trophy winner from the University of Georgia was the star of the Generals' inaugural season in the spring of 1983. Six months later, New York developer Donald J. Trump bought the lucrative Generals franchise from founder J. Walter Duncan and Chuck Fairbanks.

The Generals were on their way, as Trump began the competitive and costly process of acquiring the finest players in the game. The new football league's grid future will ride on Walker and teammate quarterback Doug Flutie—as of 1985 the highest-

paid football player in the world—as well as comparable dynasties among other contenders.

Giants

Jim Thorpe . . . Vince Lombardi . . . Tom Landry . . . Frank Gifford . . . Y.A. Tittle . . . Fran Tarkenton . . . Craig Morton . . . Larry Csonka . . . are just a few of the football legends associated with a team that was organized in 1925 for only $500.

Timothy Mara bought the National Football League franchise for New York. On the original roster was an Olympic Indian hero from Pennsylvania, Jim Thorpe. A record crowd of more than 70,000 jammed the Polo Grounds to see the Giants play Red Grange and the Chicago Bears. New York finished fourth in the 20-team league.

By 1932, the Giants' Ray Flaherty became the NFL's first official pass reception champion with 21 catches. A year later, the Giants easily won the Eastern Division of the newly divided NFL.

In 1934, the Giants defeated the Bears, 30-13, for the NFL title. The Giants won their third NFL title in 1938, icing Green Bay 23-17.

Heisman Trophy winner Herschel Walker now stars for the New Jersey Generals in the United States Football League.

Dave Jennings, star punter for the Giants.

Darroll Ray, safety for the Jets. The Jets are the latest team to find a home at the Meadowlands.

In 1952, tailback Frank Gifford was the Giants number one draft choice. Vince Lombardi joined the coaching staff in 1954 and Tom Landry was made a player-coach.

A 47-7 rout of the Chicago Bears in 1956 produced the Giants' first NFL championship in nearly two decades.

Y.A. Tittle came aboard in 1961 and Fran Tarkenton took over as quarterback in 1967. Craig Morton was obtained from Dallas in 1974 and Larry Csonka signed as a free agent in 1976 after a sensational career with the Miami Dolphins.

In 1976, the Giants finally occupied their first brand new stadium in the Hackensack Meadowlands. They no longer had to share their quarters with New York's baseball teams.

Today, they are known simply as "The Giants," appealing to fans in both the Big Apple and the Garden State.

Jets

They were organized in 1959 as the New York Titans, and like other Empire State teams, they have migrated to a more spacious setting along the Hackensack River.

In 1963, a New Jersey entertainment genius, David (Sonny) Werblin, would put the Titans-turned-Jets on the world sports map and, ultimately, orchestrate the success of the New Jersey Sports and Exposition Authority, serving as its first chairman.

The rest is history. Werblin's magic touch sparked an exodus of New York pro teams to New Jersey.

A Rutgers football player, Werblin, part of a five-man syndicate, bought the Titans in 1963, changed their image and acquired the hottest college football star of the Sixties: "Broadway Joe" Namath.

The Alabama quarterback was named Rookie of the Year in 1965 and Most Valuable Player in 1966.

Three years after the Super Bowl was established, Werblin's Jets, led by Namath, became the first American Football League team to win the coveted Vince Lombardi silver football trophy. It was a glorious 16-7 victory over the battling Baltimore Colts. Weeb Ewbank became the first coach to win the world title in both leagues.

Ewbank was named the all-time coach of the American Football League and Namath, Don Maynard and Gerry Philbin were chosen for the all-time AFL team selected by the Hall of Fame.

In September 1984, the Jets officially moved to the Meadowlands stadium. They have a five-year contract with the Sports Authority.

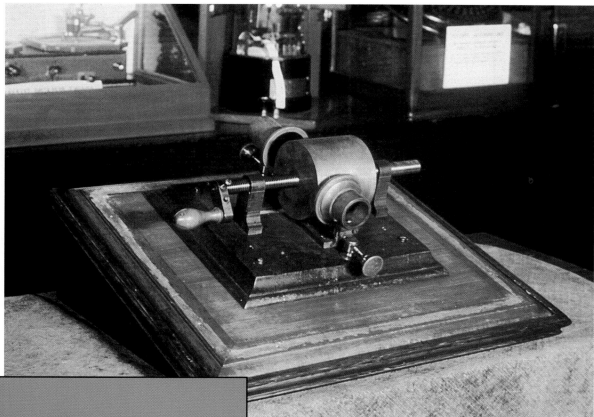

Edison's first phonograph—1877.

STATE "FIRSTS"

In the air, on the ground and in the depths of the ocean, New Jersey has pioneered many of the advances that have shaped the course of modern society.

Airline passenger service, the paved highway and the submarine, for example, have allowed humankind to explore all dimensions of the world with ease—and they all had their origins in New Jersey.

The list of New Jersey "firsts" would fill a book, revealing much of America's development since its Colonial inception.

Whether by design or fate, New Jersey has been—and continues to be—the birthplace of innovative ideas and their practical application.

New Jersey is a flourishing garden of creative interests in which searching, probing, testing and even sometimes guessing at the nature of the universe is an unending mission, the process of discovery, which ultimately pieces together those finite things that constitute reality.

From Edison's miraculous "talking machine" invented in his Menlo Park laboratory, to Einstein's quest for a Unified Theory of Relativity during the last 25 years of his life at Princeton, New Jersey has nourished and rewarded both abstract and pragmatic pursuits.

Before and after Edison opened his first labs in Jersey City and Newark in the early 1870s, and later in Menlo Park and West Orange, there have been thousands of gifted thinkers and practitioners experimenting with every conceivable notion, some of them very common and others almost incomprehensible, such as the life cycle of the universe itself.

In agriculture, aviation and communication, or medicine, manufacturing and transportation, New Jersey has compiled an unusual and remarkable record of "firsts," from the establishment of the nation's first yacht club and "America's Cup" race to the implantation of an atomic pacemaker at Newark's Beth Israel Medical Center.

The state Department of Commerce has put together a handy one-page reference that cites just 50, widely divergent New Jersey firsts. Other lists have been compiled over the years by the Department of Agriculture, various New Jersey industries, professions and historical societies.

Here's a brief rundown on some of the more interesting and rather random developments brought about in New Jersey during the last 250 years.

* * *

• Among New Jersey's more notable inventions, besides Edison's light bulb, movie camera/projector and a thousand other gadgets and improvements, there were the first flexible photographic film used in motion pictures, created by a New Jersey clergyman, the Rev. Hannibal Goodwin from Newark, and the first electronic tube that made radio and television successful, a product of Lee De Forest of Jersey City.

Some of the symbols of New Jersey's pioneering spirit include Thomas Nast's Santa Claus; the steam engine; the Thanksgiving Day resolution; the Colt revolver; Standard Time; and the steamship.

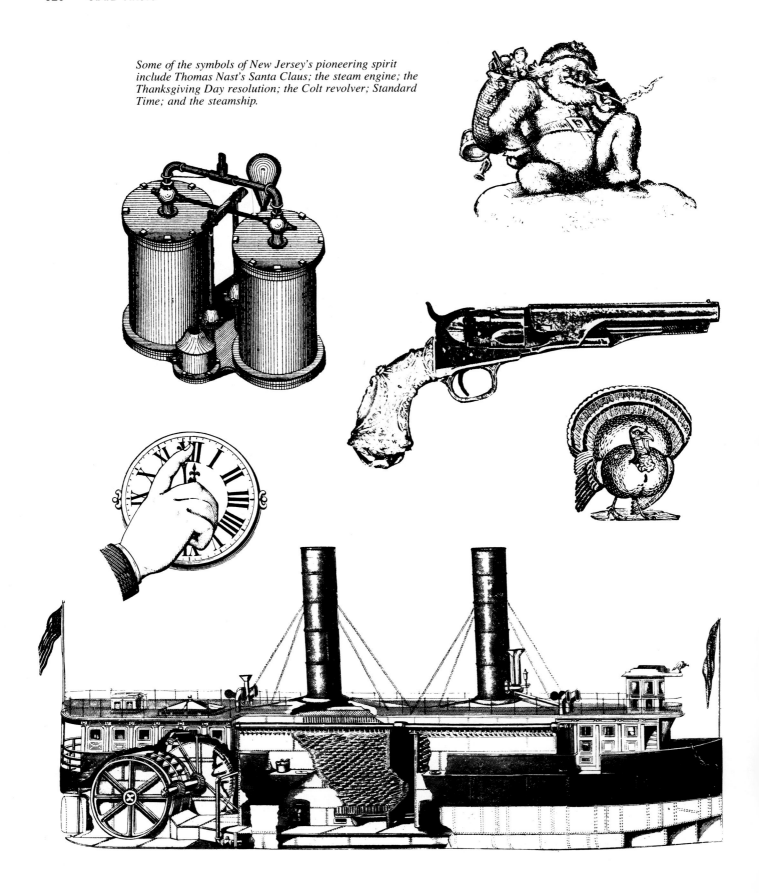

The first workable typewriter and carbon telephone transmitter, which made radio communication possible, were perfected by Edison, while the transistor was the work of a three-man team of Nobel Prize winners from Bell Laboratories in Murray Hill. Patented in 1948, the transistor revolutionized the electronic industry.

• The air conditioner was invented by Willis Haviland Carrier, who pioneered heating and cooling systems. In 1911, while working in his Newark factory, Carrier developed the basis of today's air conditioning systems in a technical paper he wrote entitled "Rational Psychometric Formulae."

• John Phillip Holland built the first submarine in Passaic County in 1878. The 14-foot, iron-skinned sub was launched in the Passaic River, descended to the bottom and then rose to the surface. The little submarine is on display in a Paterson museum. A later sub was bought by the Navy.

• Another Holland, Clifford M., engineered the world's first motor vehicle tunnel under a river, the Holland Tunnel, connecting New Jersey and New York, constructed in the 1920s and considered the greatest engineering feat of its time.

• Historians have dated the first log cabins built in what later became the United States to the 1640s in Gloucester County. The first cut nails in the U.S. were manufactured in nearby Medford, Burlington County.

• The first brewery started bottling the pale-yellow suds in 1642 in Hoboken, a waterfront town where many ideas and plans first took root.

• John Stevens, whose family founded Stevens Institute of Technology, introduced the steam ferry to New York Harbor in 1811 and experimented with the first American steam locomotive to ride on a track. The year was 1825. Twenty years earlier, Robert Fulton built the first ship drydock along the Jersey City waterfront.

John Stevens' son, Robert, invented the solid steel railroad track, or T-rail, which still keeps the trains rolling today. Robert and his brother, Edwin, ran the first commercial railroad in the United States, profitably. The first railroad charter in the United States was granted to John Stevens on Feb. 6, 1815 for his "steam wagon," which operated on a circular track in Hoboken.

Edwin Stevens helped design and build the ironclad vessels put into service by the Navy.

A third brother, John Cox Stevens, was the first commodore of the New York Yacht Club based in Hoboken, then a country resort. The nation's first yacht club was organized aboard the Stevens' schooner, Gimcrack. The Stevens family entertained friends and collaborators in its Castle Point mansion, the focal point of the institute's campus today, overlooking the Hudson River and harbor and New York skyline.

Edwin Stevens was part of a group of wealthy investors who built and owned the yacht, America. In 1851, the sleek vessel defeated all English contenders to become the first winner of the trophy that started the world famous "America's Cup" race.

• The first mechanical engineering laboratory was established at Stevens Institute, which also organized the American Society of Mechanical Engineers in 1880. The first president of Stevens, Henry Morton, is credited with the first full translation of the hieroglyphics on the Rosetta Stone.

• The first steam engine in America was brought from England in the early 1750s by Josiah Hornblower and used to pump out a flooded copper mine in Arlington.

• Paterson, the nation's first planned industrial city, became the country's home of the "Iron Horse" steam locomotive. By 1881, three locomotive companies covered some 15 acres of the city by the Passaic River Falls and produced 5,871 locomotives.

Paterson was also the place where the first Colt revolver was developed. The first smokeless gunpowder adopted by the United States government was developed by Hudson Maxim and Robert Schupphans in 1890 in Paterson.

• The first charter for a totally electric railway was granted to the Passaic-Garfield-Clifton Railway Co. in July 1890. A decade earlier, Roselle became the first town to be lighted by electricity.

• The first ball bearings for electric motors were introduced by the Electric Dynamic Co. at Bayonne in 1903. The first calculating machine to compute in pounds, shillings and pence was introduced in England by the Monroe Calculating Co. of Orange in 1922.

• As for that airline service and first paved road, Atlantic City inaugurated the first passenger flights on May 3, 1919, while the nation's first hard-surfaced road was built partly in New Jersey by the Dutch before 1664. It passed through Warren and Sussex counties, linking the famed Pahaquarry Mines with Kingston, N.Y., on the Hudson River more than 100 miles away.

• Surprisingly, aviation got off the ground in New Jersey before rail or bus travel. In 1793, a French adventurer and balloonist, Jean-Pierre Blanchard, landed a balloon at Deptford, carrying a letter from George Washington. The 46-minute ride from Philadelphia was the nation's first interstate balloon flight.

• The first public road act was formulated in New Jersey in 1673, providing a road from Middletown to Piscataway.

The first visitors to the Jersey Shore were the Indians, who left their hunting grounds to travel over the three oldest trails in America, based on fossil findings. Their footpaths were the Minnisink Trail, named after that tribe; the Upper Road, and the Old Burlington Path. The latter two, along with the Lower Road, became The Kings Highway, all in use before 1700. During that time, the first Indian reservation was set aside by the New Jersey Legislature on a 1,600-acre public tract in Evesham Township, Burlington County, on Aug. 20, 1758.

• The traffic circle and jughandle are also New Jersey transportation innovations, the first circle going around outside of Camden in 1925, and the now popular cloverleaf pattern later installed in Woodbridge for safety and timesaving. The first "double-dual" highway in the world was constructed between Newark and Elizabeth. The concrete divider down the center of highways has become the national standard. It began as the "Jersey Barrier."

• In 1891, New Jersey became the first state to grant funds for the construction of public roads.

• The Pulaski Skyway was the world's most expensive highway when built, costing $7 million a mile. The first road-sheet asphalt pavement was laid down in Newark in 1870.

• William F. Allen of South Orange was commissioned by the railroads to adopt time zones across the country. Standard Time was invented and went into effect on Nov. 18, 1883.

• The first actual mining operation in the U.S. began in 1640 in Pahaquarry Township. The first wagon road in the country was built from that mine to Kingston, N.Y., to haul ore from the mine to tidewater for transportation.

• The first public library in the country with a building of its own was in use in 1757 in Burlington. The first successful glass factory was opened by Caspar Wistar in Salem County in 1739. The first hot blast furnace in the U.S. was built in Oxford in 1834. And the first china for restaurant use was made by the Greenwood Pottery Co. of Trenton in 1862.

• In 1870, Alex Boardman erected the world's first boardwalk along the Atlantic City beachfront. The first Miss America

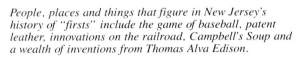

People, places and things that figure in New Jersey's history of "firsts" include the game of baseball, patent leather, innovations on the railroad, Campbell's Soup and a wealth of inventions from Thomas Alva Edison.

was chosen in Atlantic City in 1921. Salt water taffy was first produced at the Jersey Shore in the 1870s.

• It was at Long Beach in 1839 where Dr. William Newell (later governor of New Jersey) successfully tried out the "beach gun" he invented, shooting lifelines from shore to stranded ships. Newell helped found the Life Saving Service, which, in Ocean County, set up the first two official life-saving stations on the Atlantic Coast. Newell's Life Saving Service today is the U.S. Coast Guard.

* * *

• Elias Boudinot of Elizabeth initiated the resolution in Congress that led President Washington to proclaim Thanksgiving Day—Thursday, Nov. 26, 1789—as the national holiday marking the adoption by Congress of the United States Constitution. Boudinot had served as president of the Continental Congress.

• The first American flag from an American loom was made in Paterson by John Rule, father of the silk industry. The first National Historical Park was dedicated in 1933 in Morristown, site of Washington's headquarters at the Ford Mansion and Jockey Hollow, where the Continental troops survived the longest, harshest winter of the Revolutionary War.

• The first Episcopal Church in America was built in Perth Amboy in 1698 and is still in use.

• The very first Christmas tree farm originated just outside of Trenton in 1901. Farmer W.V. McGalliard owned a 10-acre tract where gravel grew more abundantly than any crops he planted. McGalliard noticed his Norway spruces were thriving in front of his house in soil similar to that in his pesky field.

He planted spruces on his unproductive farm and sold them as Christmas trees. His 25,000 Norway spruces sold for a dollar apiece. Today, there are more than 400 Christmas tree farms in the Garden State and more than 200,000 home-grown trees are available during the holiday season.

• Cartoonist Thomas Nast of Morristown drew Santa Claus as he is known today—round, jolly, whiskered with a big bag of toys. Nast's Santa first appeared as a drawing in 1863 in Harper's Weekly.

The first Christmas Day radio broadcast was from the roof of Bamberger's department store in Newark, where WOR played yule music on disc records invented by RCA, a New Jersey firm.

* * *

• The first cultivated blueberries were marketed by Elizabeth White of Whitesbog in 1916. The first "condensed soup" was cooked and canned by Campbell's Soup Co., Camden, in 1897. The first frozen foods appeared in 1933, the idea of Charles F. Seabrook of Seabrook Farms.

Other agricultural firsts were the Mason jar for preserving fruits, the Thermos jug, Welch's grape juice, certified milk and large-scale irrigation.

• In sports, the birth of baseball occurred on June 19, 1846, when the Knickerbockers and the New Yorks played the first game in Hoboken. The game ended after four innings with the New Yorks winning 23 to 1.

• The first World Series broadcast was in 1921 at radio station WJZ in Newark.

• America's first intercollegiate football game was played in New Brunswick on Nov. 6, 1869. Rutgers and Princeton universities sent their 25-member teams to the field and Rutgers won, 6 to 4, before a small group of spectators.

• The leader in communications, New Jersey, home of Bell Labs, inaugurated the first direct distance dialing from coast to coast when a call was made on Nov. 10, 1951 from Englewood to Alameda, Calif. Bell Labs also invented the solar cell, used to power telecommunication satellites.

The solar photovoltaic cell converts sunlight directly into electricity. The PV cell is being developed as the clean and inexhaustible energy supply of the 21st Century.

• Another form of communication, the drive-in movie, was first used on a 10-acre plot in Pennsauken. On June 7, 1933, a local resident by the name of Hollingshead put up a screen in a maple tree and placed a projector on the hood of a Model-A Ford. The outdoor movie introduced a new entertainment lifestyle for the world's most motorized society.

* * *

• A new pattern of living emerged in Bergen County when the world's first community was designed with the automobile in mind. Radburn, a unique suburb in Fair Lawn, was the first major departure in city planning since Venice, according to urbanologist Louis Mumford.

Unveiled as "the town of the motor age," Radburn was carved out of Fair Lawn spinach farms between 1928-32. Instead of conventional city blocks, Radburn has "superblocks." They are 10 to 15 times larger with parks in the center and no through traffic. Back doors and garages face dead-end streets where cars can come in. The front of houses and apartments face parks, gardens and pedestrian paths.

Radburn has its own recreation programs, elementary school and shopping center. Although the original plans by architects-planners Henry Wright and Clarence Stein called for a much larger self-contained community, Radburn is confined to 149 acres with a total population of about 3,000. Designated a State and National Historic Place, Radburn has directly influenced community development in Great Britain, Europe, Canada, Israel, Russia and the United States.

* * *

• In education, New Jersey was the first to establish an education trust fund; the Town of Burlington set up the procedure in 1682. The first manual training courses in the country, the forerunner of the classroom "shops" and vocational schools, was started in Montclair's elementary schools in 1882.

In medical and health care, New Jersey has also led the nation with such breakthroughs as streptomycin developed at Rutgers University by Nobel winner Dr. Selman A. Waxman, who discovered the anti-tuberculosis drug . . . Cortisone, used for arthritis and other diseases . . . Vitamin C, Vitamin B1, B12, Vitamin A . . . and the ubiquitous Band-Aid, the first adhesive and medicated plaster with a rubber base manufactured by Robert W. Johnson and George Seabury in 1870 in their East Orange plant.

The variety of products that evolved in New Jersey have made their way into just about everyone's home and place of work or worship. Some brand names, like Band-Aid, have become household words. Others are equally universal in use but are less well known. Here's a brief sampling of some of New Jersey's first contributions to a constantly changing marketplace:

Patent leather, malleable iron, cast iron pipe, Plexiglas, Teflon, Vinylite, Melamac plastics, absorbent cotton, the mechanical lighter, Linoleum, Duco lacquer, the jackhammer, adhesive tape, butyl rubber, molded pottery, White House china, zinc oxide, Neoprene, Freon, the refinery, Bakelight, the nickel factory, the volt meter, the automatic pilot (for airplanes), the communications satellite, TNT, and the window-shade roller.

The Paper Mill Playhouse in Millburn—the State Theater.

THEATER

ew Jersey is the cultural crossroads of American theater. A pioneer of the regional playhouse, the Garden State is the world leader in the production of new and revived musicals. It is also an innovator in developing minority talent and interracial audiences and is one of only three places where all of Shakespeare's works are fully staged.

"All the world's a stage," the Bard of Stratford-on-Avon aptly observed, and New Jersey is living theatrical proof of that ageless metaphor.

New Jersey's recent entertainment history begins with McCarter Theatre at Princeton University in 1930 and the Paper Mill Playhouse four years later in Millburn, joined soon after by the acclaimed New Jersey Shakespeare Festival at Drew University in Madison, the plucky Halfpenny Playhouse by the Passaic River in Kearny, the black urbane Theatre of Universal Images in downtown Newark, and the popular Whole Theatre Company in Montclair.

They make up a dynamically original matrix of classical and contemporary performances enhanced by a dozen other major showcases, such as the spunky Pushcart Players in Verona, the symbiotic George Street Playhouse and Crossroads Theatre in New Brunswick, and the experimentally engaging South Jersey Regional Theatre in Somers Point, Atlantic County.

* * *

Collectively, they form the growing and prospering New Jersey Theatre Group, the first statewide professional, nonprofit theater coalition of its kind in the United States.

The New Jersey theatrical experience embraces all aspects of artistic expression, from ballet to opera, concerts to musicals, poetry to puppets, cabarets to clowns and improvisations and films.

There are actors' theaters, directors' theaters and children's theaters, as well as playwright workshops and career seminars.

And there's a special circle of accomplished actors and directors such as Helen Hayes and Jose Ferrer practicing and polishing their craft in New Jersey, plus finely tuned touring companies linked with Lincoln Center, the John F. Kennedy Center for the Performing Arts in Washington, D.C., and the Public Broadcasting System (PBS), where the best theater on television comes alive.

Also in this durable lineup of stars and showcases are New

Jersey's favorite dinner-theaters: The Club Bene in Sayreville, the Dam Site in Tinton Falls, the McAteers in Somerset, the 76 House in Cape May County, Carbone's in Harrison, the Original Rudi's in Oak Ridge, Neil's New Yorker in Mountain Lakes, the Summit Suburban Hotel in Summit, and the Somerset Marriott Hotel in Somerset.

Paper Mill Playhouse

The largest legitimate theater in New Jersey grew humbly out of an abandoned red-brick mill built in 1790 along a splendid little stream in Millburn. In 1980 the mill burned down and New Jersey lost a landmark and, temporarily, its state theater.

The Paper Mill Playhouse has the largest number of subscribers of any nonprofit theater in America—26,000, and growing.

The Paper Mill Playhouse today is New Jersey's outstanding theater, reopened in the fall of 1982 with a stunning production of "Robert and Elizabeth," a mammoth musical about poets Robert and Elizabeth Barrett Browning. It reinforced the Paper Mill's world record of 123 musical productions since 1950.

The Paper Mill Playhouse was the dream of Antoinette Scudder, a patron of the arts, and Frank Carrington, an actor. They founded a troupe at the Newark Art Theatre in 1929 and shortly after began their search for a permanent home.

An idle old mill not far from Newark was the site selected for the Paper Mill Playhouse, established in 1934 with the support of Eleanor Roosevelt. It would become the oldest continuously operated nonprofit theater in the United States. In 1972, it became the official state theater.

The original 972-seat mill house, gutted by fire on Jan. 14, 1980, was replaced by a magnificently complete center for the performing arts, a $4.5 million edifice retaining much of the red-brick colonial charm that gave the playhouse its stable, historic image.

The new playhouse is being developed as a center for new American musical theater. Its architecture is a collaboration between the old and the new. Glass-enclosed promenades on the second floor look out on the lush flora and fauna of the South Mountain Reservation. Daylight streams in through lavish windows and brightens an already brilliant stark white art gallery.

The quaint, narrow, shoe-box shape of the mill has been supplanted by a new shorter and wider fan-like design that fits comfortably into the rather restricted wooded site.

Paper Mill started out with serious drama and sophisticated comedy, popular staples of the Depression-era '30s. The 1940s saw the "Golden Age of Operetta," giving way in the 1950s to a balanced blend of musicals, plays, operetta, children's theater, dance and concerts.

Among the stars who have performed at the Paper Mill are Helen Hayes, Jane Fonda, Pearl Bailey, Jose Ferrer, Liza Minnelli, Douglas Fairbanks Jr., Louis Armstrong, Ginger Rogers, Carol Channing, Joan Fontaine, Mike Nichols, Geraldine Page, Shelley Winters, Claudette Colbert, Jerome Hines, Edward Villella, Imogene Coca, Sir Tyrone Guthrie and many other distinguished artists.

In the records department, the Paper Mill has captured more than its share of curtain calls. In addition to the record number of musicals since 1950, the playhouse has staged 350 productions of children's plays between 1936 and 1983.

The number of plays since its founding at the old mill is approaching the 200 mark. From 1940 through 1983, the number of operettas reached 123.

The average annual attendance of 250,000 makes the Paper Mill audience the largest of any performing arts organization in New Jersey. The average annual attendance for children's programs is 50,000.

Photo Credit: Terence A. Gili

A potpourri of plays offered at the Paper Mill in Millburn includes comedies such as "You Can't Take It With You," starring Jason Robards, left, and George Rose.

Star-Ledger Photo

Caryn West and Farley Granger in "Count Dracula" at the Paper Mill Playhouse.

Some 400 actors, directors, musicians, designers, stagehands, administrators and support personnel are employed at the Millburn center in an average season.

The New Jersey Ballet is the Paper Mill's resident ballet company, one of several performing arts organizations affiliated with the state theater.

More than 3,000 individuals, corporations, foundations and government agencies contributed to the rebuilding of the Paper Mill Playhouse, itself an historic fund-raising campaign led by former Gov. Brendan Byrne (1973-81) and his wife, Jean.

McCarter Theatre Company

It stands there like an English lord's country estate, a neo-Gothic fortress housing a rich tapestry of talent tracing its roots to one of America's first regional theater companies.

Originally built in 1930 as a home for Princeton University's Triangle Club, which continues to perform there today, McCarter Theatre has developed into a major booking house for Broadway-bound productions.

The theater is named after Thomas Nesbit McCarter, Princeton Class of 1888 and an alumnus of the Triangle Club. McCarter, who donated $250,000 for the construction of the undergraduate theater, organized one of the largest utilities in the world, Public Service Electric & Gas Co., and served as its first president. He was also an attorney general for the State of New Jersey.

McCarter Theatre Company was incorporated in 1972 as a professional performing arts center for drama, dance, music, film and special events. Since its founding, membership has risen to more than 2,700 individuals and corporations with an annual constituency exceeding 200,000 patrons.

The elegant proscenium auditorium is usually filled with metropolitan denizens of every persuasion seeking a moment of genuine enrichment. A glimpse at a typical calendar of events at McCarter readily reveals why this Princeton center with its five theaters attracts a wide audience and the highest-caliber entertainers.

* * *

Imagine the impact of a Luciano Pavarotti on one end of the singing spectrum and New Jersey's own super rock star Bruce Springsteen at the other, drawing their legions of fans to the sedate Princeton campus. Or, virtuoso violinist Itzhak Perlman performing his exhausting repertoire one evening and a Mark Twain tour-de-force by Hal Holbrook on another night of special attractions.

Add to that an Ella Fitzgerald and a Hershel Bernardi, with a dash of Dina Merrill, Celeste Holme and Harry Hamlin's "Hamlet," and you've got all of the ingredients of a hit season. Except every season is like that at McCarter, which is constantly redefining the meaning of quality and limits.

The standard theater fare can be a rare mix of Chekhov, Coward and Shakespeare, or Shaw, Tennessee Williams and Euripides.

Not satisfied with the cream of the classics, McCarter nurtures new playwrights, some of the latest being James McLure's "The Day They Shot John Lennon," David Patt's "Sitting on the Right Hand of Power," Robert Auletta's "Rundown" and Wendy Kesselman's "Maggie Magalita."

Stage Two is the playwrights' outlet and the nucleus of the McCarter theatrical experience. Shakespeare himself worked a solid stable of writers, mostly poets, at his Globe Theater, developing the greatest body of tragedies, comedies and histories ever produced in one lifetime. McCarter hopes to create a similar creative environment and perhaps someday leave a comparable legacy of original American plays.

The largest of McCarter's five playhouses, which are shared with the university, is Jadwin Gym, an 8,000-seat amphitheater. The smallest is a local school gymnasium where the stage manager can design his own "variable space" for an audience of up to 125.

Photo Credit: Cliff Moore

Jay Doyle is the moaning ghost of Jacob Marley in McCarter Theatre's popular holiday staging of "A Christmas Carol."

* * *

The main McCarter Theatre with its thick Gothic doors and windows contains 1,077 seats.

The exuberant Princeton Ballet is McCarter's resident dance company. A familiar troupe in the Dance-at-McCarter series is the American Ballet Theatre II, the junior company of the world-famous American Ballet Theatre now under the direction of Mikhail Baryshnikov.

The Feld Ballet is another perennial favorite of McCarter audiences. Director Eliot Feld choreographs dances about people and relationships, and his 25 dancers animate the full range of human emotions, from jazz and folk to ballroom and square-dancing, including the classical 19th Century "white" ballet. Critic Clive Barnes found Feld to be "the most talented classic choreographer of his generation anywhere in the world." The Joffrey II Dancers also have McCarter on their itinerary.

Children's events at McCarter include the Paper Bag Players, the Shoestring Players and the Magic Garden. The holidays are filled with Dickens' legendary "A Christmas Carol" and Tchaikovsky's "The Nutcracker," performed by the Princeton Ballet Company.

Some of the recent specials have been the Royal Lipizzaner Stallions, the Big Bluegrass Jam, the Preservation Hall Jazz Band, the National Theatre of the Deaf and the Flying Karamazov Brothers.

Cinema is a special treat featuring the best American films, as well as foreign films not shown at the chain movie houses. Here's a sampling of a typical McCarter cinema listing: "Fanny and Alexander," "The Basilieus Quartet," "Gregory's Girl," "The Right Stuff," "This Is Spinal Tap" and "Silkwood."

New Jersey Shakespeare Festival

The ultimate artistic vision of the New Jersey Shakespeare Festival is to stage the entire Shakespeare canon within a time frame equal to the prime of one's life. Since 1963, with its first play, "The Taming of the Shrew," staged at the Cape May Playhouse, the New Jersey Shakespearean company has mounted 54 works by the greatest dramatist in history. Only five plays will remain to be done after 1985.

Shakespeare's second great historical tetralogy, "War of the Roses," was presented this year at the festival's 238-seat theater on the campus of Drew University in Madison, Morris County, where the festival took up residence in 1972. The four massive plays, "Henry VI" (Parts 1, 2 and 3) and "Richard III," which comprise the epic story, are rarely performed individually and almost never all in one season.

"War of the Roses" is a once-in-a-lifetime challenge for both the mature professional artist and the novice, according to artistic director Paul Barry, founder and leading actor in the festival. In this century, "War of the Roses" has been offered only once in the United States (in 1971 by the New York Shakespeare Festival) and once in Great Britain (in 1964 by the Royal Shakespeare Company).

Between 1974 and 1976, the New Jersey festival presented the four plays of Shakespeare's sweeping historical tetralogy: "Richard II," "Henry IV," "Henry V" and "Falstaff."

* * *

The production of "Roses" involved 19 professional Equity actors playing 65 featured roles over three evenings, supported by some 50 intern actors. The plays required 300 costumes, 200 weapons and 1,000 stage properties. The project required a new unit set, musicians, an assistant director and a greatly expanded production format.

While Shakespeare is the mainstay of the festival, the Bard's prolific output represents only one-third of the productions staged at the Drew University theater. By the end of the 1985 season, the festival will record its 158th production, a remarkable feat when considering the complexity and costs of such fully treated theatrical ventures.

The non-Shakespearean plays range from "Cyrano de Bergerac" and "Waltz of the Toreadors" to "A Streetcar Named Desire" and "The Country Girl."

The festival's "Hamlet" became the first color television production of that play in America for WHDH-TV, Boston, and received the Ohio State University Institute of Television Arts & Sciences' prestigious award for excellence in educational broadcasting.

Barry, who has staged most of the festival's 145 productions, has directed one of a series of new plays at Washington's Kennedy Center for the Performing Arts. He is an expert with a variety of weapons and has served as fencing choreographer to the Shakespeare festivals in New York, Oregon, Miami, McCarter Theatre and for the Hallmark television production of "Cyrano de Bergerac."

Barry's wife, Ellen, associate director of the festival, helped to coordinate such award-winning productions as "Harvey" with Helen Hayes and Jimmy Stewart, and "The School for Wives," which gave Brian Bedford a Tony Award. Ellen Barry has stage-managed dozens of professional productions, including Broadway shows for Hal Prince and Stephen Porter.

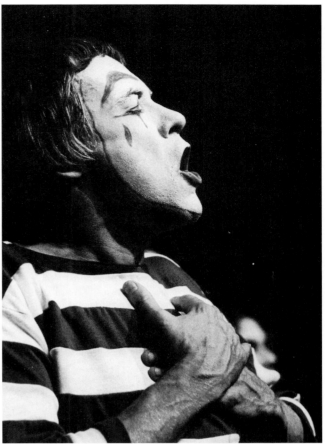

Star-Ledger Photo

Paul Barry is Littlechap, a musical "Everyman" staged at the New Jersey Shakespeare Festival, Drew University, Madison.

When the New Jersey Shakespeare Festival moved to Drew University in 1972, it extended its season from 10 to 25 weeks, and more than tripled its budget. The festival is an actor's theater, an ensemble and conservatory shaped by one actor-manager-director, composed not of stars but of classical actors attracted by the rare experience of repertory. Festival seasons typically pair the more popular plays of Shakespeare with his lesser seen works.

The festival's three primary programs are the major productions, the intern training regimen and the "Monday Night Specials." Six to eight productions are offered each season. The festival is one of the few true repertory companies remaining in the U.S. where plays are offered in nightly rotation by a resident professional group of actors.

The "Monday Night Specials" are selected productions to appeal to every patron's taste, from the Harlem Steel Ensemble and the New Jersey Brass Quintet to Gilbert & Sullivan and such celebrities as Joan Fontaine starring in "The Brownings."

The 80 or so young artists accepted annually into the company from among some 1,000 applicants from across the country call it "Barry's Boot Camp," or "School for Survival." Interns range in age from 17 to 44 and, in a typical year, can come from as many as 20 states and 100 different colleges, universities and professional schools.

Since May 1963, more than 900 young artists have completed the New Jersey Shakespeare Festival intern course. They work

15-hour days, six-day weeks, building scenery, making costumes and properties, as well as handling public relations, box office and administrative tasks.

The Barrys are guided by an old-fashioned love of literature, as expressed in one of their many programs:

"In today's society of disposable values, where 'new' has too often become synonymous with 'better,' where goods and services are deliberately designed for limited life, the Festival believes in the preservation of our cultural heritage."

The festival's goal under its six-year plan established in 1979 is to increase the number of subscribers to 7,000 and to lengthen the season from six to eight plays and from 20 to 27 weeks. With the support of the multi-billion-dollar Beneficial Corp., based in Peapack-Gladstone, Somerset County, the New Jersey Shakespeare Festival plans to create a complete conservatory and build a new 1,000-seat theater in the 1980s to carry on a tradition begun in Stratford-on-Avon some 400 years ago.

Whole Theatre Company

It's just 10 years old, but the Whole Theatre Company in Montclair already is launching world premiere productions under the direction of such esteemed artists as Jose Ferrer.

With a budget of more than $1 million for the 1984-85 season, the Whole Theatre Company is committed to presenting American and world premieres, cultivating new plays and musicals that will reach Broadway, Off-Broadway and America's regional theater circuit.

WTC began simply enough in a 95-seat annex of the First Baptist Church in Montclair with a salute to the local residents for believing in a dream conceived by a handful of actors, directors and designers. Their gratitude was expressed in a moving production of Thornton Wilder's Pulitzer Prize-winning play, "Our Town."

The Town of Montclair today enjoys one of the leading theatrical centers in America, an award-winning theater supported by more than 5,000 annual subscribers and drawing an audience of 40,000 a year from 200 communities.

The Whole Theatre Company was recognized early on for its high-quality work when the Foundation for the Extension and De-

velopment of the American Professional Theatre chose WTC to be one of its national demonstration projects. Since then, the Montclair theater has turned out to be one of the national foundation's greatest success stories.

When the new theater opened in 1978—a 200-seat configuration fashioned from a former bank building—it received the Design Award from the National Endowment for the Arts.

A professional training school, WTC is a major complex for the development of the performing arts. More than 100 actors, directors, teachers, administrators and specialists in theatrical crafts are employed by WTC.

The focus on training began in 1973 with formation of a theater school as the main filament of a full spectrum of educational services. In that first year, the WTC school conducted three acting courses.

For its 12th season in 1984, the WTC catalog was crammed with 30 courses a trimester, with more than 1,000 show biz students registered. The faculty comprises working professionals from all theatrical disciplines.

Dance classes for children, teens and adults include modern, ballet and jazz and dance for young people to develop coordination, rhythm and spatial awareness with music and art serving as stimuli.

Special workshops include one on directing, another on corporal mime and an introduction to clowning, emphasizing juggling, magic, acrobatics, mime and pratfalls.

In 1981, the Whole Theatre Company broadened its artistic visibility by producing a taped version of George Bernard Shaw's "Candida." The acclaimed drama was aired nationally on CBS Cable.

In the 1982 season, the company pushed its horizon even farther, offering two world premieres: "The U.S.O. Show" and "Off-Broadway," the latter directed by stage-screen-television star Jose Ferrer. The 1984-85 season saw the appearance of award-winning director Austin Pendleton in Romulus Linney's historic spectacle "The Sorrows of Frederick."

Its most ambitious project was the staging of the technically complicated production of Chekhov's "The Cherry Orchard." A few months later the stage was transformed into an insane asylum for Peter Weiss' "Marat/Sade." Mounted in association with William Paterson College in Wayne, the production moved with its set and entire cast of 37 for a subsequent run at the college.

William Mooney and Marilyn Chris team up in "Alone Together," presented by the Whole Theatre Company, Montclair.

Courtesy: Whole Theatre Company

Kevin Spacey, left, and George Taylor in "Sleuth" at the George Street Playhouse, New Brunswick.

Photo Credit: Suzanne Karp Krebs

Eugene O'Neill's "The Touch of the Poet" launched WTC's 10th season.

Montclair's proximity to Broadway (only a half-hour drive on Route 3 to the Hudson River) makes it an ideal workshop/showcase for Broadway stars testing new material. The very selective Colleen Dewhurst accepted an invitation from WTC's artistic director, Olympia Dukakis, for a staged reading of unexpurgated excerpts from James Joyce's controversial novel, "Ulysses." It was, of course, an instant sellout for WTC.

With subscriptions totaling more than 5,000 and annual ticket sales exceeding 40,000, Montclair's Whole Theatre Company is looking into a bright future despite a protracted recession.

WTC is planning to send more productions to other regional theaters and move the most outstanding ones to Broadway and Off-Broadway. There will be more world premieres in store for its growing number of backers, in addition to the more risky experimental productions and others presented in conjunction with New York producers.

The Montclair troupe is also expanding its programming to include art films, and will continue to tape main-stage and special shows for the expanding television marketplace.

Theatergoers also enjoy the WTC's Upstage Cafe before and after curtain call.

The Whole Theatre Company Foundation has been fortunate in recruiting the cream of American business for its board of advisers. The chairmen or presidents of the following corporations serve on the WTC Foundation board: Shering-Plough, Sandoz, Bankers Trust, Chemical Bank, Becton Dickinson, Joseph E. Seagram & Sons, Goldman-Sachs, Bank of New York, Prudential-Bache, Union Camp, Horizon Bancorp, CPC International, First Jersey National Bank and Automatic Data Processing.

George Street Playhouse

Governor Thomas H. Kean considers the George Street Playhouse "one of New Jersey's living artistic treasures."

For the more than 40,000 residents of Central Jersey who fill the little playhouse each season, George Street is a genuine gem that sparkles brighter with each new production.

The 259-seat, thrust-stage theater is conveniently situated in downtown New Brunswick, a three-century-old commercial hub on the Raritan River currently experiencing an urban renaissance sparked by Rutgers State University and Johnson & Johnson, one of the world's largest pharmaceutical houses.

As New Brunswick prospers in the renewal process, so will the hearty troupe of actors on George Street, the main thoroughfare running parallel to the state's longest inland river.

Beginning in 1974 with an audience membership numbering an even 100 and a budget of less than $54,000, the George Street Playhouse nourished that seed of a dream into a subscriber base exceeding 4,100 and an annual budget of more than a half-million dollars.

The six main productions staged at George Street are each performed eight times throughout the fall-winter months.

The community-oriented playhouse also sponsors a children's theater for Saturday performances and for touring.

A spinoff of the George Street Playhouse is the Crossroads Theatre founded in 1978. Crossroads is a professional black theater company.

Each season the playhouse premieres two works developed by the artistic director in collaboration with writers and musicians. The new productions often focus on 20th Century social and moral dilemmas.

George Street offers apprenticeships with small stipends as well as internships for college credit to those interested in working with a professional company.

New works developed during the 1980-81 season included

"Parley" by David Richmond and "Viaduct" by Aleen Malcolm. The '81-82 season saw a new musical by Judd Woldin and Richard Enquist, "Lorenzo," and "Out of the Night" by Eric Krebs, based on the book by Jan Valtin. Krebs is artistic director of the playhouse.

The 1982-83 season unveiled three new one-act plays by Ken Jenkins: "Cemetery Man," "Chug" and "Rupert's Birthday."

The '82-83 season got off to a successful start with John Steinbeck's "Of Mice and Men." Star-Ledger drama critic Bette Spero found it "as precise a presentation as the written work, which says quite a bit."

In a joint effort with Crossroads, the George Street Playhouse staged Lorraine Hansberry's historic 1959 play, "A Raisin in the Sun," as a musical. Reviewers liked "Raisin," saying it delivered the "dramatic thrust and emotional power" of the original play.

The 1984-85 season opened in a new playhouse with a critically acclaimed production of "A Streetcar Named Desire."

Crossroads Theatre Company

The George Street Playhouse created the Crossroads Theatre Company in 1978 to provide a forum for black artists and to educate audiences, both black and white, as to the significance of black theater in American culture.

The theater was initially funded by a Middlesex County CETA (Comprehensive Employment and Training Act) grant, under the auspices of the George Street Playhouse. By November 1980, Crossroads had become an independent, nonprofit theater company supported by the New Jersey State Council on the Arts.

Crossroads is only one of a handful of professional black theater companies in the United States.

Crossroads produces six plays during its September-to-May season and participates in festivals and touring programs year-round. Its outreach programs involve internships through the local colleges—Rutgers, Douglass, Livingston and Middlesex County—and the Urban League of Greater New Brunswick. In 1981, a free-ticket program for the economically disadvantaged was successfully introduced.

Crossroads was the first company approached by New Jersey Network television for a production to be presented on the newly established New Jersey Playhouse series.

In December 1981, Crossroads co-produced with New Jersey Public Television Network a new play, "A Lovesong for Miss Lydia," by Don Evans of Trenton. The play starred Earl Hyman, a renowned black stage actor; Claudia McNeil, who portrayed Mama in the Broadway and film versions of "A Raisin in the Sun," and Arthur French, an original member of the Negro Ensemble Company in New York.

With Frances Foster added to the cast, "Lovesong" was then presented at Crossroads as a world premiere. The play has been sold to the ABC Cable Co.

Crossroads is developing a playwrighting workshop, a children's theater, and is enlarging the company's touring program. It is also increasing its involvement with television production and member regional theaters around the country.

Crossroads concentrates on the work of the black (African, Afro-American and West Indian) playwright in an attempt to portray the realities of a black culture.

Crossroads' guiding philosophy is "the discovery and development of one's own culture and beauty (to) serve as a most important foundation for self-pride, constructive innovation, work incentive and a shared human and spiritual understanding."

The company's founders believe that multi-racial audiences sharing a common experience can "break down the barriers of prejudice and help to bridge the 'understanding gap' between people."

Photo Credit: Harry Rubel

Vanessa Shaw, young Cyril Johnson and Mel Johnson, Jr. star in "Raisin," a joint production of Crossroads Theatre and the George Street Playhouse, New Brunswick.

Photo Credit: Harry Rubel

Avery Brooks as Paul Robeson in "Robeson" at the Crossroads Theatre.

Among the productions staged at Crossroads since 1980 are: "To Be Young, Gifted and Black," "No Place to Be Somebody," "Paul Robeson," "The Trials and Tribulations of Staggerlee Booker T. Brown," "The Amen Corner" and "The Blood Knot."

The National Endowment for the Arts honored Crossroads in 1982 with its $20,000 Arts Recognition Award. And in announcing a major grant from the New Jersey Council on the Arts, the Sunday Star-Ledger reported: "A whopping grant of $25,000 has gone to Crossroads, a black troupe in New Brunswick and a group more earnest or artistically worthy would be hard to find."

Theater of Universal Images

Established in New Jersey's largest city in 1970, Newark's Theater of Universal Images, the state's oldest black theater group, has staged more original works by new promising playwrights than any other professional theater in New Jersey, according to the founding producer, Clarence Lilley.

The TUI's most recent season kicked off with a revival of Eugene O'Neill's "Emperor Jones," starring John Amos of East Orange. Amos portrayed Kunte Kinte in the hit TV mini-series "Roots," and also starred in the long-running TV series "Good Times" and was featured in the "Mary Tyler Moore Show."

A play, "Dutchman," by Newark poet Amiri Baraka was presented at TUI in the 1982-83 season, starring Antonio Fargas, who co-starred in the popular TV series "Starsky and Hutch," in the role of Huggy Bear.

Recent showcase features at TUI included "Don't Bother Me, I Can't Cope." Touring companies brought to Newark's TUI such hits as "Home," "For Colored Girls . . .," and "To Be Young, Gifted and Black." Classic plays such as "Don't You Wanna Be Free" and "The Sirens" have also been staged at Symphony Hall.

The TUI showcase is designed to offer four productions each season, two by major playwrights and two by promising new playwrights.

In addition to its regular theatrical season, TUI has produced a touring series, children's plays, festivals, concerts, radio dramas, film and video productions, and is operating a casting service for local professional talent.

The Theater of Universal Images has direct access to the 3,300-seat Symphony Hall, a national historic landmark and one of the largest and finest acoustical performing centers in the world.

TUI took over the television studio of WNET/13, which is one of two smaller theaters within the Symphony Hall complex. One seats 300 and the other about 250.

TUI was originally created to provide a cultural and artistic outlet to the City of Newark, the state's financial-commercial-transportation hub. Since 1970, TUI has expanded into a professional multiplex theater serving the city's predominately black and Hispanic population.

Its basic functions are to develop and make available to the community a variety of theater education services, to bring major theater touring productions to Newark, and to act as an advocate for college internships and career training opportunities.

The New Jersey Council on the Arts has consistently rated TUI as the second most effective performing theater in New Jersey in terms of its ability.

TUI has also been awarded a public access channel from Connection Communications Corp., the Newark cable TV franchise, to produce cable programming.

Pushcart to Halfpenny

Rounding out the membership of the New Jersey Theatre Group is a string of sprightly performers stretching all the way from the sandy coast of Atlantic County to the asphalt shopping strip in suburban Paramus, Bergen County.

They are the small regional theaters concocting their own brand of entertainment, bringing an inventive repertoire to communities where culture may be confined to a local movie house.

* * *

The Halfpenny Playhouse was one of the first small regional groups founded in the United States. Based in Kearny, the Halfpenny Playhouse was organized in 1963 and was the theater-in-residence at Upsala College in East Orange in 1975-76. Since then, the Halfpenny Players have become the state's first Equity company to devote itself exclusively to touring.

The Halfpenny Players have staged more than 200 dramas, comedies and musicals, ranging from "Richard III" and "Antigone" to "Oklahoma!," while presenting almost all of the works of Neil Simon, the most commercially successful playwright in America.

In its two decades of operation, the Halfpenny Players have produced more than 30 new scripts, including several innovative musical revues. An original piece, "One for Good Measure," was designed to teach the basic principles of the metric system.

Halfpenny developed a totally new concept of teaching academic subjects through the medium of the original musical revue. They have become the mainstay of Halfpenny's repertoire.

Its two most popular shows are "Jerz—A Musical Salute to the History of New Jersey," written in 1974, and "Tar Heel—A Musical Salute to the History of North Carolina," first produced in 1976. "Jerz" and "Tar Heel" have been performed more than 1,000 times. Portions of the New Jersey tribute have appeared on NBC-TV, and the entire production has been broadcast on New Jersey Network.

The City of New Brunswick commissioned the Halfpenny Playhouse in 1980 to come up with a special salute for its 300th anniversary, entitled "They Knew New Brunswick."

The Halfpenny tours serve the general audience with such works as Benet's "John Brown's Body," O'Casey's "I Knock at the Door" and Agatha Christie's "The Mousetrap."

* * *

At the heart of the Pushcart Players is the contemporary child grappling with the problems of growing up. Feelings, behav-

Antonio Fargas in "Ain't Supposed to Die a Natural Death" at the Theater of Universal Images—New Jersey's oldest black theater.

Photo Credit: Glen Frieson

ior, emotional growth and self-appreciation are a few of the subjects explored in Pushcart sketches.

Founded in 1974 in Verona, the Pushcart Players travels throughout the Mid-Atlantic region, bringing incredibly animated productions to young audiences. The ensemble brims with boundless energy and transmits catchy tunes in a sparkingly colorful atmosphere.

The surprisingly profound Pushcart Players create outrageously funny characters to convey the totally unpredicatable problems confronted by today's fast-paced youngsters.

Pushcart has traveled more than 100,000 miles to perform for nearly 800,000 children during its eight-year existence. The players have performed at Lincoln Center, the Brooklyn Center for the Performing Arts, the World Trade Center, the South Street Seaport Museum and Citicorp Center.

On television, the Pushcart Players have been seen in two prime-time specials on WCBS, entitled "This Time Feelings" and "This Time Friends."

* * *

In a quiet shore community just below Atlantic City is where the South Jersey Regional Theatre has staked out its repertorial territory. Started in 1977 as a semi-professional, non-union operation, it is now the only year-round, nonprofit Equity theater in New Jersey's southland.

The Gateway Playhouse in Somers Point, Atlantic County, serves not only the theater-going public; the players also go into the community, giving free performances to the less fortunate— those from juvenile detention homes, alternative schools, group homes, mental health facilities, and the disadvantaged and senior citizen groups throughout South Jersey.

Built in 1912 as a warehouse, Gateway was renovated in the early 1920s into a movie house known as the Seaside Theater. In 1957, it became the Gateway Musical Playhouse, an Equity summer stock company that had been operating in the nearby Gateway Casino.

The South Jersey Regional Theatre (SJRT) took up residency in 1977, ending the building's dual role for 20 years as a movie theater and summer stock company catering to shore tourists.

The regional theater has staged more than 50 productions between 1977 and 1985, offering six major vehicles each season, from opera and Off-Broadway classics to drama and traditional musical comedy.

In the summer of 1978, SJRT established a Theatre for Young Audiences through the cooperation of CETA. Four children's plays and a children's opera were presented. SJRT is resuming its youth program, eventually taking its touring productions to schools in South Jersey.

The Foundation Theatre sprouted from New Jersey's fertile farm belt in 1975 on the Pemberton campus of Burlington County College.

Appropriately, the theater made its debut with Tennessee Williams' "Summer and Smoke," and every summer since the Foundation players have been cultivating a winning crop of dramas: "The House of Blue Leaves," "The Glass Menagerie," "Scapino," "The Seagull," "The Little Foxes" and "The Crucifer of Blood."

Operating under a letter of agreement with Actors' Equity Association, the Foundation Theatre hires New Jersey actors by holding open call auditions for local professionals early each spring.

The Foundation Theater produces three plays each summer and gives complimentary tickets to disabled and disadvantaged persons. Apprenticeship programs are also offered to aspiring actors and technicians.

Hiking among New Jersey's 4,000 miles of trails.

TRAILS

At its longest and narrowest stretches, New Jersey is just 166 miles by 32 miles. But within such limited confines unwinds a delightfully complex network of nature trails—more than 4,000 miles in all—for hiking, cycling, horseback riding, cross-country skiing and snowmobiling.

More than a million people each year enjoy New Jersey's public and private trails, the most famous being the longest one in America: The Appalachian Trail, a 400-foot right-of-way meandering over 70 miles of rugged mountain terrain in Passaic and Sussex counties from the New York border to the Delaware Water Gap.

New Jersey became the first Appalachian state to assume ownership in late 1982 of its section of the legendary trail that starts in Maine and zig-zags for 2,050 miles through 14 states, terminating in Georgia.

The intricate maze of trails interlaced with waterways lures botanists and birdwatchers, anglers and hunters, artists and photographers, the young and the old, the handicapped and the physically fit, all seeking to expand their environmental consciousness.

The hiker views the world at a human pace, moving over the land by the oldest and simplest means of travel.

The rider on horseback shares the journey in a silent partnership going back thousands of years.

The canoeist, bound by geography, sees the outdoors from a unique perspective as woods and meadows glide by above eye level.

Skiers and snowshoers experience the beauty and silence of a winter landscape that cannot be reached in other ways.

And people on bicycles, trail bikes and snowmobiles take in a swiftly changing panorama.

Trails have been on earth since the first land animals wandered from one feeding area to another, following the line of least resistance while foraging or taking the most direct route to waterholes, mating grounds or places of safety.

The first humans followed the same tracks for much the same purpose. As human society grew in number and complexity, so did the network of trails. Narrow foot tracks evolved into wide, beaten paths with increased use, leading to roads for riding horses, draft animals and wheeled vehicles.

Waterways developed as transportation corridors, canals and railroads crisscrossed the state, adding still more layers of pathways to the countryside.

Unprotected rights-of-way, such as abandoned railroads, pipelines, utility lines, aqueducts and streamside paths, abound in New Jersey. The 126-mile-long shoreline from Sandy Hook to Cape May is another linear pathway used year-round.

Water trails further open opportunities for boaters using canoes, kayaks and inflatable craft on some 350 miles of tributaries that vary greatly in character from rocky whitewater streams in the highlands to lazy tidal creeks along the coast, from pastoral streams in the agricultural mid-section to the mysterious tea-colored waters of the Pinelands.

New Jersey trails are unevenly distributed, the longer, more popular ones tending to cluster in the large parks, forests and watersheds of Warren, Sussex, Passaic and Morris counties.

There are two major exceptions: The 60-mile-long Delaware and Raritan Canal State Park, which has a multiple-use towpath that links Trenton to New Brunswick. There is also a parallel railroad right-of-way along the feeder canal and Delaware River from Trenton to Bull's Island some 20 miles north of the state capital.

In south-central New Jersey, the 40-mile-long Batona Trail is the best way to explore the million-acres Pinelands preserve. There are innumerable sand roads in the Pines for walking, ski-touring, horseback riding and motorized recreation, so many, in fact, that not all have been mapped by the New Jersey Trails Council.

Star-Ledger Photo

Batona Trail through Lebanon State Park in Burlington County.

Large county parks in the more urbanized counties of northeast and central Jersey have heavily used horse and hiking trails, nature trails and more recently improved bike trails.

Short walking and bicycle paths can be found in many municipal parks. Some communities are working together to establish regional trails that cross jurisdictional lines and link existing parks, schools, historic sites and other places of interest.

The familiar "log cabin" style of architecture is a legacy from the Depression, when the federal government deployed thousands of Civilian Conservation Corps workers to restore and develop park roads and drainage systems, bridges, dams, shelters, cabins, swimming facilities and many miles of trails in the older parks such as High Point, Stokes Forest, and South Mountain and Watchung reservations in northern New Jersey.

In addition to the Appalachian and Batona trails and the Delaware-Raritan towpath, one other significant walkway is the Palisades Interstate Park Long Path along the Hudson River to the New York border.

Regional trails of considerable length are the 42-mile-long Lenape Trail through Essex County and the 27-mile Patriot's Path through Morris County.

Lenape runs from Military Park in Newark through Branch Brook Park in Belleville and Brookdale Park, to Mill's Reservation and around the Newark reservoir to the Community Park in Cedar Grove. Yellow rectangular symbols on trees and utility poles mark the Lenape Trail, which also goes through the South Mountain Reservation, with a bikeway on the abandoned Caldwell branch of the Erie Lackawanna Railway between Cedar Grove and Essex Fells.

Patriot's Path is another urban-suburban, east-west foot and bicycle trail, which connects with the Lenape Trail at the Essex Environmental Center. Patriot's and Lenape will form the east-west cross-state trail from Newark to the Delaware River.

Other significant trails include Hunterdon County's South Branch Nature Preserve, the nucleus of an evolving country trail system, and Monmouth County's Manasquan Trail, the anchor for a regional matrix of public and private pathways.

Private interests have been helpful in supplying a dense design of trails in the Ramapo-Ringwood area, in Greenwood Lake and Wawayanda state parks, and in the Pequannock Watershed, Passaic County. Most of the 700 miles of trails developed and maintained by the New York-New Jersey Trail Conference

Lenape Trail in South Mountain Reservation.

Star-Ledger Photo

and its member clubs are located in North Jersey's mountain region bordering New York.

The Batona Trail Club of Philadelphia is responsible for the popular Pinelands trail bearing its name. Batona is being extended north to the Turkey Swamp in Monmouth County and south to the Peaslee Wildlife Management Area in Cumberland County.

Hundreds of miles of additional trails are being formed from abandoned railroads in Sussex, Warren, Hunterdon, Mercer, Ocean and Cape May counties. A sewerage interceptor in Morris County has become part of the Towpath Trail. River valleys in Hunterdon, Monmouth and Ocean counties are being designated for trail uses, as is the ridgeline of the Sourland Mountains in Somerset and Hunterdon counties and the sandy roads in Ocean County.

Trails are classified for five basic uses: Water, horse, bicycle, snow and motorized.

Canoe trails are segments of freshwater streams and other waterways, a few of which have been marked and offer sanitary facilities. There are some developed launch areas and campsites along the Delaware River above the Water Gap and at state boat launches downstream of the Gap.

State facilities are also available at Kingston on the Delaware-Raritan Canal and next to Millstone River, as well as on the D&R feeder canal at Bull's Island and Washington Crossing State Park outside of Trenton.

The Manasquan River has access points in Allaire State Park off the Garden State Parkway in Monmouth County. Additional access sites and camp areas are in Wharton State Forest along the Oswego, Wading, Batsto, Lower Atsion and Mullica rivers in South Jersey. Cedar Creek is also accessible in Double Trouble State Park in Burlington County.

County and municipal parks bordering canoeable streams generally provide parking, picnic and boat launches.

* * *

A wide variety of horse trails in New Jersey is available in the bigger state and county parks, federal recreation areas and by private organizations.

While New Jersey's human population has leveled off at 7.5 million by the latest 1980 census count, the state's equine population has doubled to more than 100,000 since 1970, increasing the demand for safe riding trails.

On federal recreation lands, horse trails are available in Morris County's Jockey Hollow National Historic Park. Riding is also allowed in the Delaware Water Gap National Recreation Area on existing abandoned roads.

In South Jersey, horses are accommodated year-round in Bass River, Belleplain, Lebanon, Penn and Wharton state forests and in Double Trouble and Parvin state parks. Horses are permitted on the beach at Island Beach State Park from Oct. 1 to April 30. Prior reservations are required.

In the central part of New Jersey, equestrian trails can be found in Allaire, Cheesequake, D&R Canal and Washington Crossing state parks.

Riders can find plenty of trails in the northern hills and valleys of the Round Valley Recreation Area, Stokes State Forest and High Point, Swartswood, Allamuchy Mountain, Ringwood and Wawayanda state parks.

Campsites where horses are permitted are located in Wharton State Forest at Goshen Pond, Batona Campsite, Bodine Field, Lower Forge and Mullica River Campsite.

A $15 annual fee to the State Fish and Wildlife Management Division, with proof of liability insurance, assures riders of open horse trails at Flatbrook and Wittingham in Sussex County, Black River in Morris County, Assunpink in Monmouth County, Glassboro in Gloucester County, and Millville in Cumberland County.

Several county parks provide horse trails and some operate livery or boarding stables. In North Jersey, county trails are available at the Campgaw Reservation in Bergen County; Eagle Rock Park and South Mountain Reservation in Essex County;

Charlotte Spaulding, Walk Leader, Mary Cerulli, Coordinator, and Cheryl Short, Walk Leader, left to right, lead a group of the Essex County Trail Walkers on a three-mile hike through the South Mountain Reservation.

South Branch Nature Preserve in Hunterdon County; Tourne and Loantaka Brook parks in Morris County; Colonial in North Branch Park; Lord Stirling Park in Somerset County, and the Watchung Reservation in Union County.

In central and southern New Jersey, county horse trails are open to the public in Cooper River and Berlin parks in Camden County; Turkey Swamp in Monmouth County, and Central Park in Mercer County.

Sand roads and firebreaks in the vast Pinelands are also heavily used by equestrians.

* * *

Separate bike paths are scattered throughout the state in short segments in local or county parks, municipal lands, school properties and abandoned rail lines. Only a few are longer than three miles. The exceptions are the Cooper bikeway in Camden, which follows the Delaware River for eight miles, and 6½ paved miles of Patriot's Path traversing six municipalities.

The ubiquitous green sign tells bikers where they can ride on the 32,000 miles of roads in New Jersey, particularly in designated areas such as Island Beach State Park, Palisades Interstate Park and Sandy Hook National Recreation Area.

Four bicycle touring routes have been developed by the New Jersey Trails Council. The routes run from Cape May to High Point Park at the New York border; from the George Washington Bridge to Montague on the Delaware River, with northern and southern alternate routes; from West Trenton to the oceanfront at Mantoloking, and down the shoreline to Island Beach State Park, and a bike route from Atlantic City to Camden.

The New Jersey segment of the interstate East Coast Bicycle Trail follows the Delaware River from Port Jervis, N.Y., to Lambertville in Hunterdon County. It then swings northeast across the state to Elizabeth and over Staten Island to the New York ferry dock.

* * *

Trails for ski-touring are available on federal lands in the Delaware Water Gap National Recreation Area and Jockey Hollow National Historic Park.

State lands with ski-touring trails include Stokes Forest, High Point, Wawayanda, Ringwood, Allamuchy Mountain and Washington Crossing state parks.

Sled dog training and competitive events take place in Lebanon State Forest and on public and private lands in northern New Jersey.

Snowmobiles are allowed to use existing trails and unplowed woods roads in Stokes Forest and adjoining High Point Park, where more than 40 miles of trails are open during the winter months. Roads and trails are also available in Ringwood State Park and in Lebanon State Forest when there is sufficient snow cover.

Other snowmobile activity occurs on railroad and utility rights-of-way and on frozen lakes and open fields in designated areas.

Star-Ledger Photo

A snowy trek with the Essex County Trail Walkers.

PSE&G's synthetic natural gas plant in Linden.

UTILITIES

$\mathcal{T}$he spider-web wires and thick round pipes weaving their way around the Garden State carry the messages, the water, the wastes and the energy that make modern life possible. They line the streets and leap over mountains and burrow under rivers, connecting New Jersey's 7.5 million residents into a centralized grid of power, communications and vital natural resources.

They are New Jersey's regulated utilities, whose steel, concrete and copper lifelines reach out to every business, home and playground in need of electricity, water, natural gas, telephones and waste-moving conduits.

They are the essential links in a complex infrastructure of roads, bridges, sewers and other heavily used public facilities that travelers and consumers have come to take for granted.

The oldest utility came into being just a century ago. Most emerged in the 20th Century to serve a burgeoning metropolitan population that fanned out and settled in every habitable spot in this corridor state.

Today, New Jersey's utilities industry is a vast community of more than 52,000 workers whose annual payroll exceeds $1.3 billion. The utility workers support another 175,000 family members. Their salaries account for nearly a half-billion dollars in retail store sales.

The major regulated utilities serving New Jersey are: American Water Works Service Co., Atlantic City Electric Co., Atlantic City Sewerage Co., Continental Telephone Co., Elizabethtown Gas Co., Elizabethtown Water Co., Garden State Water Co., Hackensack Water Co., Jersey Central Power & Light Co., Lake Mohawk-Sparta Water Co., Middlesex Water Co., New Jersey Bell Telephone Co., New Jersey Natural Gas Co., Parkway Water Co., Public Service Electric & Gas Co., Rockland Electric Co., Southern Jersey Gas Co., United Telephone System and Warwick Valley Telephone Co.

The utilities are regulated by the state because they provide an essential service to the public. Making sure that service is maintained, as well as keeping the price of the product reasonable, is the responsibility of state regulators. Regulated utilities are guaranteed a fair rate of return on their investment, which is generally in the 15 percent range.

One of the largest utilities in New Jersey is not regulated, although it provides a critical service to the 1.25 million people of the Passaic Valley who depend on it. The Passaic Valley Sewerage System is the fourth largest wastewater operation in the United States, treating an average of 232 million gallons a day of flushed and discharged effluent from industry, commerce, residential and sundry other sources.

On Sept. 11, 1911, 15 municipalities entered into a compact among themselves, represented by the Passaic Valley Sewerage Commissioners. Since those Passaic River communities decided to stop using the great glacial tributary as a sewer outlet, others have joined the compact to clean up the Passaic. The member communities now number 29, from Belleville and Clifton to Paterson and Wallington.

Passaic Valley has invested more than $1 billion in sewer inceptors, pumps and a modern treatment plant in Newark to protect the Passaic River and Newark Bay. The results became clearly evident when its new half-billion-dollar secondary treatment plant went into full operation in 1985.

Some of the biggest purveyors of water, generators of electric energy, distributors of natural gas, and deliverers of vocal and visual information follow.

New Jersey Bell

No longer part of "Ma Bell's" communications family, New Jersey Bell—the state's largest private employer—is now a member of Bell Atlantic, one of the seven regional holding companies that brought together America's 22 telephone operations companies divested from American Telephone & Telegraph (AT&T) on Jan. 1, 1984.

The 29,000 men and women of New Jersey Bell provide telecommunications services to most of the state's population living and working in 3 million homes and businesses.

The public's "gateway to information and knowledge systems," New Jersey Bell placed more than 38 million calls a day over its lines in 1984.

With telephone plant assets reaching $6 billion, New Jersey Bell has pioneered telecommunications in a state where the telephone was perfected for Alexander Graham Bell by his friend Thomas Edison. The great inventor, who patented more than 1,000 ideas at his Menlo Park and West Orange laboratories, made the telephone a practical consumer product by improving the receiver so that a human voice could be distinguished.

Public Service Electric & Gas

PSE&G is the third largest combined utility in the nation and the biggest electric/gas company in New Jersey.

A $5 billion annual operation, Public Service sells natural gas or electricity to seven out of every 10 residents of the state. Its service territory begins in northern Gloucester County on the Delaware River and runs northeast to the corner of Bergen County on the Hudson River. The densely developed urban corridor is the right-of-way for both the New Jersey Turnpike and PSE&G distribution lines.

Public Service goes back to the time when trolleys were the chief transporters of people. Before Public Service joined them under one corporate symbol, there were 99 trolley companies in New Jersey and hundreds of small gas and electric firms.

PSE&G brought many of these services together in 1903, providing much of the state with gas and electric and transportation through its "street railway": The trolley car system.

A PSE&G transmission tower sends out power to the Hudson River waterfront.

Star-Ledger Photo

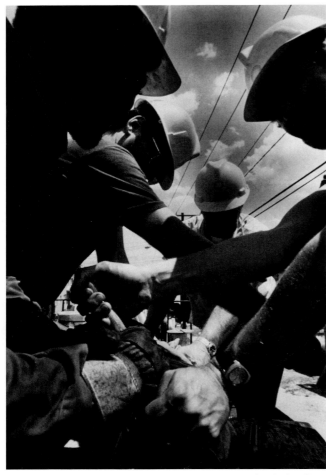

A PSE&G crew grapples with the installation of underground cable.

cal to release heat for the same purpose. Fusion reactors are expected to be spinning out voltage by the turn of the 21st Century.

PSE&G also built the pioneering Battery Energy Storage Test Facility in Hillsborough in conjunction with the U.S. Department of Energy and the Electric Power Research Institute. The project is testing a system that would permit generating stations to produce power during periods of low demand (at night) to be stored for use at times of peak requirements (noon).

Public Service is developing methods of using waste heat at its generating stations. With the financial support of the National Science Foundation, the utility has been successfully raising trout at its Mercer Generating Plant by recovering vented heat.

In cooperation with the Electric Power Research Institute and General Electric Co., PSE&G is conducting a demonstration program for a prototype advanced design electrolytic hydrogen system at its Sewaren Generating Station. The system is producing hydrogen to cool electric generators.

Meanwhile, Public Service is experimenting with electric cars and photovoltaic cells—the conversion of sunlight directly into electricity.

Imagine standing at the edge of a 250-acre tract covered only by arrays of shining solar panels silently turning sunlight into kilowatts without polluting the air, water or land.

PSE&G, working with RCA Laboratories in Princeton, believes such a space-age system will be supplying an impressive amount of New Jersey's energy needs by the 1990s.

The basic building block of the model plant is the RCA-developed amorphous silicon cell, invented by RCA scientist David Carlson in 1974. By turning to the sun, RCA and utilities can lessen their dependence on costly, limited and dirty fuels such as coal and oil.

By 1987, about 45 percent of the electricity produced for PSE&G's customers will come from nuclear power reactors. Two are operating in Salem County, while a third nearby is nearing completion. They are called Salem I and II and Hope Creek I nuclear power stations.

Public Service is the largest kilowatt user in the Pennsylvania-New Jersey-Maryland Interconnection, the nation's first power pool, which PSE&G helped found in 1927. Some 11 electric utilities in the PJM grid share power to serve more than 21 million residents of the 50,000-square-mile region, including all of Delaware, the District of Columbia and a portion of Virginia.

As a gas company, Public Service was something like an older, bigger brother to the electric industry. In 1903, there were 187,000 gas meters in service in PS territory. Today there are more than 1.4 million meters in use. In 1903, the capacity of Public Service gas plants was less than 23,000 cubic feet a day. By 1985, that figure had inflated to about 200 billion.

In 1973, Public Service built the nation's first synthetic natural gas plant in Harrison. It can produce 20 million cubic feet of gas a day. In 1974, PS built another syngas plant in Linden with a capacity of 125 million cubic feet a day.

The 1,494 miles of gas mains in use in 1903 were extended to more than 12,500 miles by 1985.

Within the next seven years, separate companies were formed for each of the activities: The Public Service Gas Co., the Public Service Electric Co., the Public Service Railway Co.

By 1924, the first two were merged to form PSE&G. By 1928, another company had been designated to operate gasoline driven buses and the trolley system. The new company was Public Service Coordinated Transport, which was taken over by the state in 1980 and now operates as New Jersey Transit.

Public Service originally was an extension of the first central generating station for electric production devised by Edison in 1882. Despite the fact that Edison had already developed the first practical incandescent light, gas was still a popular means of illumination and its use for cooking and heating was growing at the turn of the century.

When PS went into business in 1903, it had less than 19,000 electric meters in service. Today there are more than 1.7 million meters counting kilowatt hours at factories, homes, schools, hospitals and other plugged-in, peopled places.

Edison's creative spirit permeates PSE&G even today. The giant utility was the first to feed power from a fuel cell into a power grid. It has supported fusion research at Princeton University's Plasma Physics Laboratory since 1970. The opposite of a nuclear fission reaction that can produce heat to make electricity or the force of an atomic bomb, fusion is the burning of a chemi-

Jersey Central Power & Light

The corporate name suggests Jersey Central Power & Light Co. serves only the Central Jersey region. Its territory is actually larger than Public Service's, encompassing a 3,256-square-mile area of the Garden State. There are about 2 million people in JCP&L's franchised service area. That comes to 725,000 metered electric customers in 236 municipalities in 13 counties.

JCP&L is the largest subsidiary of General Public Utilities, with headquarters in Parsippany-Troy Hills, Morris County. GPU

Control room operators at the PSE&G Salem nuclear power plant in South Jersey.

Courtesy: PSE&G

is an electric utility holding company with three operating subsidiaries in New Jersey and Pennsylvania. The other companies are Metropolitan Edison, serving about 370,000 customers in central and eastern Pennsylvania, and Pennsylvania Electric, with about 519,000 hookups in the northern and western areas of the Keystone State.

GPU is one of the largest publicly owned electric utilities, with assets of $6.2 billion. GPU companies sold more than 33.4 million megawatt hours of electric power in 1984, generating revenues of about $2.7 billion.

JCP&L was founded in 1925, about 10 years after its sister company, New Jersey Power & Light Co., was organized in the northwestern counties of the state. New Jersey Power merged with JCP&L in 1973. Today, the New Jersey utility employs 3,320 men and women. Gross revenues reached $1.3 billion in 1984. Assets are valued at $2.9 billion.

Jersey Central owns all or part of 10 generating stations in New Jersey and Pennsylvania.

JCP&L pioneered the nation's first large commercial nuclear power plant at Oyster Creek, Ocean County. The 650,000-megawatt plant started up in 1969 and, in its first 10 years of service, saved the utility's customers $725 million by using nuclear fuel instead of much more expensive foreign oil.

With a lot of help from nature, JCP&L produces electricity in Blairstown from a pumped storage generating station. The Yards Creek station consists of two reservoirs, one 700 feet above the other. They are connected by a pipeline, or "penstock," through which water from the upper reservoir flows to and through the generating station at the lower reservoir.

At off-peak night hours, excess power from other JCP&L

plants pump water from the lower to the upper reservoir, where it is stored until daytime peak load periods. The water is then released to flow to the lower level to generate electric current as it passes through the power house.

Yards Creek can crank out 165 megawatts of electric energy. The system went into service in 1965.

Within its territory, JCP&L maintains some 530,000 poles and towers and 60,000 miles of wire.

Both Jersey Central and Public Service entered the solar-conservation business in 1979, offering their residential customers solar hot water systems, as well as insulation for their attics and walls to save energy and money.

Atlantic City Electric

In 1886, five investors put up $1,250 to take a chance on that new Edison invention called the electric generating system. Thus was born Atlantic City Electric, which exceeded a half-billion-dollar a year operation by 1985.

The utility's most famous customers are the glittering casinos along the world renowned boardwalk. But its biggest customer is an oil refinery on the opposite side of the state, Mobil, on the Delaware River in Paulsboro. Mobil consumed more than 136 million kilowatt hours of electricity last year.

Atlantic City Electric serves 370,000 customers in 129 municipalities in eight counties, covering 2,700 square miles. Its 2,000 employes are responsible for the delivery of 1,600 megawatts of

Star-Ledger Photo

JCP&L lineman installing new vapor street light.

Star-Ledger Photo

Linemen for Atlantic Electric work to restore power to more than 12,000 shore customers during the February blizzard in 1983.

electricity to 324,000 residential, 43,000 commercial and 1,700 industrial customers.

In 1981, Atlantic City Electric, under the helm of Chairman John Feehan, was selected as the Outstanding Electric Utility of the Year by Electric Light & Power Magazine. There have been 13 winners of the utility award.

Elizabethtown Gas

It began in 1855 as the Elizabethtown Gas Light Co., only five weeks after the City of Elizabeth was incorporated. The oldest all-gas utility in the state, Elizabethtown is two years older than Union County.

Elizabethtown started selling gas for lighting purposes only, since gas as a fuel was too expensive to compete with cheaper sources—wood and coal. At that time, gas was measured by candle power and was made primarily from coal.

In 1892, Elizabethtown purchased another company serving the city's lighting needs, Metropolitan Gas Light. To make the purchase possible, the directors of Elizabethtown elected not to pay a dividend—1892 being the only year in the company's history when stockholders didn't make money.

By 1905, a new fuel product evolved from "coal gas" and then "carbureted water gas." The new fuel was manufactured from a plant built by Elizabethtown to meet a growing demand in gas for cooking and water heating, as well as lighting.

On Dec. 19, 1922, Elizabethtown Gas Light Co. consolidated with Cranford Gas Light, Rahway Gas Light and Metuchen Gas Light to form Elizabethtown Consolidated Gas Co. When Perth

Amboy Gas Light merged with Elizabethtown on June 1, 1950, the company name was shortened to its present form.

Conversion to natural gas from the synthesized gases was completed in March 1951. Although Elizabethtown still makes synthetic gas, or syngas, to supplement its natural gas supply, its main mission is the distribution of natural gas to 195,000 metered customers. A half-million people use Elizabethtown Gas in 69 communities in seven counties: Union, Sussex, Warren, Hunterdon and parts of Middlesex, Morris and Mercer.

In extremely cold weather, Elizabethtown manufactures gas to meet peak demand. The Erie Street plant in Elizabeth is also the site of New Jersey's first liquefied natural gas (LNG) storage facility. Elizabethtown is partners in the synthetic natural gas (SNG) plant in Linden run by Public Service.

Elizabethtown today is a major marketing and gas distribution organization employing 750 people and servicing 2,000 miles of gas mains. And half of its customers use gas for heating. Elizabethtown's customers now use as much gas in five minutes as the founding company used in three months for lighting.

In June 1969, National Utilities and Industries Corp. was formed and Elizabethtown Gas became a wholly owned subsidiary of the new parent company. Elizabethtown remains the largest member of the NUI Corp. family.

NUI's revenues reached $320 million in 1984, most of that coming from Elizabethtown. The other subsidiaries are Lenape Resources, which drills for and recovers natural gas in western New York; Utility Propane, a propane distributor with more than 12,000 customers in New Jersey, and Computil, a data processing service company. Utility Propane also sells diesel fuel, gasoline and fuel oil.

Lenape Resources operates about 100 wells delivering more

than 5 million cubic feet a day of natural gas. Ninety percent of the gas goes to Elizabethtown and the balance to New Jersey Resources Corp. based in Wall Township. NUI has been trying to buy New Jersey Resources, the state's second largest gas distributor.

In addition, NUI has a 50 percent interest in two ventures involved in energy exploration in the Southwest.

Elizabethtown Water

Like the gas company, the origins of Elizabethtown Water go back to Col. John Kean in the mid-19th Century and his involvement in putting together both utilities—water in 1854 and gas a year later.

The Kean family has been the guiding force behind the Elizabethtown utilities ever since. A member of that publicly distinguished family is New Jersey's current governor, Thomas H. Kean.

When Elizabethtown Water was organized by Kean before the Civil War, there were less than 90 water distribution systems in the United States. With more than 60,000 waterworks throughout the country, "E'town" remains among the 10 largest investor-owned systems.

The colonel's original utility consisted of a coal-fired pumping station in what is today downtown Elizabeth, with a storage basin on a nearby hill at Chilton Street.

Today, Elizabethtown and its wholly owned subsidiary, the Mt. Holly Water Co., supply water to homes and businesses in 47 municipalities in six counties: Burlington, Hunterdon, Mercer, Middlesex, Somerset and Union.

The 2,200 miles of water mains weave through the 500-square-mile region, serving 1 million residents in their homes and businesses. The Raritan-Millstone water purification plant is the largest treatment facility in the state with a rated capacity of 150 million gallons a day and a still higher peaking capability of 175 million gallons.

The system also includes some 150,000 water meters and 11,000 fire hydrants.

Elizabethtown's utility plants are valued at $165 million.

"E'town" draws more than 70 million gallons a day from the Raritan River under a rights agreement with the State Department of Environmental Protection, and 32 million gallons daily from the Delaware and Raritan Canal. Supplementing that flowing supply is a network of Elizabethtown wells, which provide about 20 percent of the total daily consumption.

Elizabethtown also supplies water to municipal systems in Edison, Elizabeth, Franklin Township, Highland Park, Newark, Peapack-Gladstone, Rahway and Winfield.

Two investor-owned utilities—Commonwealth Water and Middlesex Water—also obtain portions of their supplies from Elizabethtown.

The company's work force stands at 286, an employee/customer ratio of 1 to 3,333. Elizabethtown's operating revenues reached $55 million in 1984.

Hackensack Water

From a pipeline laid down in 1874 to dams built in the early 1900s, to the construction of new impoundments in the '50s and '60s and the human-sized, walk-in pipes of today, Hackensack Water Co. processes more than 70,000 gallons a minute of potable water for nearly 1 million people in 60 towns in Bergen and Hudson counties.

Two political rivals, Garret Ackerson Jr., a Democrat, and Charles H. Voorhis, a Republican, obtained water company charters from the state Legislature in 1869. The population of Hackensack, the seat of Bergen County, was 4,000. Voorhis bought out Ackerson and new investors took over when the fledgling water company went bankrupt in the 1873 Panic. The next 100 years witnessed the growth of one of the nation's largest water purveyors.

With revenues approaching $100 million a year, Hackensack Water moves 35 billion gallons annually—or 400,000 tons a day—of thirst-quenching liquid through 1,900 miles of water mains, enough pipe to send water all the way to Denver.

The process begins at a wet spot six miles south of Bear Mountain in Rockland County, N.Y., where the Hackensack River begins. A wholly owned subsidiary of Hackensack, Spring Valley Water Co., serves almost all of Rockland County.

From the clear upstream headwaters of the Hackensack, more than 14 billion gallons of water are collected in four reservoirs: DeForest in Clarkstown, N.Y.; Lake Tappan; Oradell Reservoir, and the smaller Woodcliff Lake Reservoir.

Two large purification plants are in Oradell and Haworth. A battery of equipment—aerators, mechanical mixers, settling basins and special filters—assure a continuous flow of healthful water.

Hackensack's Ozone Pilot Project is the first full-treatment plant of its kind in the United States. Ozone, a naturally occurring form of oxygen, is a strong oxidant and a superior agent for purifying water. It is widely used in Europe for water treatment. In addition to improving water quality, ozone in water treatment results in savings to consumers.

Chlorine, a disinfectant, is a much more expensive chemical, which poses side effects if used indiscriminately.

Hackensack's sophisticated analytical instruments can detect one part of a chemical compound in 1 billion parts of water. That's the equivalent of finding one inch in 16,000 miles.

Hackensack delivers water to its North Jersey customers at a cost of a quarter-cent per gallon. Water remains nature's cheapest—and most precious—commodity.

Light from the filter gallery at Hackensack Water Company's treatment plant in Haworth brightens up the winter landscape.

Courtesy: Hackensack Water Company

A hawk at Stokes State Forest.

Courtesy: N.J. Div. of Travel & Tourism

WILDLIFE

*T*he sounds and sights of unfettered life abound just beyond everyone's backyard in New Jersey, from Turkey Swamp and Butterfly Bogs in the central region to Egg Island and Mad Horse Creek in the southern sector and Pequest and Wanaque in the northern area.

They are among the 50 Wildlife Management Areas protected by the state as sanctuaries for all of nature's creatures, including the humankind, hunters and recreationists alike.

Adding to the 150,000 acres of state game preserves are another half-dozen wildlife sanctuaries at the Gateway and Delaware Water Gap national parks, the Great Swamp in Morris County, the Brigantine Wildlife Refuge outside Atlantic City and the Hackensack Meadowlands estaurine habitat.

The wildlife terrain ranges from coastal marsh and wetlands to mountains and valleys, providing plentiful and healthful habitats for myriad species whose numbers are growing each year.

The state management areas are listed here alphabetically.

* * *

Absecon is a 3,688-acre tract in Atlantic County washed by the intercoastal waterway. Almost all salt marsh, Absecon is managed primarily for waterfowl.

During the migration season, thousands of sandpipers, knots, dowitchers, curlews, willets, plovers, turnstones and yellowlegs feed and rest in and around Absecon and Reeds bays. Also present

are gulls, terns, skimmers, American bitterns, egrets and herons. An occasional bald eagle will check out the Absecon salt marsh, along with yellow, black, clapper and Virginia rails, coots, grebes and loons.

Waterfowl hunting is permitted in season. Black duck, snow geese and bufflehead are the most abundant species, but Canada geese, widgeon and teal also stop at Absecon to nourish themselves.

Saltwater fishing and crabbing are excellent in the coastal bays and estuaries. Among the species are stripers, weakfish, fluke, flounder, white perch and bluefish. In the fall, kingfish and hickory shad make their run through the network of inlets and bays.

The northern half of the old Brigantine Bridge, just north of the Absecon inlet, is open to the public as a fishing pier. The area is ideal for boating and waterskiing, with a number of public and private launching ramps.

* * *

Amwell Lake in Hunterdon County is a picture-postcard body of water buffered by scenic farmland at the foot of the Sourland Mountains in southern Hunterdon County. The tract takes in 22 acres, half of which are water.

The state annually stocks the Y-shaped lake with rainbow, golden rainbow and brown trout. Native species include bluegill, sunfish, pumpkinseed, white catfish, brown bullhead, golden shiner and killifish.

Channel fish up to 16 pounds have been caught in Amwell Lake, which also teems with largemouth bass. Only small boats with electric motors are permitted on the lake. Boats may be launched by hand, but there is no ramp available for trailer boats.

* * *

Assunpink Lake is the main attraction within the 5,400 acres of fields, woods and hedgerows. One of the finest bird dog field trails in the Northeast zig-zags through the wildlife preserve in western Monmouth and eastern Mercer counties.

Assunpink, Stone Tavern and Rising Sun lakes were created as flood protection from the Assunpink Creek. The 225-acre Assunpink Lake is stocked with largemouth bass and channel catfish. Canada geese stop over at the lake during the fall, joining a large variety of ducks.

Bluegill outnumber the bass and pumpkinseed sunfish in the lakes. Brown bullhead and chain pickerel are also present, some having measured in at 20 inches. Other finds in the three lakes are creek chubsucker, banded killifish and golden shiner.

Pheasant, quail and rabbits are the main upland game, taking plenty of food and cover plantings and mowing and hedgerow cuttings. A small herd of deer is being developed.

The Department of Agriculture has established an Equine Activity Center for horse shows, rodeos, polo, trail riding, hunt races and programs for the handicapped.

Assunpink Lake in western Monmouth County is a haven for fauna and fowl.

Star-Ledger Photo

* * *

Baldwin Lake is a 37-acre, leg-shaped retreat just north of Pennington, outside of the state capital. Stony Brook and railroad tracks flank each side of the wildlife management area.

The 22-acre lake is surrounded by fertile farmland. Bass and sunfish are the catch of the day at Baldwin.

* * *

Beaver Swamp in Cape May County is a 2,700-acre maze of swamps, creeks, little ponds and dense forest. The land supports an adequate deer herd, as well as woodcock, quail, cottontail rabbits and squirrels.

Waterfowl are represented by wood duck, black duck, mallard and teal. For the angler, white perch are available.

* * *

Berkshire Valley, just northwest of Dover in Morris County, is traversed by the Rockaway River and Stephens Brook. The tributaries are alive with trout, stocked regularly by the state.

The 1,527 acres of fields and woodlands are natural hideaways for deer, pheasants, grouse, rabbits and squirrels. Now and then a Canada goose will investigate the valley, home for such waterfowl as mallard, wood duck and black duck.

* * *

Bevan Wildlife Management Area is one of the largest areas owned and operated by the State Division of Fish, Game and Wildlife. South of Millville in Cumberland County, Bevan covers 12,000 acres of fields and woodlands.

The planting of annual food patches, cover crops and cooperative farming with local landowners are all aimed at improving upland game: Quail, ruffed grouse, rabbit and a growing deer population.

Shaws Pond occupies the southern tip of the state preserve and Laurel Lake lies just outside the management area. The pond is a favorite of the largemouth bass.

Enjoying the streams within the habitat are teals, mallards, wood ducks and black ducks, and pickerel and catfish. The vast site is ideal for bird watching, photography and hiking.

* * *

Black River is an upland game preserve of 2,817 acres between Somerville and Netcong in Morris and Somerset counties. The Black River flows through the six-mile-long tract, which is a haven for deer, pheasant, woodcock, grouse, rabbits and squirrels.

During the open season, the state releases a number of birds for hunters. The wood duck is the principal species, joined by black and mallard.

* * *

Butterfly Bogs is a 103-acre tract that supports stands of pitch pine and scrub oak in the Pine Barrens of Ocean County. The area is maintained by the state for upland game, waterfowl and deer.

The three bogs provide 30 acres of waterfowl habitat for teal, black and wood duck, and fishing opportunities for pickerel and catfish. Red and gray foxes share the habitat with grouse, quail, cottontails and squirrels.

* * *

Capoolong Creek owes its wildlife existence to an abandoned railroad right-of-way that once served Hunterdon County. The 61 acres of land buffering Capoolong Creek create access for year-round trout fishing. The state puts brown and rainbow trout in the high-quality stream each year to supplement the smallmouth bass, rock bass and sunfish.

* * *

Cedarville Pond is another angler's oasis in flat, sandy Cumberland County. The 42 acres of woods and water off Sawmill Road in Cedarville draw the hook-and-tackle enthusiast, who is rewarded with bluegill, brown bullhead, eastern chain pickerel and largemouth bass.

* * *

Clarks Pond is really three successive ponds near Bridgeton, Cumberland County. The wildlife area serves but one purpose: Fishing, fishing and more fishing.

The shallowest of the Clarks ponds is five feet in depth and is filled with largemouth bass and eastern chain pickerel, with some bluegill, pumpkinseed and yellow bullhead.

The eight-foot-deep pond has sufficient bluegills, pumpkinseeds and brown bullheads. Not as numerous are largemouth bass, eastern pickerel, yellow perch and carp.

The deepest fishing hole, at 12 feet, contains ample pickerel, bluegill, yellow bullhead and perch, with some largemouth bass and pumpkinseed.

* * *

Clinton is the most popular of New Jersey's wildlife management areas. The 1,114 acres of fields and woodlands stretch north of the Spruce Run Reservoir.

The rugged topography, with its abundant food supply, makes it a prime deer range. The man-made impoundment has attracted mallard, geese, scaup, ringneck, canvasback and black duck.

The deep reservoir has become home for the northern pike, rainbow, brook and brown trout and the largemouth bass. Clinton is managed under a continuous farmland habitat improvement program. Among the native species are pheasant, grouse, rabbits and squirrels.

* * *

Colliers Mills in the Pine Barrens of Ocean County is one of the few places where red and gray foxes have taken over abandoned burrows and converted them into their own dens.

The substantial 12,212-acre forest of mixed hard- and softwoods (pines and oaks) is dotted with 210 acres of fields, six sizable impoundments and 250 acres of wetlands.

Five of the 13 fishing areas, led by Lake Success, Turn Mill and Colliers Mills lakes and Kennedy Pond, have a good supply of bass, perch and pickerel. Many deer roam the pine forest.

Principal native species are rabbits, squirrels, grouse and quail. The state liberates quail and pheasants in Colliers Mills for the hunting season. Game commonly harvested are mallard, teal, wood and black duck.

* * *

Delaware River Angler Access is one of the best fishing waters and also one of the most underutilized of the state's wildlife management areas. The Division of Fish, Game and Wildlife is opening the entire length of the Delaware River to fishermen.

Three sites have been opened at Holland Church, Kingwood and Mercer Pool. That stretch is between Trenton and Phillipsburg.

Shoreline fishing and parking are also provided at the Old Wharf in Trenton, where herring fishing dominates the riverbank from late March to late May. Shad run the river from April through June. Channel catfish bite during the summer months.

Some big muskellunge swim upstream from the Delaware Bay to Port Jervis, N.Y., accompanied by walleye, smallmouth bass and an assortment of panfish.

* * *

Dennis Creek is a 5,109-acre salt marsh in Cape May County for birdwatching, nature photography, hiking, water skiing, boating, crabbing, shellfishing and trapping. Coursing through the

Motorboats await passengers along Spruce Run reservoir in Clinton.

marsh are Sluice Creek and Roaring Ditch, with signs to a place called Rio Grande. Boat ramps are at Jakes Landing Road and Bidwells Ditch.

The marsh, a natural food basket, sustains numerous deer, black ducks, green-winged teal, pintail, Canada geese, widgeon, mallard, shoveler, goldeneye and hooded merganser. Tidal creeks and the Delaware Bay ripple with white perch, striped bass, weakfish, black drum, sea bass and shad, as well as sharks, flounder and crabs.

* * *

Dix is a unique mix of marsh, forest and farmland, embracing 2,395 acres in Cumberland County along the Delaware River. Mink and muskrat are two members of the rodent family that breed along the Drumbo and Division creeks and the main drainage creek (Middle) through the center of the marsh.

Rabbits are in abundance, as are pheasant and quail. Waterfowl include geese, pintail, mallard and black duck. Also in the marsh ecosystem are deer, grouse and woodcock.

Salt water fish are generally striped bass and white perch. South of Dix is a Waldenesque community called Sea Breeze.

* * *

Egg Island in Cumberland County is a study area for waterfowl brood production, clapper rail and mosquito-wildlife surveys. The high-quality tidal marsh takes in 8,325 acres, including some upland habitat.

Many shore birds nest in the brackish environment, from willets and widgeons to shovelers and gadwalls. Native species of upland game are fox, quail, rabbit and pheasant.

The nine, serpentine tidal creeks flowing into the Delaware Bay are nurseries for striped bass, white perch, weakfish and drum.

* * *

Flatbrook is named after the Big and Little Flatbrooks, two of the Garden State's most famous trout streams, which run through western Sussex County by Bevans, Walpack and Tuttles Corner. A large herd of deer on the 2,334-acre tract, plus grouse, rabbits, squirrels and woodcock account for the principal game. The marshy area is inhabited by mallards and black and wood ducks.

* * *

Fortesque attracts both wintering snow geese and naturalists and birdwatchers from the mid-Atlantic region. Another high-quality salt marsh on the Delaware Bay, Fortesque is a modest habitat, just 900 acres, but extremely productive.

The Cumberland County marsh shelters black duck, widgeon, teal, gadwall, quail, rabbits, squirrels, deer and other waterfowl and upland species. Tidal creeks with such appellations as "Sow & Pigs" and "Beadons" flow with weakfish, striped bass, white perch, kingfish, bluefish, flounder, black drum, shark and crabs.

* * *

Glassboro is a jigsaw-puzzle-shaped wildlife tract in Gloucester County. Three little lakes and ponds and a half-dozen streams criss-crossing the wilderness are enough to keep a deer herd growing for bow and gun enthusiasts.

Scattered throughout the 2,337 acres of fields and woodlands are quail, grouse, rabbits and squirrels. Additional pheasant and quail are set loose by the state during the hunting season.

* * *

Great Bay on the Atlantic Ocean at Little Egg Inlet is a birdwatchers' paradise. The 4,845 acres of salt marsh have been carved up into 19 islands by the Little Egg Harbor Bay, Great Bay and Little Egg Inlet. The only man-made intrusion is the Great Bay Boulevard that runs through the marsh, connecting the larger islands to the mainland.

The marsh comes alive with the flutter of wings during the migration season. Dozens of species have been counted, among them: Sandpipers, knots, dowitchers, curlews, willets, plovers, turnstones, yellowlegs, gulls, terns, skimmers, American bitterns, glossy ibis, oyster catchers, marsh hawks, ospreys, egrets, herons, Virginia rail, coot, grebes, loons and bald eagle. Waterfowl also thrive in the marsh, from teal and Canada geese to widgeon and clapper rail.

Fish, crabs and clams are equally abundant in the coastal bays and estuaries. Stripers, fluke, flounder, perch, bluefish and weakfish make the Great Bay an extremely productive nursery.

* * *

Greenwood Forest in Ocean County is the site of a 1,000-acre quail management preserve. The quail area is divided into 50 five-acre sections, each with its own border of hedgerows.

No vehicles are allowed in the quail protection zone. The 9,000-acre forest is distinguished by its pitch pine and scrub oak in the uplands and a white cedar swamp in the lowlands.

Some 260 acres of fields are under intensive management for wildlife. Waterfowl, including Canada geese, ducks and teal, flourish in and around 100 acres of wetlands and three impoundments, one of which is a necklace-shaped succession of little ponds.

The three lakes, covering 30 surface acres, are loaded with perch, pickerel and catfish. Annual and perennial food and cover crops feed a substantial deer herd, as well as rabbits, grouse and quail.

* * *

Hainesville is a 282-acre tract in Sussex County shaped like a boxer dog. In the belly of the dog is a 30-acre lake that looks like a blue maple leaf fed by Little Flatbrook.

The impoundment offers fine trout, sunfish and catfish. Waterfowl most commonly harvested are black and wood ducks and

Jean O'Blenis of Wyckoff, past President of the Bergen County Audubon Society, enjoys birdwatching along the Great Bay near the inlet of Little Egg Harbor.

Star-Ledger Photo

mallards. The habitat consists of mostly fields, woodlands and hedgerows for grouse, rabbits and squirrels.

During the gaming season, pheasants are released by the state. An expanding deer herd is kept in check during the hunting season by archers and gun enthusiasts.

* * *

Hamburg Mountain is a place for both hunters and skiers. High atop Hardyston and Vernon townships in Sussex County, Hamburg Mountain touches the clouds over Vernon Valley and Great Gorge, ski resorts that lease a portion of their primary slopes from the state.

The 3,636-acre mountain is heavily forested, an ideal environment for deer. Rabbits, grouse and squirrels are the principal species in the mountain wilderness, whose topography does not attract many recreationists or hunters. Just outside the public tract are three impoundments: Silver Lake, Lake Wildwood and Mud Pond.

* * *

Harrisonville Lake straddles the Salem-Gloucester County line near Woodstown. The tract is largely water, a 30-acre lake with a maximum depth of seven feet. The edge of the lake is public land, with a five-acre piece of land at the westerly end divided by Oldmans Creek.

The lake is stocked with trout during the fishing season. Species that can be caught there are largemouth bass, black crappie, bluegill, brown bullhead, carp, white perch, pumpkinseed, eastern chain pickerel and channel catfish.

* * *

Heislerville on the Delaware Bay in Cumberland County is where carp bow fishing is a popular pastime. Crabbing is also a favorite activity along the bay and Maurice River, which snakes around the easterly side of the 3,884 acres of salt marsh and fertile uplands. West Creek borders the other side of Heislerville, with Riggin Ditch slicing up the center.

The intrusion of protective technology is evident everywhere: Diked haying marshes, control of undesirable plants, and water-level management in the main impoundment at Heislerville.

There are 13 bodies of water in and around the wildlife preserve. Three ponds carved out by the state, coupled with the low Cadwalader tidal marshes, lure thousands of migrating, nesting and wintering waterfowl. The state rates black duck hunting as "superb," along with green-winged teal, widgeon, gadwall, mallard and pintail. Florida gallinule also check in at Heislerville.

Birdwatchers flock to the game preserve to view and photograph thousands of wintering snow geese. Pheasant, rabbit, quail and woodcock are plentiful, as are deer.

More numerous is the marine population: Striped bass, whitefish, perch, black drum, weakfish, kingfish, catfish, carp and bluefish, which come in from the bay to explore the many tidal creeks.

Along the Delaware Bay are two beaches—Moores and Thompsons—for sunbathing, surfing and swimming.

* * *

Higbee Beach-Pond Creek Meadow juts out on the southern tip of New Jersey in Cape May County. Pond Creek Meadow is the last fresh water area in New Jersey for migrants in their flight across Delaware Bay.

As such, it is a vital link in the Atlantic Flyway, serving as both a resting and nesting station. Seventeen species of birds populate the coastal protrusion on the Delaware Bay.

More than 100,000 people from 49 countries visited the beach-meadow wildlife preserve in 1974, the year a survey was taken by the Stone Harbor Bird Sanctuary. Upward of 50,000 hawks migrate over and through the Cape May flyway each year. Millions of songbirds use the area for cover and food.

Birders are rewarded with rare appearances by the endangered bald eagle, the peregrine falcon, the osprey and Cooper's hawk.

Another endangered species, the Eastern tiger salamander, is trying to come back in this geologically divisified refuge.

Within the 416 acres of dunes, beaches, fields, woodlands and ponds is the 4½-acre Davey's Lake. Above the lake, the wooded upland breaks the ocean breeze with its full stands of oak, holly and bayberry. The low-lying areas are stabilized by red maple, willow and black locust.

In the middle of a meadow is Sassafras Island, a wooded oasis. Woodcock take cover amidst the trees, while muskrats make their lodges in the meadows. The muskrat population remains around one lodge per acre, making Pond Creek Meadow one of the most productive in the country.

Upland, the eastern cottontail rabbit animates the countryside. Woodcock, quail, rabbits and squirrels also proliferate in the natural cover.

The beachfront extends a mile and a half along the bay to Cape May Canal. Sands from the ocean floor sweep around the southern tip, nourishing the mile-and-a-half-long beach to Cape May Canal. The beach is 150 feet at its widest.

"Cape May diamonds" can be collected on Higbee Beach. Tourists taking the tiny quartz pebbles to add to their gem collections renamed Higbee "Diamond Beach."

Behind Higbee Beach stretches dunes that rise more than 20 feet, secured by a low forest of holly, honeysuckle, Virginia creeper, red cedar, beach plum and pitch pine. Growing on the other side of the dunes in Pond Creek Meadow are foxtail, cattail and royal fern.

Two freshwater canals cut through the coastal habitat and two sand trails separate the dunes from the woodlands and fallow fields.

Residing in the brackish water and salt marsh vegetation are fiddler crabs, mollusks and killifish. Amphibians, reptiles and insects reflect the life cycle of a combined salt water and fresh water environment.

* * *

Imlaystown Lake in Monmouth County, south of Hightstown, is a lovely arm of water for a restful day of angling, situated in one of the fastest growing regions in the United States. Two square pieces of land at the western side of the lake have been set aside for launches by cartop boats with oars or electric motors.

Doctors Creek flows through the most westerly tract, replenishing the lake. Bank fishing is limited to about 10 percent of the lake shoreline because of private property ownership.

The lake, 10 feet at its deepest, comprises most of the 30-acre state wildlife management area. Fishing is good for largemouth bass, bluegill, pumpkinseed and brown bullhead. Not as abundant are Eastern chain pickerel and black crappie.

* * *

Lockwood Gorge, a magnificent setting in Hunterdon County, resembles a garnet necklace with a blue chain weaving through the middle. The 2½-mile blue line is the south branch of the Raritan River running from Califon to High Bridge.

The gorge is open to fly fishing from April through November. The 260 acres of fields and woodlands are devoted to fishing, upland game and deer. The game includes grouse, cottontail rabbits and squirrels.

More than 10 species of fish reproduce in that branch of the Raritan. Most abundant are brown and rainbow trout, rock bass, smallmouth bass and sunfish.

* * *

Logan Pond in Gloucester County, between Bridgeport and Gibbstown, is the smallest wildlife management area in New Jersey. A six-acre finger of land is surrounded by Logan Pond and Repaupo Creek.

A fly fisherman casts his line into one of the streams flowing through Lockwood Gorge.

Star-Ledger Photo

The 4½-acre pond is 12 feet deep and laden with black crappie, pumpkinseed and white perch. There are also some largemouth bass, white crappie, yellow perch, brown bullheads and carp.

Boating is not permitted because of the pond's size, but fishing lines can be cast from anywhere along the entire shoreline.

* * *

MacNamara is one of the most adventuresome backwaters on the East Coast, where canoeists and hikers can spend weeks investigating the innumerable nooks and crannies of a primitive marine environment.

Fat and skinny fingers of water reach everywhere in the MacNamara wildlife preserve in Atlantic and Cape May counties.

The Great Egg Harbor River, Tuckahoe River and Cedar Swamp Creek glide gracefully through 12,438 acres of fresh and salt water marshes, fields, woodlands and sandy Pine Barrens. Along their undulating way, they supply six lakes and a couple of ponds with enough water to turn the marsh into a wildlife utopia.

Bird watchers can lose themselves amidst flocks of gulls, egrets, herons, coots, grebes and loons, yellow, black and Virginia rails, plovers, willets, and turnstones, sandpipers, knots and dowitchers, curlews, yellowlegs and skinners, terns and American bitterns . . . and even a rare bald eagle in search of food and protective rest.

If that's not enough, there are wintering geese, mallards, clapper rail, teal, and black and wood ducks availing themselves of the nutrient-rich marshes and swamps.

Muskrats and minks scurry about the estuaries in view of the deer, with their own range farther upland.

Rabbits, quail, squirrels and woodcock prefer the higher dry land.

In the drainage basin, marine species proliferate. Largemouth bass, pickerel, yellow perch, white perch, sunfish and eel dart around the fresh water, while striped bass, fluke, flounder and white perch follow the flow of the salt water.

* * *

Mad Horse Creek is a mosaic of squiggly tidal creeks and marshes on the Delaware Bay in Salem County. The 5,816-acre salt marsh and small upland area are bounded by Hope and Stow creeks, with Mad Horse slicing through the center of the wildlife tract.

Muskrats may be trapped in season, and quail, rabbit and pheasant are fair game in the fall of the year.

Striped bass and white perch are the primary species in the brackish tributaries. Waterfowl outnumber all other species, led by black duck, mallard, blue- and green-winged teal, gadwall and Canada geese.

* * *

Manahawkin in Ocean County is a typical mid-size wildlife preserve, a miniature mirror image of New Jersey, a peninsula state saturated with rivers, lakes and bays.

One of the oldest in the state, established in 1933, Manahawkin accounts for 965 acres of fields, woodlands and salt marsh.

Manahawkin and Cedar creeks line two sides of the tract, with more than a dozen creeks and streams filling the 18 lakes and ponds in the refuge.

The water and fields nourish a growing deer herd, as well as grouse, quail, pheasant, woodcock, squirrels, and many waterfowl, from ducks and mallards to widgeons and teals, with geese coming in early in the fall season.

There's excellent crabbing in Cedar Creek and great opportunities for white perch, snapper blues and eels. Some of the ponds contain a few largemouth bass.

* * *

Manasquan is another spot of wilderness in Ocean and Monmouth counties that breaks up the suburban sameness of the most rapidly developing region in New Jersey.

The 726 acres of woodland are split by the Manasquan River, a source of good trout and eels, catfish, white perch and bluegills. Two small ponds are on the tract, one fed by a stream from the Manasquan.

Because of the development around Manasquan, game hunting is limited, although rabbits, pheasant, quail and squirrels are increasing as fast as the human population in Central Jersey.

* * *

Manchester in Ocean County, between Lakehurst and Whiting, is where the red and gray foxes run wild. They have lots of room in the 2,376-acre Pinelands preserve, as do the many deer that forage in the forest of pitch pines and scrub oaks along Routes 70 and 539.

A cedar swamp is another playground for the foxes, deer and grouse, rabbits and quail. Several streams slip quietly through the Pines, two of them being Hurricane and Ruckels brooks.

The State Division of Fish, Game and Wildlife is giving nature a helping hand by creating open five-acre fields to allow the deer to run and to supply food for the small mammals.

* * *

Marmora is a thrilling tangle of wetlands, bays and waterways all coming together in a 4,100-acre coastal hideaway south of Atlantic City in Cape May County.

The intercoastal waterway flows through the entire area, dominated by Ludlam Bay and Corson Sound.

Tens of thousands of scoters, old squaws and red-throated loons congregate at Corson Inlet during the winter months. The inlet welcomes thousands more sandpipers, knots, dowitchers, curlews, willets, plovers, turnstones and yellowlegs during the migration season.

Adding to this waterfowl wonderland are egrets, herons, skinners, gulls, terns, yellow and black rail, American bitterns, Virginia rail, coot, grebes and an occasional bald eagle on its way to a more remote habitat.

The familiar black duck, brant and bufflehead, widgeon, teal and clapper rail also occupy the salt marshes. Marmora gets even more crowded when the Canada geese arrive.

Although the bits of marshland are inaccessible to the mainland, they are natural breeding grounds for foxes, rabbits, quail, squirrels and muskrat. Less than 100 acres of the coastal refuge is upland fields.

* * *

Maskells Mill Pond is a V-shaped fishing reserve in Salem County. The state has acquired land at the far reaches of the pond and at the lower end where the V comes together. The grand total acreage is 47, which includes the 33-acre pond.

Still, the twin-legged pond is brimming with Eastern chain pickerel, yellow bullhead, pumpkinseed, bluegill and eel, and a few black crappie, largemouth bass and carp—enough to make any angler happy.

* * *

Medford is another idyllic dot of recreation near Mount Holly in Burlington County, consisting of fields and hedgerows. A single stream dips across the northwestern corner of the refuge, bearing no name.

Appropriately, this modest wildlife haven is situated next to Ark Road. The 214 acres of woods and fields are alive with ruffed grouse, quail and rabbit. The state introduces pheasant in season.

* * *

Menantico Ponds is an invigorating bundle of water holes made possible by Menantico Creek, which drains through a sandy wilderness near Millville, Cumberland County. They look like squiggly water drops racing down a cool window pane during a rainfall.

The 62 acres of lake surface and land area around Tuckahoe are accessible by auto, and small boats with electric motors are permitted.

Fishing is good for largemouth bass, Eastern chain pickerel, pumpkinseed, brown bullhead, white and yellow perch and carp. Not quite as plentiful are bluegill, white catfish and black crappie.

* * *

Nantuxent is named after a big creek that curves around an 800-acre marshland near Cedarville, Cumberland County. Joined by farmland, the total tract comes to 916 acres.

Nancy Gut, another stream, enters the combination salt and fresh water marsh, where mink, muskrat and rabbit thrive.

Pheasant and quail nest in the fields and woodlands. Deer are beginning to increase their number, although the habitat lends itself more to rodents and waterfowl such as black duck, teal, mallard, pintail and geese.

* * *

Pasadena is a square stretch of open space in the thick of the Pine Barrens of Ocean County. This is New Jersey deer country, a million acres of sand and scrub pines, much of which has been passed by time and remains as it did thousands of years ago.

Pasadena is a critical patch of the Pines, some 3,100 acres of forest and fields sustaining a variety of wildlife.

Four streams sneak around the periphery of the preserve, and railroad tracks border the westerly side.

A special management program has been established by the State Department of Environmental Protection (DEP) to improve the number and quality of wildlife. Fire lanes have been created to prevent the spread of forest fires. The lanes have been planted with rye and green cover to furnish additional food to deer and quail, grouse, rabbits and squirrels, the native species.

Small depressions have also been dug in the soft Pines surface to increase water supplies. There are only two small impoundments on the property, both in the lower corner on the Ocean-Burlington county border.

* * *

Peaslee is known for its old April cranberry bogs and the upper reaches of the Tuckahoe River trickling through this 14,000 acres of pine-oak woodlands.

The Cumberland County tract, spread out like a right angle, features a bird field trail course. Quail hunters work out their dogs in half-hour and hour-long heats.

Mannumuskin Creek and Nixons Branch are among the 20 or so waterways wandering through Peaslee. The state is restoring Bennetts Mills and most of April bogs to provide fresh water fishing, primarily pickerel and bass.

The clearing of 20 fields, totaling 150 acres of food and cover plantings, are increasing the quail, rabbit and grouse population. An already sizable deer herd is also growing larger.

* * *

Pequest River is the trout fishing center of New Jersey. The 60-foot-wide, six-foot-deep tributary flows along the northern side of the state's newest fish hatchery in Warren County.

The Pequest Warren Haven Road runs right across the middle of the 1,467 acres of woodland and fields, making the wildlife area accessible to everyone.

More than 20 species of fish have been taken from the Pequest River, the greatest number being brook, brown and rainbow trout, grass pickerel, sunfish, bullhead and rock bass. The river is managed essentially for rainbow and brown trout.

Fishing is the big sport, but a constantly improving deer herd draws bow and gun fanciers during the hunting season.

Native upland game includes rabbit, squirrel and grouse.

* * *

Port Republic on the wildlife map is a striking profile of a human face wearing a goatee and wavy wig of water sliding down to the neck. The wavy hair is Mullica River and the goatee is a jut of land sticking out of a 755-acre tract of mostly salt marsh and some upland field habitat.

Ice fishing on the Mullica River is a popular winter sport. A seemingly endless supply of striped bass and white perch make the Mullica River the angler's dream come true.

Almost as prolific are black ducks and teal in the salt marsh. Some deer scour the uplands for food, but the habitat is more ideally suited to rabbit, quail, squirrel and woodcock. Pheasant is set loose in Port Republic during the hunting season.

* * *

Prospertown Lake looks exactly like a tricky piece out of your favorite kitchen-table puzzle. The piece of blue lake fits snugly against a chunk of land along Route 537 connecting Freehold to Prospertown and Mount Holly.

The Ocean County lake covers 80 acres with a maximum depth of about eight feet. A fishing pier has been built for disabled persons in wheelchairs.

Swimming and fishing are the two recreation activities promoted at the 125-acre Prospertown park. A bathing beach is at the entrance of the lake.

Motorless boats are allowed on the lake, which is filled with largemouth bass, black crappie, bluegill, pumpkinseed and brown bullhead. There are also some Eastern chain pickerel.

* * *

Round Valley Reservoir is New Jersey's finest trout lake, a man-made impoundment in the hills of Hunterdon County. Heavily stocked with brown and rainbow trout each year, the massive body of water yields year-round species that weigh in at more than 10 pounds. The trophy-size catches have put Round Valley at the top of any sportsman's get-away agenda.

Other species that often grow to full maturity are the largemouth and smallmouth bass, bullheads, black crappie and white perch.

A boat ramp is located at the northwest end of the reservoir.

* * *

Rowands Pond in Camden County, south of Audubon, is another gem in the Garden State's landscape. A three-acre pond wrapped in 25 acres of lush woodland, Rowands is possibly the smallest public preserve managed by the state.

Too small for boating, the pond has but one function in the world of outdoorsmanship: Fishing for anyone at any time.

In season, the peaceful pond is stocked with trout. Year-round denizens are pumpkinseed, bluegill, brown bullhead, pickerel and bass.

* * *

Sawmill Creek was once a sluggish feeder stream of the polluted Hackensack River as it wound its way through the world's largest garbage dump in Bergen and Hudson counties.

Today, Sawmill Creek is a 727-acre salt marsh enjoying the greatest ecological renaissance of the 20th Century. And the stream is the source of that regeneration.

Six miles west of New York City, Sawmill Creek is the intermediary between the tidal marsh and the shallow tidal bays, creating a livable habitat for crabs, waterfowl, reptiles, rodents and fish.

Uncommon species frequenting the Sawmill marsh are the stilt sandpiper, the Hudsonian godwit, American avocet, the Wilson and the northern phalarope.

The Florida gallinule takes advantage of the Hackensack Meadowlands' summer climate. So do the least bittern, red-wing blackbird and long-billed marsh wren.

Waterfowl returning to Sawmill are the gadwall, pintail, blue- and green-wing teal, as well as the more resistant mallard, black duck and canvasback.

The waters, at times marginal, can sustain striped bass, white perch, eel, spot and carp.

Boat accesses to the marsh are at the Sky Harbor Marina in Carlstadt and Tony's Old Mill in Secaucus.

* * *

Sedge Islands are a rare collection of small and medium- to large-sized bites of land that have broken away from Long Beach Island on the Jersey Shore.

A total of 22 islands, scattered in two separate areas off the Long Beach barrier island, the Sedge assemblage is an explorer's paradise. They can be reached by boat . . . or surfboard, for the heartier.

Waders can catch crabs in the shoals around Sedge Islands. In the channels of Oyster and Double creeks, winter flounder run during the spring and fluke during the summer. Bluefish, weakfish and sea bass also swim into the channels. Striped bass have been spotted on the flats.

* * *

Stafford Forge ambles along the Westecunk and Log Swamp creeks in Ocean County, three separate, irregular tracts totaling 2,788 acres.

Halfway between Manahawkin and Tuckerton, the central tract of Stafford Forge contains four ponds and two smaller impoundments, making for excellent fishing of pickerel and catfish.

The creeks and bogs attract Canada geese during migration. Wood ducks make their home in Stafford Forge.

With no natural predators other than man and a harsh winter every few years, the deer herd in the forge is steadily growing.

Quail and rabbit are the native residents. The state supplements the upland game with pheasant during the hunting season.

* * *

Swan Bay is an aqueous sanctuary washed by the Wading and Mullica rivers, Turtle Creek and Swan Bay. Muskrats, mink and waterfowl are the dominant species on the 1,078 acres of coastal wetland.

Green wing teal, black ducks, mallards and geese have taken over the salt marsh, which is enclosed by water on three sides and bisected by Turtle Creek.

Grouse, cottontail and squirrel live in the uplands, as well as some deer wandering about all the way to the edge of the marsh.

Striped bass in the spring and fall can be taken from the Mullica River. White perch enjoy both the river and the marsh creeks.

* * *

Turkey Swamp is truly a suburban backyard escape, serenely spread out in the middle of Monmouth County's upper-middle-class tract developments of split-levels, colonials, ranches and mock tudors.

Wildlife is scattered throughout two rather large and 12 smaller pieces of old fields and new fields, swamps and pine/oak woodlands.

Just six miles south of Freehold, the 1,855 acres of uplands and lowlands are watered by three streams and the upper reaches of the Metedeconk River.

The tract adjacent to Monmouth County Park supports a sizable deer herd. A larger tract below it shelters quail, grouse, rabbits, gray squirrels and woodcock. Pheasants are liberated in the Turkey Swamp preserve in season.

* * *

Walpack is one of the oldest wildlife management areas, established by the state in 1932. In northwest Sussex County, Walpack is a long slip of fields and woodlands following the Flat Brook and Big Flat Brook, New Jersey's renowned trout streams.

The 387 acres give the native deer a long range for feeding and breeding. Waterfowl are limited to mallard and wood and black duck.

The Wanaque area features a range for wild deer in addition to secluded waterways.

Plantings, hedgerows and cuttings maintain the upland game: Grouse, woodcock, rabbit and squirrel.

* * *

Wanaque is ideally situated next to Greenwood Lake in Passaic County and just below Sterling Forest on the New Jersey-New York border.

Greenwood Lake and Wanaque River determine the shape of the 1,412-acre tract on the westerly side. Jennings Creek moves through the middle of the refuge. The waterways provide excellent trout fishing.

A natural deer range opens up to the east of Greenwood Lake. Native game—mostly rabbits and grouse—find the rugged terrain to be a safe refuge in a densely populated region.

* * *

Whiting is a wedge-shaped slice of Green Acres in the heart of New Jersey's senior citizen country—the adult communities along Route 70 in the Ocean County pines.

A dozen fields representing 70 acres have been cleared and planted for wildlife food and cover crops within this 1,200-acre reserve. To create a water supply in the center of the tract, the state carved out Bauer's Pond in the sandy surface. The water attracts black ducks, mallards and Canada geese during the fall and spring migrations.

Pine/oak woodlands and white cedar swamps provide suitable habitat for quail, grouse, rabbit, squirrel and woodcock. The grouse frequent the swamp edges and stands of scrub oaks, while the quail gather in the fields and around the perimeter of the woodlands.

Deer are plentiful, resulting in a number of deer clubs and archery hunting groups in Ocean County.

* * *

Whittingham in Sussex County is one of the few undisturbed natural habitats where beaver and otter can be observed without fear of man's technology.

Within the 1,514-acre protective zone, 400 acres will remain in their natural condition, unaffected by man's intrusive ways.

For the sports enthusiast, there are the traditional Jersey game—woodcock, grouse, rabbit, squirrel and pheasant—and standard waterfowl, ducks and mallard.

Nearby Pequest River ripples with trout, and the rocky woods shelter their share of deer.

* * *

Winslow is a long bend of land and water impacted by only one major expressway and a local road. It offers the motoring public an excellent opportunity to pass through a wildlife sanctuary, mile after green-blue mile.

The Atlantic City Expressway curves across one side of the 2,012-acre preserve in Camden and Gloucester counties. Blue Anchor Road borders the northern end and Piney Hollow Road the southern end.

Two ponds offer excellent fishing for largemouth bass and bluegills. The Great Egg Harbor River courses through the entire length of the tract.

Many deer roam the woods and marshes. Four small fields are planted annually to feed the deer, grouse, rabbits and squirrels.

Wood duck, black duck and mallard also find the Winslow habitat quite pleasant, despite the ribbon of asphalt connecting Camden and Philadephia to Atlantic City.

Courtesy: N.J. Div. of Travel & Tourism

WINERIES

It began with a plump purple grape in 1825 and spread through South Jersey like a wandering vine from which grew America's hearty wine industry.

Long before California's Napa Valley or New York's Finger Lakes wine districts, the first vineyards in the New World were producing lush grapes for robust wines in Atlantic, Burlington and Hunterdon counties.

The seeds were planted in 1825 by a dentist and Methodist minister, Dr. Thomas B. Welch, who developed an "unfermented wine" in a place appropriately named Vineland, N.J.

Welch's Grape Juice—and a new American industry—was born. Welch was the first to apply the pasteurizing technique developed by Louis Pasteur for milk and other liquids. Welch used it to pasteurize his purple Concord grapes to prevent fermentation.

In 1864, French master vintner Louis Nicholas Renault opened New Jersey's first winery in Egg Harbor after failing to establish a healthy, disease-resistant vineyard in California in the late 1850s.

Renault represented the ancient champagne house of the Duke of Montebello at Rheims, France. The expert winemaker found the South Jersey soil and climate strikingly similar to that which he knew in France. The native Jersey grape, the Lubrusca,

was all that Renault needed to start his famous French-American wine cellar.

By 1870, Renault had introduced New Jersey Champagne and became the largest distributor of the bubbly drink in America.

And Egg Harbor became known as "the wine city" because of Renault's prize-winning Jersey varieties.

Now a historical site, Renault Winery today is the oldest winery with its own vineyard in continuous operation in the United States and the largest in New Jersey.

* * *

Wine production peaked in the Garden State during the early 1940s when there were 28 wineries and the state ranked fourth nationally.

With 13 wineries and more than 25 vineyards in operation in New Jersey in 1985, vintners are rediscovering what the exacting Renault learned from the Garden State's rare environment: It's ideal for those popular French and German wines coveted by connoisseurs of the fermented grape since the reign of Charlemagne.

Quietly aging like a vintage bottle of wine, "Chateau Jersey" is coming back as a result of a farm winery law enacted by the state in September 1981. Before then, commercial wine produc-

357

tion was limited to less than 5,000 gallons a year for each wine-maker.

The number of large-scale wineries was based on New Jersey's population—one for every million residents. Only seven licenses have thus been issued, reflecting the state's 7.5 million inhabitants.

Under the 1981 law, farm wineries today can make up to 50,000 gallons of wine a year. All of the wine, however, must be processed only with New Jersey grapes or juice from New Jersey fruits: Grapes, strawberries, blueberries, raspberries, cranberries and other delicious pickings off the vine and limb.

The farm law has uncorked a small winery bonanza designed to boost agriculture and tourism. It is expected to put New Jersey back in the forefront of the finest fermented grapes bearing an American label.

Unlike California wines, New Jersey wines do not have to be refortified with acids to give them their distinctive tastes. The Jersey-grown grapes contain the acids naturally. Without sufficient acids, wines are bland.

The state's expanding wine cottage industry today bottles the full range of white and red, dry and sweet wines under such intriguing labels as Antuzzi, Balic, Delvista, Amwell Valley, Gross' Highlands, Tewksbury and Tomasello.

Some of the best have won gold, silver and bronze medals in wine-tasting competitions.

The Jersey vintners market all of the familiar shelf varieties: Beaujolais, Chianti, Chardonnay, Spumante, Sangria, Sauterne, Reisling, Rhine, Chablis Blanc, Sauvignon Blanc, Seyval Blanc, Ives Noir, Grande Rose, Cherry Royal and Pink Catawba.

Original New Jersey palate pleasers are also eye-catchers: Garden State Red, Atlantic City Casino Brand Wine, Delran Centennial White Wine, Valley of the Gods Sauterne, Waldmeister May Wine, Blueberry Duck, Apple D'Apple and a dessert wine served piping hot, Schillerwein.

One wine blended by Matthew Antuzzi in Delran and given the appellation Baco Noir was used in a Vatican ceremony to canonize an American saint.

New Jersey vintners also come from backgrounds as varied as their international mixes. The one qualification is an unquenchable love of wine and a willingness to sacrifice 80 hours a week to make a commercially acceptable alcoholic beverage.

New Jersey wineries are family operations involving grandparents, parents, children and immediate relatives, each generation learning more about the intricate and, at times, tediously patient process of winemaking.

One New Jersey winemaker is a psychologist, another an accountant. There are a veterinarian, a scientist, a salesman, a publisher and a farmer, and a few basic businessmen who want to make both good wine and a respectable income.

Americans currently consume more than 350 million gallons a year of domestic wine. As more and more Bacchian devotees indulge in their surprisingly satisfying homegrown varieties, the demand for "Chateau Jersey" will most likely rise, resulting in the conversion of more cow pastures and cornfields into neatly trimmed vineyards.

The New Jersey wineries follow.

Renault Winery

The House of Renault embraces 1,100 acres of coastal plain and a 300,000-gallon winery. When Louis Renault died in 1913 at age 93, his son, Felix, continued a family tradition that has made Renault one of the most honored wineries in the United States.

When the U.S. Congress banned alcoholic beverages in 1919, the winery was run by the John D'Agostino family, which operated under a government permit until Prohibition was repealed in

Star-Ledger Photo

An interior courtyard at Renault Winery in Egg Harbor captures the Old World charm of the 119-year-old wine cellars.

1933. For 14 years, Renault Wine Tonic, which had a 22 percent alcohol content, became the chief product and was sold in drugstores throughout the nation.

After the repeal, D'Agostino acquired two California wineries, Montebello at St. Helena and St. George at Fresno. He brought their wines to Egg Harbor City for blending and bottling. The Renault champagnes, mostly blends of California with the New Jersey Labrusca grapes, were sold around the country. Giant reproductions of Renault bottles were pasted on billboards that lined highway roadsides in New Jersey, California, Massachusetts and Florida.

When D'Agostino was killed in an auto accident in 1948, his sister Maria took charge of Renault. A talented designer, Maria D'Agostino made a showplace of the old winery through the construction of a chateau-style hospitality house. Visitors from Atlantic City and other shore resorts tour the Renault winery seven days a week.

In 1966, Miss D'Agostino added an Antique Glass Museum to display her collection of wineglasses. She assembled masterpieces of wineglass art made for kings, queens and merchant princes dating as far back as the 13th Century.

The Fountain Room is the entrance to the legendary wine center. In the middle of the room rises an ornate Italian mar-

A tour group is guided through a room where grapes are pressed and later stored in vats at Renault Winery.

ble fountain, crowned by the Greek goddess, Hebe, cupbearer to the gods and reminiscent of the winemakers along the Mediterranean Sea, where Western civilization emerged.

Leaving the Fountain Room, you walk through a gracious courtyard flanked by Old World arches and featuring a romantic wishing well. From there you can investigate the glass museum, an art gallery or the Hospitality Room, which is banked by large oaken casks like those in the winery's cavernous aging cellars. Wines can be tasted and savored in the Hospitality Room, reflecting the heritage of generations of Renault vintners.

Many of Louis Renault's original pieces of wine-making equipment are on display. There's a wine press from the late 1800s, and dosage machines and gravity filters used from the early 1800s.

Renault's vast wine cellars provide the perfect "climate" for aging. Stone and concrete construction assures constant year-round temperatures between 50 and 60 degrees. In oak and redwood casks, the wines are aged and mellowed under the watchful eye and patient care of the cellarmaster.

The European-styled Burgundy Room serves up discriminating gourmet meals in subdued lighting. In addition to luncheons and dinners, a cheese buffet is available to groups.

Renault sells sparkling wines, varietal wines, table wines, special wines and gift packs in the brick, old-world look. Collectors can also pick up a two-bottle "Pink-Pack" and an Atlantic City Casino Three-Pack Still Wine.

Among the awards bestowed upon Renault Winery were several medals in the Wineries Unlimited Wine Tasting and Judging in Lancaster, Pa. There are about 400 entries in the competition. Best in Class of Special Wines was awarded to the Renault Blueberry Champagne. A silver medal went to the Renault Garden State Red Wine, the second consecutive year the state's own brand of red wine took that category. In the white champagne category, Renault received the bronze medal.

In a wine-tasting competition sponsored by the wine trade publication, Wine Review, Renault received eight awards of the 46 wines from 17 wineries critiqued.

In reviewing the results of the consumer judging contest, Wine Review editor David Pursglove reported that "Renault's Garden State Red was deemed an excellent example of what can be done with native Eastern grapes (largely Ives) by a careful winemaker. It was dry and pleasant with only a hint of Eastern 'foxiness,' and wine professionals felt it should receive a gold medal for a well-made wine in its category."

Every fall there's a Grape Harvest Festival from mid-September through mid-October. Beginning with a "Country Day" and an old-fashioned pig roast, square dancing and hay rides, the Renault festival pays tribute to its founder during "Birthday Jamboree" with clowns, balloons, country French goodies and a giant cake with plenty of ice cream and, of course, several rounds of wine.

Opera-Art-Champagne come together in one effervescent celebration, highlighted by the Singing Ambassadors of Vineland.

"Bavarian Day" brings on a "festhaus" of music and libation with a Boombas concert by the Happy Boombadears, plus lots of hearty German food.

The charm and romance of old Italy is brought back to life on "Italian Day" when celebrants participate in a unique version of a traditional Italian pastime, Barrel Bocce.

And for those who don't mind getting their feet soaked and a bit stained, there's the "grape stomping" romp. Each participant receives the juice of the grapes he stomped, suitably bottled and labeled as a souvenir.

Saturday evenings are set aside for a shimmering candlelight tour in a monestary-like setting.

Since 1977, Renault Winery has been owned by Joseph P. Milza, a former newspaper publisher.

Antuzzi's Winery

Matthew Antuzzi, a former chemical salesman who settled in Delran, Burlington County, holds the very first winery license issued in New Jersey. Just after Prohibition was lifted, Herman Kluxen of Madison was granted the state's first and largest "Plenary Wine License with Retail Privileges." A wine license in New Jersey is as rare as an 1890 bottle from Chateau Rothschild.

Antuzzi had to sell his new home in Burlington Township to buy the Kluxen license when the Madison vintner died in 1973. To make his new winery work in Delran, Antuzzi shared a small apartment with his father, his wife, Leona, and their three children. Leona operated the winery during the day while Antuzzi earned a living as a salesman with a chemical company. Nights and weekends when Antuzzi was not on the road, he helped his wife and children in the winery.

Today when you enter Antuzzi's Winery you are greeted by a half-gallon bottle of wine bobbing over the front counter. A rope and pulley raise and lower the bottle when the front door opens to an immaculate, brightly lighted showroom.

On this particular day, it was a bottle of "Sweet Claret Wine" dancing at the end of a rope. Shelves are filled with natural fruit wines, Antuzzi's specialty. "You can get a colored flavored grape wine at the liquor store, but you can't get a natural strawberry wine," Antuzzi enthuses.

In a spacious back room are empty wine bottles stacked to the ceiling on one side and large wine vats resting contentedly on the other side. In the wide aisle a hydraulically operated assembly line pushes empty bottles forward where an automatic labeling machine slaps on the brand name and 10-cent Portuguese corks press firmly into filled bottles.

Antuzzi is brimming over with energy as he watches every step of the operation carefully. Leona places plastic bands over the necks of the filled bottles. The oldest children, Jennifer, 13, and Marie, 10, will help out by packing the finished bottles— corked end down—into cardboard cartons.

Growing up in Riverside, Calif., Antuzzi developed an early interest in winemaking. His grandfather made wine as a hobby in Italy. The elder Antuzzi's equipment was left to Matthew for

Star-Ledger Photo

Winemaking is a family affair at Antuzzi's Winery in Delran where owner Matthew Antuzzi has produced some of the country's most popular fruit wines. Antuzzi's daughter Maria places the finished bottles into cartons.

whatever use he could make of it, from a destemmer to a grape crusher and some very old barrels.

Updating grandpa's rather primitive method of fermenting grapes, Antuzzi enrolled in winemaking courses at the University of California at Davis, one of the nation's leading enology schools. Enology is the science of winemaking.

When the Madison winery license became available, Antuzzi was prepared to make the plunge into an extremely competitive business. His philosophy was to remain eastern and to be regional, following the tradition of European winemakers.

Antuzzi's first concern was to plant varieties of grapes that are "winter-hearty." His five-acre vineyard is a mix of the vitis labrusca variety and French hybrids. Labruscas produce the typically sweet Eastern wines. The French hybrids make wines with a dry taste, comparable to the California vitis vinifera style.

Antuzzi's Winery, a converted maintenance garage on Bridgeboro Road, has become the fruit wine center of New Jersey. Strawberry and blueberry are his most popular brands, although other berries are available. The fruit wines are difficult to make because the high acid content of the berries can inhibit the yeast, which converts the fruit's natural sugar into alcohol during fermentation. To achieve that "true fruit taste," nothing is added to nature's own ingredients, no colors, flavors or enhancers. Like home-canned fruits, Antuzzi's berry wines must be consumed the same year they're bottled.

The Delran winery today produces 125,000 bottles of wine, or 25,000 gallons. Some 22 flavors are offered to the public, among them Pink Catawba, Seyval Blanc, Ravat 51, Rose, Apple d'Apple, Sweet Claret, blackberry, cherry royale and Concord grape.

On April 1, 1980, a dedication wine created by Antuzzi became the official Delran Centennial Wine, a pleasurable blend of three vintage white wines made from a combination of Eastern grapes. As part of the Centennial Celebration, several bottles of Delran White were placed in a time capsule. In the year 2080, when Delran embarks on its bicentennial, residents will be able to toast their town's 200th birthday with the 1980 Centennial Wine.

For the canonization of former Bishop John Neumann, Phila-

delphia's first saint, the Vatican conducted a national search for the wine to be used in the historic mass at St. Peter's Basilica in Rome. Using the strict University of California Davis tasting rules, Antuzzi's Baco Noir was selected as the vintage that would be sent to Vatican City. Antuzzi grows 2,000 Baco Noir vines on his small farmland tract.

Antuzzi's Seyval Blanc won the Silver Medal at the Maitres des Tastevins International wine tasting competition in Washington, D.C. in 1977. His Ravat 51 also won a silver medal in the Wineries Unlimited Wine Tasting competition in Lancaster, Pa.

No detail in the making and packaging of his wine is left to chance. Antuzzi's wine packaging has received the second place showing for the best packaging of any kind in the United States.

The entire family goes on two business vacations each year to keep up with the latest developments in the rapidly changing winemaking industry in America. On their Feburary 1983 trip to California, the Antuzzis ordered the nation's first machine that bottles wine from the bottom up. Antuzzi explains:

"Oxygen is the killing factor in all wines. By filling a bottle from the bottom, you eliminate 50 percent of the oxygen, therefore improving the aging of the wine by at least 50 percent. A spout enters a bottle and as the wine pours in, the spout rises to the neck during filling. This is just one creative way of making the product better."

The bottoms-up filler is another first for "Chateau Jersey."

Tomasello Winery

The end of Prohibition marked the beginning of a winery in Hammonton, Atlantic County. It was an extension of a farm tended by Frank Tomasello, who converted most of his cropland into vineyards.

As is the family tradition among Italian farmers, Tomasello fermented a small amount of his grapes into wine for consumption in the home. Neighbors and friends who dined at the Tomasellos enjoyed the farmer's homemade brew, encouraging him to go into the winery business.

In the early days, wine production was largely an art with little in the way of scientific controls. However, with his two sons, Joseph and Charles, Tomasello developed a more scientific approach to winemaking.

Since 1933, when the winery turned out 5,000 gallons in its first year of operation, production has climbed to more than 80,000 gallons of wine made from 11 varieties of grapes, two of which are vintage dates, and six sparkling wines.

In the late 1940s, the 85-acre vineyard and winery created its first batch of champagne based on the classical French method. The Tomasellos consider their champagne among the finest in the land.

In the French Methode Champenoise, each bottle is fermented individually, instead of in bulk tank. The champagne is aged "fin tirage" (finely drawn out process) for more than a year, during which time it acquires a desirable yeasty taste. After the aging period, each bottle collects a small amount of sediment, which must be removed.

The sediment is coaxed to the opening of the bottle by placing the container upside down in a "riddling" rack. By turning, lifting and shaking, the dregs finally reach the opening end. The bottle is then removed from the rack and is frozen from just above the neck down to the opening.

When it is subsequently opened, the force of the champagne blows the frozen piece of ice and sediment out of the bottle. The matter is removed without filtration. By avoiding filtration, the bubbles in the final product are quite tiny, ensuring the champagne will remain fresh for a long period after opening. All of Tomasello's champagnes and sparkling wines are made by that highly labor intensive method.

Nearly 90 percent of Tomasello's wines are sold on the premises. The family bottles 17 brands—12 wines and five champagnes. Two are vintage dated dry French hybrid varietals, a white Villard Blanc and a full-bodied, oak-aged, red DeChaunac.

Wine aficionados get the full story of what's inside the bottle and how it got there by reading a Tomasello label. Here's what the label on the Tomasello DeChaunac American Wine 1981 says:

"This fine bodied red wine was produced from the French hybrid grape of the same name. The 1981 vintage was harvested at 19.0 degrees Brix (19 percent sugar at start of fermentation) and subsequently fermented for a period of 21 days at 63-70 degrees F. After racking, the wine was aged in quartered white oak for 270 days to impart a slight woodiness to the bouquet. The final titratable acidity was 0.65 g/100 ml. with less than 0.1 percent residual sugar. This wine can be most highly appreciated when served at 68 degrees F. It has excellent long-term storage potential."

Responsible for that precise information, which certainly tells the average wine consumer more than he or she needs to know, is Charles Tomasello, who succeeded his father as chief winemaker, viticulturist and business manager.

In 1978 and '81, the third generation of Tomasellos joined the business. Both of Charles' sons have expanded the operation by planting more French hybrids and increasing wholesale distribution. Among the latest Tomasello entries in the marketplace are a semi-dry Rhine, which resembles a Blue Nun, and a Chablis that is popular with the locals.

Amwell Valley Vineyard

Mike Fisher, born in Manchester, England and educated at the University of London, is another winemaking pioneer in Hunterdon County. Like his regional neighbor, Jim Williams, Fisher leads two lives: During the day he is the senior director of chemistry at Merck & Co. in Rahway, and the rest of his waking hours the Ph.D. scientist is pursuing his favorite hobby, winemaking.

Fisher's wife, Elsa, also splits her life in half: Secretary of a biodynamics company by day, and the rest of the time her husband's assistant at their brand new winery on Old York Road in Ringoes.

The Fishers received one of the first two licenses issued under the 1981 New Jersey Farm Winery Law, allowing them to sell up to 50,000 gallons of wine each year from grapes grown exclusively in the Garden State.

Their premier season (1983) produced 2,000 gallons from the fruit in their vineyards, which cover eight acres.

Situated on a gentle southern slope in the rolling hills of East Amwell Township in the southeast corner of Hunterdon County, Amwell Valley Vineyard commands a magnificent view of the Sourland mountain range.

An experimental planting of grapevines was undertaken in 1978, consisting of 13 varieties of French hybrids from Boordy Nursery in Riderwood, Md. Those vines, which flourished in the micro-climate of Amwell Valley, were replanted and the failures replaced.

The vineyard produces principally two varieties: Foch, which yields a dry red wine reminiscent of a Beaujolais, and Seyval, which makes a dry white wine with some of the characteristics of a Chardonnay.

The red wine is aged for a few months in white oak casks. The white is drinkable immediately after cold stabilization and clarification.

Amwell Valley Vineyard and a handful of other growers have demonstrated that French hybrid grapes can be successfully grown and good quality table wines can be produced in Hunterdon County. The area is actually more suitable for grape growing than the traditional Eastern regions such as the Finger Lakes and portions of Pennsylvania.

Some true vinifera grapes can be grown successfully in Hunterdon County: Two white varieties—Chardonnay, the grape of the famous white burgundies, and Riesling, the grape from which the best German wines are made. The jury is still out on other varieties of vinifera, especially vinifera for red wines, according to the Fishers.

Amwell Valley's wines are made in the European tradition with a liberal infusion of modern materials. September is the busiest month since both varieties mature as the fall season beckons. Foch ripens in early September and Seyval later in the month.

Measurements of sugar and acidity are taken daily as harvest time approaches. At just the right moment, the grapes must be picked and processed within hours. All grapes are picked by hand and taken directly to the crusher-stemmer. A large crew is necessary since hand-picking is a time-consuming, laborious task.

After initial fermentation is completed, the new wine is separated from the seeds and skins for the reds, and from the gross sediment for the white wines. From then on, the work slows down as the wines are carefully purified and matured. Bottling takes place in early spring and both wines are ready to drink within a month after corking.

The entire operation is carried out in a small, simple building using minimal equipment: An Italian-style basket press, a mechanical crusher-stemmer and electric transfer pumps. The juice is fermented in food-grade polyethylene tanks, which are inert and hygienic. They are also easy to clean.

Much of the purification takes place in similar tanks, although the red wines benefit from a brief rest in an oak barrel. Final brightness is achieved by filtration.

Gross' Highland Winery

A tradition of authentic European winemaking begun in 1934 by a German immigrant has made Gross' Highland Winery in Absecon, near Atlantic City, the largest direct-to-the-consumer winery in the East.

More than 20 varieties of dinner, dessert and sparkling wines are produced, bottled and sold at the Absecon winery and its outlet in Manasquan, Monmouth County, the first satellite winery in New Jersey.

The present storage capacity for wines is 185,000 gallons. Stainless steel is evident everywhere throughout the fermentation and storage cellars.

At the 83-acre Absecon winery, visitors can see modern wine- and champagne-making equipment, cool damp wine cellars and the fragrant bouquet of peacefully fermenting wines. In the spring, one can witness a remarkable bottling machine that fills, labels and caps each bottle in one smooth, continuous operation.

In the fall, the great automatic harvester gently combs the vineyards while the wine press extracts the juice of nature's bountiful gift. Visitors are given an informative audio-visual presentation that graphically explains the entire winemaking process. There's also a gift shop with glassware from around the world at this year-round tourist attraction.

The story of Highland Winery began when a young John Gross arrived in New York City from Germany in 1902. At 15, he brought little with him except his dreams and knowledge of winemaking. His grandfather was a commercial winemaker and operated a major cooperative winery in Germany. It was there the boy learned the ages-old art of winemaking as practiced by the Bavarian master vintners.

Young John was up early in the mornings for hand harvesting and during the mild spring afternoons he closely watched the crucial wine-tasting ritual.

Gross' Highland Winery in Absecon produces more than 20 varieties of dessert, dinner and sparkling wines.

Star-Ledger Photo

When John came to America, he wanted to continue the much-respected winemaking tradition of the Gross family. Lacking sufficient funds to start his own business, John worked for a while in New York City's famous Ruppert's Brewery. Later, he moved to Philadelphia to work for other breweries.

When he saved enough money, John bought a modest eight-acre farm in Absecon. He soon became friends with the small commercial winemakers already settled in the area. He also exchanged correspondence with other winery owners in New York State.

In August 1934, Gross opened his little winery. Now the center of Gross' winery complex, the original structure is three stories with 18-inch-thick brick walls. In its cool deep cellars, oak casks contained wine. Facilities for bottling and champagne production were, as they are today, confined to the main levels.

Before Prohibition, 28 wineries operated in Atlantic County. After the controversial law was repealed, only two could afford to reopen. Gross had earned a reputation for marketing high-quality wine and his winery survived Prohibition.

His first move was to begin a vineyard expansion program spanning six years. He contracted local grapegrowers to provide him with the fruit until his own vineyards were mature. Twenty-two years after opening, Gross' Winery had reached 7,000 gallons annually. Gross succeeded in developing a number of specialized wines for his southern New Jersey market.

At the time of his death in 1956, Gross had seen his dream come true. It is a thriving enterprise today under the direction of Bernard (Skip) D'Arcy, who has brought production up to 185,000 gallons a year.

As the wine industry changed with the growth of the food industry, Gross' winery played an important role in experimenting with stainless steel tanks and quality control lab techniques. Automatic harvesting was only one innovation in the wine industry spearheaded at Gross' winery.

Visitors are welcomed to Highland Winery every day except Sunday. The winery is located on Jim Leeds Road, just a few miles from Atlantic City.

DelVista

When Ray Williams gave his brother Jim a home winemaking kit for Christmas in 1970, little did he know that he was planting the seeds of one of New Jersey's newest and most promising wineries.

Jim Williams is, during weekdays, a psychologist at Bell Laboratories in Piscataway. Evenings and weekends he turns into a different kind of doctor, specializing in the delicate art of winemaking.

Jim and his wife, Jonetta, started savoring wines in the early 1960s. As they tasted more and more wines, their palates became more sophisticated, eventually acquiring a preference for the dry premium varieties. Until about 1969, the Williamses considered themselves "European wine snobs." Williams had taken numerous correspondence courses in French, German and Italian wines. Then the couple discovered California premium wines while staying in San Francisco on business matters.

That led to the sampling of other American wines produced in New York and other states. When Williams got the winemaking kit from his brother, he learned that one of the places where he could find information and obtain supplies to make his home brews was at the Wine Arts store right in his town, Watchung.

After browsing through the Wine Arts store, Williams, who works with top scientists and engineers at Bell Labs, came across some "impressive technology" to make wine at home. His first batch convinced him he could make a pleasant tasting wine.

The early wines were made from concentrates from California, France and Spain. Williams made everything from apple to zinfandel and tried his hand at sherry, port and sparkling wines. The more he made the better they tasted until his friends and neighbors asked if they could buy his wine. Due to state and federal regulations, Williams would not sell his special mixes.

The Williamses even planted 25 grape vines to try to produce their own fruit, but the Watchung site wasn't satisfactory. By 1977, the wine tasting group the Williamses belonged to invited Eric Miller from Ben Marl Vineyards in the New York Hudson Valley to give a talk and introduce their wines. The Williamses were surprised by the quality of the Hudson Valley wines and believed they could produce as good a wine. They also believed New Jersey had even better grape-growing conditions than New York.

After reading everything they could find concerning the types of soil and sites where the best wine grapes grow, they began their search for a New Jersey site.

Nine months passed before they happened upon the abandoned Ken Hatcheries, one of the largest chicken operations in New Jersey. The original farmhouse was built in the late 1700s or early 1800s. The property is believed to be part of the original Lowrey tract once occupied by Samuel Fleming, the founder of Flemington along the Delaware River in Hunterdon County. Lowrey, from Ireland, later married Fleming's daughter.

The Lowrey tract had an appropriate, well-drained soil, a shaley loam, common in German wine producing regions. The tract also had a good southern exposure, situated on a plateau overlooking the Delaware River. The river, as it courses down the valley, moderates climate extremes needed for a healthy vineyard. The property also contained an old building that could be converted into a winery.

In the spring of 1978, the Williamses planted their first four acres on the 10-acre tract, three acres of French hybrids and one acre of vinifera (European varieties).

Jonetta Williams tends the vineyards at the Del Vista winery where yields of up to 2,000 bottles are registered in the spring.

Jim Williams, owner of Del Vista Vineyards in Frenchtown, inspects a sample of his wine.

The time came to name the Williams' Delaware Valley vineyard. Their son, Jason, suggested calling it "Fermentation Hill," but Williams settled on DelVista (a conjunction of Delaware and vista) Vinyards (for wine-yards). The "e" was purposely left out of vineyards, but much of the mail the Williamses have gotten since DelVista was incorporated arrives with the "e" back in the company name.

The Williamses learned that nearby Frenchtown was the site where the wine grape "Delaware" originated in the middle 1800s, placing that Colonial settlement on the viticulture map. Paul Prevost, for whom Frenchtown was named, was a fugitive from the French Revolution who bought a large tract of land in Alexandria Township to start a new life. The Delaware grape variety was found growing in Prevost's garden, an apparent cross between grapes he brought from France and the native varieties. Ironically, it received its name from Delaware, Ohio, from where it was later propagated.

The Williams' strategy from inception was to experiment, like Ben Marl, to determine which grape varieties would make the best wines in that region of the Delaware Valley. In the vinifer varieties, DelVista Vinyards is concentrating on Chardonnay, Riesling, Sylvaner, Pinot Noir, Zinfandel, Cabernet and some Merlot and Gewarztraminer.

French hybrids include Seyval Blanc, Aurore, Vidal Blanc, Villard Blanc, Verdelet, Sigfried, Rayon D'Or (whites), GW-9 and Chelois, DeChaunac and Chancellor (reds). And, of course, the Williamses offer the American Delaware variety.

Williams' approach to winemaking is to make the wines in the mostly European style that he and his wife prefer—primarily dry, crisp whites and full-bodied complex reds, except for the Nouveau. DelVista leaves the skins on the reds for at least a week, subjecting them to malolatic (special yeast) fermentation to lower their acids and increase their complexity. The final products are table wines intended to go with foods, bringing out their best qualities.

The Nouveau is a different style altogether and fills the gap between the crisp whites and the full-bodied reds. It is medium-bodied and fruity and is made in the French style, utilizing a combination of whole berry fermentation and carbonic maceration.

The Nouveau is made by crushing and pressing just enough grapes to add about two gallons to each of the 50-gallon drums in which the whole berries are fermented. Wine yeast is added to the juice and then the berries, stems and all, are poured into the drums until each drum is about three-fourths full. Carbon dioxide gas is released into the drum and the lid is tightly closed.

Periodically, the carbon dioxide gas is replenished. The gas actually breaks down the grape tissue, a process known as carbonic maceration, and reduces some of the wine's acidity. After about three weeks, the liquid is separated and the remaining grapes are pressed. The wine matures rapidly and is ready to drink within a few months.

The Williams family shares the winemaking responsibilities. Jonetta manages the vineyard, supervising the part-time labor force, and takes care of the advertising. When away from his Bell Labs office, Williams serves as the winemaker and is responsible for the overall financial planning and record keeping. Their son, Jason, had worked in the vineyard until he started college in the fall of 1982. Janise, their daughter, still helps with various vineyard and winery activities.

Their first harvest in the fall of 1982 yielded 2,000 bottles of wine in the spring of 1983. DelVista's 10-acre vineyard eventually will produce 50,000 gallons a year.

Tewksbury Wine Cellars

Dr. Daniel Vernon is a veterinarian who shares his love of animals with winemaking, not necessarily incompatible interests in the green farm belt of Hunterdon County.

Tewksbury Wine Cellars is a small, 10,000-gallon winery near Oldwick, an antique village in the heart of Hunterdon's fox country.

With his wife, Lynn, Vernon has planted more than 8,000 grapevines on 20 acres of their 50-acre vineyard. Tewksbury's varieties include Chardonnay, Gamay Beaujolais and Gerwurztraminer, which produce the magnificent white wines of Burgundy, the fruity young reds of Beaujolais and the intensely spicy whites of the Alsace.

Because the classic wine grapes of Europe have never been developed on a commercial scale in New Jersey, the Vernons are experimenting with rootstocks and cultural techniques with the hope of eventually arriving at both varieties and viticultural practices that result in truly exceptional wines.

Tewksbury's first harvest from its own vines was in 1981, followed by increasing yields from new plantings until the intended capacity of 10,000 gallons was reached in 1984.

In the meantime, the Vernons have purchased grapes locally from a small vineyard in Hunterdon County and from neighboring New York and Pennsylvania.

The Vernons want to establish a wine cellar in Oldwick comparable to those found in some little European villages catering to visitors and tourists. Those local wineries the Vernons found while vacationing in Europe, offered wine that was fresher and livelier than those imported to America. It was, they learned, made for a regional market.

Wines that must travel great distances and are likely to be stored in warehouses or shops at improper temperatures are made differently, especially young ones, which most are. They need a large dose of preservative, are more finely filtered and are often pasteurized, the Vernons learned in their travels to the remote villages of Germany, France and Spain.

None of that is harmful to the consumer, so far as is known, but it does deprive the wine of color, freshness, body and bouquet, the veterinarian discovered in comparative taste tests.

Tewksbury Cellars wines are produced for the local market and are stored under favorable conditions.

Fennelly Farm Vineyard

It is the northernmost of the new genre of fine wine grape vineyards started in northern New Jersey in the latter part of the 1970s.

Since 1978, Betsy and Donald Fennelly have planted eight and a half acres of their 86-acre Lebanon Township farm in white wine grapes: 70 percent vitis vinifera (European Riesling and Chardonnay), and 30 percent French-American hybrids, principally Seyval Blanc.

An accountant with the international accounting firm of Arthur Young & Co., Fennelly is developing high quality white wines to be vinified in the French style, favoring moderate alcohol levels, high acidity and low residual sugar.

"The climate and the terrain of northern New Jersey approximate those of some of the great white wine districts of France and Germany and we're convinced that the taste and discrimination of American wine drinkers are changing rapidly towards a preference for wines made in that style," Fennelly predicts.

Co-founders of the Hunterdon County Wine Growers Associa-

A small cluster of grapes starts on the vine early in the season at Tewksbury Wine Cellars in Tewksbury.

Star-Ledger Photo

Cellarmaster John Altmaier of Tewksbury Wine Cellars taps into the stored barrels of wine.

Star-Ledger Photo

tion, the Fennellys worked closely in the development of the New Jersey Farm Winery Bill.

"The new law led New Jersey out of the dark ages of wine production in which it had been languishing since the enactment of Prohibition," Fennelly says.

Balic, Lee and Laird

Savo Balic's dream is attending a Governor's state dinner at the Drumthwacket mansion in Princeton and watching the guests toast the evening with champagne or wine from a New Jersey vineyard.

Balic Winery in Mays Landing, Atlantic County, began as a grape farm in 1965. The 35 acres of red and white grapes started producing wines in 1975.

A former construction worker, Balic, in his late 50s, today grows nine varieties of grapes and bottled 15,000 gallons of wine in 1984. Like all but one of New Jersey's wineries, Balic is open to the public six days a week.

With his wife and children involved in the harvesting and packaging, Balic offers a fine selection of dry, sweet, red and white wines, as well as champagnes, including premium effervescents fermented in the bottle and costing half as much as the famous French imports.

Balic would like to see the state promote "Chateau Jersey" as vigorously as California and New York advertise their wines nationally.

"If our leading state officials displayed New Jersey wines during political and social functions, the public would become aware of just how good our wines are compared to the imports," Balic enthuses. "New Jersey's got the product. All it needs now is a little exposure from the right people."

Balic's winery list includes Burgundy, Ives Noir, De Chaunac, Rose, Sauterne, Vidal Blanc, Chablis and Red Velvet.

* * *

In Mansfield, Burlington County, is **Jacob Lee's Bonded Winery**, which specializes in sweet wines. The six-acre vineyard yields 25 to 30 tons of grapes, or 10,000 to 15,000 gallons of wine yearly. It is the only winery that does not offer tours to the public.

* * *

Finally, there is America's oldest native distilled spirit beverage made not from grapes, but New Jersey apples. In March 1964, the New Jersey Senate passed a resolution "saluting the Apple Jack Brandy industry as the oldest native distilled beverage industry in the United States."

Records reveal that William Laird, a county Fyfe Scotsman, settled in Monmouth County, and produced Apple Jack as early as 1698.

Laird's Apple Jack in Scobeyville is America's oldest family of brandy distillers. The Colts Neck Inn near Laird's apple orchards was built by a member of the family in 1717. It was a stopping place for stagecoaches and dispatch riders traveling between Freehold and Amboy.

Laird's Apple Jack Brandy is made only during the peak of the apple harvest each year from early September to mid-November when the quality and sweetness of the apples are at their best.

The apples are scrutinized one by one, washed and pressed into pure, sweet apple juice. The juice is then allowed to ferment naturally. No yeasts, cultures or starters are employed in the process.

The pure fermented juice is then distilled. After distillation, the "new" apple jack is put in charred oak barrels to tenderly age for up to eight years.

Laird's Apple Jack is unique because it retains the delicate flavor of the whole tree-ripened apples. It imparts that flavor to mixed drinks, cocktails, punches, eggnogs and food recipes.

A Siberian tiger rests in the cool grass at the Great Adventure Safari Park in Jackson Township.

ZOOS

One is an exotic safari park in the primeval pine forest of Ocean County, the largest authentic wild preserve outside Africa.

Another is a little "Live Animal Room" animating an arts and sciences museum in suburban Morris County.

Still another is a living 1860s barnyard hiding out in a packed bedroom community of Bergen County.

One other specializes in turtles, from hand-held to giant tortoises, in the urban heart of New Jersey, Essex County.

There's even a Popcorn Park Zoo along the Jersey Shore for abandoned, injured or handicapped wildlife taken in by the Humane Society.

And in North Jersey, animal visitations to hospitals and nursing homes are part of a medical treatment program.

One of the last free-admission zoos in the United States features four continents of animals, from rare tropical birds to the familiar farm creatures.

Collectively, they are the Garden State's animal parks and zoos—nine in all—operated by public agencies and private corporations and families setting aside natural habitats for endan-

Beast meets machine in the Safari Park at Great Adventure.

Star-Ledger Photo

gered species and for educational and environmental experiences and just sheer enjoyment for the humankind.

From the private Space Farms Zoo in rural and rocky Sussex County to the public Cohanzick Zoo in South Jersey's flat dairyland, the miniature animal kingdoms are like green oases giving wildlife a final foothold in a creeping concrete corridor.

With less than 2,000 acres—the size of a modest ranch in Texas—New Jersey's zoos and animal parks are home for more than 300 species and 3,000 animals.

From addax and audad to wallaby and zebra, almost every variety of wildlife has adapted to New Jersey's diversified environment.

There are gnus, emus and kudus . . . oryxes, gemsboks and elands . . . and camels, collared peccary and coati-mundis.

Many are treated royally in heated pools and barns and glass-enclosed nurseries. All are carefully watched over by veterinarians, zoologists and humane specialists to be sure each animal survives throughout its natural life cycle in good health.

Some are television stars, such as the Exxon tiger and Princeton University mascot, a rare Siberian strain leading a contented life at Terry Lou Zoo in an upper-class neighborhood of Scotch Plains.

At Van Saun Park Zoo in Paramus—the shopping center crossroads of New Jersey—the popular pets are elevated, one at a time, to "Animal of the Month" with posters and fliers and the accompanying publicity. Eventually, all of the species, no matter how small, will have their celebrated moment in the human calendar of events at Van Saun Park.

As an enterprise, however, the zoos themselves are threatened activities in a state with the highest population and development density in America. Like the vanishing farmlands, animal parks can become victims of human encroachment.

If New Jersey's animal parks are to remain viable refuges for wildlife and their human observers, land-use planners will have to hold back intrusions that can create incompatible and insoluable conflicts between natural habitats and permanent people structures and activities.

Ranging from a 1,100-acre zoo in Cumberland County to a 27-by-31-foot room in Morris Township, New Jersey's animal parks are listed here.

Great Adventure Safari Park

A six-mile drive through Great Adventure's 450-acre wilderness takes in Africa's Serengeti Plains and Veldt (grasslands), Australia's outback, the sub-Mediterranean deserts and the great American plains.

Many of the animals roaming protectively in the safari park are almost non-existent in their native lands.

The Australian section is a first for a drive-through safari.

Shaped like a long, bent leg, the safari park in Jackson Township is divided into 12 distinct habitats: The Australian section, the Serengeti, the Veldt, the American Plains, the Mediterranean, baboons, Siberian tigers, leopards, bird sanctuary, European brown bear, African lions and American black bear.

In the 42-acre **American Plains**, motorists can see a Roosevelt elk shed his large antlers, and when mating time comes, the male with his new antlers sounds his call, or bugle, as it's known.

The big, grayish-brown member of the deer family runs about with white elk, red deer, white-tailed deer, 2,000-pound bisons and, from South America, the rather inelegant-looking llama. A member of the camel family, the llama is used as a pack animal.

Also in the American Plains is the smaller member of the ostrich family, the rhea. The tall, flightless birds have curious mating habits. Males have two or three mates, all of whom lay their eggs in one nest. When the nest fills up with 20 to 30 eggs, the male and females sit on them.

The **African Veldt**, with its resilient bushes and trees scattered sparsely throughout the grasslands, is home for the elephant, white rhino and ostrich.

The African elephant is the largest land mammal on earth, weighing about 6 tons when mature and reaching 11 feet at the shoulders. An elephant eats 18 hours a day, consuming 30 to 50 gallons of water in the process.

The elephant's gestation period is the longest of any mammal, 21 months, and the calves aren't fully weaned until five years of age.

The "white" rhino gets its name from the African word

An automobile yields to a mature rhino at Great Adventure.

Courtesy: Six Flags Great Adventure

"vide," meaning wide, a reference to his huge mouth and square jaw. The rhino is peaceful, unless provoked.

Despite its tank-like size, a rhino can move fast and is ready for combat with a pair of thick horns protruding 60 inches from the snout.

The ostrich is the largest bird today. Fully grown, it stands nine to 10 feet high and can reach 300 pounds. Its 15-foot strides make it one of the fastest creatures in the world at 40 mph.

Ostriches are omnivorous, feeding on fruit, plants, small mammals, reptiles and insects. Females are grayish with no white and males are black with white-tipped plumes.

The 75-acre **Serengeti Plains** is the largest section in the Ocean County park, offering the widest variety of beautiful and exotic animals. The tallest of all creatures, the giraffe, stands out in its quest for high-limbed leafy snacks, which are taken with the assistance of an 18-inch long tongue.

The sable antelope has a velvety brownish-black coat with contrasting white belly and its long horns curve gracefully backward. Kudus are a relative of the sable antelope, and have a fine tan coat delicately marked with thin, white, vertical stripes and a pair of long, gently spiralling horns.

The eland is a larger antelope with similar markings but with shorter, twisting horns. Also strikingly beautiful is a member of the Oryx family, the gemsbok, with its long, nearly straight sharp horns and an attractive white-masked head with dark markings.

Equally attractive are the addax, beisa oryx and scmitar-horned oryx, all cousins to the gemsbok. Blackbucks are the most graceful and agile animals in the Serengeti Plains. Chestnut brown with horns that twist up and backward in a corkscrew curve, blackbucks leap gracefully across the plain.

Also residing in the Serengeti are the white-tailed gnu and the white-bearded gnu, odd-looking creatures that seem to have the head of a buffalo, the tail of a horse and feet of an antelope. Rounding out the plains population are the hartebeests, camaroon goat, water buck, peacock, guinea fowl, ankoli cattle, East African crown cranes and maribu storks.

Herds of zebra also graze in the Serengeti. The zebra's body is whitish with dark stripes, not the other way around.

The **Australian** habitat was established in 1979, the terrain modified to emulate the natural environment of the kangaroo, wallaby, wallaroo and emu. Kangaroos are marsupials, just like those familiar New Jersey opossums.

* * *

Less than 420 **Siberian tigers** are left in the world today and of those, 120 are in the wild. The Siberian section contains more than can be found in any other spot on earth.

They come from the cold and snowy forest of northern Manchuria and southeastern Siberia. They are a larger and heavier breed than Bengal tigers, growing to lengths of 13 and 14 feet at weights up to 650 pounds.

During floods in their native habitat, Siberians have been known to consume animals as large as crocodiles. Of tremendous strength, the sleek cat can drag prey weighing up to 1,200 pounds for a distance of a quarter of a mile.

Segregated from the other animals are the **African lions**, numbering 35 strong in the Great Adventure Safari Park. Lions form families called prides, usually limited to 15-20 members. Fed 10 pounds of fresh meat a day supplemented with vitamins, lions can be more dangerous in captivity than they are in the wild.

Many wild sheep and goats wander about the **Mediterranean Reserve**, along with the dromedary, the flat-footed breed of one-humped camel found in the sandy wastelands of Arabia.

The **American black bear** is the smallest of American bears. When black bears are born they weigh only nine or 10 ounces, but can top the scales at 500 pounds as adults and, when standing upright, reach seven feet tall.

The **European brown bears** often weigh up to 550 pounds with a length of seven feet from nose to tail. Their size and formidable array of claws, backed by an aggressive attitude toward other animals, command respect.

The **leopards** are mysterious spotted cats. Fierce and dangerous, they are nocturnal and live mainly in trees. The Great Adventure leopards are the only major group in captivity.

Ordinarily, leopards are tawny to yellowish, with black spots, but some (called black panthers) are entirely jet black. When examined closely, however, muted black spots can be detected. Leopards are up to seven feet long and often exceed 150 pounds. They evolved in Africa and Asia.

Once an ancient marshland, the **bird sanctuary** is an ideal bog for the big birds who are happiest in watery surroundings. They include white swans, ducks, geese and mallards.

Perhaps the favorites are the sometimes people-like **baboons**, who are tremendously curious about humans. Extremely social creatures, their family groups number as many as 80.

Although generally good-natured, baboons are totally unpredictable and can suddenly become infuriated for no apparent reason and attack anyone or anything within reach.

Baboons are simians, a term used to describe apes, gorillas and chimps. The biggest, strongest male is very definitely the boss and is challenged daily to retain his position as "king."

Turtle Back Zoo

Opened in 1963 as a "children's zoo," Turtle Back today is one of America's great urban animal parks, a natural landmark in West Orange.

The 16-acre preserve along Northfield Avenue is home for more than 200 species of animals numbering approximately 650. As its name implies, it houses one of the largest collections of turtles in the United States, from two giant tortoises weighing some 300 pounds to snappers, diamond-back terrapins and Eastern boxes.

Turtle Back's hilly terrain is perfect for the 50 species of turtles—more than 200 at last count—meandering around the grounds shaded by redwoods, ferns, flowering bulbs and a grove of Norway spruce.

Newborn and tame animals are cared for in a glass-enclosed nursery. California sea lions swim in a heated pool and youngsters can pet and feed sheep and goats in a contact area. Among the

Star-Ledger Photo

*A parrot at Turtle Back Zoo,
West Orange.*

*Eilish Morley, left and Eileen Martin, both of Allendale,
cautiously pet a skunk at Turtle Back Zoo in West Orange.*

Star-Ledger Photo

residents from the far corners of the globe are Siberian tigers, leopards, llamas, a yak, penguin, vulture, South American tapir, an Oriental short-clawed otter and a sitatunga, or African antelope.

A miniature antique train takes zoo visitors on a mile-long ride along the scenic wooded backdrop that lines the southern border of the park.

Live animal lectures are available to any group, from preschool to college, business or service interests.

A survey of several classes of animals representing reptiles, birds and mammals is the basis of a general animal talk.

A "Touch and Feel Tank" focuses on the marine invertebrate life thriving along the New Jersey coast. The talk culminates with teachers and students getting their hands into the zoo's "Touch and Feel Tank." The 250-gallon tank contains an assortment of sea denizens, including starfish, sea urchins, hermit crabs, snails and clams.

Another 40-minute presentation looks at amphibians. Three orders of amphibians are examined, utilizing four animals from the zoo's collection.

Reptiles are spotlighted in a 40-minute show using photographs, slides, preserved specimens and representatives of the three orders of reptilian life, with emphasis on six specific creatures.

Also on the agenda is the avian structure and a survey of bird types, featuring four or five species.

Primitive to advanced mammals are the subject of another lecture, starring such mammalian members as the armadillo and prairie dog.

For junior high students and up, there's a discussion on vertebrate reproduction, from fish to mammals.

In the field of animal ecology, the concepts and problems of animals and their relationship to their environment, particularly Essex County and New Jersey, are covered in a 45-minute review for students from the fourth grade and up.

Captive animal management is the theme of a slide presentation and tour of Turtle Back Zoo for junior high schoolers and up.

Some specialized programs concentrate on hawks, owl snakes, turtles, sea lions, Essex County mammals, New Jersey amphibians, birds, reptiles, animal adaptation and endangered species.

The zoo's education center also conducts guided tours along nature trails offering spectacular views of wildlife.

Space Farms Zoo and Museum

In the beginning, Ralph Space split his time between repairing Model-T cars in his Sussex garage and working for the state as a trapper.

In those good old days when Sussex County was strictly for farmers and "wild varmits," Space, when not fixing Model-Ts, caught coyotes, foxes and wolves terrorizing cows and horses grazing in open pastures.

It was only natural, therefore, that Space's interests in cars and animals would someday lead to a collection of creatures and old equipment saved during years of hard work.

Those rather interesting aspects of Sussex County's development into an agricultural-recreational center are reflected in this mechanic-trapper's Space Farms Zoo and Museum, featuring antique autos and a selection of "critters" ranging from Hokkaido bears and wild turkeys to bobcats, badgers and beavers.

Space Farms today boasts the largest private collection of North American wild animals, more than 500 specimens representing well over 100 species. They are managed in a 45-acre tract that is the center of a 425-acre preserve owned by three generations of the Space family.

Before the area was improved by Space, it had been a "bog lot," a swampy mosquito nest not even fit for farming. The land was drained and restored and now supports a growing population of wildlife: Scottish Highland cows, elk, deer, sheep, goats, fowl, tigers, lions, monkeys, ponies, Texas Longhorn cattle, jaguars, fish and minks.

Space Farms raises more than 20,000 minks a year on a 20-acre ranch. The balance of the farmland produces food for the hooved animals and the vegetarians in the zoo. More than 150 tons of grain and 100 tons of hay are required each year to sustain a healthy lifestyle for the animals.

The museum complex takes in eight buildings chock-full of carriages, coaches, wagons, old cars, motorcycles, sleighs, tools, toys, utensils, dolls, Indian relics, glass, porcelain, guns, clocks and hundreds of other items reflecting America's heritage.

Bits and pieces of Sussex County's history are preserved in a blacksmith shop, general store and farm shed. Also within the museum area are an animal nursery, snake den, eagle monument, gift shop and restaurant.

All of that comes with a touch of animal humor provided by Ralph, his son, Fred, and the two grandchildren, Eric and Parker. Here's a sampling of easy one-liners, compliments of the Space family: Cross a centipede with a parrot and you'll get a walkie-talkie. Or, cross a salmon with a feather and you'll get a fish that's tickled pink.

Had enough? Just one more: Cross a mink with an octopus and you'll get a coat of arms.

Cohanzick Zoo

The only municipal park in New Jersey, the Cohanzick Zoo bills itself as a family-size zoo set amid a 1,100-acre recreation retreat in Bridgeton, Cumberland County. And it's free to the public, thanks to the persevering fund-raising efforts of the Cohanzick Zoological Society.

Cohanzick is derived from the name of the Indian tribe, the Cohansey, part of the Lenni Lenape, or Delaware, Indians occupying New Jersey, Delaware and part of Pennsylvania before Columbus discovered the New World.

Although just 52 mammals and 100 birds make up the zoo's population, the Cohanzick is only one of 10 zoos in the United States to successfully breed ocelets. Mountain lions are also bred in the community compound, whose feline members include African lions, jaguars, lynxes and other wild cats.

Started 35 years ago as a drop-off shelter for unwanted animals, the Cohanzick Zoo today provides a refuge for several dozen species of animals grouped by continents—African, Asian, South American and North American.

Having recently completed a new tropical bird aviary, the Cohanzick Zoological Society is currently preparing plans for a modern 90-acre zoo. The money to feed and maintain the preserve comes mostly from the sale of refreshments and souvenirs at the zoo.

Terry Lou Zoo

New Jersey's biggest privately owned zoo devoted exclusively to the care and raising of animals, Terry Lou Zoo is situated in one of the most unlikely places in the Garden State, a fashionable neighborhood which at the turn-of-the-century was a pastoral farmland.

Within this seven-acre natural paradise dwells a pair of exquisite Siberian tigers, "Junette" and "Bradsha." They are a breeding pair and their first-born is a feline celebrity, star of the Exxon tiger commercials and the mascot for Princeton University athletic events. Other offspring of the breeding tigers have been sold to zoos throughout the country.

Frank and Louise Terry operate Terry Lou Zoo, which is comfortably stocked with 287 birds and animals: Ringtail lemurs (a vanishing species), llamas from the Andes of South America, buffalo from the Northwest, mares with frolicking colts, zebras, kangaroos, giraffes, camels, lions, tigers and chimps.

The Terrys' philosophy is to encourage an interest in wild animals to the point where zoos will not be thought of in the company of amusements, but in the company of educational institutions such as museums and schools.

Although a small animal farm, the Scotch Plains preserve is a major investment. A giraffe, for example, is worth $8,000, and a bison eats five bales of hay and 250 pounds of grain a week.

Consumed in one week at Terry Lou Zoo are 560 pounds of meat, 280 pounds of bananas, 200 pounds of cracked corn, 1¼ tons of grain, 100 pounds of turkey pellets, 35 bales of hay, 75 pounds of monkey chow, 50 pounds of sunflower and wild bird seeds, plus daily vitamins and assorted fruits and vegetables.

Frank Terry comes from a long line of Union County farmers and original settlers of Scotch Plains. Terry wanted to save a piece of the original rural atmosphere and thought an animal park was the best way to do it.

Once a camping ground of the Lenni-Lenape Indians, the choice woodlands played its part in the Revolutionary War. Created by a grant from the King of England, the farm was the site of the famous "Aunt Betsy Frazee baking incident" in which British soldiers were refused food by a patriotic settler.

Terry Lou Zoo today is home for 115 mammals, 157 birds and 15 reptiles, many of which are unpenned. Children are encouraged to pet and "make friends" with most of the animals. Staff members are on the grounds to answer all questions about rare breeds.

Morris Museum Live Animal Room

It's just a 27-by-31-foot room, but it's the most popular space at the Morris Museum in Morris Township. It's where some 40 animals, including reptiles, enjoy all of the creature comforts of a man-made environment.

Since its inception in 1913, the Morris Museum has cultivated a deepening interest in the natural sciences. Although the museum began to develop a small reptile collection in the early 1950s, it wasn't until the museum moved to Madison Avenue in 1956 that live animals acquired a bigger role in the then Morris Junior Museum.

In those days, under the tutelage of John Ripley Forbes of the Natural Science for Youth Foundation, live animals became a vital facet of most children's museums throughout the country. Typical animals in the Morris collection at that time included small local snakes, a few turtles, amphibians, some mammals and an exceptional exhibit of tropical finches, all of which were used for educational purposes.

The Morris Museum moved to its present location on Normandy Heights Road in 1964—and the miniature animal kingdom moved, too. In the 1970s, the Morris Museum expanded its program by accepting injured and orphaned animals from New Jersey.

Today, most of the museum's animals come to it through state referrals or as "unwanted" pets. The museum usually keeps only those animals not healthy or well-adapted enough to survive in their natural habitats.

In 1985, the residents of the "Live Animal Room" included a skunk; a rabbit; an owl monkey; mice; seven species of snakes; an iguana and other lizards; six turtle species (box, map, sliders, painted, snapping, elongated tortoise); a dove, and several amphibians: Tiger salamander, American toad, giant toad and green frogs.

One of the museum's greatest functions is its educational work in the form of lectures and exhibits. A total of 21,000 school children visit and receive lectures on a variety of subjects each year.

Live animals have a universal appeal to young and old and are an excellent educational tool, adding another dimension to the teaching of animal care, conservation and environmental education, according to Elizabeth Johnson, natural science curator.

"From the beginning, live animals have helped the museum staff to teach concern and respect for animals and the environment," Johnson says. "They are used daily in our docent (teaching) programs, and the 'Live Animal' lecture is still the most popular in the museum." Upward of 450 live animal talks are given annually, besides the number of animal lectures in conjunction with the natural science workshops.

Through its extension programs, members of the museum staff take various animals on bimonthly visits to children in pediatrics at Morristown Memorial Hospital and to residents of nursing homes. Most of the high school volunteers working in the museum's natural science programs go on to pursue careers in biology, veterinary science or environmental studies.

"Because animal/environmental conservation is of great importance to our natural sciences department, the animals will be with us for a long time," Johnson says. "Live animals fill an invaluable educational niche in these environmentally precarious times, especially since today's children will be the future custodians of our natural resources."

Van Saun Park Zoo

Education and the environment are also the themes of an 18-acre animal farm safely enveloped within a 140-acre county park in Paramus, Bergen County, site of the busiest intersection in New Jersey: Routes 4 and 17, the shoppers' crossroads.

Its pastoral setting is accented by rock gardens, floral displays, a picturesque waterfowl pond and naturally decorated wildlife exhibits. Paths are wide and shady and benches are anchored everywhere for animal observations.

Van Saun Park Zoo is open 365 days a year, weather permitting. Admission is free to all, making it one of the last free zoos in America.

More than 25,000 school children participate in classes and lectures, the topics ranging from A to Z, animal behavior to zookeeper.

Van Saun Park Zoo has an extensive collection of domestic animals—sheep, goats, beef cattle, dairy cows, swine, donkeys and chickens—all exhibited in a replica 1860s farmyard setting among antique farm equipment and buildings. Sheep shearing and milking demonstrations are conducted by the zoo's staff during certain times of the year.

Some of the species at the zoo are ostriches, mouflon (wild sheep), collared peccaries (wild pigs), guanaco (wild llama), Arctic foxes, black-handed spider monkeys and waterfowl. There are also a North American river exhibit, a toco toucan exhibit, an ocelot exhibit and a spacious walk-through aviary housing North American marsh and wading birds.

Projects under development are a North American Plains exhibit, a South American Pampas exhibit, jaguars, a mountain lion, prairie dogs, sea lions and macaws.

Van Saun Park Zoo was founded in 1960 by the Bergen County Park Commission as a children's zoo. Little changed until 1975, when the park's first professional zoologist was hired.

A professional staff of animal keepers was employed to care for the growing and diverse collections of wild and domestic animals. In 1979, a zoo architectural firm developed a master plan for the then eight-acre facility.

The year 1982 witnessed the most dramatic changes at Van Saun Park. The first birth of an endangered species occurred early in the year.

Construction of major animal holding areas, storage buildings and a modern, fully equipped commissary were undertaken. A collection of New World (North and South American) animals would become the central theme to exhibit the dimorphic differences between the familiar North American species and those lesser known neighbors to the south.

The Paramus zoo today holds approximately 350 animals, with plans for another 150-200 creatures by 1986.

Wyckoff Wildlife Center

More than 100 turtles, snakes, frogs, toads, fish, waterfowl and bees' nests—all native North Jersey specimens—are protected in an 81-acre park in Wyckoff, Bergen County. The wildlife center attracts more than 280,000 people a year. Open year-round, the center is free to the public.

An exhibit hall contains live native animals, natural history displays and a monthly art show. An observatory overlooks a pond supporting various species of waterfowl. A deer pen is located at the start of a two-thirds-mile-long, self-guiding trail.

The center serves as the meeting headquarters for the Bergen County Federation of Garden Clubs, the Fyke Nature Association, the Ridgewood Audubon Club, the Antique Bottle Collectors Association and the Ridgewood Camera Club.

Weeping willows overhang a swan pond, one of the attractions at Van Saun Park Zoo in Paramus.

Star-Ledger Photo

Weekend programs are open to the public and cover such subjects as "The Aquatic Life of Lakes and Streams" ... "Wildflowers of the Woods and Fields" ... "From the Ocean to the Sky" ... "Herbs: Then and Now" ... "Beginner's Orienteering" (map-making) ... "Wilderness at Our Doorstep" ... "Life Cycle of the Bass" ... "The American Island" ... "The Historic Blacksmith" ... "Garden Soil Preparation" ... "Castles of Clay" ... "Bird Banding" and "A Food and Fuel Self-Sufficient Lifestyle in the City."

Many programs are designed for active participation by school, youth and other groups. Among them:

• Sense Impressions—Discovering the natural world through creative activities that sharpen one's sensory perceptions, emphasizing form, color, texture, shape, sound and smell during a one-hour walk along the natural trail.

• Secret of Trees—Learning about tree life cycles and how to identify common species. How a tree grows and why leaves turn color in autumn, and finding out about current and historical uses of trees.

• Indian Natural Heritage—Going shopping the Indian way, in nature's store. Learning how the Indians of New Jersey used plants, animals and other natural materials to survive.

• Animal Homes and Hideouts—Discovering where the animals live and exploring their habitats along the woodland trail.

• Feathers and Wings—Exploring such questions as how a bird flies and what different birds eat.

• Mammals of New Jersey—An examination of live mammals within the wildlife center.

Popcorn Park Zoo

The only free, federally licensed zoo in the United States, Popcorn Park Zoo is also the only public zoo in Ocean County. It is the New Jersey Humane Society's response to saving homeless pets and injured animals from dying in the streets and backlots of the cities and suburbs.

Established in 1977 on an 11-acre site in the Pinelands of Lacey Township, Popcorn Zoo is the final resort for creatures with no place to go. More than 100 animals are sheltered in the refuge, all of them victims of a fast-moving society.

Take Lacey the Lion, which was purchased by a magician when still a pup but developed illnesses during its short-lived show business career. The Ohio magician left the lion with a veterinarian whenever it was sick and needed treatment.

Soon the doctor bills piled up and the lion became collateral for the vet seeking payment. A woman working for the Humane Society learned of the lion's medical plight and found a home for the confused cat at the Popcorn Zoo.

The two black bears at the Lacey park were recruited by a gas station operator in Maine to attract customers. Business picked up but the bears suffered in confined quarters behind the gas station where they were kept during the night.

Like Lacey the Lion, they were checked in at Popcorn Zoo and seem to be enjoying their new life entertaining the local animal lovers.

Three wolves at Central Park Zoo grew old and the pack rearranged its leadership, ousting the senior members. Not a pleasant sight for a big city zoo, so the three wolves wound up at the Jersey Shore shelter for the rest of their days.

Then there's the story of the poisonous puff adder. The Monmouth County Prosecutor's Office raided a house in connection with a murder case. Detectives found an arsenal of handguns, rifles, machine guns, bombs ... and a snake and a Great Dane. The Lacey shelter had no problem finding a good home for the big dog, but nobody wanted to adopt a killer snake.

The Philadelphia Zoo heard about the prosecutor's raid and offered to take the puff adder as part of its large snake collection.

Not all snakes pose problems for Popcorn's zookeepers. A seven-foot Burmese python was saved from the garbage dump when the shelter took it off the hands of a Harrison resident, who bought it on a whim and couldn't care for it in his home.

Raccoons are constantly being rescued from steel traps and those that recover are released back into the wilds. Six white-tailed deer that got in the way of cars are recuperating at the zoo, as are a couple of foxes, several skunks, opossums and other casualties losing their habitats to development, such as ducks, geese, swans, rabbits, chickens, plus lots of orphaned cats and dogs.

Popcorn is New Jersey's random zoo, a place whose gates are open to all creatures in need of a helping hand.

Production Manager: Mary D. Morano
Art Director: Anne U. Ricigliano
Ass't. Art Director: Maryalice Lento
Senior Editor: Catherine M. Doherty
Book Manufacturing: Jean Karash
                    Joyce Turner

Endpapers: Brant Beach
           Long Beach Island

Photo Credit:
Mary D. Morano